Fodor's 06

WALT DISNEY WORLD®, UNIVERSAL ORLANDO® & CENTRAL FLORIDA

Fodor's Travel Publications   New York, Toronto, London, Sydney, Auckland

www.fodors.com

FODOR'S WALT DISNEY WORLD®, UNIVERSAL ORLANDO® & CENTRAL FLORIDA 2006
Editor: Emmanuelle Alspaugh

Editorial Production: Tom Holton
Editorial Contributors: Felice Aarons, Jennie Hess, Gary McKechnie, Alicia Rivas, and Rowland Stiteler
Maps: David Lindroth, *cartographer;* Bob Blake and Rebecca Baer, *map editors*
Design: Fabrizio La Rocca, *creative director;* Guido Caroti, *art director;* Moon Sun Kim, *cover designer;* Melanie Marin, *senior picture editor*
Illustrations: Robert Dress
Production/Manufacturing: Robert B. Shields
Cover Photo (Magic Carpets of Aladdin ride, Magic Kingdom® Park): © Disney

SPECIAL SALES
This book is available for special discounts for bulk purchases for sales promotions or premiums. Special editions, including personalized covers, excerpts of existing books, and corporate imprints, can be created in large quantities for special needs. For more information, write to Special Markets/Premium Sales, 1745 Broadway, MD 6-2, New York, New York 10019, or e-mail specialmarkets@randomhouse.com.

IMPORTANT TIP & AN INVITATION
Although all prices, opening times, and other details in this book are based on information supplied to us at press time, changes occur all the time in the travel world, and Fodor's cannot accept responsibility for facts that become outdated or for inadvertent errors or omissions. So **always confirm information when it matters,** especially if you're making a detour to visit a specific place. Your experiences—positive and negative—matter to us. If we have missed or misstated something, **please write to us.** We follow up on all suggestions. Contact the Walt Disney World, Universal Orlando & Central Florida editor at editors@fodors.com or c/o Fodor's at 1745 Broadway, New York, New York 10019.

PRINTED IN THE UNITED STATES OF AMERICA

10 9 8 7 6 5 4 3 2 1

Be a Fodor's Correspondent

Your opinion matters. It matters to us. It matters to your fellow Fodor's travelers, too. And we'd like to hear it. In fact, we *need* to hear it.

When you share your experiences and opinions, you become an active member of the Fodor's community. That means we'll not only use your feedback to make our books better, but we'll publish your names and comments whenever possible.

Here's how you can help improve Fodor's for all of us.

Tell us when we're right. We rely on local writers to give you an insider's perspective. But our writers and staff editors—who are the best in the business—depend on you. Your positive feedback is a vote to renew our recommendations for the next edition.

Tell us when we're wrong. We're proud that we update most of our guides every year. But we're not perfect. Things change. Hotels cut services. Museums change hours. Charming cafés lose charm. If our writer didn't quite capture the essence of a place, tell us how you'd do it differently. If any of our descriptions are inaccurate or inadequate, we'll incorporate your changes in the next edition and will correct factual errors at fodors.com *immediately.*

Tell us what to include. You probably have had fantastic travel experiences that aren't yet in Fodor's. Why not share them with a community of like-minded travelers? Maybe you chanced upon a beach or bistro or B&B that you don't want to keep to yourself. Tell us why we should include it. And share your discoveries and experiences with everyone directly at fodors.com. Your input may lead us to add a new listing or highlight a place we cover with a "Highly Recommended" star or with our highest rating, "Fodor's Choice."

Give us your opinion instantly at our feedback center at www.fodors.com/feedback. You may e-mail us your nominations, comments, and complaints at editors@fodors.com. Or send a letter to the Walt Disney World, Universal Orlando & Central Florida Editor, Fodor's, 1745 Broadway, New York, NY 10019.

You and travelers like you are the heart of the Fodor's community. Make our community richer by sharing your experiences. Be a Fodor's correspondent.

Happy traveling!

Tim Jarrell, Publisher

CONTENTS

ABOUT THIS BOOK

Our Ratings

In theme-park chapters, ★, ★★, or ★★★ rates the appeal of the attraction to the audience noted. "Young children" refers to kids ages 5–7; "very young children" are those (ages 4 and under) who probably won't meet the height requirements of most thrill rides anyway. Since youngsters come with different confidence levels, exercise your own judgment when it comes to the scarier rides.

In non-theme-park chapters, such as the Space Coast, black stars in the margin highlight sights and properties we deem **Highly Recommended,** places that our writers, editors, and readers praise again and again for consistency and excellence.

And finally, the very best attractions, properties, and experiences get our highest rating, the orange **Fodor's Choice** symbol, throughout this book.

By default, there's another category: any place we include in this book is by definition worth your time, unless we say otherwise. And we will.

Disagree with any of our choices? Care to nominate a place or suggest that we rate one more highly? Visit our feedback center at www.fodors.com/feedback.

Budget Well

Hotel and restaurant price categories from ¢ to $$$$ are defined in the opening pages of chapters 5, 6, and 10. For attractions, we always give standard adult admission fees; reductions are usually available for children, students, and senior citizens. Want to pay with plastic? **AE, D, DC, MC, V** following restaurant and hotel listings indicate if American Express, Discover, Diner's Club, MasterCard, and Visa are accepted.

Restaurants

Unless we state otherwise, restaurants are open for lunch and dinner daily. We mention dress only when there's a specific requirement and reservations only when they're essential or not accepted—it's always best to book ahead.

Hotels

Hotels have private bath, phone, TV, and air-conditioning and operate on the European Plan (a.k.a. EP, meaning without meals), unless we specify that they use the Continental Plan (CP, with a Continental breakfast), Breakfast Plan (BP, with a full breakfast), or Modified American Plan (MAP, with breakfast and dinner) or are all-inclusive (including all meals and most activities). We always list facilities but not whether you'll be charged an extra fee to use them, so when pricing accommodations, find out what's included.

Many Listings

★	Fodor's Choice
★	Highly recommended
⊠	Physical address
✛	Directions
⌂	Mailing address
☎	Telephone
🖷	Fax
⊕	On the Web
✆	E-mail
🖃	Admission fee
⊘	Open/closed times
▶	Start of walk/itinerary
▭	Credit cards

Hotels & Restaurants

🏨	Hotel
⇥	Number of rooms
♨	Facilities
🍽	Meal plans
✕	Restaurant
⌕	Reservations
🏛	Dress code
✕🏨	Hotel with restaurant that warrants a visit

Outdoors

🏌	Golf
⛺	Camping

Other

ℹ	Contact information
⇨	See also
⊠	Branch address
☞	Take note

Rides

🕶	Thrill ride
🕶	Thrill ride with water
🕶	3-D film
🕶	Simulator ride
😀	Live show or animatronics show

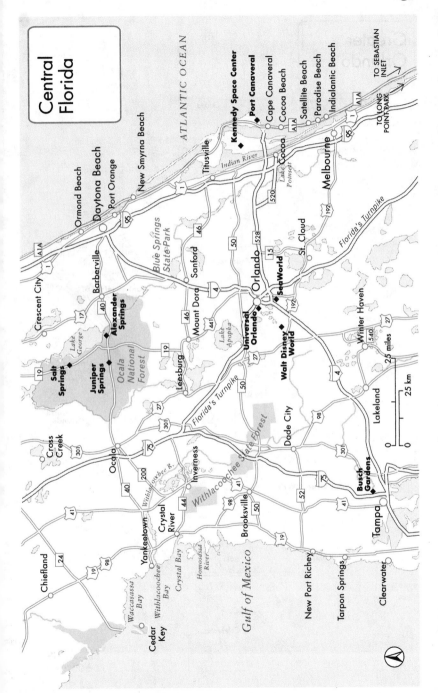

Central
Florida

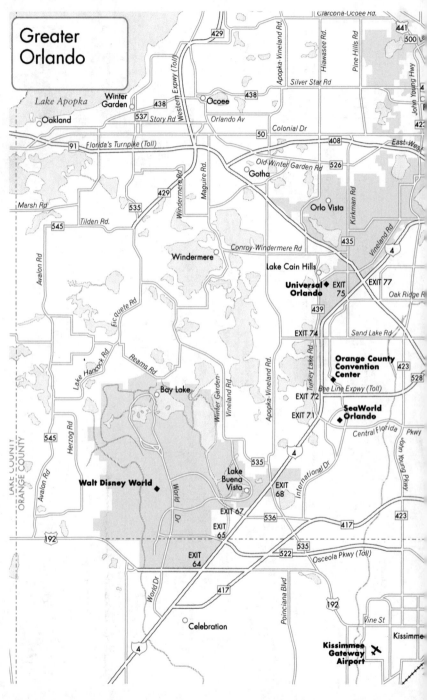

Greater Orlando

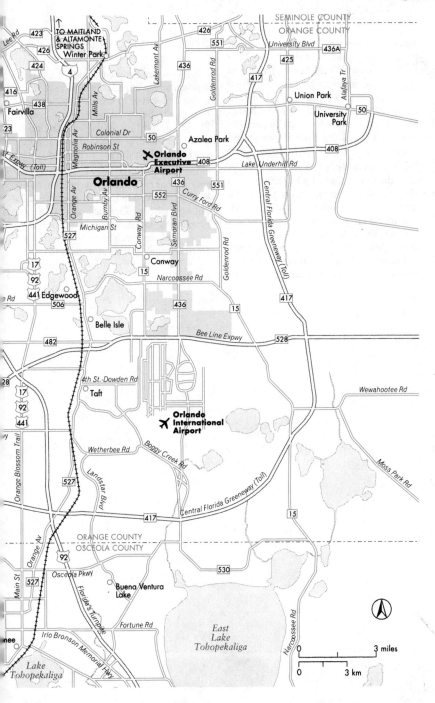

ABOUT OUR WRITERS

Jennie Hess is a travel and feature writer based in Orlando. Formerly a publicist for Walt Disney World Resort, Jennie still enjoys exploring every corner of the evolving kingdom and gathering theme-park details faster than Pooh can sniff out honey. She gets us the inside scoop on Disney, plus insights gleaned from her husband and two sons.

Florida native Gary McKechnie has encyclopedic knowledge of what he thinks is the greatest state in the Union. During his student days, he worked as a Walt Disney World ferryboat pilot, Jungle Cruise skipper, steam-train conductor, double-decker bus driver, and improv comedian at Epcot. His book *Great American Motorcycle Tours* won a silver medal in the 2001 Lowell Thomas Travel Journalism Competition.

Alicia Rivas, our Shopping and Smart Travel Tips updater, is a freelance broadcast journalist and writer. Though technically a transplant, she considers herself a Central Florida native. Rivas worked at Epcot while she was in college, and she still considers it the best job she's ever had.

Good meals stick to your ribs; great meals stick in your mind. That's the belief of Rowland Stiteler, who has served as editor and dining critic of *Orlando* and *Central Florida* magazines. During the past seven years he's researched more than 300 Florida hotels and restaurants for travel publications and the convention and resort industry.

Orlando can be a pretty bewildering place, filled with an endless stream of attractions. Walt Disney World alone can flummox the planner in you, with its 47 square mi (that's twice the area of Manhattan). But don't let the selection and the enormousness of it all stop you in your tracks.

Let's start with Walt Disney World. Many people are surprised to learn that it isn't a theme park. It's really a whole "world" of assorted diversions, including several theme parks, water parks, resort hotels, golf courses, and shopping-dining-entertainment complexes.

Then there's Universal Orlando, which is made up of two theme parks: Universal Studios Florida and Islands of Adventure, as well as CityWalk, a complex of restaurants, nightclubs, and stores.

And that's just the beginning. There's still SeaWorld, Discovery Cove, and Busch Gardens to explore.

The Magic Kingdom

What most people imagine to be Walt Disney World—the Magic Kingdom—actually is a small, but emblematic, part of it. Similar to California's Disneyland, the Magic Kingdom is the wellspring of Mickeymania and the most popular individual theme park in the United States, welcoming millions every year. For many of those who have grown up with Cinderella, Snow White, Peter Pan, Dumbo, and Pinocchio, it's one of those magical places, "so full of echoes, allusions, and half-memories as to be almost metaphysical," according to renowned travel writer Jan Morris. It's the site of such world-famous attractions as Space Mountain, Pirates of the Caribbean, Splash Mountain, and "it's a small world," as well as new thrills like Stitch's Great Escape and Mickey's Philharmagic.

Epcot

Designed to promote enthusiasm for discovery and learning, WDW's Epcot is a sweeping combination of amusement park and world's fair. In Future World, anchored by the trademark 17-story silver geosphere known as Spaceship Earth, the focus inside 10 landmark pavilions is on the fascinating discoveries of science and technology. Don't miss the funny, often startling, 3-D film and special-effects attraction *Honey, I Shrunk the Audience,* and if you can handle an intense simulation blast-off, try out the Mission: SPACE ride to Mars. In the second major area of Epcot, the World Showcase, you can tour 10 different countries without the jet lag, stopping at each for a ride, a film, or a shopping or dining expedition.

Disney–MGM Studios

With a cast that reads like the credits of the biggest blockbuster ever made—to Walt's name add George Lucas, Jim Henson, the Duke, Bogie, and Julie Andrews—this is Disney's re-creation of Hollywood as it might have been in the good old days. Amazing attractions are the key to "The Studios' " success: there's the Rock 'n' Roller Coaster Starring Aerosmith, the Twilight Zone Tower of Terror, the classic Great Movie Ride, and two stunt shows. Other not-to-be-missed attractions include the closing show, *Fantasmic!,* and the Magic of Disney Animation, a behind-the-scenes look at those remarkable Disney animators working at their art. MGM still has a fully operational film and television production center as well as back-lot tours that reveal tricks of the film business.

Disney's Animal Kingdom
Walking into the Animal Kingdom is like entering a lush, tropical rainforest. Tall trees, vines, and thickets surround the walkways, providing shade and moisture to temper the Florida heat. In the center of the park, the huge, sculpted Tree of Life rises 145 feet, towering over all the other trees in the park. Walkways encircle the tree, leading to attractions, including a water ride, a safari ride, and several shows, in the Asia, Africa, and Dinoland areas of the park. With a 100-acre savanna and wildlife preserve, the Animal Kingdom is the largest of all the Disney parks, though guests can only access a portion of the land. The rest is reserved for the park's resident elephants, zebras, lions, and other animals.

Typhoon Lagoon & Blizzard Beach
What could be better than a water park on a hot summer day? Disney has been in the business of dousing water on all and sundry for quite some time. Typhoon Lagoon and Blizzard Beach are two separate water parks that are always jam-packed when the weather's steamy. The best ride—or is it the worst?—is the wild, 55-mph dead-drop to a splashy landing from Blizzard Beach's Summit Plummet, which feels as fast as it sounds. If you have water babies in tow, look for Typhoon Lagoon's scaled-down Ketchakiddie Creek and Blizzard Beach's Tyke's Peak.

Downtown Disney
A vast lakeside complex of shops, nightclubs, restaurants, theaters, and other entertainment venues, Downtown Disney is where to go for afternoon shopping and late-night partying. It's divided into three main areas: the West Side is where you'll find DisneyQuest, the House of Blues, and the Cirque du Soleil theater (presenting *La Nouba,* the only permanent Cirque show beyond Las Vegas), among other attractions. The Markeplace, on Downtown Disney's east side, has a million kid-friendly shops and restaurants, including the Rainforest Café, Ghirardelli Soda Fountain & Chocolate Shop, the LEGO Imagination Center, Once Upon a Toy, and Disney Pin Traders. In between the West Side and the Marketplace is Pleasure Island, with the Mannequins Dance Palace (21 and over), Comedy Warehouse, and Pleasure Island Jazz Company.

Disney's BoardWalk
Looking like a 1960s postcard of Atlantic City, this crescent-shape boardwalk beside a lake is a pleasant place for families. Sidewalk artists set up their easels, pedal cars roll up and down the strand, diners sit at sidewalk cafés and breweries, and shoppers browse through stores. For a quiet evening meal, consider Spoodles, a top-rated Mediterranean restaurant. After dinner you might stroll over to Seabreeze Point for a fantastic view of Epcot's nightly IllumiNations fireworks show. Then you can always check out the dueling pianos at Jellyrolls or the DJ-powered dancefest at the Atlantic Dance Hall.

Universal Studios

Universal's classic theme park pays tribute to the movie business with well-designed street scenes from Hollywood and New York, and rides devoted to making you feel like you're actually in a movie. Look for The Mummy Returns and Shrek 4-D, as well as *Back to the Future*— The Ride and *Men In Black:* Alien Attack.

Islands of Adventure

If you have teenagers or adult thrill seekers in your party, do not miss a day at Islands of Adventure. It has absolutely the best roller coasters in Central Florida, and the fantastical designs of its five lands give Disney a run for the money. The screamfest begins at the Incredible Hulk Coaster and continues at the double coaster known as Dueling Dragons. People are still shrieking like babies at the Amazing Adventures of Spider-Man 3-D show. There are plenty of ways to get soaked, too: Dudley Do-Right's Ripsaw Falls is a flume ride with a serious drop and a splash landing that even gets onlookers wet. Little ones have a land all to themselves: Seuss Landing, where they can enter the world of *One Fish, Two Fish, Red Fish, Blue Fish* and *The Cat in the Hat.* All in all, they've done it all—and they've done it all right.

Universal CityWalk

With nightspots ranging from a red-hot Latin music club to a cool and smooth jazz lounge, the CityWalk entertainment complex has enough diversity to please any couple or family. Clubgoers should check out "the groove" nightclub or Latin Quarter, and bar hoppers should make it to Jimmy Buffett's Margaritaville. When deciding between here and Disney's Pleasure Island, keep in mind that each is equally entertaining, but CityWalk's $9.49 admission is less than half of Disney's $21 cover.

SeaWorld Orlando

It's the animals who are the stars here. Sleek dolphins perform like gymnastic champions, and orcas sail through the air like featherweight Nijinskys. The world's largest zoological park, SeaWorld is devoted to mammals, birds, fish, and reptiles that live in the oceans and their tributaries. Every attraction is designed to explain the marine world and its vulnerability to human use. Yet the presentations are always enjoyable, and almost always memorable. The highlight is Shamu Stadium, where you can see Shamu and his sidekicks propel their trainers high up into the air.

Discovery Cove

An oasis of artificial reefs, white-sand beaches, tropical fish, dolphins, and exotic birds, this limited-admission park is Orlando's most unusual retreat. The major attraction is one-on-one time with a real, live dolphin, which you get to touch, feed, swim with, and even kiss. At $249 per ticket, this is Orlando's most expensive theme park, but the sting of the price is soothed when you realize the price covers meals, towels, a locker, a mask, a snorkel, a wetsuit or swim vest, and admission to sister parks SeaWorld Orlando or Busch Gardens.

Busch Gardens

Wildlife at its chest-thumping best is the specialty here: Busch Gardens Tampa is one of America's leading legitimate zoos as well as a great theme park. Going eyeball-to-eyeball with a Western Lowland gorilla will please any budding biologist. Plus, there are spectacular roller coasters and other thrill rides: the twisting Kumba; the inverted Montu, whose cars are suspended from the track rather than placed on top of it; the Tanganyika Tidal Wave, whose 55-foot drop is an outrageous way to test zero gravity; and Gwazi, twin racing wooden coasters.

Wet 'n Wild

Kids go nuts when they see the elaborate and ingenious waters slides at Wet 'n Wild, the biggest and best water park in Orlando (and perhaps America). You can calm things down with a peaceful cruise down a quiet river or jazz things up by knee-skiing around a lake or plunging down a 200-foot-long slide. All in all, it rivals a day on the beach.

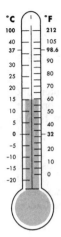

Timing can spell the difference between a good vacation in the theme parks and a great one. Since the Orlando area is an obvious destination for families, the area is at its most crowded during school vacation periods. If you're traveling without youngsters or with just preschoolers, avoid school holidays. Attendance is light (the parks are busy but not packed) from early September until just before Thanksgiving, as well as in early February and early May. The least crowded period of all is from just after the Thanksgiving weekend until the beginning of the Christmas holidays. If you have school-age children, however, the question of when to go is more complicated.

With schoolchildren, it's nice to avoid prime break times, but it's not always possible—or necessary. During certain periods, especially Christmas to New Year's Day, the parks are oppressively crowded, with discouraging lines. However, busy periods bring longer hours and sometimes added entertainment and parades, such as the evening SpectroMagic parade in Disney's Magic Kingdom, that you can't see in quiet seasons.

So if possible, avoid Christmas, March (when most colleges have spring break), the Easter weeks, and mid-June to mid-August, especially around July 4 (it's not fun waiting in lines in the hot sun, anyway). Try to vacation in May or early June (excluding Memorial Day weekend), as soon as the school year ends; in late August, if you must go in summer; or at Thanksgiving, which is not as busy as other holidays. You might even consider taking the kids out of school for a couple of days to avoid the crowds. Consult your children's teachers about the best time. Working with teachers can make missing school easier on your child. Plus, there are ways of making the trip educational. For example, your child could write about the different countries featured at Epcot in lieu of a missed homework assignment.

Finally, before you finalize your travel schedule, call the theme parks you plan to visit in order to find out about any planned maintenance that will close major attractions you want to see.

Climate

Below are average daily maximum and minimum temperatures for Orlando.

🖪 Forecasts **Weather Channel Connection** ☎ 900/932–8437, 95¢ per minute from a Touch-Tone phone.

ORLANDO

Month	°F	°C	Month	°F	°C	Month	°F	°C
Jan.	70F	21C	May	88F	31C	Sept.	88F	31C
	49	9		67	19		74	23
Feb.	72F	22C	June	90F	32C	Oct.	83F	28C
	54	12		74	23		67	19
Mar.	76F	24C	July	90F	32C	Nov.	76F	24C
	56	13		74	23		58	14
Apr.	81F	27C	Aug.	90F	32C	Dec.	70F	21C
	63	17		74	23		52	11

ON THE CALENDAR

WINTER	
December	Early in the month, Orlando's Loch Haven Park stages a Pet Fair & Winterfest (☎ 407/514–2266).
	Christmas in the Park (☎ 407/645–5311) in downtown Winter Park is the first weekend in December. Central Park becomes a brilliant place with the Lighting of the Tiffany, when a collection of Tiffany windows is rolled into the park for viewing. The Bach Festival adult and children's choirs provide holiday music.
	From December 8 to 14, Disney's Wide World of Sports hosts the Pop Warner Little Scholars Super Bowl and the Pop Warner National Cheer & Dance Championships (☎ 407/828–3267). These events bring hundreds of aspiring young football players and cheerleaders to Orlando from across the nation.
	For a Disney Christmas, Walt Disney World gears up by decorating Main Street in perfect Victorian style, complete with a magnificent Christmas tree in Town Square, special afternoon parades, and holiday entertainment.
	On select December evenings before Christmas, Mickey's Very Merry Christmas Party (☎ 407/824–4321) special-ticket event in the Magic Kingdom can really get you into the holiday spirit.
	At Epcot the Candlelight Processional and Holidays Around the World (☎ 407/824–4321) keep things festive.
	Downtown Disney (☎ 407/824–4321) has some terrific holiday shopping, especially at Disney's Days of Christmas shop; nightly tree-lighting festivities; and appearances by the North Pole's most important citizen.
	Universal's Grinchmas (☎ 407/363–8000) takes place from mid-November until December 31, with real snow and Whos aplenty.
	A Norman Rockwell Holiday Showcase at SeaWorld runs from mid-November to after New Year's. The old-time Christmas comes complete with strolling musicians as well as visits from Santa and the Budweiser Clydesdales decked out in their full regalia.
January	The Capitol One Bowl (☎ 407/423–2476) takes place at the Orlando Citrus Bowl on January 1.
	In early January, the Walt Disney World Marathon and Half Marathon (☎ 407/939–7810 ⊕ www.disneyworldsports.com) send runners on a 26.25-mi odyssey (or half an odyssey for those with less stamina) around the World.

The City of Eatonville, the country's oldest incorporated black community, hosts the annual Zora Neale Hurston Festival of the Arts (☎ 800/972–3310 ⊕ www.zoranealehurston.cc).

At the end of January, Scottish Highland Games (☎ 407/426–7268 ⊕ www.flascot.com) are held at Central Winds Park in Winter Springs.

On the third weekend of January, February, and November, Renninger's Antique Extravaganza (☎ 352/383–8303 ⊕ www.renningersflorida.com) draws about 1,500 dealers and about 50,000 shoppers to Mount Dora.

The Rolex 24 (☎ 386/253–7223 ⊕ www.daytonaintlspeedway.com) at Daytona International Speedway usually lands on the last weekend of January or first weekend in February.

February

Kicking off a busy February, the Mount Dora Art Festival (☎ 352/383–2165 ⊕ www.mountdora.com) opens Central Florida's spring art-fair season.

The Renningers/Townsend Battle (☎ 407/422–2956), a Civil War reenactment, takes place in early February.

The Orlando Museum of Art's annual Antiques Show and Sale (☎ 407/672–3838 www.omart.org) is a significant show with more than 30 national dealers.

A tradition since 1935, the Bach Music Festival (☎ 407/646–2182 ⊕ www.bachfestivalflorida.org) usually spans late February to early March.

February also brings the granddaddy of Nascar races, the Daytona 500 (☎ 386/253–7223 ⊕ www.daytonaintlspeedway.com).

Kissimmee's Silver Spurs Rodeo (☎ 407/847–5000 ⊕ www.silverspursrodeo.com) is one of the oldest and largest rodeos in the South, drawing cowboys from all over North America.

Bike Week (⊕ www.daytonachamber.com) in Daytona Beach may be the single biggest annual event in Central Florida. Held from the end of February to early March, the 10-day festival attracts hundreds of thousands of motorcycle enthusiasts from all over the world.

SPRING

March

March means Universal Studios' Mardi Gras (☎ 407/363–8000), one of the events that has given Universal the reputation for hosting the best parties. Actual Mardi Gras floats from New Orleans are shipped to Universal for the huge post–Fat Tuesday celebration.

Pleasure Island Mardi Gras (☎ 407/939–2648) at Downtown Disney is another area alternative to the Big Easy itself.

The **Florida Film Festival** (☎ 407/629–8587 ⊕ www.floridafilmfestival.com) is now in early March. The 10-day festival is a qualifying festival for the Oscars in the category of live-action short films.

One weekend in early March the **Kissimmee Bluegrass Festival** (☎ 813/783–7205) showcases bluegrass bands and gospel music at the Silver Spurs Rodeo Arena.

SeaWorld's All American Barbecue Festival (☎ 407/351–3600) is a four-day, old-fashioned family-barbecue celebration, complete with entertainment from top country artists.

Midmonth, the **Bay Hill Invitational** (☎ 407/876–2888 ⊕ www.bayhillinvitational.bizland.com), a regular PGA Tour stop, is held at Orlando's Bay Hill Club.

The **Winter Park Sidewalk Art Festival** (☎ 407/672–6390 ⊕ www.wpsaf.org) takes over Winter Park in mid-March. One of the most prestigious juried shows in the country, the three-day festival attracts well over 300,000 visitors.

March is also the season for **baseball spring training** all over Florida. **Disney's Wide World of Sports** (☎ 407/939–7810 ⊕ www.disneyworldsports.com) hosts the Atlanta Braves.

April	From early April through early May, the **Orlando-UCF Shakespeare Festival** (☎ 407/423–6905 ⊕ www.shakespearefest.org) pays tribute to the Bard at Orlando's Lake Eola Amphitheater.
	From the end of April until early May, the **Orlando International Fringe Festival** (☎ 407/648–0077 ⊕ www.orlandofringe.com) brings 200 artists and theater troupes to perform in downtown Orlando.
	The **41st Annual Easter Surf Festival** (☎ 888/757–8737 ⊕ www.eastersurffest.com) is a four-day Cocoa Beach event held over Easter weekend and attracting top-ranked surfers.
May	Topiaries of Disney characters and beautiful floral designs grace Epcot during its **International Flower & Garden Festival** (☎ 407/824–4321), which runs from mid-April through the first week in June. There are also how-to seminars and nightly entertainment.
	SeaWorld's **Viva La Musica** (☎ 407/351–3600) is a celebration of Hispanic music, food, and culture; the festival is held in May and again in September.

SUMMER

June	The city of Orlando hosts the **Cultural Heritage Festival** (☎ 407/423–6905) during the first weekend in June.
	Gay Day (⊕ www.gayday.com) activities take place at several major Central Florida attractions, including the Magic Kingdom, SeaWorld Orlando, and Universal Studios Florida. Although they

aren't sanctioned as official park events, attendance has grown each year, and they now attract more than 100,000 gay and lesbian visitors to the area.

Summer Nights (☎ 407/351–9453) kick off at Wet 'n Wild with late park hours, live entertainment, contests, and giveaways.

Late in June and early in July is the Silver Spurs Rodeo (☎ 407/847–5000 ⊕ www.silverspursrodeo.com); there's another in early February.

July	The Fourth of July is a big day in and around Orlando with fireworks everywhere. Independence Day pyrotechnic displays at WDW (☎ 407/939–7814) are legendary; theme-park crowds reach their peak for this holiday. In downtown Orlando, the masses gather around Lake Eola (☎ 407/363–5871) for the city's fireworks. Lakefront Park (☎ 407/932–7223) in Kissimmee has fireworks as part of an old-fashioned celebration that also includes games, rides, entertainment, and food.
	Three days of racing surround Fourth of July celebrations in Daytona, culminating with the Pepsi 400 (☎ 386/253–7223), which usually lands on July 5.
August	The 10th annual Christmas in August Craft Fair (☎ 407/860–0092) is held at the Central Florida Fairgrounds.

FALL

October	Legendary bull riders and cowboys compete at the Silver Spurs Rodeo and RibFest (☎ 407/847–4052 or 407/847–3174) held the first weekend in October in Kissimmee.
	Early in October the Universal Art Show (☎ 407/295–3247) is held on Orlando's Central Florida Fairgrounds.
	Mid-October is the time for the Walt Disney World Golf Classic (☎ 407/824–2250), played on two of Walt Disney World's 18-hole golf courses.
	At the Epcot International Food & Wine Festival (☎ 407/824–4321), early October through mid-November, you'll find delicacies, fine wines, and special entertainment from around the world, with wine-tasting seminars and culinary demonstrations daily.
	The Winter Park Autumn Art Festival (☎ 407/644–8281) takes place at Lake Island Park.
	The prestigious Winter Park Concours d'Elegance (☎ 407/644–8282 ⊕ www.dupontregistry.com) is an exotic car show sanctioned by the Dupont Registry.
	For Halloween there are several October weekends of Halloween Horror Nights at Universal Studios, one of the top events of the year

in Orlando. Universal creative talents exercise the dark side of their imagination, and there are several truly frightening haunted houses placed throughout the park grounds, open only during the special ticketed events.

At the Magic Kingdom, Mickey's Not-So-Scary Halloween Party plays several evenings throughout October and is ideal for younger children.

Shamu's Halloween Spooktacular promises ghoulishly fun shows, trick-or-treat stations, costume parades, and street performers.

November

The American Indian Powwow (☎ 407/295–3247) kicks off the month at the Central Florida Fairgrounds.

Early in the month there's Festival in the Park, an arts-and-crafts show on the shores of downtown Orlando's Lake Eola.

The Space Coast Birding & Wildlife Festival (☎ 321/268–5000 ⊕ www.spacecoastbirding.com) in Titusville occurs in early November. Field trips, seminars, and art exhibits are all organized.

November 8–10 is the Festival of the Masters (☎ 407/934–6743) with 150 top artists exhibiting their creations at Downtown Disney.

Daytime drama fans love Super Soap Weekend (☎ 407/824–4321) at Disney–MGM Studios, where they can schmooze for two days with their fave ABC soap stars and participate in soap-related festivities.

Universal's CityWalk hosts its annual BeerFest (☎ 407/363–8000), complete with tastings of lagers from throughout the world.

PLEASURES & PASTIMES

Water Play Once visitors are land-locked in Central Florida and at least an hour's drive from the nearest ocean, they are often overcome with the instinct to seek an alternative body of water and jump in. No problem. Wet options abound in this land of lakes, water parks, natural springs, fountains, elaborate resort swimming pools, and theme-park attractions designed to spray, splash, and soak all who dare enter. Disney's Typhoon Lagoon can convince you that you're stranded on a tropical island, and Blizzard Beach is awash with faux–ice-water fun. Beyond Disney, Wet 'n Wild and Water Mania are fresh-water attractions with plenty of slides and rafting experiences. There are dozens of natural hot springs in central and north Florida, including Wekiwa Springs in Longwood, about 40 minutes' drive north of Disney, and DeLeon Springs, in DeLand, about an hour northeast of Disney. You can go airboating on Lake Toho in Kissimmee and waterskiing on any number of Orlando-area lakes. If you have only enough time for a theme-park blitz, hit the parks' flume rides for a refreshing dunk, or look for some spray from the nearest dancing fountain.

Thrill Rides You don't have to be an astronaut or leave the atmosphere to experience G-forces during a visit to Florida. Defying gravity is a thrilling way to pass the time on the many roller-coaster slopes and multiple inversions that dot the parks from Universal to SeaWorld to Disney. Islands of Adventure is packed with the highest-tech rides, exposing you to near-collisions on dueling coasters and stomach-churning action on the high-speed Incredible Hulk coaster. All 53-inches-tall coaster enthusiasts are dreaming of the extra inch that's their ticket onto SeaWorld's Kraken, the area's highest coaster at 15 stories. Until that anticipated growth spurt, they can test their mettle on the Magic Kingdom's legendary indoor Space Mountain for twists, turns, and drops in the dark. The most elaborately themed ride is Disney–MGM's Rock 'n' Roller Coaster Starring Aerosmith, another indoor coaster with limolike ride vehicles that hug the curves and blast tunes on a speaker system worth screaming about.

Dining Around the World The world is your oyster, your spring roll, or even your seared maize cake in the wonderful world of Orlando-area dining. Years before Wolfgang Puck came to town with one of his famous cafés and Emeril Lagasse opened his thriving Emeril's Orlando with a bam!, dining options were diverse throughout the metropolitan area. Even the theme parks offer a degree of culinary savvy, whipping up counter-service fare beyond the expected burgers, dogs, and fries and often including vegetarian options. Throughout Orlando, Winter Park, and the Disney and Kissimmee area, food lovers have their pick of African, Thai, Cuban, French, Indian, and other ethnic cuisines. Many local eateries boast impressive wine cellars. Whether your stomach aches for comfort food or your taste buds beg for the freshest ingredients combined with flair, there's a buffet in town to die for or a restaurant serving a little slice of heaven.

Golf for Everyone
Whether you're a serious golfer or just one who likes to putt around, you have options: indulge on a championship course, take in a scenic nine holes, or aim for par at one of many themed minigolf attractions. In the city that Tiger Woods, Arnold Palmer, and many famous PGA pros call home, you must have a member's invitation to play at Arnold Palmer's Bay Hill Golf Resort. But you won't have to pull strings to play on one of Disney's five 18-hole courses or its 9-hole walking course. The picturesque Winter Park Municipal Golf Club is on the National Register of Historic Places and has some of the lowest greens fees in town. Countless resort courses and clubs offer excellent year-round challenges. Colorful minigolf courses with pirate, jungle, and other themes dot the area from International Drive to Lake Buena Vista and Kissimmee. At Disney you can golf with the hippos from *Fantasia* at Disney's Fantasia Gardens minigolf course or even with a "snowman" at the chill-inspiring Winter Summerland course next to, you guessed it, Blizzard Beach.

Bird-Watching
It's a strange and fascinating sight to see an anhinga, also known as a snakebird, dive for its dinner in one of Central Florida's many lakes. The large water bird, which has no oil glands to waterproof its feathers, plunges underwater, its long, snakelike neck breaking the surface here and there until fishing is done. Back on shore, it spreads its wings to dry in the sun. Orlando's abundant wildlife also includes other birds, from the great blue heron and white ibis to hawks and American bald eagles. At the Audubon Center for Birds of Prey in Maitland, you can see injured or orphaned birds such as owls, falcons, eagles, and kites being cared for and rehabilitated. Many are released back into the wild after recuperating. And two terrific aviaries at Disney's Animal Kingdom show off a variety of bird species native to Africa and Asia, including the carmine bee-eater, hottentot teal, hammerkop, the yellow-throated laughing thrush, and timor sparrow finch.

FODOR'S CHOICE

The sights, restaurants, hotels, and other travel experiences on these pages are our editors' top picks—our Fodor's Choices. They're the best of their type in the area covered by the book—not to be missed and always worth your time. In the destination chapters that follow, you will find all the details.

LODGING

$$$$ **Disney's BoardWalk Inn and Villas,** Walt Disney World. This elegant re-creation of an early-1900s beach resort even extends its homage to the swimming pool, where the 200-foot water slide resembles an old wooden roller coaster.

$$$$ **Disney's Grand Floridian Resort & Spa,** Walt Disney World. If it weren't for its modern amenities, you might think you were in one of the great hotels of the 19th century when you visit this Victorian-style charmer, Disney's flagship resort.

$$$$ **Disney's Wilderness Lodge,** Walt Disney World. This majestic hotel surrounded by towering pines is patterned after the Rocky Mountain lodges of the Teddy Roosevelt era.

$$$$ **Disney's Yacht and Beach Club Resort,** Walt Disney World. The refined elegance of Cape Cod makes its way to Disney World via these two similar properties near Epcot and Disney–MGM Studios.

$$$$ **Hyatt Regency Grand Cypress Resort,** near Lake Buena Vista. The word "grand" in the hotel's name is no misrepresentation—within its 2⅓ square mi are a nature preserve, an enormous pool, and a bird-filled, 18-story atrium.

$$$$ **Reunion Resort & Club of Orlando,** near Celebration. The serene landscape and enormous suites and vacation homes of this gated resort will help you relax after eight hours of pounding the theme-park pavement.

$$$$ **Ritz-Carlton Orlando Grande Lakes,** in the I-Drive Area. With an elaborate pool area that rivals Orlando's best water parks, a huge European-style spa, and what seems like miles of marble floors, this opulent resort has something for everyone and then some.

$$$ **Gaylord Palms Resort,** Kissimmee. The 4-acre, glass-enclosed atrium contains environments recalling old St. Augustine, Key West, and the Everglades, all exceptionally detailed.

$$$ **Royal Pacific Resort,** Universal Studios. The South Pacific theme extends to the beautiful, lagoon-style pool and grounds filled with tropical flora.

RESTAURANTS	
$$$$	**Victoria and Albert's,** Walt Disney World. It's expensive, but menu offerings like grilled prime fillet over onion risotto and cabernet jus are well worth the price.
$$$–$$$$	**Jiko,** in the Animal Kingdom Lodge. Excellent, creative, African-inspired cuisine, an exceptional South African wine list, and superb service make this Disney restaurant one not to miss.
$$–$$$$	**Le Coq au Vin,** in Central Orlando. New York critics periodically pay homage to this fine little eatery's French country cooking, especially preparations such as the house namesake dish.
$$–$$$$	**Les Chefs de France,** at Epcot. Very good French food is served daily at this Epcot charmer, which many call Disney's best.
$$–$$$	**Boma,** in the Animal Kingdom Lodge. More than a dozen creative dishes, like spiced chicken and banana leaf–wrapped salmon, lined up on an attractive buffet make this restaurant a casual favorite.
$–$$$	**Seasons 52,** in the Sand Lake Road Area. Healthy, contemporary cuisine is served at this snazzy restaurant and wine bar.
$–$$	**"Once Upon a Time" Character Breakfast at Cinderella's Royal Table,** Magic Kingdom. Getting the reservation requires more strategy than traversing the theme parks, but it's an exceptional opportunity for children infatuated with the Disney princesses.
AFTER HOURS	
	Comedy Warehouse, Downtown Disney Pleasure Island. Talented improv performers deliver quick one-liners and longer sketches— and there's not an off-color joke in the bunch.
	House of Blues, Downtown Disney West Side. In this antidote to Orlando's bubblegum pop slop, real musicians play real music, accompanying real food made by real Southerners.
	Cirque du Soleil–La Nouba, Downtown Disney West Side. Probably the best thing you can do at WDW as a couple or as a family with children over eight. You are likely to alternately hold your breath and exclaim in wonder.
ANIMAL ENCOUNTERS	
	Kilimanjaro Safaris, Disney's Animal Kingdom. You might see more wild animals in authentic-looking habitats on this themed 20-minute jumbo jeep ride than you might if you went all the way to Africa.
	Myombe Reserve, Busch Gardens. The windows inside the quiet caves here bring you a little closer to the secret world of gorillas and chimps.

Pets Ahoy, SeaWorld. Starring pets rescued from local animal shelters, this is a show that's fun for everyone.

Rhino Rally, Busch Gardens. Mixing the kind of rapid-fire jokes you hear on Disney's Jungle Cruise with white-water rapids and an ersatz safari experience makes this attraction a thrill a second.

Shamu Rocks America, SeaWorld. How in the world can an Arctic whale make you proud to be an American? Who knows? At this spectacular, Shamu does his bit for the USA.

FIREWORKS & PARADES

IllumiNations, Epcot. An amazing fireworks show accompanied by lasers, fountains, and original music.

SpectroMagic Parade, Magic Kingdom. This extravaganza makes for a true "When You Wish upon a Star" finale to any day.

RIDES

The Amazing Adventures of Spider-Man, Islands of Adventure. Easily the best ride in town. The huge leaps in technology and the sensory tricks make this worth the wait—and you will, unless you get up bright and early and head straight over.

Soarin', Epcot. Take off on a virtual flight over California's beautiful landscapes.

Summit Plummet, Blizzard Beach. Dangle your legs on Florida's only "ski lift" as you ride to the top of Mt. Gushmore, a 350-foot-long water slide.

Test Track, Epcot. A wild ride on a General Motors proving ground as your car revs up to 60 mph on a hairpin curve.

Twilight Zone Tower of Terror, Disney–MGM Studios. Scare up some nerve and defy gravity inside this deserted hotel. You'd be better off taking the stairs—if there were any to take. As they say, the 13th story is a killer.

ROLLER COASTERS

Big Thunder Mountain Railroad, Magic Kingdom. This old classic coaster isn't too scary; it's just a really good, bumpy, swervy thrill.

Dueling Dragons, Islands of Adventure. With multiple inversions and relative fly-by speeds of up to 120 mph, these floorless coasters can really churn up your stomach.

Dudley Do-Right's Ripsaw Falls, Islands of Adventure. You will get completely soaked on this log flume ride, which has an even scarier dive than at Splash Mountain.

Incredible Hulk Coaster, Islands of Adventure. Many consider this to be Central Florida's best coaster. It's long, it's terrifying, and you go upside down no less than seven times.

Kraken, SeaWorld. Seven inversions and moments of weightlessness attract big crowds to this floorless, 149-foot-tall roller coaster.

Rock 'n' Roller Coaster Starring Aerosmith, Disney–MGM Studios. WDW's high-speed, multiple-inversion roller coaster, with the pumped-up volume of Aerosmith, is a hit.

Sheik Ra, Busch Gardens. Florida's newest, tallest, and fastest roller coster will give you the thrill of your life.

Space Mountain, Magic Kingdom. All you see are stars and blackness as you zip along in the Magic Kingdom's scariest ride.

Splash Mountain, Magic Kingdom. Heading over the final 52½-foot drop here, one of the steepest of any flume ride in existence, makes you feel like Wile E. Coyote about to bite the dust again.

SHOWS, FILMS & TOURS

Animal Planet Live!, Universal Studios. A perfect family show starring a menagerie of animals whose unusually high IQs are surpassed only by their cuteness and cuddle-ability.

Eighth Voyage of Sindbad, Islands of Adventure. Running, jumping, diving, punching—is it another Schwarzenegger action film? No, it's a cool, live stunt show with a love story thrown in.

Festival of the Lion King, Disney's Animal Kingdom. Singers and dancers dressed in fantastic costumes interact with audience members and even invite children into a simple circular parade.

Honey, I Shrunk the Audience, Epcot. This side-splitting, chill-inducing 3-D and special-effects show is a wild sensation that ranks among the best in the World.

The Magic of Disney Animation, Disney–MGM Studios. This tour takes a behind-the-scenes look at the making of Disney's great animated films.

Mickey's PhilharMagic, Magic Kingdom. When Donald borrows Mickey's magical sorcerer's hat, you're launched into a wild 3-D presentation with characters from favorite Disney films.

Tree of Life—It's Tough to Be a Bug!, Disney's Animal Kingdom. Adults and children who don't mind surprises in a dark theater shouldn't miss the music, special effects, and puns found here.

Universal Horror Make-Up Show, Universal Studios. This sometimes gross, often raunchy, but always entertaining demonstration merges the best of stand-up comedy with creepy effects.

GOLF

Osprey Ridge, in Walt Disney World. With its pristine pine groves, this Tom Fazio–designed course is among the most pleasant in WDW, but it's also one of the most challenging, as its tees and greens are as much as 20 feet above the fairways.

Winter Summerland Miniature Golf Course, in Walt Disney World. You putt through sand castles and snow that never melts at this fantasy-driven minigolf course for all levels.

MUSEUMS

Charles Hosmer Morse Museum, in Winter Park. Stunning stained-glass windows, lamps, and watercolors designed by Louis Comfort Tiffany are the draw.

Orlando Science Center, in Downtown Orlando. Science meets entertainment in 12 themed display halls with interactive exhibits that cover health, energy, nature, and the solar system, among other educational subjects.

SPORTS & THE OUTDOORS

Bob's Balloons, in Lake Buena Vista. What better way to end your trip than with a hot-air balloon ride over Disney World and a nearby nature preserve?

Disney's Wide World of Sports Complex, in Walt Disney World. Sign up to play in a multiple-sport challenge or just come to watch a game at this comprehensive sports center.

Grand Cypress Equestrian Center, near Lake Buena Vista. You can take a Western trail ride through the Florida scrub or attend a dressage show at this center at the Hyatt Grand Cypress Resort.

Sky Venture, in the I-Drive area. Here, to get the thrill of sky diving, you don't have to jump out of an airplane or even get very far off the ground.

PARKS & GARDENS

Historic Bok Sanctuary, in Lake Wales. When you're ready for a peaceful retreat from the parks, take a walk along the quiet path through these colorful gardens, shaded by the arching boughs of ancient trees, atop peninsular Florida's highest point.

Wekiwa Springs State Park, in Apopka. Bring a picnic and spend the day canoeing, swimming, and looking for water turtles at this 6,400-acre state park.

SHOPPING

Belz Factory Outlet World, in the I-Drive area. New stores and regular expansions keep the grandfather of all outlet malls on top.

Downtown Disney, in Walt Disney World. Reserve an evening for some lakeside shopping and strolling. You can't beat the World of Disney store for selection and presentation.

Florida Mall, in the I-Drive Area. Central Florida's biggest mall, with all the major chains, plus great restaurants and movie theaters, attracts crowds of international travelers.

Main Street, U.S.A., Magic Kingdom. Shopping at the souvenir and novelty stores along America's most beloved Main Street, with its pastel, gingerbread buildings and cheerful street vendors, is a classic WDW experience.

Mall at Millenia, in the I-Drive Area. This upscale mall is the place to get your Jimmy Choo shoes, Prada bags, and BCBG Max Azria dresses.

World Showcase, Epcot. Each pavilion offers a slew of exotic goods and gifts. You might walk away with a German-made cuckoo clock, a silk Chinese robe, or Canadian maple syrup.

THE SPACE COAST

Kennedy Space Center Visitor Complex, in Titusville. Don't miss the bus tours here—a must if you want a close-up view of the enormous space shuttle.

Merritt Island National Wildlife Refuge, in Titusville. This preserve owes its existence to Kennedy Space Center—it's a buffer zone between civilization and space central. The wildlife and the endless Florida plains make for complete tranquillity.

Ron Jon Surf Shop, in Cocoa Beach. Self-promotion turned this 24-hour surf store into an East Coast icon.

Surfing off Cocoa Beach. The "Small Wave Capital of the World" is a great place to laze on the beach or buy a board and learn how to kick a tube.

SMART TRAVEL TIPS

AIR TRAVEL TO & FROM ORLANDO

All major and most discount airlines, including Southwest, JetBlue, Spirit, Ted, and ATA fly to Orlando International Airport, which serves as a hub for Delta and Air-Tran. You can also fly direct from the United Kingdom or Canada. Qantas and Air New Zealand do not fly into Orlando, so travelers have to fly into Los Angeles and take a domestic flight to Orlando. German travelers will be happy to know that Thomas Cook airlines offers twice-weekly nonstop flights from Frankfurt to Orlando.

BOOKING

When you book, look for nonstop flights and remember that "direct" flights stop at least once. Try to avoid connecting flights, which require a change of plane. To find more booking tips and to check prices and make online flight reservations, log on to www.fodors.com.

CARRIERS

More than 20 scheduled airlines and more than 30 charter firms operate in and out of Orlando International Airport, providing direct service to more than 100 cities in the United States and overseas. Air service to Orlando is constantly being expanded, along with the airport; check OIA's Web site for the most complete list of options.

🛪 Major Airlines **Air Tran** ☎ 800/247-8726 ⊕ www.airtran.com. **Alaska Airlines** ☎ 800/252-7522 ⊕ www.alaskaair.com. **American** ☎ 800/433-7300 ⊕ www.aa.com. **Continental** ☎ 800/523-3273 ⊕ www.continental.com. **Delta** ☎ 800/221-1212 ⊕ www.delta.com. **Northwest/KLM** ☎ 800/225-2525 ⊕ www.nwa.com. **United Airlines** ☎ 800/241-6522 ⊕ www.united.com. **US Airways** ☎ 800/428-4322 ⊕ www.usairways.com.

🛪 Smaller Airlines **ATA** ☎ 800/225-2995 ⊕ www.ata.com. **Frontier** ☎ 800/432-1359 ⊕ www.frontierairlines.com. **JetBlue** ☎ 800/538-2583 ⊕ www.jetblue.com. **Midwest Express** ☎ 800/452-2022 ⊕ www.midwestairlines.com. **Song** ☎ 800/359-7664 ⊕ www.flysong.com. **Southwest** ☎ 800/435-9792 ⊕ www.iflyswa.com. **Spirit** ☎ 800/772-7117 ⊕ www.spiritair.com.

🛪 From the U.K. **American** ☎ 0208/572-5555 in London, 845/7789-789 ⊕ www.aa.com via Miami or

Chicago. **British Airways** ☎ 0845/773-3377 ⊕ www.ba.com. **Continental** ☎ 0800/776-464 ⊕ www.continental.com. **Delta** ☎ 0800/414-767 ⊕ www.delta.com. **United** ☎ 0845/844-4777 ⊕ www.united.com. **Virgin Atlantic** ☎ 01293/747-747 ⊕ www.virgin-atlantic.com.

CHECK-IN & BOARDING

Always **find out your carrier's check-in policy.** Plan to arrive at the airport about two hours before your scheduled departure time for domestic flights and 2½ to 3 hours before international flights. You may need to arrive earlier if you're flying from one of the busier airports or during peak air-traffic times. At Orlando International Airport (OIA), all baggage and vehicles are subject to search while on airport property, so be prepared to cooperate if authorities ask to search your belongings. OIA has been ranked number one in the nation repeatedly by J. D. Powers and Associates for customer satisfaction in terms of security and service. The Orlando–New York route is the busiest for OIA. To avoid delays at airport-security checkpoints, try not to wear any metal. Jewelry, belt and other buckles, steel-toe shoes, barrettes, and underwire bras are among the items that can set off detectors.

Assuming that not everyone with a ticket will show up, airlines routinely overbook planes. When everyone does, airlines ask for volunteers to give up their seats. In return, these volunteers usually get a several-hundred-dollar flight voucher, which can be used toward the purchase of another ticket, and are rebooked on the next flight out. If there are not enough volunteers, the airline must choose who will be denied boarding. The first to get bumped are passengers who checked in late and those flying on discounted tickets, so get to the gate and check in as early as possible, especially during peak periods.

Always **bring a government-issued photo ID.** to the airport; even when it's not required, a passport is best.

CUTTING COSTS

Since Orlando receives a high volume of visitors, a lot of deals are offered via the Internet and airlines. Last-minute flights purchased over the Internet can be very cheap, but generally the least expensive airfares to Orlando must be purchased in advance and are nonrefundable. The cheapest tickets are also for round-trip travel, though airlines generally allow you to change your return date for a fee. It's smart to call a number of airlines and check the Internet; when you are quoted a good price, book it on the spot—the same fare may not be available the next day, or even the next hour. Always check different routings and look into using alternate airports. Also, price off-peak flights, which may be significantly less expensive than others. Travel agents, especially low-fare specialists (⇨ Discounts & Deals), are helpful.

Consolidators are another good source. They buy tickets for scheduled flights at reduced rates from the airlines, then sell them at prices that beat the best fare available directly from the airlines. (Many also offer reduced car-rental and hotel rates.) Sometimes you can even get your money back if you need to return the ticket. Carefully read the fine print detailing penalties for changes and cancellations, purchase the ticket with a credit card, and confirm your consolidator reservation with the airline.

🔳 **Consolidators AirlineConsolidator.com** ☎ 888/468-5385 ⊕ www.airlineconsolidator.com, for international tickets. **Best Fares** ☎ 800/880-1234 or 800/576-8255 ⊕ www.bestfares.com; $59.90 annual membership. **Cheap Tickets** ☎ 800/377-1000 or 800/652-4327 ⊕ www.cheaptickets.com. **Expedia** ☎ 800/397-3342 or 404/728-8787 ⊕ www.expedia.com. **Hotwire** ☎ 866/468-9473 or 920/330-9418 ⊕ www.hotwire.com. **Now Voyager Travel** ✉ 1717 Avenue M, Brooklyn, NY 11230 ☎ 212/459-1616 🖷 718/504-4762 ⊕ www.nowvoyagertravel.com. **Onetravel.com** ⊕ www.onetravel.com. **Orbitz** ☎ 888/656-4546 ⊕ www.orbitz.com. **Priceline.com** ⊕ www.priceline.com. **Travelocity** ☎ 888/709-5983, 877/282-2925 in Canada, 0870/876-3876 in U.K. ⊕ www.travelocity.com.

ENJOYING THE FLIGHT

En route to Orlando, wear lighter clothing and carry a midweight jacket if you're coming from a colder climate. If you're traveling with children, be sure to bring snacks, games, toys, and books to keep them entertained during the flight.

State your seat preference when purchasing your ticket, and then repeat it when you confirm and when you check in. For more legroom, you can request one of the few emergency-aisle seats at check-in, if you're capable of moving obstacles comparable in weight to an airplane exit door (usually between 35 pounds and 60 pounds)—a Federal Aviation Administration requirement of passengers in these seats. Seats behind a bulkhead also offer more legroom, but they don't have underseat storage. Don't sit in the row in front of the emergency aisle or in front of a bulkhead, where seats may not recline.

Ask the airline whether a snack or meal is served on the flight. If you have dietary concerns, request special meals when booking. These can be vegetarian, low-cholesterol, or kosher, for example. It's a good idea to pack some healthful snacks and a small (plastic) bottle of water in your carry-on bag. On long flights, try to maintain a normal routine, to help fight jet lag. At night, get some sleep. By day, eat light meals, drink water (not alcohol), and **move around the cabin** to stretch your legs. For additional jet-lag tips consult *Fodor's FYI: Travel Fit & Healthy* (available at bookstores everywhere).

Most airlines prohibit smoking on all their flights, but some allow smoking on certain routes or certain departures. Ask your carrier about its policy.

FLYING TIMES

Flying time is 2½ hours from New York, 3½ hours from Chicago, and 5 hours from Los Angeles.

HOW TO COMPLAIN

If your baggage goes astray or your flight goes awry, complain right away. Most carriers require that you **file a claim immediately.** The Aviation Consumer Protection Division of the Department of Transportation publishes *Fly-Rights,* which discusses airlines and consumer issues and is available online. You can also find articles and information on mytravelrights.com, the

Web site of the nonprofit Consumer Travel Rights Center.

🔲 Airline Complaints **Aviation Consumer Protection Division** ✉ U.S. Department of Transportation, Office of Aviation Enforcement and Proceedings, C-75, Room 4107, 400 7th St. SW, Washington, DC 20590 ☎ 202/366-2220 ⊕ airconsumer.ost.dot.gov. **Federal Aviation Administration Consumer Hotline** ✉ For inquiries: FAA, 800 Independence Ave. SW, Washington, DC 20591 ☎ 800/322-7873 ⊕ www.faa.gov.

RECONFIRMING

Check the status of your flight before you leave for the airport. You can do this on your carrier's Web site, by linking to a flight-status checker (many Web booking services offer these), or by calling your carrier or travel agent. Always confirm international flights at least 72 hours ahead of the scheduled departure time.

AIRPORTS & TRANSFERS

The Orlando airport is relatively easy to navigate thanks to excellent signs. The airport is divided into terminals A and B. Monorails shuttle you from gate areas to the core area, where you'll find baggage claim. If you land in the A section, go to the A baggage claim area, and if you land in the B section, go to the B baggage claim area. The complex is southeast of Orlando and northeast of Walt Disney World.

🔲 Airport Information **Orlando International Airport (MCO)** ☎ 407/825-2001 ⊕ www. orlandoairports.net. **Orlando Executive Airport (ORL)** ☎ 407/894-9831.

AIRPORT TRANSFERS

Taxis take only a half hour to get from the airport to hotels in the WDW area; they charge about $30 plus tip to the International Drive area, about $10 more to the U.S. 192 area. Depending on the number of people in your party, this may cost less than paying by the head for an airport shuttle. Mears Transportation Group meets you at the gate, helps with the luggage, and whisks you away in either an 11-passenger van, a town car, or a limo. Vans run to Walt Disney World and along U.S. 192 every 30 minutes; prices range from $17 one-way for adults ($13 for children 4–11) to $29 round-trip for adults

($21 children 4–11). Limo rates run $44–$70 for a town car that accommodates three or four to $125 for a stretch limo that seats six. Town & Country Transportation charges $35–$55 one-way for up to seven people.

If you're staying at a Disney hotel, make arrangements to use Disney's free Magical Express service, which includes shuttle transportation to and from the airport, luggage delivery, and airline check-in at the hotel. The service was introduced for the Happiest Celebration on Earth event beginning May 2005 and ending in September 2006. If you're traveling after the event ends, be sure to call and find out if the service is still being offered, and if so, if it's still free.

Public buses, operated by Lynx transportation authority, operate between the airport and the main bus terminal in downtown Orlando. The cost is $1.25.

🚌 Buses & Shuttles **Disney's Magical Express** for Disney hotel guests only ☎ 407/827–6777 **Lynx** ✉ 1200 W. South St., Orlando ☎ 407/841–8240 or 800/344–5969 ⊕ www.golynx.com. **Mears Transportation Group** ☎ 407/423–5566 ⊕ www. mearstransportation.com.

🚕 Taxis & Limos **Ace Metro Cab** ☎ 407/855–1111. **Town & Country Transportation** ☎ 407/828–3035. **Yellow Cab Co.** ☎ 407/699–9999.

BUSINESS HOURS

THEME PARKS

The major area theme parks, including those in Walt Disney World, are open 365 days a year. Opening times vary but generally hover around 9 AM. Certain attractions within the parks may not open until 10 or 11 AM, however, and parks usually observe shorter hours during the off-seasons in January, February, April, May, September, and October. In summer and on school holidays, most parks stay open until 10 or 11 PM; in the off-season they close between 6 and 7 PM. You can check exact opening and closing times by calling the parks directly or checking their Web sites.

SHOPS

Malls and shopping centers are open Monday through Saturday from 10 AM to 9 PM, and Sunday from noon to 6 PM. The shops at Downtown Disney and CityWalk stay open as late as 11 PM in summer and during holidays, while the boutiques on trendy Park Avenue in Winter Park generally close around 6 PM. Convenience stores and several grocery store chains are open 24 hours.

BUS TRAVEL TO & FROM ORLANDO

Greyhound is the only major bus line providing service to the Orlando area. Round-trip tickets from other Florida cities, such as Jacksonville, start at about $50, and traveling time is 2½ hours, longer than the same trip by car. The Greyhound terminal is in an industrial area of Orlando, outside of downtown proper. There is no shuttle service available from the terminal to area attractions, but you can call for a taxi or wait at the taxi stand outside the terminal.

🚌 Bus Information **Greyhound Bus Lines of Orlando** ✉ 555 N. John Young Pkwy. ☎ 800/231–2222.

BUS TRAVEL WITHIN ORLANDO

Public buses run by Lynx transportation authority can get you around the International Drive area, Kissimmee, and Orlando proper. To find out which bus to take, ask the information desk at your hotel or contact Lynx customer service. Lymmo, operated by Lynx, is a free bus service that circulates through downtown Orlando daily until 10 PM (until midnight on Friday and Saturday).

Many hotels run shuttles for guests, although these buses may not run to the places you want to see on the days or at the times you prefer, whether that's back to your hotel at midday or out to the theme parks in late afternoon. Some buses also pick up or drop off guests at several hotels, adding to your ride time and delaying your arrival.

Your hotel may have contracted service with Mears Transportation, or the concierge may be able to call a Mears shuttle for you. During certain times of the year, you can get a good deal on special excursion fares that include both transportation and admission to Busch Gardens, which is more than a half hour's drive away. Sometimes you can negotiate a room rate that includes free transportation, even when it's not routinely available.

If you're staying on International Drive or Universal Boulevard between Vineland Avenue and the Florida Turnpike, and you plan to spend a day visiting just I-Drive attractions, then consider using the I-Ride Trolley to get around. For 75¢ the trolley takes you to SeaWorld, Wet 'n Wild, the Mercado, the Orange County Convention Center, Orlando Premium Outlets, and Belz Factory Outlet stores, and it will put you within walking distance of dozens of other attractions, shops, and restaurants.

FARES & SCHEDULES

One-way public bus fare is $1.25, and exact change in coins or a dollar bill is required. Transfers and bus travel in downtown Orlando are free. Daily ($3) and weekly ($10) bus passes let you ride as many times as you want while the pass is valid. A one-way fare on a Mears bus between major hotel areas and the Disney parks usually costs $8–$10 per adult, and a couple of dollars less for children ages 4–11. I-Ride trolleys run daily 8 AM–10:30 PM. Exact change is necessary for the adult fare (75¢); children under 12 ride free. Passes let you ride as many times as you want for a set price: $2 for one day, $3 for three days, $5 for five days, and $7 for one week.

🚌 Between Hotels & Attractions **Lynx Information Office** ✉ 1200 W. South St., Orlando ☎ 407/841-8240 or 800/344-5969 (LYNX) ⊕ www.golynx.com. **Mears Transportation Group** ☎ 407/423-5566 ⊕ www.mearstransportation.com. **I-Ride Trolley** ☎ 407/248-9590 or 866/243-7483 ⊕ www.iridetrolley.com.

CAMERAS & PHOTOGRAPHY

Central Florida presents lots of opportunities for a great photo, from shots of the family hugging Disney characters to panoramas of beautifully manicured lakeside parks to up-close snaps of gators and crocs. Be sure to keep the sun behind you when you compose a photo.

The *Kodak Guide to Shooting Great Travel Pictures* (available at bookstores everywhere) is loaded with tips.

🎞 Photo Help **Kodak Information Center** ☎ 800/242-2424 ⊕ www.kodak.com.

EQUIPMENT PRECAUTIONS

Don't pack film or equipment in checked luggage, where it is much more susceptible to damage. X-ray machines used to view checked luggage are extremely powerful and therefore likely to ruin your film. Try to ask for hand inspection of film, which becomes clouded after repeated exposure to airport X-ray machines, and keep videotapes and computer disks away from metal detectors. Always keep film, tape, and computer disks out of the sun. Carry an extra supply of batteries, and be prepared to turn on your camera, camcorder, or laptop to prove to airport security personnel that the device is real.

CAR RENTAL

If you want to visit major theme parks outside Walt Disney World, or move from park to resort to park on Disney property in a single day, or stay in a Disney resort that's served only by buses, or venture off the beaten track, or eat where most tourists don't, **rent a car.** Rates here are among the lowest in the United States, but vary seasonally. They can begin as low as $30 a day and $149 a week for an economy car with air-conditioning, automatic transmission, and unlimited mileage. This does not include tax on car rentals, which is 6.5%. Avis and Budget have car lots on airport property, a short walk from baggage claim. Bus transportation to other car rentals is usually fast and efficient.

🚗 Major Agencies **Alamo** ☎ 800/327-9633 ⊕ www.alamo.com. **Avis** ☎ 800/331-1212, 800/879-2847 or 800/272-5871 in Canada, 0870/606-0100 in U.K., 02/9353-9000 in Australia, 09/526-2847 in New Zealand ⊕ www.avis.com. **Budget** ☎ 800/527-0700, 0870/156-5656 in U.K. ⊕ www.budget.com. **Dollar** ☎ 800/800-4000, 0800/085-4578 in U.K. ⊕ www.dollar.com. **Hertz** ☎ 800/654-3131, 800/263-0600 in Canada, 0870/844-8844 in U.K., 02/9669-2444 in Australia, 09/256-8690 in New Zealand ⊕ www.hertz.com. **National Car Rental** ☎ 800/227-7368, 0870/600-6666 in the U.K. ⊕ www.nationalcar.com.

CUTTING COSTS

For a good deal, book through a travel agent who will shop around. Also, price local car-rental companies—whose prices may be lower still, although their service and maintenance may not be as good as those of major rental agencies—and research rates on the Internet. Consolidators that specialize in air travel can offer good rates on cars as well (⇨ Air Travel). Remember to ask about required deposits, cancellation penalties, and drop-off charges if you're planning to pick up the car in one city and leave it in another. If you're traveling during a holiday period, also make sure that a confirmed reservation guarantees you a car.

🔁 **Local Agencies Prestige Car Rental** ☎ 407/932-1735. **Carl's Rent A Van** ☎ 407/856-8866. **All Save Auto Rental** ☎ 888/598-7368 ⊕ www.allsaveauto.com. **Choice Auto Rental** ☎ 407/251-7222 ⊕ www.choicerentalcars.com.

INSURANCE

When driving a rented car you are generally responsible for any damage to or loss of the vehicle. You also may be liable for any property damage or personal injury that you may cause while driving. Before you rent, see what coverage you already have under the terms of your personal auto-insurance policy and credit cards.

For about $9 to $25 a day, rental companies sell protection, known as a collision- or loss-damage waiver (CDW or LDW), that eliminates your liability for damage to the car; it's always optional and should never be automatically added to your bill. In most states you don't need a CDW if you have personal auto insurance or other liability insurance. However, **make sure you have enough coverage to pay for the car.** If you do not have auto insurance or an umbrella policy that covers damage to third parties, purchasing liability insurance and a CDW or LDW is highly recommended.

REQUIREMENTS & RESTRICTIONS

In Florida, some agencies require that you be at least 21 to rent a car. Others require that you be 25.

SURCHARGES

Before you pick up a car in one city and leave it in another, ask about drop-off charges or one-way service fees, which can be substantial. Also inquire about early-return policies; some rental agencies charge extra if you return the car before the time specified in your contract, while others give you a refund for the days not used. To avoid a hefty refueling fee, fill the tank just before you turn in the car, but be aware that gas stations near the rental outlet may overcharge. It's almost never a deal to buy the tank of gas that's in the car when you rent it; the understanding is that you'll return it empty, but some fuel usually remains. Surcharges may apply if you're under 25 or if you take the car outside the area approved by the rental agency. You'll pay extra for child seats (about $8 a day), which are compulsory for children under five, and usually for additional drivers (up to $25 a day, depending on location).

CAR TRAVEL

The Beeline Expressway (Route 528) is the best way to get to the International Drive area and Walt Disney World from the Orlando International Airport, though you should expect to pay about $1.50 in tolls. Depending on the location of your hotel, follow the expressway west to International Drive, and either exit at SeaWorld for the International Drive area or stay on the Beeline to I–4 and head west for Walt Disney World and U.S. 192/Kissimmee or east for Universal Studios and downtown Orlando. Call your hotel for the best route.

I–4 is the main artery in Central Florida, linking the Gulf coast in Tampa to the Atlantic coast in Daytona Beach. Although I–4 is an east–west highway, it actually follows a north–south track through the Orlando area. So **think north when I–4 signs say east and think south when the signs say west.**

In 2002 the Florida Department of Transportation changed the exit numbers of several major interstates, including I–4, which intersects Orlando and Walt Disney World. The WDW exits are 64B, 65, 67, and 68, but older maps may still cite the old exits, 25, 24D, 26D, and 27, respectively.

Two other main roads you're likely to use are International Drive, also known as I-Drive, and U.S. 192, sometimes called the Spacecoast Parkway or Irlo Bronson Memorial Highway. You can get onto International Drive from I–4 Exits 72 (formerly

28), 74A (formerly 29), and 75B (formerly 30B). U.S. 192 cuts across I–4 at Exits 64A (formerly 25A) and 64B (formerly 25B).

EMERGENCY SERVICES

If you have a cell phone, dialing *347 (*FHP) will get you the Florida Highway Patrol. Most Florida highways are also patrolled by Road Rangers, a free roadside service that helps stranded motorists with minor problems and can call for a tow truck when there are bigger problems. Disney's Car Care Center near the Magic Kingdom is a full-service operation that will provide most emergency services, except towing, while it is open (weekdays 7 AM–6 PM, Saturday 7:30 AM–4 PM). On Disney property you can flag a security guard any day until 10 PM for help with minor emergencies, such as a flat tire, dead battery, empty gas tank, or towing.

🚗 **Florida Highway Patrol** ☎ *347. **Walt Disney World Car Care Center** ☎ 407/824-0976.

PARKING

For information on parking at the theme parks, *see* Parking *in* the A to Z sections of the individual parks *in* chapters 1, 2, and 3.

Parking in downtown Orlando is available both on the street and in garages. Meters on the street take nickels, dimes, and quarters, and parking rules are strictly enforced. Fines start at $15 and can go as high as $45. Meter debit cards are available for purchase at city hall. There are several large parking garages downtown. Most charge 50¢ for the first half hour and $1 for each additional hour. Overnight parking is available only at the Central Boulevard garage and the Market Street and Library garage, both of which offer a flat rate of $4 to park 5 PM–5:30 AM. Private parking is widely available at properties on I-Drive and in Kissimmee and outlying towns.

RULES OF THE ROAD

All front-seat passengers are required to wear seat belts. All children under 4 years old must be in approved child-safety seats. Children older than 4 must wear a seat belt. Florida's Alcohol/Controlled Substance DUI Law is one of the toughest in the United States. A blood alcohol level of .08 or higher can have serious repercussions even for the first-time offender.

In Florida, you may turn right at a red light after stopping, unless otherwise posted. When in doubt, wait for the green. Be alert for one-way streets, "no left turn" intersections, and blocks closed to car traffic. Watch for middle lanes with painted arrows that point left. These are turn lanes. They are to help you make a left turn without disrupting the flow of traffic behind you. Turn your blinker on, pull into this lane, and come to a stop, if necessary, before making a left turn. Never use this lane as a passing lane.

Expect heavy traffic during rush hours, which are on weekdays 6–10 AM and 4–7 PM. To encourage carpooling, some freeways have special lanes for so-called high-occupancy vehicles (HOV)—cars carrying more than one passenger. The use of radar detectors is legal in Florida and its neighboring states, Alabama and Georgia. Although it is legal to talk on your cell phone while driving in Florida, it is not recommended. Dial *511 on a cell phone to hear an I–4 traffic advisory.

CHILDREN IN ORLANDO

Are your children old enough for a Central Florida vacation? There's no question that at 10, or even 8 or 9, many children have the maturity to understand and enjoy the information and entertainment at the theme parks.

Younger children are another matter. It's not that they won't enjoy it, because all the theme parks get high marks from young travelers. But you'll be spending a lot of money and probably battling huge crowds to see the place yourself, and you and your children may have totally different ideas about what's fun. While you're envisioning the Hulk, Twilight Zone Tower of Terror, and Space Mountain, your youngsters may want to ride Dumbo 100 times, splash in the fountains outside Ariel's Grotto, and collect signatures from people dressed up in funny outfits. And they may well be terrified by the very attractions that adults typically travel to the Orlando area to experience. Although the Baby Swap system works well, allowing you and your partner to take turns experiencing an attraction, you both end up riding with total strangers.

Consider how you feel about forcing your kids to wait repeatedly in the hot Florida sun, or making them go on rides or see shows that are too loud or scary for them. Don't forget cost: do you really want to spend $50 a day for your child to do this? Think about how having young children along slows you down, and you may decide to hold off until your kids are older.

The alternative, of course, is to bite the bullet and go anyway. But **create an itinerary that builds in your children's interests as well as your own,** understanding that they will delight in details that you might overlook. You might find it helpful to consult www.disneyworld.com, where attractions are labeled by age group. Allow yourself to appreciate the park from your children's point of view, and be flexible. If the line for Jungle Cruise is 40 minutes, just skip it for the time being. It might be shorter a few hours later. This strategy may result in more walking back and forth, but it's probably worth it to keep young children out of long, tiresome lines. And **plan for plenty of family time away from the theme parks.** For a night or two, step out for the fireworks or some other after-dark thrills in or away from the theme parks. Give yourself more time than you think you need, and buy park-hopper tickets so that you can always go back and see what you've missed another day. *Fodor's Walt Disney World with Kids* (available in bookstores everywhere) can help you plan your days together.

Crowds are often a problem and can overwhelm preschoolers. Do what you can to avoid the times of the year that are likely to be the most crowded (during school holidays, for example) and then plan your itinerary around the days of the week and times of day when the parks and attractions are the least busy. For more information on the busiest and least-crowded times to visit the theme parks, *see* the When to Go section at the front of the book, and the Tip Sheets in chapters 1, 2, and 3.

So that you won't have to concern yourself with lugging items such as strollers, cribs, high chairs, and backpack carriers, ask your hotel whether what you need can be provided. If it can't, consider calling A Baby's Best Friend before you leave, or visit their Web site, which now allows you to reserve online. The company's employees will deliver high-quality equipment to your accommodations prior to your arrival and pick them up after your departure.

If you are renting a car, don't forget to arrange for a car seat when you reserve. For general advice about traveling with children, consult *Fodor's FYI: Travel with Your Baby* (available in bookstores everywhere).

🔲 Rental Baby Equipment **A Baby's Best Friend** ☎ 407/891-2241 or 888/461-2229 🌐 www.abbf.com.

BABYSITTING

Disney's Kid's Night Out program provides infant care and in-room babysitting. Fees start at $14 an hour for one child, and increase by $2.50 for each additional child. There is a four-hour minimum, plus a transportation fee for the sitter to travel to your hotel room. When you make a reservation, you must provide a credit-card number. There is a 24-hour cancellation policy; if you cancel with less than 24 hours' notice, your credit card is charged the four-hour fee ($56).

🔲 Agencies **Kid's Night Out** ☎ 407/828-0920 or 800/696-8105 🌐 www.kidsniteout.com.

BABY SWAP

Parents with small children under the height limit for major attractions have to take turns waiting in the long lines, right? Wrong. In what's unofficially known as the Baby Swap, both of you queue up, and when it's your turn to board, one stays with the youngsters until the other returns; the waiting partner then rides without waiting again. Universal Studios calls it a Baby Exchange and has areas set aside for it at most rides.

CHARACTER MEALS

At special breakfasts, brunches, lunches, and dinners in many Walt Disney World restaurants, Mickey, Donald, Goofy, Chip 'n' Dale, Cinderella, and other favorite characters sign autographs and pose for snapshots. Universal's Islands of Adventure has a character luncheon, so your children can enjoy pizza or chicken fingers with their favorite Seuss characters. Talk with your children to find out which characters they most want to see; then call the Disney dining reservations line and speak with the representative about what's available.

Reservations are not always necessary, but these hugging-and-feeding frenzies are wildly popular, so **show up early.** It's a good idea to have your character meal near the end of your visit, when your little ones will be used to seeing these large and sometimes frightening figures; they're also a good way to spend the morning on the day you check out.

DINING

Many Central Florida restaurants have children's menus. And franchised fast-food eateries abound, providing that reassuring taste of home. The McDonald's on International Drive has an elaborate multilevel playground that seems almost bigger than the restaurant. The Rainforest Café chain, with its rainstorms and jungle details, is another child-pleaser. Stagestruck children like the belly dancer in the Marrakesh Restaurant, in Morocco in Epcot's World Showcase. Whispering Canyon Café in Disney's Wilderness Lodge and 'Ohana in the Polynesian have what it takes to please both parents and their offspring.

EDUCATIONAL PROGRAMS

For any behind-the-scenes tours and programs, be sure to **reserve ahead.**

Many of Walt Disney World's backstage tours are good for children. For full descriptions of each, *see* Guided Tours *in* the A to Z sections of the individual theme parks *in* chapter 1. Two favorites are "Dolphins In Depth" at Epcot, costing $150 for three-and-a-half hours, and Disney's "Family Magic Tour" at the Magic Kingdom, costing $25 for two hours.

SeaWorld's Behind the Scenes Tours offer an up-close look at rescue procedures and caring for killer whales. One-hour tours are $15 for adults, $12 for children ages 3–9, in addition to park admission price. The

seven-hour "Trainer For A Day" program costs $399. There are also more than 16 year-round adventure camps, from half-day to week-long sessions (prices start at $50). The bring-your-own-sleeping-bag "Education Sleepovers" provide kids with the chance to sleep near the sharks or penguins.

Busch Gardens' Multiday Zoo Camps keep children learning here from June through October. There's a different program for each age group, from 3rd grade through 12th, and each program lasts a week (prices start at around $200 per session). Busch Gardens also offers field study trips for kids, which combine a short classroom study with a safari outing. The trips last about an hour an a half and cost $20 above and beyond park admission. 🄙 **Walt Disney World Resort** ☎ 407/824-4321 ⊕ www.disney.com. **SeaWorld** ☎ 407/363-2380 or 800/406-2244 ⊕ www.seaworld.org. **Busch Gardens** ☎ 813/987-5555 ⊕ www.buschgardens.com.

FLYING

If your children are two or older, ask about children's airfares. As a general rule, infants under two not occupying a seat fly at greatly reduced fares or even for free. But if you want to guarantee a seat for an infant, you have to pay full fare. Consider off-peak days and times; most airlines will grant an infant a seat without a ticket if there are available seats. When booking, confirm carry-on allowances if you're traveling with infants. In general, for babies charged 10% to 50% of the adult fare you are allowed one carry-on bag and a collapsible stroller; if the flight is full, the stroller may have to be checked or you may be limited to less.

Experts agree that it's a good idea to use safety seats aloft for children weighing less than 40 pounds. Airlines set their own policies: if you use a safety seat, U.S. carriers usually require that the child be ticketed, even if he or she is young enough to ride free, because the seats must be strapped into regular seats. And even if you pay the full adult fare for the seat, it may be worth it, especially on longer trips. Do **check your airline's policy about using safety seats during takeoff and landing.** Safety seats are not allowed everywhere in the plane, so get your seat assignments as early as possible.

When reserving, request children's meals or a freestanding bassinet (not available at all airlines) if you need them. But note that bulkhead seats, where you must sit to use the bassinet, may lack an overhead bin or storage space on the floor.

LODGING

Walt Disney World has strong children's facilities and programs at the BoardWalk, Contemporary, Dolphin, Grand Floridian, Polynesian, Swan, Wilderness Lodge, and Yacht and Beach Club resorts. The Polynesian Resort's Neverland Club has an enchanting Peter Pan–theme clubhouse and youngsters-only dinner show. Parents also rave about the Sand Castle Club at the Yacht and Beach Club resorts. The Board-Walk's child-care facility, Harbor Club, provides late-afternoon and evening babysitting.

Many hotels have supervised children's programs with trained counselors and planned activities as well as attractive facilities; some even have mascots. Standouts are the Hyatt Regency Grand Cypress, near Downtown Disney, and the Camp Holiday programs at the Holiday Inn Sun-Spree Resort Lake Buena Vista and Holiday Inn Hotel & Suites Main Gate East.

The Hilton, near Downtown Disney's Marketplace, has the Vacation Station, a hotel within a hotel for the little ones. East of International Drive, the connected JW Marriott and Ritz-Carlton Grand Lakes resorts have rooms with adjoining kids' suites, complete with miniature furniture and toys. Additionally, the JW Marriott has a 24,000-square-foot "lazy river" pool, and the Ritz-Carlton has a Kids Club with a play area and daily scheduled activities.

Nickelodeon Family Suites by Holiday Inn, in Lake Buena Vista, offers suites with separate kid-friendly bedrooms decorated with images of cartoon characters. Plus, there are scheduled breakfasts and shows featuring Nick characters.

STROLLER RENTALS

Stroller rentals are available in theme parks and cost $8 to $15 a day depending on the size of the stroller you want. Renting a stroller means that you have one less thing to struggle with while traveling. Theme-park strollers are lightweight and highly maneuverable. Bringing your own stroller does have its advantages, though. You save money on rentals, and you have a stroller in places where rentals aren't available, such as in downtown Orlando.

If you do rent a stroller, there is always the possibility that it will be taken. Although it is tempting, **don't leave packages in your stroller.** Experienced park goers tape a large card with their name to the stroller; now many of the parks provide the tags.

In addition, you might want to attach some small personal item to mark yours, such as a bandanna, a T-shirt, or even a clear plastic bag with diapers inside; the theory is that people who wouldn't think twice about taking theme-park property that they will subsequently return hesitate to make off with something that belongs to a fellow parent. If your stroller does disappear, you can easily pick up a replacement; ask any park staffer for the nearest location. If you wish to park-hop on the same day there's no need to rent another stroller. Simply turn the old one in when leaving the first park and get a new one upon entrance to the next park. Your deposit receipt is good all day at all Disney theme parks.

WHAT TO BRING

A backpack is a good idea. Sunscreen, sunglasses, and a hat are recommended year-round, as well as a water bottle that you can refill at drinking fountains, and an assortment of small, uncrushable snacks to tide you over between meals (or even as meals themselves). Peanut-butter sandwiches, for instance, travel well, though kids may miss the jelly. Some parents bring frozen juice boxes. They take a few hours to thaw, so kids have chilled juice all morning. A bathing suit or a change of clothes can also be helpful, since youngsters like to splash around in theme-park fountains. Clean, dry socks are incredibly soothing to sore feet in the middle of the day. A pen or Sharpie marker is essential for gathering those precious character autographs.

CONCIERGES

Concierges, found in many hotels, can help you with theater tickets and dinner reservations: a good one with connections may be able to get you seats for a hot show or prime-time dinner reservations at the restaurant of the moment. You can also turn to your hotel's concierge for help with travel arrangements, sightseeing plans, services ranging from aromatherapy to zipper repair, and emergencies. **Always tip** a concierge who has been of assistance (⇨ Tipping).

CONSUMER PROTECTION

Whether you're shopping for gifts or purchasing travel services, **pay with a major credit card** whenever possible, so you can cancel payment or get reimbursed if there's a problem (and you can provide documentation). If you're doing business with a particular company for the first time, contact your local Better Business Bureau and the attorney general's offices in your state and (for U.S. businesses) the company's home state as well. Have any complaints been filed? Finally, if you're buying a package or tour, always consider travel insurance that includes default coverage (⇨ Insurance).

🄵 **BBBs Council of Better Business Bureaus** ✉ 4200 Wilson Blvd., Suite 800, Arlington, VA 22203 ☎ 703/276-0100 🖷 703/525-8277 ⊕ www.bbb.org.

BBB of Central Florida, Inc. ✉ 151 Wymore Rd., Suite 100, Altamonte Springs, 32714 ☎ 407/621-3300 🖷 407/786-2625 ⊕ www.orlando.bbb.org.

CRUISE TRAVEL

With Disney's reach extending all the way to the high seas on two cruise ships, the *Disney Magic* and the *Disney Wonder,* there's an alternative vacation for "sail" beyond the Orlando kingdom. Disney Cruise Line offers several excursions from Port Canaveral, Florida, to eastern and western Caribbean destinations, with stops at a nice mix of ports and at Disney's own private island, Castaway Cay.

Aboard the *Magic,* Mickey's silhouette is on the funnels and Goofy clings to the stern. Styled like a classic liner, the ship sails on a seven-night eastern Caribbean cruise, stopping at St. Maarten and St. Thomas with excursions to St. John and Castaway Cay. On alternate weeks, the *Magic* follows a western Caribbean itinerary to ports of call in Key West, Grand Cayman, and Cozumel, with the grand finish at Castaway Cay.

The art nouveau–inspired *Wonder* travels on three- or four-night Bahamian cruises, popular with first-time cruisers. Plus, you can combine this ocean getaway with a stay at Walt Disney World Resort for a seven-night seamless land-and-sea vacation. You check in just once: your room key at your Disney resort hotel becomes both your boarding pass at Disney's terminal at Port Canaveral and the key to your stateroom. The *Wonder* calls at Nassau en route to Castaway Cay, where there are separate beaches for adults, families, and teens, as well as good snorkeling. Parents: enjoy some private time on the island while your well-tended kids forget you're even around. Then share some family time on the beach or in the water. Seven-night sea cruises start at $829 for adults, $399 for children age 3 to 12, and $139 for kids under 3; seven-night land-and-sea packages are $829 for adults, $399 for children age 3 to 12, and $139 for kids under 3. Call ☎ 888/325-2500 or book online at ⊕ www.disneycruise.com.

On both ships, several areas are set aside for just the grown-ups, including one of the three pools. Poolside games, wine tastings, and other activities are on the schedule daily. The ship's spa is a don't-miss for those who need some on-board pampering, but book as soon as you've checked in or risk missing the opportunity.

On both the *Magic* and the *Wonder,* there's nearly an entire deck reserved for kids only. The well-run Oceaneer Club (both ships) is part of the cruise package, providing nonstop activities for kids ages 3 to 7, and giving parents the opportunity to enjoy some R&R. Kids ages 8 to 12 love the high-tech, game-filled Oceaneer Lab, and teens can chill out at the Stack, for music, big-screen TV, and meeting new friends. Babysitting is available at extra charge for children under 3 at Flounder's Reef Nursery.

Disney on-board dining is an experience in itself. At Animator's Palate (both ships), the color scheme goes from black-and-white to Technicolor as the meal progresses. Dining is slightly more formal at Lumiere's (Magic) and Triton's (Wonder). And the mood is casual-festive at the Caribbean-themed Parrot Cay (both ships). Disney schedules you for a different restaurant each night, so you sample all three. Your assigned wait staff travels with you. The intimate Palo (both ships), with its sweeping ocean view from one of the ship's highest points, is for adults only (reserve early as it's a hot ticket). Character breakfasts, champagne brunch, and high tea are options aboard the Magic. Tea with Wendy Darling of Peter Pan is offered to families and children. There's also a captain's gala cocktail party and dinner on the seven-night cruise.

Each night, lavish shows entertain families with tales of princesses, heroes, and pirates, with eye-popping special effects. "The Golden Mickeys" show is a high-tech salute to the animation of Walt Disney in the form of a Hollywood-style award ceremony, while "Who Wants to Be a Mouseketeer?" is a take-off of the TV show "Who Wants to Be a Millionaire." Each ship has a cinema showing Disney classics and first-run films, and there are nightclubs for grown-ups.

To learn how to plan, choose, and book a cruise-ship voyage, consult *Fodor's FYI: Plan & Enjoy Your Cruise* (available in bookstores everywhere).

🚢 **Cruise Line Disney Cruise Line** ☎ 800/951-3532 ⊕ www.disneycruise.com.

CUSTOMS & DUTIES

IN AUSTRALIA

Australian residents who are 18 or older may bring home A$900 worth of souvenirs and gifts (including jewelry), 250 cigarettes or 250 grams of cigars or other tobacco products, and 2.25 liters of alcohol (including wine, beer, and spirits). Residents under 18 may bring back A$450 worth of goods. If any of these individual allowances are exceeded, you must pay duty for the entire amount (of the group of products in which the allowance was exceeded). Members of the same family traveling together may pool their allowances. Prohibited items include meat products. Seeds, plants, and fruits need to be declared upon arrival.

🛂 **Australian Customs Service** ✍ Locked Bag 3000, Sydney International Airport, Sydney, NSW 2020 ☎ 02/6275-6666 or 1300/363263, 02/9364-7222 or 1800/020-504 quarantine-inquiry line ☎ 02/8339-6714 ⊕ www.customs.gov.au.

IN CANADA

Canadian residents who have been out of Canada for at least seven days may bring in C$750 worth of goods duty-free. If you've been away fewer than seven days but more than 48 hours, the duty-free allowance drops to C$200. If your trip lasts 24 to 48 hours, the allowance is C$50 if the goods are worth more than C$50, you must pay full duty on all of the goods. You may not pool allowances with family members. Goods claimed under the C$750 exemption may follow you by mail; those claimed under the lesser exemptions must accompany you. Alcohol and tobacco products may be included in the seven-day and 48-hour exemptions but not in the 24-hour exemption. If you meet the age requirements of the province or territory through which you reenter Canada, you may bring in, duty-free, 1.5 liters of wine *or* 1.14 liters (40 imperial ounces) of liquor *or* 24 12-ounce cans or bottles of beer or ale. Also, if you meet the local age requirement for tobacco products, you may bring in, duty-free, 200 cigarettes and 50 cigars. Check ahead of time with the Canada Border Services Agency or the Department of Agriculture for policies regarding meat products, seeds, plants, and fruits.

You may send an unlimited number of gifts (only one gift per recipient, however) worth up to C$60 each duty-free to Canada. Label the package UNSOLICITED GIFT—VALUE UNDER $60. Alcohol and tobacco are excluded.

🛂 **Canada Border Services Agency** ✉ 2265 St. Laurent Blvd., Ottawa, Ontario K1G 4K3 ☎ 800/461-

9999 in Canada, 204/983–3500, 506/636–5064
⊕ www.ccra.gc.ca.

IN NEW ZEALAND

All homeward-bound residents may bring back NZ$700 worth of souvenirs and gifts; passengers may not pool their allowances, and children can claim only the concession on goods intended for their own use. For those 17 or older, the duty-free allowance also includes 4.5 liters of wine or beer; one 1,125-ml bottle of spirits; and either 200 cigarettes, 250 grams of tobacco, 50 cigars, *or* a combination of the three up to 250 grams. Meat products, seeds, plants, and fruits must be declared upon arrival to the Agricultural Services Department.

New Zealand Customs ⊠ Head office: The Customhouse, 17–21 Whitmore St., Box 2218, Wellington ☎ 09/300–5399 or 0800/428–786 ⊕ www.customs.govt.nz.

IN THE U.K.

From countries outside the European Union, including the U.S., you may bring home, duty-free, 200 cigarettes, 50 cigars, 100 cigarillos, or 250 grams of tobacco; 1 liter of spirits or 2 liters of fortified or sparkling wine or liqueurs; 2 liters of still table wine; 60 ml of perfume; 250 ml of toilet water; plus £145 worth of other goods, including gifts and souvenirs. Prohibited items include meat products, seeds, plants, fruits, and dairy products.

HM Customs and Excise ⊠ Portcullis House, 21 Cowbridge Rd. E, Cardiff CF11 9SS ☎ 0845/010–9000, 0208/929–0152 advice service, 0208/929–6731, 0208/910–3602 complaints ⊕ www.hmce.gov.uk.

DISABILITIES & ACCESSIBILITY

Central Florida attractions are among the most accessible destinations in the world for people who have disabilities. The hospitality industry continues to spend millions on barrier-removing renovations. Though some challenges remain, most can be overcome with planning.

The main park-information centers can answer specific questions and dispense general information for guests with disabilities. Both Walt Disney World and Universal Studios publish guidebooks for guests with disabilities; allow six weeks for delivery.

LODGING

Despite the Americans with Disabilities Act, the definition of accessibility seems to differ from hotel to hotel. Some properties may be accessible by ADA standards for people with mobility problems but not for people with hearing or vision impairments, for example.

If you have mobility problems, ask for the lowest floor on which accessible services are offered. If you have a hearing impairment, check whether the hotel has devices to alert you visually to the ring of the telephone, a knock at the door, and a fire/emergency alarm. Some hotels provide these devices without charge. Discuss your needs with hotel personnel if this equipment isn't available, so that a staff member can personally alert you in the event of an emergency.

If you're bringing a guide dog, get authorization ahead of time and write down the name of the person with whom you spoke.

Hotels and motels at Walt Disney World are continually being renovated to comply with the Americans with Disabilities Act. Call the WDW Special Request Reservations line for up-to-the-minute information.

For guests using wheelchairs, staying at Disney-owned resort hotels is particularly convenient, since the Disney transportation system has dozens of lift-equipped vehicles. Most resorts here in every price range have rooms with roll-in showers or transfer benches in the bathrooms. Especially worthwhile and convenient are the luxurious Grand Floridian and the Port Orleans–French Quarter.

One of the most accommodating off-Disney resorts is the Marriott Orlando World Center; its level of commitment is especially apparent on Sunday morning, when the Solaris Restaurant hosts one of the most delicious, hospitable, and wheelchair-accessible Sunday brunches in Central Florida. Newer hotels, such as the JW Marriott Orlando Grand Lakes, are fully accessible.

In most properties, only elevators are braille-equipped, but some have programs to help employees understand how best to assist guests with visual impairments. Particularly outstanding is the Wyndham Palace Resort & Spa. The Embassy Suites hotels offer services such as talking alarm clocks and braille or recorded menus.

Most area properties have purchased the equipment necessary to accommodate guests with hearing impairments. Telecommunications devices for the deaf, flashing or vibrating phones and alarms, and closed captioning are common; an industry-wide effort to teach some employees sign language is under way. The Grosvenor Resort, on Hotel Plaza Boulevard, has excellent facilities but no Teletype reservations line.

fi **WDW Wheelchair-Accessible Lodgings** All-Star Music Resort ☎ 407/939-6000. **All-Star Movies Resort** ☎ 407/939-7000. **All-Star Sports Resort** ☎ 407/939-5000. **Beach Club Resort and Villas** ☎ 407/934-8000. **BoardWalk Inn and Villas** ☎ 407/939-5100. **Grand Floridian Resort & Spa** ☎ 407/824-3000, 407/934-7639 Walt Disney World Central Reservations, 407/828-6799 TTY. **Port Orleans Resort-French Quarter** ☎ 407/934-5000. **Wilderness Lodge** ☎ 407/824-3200. **Yacht Club Resort** ☎ 407/934-7000.

fi **Wheelchair-Accessible Lodgings Elsewhere** **Embassy Suites Hotel International Drive South** ☎ 800/433-7275, 407/352-1400 front desk, which can help callers with hearing problems ⊕ www. embassysuitesorlando.com. **Embassy Suites Hotel Lake Buena Vista Resort** ☎ 407/239-1144 or 800/ 362-2779, 800/451-4833 TTY ⊕ www. embassysuitesorlando.com.

fi **Good Hotels for Vision-Impaired Guests** Embassy Suites Hotel International Drive South ☎ 800/433-7275, 407/352-1400 TTY ⊕ www. embassysuitesorlando.com. **Embassy Suites Hotel Lake Buena Vista Resort** ☎ 407/239-1144 or 800/ 362-2779, 800/451-4833 TTY ⊕ www. embassysuitesorlando.com. **Wyndham Palace Resort & Spa in the WDW Resort** ☎ 407/827-2727 or 800/327-2990 ⊕ www.wyndham.com.

RESERVATIONS

When discussing accessibility with an operator or reservations agent, ask hard questions. Are there any stairs, inside *or* out? Are there grab bars next to the toilet

and in the shower/tub? How wide is the doorway to the room? To the bathroom? For the most extensive facilities meeting the latest legal specifications, opt for newer accommodations. If you reserve through a toll-free number, consider also calling the hotel's local number to confirm the information from the central reservations office. Get confirmation in writing when you can.

fi **WDW Special Request Reservations** ☎ 407/ 354-1853.

SIGHTS & ATTRACTIONS

Guests with disabilities can **take advantage of many discounts:** 50% at Busch Gardens for wheelchair users and the visually or hearing impaired; at least 50% at SeaWorld for guests with visual or hearing impairments; and 20% at Universal Studios for those with a disability that limits enjoyment of the park.

At Walt Disney World, a new standard of access was set with the opening of Disney's Animal Kingdom; all attractions, restaurants, and shops are wheelchair accessible. Disney–MGM Studios comes in a close second, followed by Epcot, some of whose rides have a tailgate that drops down to provide a level entrance to the ride vehicle. Though the Magic Kingdom, now in its third decade, was designed before architects gave consideration to access issues, renovation plans are under way. Even so, the 20 or so accessible attractions combine with the live entertainment around the park to provide a memorable experience. Universal Studios and SeaWorld are both substantially barrier-free.

In some attractions, you may be required to transfer to a wheelchair if you use a scooter. In others, you must be able to leave your own wheelchair to board the ride vehicle and must have a traveling companion assist, as park staff cannot do so. Attractions with emergency evacuation routes that have narrow walkways or steps require additional mobility. Turbulence on other attractions poses a problem for some guests.

Rest rooms at all of these parks have standard accessible stalls. More spacious facilities are available in first-aid stations.

Walt Disney World's *Guidebook for Guests with Disabilities* describes the theme and story of various attractions in its three parks. The guidebook is available in the park at Guest Relations, ticket booths, or the wheelchair rental location; you can also call ahead and request one by mail.

WDW and Universal have produced descriptive cassette tapes that can be borrowed, along with portable tape recorders (deposit required); SeaWorld, with a week's notice, provides an escort or interpreter to take people with visual or hearing impairments through the park. Service animals, although welcome, must be leashed or in a harness; they may board many rides, but not all—usually not those with loud noises, pyrotechnics, and other intense effects that may startle the animals.

WDW has several free devices available for the hearing impaired. The Hand-held Captioning Device is available at the attractions themselves. Assistive Listening Devices (deposit $25) are available at the Guest Relations window of all theme parks. Stage shows with sign language interpreters are listed in the calendar of events. At Epcot, you can rent personal translator units that amplify the sound tracks of seven shows ($4; $40 deposit). At Epcot and in the Magic Kingdom (and in Disney–MGM Studios by special arrangement) four-hour guided tours in sign language are available. Advance reservations are a must; provide two weeks' notice if possible ($5 adults, $3.50 children 3–9).

Both Universal Studios and SeaWorld can also provide guides fluent in sign language with advance notice; Universal has scripts available for all its shows. Busch Gardens does not offer assistance in sign.

🖪 Theme-Park Information for Guests with Disabilities **Walt Disney World** ☎ 407/560-6233, 407/827-5141 TTY. **Universal Studios** ☎ 407/224-4414, 407/363-8265 TTY. The TDD (Telecommunications Device for the Deaf) number is 407/363-8000. **SeaWorld** ☎ 407/363-2414 or 407/351-3600, 407/363-2617 TTY, TDD 800/837-4268.

TRANSPORTATION

Outside Disney property there are some lift-equipped vans for rent and some shuttle services available, but you'll need to plan your itinerary beforehand. Inside Disney, every other bus on each route is lift-equipped and there's never more than a 30-minute wait for hotel-to-theme park trips. Consult transportation companies for more information.

Designated parking is available for guests with disabilities. At most parks it's near the turnstile area. The Magic Kingdom's special lot is near the Transportation and Ticket Center, where ferries depart for the Magic Kingdom. From there the monorails depart for Epcot. Monorail entrances are level, but the ramp is quite steep.

The U.S. Department of Transportation Aviation Consumer Protection Division's online publication *New Horizons: Information for the Air Traveler with a Disability* offers advice for travelers with a disability, and outlines basic rights. Visit DisabilityInfo.gov for general information.

🖪 Information & Complaints **Aviation Consumer Protection Division** (⇨ Air Travel) for airline-related problems ⊕ airconsumer.ost.dot.gov/publications/horizons.htm for airline travel advice and rights. **Departmental Office of Civil Rights** ✉ for general inquiries, U.S. Department of Transportation, S-30, 400 7th St. SW, Room 10215, Washington, DC 20590 ☎ 202/366-4648, 202/366-8538 TTY ⊕ 202/366-9371 ⊕ www.dotcr.ost.dot.gov. **Disability Rights Section** ✉ NYAV, U.S. Department of Justice, Civil Rights Division, 950 Pennsylvania Ave. NW, Washington, DC 20530 ☎ ADA information line 202/514-0301, 800/514-0301, 202/514-0383 TTY, 800/514-0383 TTY ⊕ www.ada.gov. **U.S. Department of Transportation Hotline** ☎ for disability-related air-travel problems, 800/778-4838 or 800/455-9880 TTY.

TRAVEL AGENCIES

In the United States, the Americans with Disabilities Act requires that travel firms serve the needs of all travelers. Some agencies specialize in working with people with disabilities.

🖪 Travelers with Mobility Problems **Access Adventures/B. Roberts Travel** ✉ 206 Chestnut Ridge Rd., Scottsville, NY 14624 ☎ 585/889-9096 ⊕ www.brobertstravel.com ✉ dltravel@prodigy.net, run by a former physical-rehabilitation counselor. **Accessible Vans of America** ✉ 37 Daniel Rd. W, Fairfield, NJ 07004 ☎ 877/282-8267 or 888/282-8267, 973/808-9709 reservations ⊕ 973/808-9713

⊕ www.accessiblevans.com. **CareVacations** ✉ No. 5, 5110–50 Ave., Leduc, Alberta, Canada, T9E 6V4 ☎ 780/986–6404 or 877/478–7827 ⊟ 780/986–8332 ⊕ www.carevacations.com, for group tours and cruise vacations. **Flying Wheels Travel** ✉ 143 W. Bridge St., Box 382, Owatonna, MN 55060 ☎ 507/451–5005 ⊟ 507/451–1685 ⊕ www.flyingwheelstravel.com.

🔁 Travelers with Developmental Disabilities **New Directions** ✉ 5276 Hollister Ave., Suite 207, Santa Barbara, CA 93111 ☎ 805/967–2841 or 888/967–2841 ⊟ 805/964–7344 ⊕ www.newdirectionstravel.com. **Sprout** ✉ 893 Amsterdam Ave., New York, NY 10025 ☎ 212/222–9575 or 888/222–9575 ⊟ 212/222–9768 ⊕ www.gosprout.org.

WHEELCHAIRS

Probably the most comfortable course is to bring your wheelchair from home. Access may be difficult except in theater-style shows, however, if your chair is wider than 24½ inches and longer than 32 inches (44 inches for scooters); consult attraction hosts and hostesses. Thefts of personal wheelchairs while their owners are inside attractions are rare but have been known to occur. Take the precautions you would in any public place.

Wheelchair rentals are available from area medical-supply companies that will deliver to your hotel and let you keep the chair for the duration of your vacation. You can also rent by the day in major theme parks ($7 a day for wheelchairs, plus a $1 refundable deposit); $30 daily for the limited number of scooters, plus a $10 refundable deposit).

In Disney parks, since rental locations are relatively close to parking, it may be a good idea to send someone ahead to get the wheelchair and bring it back to the car; at day's end, a Disney host or hostess may escort you to your car and then return the wheelchair for you. Rented wheelchairs that disappear while you're on a ride can be replaced throughout the parks—ask any staffer for the nearest location. Attaching a small personal item to the wheelchair may prevent other guests from taking yours by mistake.

DISCOUNTS & DEALS

There are plenty of ways to save money while you're in the Orlando area. Coupon books, such as those available from Entertainment Travel Editions for around $30, can be good sources for discounts on rental cars, admission to attractions, meals, and other typical purchases.

Be a smart shopper and compare all your options before making decisions. A plane ticket bought with a promotional coupon from travel clubs, coupon books, and direct-mail offers or purchased on the Internet may not be cheaper than the least expensive fare from a discount ticket agency. And always keep in mind that what you get is just as important as what you save.

BEST WAYS TO SAVE

1. Shop around for discounted theme-park tickets, which are widely available. Be sure to **look into combination tickets** and second-day free tickets that get you admission to multiple theme parks or two days' admission for the price of one to a single park. The Orlando FlexTicket is just one example of the various combination tickets available. You can also visit the Orlando/Orange County Convention and Visitors Bureau on International Drive or stop in one of the many ticket booths around town, including the Tourism Bureau of Orlando, Know Before You Go, and the Tourist Information Center of Orlando. Be wary of extra-cheap tickets (they may be expired) and discounts that require you to take time-share tours—unless you're interested in a time-share, of course.

If you're a member of the American Automobile Association, be sure to ask at your local club about getting discounted tickets. You may also find you're eligible for purchases within the parks on things like food and merchandise. Find out if your company belongs to the Universal Fan Club or the Magic Kingdom Club, which offer discount schemes to members' employees. At Busch Gardens, go for the Twilight Tickets, available after 3 PM.

2. Buy your tickets as soon as you know you're going. Prices typically go up two or three times a year, so you might beat a price hike—and save a little money.

3. Stay at hotels on U.S. 192 around Kissimmee and on International Drive that

offer free transportation to and from the park. Getting to and from the parks may take a little extra time, but you won't have to pay to rent a car—or to park it.

4. In deciding whether or not to rent a car, do the math. Weigh the cost of renting against what it will cost to get your entire party to and from the airport and the theme parks and any other places you want to go. If you are traveling with a group of more than four, renting a car may be cheaper than other options.

5. Choose accommodations with a kitchen. You can stock up on breakfast items in a nearby supermarket, and save time—and money—by eating your morning meal in your hotel room.

6. Watch your shopping carefully. Theme-park merchandisers are excellent at displaying the goods so that you (or your children) can't resist them. You may find that some articles for sale are also available at home—for quite a bit less. One way to cope is to give every member of your family a souvenir budget—adults and children alike.

7. Avoid holidays and school vacation times, or go off-season. You can see more in less time and lodging rates are lower.

8. If you plan to eat in a full-service restaurant, have a large, late breakfast, and then eat lunch late in the day in lieu of dinner. Lunchtime prices are almost always lower than dinnertime prices. Also look for "early bird" menus, which offer dinner entrées at reduced prices during late afternoon and early evening hours.

For further discount information, if applicable, *see* Disabilities and Accessibility and Senior-Citizen Travel.

Central Florida Tickets and Travel ✉ 3501 W. Vine St., Suite 319, Kissimmee, 34741 ☎ 407/932-2080 ⊕ www.centralfloridatravel.com. **Entertainment Travel Editions** ☎ 800/445-4137 ⊕ www.entertainment.com. **Know Before You Go** ☎ 407/352-9813. **Orlando/Orange County Convention and Visitors Bureau** ✉ 8723 International Dr., Orlando, FL 32819 ☎ 407/363-5871. **Tourism Bureau of Orlando** ☎ 407/363-5800. **Tourist Information Center of Orlando** ☎ 407/363-5871.

DISCOUNT RESERVATIONS

To save money, look into discount reservations services with Web sites and toll-free numbers, which use their buying power to get a better price on hotels, airline tickets (⇨ Air Travel), even car rentals. When booking a room, always **call the hotel's local toll-free number** (if one is available) rather than the central reservations number—you'll often get a better price. Always ask about special packages or corporate rates.

Airline Tickets Air 4 Less ☎ 800/AIR4LESS, low-fare specialist.

Hotel Rooms Accommodations Express ☎ 800/444-7666 or 800/277-1064 ⊕ www.accommodationsexpress.com. **Central Reservation Service (CRS)** ☎ 800/555-7555 or 800/548-3311 ⊕ www.crshotels.com. **Hotels.com** ☎ 800/246-8357 ⊕ www.hotels.com. **Quikbook** ☎ 800/789-9887 ⊕ www.quikbook.com. **Turbotrip.com** ☎ 800/473-7829 ⊕ www.turbotrip.com.

PACKAGE DEALS

Don't confuse packages and guided tours. When you buy a package, you travel on your own, just as though you had planned the trip yourself. Fly–drive packages, which combine airfare and car rental, are often a good deal. In cities, ask the local visitor's bureau about hotel and local transportation packages that include tickets to major museum exhibits or other special events.

EMERGENCIES

All the major theme parks have first-aid centers. Hospital emergency rooms are open 24 hours a day. For minor emergencies visit the Main Street Physicians clinic (open February through August, weekdays 8 to 8, weekends 8 to 5, and September through January, weekdays 8–7, weekends 8–4) or its minor-emergency mobile service, which offers hotel-room visits by physicians for minor medical care and dispenses nonnarcotic medication. There are several Centra Care centers. One is closer to Orlando (a block east of Kirkman Road) and is open daily 8 AM–midnight. Another Centra Care center is near Downtown Disney and is open weekdays 8 AM–midnight; and another is in Lake

Buena Vista, open weekdays 8–8, weekends 9–9. The latter provides free shuttle service from any of the Disney theme park's first-aid stations.

🚹 **Police or ambulance** ☎ 911.

🚹 **Doctors & Dentists Dental Emergency Service** ☎ 407/331-2526.

🚹 **Hospitals & Clinics Orlando Regional Medical Center/Sand Lake Hospital** ✉ 9400 Turkey Lake Rd., I-Drive Area ☎ 407/351-8500. **Florida Hospital Celebration Health** ✉ 400 Celebration Pl., Celebration ☎ 407/764-4000. **Main Street Physicians** ✉ 8324 International Dr. ☎ 407/370-4881. **Centra Care** ✉ 4320 W. Vine St., Kissimmee ☎ 407/390-1888. **Centra Care** ✉ 12500 S. Apopka Vineland Rd., Lake Buena Vista ☎ 407/934-2273.

🚹 **24-Hour Pharmacies Walgreens** ✉ 5501 S. Kirkman Rd., Universal Studios Area ☎ 407/248-0315.

CVS ✉ 5308 W. Irlo Bronson Memorial Hwy, Disney area ☎ 407/390-9185.

GAY & LESBIAN TRAVEL

Gay Day Orlando, held the first Saturday in June, includes a week's worth of activities. Contact the Gay, Lesbian & Bisexual Community Center of Central Florida (GLBCC) or visit Gay Day's official Web site for more information.

For details about the gay and lesbian scene, consult *Fodor's Gay Guide to the USA* (available in bookstores everywhere).

🚹 **Local Information Gay and Lesbian Community Services** ✉ 946 N. Mills Ave., Orlando, FL 32803 ☎ 407/228-8272 ⊕ www.glbcc.org. **Gay Day at Walt Disney World** ⊕ www.gayday.com.

🚹 **Gay- & Lesbian-Friendly Travel Agencies Different Roads Travel** ✉ 1017 North La Cienega Blvd, Suite 308, West Hollywood, CA 90069 ☎ 800/429-8747 (Ext. 14) 🖷 310/855-0323 ✉ lgernert@tzell. com. **Kennedy Travel** ✉ 130 W. 42nd St., Suite 401, New York, NY 10036 ☎ 212/840-8659 or 800/237-7433 🖷 212/730-2269 ⊕ www.kennedytravel.com. **Now, Voyager** ✉ 4406 18th St., San Francisco, CA 94114 ☎ 415/626-1169 or 800/255-6951 🖷 415/626-8626 ⊕ www.nowvoyager.com. **Skylink Travel and Tour/Flying Dutchmen Travel** ✉ 1455 N. Dutton Ave., Suite A, Santa Rosa, CA 95401 ☎ 707/546-9888 or 800/225-5759 🖷 707/636-0951, serving lesbian travelers.

GUIDEBOOKS

Plan well and you won't be sorry. Guidebooks are excellent tools—and you can take them with you. You may want to check out the color photo–illustrated *Fodor's Exploring Florida* and *Compass American Guide: Florida,* thorough on culture and history; or *Fodor's Road Guide USA: Florida* for comprehensive restaurant, hotel, and attractions listings. All are available at online retailers and bookstores everywhere. *Fodor's Walt Disney World & Universal Orlando with Kids,* by Kim Wright Wiley, is the most comprehensive guide to WDW for families with small children.

HOLIDAYS

Major national holidays are New Year's Day (Jan. 1); Martin Luther King Day (3rd Mon. in Jan.); Presidents' Day (3rd Mon. in Feb.); Memorial Day (last Mon. in May); Independence Day (July 4); Labor Day (1st Mon. in Sept.); Columbus Day (2nd Mon. in Oct.); Thanksgiving Day (4th Thurs. in Nov.); Christmas Eve and Christmas Day (Dec. 24 and 25); and New Year's Eve (Dec. 31).

INSURANCE

The most useful travel-insurance plan is a comprehensive policy that includes coverage for trip cancellation and interruption, default, trip delay, and medical expenses (with a waiver for preexisting conditions).

Without insurance you'll lose all or most of your money if you cancel your trip, regardless of the reason. Default insurance covers you if your tour operator, airline, or cruise line goes out of business—the chances of which have been increasing. Trip-delay covers expenses that arise because of bad weather or mechanical delays. Study the fine print when comparing policies.

U.K. residents can buy a travel-insurance policy valid for most vacations taken during the year in which it's purchased (but check preexisting-condition coverage).

Always **buy travel policies directly from the insurance company;** if you buy them from a cruise line, airline, or tour operator that goes out of business you probably won't be covered for the agency or operator's default, a major risk. Before making any purchase, review your existing health and home-owner's policies to find what they cover away from home.

🛈 Travel Insurers In the U.S.: **Access America** ✉ 2805 N. Parham Rd., Richmond, VA 23294 ☎ 800/284-8300 🖷 804/673-1469 or 800/346-9265 🌐 www.accessamerica.com. **Travel Guard International** ✉ 1145 Clark St., Stevens Point, WI 54481 ☎ 715/345-0505 or 800/826-1300 🖷 800/955-8785 or 715/345-1990 🌐 www.travelguard.com.

FOR INTERNATIONAL TRAVELERS

For information on customs restrictions, *see* Customs & Duties.

CAR RENTAL

When picking up a rental car, non-U.S. residents need a reservation voucher for any prepaid reservations that were made in the traveler's home country, a passport, a driver's license, and a travel policy that covers each driver.

CAR TRAVEL

In Orlando gasoline costs at this writing ranged from $1.70 to $2.49 a gallon. Gas stations closest to Walt Disney World always charge roughly 20¢ more per gallon than elsewhere. Stations are plentiful. Most stay open late; some are open 24 hours.

Highways are well paved. Interstate highways—limited-access, multilane highways whose numbers are prefixed by "I–"—are the fastest routes. Interstates with three-digit numbers encircle urban areas, which may have other limited-access expressways, freeways, and parkways as well. Tolls may be levied on limited-access highways. So-called U.S. highways and state highways are not necessarily limited-access but may have several lanes.

Along larger highways, roadside stops with rest rooms, fast-food restaurants, and sundries stores are well spaced. State police and tow trucks patrol major highways and lend assistance. If your car breaks down on an interstate, pull onto the shoulder and wait for help, or have your passengers wait while you walk to an emergency phone (available in most states). If you carry a cell phone, dial *55, noting your location on the small green roadside mileage markers.

Driving in the United States is on the right. Do obey speed limits posted along roads and highways. Watch for lower limits in small towns and on back roads. Florida requires all front-seat passengers, regardless of age, to wear seat belts. On weekdays between 6 and 10 AM and again between 4 and 7 PM expect heavy traffic. To encourage carpooling, some freeways have special lanes for so-called high-occupancy vehicles (HOV)—cars carrying more than one passenger.

Bookstores, gas stations, convenience stores, and rest stops sell maps (about $3) and multiregion road atlases (about $10).

CURRENCY

The dollar is the basic unit of U.S. currency. It has 100 cents. Coins are the copper penny (1¢); silvery nickel (5¢), dime (10¢), quarter (25¢), and half-dollar (50¢); and the golden $1 coin, replacing a now-rare silver dollar. Bills are denominated $1, $5, $10, $20, $50, and $100, all mostly green and identical in size; designs and background tints vary. In addition, you may come across a $2 bill, but the chances are slim. The exchange rate at this writing is U.S. $1.34 per Euro, U.S. $1.94 per British pound, U.S. $.88 per Canadian dollar, U.S. $.76 per Australian dollar, and U.S. $.71 per New Zealand dollar.

ELECTRICITY

The U.S. standard is AC, 110 volts/60 cycles. Plugs have two flat pins set parallel to each other.

EMERGENCIES

For police, fire, or ambulance, **dial 911** (0 in rural areas).

INSURANCE

Britons and Australians need extra medical coverage when traveling overseas.

🛈 Insurance Information In the U.K.: **Association of British Insurers** ✉ 51 Gresham St., London EC2V 7HQ ☎ 020/7600-3333 🖷 020/7696-8999 🌐 www.abi.org.uk. In Australia: **Insurance Council of Australia** ✉ Insurance Enquiries and Complaints, Level 12, Box 561, Collins St. W, Melbourne, VIC 8007 ☎ 1300/780808 or 03/9629-4109 🖷 03/9621-2060 🌐 www.iecltd.com.au. In Canada: **RBC Insurance** ✉ 6880 Financial Dr., Mississauga, Ontario L5N 7Y5

☎ 800/668-4342 or 905/816-2400 🖷 905/813-4704 ⊕ www.rbcinsurance.com. In New Zealand: **Insurance Council of New Zealand** ✉ Level 7, 111-115 Customhouse Quay, Box 474, Wellington ☎ 04/472-5230 🖷 04/473-3011 ⊕ www.icnz.org.nz.

MAIL & SHIPPING

You can buy stamps and aerograms and send letters and parcels in post offices. Stamp-dispensing machines can occasionally be found in airports, bus and train stations, office buildings, drugstores, and the like. You can also deposit mail in the stout dark-blue steel bins at strategic locations everywhere and in the mail chutes of large buildings; pickup schedules are posted. You can deposit packages at public collection boxes as long as the parcels are affixed with proper postage and weigh less than one pound. Packages weighing one or more pounds must be taken to a post office or handed to a postal carrier.

For mail sent within the United States, you need a 37¢ stamp for first-class letters weighing up to 1 ounce (23¢ for each additional ounce) and 23¢ for postcards. You pay 80¢ for 1-ounce airmail letters and 70¢ for airmail postcards to most other countries; to Canada and Mexico, you need a 60¢ stamp for a 1-ounce letter and 50¢ for a postcard. An aerogram—a single sheet of lightweight blue paper that folds into its own envelope, stamped for overseas airmail—costs 70¢.

To receive mail on the road, have it sent c/o General Delivery at your destination's main post office (use the correct five-digit ZIP code). You must pick up mail in person within 30 days and show a driver's license or passport.

PASSPORTS & VISAS

When traveling internationally, carry your passport even if you don't need one (it's always the best form of ID) and **make two photocopies of the data page** (one for someone at home and another for you, carried separately from your passport). If you lose your passport, promptly call the nearest embassy or consulate and the local police.

Visitor visas aren't necessary for Canadian or European Union citizens, or for citizens of Australia who are staying fewer than 90 days.

🇦🇺 Australian Citizens **Passports Australia** ☎ 131-232 ⊕ www.passports.gov.au. **United States Consulate General** ✉ MLC Centre, Level 59, 19-29 Martin Pl., Sydney, NSW 2000 ☎ 02/9373-9200, 1902/941-641 fee-based visa-inquiry line ⊕ usembassy-australia.state.gov/sydney.

🇨🇦 Canadian Citizens **Passport Office** ✉ To mail in applications: 200 Promenade du Portage, Hull, Québec J8X 4B7 ☎ 819/994-3500 or 800/567-6868, 866/255-7655 TTY ⊕ www.ppt.gc.ca.

🇳🇿 New Zealand Citizens **New Zealand Passports Office** ✉ For applications and information, Level 3, Boulcott House, 47 Boulcott St., Wellington ☎ 0800/22-5050 or 04/474-8100 ⊕ www.passports.govt.nz. **Embassy of the United States** ✉ 29 Fitzherbert Terr., Thorndon, Wellington ☎ 04/462-6000 ⊕ usembassy.org.nz. **U.S. Consulate General** ✉ Citibank Bldg., 3rd fl., 23 Customs St. E, Auckland ☎ 09/303-2724 ⊕ usembassy.org.nz.

🇬🇧 U.K. Citizens **U.K. Passport Service** ☎ 0870/521-0410 ⊕ www.passport.gov.uk. **American Consulate General** ✉ Danesfort House, 223 Stranmillis Rd., Belfast, Northern Ireland BT9 5GR ☎ 028/9032-8239 🖷 028/9024-8482 ⊕ usembassy.org.uk. **American Embassy** ✉ For visa and immigration information or to submit a visa application via mail (enclose an SASE), Consular Information Unit, 24 Grosvenor Sq., London W1 1AE ☎ 09055/444-546 for visa information (per-minute charges), 0207/499-9000 main switchboard ⊕ usembassy.org.uk.

TELEPHONES

All U.S. telephone numbers consist of a three-digit area code and a seven-digit local number. Within many local calling areas you dial only the seven-digit number. Within some area codes you must dial "1" first for calls outside the local area. To call between area-code regions, dial "1" then all 10 digits; the same goes for calls to numbers prefixed by "800," "888," "866," and "877"—all toll-free. For calls to numbers preceded by "900" you must pay—usually dearly.

For international calls, dial "011" followed by the country code and the local number. For help, dial "0" and ask for an overseas operator. The country code for Australia is 61, for New Zealand 64, for the United Kingdom 44. Calling Canada is the same as calling within the United States. Most local phone books list country codes and U.S. area codes. The country code for the United States is 1.

For operator assistance, dial "0." To obtain someone's phone number, call directory assistance at 555–1212 or occasionally 411 (free at many public phones). To have the person you're calling foot the bill, phone collect; dial "0" instead of "1" before the 10-digit number.

At pay phones, instructions often are posted. Usually you insert coins in a slot (usually 25¢–50¢ for local calls) and wait for a steady tone before dialing. When you call long-distance, the operator tells you how much to insert; prepaid phone cards, widely available in various denominations, are easier. Call the number on the back, punch in the card's personal identification number when prompted, then dial your number.

MEDIA

All major U.S. television networks have affiliates in Orlando, and there are several Spanish-language radio and television stations as well.

NEWSPAPERS & MAGAZINES

The *Orlando Sentinel* is the area outlet for news; *Orlando Magazine* is a monthly publication. The *Orlando Weekly* is the alternative newspaper for the city, covering and criticizing local politics when it's not recommending bars and clubs. The free weekly is found in distinctive red racks throughout the city.

RADIO

WMFE (90.7 FM) is the local National Public Radio affiliate. **WDBO** (580 AM) is an excellent source for news and traffic. **WFLA** (540 AM) has weak news but several popular talk shows. **WRUM** (100.3 FM) is a Spanish music station. You'll find country music at **WPCV** (97.5 FM) and **WWKA** (92 FM).

TELEVISION

WFTV (channel 9) is the local ABC affiliate; **WKMG** (channel 6) is the CBS affiliate; **WESH** (channel 2) is the NBC affiliate; and **WOFL** (channel 35) is the Fox affiliate.

MONEY MATTERS

Be prepared to spend and spend—and spend some more. Despite relatively low airfares and car-rental rates, cash seems to evaporate out of wallets, and credit-card balances seem to increase on exposure to the hot Orlando sun. Theme-park admission is roughly $60 per day per person—not counting all the $2 soft drinks and $20 souvenirs. Hotels range so wildly—from $60 a night to 10 or more times that—that you have to do some hard thinking about just how much you want to spend. Meal prices away from the theme parks are comparable to those in other midsize cities, ranging from $5 per person at a fast-food chain to $40 entrées at a fancy restaurant.

ATMS

There are ATMs in the entry areas of all theme parks as well as here and there around town. Often there's a $1.50–$2.50 charge if you're not a customer of the specific bank that maintains the ATM.

CREDIT CARDS

Throughout this guide, the following abbreviations are used: **AE**, American Express; **D**, Discover; **DC**, Diners Club; **MC**, MasterCard; and **V**, Visa.
🔁 Reporting Lost Cards **American Express** ☎ 800/441-0519. **Diners Club** ☎ 800/234-6377. **Discover** ☎ 800/347-2683. **MasterCard** ☎ 800/622-7747. **Visa** ☎ 800/847-2911.

PACKING

Comfortable walking shoes or sneakers are essential. The entire area is extremely casual, day and night, so men need a jacket and tie in only a handful of restaurants. For sightseeing and theme-park visits, pack cool, comfortable clothing. On hot summer days the perfect theme-park outfit begins with shorts with large pockets made of a breathable, quick-drying material, topped by a T-shirt of similar material. Women may want to consider wearing a bathing-suit top under their T-shirts. Most theme parks either have water rides that leave you drenched or interactive fountains that are so tempting on hot days—that is, most of the time—that you're hard put to pass them by. Experienced theme-park visitors also suggest using a waist pack rather than a tote bag or purse. Sunglasses and a hat are a must—as is sunscreen. Don't ruin your trip by getting sunburned on the first day.

In winter be prepared for a range of temperatures: take clothing that you can layer, including a sweater and warm jacket. It can get quite cool in December and January. For summer, you'll want a sun hat, and a poncho and folding umbrella in case of sudden thunderstorms.

In your carry-on luggage, pack an extra pair of eyeglasses or contact lenses and enough of any medication you take to last a few days longer than the entire trip. You may also ask your doctor to write a spare prescription using the drug's generic name, as brand names may vary from country to country. In luggage to be checked, **never pack prescription drugs, valuables, or undeveloped film.** And don't forget to carry with you the addresses of offices that handle refunds of lost traveler's checks. Check *Fodor's How to Pack* (available at online retailers and bookstores everywhere) for more tips.

To avoid customs and security delays, carry medications in their original packaging. Don't pack any sharp objects in your carry-on luggage, including knives of any size or material, scissors, nail clippers, and corkscrews, or anything else that might arouse suspicion.

To avoid having your checked luggage chosen for hand inspection, don't cram bags full. The U.S. Transportation Security Administration suggests packing shoes on top and placing personal items you don't want touched in clear plastic bags.

CHECKING LUGGAGE

You're allowed to carry aboard one bag and one personal article, such as a purse or a laptop computer. Make sure what you carry on fits under your seat or in the overhead bin. Get to the gate early, so you can board as soon as possible, before the overhead bins fill up.

Baggage allowances vary by carrier, destination, and ticket class. On international flights you're usually allowed to check two bags weighing up to 70 pounds (32 kilograms) each, although a few airlines allow checked bags of up to 88 pounds (40 kilograms) in first class. Some international carriers don't allow more than 66 pounds (30 kilograms) per bag in business class and 44 pounds (20 kilograms) in economy. On domestic flights, the limit is usually 50 to 70 pounds (23 to 32 kilograms) per bag. In general, carry-on bags shouldn't exceed 40 pounds (18 kilograms). Most airlines won't accept bags that weigh more than 100 pounds (45 kilograms) on domestic or international flights. Expect to pay a fee for baggage that exceeds weight limits. Check baggage restrictions with your carrier before you pack.

Airline liability for baggage is limited to $2,500 per person on flights within the United States. On international flights it amounts to $9.07 per pound or $20 per kilogram for checked baggage (roughly $640 per 70-pound bag), with a maximum of $634.90 per piece, and $400 per passenger for unchecked baggage. You can buy additional coverage at check-in for about $10 per $1,000 of coverage, but it often excludes a rather extensive list of items, shown on your airline ticket.

Before departure, itemize your bags' contents and their worth, and label the bags with your name, address, and phone number. (If you use your home address, cover it so potential thieves can't see it readily.) Include a label inside each bag and **pack a copy of your itinerary.** At check-in, make sure each bag is correctly tagged with the destination airport's three-letter code. Because some checked bags will be opened for hand inspection, the U.S. Transportation Security Administration recommends that you leave luggage unlocked or use the plastic locks offered at check-in. TSA screeners place an inspection notice inside searched bags, which are re-sealed with a special lock.

If your bag has been searched and contents are missing or damaged, file a claim with the TSA Consumer Response Center as soon as possible. If your bags arrive damaged or fail to arrive at all, file a written report with the airline before leaving the airport.

📋 Complaints **U.S. Transportation Security Administration Contact Center** ☎ 866/289–9673 🌐 www.tsa.gov.

PETS

It's probably best to leave Rover at home, but if you just can't part with your animal, all the parks have kennel facilities. They provide a cage, water, and sometimes food. Some of the kennels, such as the one at Epcot, offer dog-walking services for an additional fee. On-site Disney resort guests may board their pets for $9 per night; others pay $11 per night. The day rate is $6. The Holiday Inn Maingate West is one of the few area hotels that allows pets to stay in your room. The fee is $75 per pet, of which $25 is refundable if no damage results to the room. The Portofino Bay Hotel, the Hard Rock Hotel, and the Royal Pacific Resort at Universal allow your pet to stay in your room at no extra cost, and they even offer pet room service. However, you must provide a pet health certificate that is no more than 10 days old.

📋 **Hard Rock Hotel** ✉ 1000 Universal Studios Plaza, Universal Studios, 32819 ☎ 407/503–7625 or 800/232–7827 🖶 407/503–7655 🌐 www. loewshotels.com. **Holiday Inn Maingate West** ✉ 7601 Black Lake Rd., Kissimmee 34747 ☎ 407/ 396–1100 or 800/365–6935 🖶 407/396–0689 🌐 www.sixcontinentshotels.com. **Portofino Bay Hotel** ✉ 5601 Universal Blvd., Universal Studios 32819 ☎ 407/503–1000 or 888/322–5541 🌐 www. loewshotels.com.

PLANNING YOUR TRIP

Careful planning is key to the most hassle-free visit to the Orlando area. The first step is to **figure out everything you want to see and do in the area.** Will you be staying put, or do you want to spend some time at the beach? Once you've settled on your sightseeing priorities, you can figure out how long you want to stay, make reservations, and buy tickets.

HOW LONG TO STAY

There are a couple of ways to approach this question. If your objective is to enjoy the complete Orlando resort experience, seven days is a comfortable period to

allow; this gives you time to see all of the parks at Universal and WDW and to take in one water park, to sample the restaurants and entertainment, and to spend a bit of time around the pool. Eight days would be better. Figure on an additional day for every other area theme park you want to visit, and then add your travel time to and from home.

If you're coming to the area mostly to go on the rides and see the theme parks, allow one day per theme park. This supposes that you're willing to start out early every day, move quickly, breeze through shops, and hurry through meals. Then add your travel time to and from home.

In either case, add time for exploring Orlando, and for shopping. Orlando has some great high-end and discount shopping. Tenants at the Mall at Millenia include Bloomingdale's, Macy's, Neiman Marcus, Tiffany & Co., and Chanel. The Florida Mall has a Nordstrom and Saks. **Add an extra day or two if you're traveling with small children,** who may have limited patience for marathon touring, or if you're staying off Disney property. Also add in extra time if you're visiting during a busy period, when long lines will make it nearly impossible to see all the most popular attractions unless you have enormous stamina and are willing to be on the go from early in the morning until park closing. You could easily spend more than two weeks in the area and still not see it all.

CREATING AN ITINERARY

Once you know what you want to see and do, **lay out a day-by-day touring plan,** using the Blitz Tours, Tip Sheets, and Strategies for Your Visit sections in chapters 1, 2, and 3. Also look at the italicized Crowds and Strategy information following each review. Don't try to plot your route from hour to hour; instead break the day up into morning, afternoon, and evening sections. Make a note of the busiest days in each park you've planned to visit, and schedule yourself accordingly. Then, beginning with the dates on which you plan to visit, **decide which parks you will see on each day.**

Think creatively. If you're staying on Walt Disney World property in a not-too-busy period and have at least five days, **consider spending afternoons at one of the water parks,** at your hotel swimming pool, or at a spa or sports facility. If you buy a multi-day Park Hopper pass, which is good for unlimited visits to WDW's major parks, you can also **visit two or more theme parks in a day**—say, do the Magic Kingdom in the morning, when the park isn't as crowded, and spend an afternoon in Epcot's Future World, that area's least busy time. Put each day's plan on a separate index card, and carry the card with you as you explore Orlando.

Finally, **make a list of all the things you want to do that require reservations.** Note on the list how far in advance you can book for each. Then, based on your travel schedule, designate the date on which you should call for the reservations you want. Some reservations can be made as soon as you book your hotel or before; others will have to wait until you're in the area.

BUYING YOUR TICKETS

If you aren't signing up for an escorted tour or travel package, buy your tickets in advance. This will save you time in Orlando, and you may beat a price hike and save a little money as well.

The Orlando airport has Universal Studios, SeaWorld, and Walt Disney World gift shops, where tickets, maps, and information are available. Buying tickets here while waiting for your bags to be unloaded will save time later. Local Disney Stores also sell certain multiday passes. Plenty of other outlets around Orlando sell theme-park tickets, including stores and, most likely, your hotel.

REST ROOMS

Rest rooms at Walt Disney World, Universal, and SeaWorld are widely available, frequently cleaned, and there are usually enough stalls so that you rarely have to wait in line; most, including men's rooms, have baby-changing stations. Some park areas, such as the Woody Woodpecker Kid Zone at Universal, even feature kid-size potties and sinks. Plus, rest rooms at the airport and at most attractions use the automatic infrared flush trigger, so you never have to touch the toilet.

SENIOR-CITIZEN TRAVEL

Bear in mind that school vacation times can spell ordeal rather than adventure if you have limited energy or patience. Your endurance will go further if you arrive in the theme parks at opening time or before. Take in first those attractions that you most want to see. This way you can take it easy when the day warms up. Then relax in the shade, have a nice long lunch, see some shows in air-conditioned theaters, and maybe even go back to your hotel to relax around the pool, read, or nap. Refreshed, you can return to one of the theme parks, when they're open late, or explore Pleasure Island or Orlando's other after-dark options.

To qualify for age-related discounts, mention your senior-citizen status up front when booking hotel reservations (not when checking out) and before you're seated in restaurants (not when paying the bill). Be sure to have identification on hand. When renting a car, ask about promotional car-rental discounts, which can be cheaper than senior-citizen rates.

🏫 Educational Programs **Elderhostel** ✉ 11 Ave. de Lafayette, Boston, MA 02111-1746 ☎ 877/426-8056, 978/323-4141 international callers, 877/426-2167 TTY 🖷 877/426-2166 ⊕ www.elderhostel.org.

SHOPPING

SMART SOUVENIRS

Although it is easy to burn through wads of cash in the gift stores, some of the most popular and unique items are quite affordable. Disney's trading pins are a big hit with kids and can be bought for $6 in all the theme parks. You'll find the largest assortment of pins at Disney's Pin Traders at the Downtown Disney Marketplace. Probably the single most popular item at Disney is the autograph book, which costs less than $20.

SIGHTSEEING TOURS

IN THE THEME PARKS

Guided tours are available in all the area's major theme parks. *See* theme park A to Z sections for tour descriptions, fees, and additional information.

AROUND ORLANDO

Helicopter rides are a great way to get an overall view of the Orlando area. You'll be surprised at the vast number of lakes and open spaces; costs range from $20 per person to $350. If you'd rather see the lakes up close, consider a boat tour. One-hour tours generally cost $8 per adult and $4 per child under 12. Airboat tours on Saint John's River start at $35 per adult and $20 per child under 12 for 90 minutes.

🛈 Boat Tours **Scenic Boat Tours** ☎ 407/644-4056 ⊕ www.scenicboattours.com. **A-Awesome Airboat Ride** ☎ 407/568-7601 ⊕ www.airboatride.com.

🛈 Helicopter Rides **Air Florida** ✉ 8990 International Dr., Orlando ☎ 407/354-1400 ⊕ www. airfloridahelicopters.com.

STUDENTS IN ORLANDO

The major theme parks do not offer discount prices for students.

🛈 IDs & Services **STA Travel** ✉ 10 Downing St., New York, NY 10014 ☎ 212/627-3111, 800/777-0112 24-hr service center 🖷 212/627-3387 ⊕ www.sta. com. **Travel Cuts** ✉ 187 College St., Toronto, Ontario M5T 1P7, Canada ☎ 800/592-2887 in the U.S., 416/979-2406 or 866/246-9762 in Canada 🖷 416/979-8167 ⊕ www.travelcuts.com.

TAXES

Tourists pay a 5% bed tax on top of the sales tax, which means you will pay an extra 11%–12% of the rate for your hotel stay. There are no airport departure taxes.

SALES TAX

Orlando-area sales tax varies from 6% to 7%; it's 6.5% in Orange, 6% in Volusia County, 7% in Osceola and Seminole counties. You will pay different sales tax within Walt Disney World depending on where you are in the complex. At other major area theme parks, which are all in Orange County, you pay 6.5%. Sales taxes are levied on clothing, souvenirs, restaurants meals, and snack items.

TAXIS

Taxi fares start at $3.25 for the first mile and add $1.75 for each mile thereafter. Sample fares: to WDW's Magic Kingdom, about $25 from International Drive, $14 to $18 from U.S. 192. To Universal Studios, $10 to $14 from International Drive, $27 to $34 from U.S. 192. To downtown, $22 to $28 from International Drive, $32 to $44 from U.S. 192. For information on getting to or from the airport by taxi, *see* Airports and Transfers.

🛈 Taxi Companies **A-1 Taxi** ☎ 407/328-4555. **Checker Cab Company** ☎ 407/699-9999. **Star Taxi** ☎ 407/857-9999.

TIME

Florida is in the Eastern U.S. time zone and adopts Daylight Saving Time between April and October (clocks are set one hour ahead).

TIPPING

Whether they carry bags, open doors, deliver food, or clean rooms, hospitality employees work to receive a portion of your travel budget. In deciding how much to give, **base your tip on what the service is and how well it's performed.**

In transit, tip an airport valet $1 to $3 per bag, a taxi driver 15% to 20% of the fare.

For hotel staff, recommended amounts are $1 to $3 per bag for a bellhop, $2 per night per guest for housekeeping, $5 to $10 for special concierge service, $1 to $3 for a doorman who hails a cab or parks a car, 15% of the greens fee for a caddy, 15% to 20% of the bill for a massage, and 15% of a room service bill, which is often already included, so be sure to check.

In a restaurant, give 15% to 20% of your bill before tax to the server, 5% to 10% to the maître d', 15% to a bartender, and 15% of the wine bill for a wine steward who makes a special effort in selecting and serving wine.

TOURS & PACKAGES

Because everything is prearranged on a prepackaged tour or independent vacation, you spend less time planning—and often get it all at a good price.

BOOKING WITH AN AGENT

Travel agents are excellent resources. But it's a good idea to collect brochures from several agencies, as some agents' suggestions may be influenced by relationships with tour and package firms that reward them for volume sales. If you have a special interest, find an agent with expertise in that area. The American Society of Travel Agents (ASTA) has a database of specialists worldwide. You can log on to the group's Web site to find an ASTA travel agent in your neighborhood.

Make sure your travel agent knows the accommodations and other services of the place being recommended. Ask about the hotel's location, room size, beds, and whether it has a pool, room service, or programs for children, if you care about these. Has your agent been there in person or sent others whom you can contact?

Do some homework on your own, too: local tourism boards can provide information about lesser-known and small-niche operators, some of which may sell only direct.

BUYER BEWARE

Each year consumers are stranded or lose their money when tour operators—even large ones with excellent reputations—go out of business. So check out the operator. Ask several travel agents about its reputation, and try to **book with a company that has a consumer-protection program.** (Look for information in the company's brochure.) In the United States, members of the United States Tour Operators Association are required to set aside funds ($1 million) to help eligible customers cover payments and travel arrangements in the event that the company defaults. It's also a good idea to choose a company that participates in the American Society of Travel Agents' Tour Operator Program; ASTA will act as mediator in any disputes between you and your tour operator.

Remember that the more your package or tour includes, the better you can predict the ultimate cost of your vacation. Make sure you know exactly what is covered, and beware of hidden costs. Are taxes, tips, and transfers included? Entertainment and excursions? These can add up.

 Tour-Operator Recommendations **American Society of Travel Agents** (⇨ Travel Agencies). **CrossSphere–The Global Association for Packaged Travel** ✉ 546 E. Main St., Lexington, KY 40508 ☎ 859/226–4444 or 800/682–8886 🖷 859/

226–4414 ⊕ www.CrossSphere.com. **United States Tour Operators Association** (USTOA) ✉ 275 Madison Ave., Suite 2014, New York, NY 10016 ☎ 212/599–6599 🖷 212/599–6744 ⊕ www.ustoa.com.

TRAIN TRAVEL

Amtrak stops in downtown Orlando and in picturesque Winter Park, about 15 mi north of Walt Disney World. A taxi ride from the Orlando station to the Disney area costs around $50. Although you won't find car-rental agencies at the stations, some agencies will send a shuttle to pick you up or reimburse your cab fare to their location.

If you want to have your car in Florida without driving it there, consider a 900-mi shortcut with Amtrak's Auto Train, which departs for Florida from Lorton, Virginia, near Washington, D.C. Its southern terminus—Sanford, Florida—is 23 mi north of Orlando.

FARES & SCHEDULES

Round-trip Amtrak fare in coach from New York to Orlando costs $188, round-trip fare from Jacksonville costs $36, and round-trip fare from Houston costs $168.

The Auto Train runs daily, with one departure at 4 PM (car boarding ends one hour earlier). You'll arrive in Sanford around 8:30 the next morning. Fares vary depending on class of service and time of year, but expect to pay between $229 and $445 for a basic sleeper seat and car passage each way. For a group of four and one car, the cost is about $800 total. You must be traveling with an automobile to ride on the Auto Train.

 Train Information **Amtrak** ☎ 800/872–7245. **Auto Train** ☎ 407/321–3873 or 877/754–7495.

TRANSPORTATION AROUND WDW, UNIVERSAL & ORLANDO

If you're staying on Disney property, plan to use Disney's transportation system, which consists of buses, ferries, launches, and a monorail—all fast, clean, and comfortable—to travel between the parks and your hotel.

Universal is not as spread out as WDW, so if you stay on property you can walk to most attractions and restaurants. A pleasant boat ride connects the Portofino Bay Hotel and Citywalk.

If your hotel is on International Drive and you plan to spend a day visiting the area, avoid driving in horrendous traffic by taking the I-Ride Trolley (⇨ Bus Travel Around Orlando) to I-Drive's attractions, shops, and restaurants.

Although public buses (⇨ Bus Travel Around Orlando) are available, a car is the fastest and most convenient way to travel if you plan to visit several theme parks and downtown Orlando. Once you're in downtown Orlando, however, park and ride the free Lymmo bus.

TRAVEL AGENCIES

A good travel agent puts your needs first. Look for an agency that has been in business at least five years, emphasizes customer service, and has someone on staff who specializes in your destination. In addition, **make sure the agency belongs to a professional trade organization.** The American Society of Travel Agents (ASTA) has more than 10,000 members in some 140 countries, enforces a strict code of ethics, and will step in to mediate agent-client disputes involving ASTA members. ASTA also maintains a directory of agents on its Web site; ASTA's TravelSense.org, a trip planning and travel advice site, can also help to locate a travel agent who caters to your needs. (If a travel agency is also acting as your tour operator, *see* Buyer Beware *in* Tours & Packages.)

🔢 Local Agent Referrals American Society of Travel Agents (ASTA) ✉ 1101 King St., Suite 200, Alexandria, VA 22314 ☎ 703/739-2782 or 800/965-2782 24-hr hotline 🖷 703/684-8319 ⊕ www.astanet.com and www.travelsense.org. **Association of British Travel Agents** ✉ 68-71 Newman St., London W1T 3AH ☎ 020/7637-2444 🖷 020/7637-0713 ⊕ www.abta.com. **Association of Canadian Travel Agencies** ✉ 130 Albert St., Suite 1705, Ottawa, Ontario K1P 5G4 ☎ 613/237-3657 🖷 613/237-7052 ⊕ www.acta.ca. **Australian Federation of Travel Agents** ✉ Level 3, 309 Pitt St., Sydney, NSW 2000 ☎ 02/9264-3299 or 1300/363-416 🖷 02/9264-1085 ⊕ www.afta.com.au. **Travel Agents' Association of New Zealand** ✉ Level 5, Tourism and Travel House, 79 Boulcott St., Box 1888,

Wellington 6001 ☎ 04/499-0104 🖷 04/499-0786 ⊕ www.taanz.org.nz.

VISITOR INFORMATION

For Disney parks, hotels, dining, and entertainment reservations, contact Walt Disney World Information and Disney Reservation Center. To sit in the audience at a show being taped at Disney–MGM Studios call Production Information.

To get general information packages on the attractions of the Greater Orlando area, contact the convention and visitors bureaus below. For information on destinations outside the immediate Orlando-Kissimmee area, contact the Florida Tourism Industry Marketing Corporation.

🔢 Disney Information Walt Disney World Information 🏛 Box 10000, Lake Buena Vista, FL 32830 ☎ 407/824-4321, 407/827-5141 TDD ⊕ www.disney.com. **Disney Reservation Center** ☎ 407/934-7639, 407/939-3463 for dining. **Production Information** ☎ 407/560-4651.

🔢 Details on Other Theme Parks Universal Studios Escape ✉ 1000 Universal Studios Plaza, Orlando, FL 32819-8000 ☎ 407/363-8000, 407/363-8265 TDD ⊕ www.uescape.com. **SeaWorld Orlando** ✉ 7007 SeaWorld Dr., Orlando, FL 32821 ☎ 407/351-3600 ⊕ www.seaworld.com. **Busch Gardens** 🏛 Box 9158, Tampa, FL 33674 ☎ 813/987-5283 ⊕ www.buschgardens.com.

🔢 About Greater Orlando Orlando/Orange County Convention & Visitors Bureau ✉ 8723 International Dr., Orlando, FL 32819 ☎ 407/363-5871. **Kissimmee/St. Cloud Convention and Visitors Bureau** ✉ 1925 Irlo Bronson Hwy., Kissimmee, FL 34744 ☎ 407/847-5000 or 800/327-9159. **Winter Park Chamber of Commerce** 🏛 Box 280, Winter Park, FL 32790 ☎ 407/644-8281.

🔢 About the State of Florida Visit Florida ✉ 661 E. Jefferson St., Suite 300, Box 1100, Tallahassee, FL 32302 ☎ 850/488-5607 🖷 850/224-9589 ⊕ www.visitflorida.com. In the U.K.: **ABC Florida** 🏛 Box 35, Abingdon, Oxon OX14 4TB ☎ 0891/600-555; enclose £2 for a vacation pack, or call at 50p per minute.

🔢 Government Advisories U.S. Department of State ✉ Overseas Citizens Services Office, 2100 Pennsylvania Ave. NW, 4th fl., Washington, DC 20520 ☎ 202/647-5225 interactive hotline, 888/407-4747 ⊕ www.travel.state.gov. **Consular Affairs Bureau of Canada** ☎ 800/267-6788 or 613/944-6788 ⊕ www.voyage.gc.ca. **U.K. Foreign and Com-**

monwealth Office ✉ Travel Advice Unit, Consular Division, Old Admiralty Bldg., London SW1A 2PA ☎ 0870/606-0290 or 020/7008-1500 ⊕ www.fco.gov.uk/travel. **Australian Department of Foreign Affairs and Trade** ☎ 300/139-281 travel advice, 02/6261-1299 Consular Travel Advice ⊕ www.smartraveller.gov.au or www.dfat.gov.au. **New Zealand Ministry of Foreign Affairs and Trade** ☎ 04/439-8000 ⊕ www.mft.govt.nz.

FURTHER READING

The most perceptive book on Walt Disney and his works is *The Disney Version,* by Richard Schickel (Ivan R. Dee, third edition 1997). A comprehensive history of the great Disney animation tradition is provided in *Disney Animation: The Illusion of Life,* by Frank Thomas and Ollie Johnston (Hyperion, revised edition 1995). For a good read about Disney and other animators, look for *Of Mice and Magic* (New American Library, revised edition 1990), by Leonard Maltin. *Walt Disney: An American Original* (Hyperion, reprint edition 1994), by Bob Thomas, is full of anecdotes about the development of WDW. Rollins College professor Richard Fogelsong questions the "economic marriage" between Disney and Orlando in his book *Married to the Mouse* (Yale University Press, reprint edition 2003).

WEB SITES

Be sure to visit Fodors.com (⊕ www.fodors.com), a complete travel-planning site. You can research prices and book plane tickets, hotel rooms, rental cars, vacation packages, and more. In addition, you can post your pressing questions in the Travel Talk section.

Check theme-park Web sites, including disneyworld.com, universalorlando.com, and seaworldorlando.com, to get the latest prices and operating hours. Unofficial theme-park Web sites with excellent up-to-date information include allearsnet.com and wdwinfo.com To get feedback from fellow visitors who have been there, done that, check out the lively bulletin boards at disneyinfo.com and at fodors.com. To tap into the thrill-riding community, check out thrillride.com. Orlando is heavily represented, although you can also read about other theme parks nationwide.

WEDDINGS

Planning on living happily ever after? Then maybe you should tie the knot at Walt Disney World, as do some 1,000 couples every year. At the Fairy Tale Wedding Pavilion near the Grand Floridian Resort, the bride can ride in a Cinderella coach, have rings borne to the altar in a glass slipper, and invite Mickey and Minnie to attend the reception. Or exchange vows in the presence of sharks and dolphins at SeaWorld's *Ports of Call* events and banquet complex. Although it may prove impossible for Shamu to make a guest appearance, the maritime surroundings do make the pavilion tranquil.

🎫 WDW Wedding Information **Fairy Tale Wedding Pavilion** ☎ 407/828-3400 🖶 407/828-3744. *Ports of Call* ☎ 407/363-2200. **SeaWorld Weddings** ☎ 407/363-2273.

Walt Disney World

1

FODOR'S CHOICE

Big Thunder Mountain Railroad, *in the Magic Kingdom*

Fantasmic!, *in Disney–MGM Studios*

Festival of the Lion King, in the Animal Kingdom

Haunted Mansion, *in the Magic Kingdom*

IllumiNations, *in Epcot*

Kilimanjaro Safaris, *in the Animal Kingdom*

The Magic of Disney Animation, *in Disney–MGM Studios*

Mickey's PhilharMagic, *in the Magic Kingdom*

Mission: SPACE, *in Epcot*

Rock 'n' Roller Coaster Starring Aerosmith, *in Disney–MGM Studios*

Soarin' *in Epcot*

Space Mountain, *in the Magic Kingdom*

Splash Mountain, *in the Magic Kingdom*

SpectroMagic Parade, *in the Magic Kingdom*

Summit Plummet, *in Blizzard Beach*

Tree of Life—*It's Tough to Be a Bug!, in the Animal Kingdom*

Twilight Zone Tower of Terror, *in Disney–MGM Studios*

Updated by
Jennie Hess

NO MOSS EVER GROWS under the Mouse's trademark yellow clogs (unless it's artfully re-created moss for some lush forest landscape). Since its opening in 1971, Walt Disney World has made it a point to stay fresh, current, and endlessly amusing. Disney Imagineers and producers constantly choreograph new shows and parades, revamp classic theme rides, and periodically replace an entire attraction. Yet amid all the hoopla, much remains reassuringly the same, rekindling fond memories among the generations who return.

Millions of visitors, even those who place Pirates of the Caribbean and Space Mountain among the wonders of the world, are hard-pressed to define Walt Disney World. When you take a Walt Disney World exit off I–4, you're almost on the grounds, even though there's no Cinderella Castle in sight. It's a very big place, and it's crammed with pleasures: from swooping above the Magic Kingdom's starlit London in Peter Pan's Flight to simply sitting under the shade of a Callary pear tree frosted with blooms in Epcot; from whooping and hollering down water slides at the cleverly designed water parks to enjoying jazz at Pleasure Island.

The sheer enormity of the property—30,000 acres near Kissimmee, Florida—suggests that WDW is more than a single theme park with a fabulous castle in the center. The property's acreage translates to 47 square mi—twice the size of Manhattan or Bermuda, and about the same size as San Francisco. On a tract that size, 107 acres is a mere speck, yet that's the size of the Magic Kingdom. When most people imagine Walt Disney World, they think of only those 107 acres, but there's much, much more.

Epcot, the second major theme park and at 300 acres more than twice as big as the Magic Kingdom, is a combination of a science exploratorium and a world's fair, sprinkled with thrills throughout. Disney–MGM Studios is a park devoted to the world of live-action and animated movies and television shows. The Animal Kingdom, the fourth major theme park, salutes creatures real, imaginary, and extinct. Add two water parks, more than two dozen hotels, a sports complex, and countless shops, restaurants, and nightlife venues, and you start to get the picture. And still there are thousands of undeveloped acres. Deer patrol grassy plains and pine forests, and white ibis inhabit swamps patched by thickets of palmettos.

Best of all, Disney has proved that it can manage its elephantine resort and make customers so happy that they return year after year. Perhaps the company's most practical innovation, the FASTPASS system lets you experience the top attractions with little or no wait. Just feed your theme-park admission ticket into a FASTPASS machine and book your reservation time to visit an attraction.

Disney's tradition of constant and excellent upkeep has persevered through years of ups and downs within the company. Although minor slips in maintenance and cleanliness have been reported as of late, Disney insiders have seen few negative changes in spite of the company's recent economic woes and political turmoil. Whatever is happening in the background, all is still well on the kingdom's grounds.

Walt Disney's original decree that his parks be ever changing, along with some healthy competition from Universal Studios, SeaWorld, and other area attractions, keeps the Disney Imagineers and show producers on their toes as they dream up new entertainment and install higher-tech attractions. To avoid missing anything, do plenty of research before you go, make a plan, then try to relax—and have a wonderful time.

MAGIC KINGDOM

The Magic Kingdom is the heart and soul of the Disney empire. Comparable (in scope) to California's Disneyland, it was the first Disney outpost in Florida when it opened in 1971, and it's the park that launched Disney's presence, with modifications, in France, Japan, and now Hong Kong.

For a landmark that wields such worldwide influence, the Magic Kingdom may seem small: at 107 acres, it's smaller than Disney World's other Big Three parks. But looks can be deceiving: the unofficial theme song— "It's a Small World After All"—doesn't hold true when it comes to the

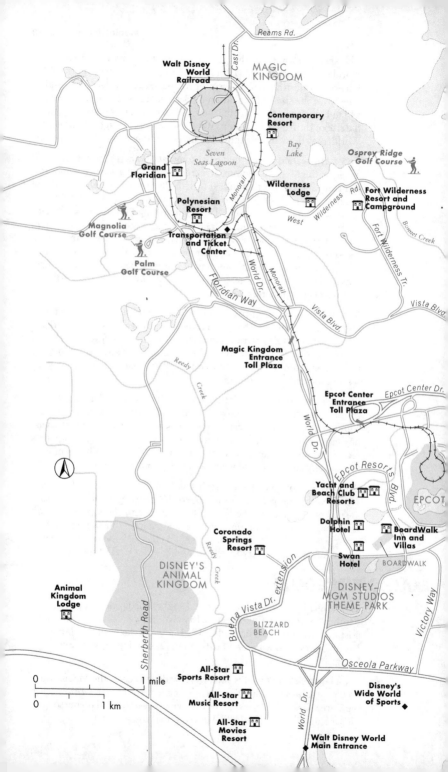

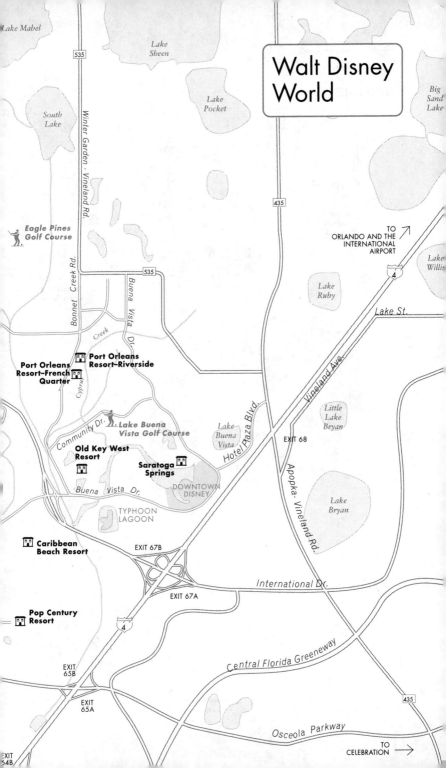

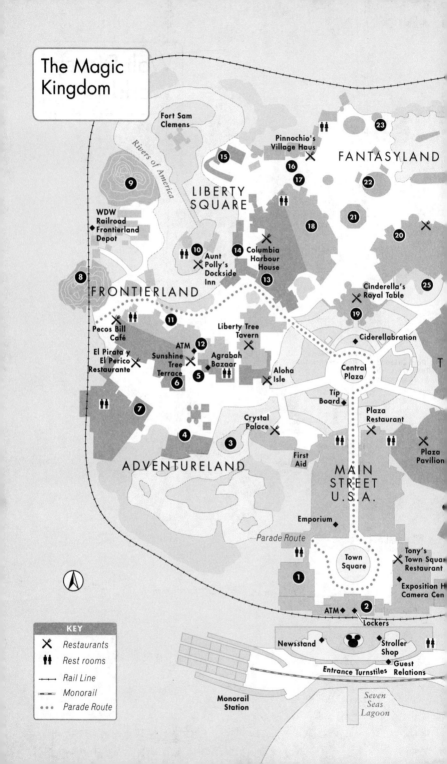

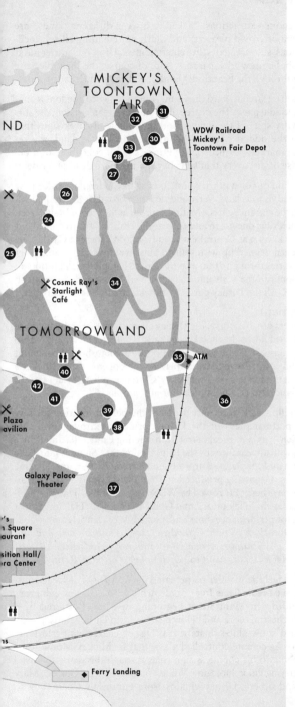

MICKEY'S TOONTOWN FAIR

WDW Railroad
Mickey's
Toontown Fair Depot

ND

Cosmic Ray's
Starlight
Café

TOMORROWLAND

ATM

Plaza
avilion

Galaxy Palace
Theater

's
n Square
aurant

sition Hall/
era Center

Ferry Landing

Magic Kingdom's attractions. Packed into seven different "lands" are nearly 50 major crowd pleasers, and that's not counting all the ancillary attractions: shops, eateries, live entertainment, Disney-character meet-and-greet spots, fireworks, parades, and, of course, the sheer pleasure of strolling through the beautifully landscaped and manicured grounds.

Many rides are geared toward the young, but the Magic Kingdom is anything but a kiddie park. The degree of detail, the greater vision, the surprisingly witty spiel of the guides, and the tongue-in-cheek signs that crop up in the oddest places—for instance, in Fantasyland, the restrooms are marked "Prince" and "Princess"—all contribute to a delightful sense of discovery that's far beyond the mere thrill of a ride.

The park is laid out on a north–south axis, with Cinderella Castle at the center and the various lands surrounding it in a broad circle. Upon passing through the entrance gates, you find yourself at the foot of Main Street, U.S.A., which runs due north and ends at the Hub, a large tree-lined circle, properly known as Central Plaza, in front of Cinderella Castle. The castle has been gussied up with stained-glass window effects and other royal accessories through 2006 as part of the "Happiest Celebration on Earth" in honor of the 50th anniversary of Walt's first park, Disneyland in California. All the Disney parks worldwide are in on the festivities.

Entertainment

The headliners are, of course, the Disney characters, especially if you're traveling with children. In what Disney calls "character greetings, " these lovable creatures sign autographs and pose for snapshots throughout the park—line up in Town Square when the gates open, or snag Mickey's autograph at the Judge's Tent in Mickey's Toontown Fair. Ariel's Grotto in Fantasyland also is a great place for autographs.

The Cinderella Castle forecourt provides the perfect location for several daily performances of the Disney princess extravaganza, **Cinderellabration,** a gala musical coronation starring Cinderella and Prince Charming, with appearances by the Fairy Godmother, Snow White, Belle from *Beauty and the Beast,* Aurora from *Sleeping Beauty,* and Jasmine from *Aladdin.* Originally produced at Tokyo Disneyland in 2003, *Cinderellabration* is being borrowed by WDW as part of the "Happiest Celebration on Earth." Pick up a Times Guide flyer at City Hall or in most park shops for performance times and a schedule of character meet-and-greets. ☞ **Duration:** *18 min.* **Crowds:** *Heavy, as with all new and limited-time shows.* **Strategy:** *Arrive 30–40 min early.* **Audience:** *All ages. Boys and older kids may want to skip it in favor of rides.* **Rating:** ★★.

Get ready to feel the wonder perpetuated by Walt Disney's legacy during the **Share a Dream Come True** parade, which proceeds through Frontierland and down Main Street beginning at 3 PM. Bolstered by a powerful orchestral score and beloved songs from Disney films, the six giant themed snow-globe floats reveal Disney characters performing "under glass"—climate-controlled glass, that is. Mickey Mouse leads off in a tribute to his countless film roles through the years, followed by floats carrying Pinocchio, Snow White, Cinderella, Belle, Dumbo, Mary Poppins, and others; Disney villains from Fantasia's Chernabog to

Best of the Park

Arrive at the parking lot 45 minutes before scheduled opening, and once in the park, dash left, or hop the **Walt Disney World Railroad,** to Frontierland, where you can claim an early FASTPASS time for **Splash Mountain.** After you've received your ticket, head over for **Big Thunder Mountain Railroad,** then ride **Pirates of the Caribbean.** By now, your FASTPASS ticket should be valid to ride Splash Mountain. Next head over to Liberty Square and get a FASTPASS for the **Haunted Mansion.** See the **Country Bear Jamboree** show or ride **it's a small world** until your time to visit the mansion is up. When you're finished, sprint over to Tomorrowland and pick up your next FASTPASS, this time for **Space Mountain** or **Stitch's Great Escape.** Try to time this so that you can have some lunch and then see **Cinderellabration** at the castle. If you have longer to wait, head to the **Timekeeper** or the **Carousel of Progress** if they're operating. By now, it'll be time for you to experience Space Mountain or Stitch. Afterward, pick up a FASTPASS for **Buzz Lightyear's Space Ranger Spin.** Then ride the **Tomorrowland Transit Authority** or squeeze in any attractions above that you may have missed.

If you haven't seen the 3 PM parade on previous visits, start looking for a viewing spot at 2:30 (many begin even earlier). Once you settle on a curb, send a member of your group to pick up the next set of FASTPASS tickets for the **Many Adventures of Winnie the Pooh.** If the crowds aren't too thick, the second floor of the train station makes a really nice parade viewing spot. After the parade, hop the train to Mickey's Toontown Fair and pose by the colorful house fronts for some fun photos. From there, stroll into Fantasyland for your FASTPASS appointment with Pooh. Afterward, get your FASTPASS appointment for **Mickey's PhilharMagic** or **Peter Pan's Flight.** While you wait, take a spin on **Cinderella's Golden Carrousel** and check out the **Cinderella Castle** mosaics.

You probably have time to get dinner and return to your hotel for a couple hours' rest before the **SpectroMagic** parade and **Wishes** fireworks show. If you watch the fireworks from Town Square, you can be ready to grab a monorail seat back to the parking lot as soon as it ends. On the other hand, if you want to ride Splash Mountain or Space Mountain again, lines will be short now, and you can see the fireworks from pretty much anywhere in the park.

On Rainy Days

If you visit during a busy time of year, pray for rain. Rainy days dissolve the crowds here. Unlike those at Disney–MGM and Epcot's Future World, however, many of the Magic Kingdom's attractions are outdoors. If you don't mind getting damp, pick up a poncho with Mickey insignia ($6 adults, $5 children) in almost any Disney merchandise shop and soldier on.

With Small Children
At Rope Drop, go directly to Fantasyland and start your day by getting a FASTPASS return-time ticket at the **Many Adventures of Winnie the Pooh.** Then, go on a ride with **Dumbo the Flying Elephant.** Next, check show times for **Mickey's PhilharMagic** 3-D extravaganza and plan to see it before moving on to a new land. While you wait for the show and your appointment with Pooh, take a whirl on **Cinderella's Golden Carrousel** and, moving clockwise, other attractions without prohibitive waits. You can also head for a character greeting (check your guide map for times). By now it should be time to use your FASTPASS ticket at the Many Adventures of Winnie the Pooh. When you've finished, get a FASTPASS for **Peter Pan's Flight.** Next head to **it's a small world.** If you have time before Peter Pan, visit **Ariel's Grotto** to pose for snapshots with the Little Mermaid, see a performance of **Cinderellabration** in front of the castle, or visit Pooh's new playground.

If you want a sit-down lunch, proceed to **Cinderella's Royal Table** at Cinderella Castle or **Liberty Tree Tavern** in Liberty Square (be sure to reserve seating in advance). **The Crystal Palace** buffet is a great option complete with character visits. Depending on your lunch location, either take the train or walk to Mickey's Toontown Fair. Lunch can digest while the children get their autographs and photos with Mickey Mouse. Then on to the **Barnstormer** to test their coaster mettle. Taking the **Walt Disney World Railroad** is the most relaxing way to return to Frontierland, where you can pick up your FASTPASS timed ticket for **Splash Mountain.** Then claim a piece of pavement across the street from the Country Bear Jamboree for the 3 PM parade so you can make a quick exit to line up for **Big Thunder Mountain Railroad**—if your kids can handle the thrills and are tall enough. For the shortest lines, go *during* the parade. By now, it should be time for your FASTPASS reservation for Splash Mountain. After the ride, check out either the **Country Bear Jamboree** or the **Haunted Mansion.**

Late afternoon is a nice time to hitch a raft to **Tom Sawyer Island.** When you return, head straight for Adventureland. Proceed directly across the Adventureland plaza to the **Jungle Cruise.** Pick up another FASTPASS here if the line is long. Then do **Pirates of the Caribbean** and the **Magic Carpets of Aladdin.** If you still have some time and energy left, scramble around the **Swiss Family Treehouse** and then head back for your FASTPASS entry to the Jungle Cruise.

Now stroll across the Main Street hub to Tomorrowland and pick up a FASTPASS ticket for **Buzz Lightyear's Space Ranger Spin.** While you wait, try to see **Stitch's Great Escape** or plan to return later for a FASTPASS. Then climb aboard **Tomorrowland Transit Authority** and, if the line's not prohibitive, **Astro-Orbiter.** By now it's time to join Buzz on his intergalactic mission and, if there's time afterward, to take a spin at the **Mad Tea Party.**

If you're really determined to see it all, have dinner at the closest restaurant, then hike toward the front of the park to grab a rocker on the porch of **Tony's Town Square Restaurant** or stake out a curb about an hour before the evening **SpectroMagic** parade and **Wishes** fireworks show for a spectacular end to your day.

Cruella de Vil; and a magical finale double snow globe of Cinderella Castle with Tinkerbell and other character favorites. ☞ *Show times: Daily at 3* PM *except during holiday performances of Mickey's Very Merry Christmas Parade.* **Duration:** *About 15 min.* **Crowds:** *Heavy.* **Strategy:** *Arrive 20–30 min in advance.* **Audience:** *All ages. Older kids may want to skip it in favor of rides, which will have shorter lines until the parade ends.* **Rating:** ★★.

FodorsChoice ★ The magic truly comes out at night when the **SpectroMagic** parade rolls down Main Street, U.S.A., in a splendidly choreographed surge of electroluminescent, fiber-optic, and prismatic lighting effects that bring to life peacocks, sea horses, fountains, fantasy gardens, and floats full of colorful Disney characters. Plenty of old-fashioned twinkle lights are thrown in for good measure, and familiar tunes are broadcast over 204 speakers with 72,000 watts of power. Mickey, as always, is the star. But Practical Pig, from one of Disney's prewar Silly Symphony cartoons, steals the show. With the flick of a paintbrush, he transforms more than 100 feet of multicolor floats into a gleaming white-light dreamscape. ☞ *Duration: 20 min.* **Crowds:** *Heavy.* **Strategy:** *Take your place on the curb at least 40 min before the parade begins.* **Audience:** *All ages.* **Rating:** ★★★.

When the lights dim on Main Street and orchestral music fills the air, you know the **Wishes** fireworks show is about to begin. The Kingdom's newest nighttime extravaganza is longer and even more impressive than the Fantasy in the Sky fireworks show, which it replaced in late 2003. In Wishes, Jiminy Cricket returns to convince you that your wishes really can come true, and he is supported by Disney characters from such classic films as *Pinocchio, Fantasia, Cinderella,* and *The Little Mermaid.* Songs from the movies play over loudspeakers as more than 650 individual fireworks paint the night sky. Oh, and don't worry that Tinker Bell may have been sealed in her jar for the night—she comes back to fly above the crowd in grand pixie-dust style. ☞ *Duration: 12 min.* **Crowds:** *Heavy.* **Strategy:** *Find a place near the front of the park so you can make a quick exit at the end of the show.* **Audience:** *All ages.* **Rating:** ★★★.

Numbers in the margin correspond to points of interest on the Magic Kingdom map.

Main Street, U.S.A.

With its pastel Victorian-style buildings, antique automobiles ahoohga-oohga-ing, sparkling sidewalks, and an atmosphere of what one writer has called "almost hysterical joy, " Main Street is more than a mere conduit to the other enchantments of the Magic Kingdom. It's where the spell is first cast.

Like Dorothy waking up in a Technicolor Oz or Mary Poppins jumping through the pavement painting, you emerge from beneath the Walt Disney World Railroad Station into a realization of one of the most tenacious American dreams. The perfect street in the perfect small town in a perfect moment of time is burnished to jewel-like quality, thanks to a four-fifths-scale reduction, nightly cleanings with high-pressure hoses, and constant repainting. And it's a very sunny world thanks to an out-pouring of welcoming entertainment: live bands, barbershop quartets, and background music from Disney films and American musicals played over loudspeakers. Old-fashioned horse-drawn trams and omnibuses with their horns tooting chug along the street. Street vendors in Victorian costumes sell balloons and popcorn. And Cinderella's famous castle floats whimsically in the distance where Main Street disappears.

Although attractions with a capital "A" are minimal on Main Street, there are plenty of inducements—namely, shops—to while away your time and part you from your money. The largest of these, the Emporium, is often the last stop for souvenir hunters at day's end, so avoid the crowds and buy early. You can have your purchases delivered to your hotel or mailed home.

The Harmony Barber Shop is a novel stop if you want to step back in time for a haircut ($14 for children 12 and under; $17 for all others). Kids get complimentary Mickey Ears and a certificate if it's their first haircut ever. The Main Street Exposition Hall in Town Square is actually a shop, exhibit, and theater in one, where you can see cameras of yesteryear and today, and Disney animated short films such as *Steamboat Willie,* from 1928. (Walt Disney said that he loved his creation more than any woman, which could make you wonder how his wife, Lillian, felt about this. It was she who persuaded her husband to change the character's name from Mortimer.) The shops in Exposition Hall are a good place to stock up on batteries, memory cards, and disposable cameras.

Main Street is also full of Disney insider fun for those in the know. For instance, check out the proprietors' names above the shops: Roy O. Disney, etched above the Main Street Confectionary, is the name of Walt's brother. Dick Nunis, former chairman of Walt Disney Attractions, has an honored spot above the bakery. At the Main Street Athletic Club, Card Walker—the "Practitioner of Psychiatry and Justice of the Peace"—is the former chairman of the company's executive committee. At last glance, Michael Eisner still didn't have his own shop; considering the company's recent political upheaval and Eisner's planned departure in 2006, perhaps he never will.

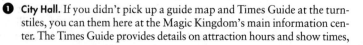

groovy souvenirs / Get your collectible Disney character pins at the **pin cart** across from the Chapeau on Main Street. The cart has the best pin selection in the park. Mickey-shape pasta from the **Main Street Market House** makes a wonderful gift for anyone, though you have to pack it carefully. Serious collectors of Disney memorabilia stop at the bright yellow, gingerbread **Main Street Gallery,** next to City Hall. If the sky looks dark, head to the **Emporium** for Disney's classic Mickey rain ponchos, essential on a rainy day. This is also the place to buy a stuffed character toy.

❶ **City Hall.** If you didn't pick up a guide map and Times Guide at the turn-stiles, you can them here at the Magic Kingdom's main information center. The Times Guide provides details on attraction hours and show times,

When to Go

Most families hit the Magic Kingdom early in their visit, so try to go toward the end of the week instead. Avoid weekends, since that's when local residents tend to visit the park.

Arrive at the turnstiles at least 30 minutes before Rope Drop to get your bearings and explore the shops on Main Street.

If you're staying at a Disney resort, arrive at park opening and stay until early afternoon, then head back to the hotel for a nap or swim. You can return to the park in the mid- to late afternoon, refreshed and ready to soak up more magic.

Times for after-dark entertainment depend on the day of the week, holidays, and peak times. Check the schedule before entering the park so you can set priorities and plan your day to avoid missing the nighttime festivities.

When You're There

Check Disney's Tip Board at the end of Main Street for good information on wait times—fairly reliable except for those moments when everyone follows the "See It Now!" advice and the line immediately triples.

Staying hydrated is critical on steamy, Central Florida afternoons. Take your own water bottles and refill them at park fountains throughout the day. A 20–24 ounce bottle of water sells for $2 in the parks; smaller bottles go for $1.25.

Do your shopping in midafternoon, when attraction lines resemble a napping anaconda. During the afternoon parade, store clerks have been spotted twiddling their thumbs, so this is the time to seek sales assistance. If you go at the end of the day, you'll be engulfed by rush-hour crowds.

See or ride one of the star attractions while the parade is going on, if you're willing to miss it, since lines ease considerably. But be careful not to get stuck on the wrong side of the parade route when the hoopla starts, or you may never get across.

Designate a very specific meeting place—such as a particular bench—after restroom stops, when it's easy to miss someone.

At the start of the day, set up a rendezvous point and time, just in case you and your companions get separated. Good places are by the Cinderella Fountain in Fantasyland, the bottom of the staircase at the Main Street railroad station, the benches of City Hall, and the archway entrance to Adventureland.

which vary from day to day. Restaurant hours, character greeting times and locations, and other key park details are included.

② **Walt Disney World Railroad.** If you click through the turnstile just before 9 AM with young children in tow, wait at the entrance before crossing beneath the train station. In a few moments you'll see the day's first steam-driven train arrive laden with the park's most popular residents: Mickey Mouse, Donald Duck, Goofy, Pluto, and characters from every corner of the World. Once they disembark and you've collected the stars' signatures, step right up to the elevated platform above the Magic Kingdom's entrance for a ride into living history. Walt Disney was a railroad buff of the highest order—he constructed a one-eighth-scale train in his backyard and named it *Lilly Belle*, after his wife, Lillian. Another *Lilly Belle* rides the rails here, as do *Walter E. Disney, Roy O. Disney,* and *Roger Broggie* (named for a Disney Imagineer and fellow railroad aficionado). All the locomotives date from 1928, coincidentally the same year Mickey Mouse was created. Disney scouts tracked down these vintage carriers in Mexico, where they were used to haul sugarcane in the Yucatán, brought them back, and completely overhauled them to their present splendor. And splendid they are, with striped awnings, brightly painted benches, authoritative "choo-choo" sounds, and hissing plumes of steam. Their 1½-mi track runs along the perimeter of the Magic Kingdom, with much of the trip through the woods. Stops are in Frontierland and Mickey's Toontown Fair. The ride provides a good introduction to the layout of the park and a quick trip with small children to Toontown in the morning; otherwise, it's great as relief for tired feet and dragging legs later in the day. The four trains run at five- to seven-minute intervals. ☞ *Duration: 21 min. Crowds: Can be substantial beginning in late morning through late afternoon. Strategy: Board with small children for an early start in Toontown, or hop aboard in midafternoon if you don't see a line. Or ride to Frontierland in the early morning to get a jump-start on the Splash Mountain line. Audience: All ages. Rating:* ★★.

Adventureland

From the scrubbed brick, manicured lawns, and meticulously pruned trees of the Central Plaza, an artfully dilapidated wooden bridge leads to the jungles of Adventureland. The landscape artists went wild here: South African cape honeysuckle droops, Brazilian bougainvillea drapes, Mexican flame vines cling, spider plants clone, and three different varieties of palm trees sway, all creating a seemingly spontaneous mess. The bright, all-American sing-along tunes that fill the air along Main Street and Central Plaza are replaced by the recorded repetitions of trumpeting elephants, pounding drums, and squawking parrots. The architecture is a mishmash of the best of Thailand, the Middle East, the Caribbean, Africa, and Polynesia, arranged in an inspired disorder that recalls comic-book fantasies of far-off places.

③ **Swiss Family Treehouse.** Inspired by the classic novel by Johann Wyss about the adventures of the Robinson family, who were shipwrecked on the way to America, the tree house shows what you can do with a big tree and a lot of imagination. The rooms are furnished with patchwork quilts and mahogany furniture. Disney detail abounds: the kitchen sink is a giant clamshell; the boys' room, strewn with clothing, has two hammocks instead of beds; and an ingenious system of rain barrels and bamboo pipes provides running water in every room. As you clamber around the narrow wooden steps and rope bridges that connect the rooms in this split-level dwelling, take a look at the Spanish moss. It's real, but the tree itself—some 90 feet in diameter, with more than 1,000 branches—was constructed by the props department. The 300,000 leaves are vinyl. It all adds up to a species of tree unofficially called *Disneyodendron eximus,* or "out-of-the-ordinary Disney tree." ☞ *Duration: Up to you. Crowds: Artfully camouflaged so you may not see them—and the lines move slowly. Strategy: Visit while waiting for your Jungle Cruise FAST-PASS appointment. Audience: All ages; toddlers unsteady on their feet may have trouble with the stairs.* **Rating: ★★**.

④ Jungle Cruise. On this Disney classic, you cruise through three continents and along four rivers: the Congo, the Nile, the Mekong, and the Amazon. The canopied launches are loaded, the safari-suited guides make a point of checking their pistols, and the *Irrawady Irma* or *Mongala Millie* is off for another "perilous" journey. The guide's shtick is surprisingly funny in a wry and cornball way. Along the way, you'll encounter Disney's famed audio-animatronics creatures of the African veldt: bathing elephants, slinky pythons, an irritated rhinoceros, a tribe of hungry headhunters, and a bunch of hyperactive hippos (good thing the guide's got a pop pistol). Then there's Old Smiley, the crocodile, who's always waiting for a handout—or, as the guide quips, "a foot out." The animals are well-designed, but anyone who's seen the real thing at the Animal Kingdom or even a good zoo won't be impressed. The Jungle Cruise isn't really worth a FASTPASS. ☞ *Duration: 10 min. Crowds: Huge, from late morning until dinnertime. Strategy: Go during the afternoon parade, but not after dark—you miss too much. Audience: All ages.* **Rating: ★**.

need a break? If you're looking for real refreshment and an energy boost, stop by **Aloha Isle,** where you'll find some of the tastiest and most healthful goodies. Try the fresh pineapple spears, or sip a smoothie or just some fruit juice, while you relax on one of the benches scattered throughout Adventureland.

⑤ The Magic Carpets of Aladdin. Brightening the lush Adventureland landscape is this jewel-toned ride around a giant genie's bottle. You can control your own four-passenger, state-of-the-art carpet with a front-seat lever that moves it up and down and a rear-seat button that pitches it forward or backward. Part of the fun is trying to dodge the right-on aim of a water-spewing "camel." Though short, the ride is a big hit with kids, who are also dazzled by the colorful gems implanted in the pavement around the attraction. ☞ *Duration: About 3 min. Crowds: Heavy due to the attraction's newness, but lines move fairly quickly. Strategy: Visit while waiting for your Jungle Cruise FASTPASS appointment. Audience: All ages; parents must ride with toddlers.* **Rating: ★★★**.

6 Enchanted Tiki Room. In its original incarnation as the Enchanted Tiki Birds, this was Disney's first audio-animatronics attraction. Now updated, it includes the avian stars of two popular Disney animated films: Zazu from *The Lion King* and Iago from *Aladdin*. The boys take you on a tour of the original attraction while cracking lots of jokes. A holdover from the original is the ditty "In the Tiki, Tiki, Tiki, Tiki, Tiki Room," which is second only to "It's a Small World" as the Disney song you most love to hate. Speaking of which, many people really do hate this attraction, finding the talking birds obnoxious and the music way too loud and peppy. ☞ *Duration: 12 min.* **Crowds:** *Waits seldom exceed 30 min.* **Strategy:** *Go when you need a sit-down refresher in an air-conditioned room.* **Audience:** *All ages.* **Rating:** ★.

7 Pirates of the Caribbean. This boat ride is classic Disney with a set and cast of characters created with incredible attention to detail. One of the pirate's "Avast, ye scurvy scum!" is the sort of greeting you'll want to practice on your companions. And if you've seen *Pirates of the Caribbean,* the movie, you'll even recognize some scenes. This might be the only ride in the world that inspired a film rather than the other way around.

The gracious arched entrance soon gives way to a dusty dungeon, redolent of dampness and of a spooky, scary past. Lanterns flicker as you board the boats and a ghostly voice intones, "Dead men tell no tales." Next, a deserted beach, strewn with shovels, a skeleton, and a disintegrating map indicating buried treasure, prefaces this story of greed, lust, and destruction. Emerging from a pitch-black tunnel after a mild, tummy-tickling drop, you're caught in the middle of a furious battle. A pirate ship, cannons blazing, attacks a stone fortress. Audio-animatronics pirates hoist the Jolly Roger while brave soldiers scurry to defend the fort—to no avail. Politically correct nerves may twinge as the women of the town are rounded up and auctioned. "Strike your colors, ye brazen wench, no need to expose your superstructure!" shouts one pirate. The wild antics of the pirates result in a conflagration; the town goes up in flames, and all go to their just reward amid the catchy chorus. There's a moral in there somewhere, if you want to look for one—or you can just enjoy the show. ☞ *Duration: 10 min.* **Crowds:** *Waits seldom exceed 30 min, despite the ride's popularity.* **Strategy:** *A good destination, especially in the heat of the afternoon.* **Audience:** *All ages.* **Rating:** ★★★.

groovy souvenirs Among the all-time best Magic Kingdom souvenirs are the pirate hats, swords, and plastic hooks-for-hands at the **Pirate's Bazaar** near the Pirates of the Caribbean exit. Nearby, the **Agrabah Bazaar** has Aladdin-wear, including costumes and jewelry, plus safari hats, carvings, and masks. Jasmine and other Aladdin characters are sometimes on hand to sign autographs next to the store.

Frontierland

Frontierland, in the northwest quadrant of the Magic Kingdom, evokes the American frontier. The period seems to be the latter half of the 19th century, and the West is being won by Disney cast members dressed in checked shirts, leather vests, cowboy hats, and brightly colored neckerchiefs. Banjo and fiddle music twangs from tree to tree, and snackers walk around munching turkey drumsticks so large that you could best an outlaw single-handedly with one.

The screams that periodically drown out the string music are not the result of a cowboy surprising an Indian. They come from two of the Magic Kingdom's more thrilling rides: Splash Mountain, an elaborate flume ride; and Big Thunder Mountain Railroad, one of the park's two roller coasters. In contrast to lush Adventureland, Frontierland is planted with mesquite, twisted Peruvian pepper trees, slash pines, and cacti.

The Walt Disney World Railroad makes a stop at Frontierland. It tunnels past a colorful scene in Splash Mountain and drops you off between Splash Mountain and Thunder Mountain.

FodorsChoice

8 **Splash Mountain.** At Rope Drop, one of the attractions to which the hordes are dashing is this incredibly popular log-flume ride, based on the animated sequences in Disney's 1946 film *Song of the South*. Here the audio-animatronics creations of Brer Rabbit, Brer Bear, Brer Fox, and a menagerie of other Brer beasts frolic in bright, cartoonlike settings. No matter what time you get there, you *will*, repeat *will*, wait in line. So the Disney folks have made the waiting area here as entertaining and comfortable as possible. When you finally do settle into the eight-person hollowed-out logs, Uncle Remus's voice growls, "Mark mah words, Brer Rabbit gonna put his foot in Brer Fox's mouth one of these days." And this just might be the day.

As the boat carries you through a lily pond and up the mountain, Brer Rabbit's silhouette hops merrily ahead to the tune of the ride's theme song, "Time to Be Moving Along." Every time some critter makes a grab for the bunny, your log boat drops out of reach. But Brer Fox has been studying his book *How to Catch a Rabbit,* and our lop-eared friend looks as if he's destined for the pot. Things don't look so good for the flumers, either. You get one heart-stopping pause at the top of the mountain—just long enough to grab the safety bar—and then the boat plummets down into a gigantic, very wet briar patch. In case you want to know what you're getting into, the drop is 52½ feet—that's about five stories—at a 45-degree angle, enough to reach speeds of 40 mph and make you feel weightless. Try to smile through your clenched teeth: as you begin to drop, a flashbulb pops. You can purchase a photographic memento of the experience before exiting the ride. Brer Rabbit escapes—and so do you, wet and exhilarated—to the tune of "Zip-a-Dee-Doo-Dah, " the bouncy, best-known melody from the film. If you want to get really wet—and you will get splashed from almost every seat—ask the ride attendant to seat you in the front row. ☞ *Duration: 11 min. Crowds: Yes! Strategy: FASTPASS appointment. Otherwise, if you're not in line by 9:45 AM, plan to ride during meal or parade times. Parents who need to Baby Swap can take the young ones to a play area in a cave under the ride. Audience: All except very young children, who may be terrified by the final drop. No pregnant women or guests wearing back, neck, or leg braces. Minimum height: 40″. Rating:* ★★★.

Fodor's Choice

⑨ Big Thunder Mountain Railroad. Set in gold-rush days, the theme of this thrilling roller coaster is a runaway train. It's a bumpy ride with several good drops and moments when you feel like you're going to fly right off the tracks, but there are no inversions and at least you can see where you're going (unlike in Space Mountain). Overall it's more fun than scary and you'll see kids as young as seven lining up to ride. The design is fabulous, too. The train rushes and rattles past 20 audio-animatronics figures—including donkeys, chickens, a goat, and a grizzled old miner surprised in his bathtub—as well as $300,000 worth of genuine antique mining equipment, tumbleweeds, a derelict mining town, hot springs, and a flash flood.

The ride was 15 years in the planning and took two years and close to $17 million to build. This 1979 price tag, give or take a few million, equaled the entire cost of erecting California's Disneyland in 1955. The 197-foot mountain is based on the monoliths of Utah's Monument Valley, and thanks to 650 tons of steel, 4,675 tons of concrete, and 16,000 gallons of paint, it closely resembles the real thing. ☞ *Duration: 4 min. Crowds: Large. Strategy: Use FASTPASS unless the wait is less than 10 min. The ride is most exciting at night, when you can't anticipate the curves and the track's rattling sounds as if something's about to give. Audience: All except young children. No pregnant women or guests wearing back, neck, or leg braces. Minimum height: 40".* **Rating:** ★★★.

⑩ Tom Sawyer Island. An artfully ungrammatical sign tells you what to expect: "IF'N YOU LIKE DARK CAVES, MYSTERY MINES, BOTTOMLESS PITS, SHAKY BRIDGES 'N' BIG ROCKS, YOU HAVE CAME TO THE BEST PLACE I KNOW." Aunt Polly would have walloped Tom for his orthography, but she couldn't have argued with the sentiment. Actually two tiny islands connected by an old-fashioned swing bridge, Tom Sawyer Island is a natural playground, all hills and trees and rocks and shrubs.

The main island, where your raft docks, is where most of the attractions are found. The Mystery Cave is an almost pitch-black labyrinth where the wind wails in a truly spooky fashion. Children love Injun Joe's Cave, all pointy stalactites and stalagmites and with lots of columns and crevices from which to jump out and startle siblings. And, in a clearing at the top of the hill, there's a rustic playground. As you explore the shoreline on the dirt paths, keep an eye out for the barrel bridge—every time someone takes a step, the whole contraption bounces.

On the other island is Fort Sam Clemens, a log fortress from which you can fire air guns with great booms and cracks at the passing *Liberty Belle* riverboat. It's guarded by a snoring audio-animatronics sentry, working off his last bender. Both islands are sprinkled with lookouts for great views to Thunder Mountain and Frontierland. ☞ *Duration: Up to you. Crowds: Seldom overwhelming, but it wouldn't matter—here, the more the merrier. Strategy: Try it as a refreshing afternoon getaway. Audience: All ages.* **Rating:** ★★.

⑪ Country Bear Jamboree. Wisecracking, cornpone, lovelorn audio-animatronics bears joke, sing, and play country music and 1950s rock-and-roll in this stage show. The emcee, the massive but debonair Henry, leads the stellar cast of Grizzly Hall, which includes the robust Trixie, who laments love lost while perching on a swing suspended from the ceiling; Bubbles, Bunny, and Beulah, harmonizing on "All the Guys That Turn Me On Turn Me Down"; and Big Al, the off-key cult figure who has inspired postcards, stuffed animals, and his own shop next door. Don't miss the bears' seasonal show in late November and December, when they deck the halls for a special concert. ☞ *Duration: 17 min.* *Crowds: Large, considering the relatively small theater.* *Strategy: Visit before 11 AM, during the afternoon parade, or after most small children have left for the day. Stand to the far left in the anteroom, where you wait, to end up in the front rows; to the far right if you want to sit in the last row, where small children can perch on top of the seats to see better.* *Audience: All ages; even timid youngsters love the bears.* *Rating:* ★★★.

groovy souvenirs

Cowboy hats and Davy Crockett coonskin caps at **Big Al's,** across from the County Bear Jamboree, are fun to try on even if you don't want to take one home. And families with a passion for pin trading can choose from among a selection of 400 Disney pins, including limited-edition pieces, at the **Frontier Trading Post.** The **Prairie Outpost & Supply** carries gourmet goodies for all tastes.

⑫ Frontierland Shootin' Arcade. At this classic shooting arcade, laser beams substitute for bullets, as genuine Hawkins 54-caliber buffalo rifles have been refitted to emit electronic beams. When they strike, tombstones spin and epitaphs change, ghost riders gallop out of clouds, and skulls pop out of graves, accompanied by the sounds of howling coyotes, creaking bridges, and the cracks of the rifles blasted over the digital audio system. ☞ *Cost: 50¢ per 25 shots.* *Strategy: Bring a pocketful of change.* *Audience: Older children and adults.* *Rating:* ★.

Liberty Square

The rough-and-tumble Western frontier gently folds into colonial America as Liberty Square picks up where Frontierland leaves off. The weathered siding gives way to solid brick and neat clapboard. The mesquite and cactus are replaced by stately oaks and masses of azaleas. The theme is colonial history, which Northerners will be happy to learn is portrayed here as solid Yankee. The small buildings, topped with weather vanes and exuding comfortable prosperity, are pure New England.

A replica of the Liberty Bell, crack and all, seems an appropriate prop to separate Liberty Square from Frontierland. There's even a Liberty Tree, a more than 150-year-old live oak found elsewhere on Walt Disney World property and moved to the Magic Kingdom. Just as the Sons of Liberty hung lanterns on trees as a signal of solidarity after the Boston Tea Party, the Liberty Tree's branches are decorated with 13 lanterns representing the 13 original colonies. Around the square are tree-shaded tables for an alfresco lunch and plenty of carts and fast-food eateries to supply the goods.

⑬ Hall of Presidents. This multimedia tribute to the Constitution caused quite a sensation when it opened decades ago, because it was here that the first refinements of the audio-animatronics system of computerized robots could be seen. Now surpassed by Epcot's American Adventure, it's still well worth attending, as much for the spacious, air-conditioned theater as for the two-part show.

It starts with a film, narrated by writer Maya Angelou, that discusses the Constitution as the codification of the spirit that founded America. You learn about threats to the document, ranging from the 18th-century Whiskey Rebellion to the Civil War, and hear such famous speeches as Benjamin Franklin's plea to the Continental Congress delegates for ratification and Abraham Lincoln's warning that "a house divided against itself cannot stand." The shows conveying Disney's brand of patriotism may be a little ponderous, but they're always well researched and lovingly presented; this film, for instance, was revamped to replace a lingering subtext of Cold War fear with the more progressive assertion that democracy is a work in progress, that liberty and justice still do not figure equally in the lives of all Americans.

The second half is a roll call of all 42 U.S. presidents. (Because Grover Cleveland's two terms were nonconsecutive, they are counted separately.) Each chief executive responds with a nod—even those who blatantly attempted to subvert the Constitution—and those who are seated rise (except for wheelchair-bound Franklin Delano Roosevelt, of course). The detail is lifelike, right down to the brace on Roosevelt's leg. The robots can't resist nodding, fidgeting, and even whispering to each other while waiting for their names to come up. ☞ *Duration: 30 min.* **Crowds:** *Light to moderate.* **Strategy:** *Go in the afternoon, when you'll appreciate the air-conditioning.* **Audience:** *Older children and adults.* **Rating:** ★★.

---

need a break?

Sleepy Hollow offers quick pick-me-ups in the decadent form of fruit cobblers, brownies, and other baked treats. Espresso drinks, root beer floats, and caramel corn are also on the menu.

---

⑭ Liberty Square Riverboat. An old-fashioned steamboat, the *Liberty Belle* is authentic, from its calliope whistle and the gingerbread trim on its three decks to the boilers that produce the steam that drives the big rear paddle wheel. In fact, the boat misses authenticity on only one count: there's no mustachioed captain to guide it during the ride around the Rivers of America. That task is performed by an underwater rail. The trip is slow and not exactly thrilling, except, perhaps, to the kids getting "shot at" by their counterparts at Fort Sam Clemens on Tom Sawyer Island. But it's a relaxing break for all concerned, and children like exploring the boat. ☞ *Duration: 15 min.* **Crowds:** *Moderate, but capacity is high, so waits are seldom trying.* **Strategy:** *Go when you need a break from the crowds.* **Audience:** *All ages.* **Rating:** ★.

⑮ Haunted Mansion. The special effects here are a howl. Or perhaps a scream is more like it. Or for most, both. You're greeted at the creaking iron gates of this Hudson River Valley Gothic mansion by a lugubrious attendant, who has one of the few jobs at Walt Disney World for which smiling is frowned upon, and ushered into a spooky picture gallery. A disembodied voice echoes from the walls: "Welcome, foolish mortals, to the Haunted Mansion. I am your ghost host." A scream shivers down, and you're off into one of Disney's classic attractions.

Consisting mainly of a slow-moving ride in a black, cocoonlike "doom buggy," the Haunted Mansion is only scary for younger children, and that's mostly because of the darkness. Everyone else will just laugh at the special effects. Watch the artfully strung liquid cobwebs pass you by; the suit of armor that comes alive; the shifting walls in the portrait gallery that make you wonder if they are moving up or if you are moving down; the ghostly ballroom dancers; and, of course, Madame Leota's talking disembodied head in the crystal ball. Just when you think the Imagineers have exhausted their bag of ectoplasmic tricks, along comes another one; you suddenly discover that your doom buggy has gained an extra passenger. As you approach the exit, your ghoulish guide intones, "Now I will raise the safety bar and the ghost will follow you home." Thanks for the souvenir, pal. And speaking of souvenirs, if you can't resist resurrecting the mansion's residents, you can get a plastic model of the mansion, complete with tiny ghosts and guests, or Disney's Haunted Mansion Clue board game, at the park's Disney & Co. shop and at Once Upon a Toy in Downtown Disney.

An interesting piece of Disney trivia: one of the biggest jobs for the maintenance crew here isn't cleaning up but keeping the 200-odd trunks, chairs, harps, dress forms, statues, rugs, and knickknacks appropriately dusty. Disney buys its dust in 5-pound bags and scatters it throughout the mansion with a special gadget resembling a fertilizer spreader. According to local lore, enough dust has been dumped since the park's 1971 opening to completely bury the mansion. Where does it all go? Perhaps the voice is right in saying that something will follow you home. ☞ *Duration: 8 min. Crowds: Substantial, but high capacity and fast loading usually keep lines moving. Strategy: Take advantage of FASTPASS here unless the line is short. Nighttime adds an extra fright factor, and you may be able to queue right up during the evening parade in peak season. Audience: All but very young children who are easily frightened. Rating:* ★★★.

Fantasyland

Walt Disney called this "a timeless land of enchantment." Fantasyland does conjure up pixie dust. Perhaps that's because the fanciful gingerbread houses, gleaming gold turrets, and, of course, rides based on Disney-animated movies are what the Magic Kingdom is all about.

With the exception of the slightly spooky Snow White's Scary Adventures, the attractions here are whimsical rather than heart-stopping. Like the animated classics on which they're based, these rides, which could ostensibly be classified as rides for children, are packed with enough delightful detail to engage the adults who accompany them. It's hard to remain unmoved by the view of moonlit London in Peter Pan's Flight. If you're traveling without children, stick with Peter Pan, the unforgettable "it's a small world," and Mickey's PhilharMagic 3-D extravaganza. Unfortunately, Fantasyland is always the most heavily trafficked area in the park, and its rides are almost always crowded.

BEHIND THE SCENES

AS YOU STROLL DOWN *Main Street, U.S.A., Disney cast members are dashing through tunnels in a bustling underground city, the nerve center of the Magic Kingdom. The 9-acre corridor system beneath the park leads to behind-the-scenes areas where employees create their Disney magic. It also ensures that you'll never see a frontiersman ambling through Tomorrowland. There's the Costuming department with miles of racks, and Cosmetology, where Cinderella can touch up her hair and makeup. At the heart of this domain is the Digital Animation Control System (DACS), which directs virtually everything in the Magic Kingdom.*

The only way to see what goes on in Disney's tunnels is by taking one of two backstage tours: the Keys to the Kingdom lasts more than four hours and costs $58, including lunch but not mandatory park admission; and Backstage Magic lasts seven hours and costs $199 including peeks at Epcot and Disney–MGM Studios, as well as lunch (park admission not included or required). These tours are restricted to people age 16 and older. Security measures prevent access to most of the concrete tunnels, so it's unlikely you'll bump into Mickey without his head on. (And don't expect to take photos. Disney guards its underground treasures carefully!) If you visit in December, you can take the three-hour Yuletide Fantasy tour ($59)—an insider's look at how Disney's elves transform its parks and resorts. Reserve a spot several months in advance. For details, call ☎ 407/939-8687.

You can enter Fantasyland on foot from Liberty Square, but the classic introduction is through Cinderella Castle. To get in an appropriately magical mood—and to provide yourself with a cooling break—turn left immediately after you exit the castle's archway. Here you'll find a charming and often overlooked touch: Cinderella Fountain, a lovely brass casting of the castle's namesake, who's dressed in her peasant togs and surrounded by her beloved mice and bird friends.

Photographers will want to take advantage of one of the least-traveled byways in the Magic Kingdom. From the southern end of Liberty Square, turn left at the Sleepy Hollow snack shop. Just past the outdoor tables is a shortcut to Fantasyland that provides one of the best unobstructed ground-level views of Cinderella Castle in the park. It's a great spot for a family photo.

16 it's a small world. Visiting Walt Disney World and not stopping for this tribute to terminal cuteness—why, the idea is practically un-American. Freshly renovated in 2004, this new-and-improved ride has stereo sound for the first time, so you can discern the famous song as it emanates from each scene—it's quite an improvement over the old mono soundtrack.

The attraction is essentially a boat ride through several candy-color lands, each representing a continent and each crammed with musical moppets, all madly singing. Disney raided the remains of the 1964–65 New York World's Fair for sets, and then appropriated the theme song of international brotherhood and friendship for its own. Some claim that it's the revenge of the audio-animatrons, as simplistic dolls differentiated mostly by their national dress—Dutch babies in clogs, Spanish flamenco dancers, German oompah bands, Russians playing balalaikas, sari-wrapped Indians waving temple bells, Tower of London guards in scarlet beefeater uniforms, Swiss yodelers and goatherds, Japanese kite fliers, Middle East snake charmers, and young French cancan dancers, to name just a few—parade past, smiling away and wagging their heads in time to the song. But somehow, by the time you reach the end of the ride, you're grinning and wagging, too, with the one-verse theme song indelibly impressed in your brain. Now all together: "It's a world of laughter, a world of tears. It's a world of hope and a world of fears. . . ." ☞ *Duration: 11 min. Crowds: Steady, but lines move fast. Strategy: Go back later if there's a long wait, since crowds ebb and flow here. Tots may beg for a repeat ride; it's worth another go-round to see all that you missed on the first trip through. Audience: All ages. Rating:* ★★.

❼ Peter Pan's Flight. This truly fantastic indoor ride was inspired by Sir James M. Barrie's 1904 novel about the boy who wouldn't grow up, which Disney animated in 1953. Aboard two-person magic sailing ships with brightly striped sails, you soar into the skies above London en route to Neverland. Along the way you can see Wendy, Michael, and John get sprinkled with pixie dust while Nana barks below, wave to Princess Tiger Lily, meet the evil Captain Hook, and cheer for the tick-tocking, clock-swallowing crocodile who breakfasted on Hook's hand and is more than ready for lunch. Despite the absence of high-tech special effects, children love this ride. Adults enjoy the dreamy views of London by moonlight, a galaxy of twinkling yellow lights punctuated by Big Ben, London Bridge, and the Thames River. The only negative is the rides brevity. Avoid the stand-by line or upon exiting you may find yourself more than a little annoyed at having waited for an hour for a 2½ minute ride. ☞ *Duration: 2½ min. Crowds: Always heavy, except in the evening and early morning. Strategy: Get a FASTPASS, and enjoy other Fantasyland attractions while you wait. Audience: All ages. Rating:* ★★.

FodorśChoice

❽ Mickey's PhilharMagic. Mickey Mouse may be the headliner here, but it's Donald Duck's misadventures—reminiscent of Mickey's as the sorcerer's apprentice in *Fantasia*—that set the comic pace in this gorgeous, 3-D animated film. As you settle into your theater seat, the on-screen action takes you behind the curtains at a grand concert hall where Donald and Mickey are preparing for a musical performance. But when Donald misuses Mickey's magical sorcerer's hat, he suddenly finds himself on a whirlwind journey that includes a magic carpet ride and an electrifying dip under the sea. And you go along for the ride. On the way you meet favorite Disney characters including Ariel, Simba, Aladdin and Jasmine, and Peter Pan and Tinker Bell. The film startles with its special-effects technology—you'll smell a fresh-baked apple pie, feel the rush of air as champagne corks pop, and get lost in the action on one of the largest screens ever created for a 3-D film: a 150-foot-wide canvas. The film is beautifully scored, with popular tunes like "Be Our Guest" and "Part of Your World," and it marks the first time that classic Disney characters appear in a computer-generated animation attraction. ☞ *Duration: 12 min. Crowds: Heavy. Strategy: Grab a FASTPASS or arrive early or during a parade. Audience: All ages. Rating:* ★★★.

⑲ Cinderella Castle. This quintessential Disney icon, with its royal blue turrets, gold spires, and glistening white towers, was inspired by the castle built by the mad Bavarian king Ludwig II at Neuschwanstein, as well as by drawings prepared for Disney's animated film of the French fairy tale. Although often confused with Disneyland's Sleeping Beauty Castle, at 180 feet this castle is more than 100 feet taller; and with its elongated towers and lacy fretwork, it is immeasurably more graceful. It's easy to miss the elaborate murals on the walls of the archway as you rush toward Fantasyland from the Hub, but they're worth a stop. The five panels, measuring some 15 feet high and 10 feet wide, were designed by Disney artist Dorothea Redmond and created from a million bits of multicolor Italian glass, silver, and 14-karat gold by mosaicist Hanns-Joachim Scharff. Following the images drawn for the Disney film, the mosaics tell the story of the little cinder girl as she goes from pumpkin to prince to happily ever after.

The fantasy castle has feet, if not of clay, then of solid steel beams, fiberglass, and 500 gallons of paint. Instead of dungeons, there are service tunnels for the Magic Kingdom's less-than-magical quotidian operations, such as Makeup and Costuming. These are the same tunnels that honeycomb the ground under much of the park. And upstairs doesn't hold, as rumor has it, a casket containing the cryogenically preserved body of Walt Disney. Within the castle's archway is the **King's Gallery,** one of the Magic Kingdom's priciest shops. Here you'll find exquisite hand-painted models of carousel horses, delicate crystal castles, and other symbols of fairy-tale magic, including Cinderella's glass slipper in many colors and sizes.

If you have reservations to dine at **Cinderella's Royal Table,** you enter the castle by way of an ascending spiral staircase where costumed waiters attend to your meal. Cinderella, her Fairy Godmother, and other princesses join you at what is one of the most popular character-greeting experiences offered at Walt Disney World.

⑳ Snow White's Scary Adventures. What was previously an unremittingly scary indoor spook-house ride where the dwarves might as well have been named Anxious and Fearful is now a kinder, gentler experience with six-passenger cars and a miniversion of the movie. There's still the evil queen, the wart on her nose, and her cackle, but joining the cast at long last are the Prince and Snow White herself. Although the trip is packed with plenty of scary moments, an honest-to-goodness kiss followed by a happily-ever-after ending might even get you "heigh-ho"-ing on your way out. ☞ *Duration: 3 min. Crowds: Steady from late morning until evening. Strategy: Go very early, during the afternoon parade, or after dark. Audience: All ages; may be frightening for young children. Rating:* ★.

㉑ Cinderella's Golden Carrousel. It's the whirling, musical heart of Fantasyland. This ride encapsulates the Disney experience in 90 prancing horses and then hands it to you on a 60-foot moving platter. Seventy-two of the dashing wooden steeds date from the original carousel built in 1917 by the Philadelphia Toboggan Company; additional mounts were made of fiberglass. All are meticulously painted—it takes about 48 hours per horse—and each one is completely different. One wears a collar of bright yellow roses; another a quiver of Native American arrows. The horses gallop ceaselessly beneath a wooden canopy, gaily striped on the outside and decorated on the inside with 18 panels depicting scenes from Disney's 1950 film *Cinderella*. As the platter starts to spin, the mirrors sparkle, the fairy lights glitter, and the band organ plays favorite tunes from Disney movies. If you wished upon a star, it couldn't get more magical. ☞ **Duration:** *2 min.* **Crowds:** *Lines during busy periods but they move fairly quickly.* **Strategy:** *Go while waiting for your Peter Pan's Flight FASTPASS reservation, during the afternoon parade, or after dark.* **Audience:** *A great ride for families and for romantics, both young and old.* **Rating:** ★★.

㉒ Dumbo the Flying Elephant. Hands down, this is one of Fantasyland's most popular rides. Although the movie has one baby elephant with gigantic ears who accidentally downs a bucket of water spiked with champagne and learns he can fly, the ride has 16 jolly Dumbos flying around a central column, each pachyderm packing a couple of kids and a parent. A joystick controls each of Dumbo's vertical motions, so you can make him ascend or descend at will. Alas, the ears do not flap. Keep an eye out for Timothy Mouse atop the ride's colorful balloon. ☞ **Duration:** *2 min.* **Crowds:** *Perpetual, except in very early morning, and there's little shade—in summer, the wait is truly brutal.* **Strategy:** *If accompanying small children, make a beeline here at Rope Drop; if you're lucky enough to time your ride during end-of-day fireworks over the castle, you'll be living one of Disney's happy endings.* **Audience:** *Toddlers and young children—the modest thrills are just perfect for them.* **Rating:** ★★.

㉓ Ariel's Grotto. A "beneath the sea" motif distinguishes this starfish-scattered meet-and-greet locale. Ariel the Little Mermaid appears here in person, her carrot-red tresses cascading onto her glittery green tail. Just across the ropes from the queue area are a group of wonderfully interactive fountains that little kids love splashing around in. ☞ **Duration:** *Up to you.* **Strategy:** *Check your map for appearance times, and arrive at least 20 min ahead.* **Audience:** *Young children, especially little girls.* **Rating:** ★★.

㉔ The Many Adventures of Winnie the Pooh. The famous honey lover and his exploits in the Hundred Acre Wood are the theme for this ride. You can read passages from A. A. Milne's famous stories as you wait in line. Once you board your honey pot, Pooh and his friends wish you a "happy windsday." Pooh flies through the air, held aloft by his balloon, in his perennial search for "hunny," and you bounce along with Tigger, ride with the Heffalumps and Woozles, and experience a cloudburst. When the rain ends at last, everyone gathers again to say "Hurray!" This ride replaced the late lamented Mr. Toad's Wild Ride; look for the painting of Mr. Toad handing the deed to Owl. ☞ *Duration: About 3 min. Crowds: Large. Strategy: Use the FASTPASS setup; if the youngsters favor immediate gratification, go early in the day, late in the afternoon, or after dark. Audience: All ages. Rating:* ★★★.

㉕ Story Time with Belle. Disney's beloved bookworm makes an appearance at the Fairytale Garden several times daily and brings *Beauty and the Beast* to life, using her audience as members of the cast. Storytelling was never so much fun. *Duration: 25 min, several times daily (check guide map schedule). Crowds: Heaviest in midday. Strategy: See during the Fantasyland stage show or during the parade. Audience: All ages. Rating:* ★.

㉖ Mad Tea Party. This carnival staple is for the vertigo addict looking for a fix. The Disney version is based on its own 1951 film *Alice in Wonderland,* in which the Mad Hatter hosts a tea party for his un-birthday. You hop into oversize, pastel-color teacups and whirl around a giant platter. Add your own spin to the teacup's orbit with the help of the steering wheel in the center. If the centrifugal force hasn't shaken you up too much, check out the soused mouse that pops out of the teapot centerpiece and compare his condition with your own. ☞ *Duration: 2 min. Crowds: Steady from late morning on, with slow-moving lines. Strategy: Skip this ride if the wait is longer than 30 min. Rating:* ★.

Mickey's Toontown Fair

This concentrated tribute to the big-eared mighty one was built in 1988 to celebrate the Mouse's Big Six-O. Owing to its continual popularity with the small-fry set, it is now an official Magic Kingdom land, a 3-acre niche set off to the side of Fantasyland. As in a scene from a cartoon, everything is child size. The pastel houses are positively Lilliputian, with miniature driveways, toy-size picket fences, and signs scribbled with finger paint. Toontown Fair provides great one-stop shopping (better known as meet-and-greets) for your favorite Disney characters—hug them, get autographs, and take photos. The best way to arrive is on the Walt Disney World Railroad, the old-fashioned choo-choo that also stops at Main Street and Frontierland.

㉗ The Barnstormer at Goofy's Wiseacre Farm. Traditional red barns and farm buildings form the backdrop at Goofy's Wiseacre Farm. But the real attraction is the Barnstormer, a roller coaster whose ride vehicles are 1920s crop-dusting biplanes—designed for children but large enough for adults as well. Hold on to your Mouse ears—this attraction promises tummy-tickling thrills to young first-time coaster riders. If you are uncertain whether your offspring are up to Big Thunder Mountain Railroad, this is the test to take. ☞ *Duration: 1 min. Crowds: Heaviest in midmorning. Strategy: Visit in the evening, when many tykes have gone home. Audience: Younger children. Restrictions: No riders under age 3. Rating:* ★★★.

㉘ Toon Park. This spongy green area is filled with foam topiary in the shapes of goats, cows, pigs, and horses. Children can jump and hop on inter-

HIDDEN MICKEYS

SEARCHING FOR MICKEY? *Character meals and meet-and-greets aren't the only places you can find the "big cheese." If you keep your eyes peeled, you might spot images of Mickey Mouse hidden in murals, statues, and floor tiles in queue areas and rides.*

Hidden Mickeys began as an inside joke among Disney Imagineers. When putting the finishing touches on an attraction, they'd subtly slip a Mickey into the motif to see if coworkers and friends would notice. Today, hunting for Hidden Mickeys (and Minnies) has become quite popular and can be a great way to pass the time while standing in line. For example, as you wait to board Norway's Maelstrom ride in Epcot, you can scan the big mural for the Viking wearing mouse ears.

The most common image you'll spy is the outline of Mickey's face. While riding Big Thunder Mountain Railroad in the Magic Kingdom, you'll pass three rusty gears on the ground that form Mickey's head and ears. (Look to your right as your train nears the station.) But also watch for Mickey in profile. After the final drop in Splash Mountain, he lounges on his back in a cloud to the right of the Steamboat where the characters "zip-a-dee-doo-dah."

You can request a list of Hidden Mickeys at guest services in the theme parks or at Disney hotels, and the non-Disney Web site ⊕ www.hiddenmickeys.org has a list and photos. Before you begin your search, keep in mind that some of the images can be quite difficult to discern. (You practically need a magnifying glass to make out the profile of Minnie Mouse in the Hollywood mural at the Great Movie Ride in Disney–MGM Studios; she's above the roof of the gazebo.) If you're traveling with young children, don't count on using Hidden Mickeys as a distraction tactic. Preschoolers might actually become frustrated trying to find him. (And besides, "Let's look for Mickey" means something quite different to a four-year-old.) But school-age kids might welcome the challenge of finding as many Hidden Mickeys as they can and checking them off their list. Here are some more clues to help you get started on your mouse hunt:

In the Magic Kingdom

Snow White's Scary Adventures. In the queue-area mural, look for shorts hanging on the clothesline and at three of the stones in the chimney.

Haunted Mansion. There's a Mouse-eared place setting on the table in the ballroom.

In Epcot

Spaceship Earth. Mickey smiles down from a constellation behind the loading area.

The American Adventure. Check out the painting of the wagon train, and look above the front leg of the foremost oxen.

At Disney–MGM Studios

Twilight Zone Tower of Terror. In the boiler room, look for a whimsical water stain on the wall right after the queue splits.

Rock 'n' Roller Coaster. A pair of Mickeys hide in the floor tile right before the doors with the marbles.

In the Animal Kingdom

DINOSAUR. Stare at the bark of the painted tree in the far left background of the wall mural at the building's entrance.

Rafiki's Planet Watch. The main Conservation Station building contains more than 25 Hidden Mickeys. Look in the eyes of animals in the entrance mural, on insects' wings and bodies, and in the tree trunks of the rain forest.

— Ellen Parlapiano

active lily pads to hear animal topiaries moo, bleat, and whinny. ☞ *Duration: Up to you. Crowds: Moderate and seldom a problem. Strategy: Go anytime. Audience: Young children mainly, but everyone enjoys watching them. Rating:* ★.

㉙ Donald's Boat. A cross between a tugboat and a leaky ocean liner, the *Miss Daisy* is actually a water-play area, with lily pads that spray without warning. Although it's intended for kids, there's no reason why grownups can't also take the opportunity to cool off on a humid Central Florida afternoon. ☞ *Duration: Up to you. Crowds: Can get heavy in late morning and early afternoon. Strategy: Go first thing in the morning or whenever the kids need some free-play time. Audience: Young children and their families. Rating:* ★★.

> **need a break?**   The **Toontown Farmer's Market** sells simple, healthful snacks and fruit, plus juices, espresso drinks, and soda. If you're lucky, you can find a place on the park bench next to the cart and give your feet a rest.

㉚ Mickey's Country House. Begin here to find your way to the big cheese himself. As you walk through this slightly goofy piece of architecture right in the heart of Toontown Fairgrounds, notice the radio in the living room, "tooned" to scores from Mickey's favorite football team, Duckburg University. Down the hall, Mickey's kitchen shows the ill effects of Donald and Goofy's attempt to win the Toontown Home Remodeling Contest—with buckets of paint spilled and stacked in the sink and paint splattered on the floor and walls. The Judge's Tent just behind Mickey's house is where the mouse king holds court as he doles out hugs and autographs and mugs for photos with adoring fans. ☞ *Duration: Up to you. Crowds: Moderate. Strategy: Go first thing in the morning or during the afternoon parade. Audience: All ages, although teens may be put off by the terminal cuteness of it all. Rating:* ★★.

㉛ Judge's Tent. If you want to spend a few moments with the big cheese himself, load your camera, dig out a pen, and get in line here. You can catch Mickey in his personal dressing room for the ideal photo opportunity and autograph session. ☞ *Duration: Plan to wait it out if an audience with Mickey is a priority. Strategy: If you can't get there early, try a lunchtime visit. Audience: Young children and families. Rating:* ★★★.

㉜ Toontown Hall of Fame. Stop here to collect an autograph and a hug from such Disney characters as Pluto and Goofy, and check out the blue ribbon–winning entries from the Toontown Fair. **County Bounty** sells stuffed animals and all kinds of Toontown souvenirs, including autograph books. ☞ *Duration: Up to you. Crowds: Can get heavy in late morning and early afternoon. Strategy: Go first thing in the morning or after the toddlers have gone home. Audience: Young children. Rating:* ★★.

㉝ Minnie's Country House. Unlike Mickey's house, where ropes keep you from going into the rooms, this baby-blue-and-pink house is a please-touch kind of place. In this scenario, Minnie is editor of *Minnie's Car-*

toon Country Living magazine, the Martha Stewart of the mouse set. While touring her office, crafts room, and kitchen, you can check the latest messages on her answering machine, bake a "quick-rising" cake at the touch of a button, and, opening the refrigerator door, get a wonderful blast of arctic air while checking out her favorite ice cream flavor: cheese-chip. ☞ *Duration: Up to you. Crowds: Moderate. Strategy: Go first thing in the morning or during the afternoon parade. Audience: All ages, although teens may find it too much to take. Rating:* ★★.

Tomorrowland

The "future that never was" spins boldly into view as you enter Tomorrowland, where Disney Imagineers paint the landscape with whirling spaceships, flashy neon lights, and gleaming robots. This is the future as envisioned by sci-fi writers and moviemakers in the 1920s and '30s, when space flight, laser beams, and home computers belonged in the world of fiction, not fact. Retro Jetsonesque styling lends the area lasting chic.

34 **Tomorrowland Indy Speedway.** This is one of those rides that incite instant addiction in children and immediate hatred in their parents. The reasons for the former are easy to figure out: the brightly colored Mark VII model cars that swerve around the four 2,260-foot tracks with much vroom-vroom-vrooming. Kids will feel like they're Mario Andretti as they race around. Like real sports cars, the gasoline-powered vehicles are equipped with rack-and-pinion steering and disc brakes; unlike the real thing, these run on a track. However, the track is so twisty that it's hard to keep the car on a straight course—something the race car fanatics warming the bleachers love to watch. You may spend a lot of time waiting, first to get your turn on the track, then to return your vehicle after your lap. All this for a ride in which the main thrill is achieving a top speed of 7 mph. ☞ *Duration: 5 min. Crowds: Steady and heavy from late morning to evening. Strategy: Go in the evening or during a parade; skip on a first-time visit unless you've been through all the major attractions. Audience: Older children. Minimum height: 52″ to drive. Rating:* ★.

35 **Tomorrowland Arcade.** With so much to cover in the Kingdom, it's hard to imagine giving up time and cash to a bank of video games. But this arcade adjacent to Space Mountain is a draw for older children and teens who may be sorely missing their Xboxes at home, especially when afternoon lines at the attractions are forbidding. Most recent game additions include a Brave Firefighters two-player video game, Dell Electronics' 360-degree motion Turret Tower, and updated Skeeball Lightning. Formula One racing games are also hot, and there's rarely a line to play. The nearby ATM is useful when the games begin to deplete your stash of cash. ☞ *Duration: Up to you. Crowds: Not usually a problem. Strategy: Just as tots need down time, so do teens. Allow them time to play while you shop or relax on a nearby bench. Audience: Teens. Rating:* ★★.

Fodor'sChoice

36 Space Mountain. The needlelike spires and gleaming white concrete cone of this attraction are almost as much of a Magic Kingdom landmark as Cinderella Castle. Towering 180 feet high, the structure has been called "Florida's third-highest mountain." Inside is what is arguably the world's most imaginative roller coaster. Although there are no loop-the-loops, gravitational whizbangs, or high-speed curves, the thrills are amply provided by Disney's masterful brainwashing as you take a trip into the depths of outer space—in the dark.

The wait to ride Space Mountain can be an hour or more if you don't have a FASTPASS, so do your best to get one. As you walk to the loading area, you'll pass whirling planets and hear the screams and shrieks of the riders and the rattling of the cars, pumping you up for your own ride. Once you wedge yourself into the seat and blast off, the ride lasts only 2 minutes and 38 seconds, with a top speed of 28 mph, but the devious twists and invisible drops in the dark make it seem twice as long. Stow personal belongings securely or have a non-rider hold onto them. ☞ *Duration: 2½ min. Crowds: Large and steady, with long lines from morning to night despite high capacity. Strategy: Get a FAST-PASS ticket, or go either at the beginning of the day, the end, or during a parade. Audience: All except young children. No pregnant women or guests wearing back, neck, or leg braces. Minimum height: 44″. Rating:* ★★★.

37 Walt Disney's Carousel of Progress. Originally seen at New York's 1964–65 World's Fair, this revolving theater traces the impact of technological progress on the daily lives of Americans from the turn of the 20th century into the near future. Representing each decade, an audio-animatronics family sings the praises of modern-day gadgets that technology has wrought. Fans of the holiday film *A Christmas Story* will recognize the voice of its narrator, Jean Shepard, who injects his folksy, all-American humor as father figure through the decades. This attraction may be closed when the park's not crowded; check your Times Guide flyer, or ask a Disney staffer. ☞ *Duration: 20 min. Crowds: Moderate. Strategy: Skip on a first-time visit unless you're heavily into nostalgia. Audience: All ages. Rating:* ★.

38 Tomorrowland Transit Authority. A reincarnation of what Disney old-timers may remember as the WEDway PeopleMover, the TTA takes a nice, leisurely ride around the perimeter of Tomorrowland, circling the Astro-Orbiter and eventually gliding through the middle of Space Mountain. Some fainthearted TTA passengers have no doubt chucked the notion of riding the roller coaster after being exposed firsthand to the screams emanating from within the mountain—although these make the ride sound worse than it really is. Disney's version of future mass transit is smooth and noiseless, thanks to an electromagnetic linear induction motor that has no moving parts, uses little power, and emits no pollutants. ☞ *Duration: 10 min. Crowds: Not one of the park's most popular attractions, so lines are seldom long and they move quickly. Strategy: Go if you want to preview Space Mountain, if you have very young children, or if you simply want a nice, relaxing ride that provides a great bird's-eye tour of Tomorrowland. Audience: All ages. Rating:* ★.

39 **Astro-Orbiter.** This gleaming superstructure of revolving planets has come to symbolize Tomorrowland as much as Dumbo represents Fantasyland. Passenger vehicles, on arms projecting from a central column, sail past whirling planets; you control your car's altitude but not the velocity. The queue is directly across from the entrance to the TTA. ☞ *Duration: 2 min. Crowds: Often large, and the line moves slowly. Strategy: Visit while waiting out your Space Mountain FASTPASS appointment or skip on your first visit if time is limited, unless there's a short line. Audience: All ages. Rating:* ★★.

40 **Stitch's Great Escape** (a.k.a. Experiment 626). Once again, Disney seizes upon a hit film to create a crowd-pleasing attraction. This time the film is *Lilo & Stitch,* and the attraction is built around a back-story to the film, about the mischievous alien, Stitch, before he meets Lilo in Hawaii. You are invited, as a new security recruit for the Galactic Federation, to enter the high-security teleportation chamber, where the ill-mannered Stitch is being processed for prison. In the form of a 3½-foot-tall audio-animatronics figure, Stitch escapes his captors and wreaks havoc on the room during close encounters with the audience in near-darkness. Sensory effects and tactile surprises are part of the package. Beware the chili-dog "belch" and a spray that prompts more than a few gasps of surprise (hint: Stitch is the first Audio-Animatronics figure to spit). Stitch's Great Escape replaces the former ExtraTERRORestrial Alien Encounter and takes place in the same theater-in-the-round setting. Preteens seem to like this show best, while young children find it too scary, and for adults it's not as satisfying as, say, Mickey's Philharmonic. It's really not worth waiting in line for an hour unless you have some serious Stitch fans in your party. ☞ *Duration: 15 min. Crowds: Large because it's a new attraction. Strategy: Use FASTPASS if you've already been on Splash Mountain, Space Mountain, and Big Thunder Mountain, or see it during a parade. Audience: All but young children, who may be frightened by shoulder restraints, periods of darkness, and startling noises. Rating:* ★★.

41 **Buzz Lightyear's Space Ranger Spin.** Based on the wildly popular *Toy Story,* this ride gives you a toy's perspective as it pits you and Buzz against the evil Emperor Zurg. You're seated in a fast-moving two-passenger Star Cruiser vehicle with a laser gun in front of each rider and a centrally located lever for spinning your ship to get a good vantage point. You shoot at targets throughout the ride to help Disney's macho space toy, Buzz, defeat the emperor and save the universe—you have to hit the targets marked with a "Z" to score, and the rider with the most points wins. As Buzz likes to say, "To infinity and beyond!" The larger-than-life-size toys in the waiting area are great distractions while you queue. ☞ *Duration: 5 min. Crowds: Substantial, but lines move fast. Go first thing in the morning, get your FASTPASS appointment time, then return when scheduled. If you're with children, time the wait and ride twice if it's only 15 or 20 min. Youngsters like a practice run to learn how to hit the targets. Audience: Kids 3 to 100. Rating:* ★★★.

42 **Timekeeper.** Walt Disney World buffs may remember this attraction as the former America the Beautiful, a CircleVision 360-degree tribute to the natural wonders of the United States. It's now a time-traveling adventure hosted by TimeKeeper, a C-3PO clone whose frenetic personality is given voice by the great Robin Williams, and Nine-Eye, a slightly frazzled droid, who's a graduate of MITT (the Metropolis Institute of Time Travel). Along the way, you meet famous inventors and visionaries of the machine age, such as Jules Verne and H. G. Wells. Don't plan on a relaxing voyage, however; there are no seats in the theater—only lean rails. Timekeeper sometimes closes when the park's not crowded; check the Times Guide flyer, or ask a Disney staffer. ☞ *Duration: 11 min. Crowds: Moderate, but lines move steadily, since theater capacity is nearly 900. Strategy: Go when you're waiting for your Buzz Lightyear FASTPASS appointment. Audience: All ages, although you'll have to hold youngsters or piggyback them so they can see. Rating:* ★★.

Magic Kingdom A to Z

To research prices, get advice from other travelers, and book travel arrangements, visit www.fodors.com.

BABY CARE

The Magic Kingdom's soothing, quiet **Baby Care Center** is next to the Crystal Palace, which lies between Main Street and Adventureland. Furnished with rocking chairs, it has a low lighting level that makes it comfortable for nursing, though it can get crowded in midafternoon in peak season. There are adorable toddler-size toilets (these may be a high point for your just-potty-trained offspring) as well as supplies such as formula, baby food, pacifiers, disposable diapers, and even children's pain reliever. Changing tables are here, as well as in all women's rooms and most men's rooms. You can also buy disposable diapers in the Emporium on Main Street. The **Stroller Shop** near the entrance to the Magic Kingdom, on the east side of Main Street, is the place for stroller rentals ($7 single, $14 double; plus $1 deposit refundable in the form of a Disney dollar that is redeemable only at Disney properties).

CAMERAS

Disposable cameras and film, and memory cards for digital cameras, are widely available in shops throughout the theme parks and hotels. The **Camera Center,** in the Town Square Exposition Hall, is staffed by cast members who'll position you and your group for a photo in front of Cinderella Castle or one of many other scenes from popular Disney films, such as Pooh's Hundred Acre Wood or the ballroom from *Beauty and the Beast.* A 5″×7″ photo costs $12.95 for the first print and $9.95 for each additional copy. An 8″×10″ costs $16.95 and $12.95 for each additional copy. This is also the place for minor camera repairs. If you'd like to purchase family photos shot by Disney photographers in the park, ask them for the Disney PhotoPass so you can view and order them online at any time.

DISABILITIES & ACCESSIBILITY

ATTRACTIONS   Overall, the Magic Kingdom gets decent marks from visitors with disabilities. Before your trip, call and request a copy of the "Guidebook for Guests with Disabilities" to help with planning your visit. The guide-book, assistive listening systems, reflective captioning equipment, Braille and audio guides, and sign-language interpretation schedules are available in the park at Guest Relations. Call Walt Disney World Information at least two weeks in advance for a schedule of sign language–interpreted shows. Interpreters rotate daily between Disney's four major theme parks.

To board the **Walt Disney World Railroad** at the Main Street Station, you must transfer from your wheelchair, which can be folded to ride with you or left in the station. Alternatively, board at Frontierland or Mickey's Toontown Fair. The **Main Street Vehicles** can be boarded by those with limited mobility as long as they can fold their wheelchair and climb into a car. There are curb cuts or ramps on each corner.

In Adventureland, the **Magic Carpets of Aladdin** has ramped access for guests in wheelchairs and a customized control pendant for manipulating the "carpet's" height and pitch movement. The **Swiss Family Tree-house**, with its 100 steps and lack of narration, gets low ratings among those with mobility and visual impairments. At the **Jungle Cruise,** several boats have lifts that allow access to visitors in wheelchairs; people with hearing impairments who lip-read will find the skippers' punny narration, delivered with a handheld mike, difficult to follow, although sitting up front may make it easier to see. Boarding **Pirates of the Caribbean** requires transferring from a nonfolding to a folding wheelchair, available at the entrance; the very small flume drop may make the attraction inappropriate for those with limited upper-body strength or wearing neck or back braces. Because of gunshot and fire effects, service animals should stay behind.

Frontierland is the only area of the park, aside from Main Street, that has sidewalk curbs; there are ramps by the Mile Long Bar and east of Frontierland Trading Post. To ride **Big Thunder Mountain Railroad** and **Splash Mountain,** you must be able to step into the ride vehicle and walk short distances, in case of an emergency evacuation; those with limited upper-body strength should assess the situation on-site, and those wearing back, neck, or leg braces shouldn't ride. Service animals aren't allowed on these rides. **Tom Sawyer Island,** with its stairs, bridges, inclines, and narrow caves, is not negotiable by those using a wheelchair. The **Country Bear Jamboree** is completely wheelchair accessible; if you lip-read, ask to sit up front. The **Frontierland Shootin' Arcade** has two guns set at wheelchair level.

The **Hall of Presidents** and *Liberty Belle* Riverboat, in Liberty Square, are completely wheelchair accessible. At the **Haunted Mansion,** those in wheelchairs must transfer to the "doom buggies" and take one step; however, if you can walk as much as 200 feet, you'll enjoy the great preshow as well as the sensations and eerie sounds of the rest of the ride.

Mickey's PhilharMagic has special viewing areas for guests in wheelchairs. **it's a small world** can be boarded without leaving your wheelchair, but only if it's standard size; if you use a scooter or an oversize chair, you must transfer to one of the attraction's standard chairs, available at the ride entrance. To board **Peter Pan's Flight, Dumbo the Flying Elephant, Cinderella's Golden Carrousel,** the **Mad Tea Party,** and **Snow White's Scary Adventures,** guests using wheelchairs must transfer to the ride vehicles. The Dumbo and Peter Pan rides are not suitable for service animals. For **The Many Adventures of Winnie the Pooh,** people who use wheelchairs wait in the main queue and are then able to roll right onto an individual honey pot to ride, with one member of their party accompanying them. There are amplifiers for guests with hearing impairments.

Mickey's Toontown Fair is completely accessible.

In Tomorrowland, **Stitch's Great Escape** requires guests in motorized scooters to transfer to an on-site standard wheelchair for the show's duration. **Timekeeper** and the **Carousel of Progress** are barrier-free for those using wheelchairs. To board **Buzz Lightyear's Space Ranger Spin, Astro-Orbiter,** and the **Tomorrowland Transit Authority,** you must be able to walk several steps and transfer to the ride vehicle. The TTA has more appeal to guests with visual impairments. To drive **Tomorrowland Indy Speedway** cars, you must have adequate vision and be able to steer, press the gas pedal, and transfer into the low car seat. The cautions for **Big Thunder Mountain Railroad** and **Splash Mountain** also apply to **Space Mountain.** In the **Tomorrowland Arcade,** the machines may be too high for guests using wheelchairs.

🖫 **WDW Guest Information** ☎ 407/824-4321, 407/939-7807, or 407/827-5141 TTY.

RESTAURANTS &
SHOPS
All restaurants and shops throughout the park have level entrances or are accessible by ramps.

WHEELCHAIR
RENTALS
Go to the gift shop to the left of the ticket booths at the **Transportation and Ticket Center** or the **Stroller Shop** inside the main entrance to your right. Wheelchairs are rented for $7 plus a $1 deposit refunded as Disney dollar; motor-powered chairs are rented for $30, plus a $10 refundable deposit. If your rental needs replacing, ask any host or hostess.

FIRST AID
The Magic Kingdom's First Aid Center, staffed by registered nurses, is alongside the Crystal Palace.

GETTING AROUND
Once you're in the Magic Kingdom, distances are generally short, and the best way to get around is on foot. The Walt Disney World Railroad, the Main Street vehicles, and the Tomorrowland Transit Authority do help you cover some territory and can give your feet a welcome rest, but they're primarily entertainment, not transportation.

GUIDED TOURS
A number of **guided tours** are available. Arrive 15 minutes ahead of time to check in for all tours. Some companies, such as American Express, offer discounts for some of the tours; make sure to ask ahead about special discounts.

The 4½-hour **Keys to the Kingdom Tour** is a good way to get a feel for the layout of the Magic Kingdom and what goes on behind the scenes. The walking tour, which costs $58, includes lunch but not admission to the park itself. No one younger than 16 is allowed. Tours leave from City Hall daily at 8:30, 9, and 9:30 AM. Included are visits to some of the "backstage" zones: the parade staging area and the wardrobe area and other parts of the tunnels that web the ground underneath the Magic Kingdom.

The **Family Magic Tour** is a two-hour "surprise" scavenger hunt in which your tour guide encourages you to find things that have disappeared. Disney officials don't want to reveal the tour's components—after all, it's the Family "Magic" Tour—but they can say that a special character-greeting session awaits you at the end of the adventure. Tours leave City Hall at 10 AM daily ($25 for adults and children 3 and up).

Railroad enthusiasts will love the **Magic Behind Our Steam Trains,** which gives you an inside look at the daily operation of the WDW railroad. This tour became so popular that it was lengthened from two to three hours and is now offered on four days instead of three. Tours begin at 7:30 AM on Monday, Tuesday, Thursday, and Saturday. Those over 10 years old may participate. The cost is $40 per person, plus park admission. No discounts are offered.

Backstage Magic takes you on a tour of the Magic Kingdom, Epcot, Disney–MGM Studios, and the resort's behind-the-scenes Central Shop area, where repair work is done. The cost for the seven-hour tour, which is for those 16 and older, is $199 per person. Tours depart at 9 AM on weekdays. The fee includes lunch but does not include park admission, which is not required for the tour itself.

A seasonal tour that holiday fans will enjoy is **Yuletide Fantasy,** a 3-½–hour visit through the theme parks and several resorts to see how Disney's elves weave decorations and holiday traditions throughout the 47-square-mile property. One day it's a tropical paradise, the next it's a winter wonderland. The $59 tour departs daily and is for those 16 and older.
🚹 Guided Tours ☎ 407/939-8687.

LOCKERS
Lockers are available in an arcade underneath the Main Street Railroad Station ($5; plus $2 deposit). If you're park-hopping, you can use your locker receipt to acquire a locker at the next park you visit for no extra charge.

LOST THINGS & PEOPLE
Name tags are available at City Hall or at the Baby Care Center next to the Crystal Palace, if you're worried about your children getting lost. Instruct them to talk to anyone with a Disney name tag if they lose you. If that does happen, immediately ask any cast member and try not to panic; children who are obviously lost are usually taken to City Hall or the Baby Care Center, where lost-children logbooks are kept, and everyone is well trained to effect speedy reunions. City Hall also has a Lost & Found and a computerized Message Center, where you can leave notes for your traveling companions, both those in the Magic Kingdom and those visiting other parks. After a day, found items are taken to the Transportation and Ticket Center.
🚹 **Magic Kingdom Lost & Found** ✉ City Hall ☎ 407/824-4521. **Main Lost & Found** ✉ Magic Kingdom, Transportation and Ticket Center ☎ 407/824-4245.

MONEY MATTERS

ATMs are by the lockers underneath the Main Street railroad station, inside the Tomorrowland Arcade, and in the breezeway between Adventureland and Frontierland. For currency exchange, go to the Guest Relations window in the turnstile area or to City Hall.

PACKAGE PICKUP

Ask the shop clerk to send any large purchase you make to Guest Relations, so you won't have to carry it around all day. Allow three hours for the delivery. The package pickup area is in Town Square near the firehouse next to the Emporium.

VISITOR INFORMATION

City Hall is the Magic Kingdom's principal information center. Here you can search for misplaced belongings or companions, ask questions of the omniscient staffers, and pick up the "Magic Kingdom Guide Map," and the "Times Guide & New Information" flyer, with its schedule of daily events and character-greeting and attraction information.

At the end of Main Street, on the left as you face Cinderella Castle, just before the Hub, is the **Tip Board,** a large board with constantly updated information about attractions' wait times.

Signs at the centrally located WDW Ticket and Transportation Center, where you board the monorail or ferry to the park, keep you posted about park hours and activities such as parades and fireworks. And cast members are available at almost every turn to help you. In fact, providing information to visitors is part of the job description of the young men and women who sweep the pavement and work hard to keep litter in its place. 🔳 **City Hall** ☎ 407/824-4521.

EPCOT

Walt Disney World was created because of Walt Disney's dream of EPCOT, an "Experimental Prototype Community of Tomorrow." Disney envisioned a future in which nations coexisted in peace and harmony, reaping the miraculous harvest of technological achievement. He suggested the idea as early as October 1966, saying that EPCOT would "take its cue from the new ideas and new technologies that are now emerging from the creative centers of American industry." He wrote that EPCOT, never completed, always improving, "will never cease to be a living blueprint of the future . . . a showcase to the world for the ingenuity and imagination of American free enterprise."

But the permanent settlement that he envisioned wasn't to be and, instead, has taken an altered shape in Disney's Celebration, an urban planner's dream of a town near fast-growing Kissimmee. Epcot, which opened in 1982, 16 years after Disney's death, is a showcase, ostensibly, for the concepts that would be incorporated into the real-life Epcots of the future. It's composed of two parts: Future World, where most pavilions are colorful collaborations between Walt Disney Imagineering and major U.S. corporations and are designed to demonstrate technological advances; and the World Showcase, where exhibition areas are microcosms of 11 countries from four continents.

Epcot today is both more and less than Walt Disney's original dream. Less because a few of the Future World pavilions remain stuck in a 1964 World's Fair mentality and because the World Showcase presents views of its countries that are, as an Epcot guide once put it, "as Americans perceive them"—highly idealized. But these are minor quibbles in the face of the major achievement: Epcot is that rare paradox—an educational theme park—and a very successful one, too. Every year, Epcot experiences change and inspires greater interest among the younger set, and the amount of imagination concentrated in its 230 acres is astounding.

Although several of the newer attractions, such as Mission: SPACE and Test Track, provide high-octane kicks, the thrills are mostly for the mind. Epcot is best for older children and adults. But that doesn't mean the little ones can't have a great time here. Much of the park's entertainment and at least half of its attractions provide fun diversions for younger children overstimulated by the Magic Kingdom's pixie dust. If you do bring young ones, don't miss the Kid Zones sprinkled throughout the World Showcase, where they can make puppets, draw pictures, and even create a Moroccan fez. And bring their swimsuits and a towel so they can play in the interactive fountains in front of Mission: SPACE and by the walkway from Future World to the World Showcase.

The northern half of Epcot, Future World, is where the monorail drops you off and where the official entrance is located. The southern half, World Showcase, surrounds the 40-acre World Showcase Lagoon and has an entrance used by Epcot Resort guests—the International Gateway. You can reach the gateway, between the France and United Kingdom pavilions, via water launches or a walkway from the Dolphin and Swan hotels, Disney's Yacht and Beach Club resorts, and Disney's BoardWalk resort.

Entertainment

Some of the most enjoyable entertainment takes place outside the pavilions and along the promenade. Live shows with actors, dancers, singers, mime routines, and demonstrations of folk arts and crafts are presented at varying times of day; get times in your Epcot guide map or at the World-Key terminals at Guest Relations and Germany. Or look for signs posted at the pavilions. The enigmatic **Imaginum** (Living Statues) of Italy, the United Kingdom's **British Invasion**, Morocco's **MoRockin'**, and China's incredible **Dragon Legend Acrobats** keep audiences coming back.

A group that calls itself the **JAMMitors** plays up a storm several days during the week (check Epcot entertainment schedule) at various Future World locations, using the tools of the janitorial trade—garbage cans, wastebaskets, brooms, mops, and dustpans. If you hear drumming from the vicinity of Japan, scurry on over to watch the traditional Japanese **Matsuriza** Taiko drummers in action.

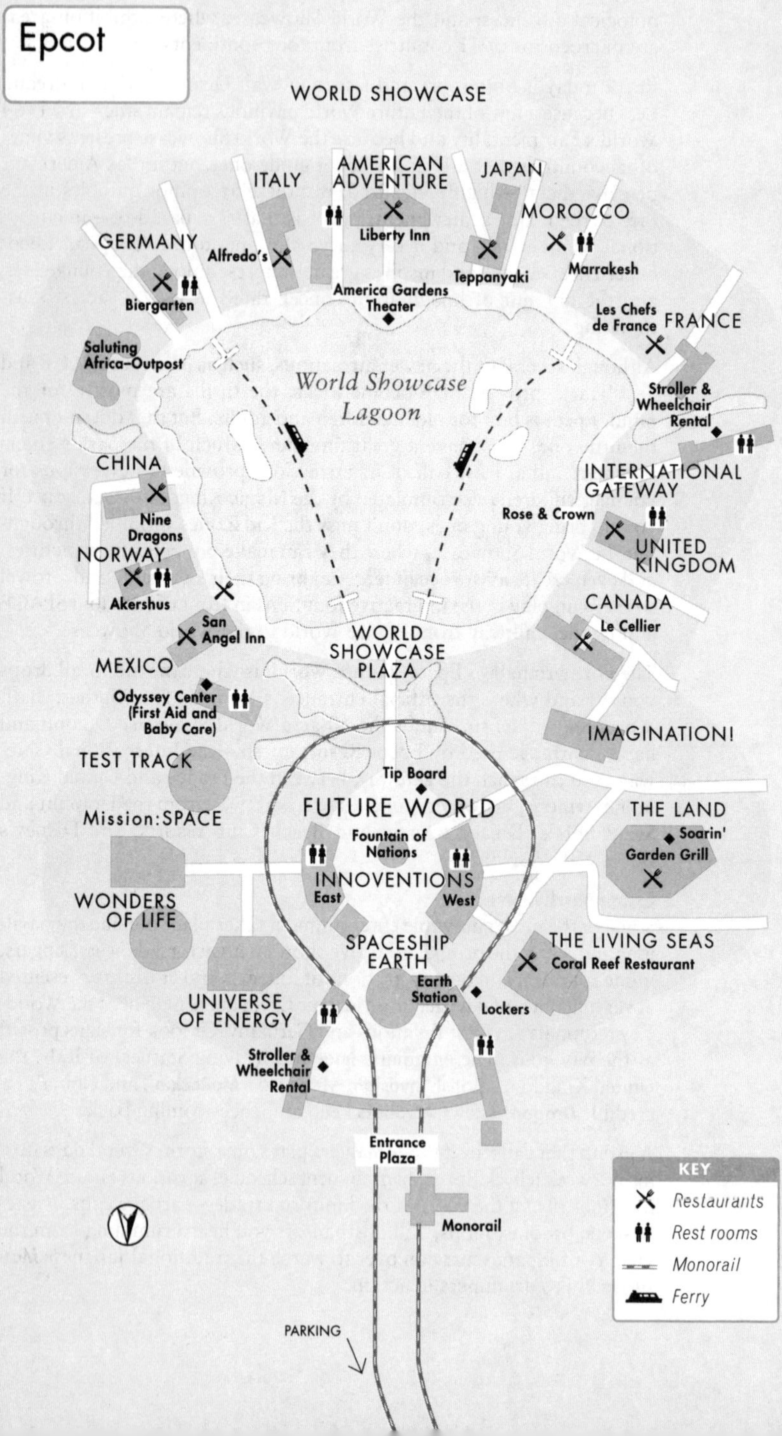
Epcot
WORLD SHOWCASE
ITALY
AMERICAN ADVENTURE
JAPAN
MOROCCO
GERMANY
Alfredo's
Liberty Inn
Teppanyaki
Marrakesh
Biergarten
America Gardens Theater
Les Chefs de France
FRANCE
Saluting Africa–Outpost
World Showcase Lagoon
Stroller & Wheelchair Rental
CHINA
INTERNATIONAL GATEWAY
Nine Dragons
Rose & Crown
UNITED KINGDOM
NORWAY
Akershus
CANADA
San Angel Inn
Le Cellier
WORLD SHOWCASE PLAZA
MEXICO
Odyssey Center (First Aid and Baby Care)
IMAGINATION!
TEST TRACK
Tip Board
FUTURE WORLD
THE LAND
Mission:SPACE
Fountain of Nations
Soarin'
Garden Grill
INNOVENTIONS
East
West
WONDERS OF LIFE
SPACESHIP EARTH
THE LIVING SEAS
Coral Reef Restaurant
Earth Station
Lockers
UNIVERSE OF ENERGY
Stroller & Wheelchair Rental
Entrance Plaza
KEY
Restaurants
Rest rooms
Monorail
Ferry
Monorail
PARKING

Fodor's Choice
★
The marvelous nighttime spectacular, **IllumiNations: Reflections of Earth,** takes place over the World Showcase Lagoon every night before closing. Be sure to stick around for the lasers, lights, fireworks, fountains, and music that fill the air over the water. Although there's generally good viewing from all around the lagoon, some of the best spots are in front of the Italy pavilion, on the bridge between France and the United Kingdom, on the promenade in front of Canada, and on the bridge between China and Germany, which will give you a clear shot, unobstructed by trees. After the show, concealed loudspeakers play the theme music manipulated into salsa, polka, waltz, and even—believe it or not—Asian rhythms. ☞ *Duration: 13 min. Crowds: Heavy. Strategy: For best views (and if you have young children), find your place 45 min in advance. Audience: All ages. Rating:* ★★★.

Future World

Future World is made up of two concentric circles of pavilions. The inner core is composed of the Spaceship Earth geosphere and, just beyond it, a plaza anchored by the wow-generating computer-animated Fountain of Nations, which is as mesmerizing as many a more elaborate ride or show. Bracketing it are the crescent-shape Innoventions East and West.

Seven pavilions compose the outer ring. On the east side they are, in order, the Universe of Energy, Wonders of Life, Mission: SPACE, and Test Track. With the exception of the Wonders of Life, the east pavilions present a single, self-contained ride and an occasional postride showcase; a visit rarely takes more than 30 minutes, but it depends on how long you spend in the postride area. On the west side there are Living Seas, The Land, and Imagination! Like the Wonders of Life, these blockbuster exhibits contain both rides and interactive displays; you could spend at least 1½ hours at each of these pavilions, but there aren't enough hours in the day, so prioritize.

Spaceship Earth

Balanced like a giant golf ball waiting for some celestial being to tee off, the multifaceted silver geosphere of Spaceship Earth is to Epcot what Cinderella Castle is to the Magic Kingdom. As much a landmark as an icon, it can be seen on a clear day from an airplane flying down either coast of Florida. Spaceship Earth contains the Spaceship Earth Ride.

Everyone likes to gawk at the golf ball, but there are some truly jaw-dropping facts about it: it weighs 1 million pounds and measures 164 feet in diameter and 180 feet in height ("Aha!" you say. "It's not really a sphere!"). Altogether it encompasses more than 2 million cubic feet of space, and it's balanced on six pylons sunk 100 feet into the ground. The anodized aluminum sheath is composed of 954 triangular panels, not all of equal size or shape. And, last, because it is not a geodesic dome, which is only a half sphere, the name "geosphere" was coined; no other like it existed when it was built.

Spaceship Earth Ride. This ride transports you past a series of tableaux that explore human progress and the continuing search for better forms of communication. Scripted by science-fiction writer Ray Bradbury and narrated by Jeremy Irons, the journey begins in the darkest tunnels of time, proceeds through history, and ends poised on the edge of the future.

Audio-animatronics figures (somewhat dated compared to more recent technology) present Cro-Magnon man daubing mystic paintings on cave walls, Egyptian scribes scratching hieroglyphics on papyrus, Roman centurions building roads, Islamic scholars mapping the heavens, and 11th- and 12th-century Benedictine monks hand-copying ancient manuscripts in order to preserve the wisdom of the past. One monk, not as tireless as history would have us believe, is conked out at his carrel, his candle smoking in the gusts of his snores. As you move into the Renaissance, Michelangelo paints the Sistine Chapel, Gutenberg invents the printing press, and in rapid succession, the telegraph, radio, television, and computer come into being. The pace speeds up, and you're bombarded with images from the age of communication before entering serene space. In one corner is a photograph of the Earth taken by an astronaut on one of the *Apollo* moon shots. Toward the conclusion of the ride, you arrive in a "Global Neighborhood" that ties all of the earth's peoples together through an interactive global network. ☞ **Duration:** *15 min.* **Crowds:** *Longest during the morning and shortest just before closing.* **Strategy:** *Ride while you're waiting for your Mission: SPACE or Test Track appointments.* **Audience:** *All ages.* **Rating:** ★★.

Innoventions

In Innoventions—the two-building, 100,000-square-foot attraction at the center of Future World—new technology that affects daily living is highlighted by constantly changing exhibits, live stage demonstrations, and hands-on displays. Each major exhibition area is presented by a leading technology company or association. Innoventions East focuses heavily on home products for the not-too-distant future. Here you can explore the House of Innoventions, presented by Whirlpool and several other companies, and filled with innovative lifestyle conveniences that include a hot tub with a built-in, 43", high-definition plasma video screen with surround-sound. There's also an oven with built-in refrigerator and warming capabilities that can be programmed to prepare a meal 24 hours ahead. The area's Disney.com Internet Zone is loaded with family-friendly activities, and the Segway Human Transporter offers a cutting-edge alternative to walking. The transporter is so popular that it is used by some Disney personnel to wheel across the park and has been incorporated into a new Epcot guided tour.

At Innoventions West, IBM's ThinkPlace exhibits a wearable computer and showcases a high-tech playground for children called the Little Thinkers Playground. Lutron demonstrates an Ultimate Home Theater with fiber-optic lighting and even a romantic "star-field" ceiling. Disney Interactive Video Games of Tomorrow offers an interactive preview of games to come. You'll be hard-pressed to pull your kids out of here. Everyone in the family can take the interactive challenge at "Where's the Fire?" presented by Liberty Mutual, where team members wield hand-held "zappers" to eliminate fire hazards projected onto screens in different rooms of two deconstructed homes. Each correct "zap" earns team points that are tallied at game's end. When you finally do exit, if you're

Best of the Park Plan to arrive in the parking lot 30 minutes before the official park opening. As soon as you're admitted, race over to **Mission: SPACE** and either wait in line to ride it or get a FASTPASS appointment. After you ride Mission: SPACE, be sure to get a FASTPASS ticket for Test Track. Then, ready to have your mind expanded, backtrack to **Spaceship Earth.** Upon leaving Spaceship Earth, people naturally head for the first pavilion they see: either Universe of Energy or the Living Seas. Skip them for now and go directly to the **Wonders of Life,** if the pavilion is open, and segue without a pause from Body Wars to *The Making of Me* to Cranium Command.

Next head to Future World's western pavilions and go straight to **Soarin'** at the Land. If the wait is long, grab a FASTPASS, then take the boat ride and see **Circle of Life.** Ride Soarin', then proceed to the **Imagination!** pavilion and get another FASTPASS ticket for *Honey, I Shrunk the Audience.* Visit **Journey into Imagination with Figment,** and if you have time left, meander through Image Works before returning to *Honey, I Shrunk the Audience.* By this time there may be a line at **Living Seas,** but if there isn't, go on in and stay as long as you like. Outside, things should be getting crowded.

Head counterclockwise into the World Showcase, toward **Canada,** while everyone else is hoofing it toward Mexico. If it's lunchtime, you may be able to get a table right away at **Le Cellier,** one of Epcot's lesser-known dining gems. Then try to catch a performance of the British Invasion in the United Kingdom before crossing the bridge into **France,** where you can snap up an éclair or napoleon at **Boulangerie Pâtisserie.** Shop in Morocco and Japan; then see the **American Adventure Show,** timing it to a Voices of Liberty or American Vybe performance. If there are lines at **Norway** by the time you get there, grab a FASTPASS for the Maelstrom ride, then head for **Innoventions** or **Ellen's Energy Adventure** at the Universe of Energy.

Now's the time to head back to Norway and Maelstrom, followed by an early dinner at France, Italy, Mexico, or another inviting spot. See any attractions you missed, remembering that parts of Future World sometimes close ahead of the rest of the park. Stick around for **IllumiNations,** and stake out a spot early by the lagoon wall at Italy, on the International Gateway Bridge between France and the United Kingdom, or at an outdoor U.K. table. Make sure the wind is to your back so fireworks and special-effects smoke don't waft your way and obscure the scene. Take your time on the way out—the park seems especially magical after dark.

On Rainy Days Although attractions at Future World are largely indoors, Epcot's expansiveness and the pleasures of meandering around the World Showcase on a sunny day make the park a poor choice in inclement weather. Still, if you can't go another day, bring a poncho and muddle through. You'll feel right at home in the United Kingdom.

---

a collector of the myriad Disney pins that are sold in nearly all the theme-park shops, you'll want to stop by the Pin Station at Innoventions Plaza—it's headquarters for either purchasing or trading pins with fellow collectors. ☞ *Duration: Up to you.* **Crowds:** *Largest around the popular computer displays.* **Strategy:** *Go before 10 AM or after 2 PM.* **Audience:** *All but toddlers. Several games are designed with preschoolers in mind.* **Rating:** ★★★.

> **need a break?**

The **Fountain View Espresso and Bakery** sells freshly brewed coffees, scrumptious croissants, fruit tarts, and éclairs. You can eat at the circular counter or grab a table. The umbrella-covered tables on the patio have a fine view of the fountain. In the afternoon, this is a great place to sip a beverage and watch the Fountain of Nations water ballet show without having to crane your neck while standing in the blazing sun.

Ice Station Cool

Stooping low in the ice tunnel–like entrance to this re-created igloo, you see statues of one Refreshus Maximus, frozen in his hunt for refreshment. Beyond, you come to a room full of soda machines where you can sample Coca-Cola products from around the world, such as Vegitabeta from Japan, Smart Watermelon from China, and Kinley Lemon from Israel. There's no free American Coke here, but there's plenty of Coca-Cola memorabilia to buy. ☞ *Duration: As long as you like.* **Crowds:** *Move pretty quickly.* **Strategy:** *Visit in midafternoon on a very hot day.* **Audience:** *All ages.* **Rating:** ★.

Universe of Energy

The first of the pavilions on the left, or east, side of Future World, the Universe of Energy occupies a large, lopsided pyramid sheathed in thousands of mirrors—solar collectors that power the attraction inside. Though it's a technologically complex show with a ride, film, and large audio-animatronics dinosaurs, the attraction could use some updating. One of the ride's special effects includes enough cold, damp fog to make you think you've been transported to the inside of a defrosting refrigerator. ("We don't want to go through that fog again, " one child announced after emerging from a particularly damp vision of the Mesozoic era.)

Ellen's Energy Adventure. In the Universe of Energy show, comedian Ellen DeGeneres portrays a woman who dreams she's a contestant on *Jeopardy!* only to discover that all the categories involve a subject she knows nothing about—energy. Her challengers on the show, hosted by Alex Trebek himself, are Ellen's know-it-all former college roommate

When to Go

Epcot is now so vast and varied that you really need two days to explore it all. The best days to go are early in the week, since most people tend to go to Disney's Animal Kingdom and the Magic Kingdom first.

Arrive at the turnstiles 15 minutes before opening, so you can avoid some of the lines. Make Mission: SPACE, Test Track, and Soarin' your first stops.

When You're There

Plan to have at least one relaxed meal. With children, you may want to make reservations (try to make them 3 to 4 months in advance) for the Princess Storybook Breakfast at Norway's Akershus, or for lunch or dinner at The Land's Garden Grill, a revolving restaurant that features character appearances by Mickey and friends. Or opt for an early seafood lunch at the Coral Reef in the Living Seas. A late lunch or an early dinner at one of the World Showcase restaurants is another great option.

Upon entering, check Epcot's Tip Board past Spaceship Earth and just outside Innoventions, and modify your strategy if there's a short line at a top attraction.

Walk fast, see the exhibits when the park is at its emptiest, and slow down and enjoy the shops and the live entertainment when the crowds thicken.

Set up a rendezvous point and time at the start of the day, just in case you and your companions get separated. Some good places in Future World include in front of Gateway Gifts near Spaceship Earth and in front of the Fountain of Nations; in World Showcase, in front of your country of choice.

(played to the irritating hilt by Jamie Lee Curtis) and Albert Einstein. Enter Bill Nye, the Science Guy, Ellen's nice-guy neighbor and all-around science whiz, who guides Ellen (and you) on a crash course in Energy 101.

First comes the history of the universe—in one minute—on three 70-mm screens, 157 feet wide by 32 feet tall. Next the theater separates into six 96-passenger vehicles that lurch into the forest primeval. Huge trees loom out of the mists of time, ominous blue moonbeams waver in the fog, sulfurous lava burbles up, and the air smells distinctly of Swamp Thing. Through this unfriendly landscape apatosauruses wander trailing mouthfuls of weeds, a tyrannosaurus fights it out with a triceratops, pterodactyls swoop through the air, and a truly nasty sea snake emerges from the swamp to attack the left side of the tram. A terrified Ellen is even cornered by a menacing elasmosaurus.

The ride concludes with another film in which Ellen learns about the world's present-day energy needs, resources, and concerns. It's shown on three screens, each 30 feet tall, 74 feet wide, and curved to create a 200-degree range of vision. Does Ellen win in her *Jeopardy!* dream? You'll have to travel back in time for the answer. ☞ *Duration: 30 min. Crowd: Steady but never horrible; 600 people enter every 15 min. Strategy: To be at the front of the ride and have your experience of the primeval landscape unspoiled by rows of modern heads in front of you, sit in the seats to the far left and front of the theater; to get these seats, be sure to position yourself similarly in the preshow area.* **Audience:** *All ages.* **Rating:** ★★.

Wonders of Life

A towering statue of a DNA double helix outside the gold-crowned dome of the Wonders of Life welcomes you to this well-done pavilion, which focuses on health and fitness. The messages come via two terrific films; one of Disney's first flight-simulator rides; a multimedia presentation; and dozens of interactive gadgets that whiz, bleep, and blink. The pavilion is open only during peak travel periods, so check the "Times Guide" before heading over.

Body Wars. The flight-simulator technology that's used to train commercial and military pilots adapts perfectly to thrill attractions, though this 15-year-old ride could be even better with some high-tech tweaking. By synchronizing the action on a movie screen with the movement of a ride vehicle, you're tricked into thinking you're moving in wild and crazy fashion even though you never leave your seat. Probably the mildest flight simulator in Central Florida, Body Wars still offers a worthwhile experience, thanks to the fascinating film and the ingenious idea. You and your fellow scientists enter a simulator chamber that, like something out of a science-fiction plot, will be miniaturized and injected into the body's bloodstream to remove a splinter, which appears on-screen like a massive rock formation. Soon, you're shooting through the heart, wheezing through the lungs, and picking up a jolt of energy in the brain as you race against time to complete your mission. ☞ *Duration: 5 min.* **Crowds:** *Rarely a long line now that Test Track and Mission: SPACE are the biggest draws.* **Strategy:** *Go anytime.* **Audience:** *All but some young children, who may be frightened by the sensation of movement the film induces and by the lurching and pitching of the simulator chamber. Not recommended for pregnant women or guests with heart, back, or neck problems or motion sickness. Minimum height: 40".* **Rating:** ★★★.

The Making of Me. Show times at Wonders of Life are staggered to pick up as soon as another lets out, so with a little luck you can segue right into this valuable film on human conception and childbearing. Starring Martin Short as a man who, in search of his origins, journeys back in time to his parents' childhood, youth, marriage, and, eventually, their decision to have him, the film uses both animation and actual footage from a live birth to explain where babies come from. Some scenes are explicit, but all the topics are handled with gentle humor—as when the sperm race for the egg to the tune of "The Ride of the Valkyries"—and with great delicacy. Many adults find the film affecting enough to get out the handkerchiefs for a quick swipe at overflowing eyes, and the film gives children a great opening for talking with their parents about the beginning of life. ☞ *Duration: 14 min. Crowds: Manageable lines, though the theater is small.* **Strategy:** *Line up 5–10 min before show-time.* **Audience:** *All ages.* **Rating:** ★★★.

Cranium Command. Combining a fast-paced movie with an elaborate set, Disney's audio-animatronics, and celebrity cameos, this engaging show takes a clever look at how the cranium manages to make the heart, the uptight left brain, the laid-back right brain, the stomach, and an ever-alert adrenal gland all work together as their host, a 12-year-old boy, dodges the slings and arrows of a typical day. The star is Buzzy, a bumbling audio-animatronics Cranium Commando given one last chance to take the helm of an adolescent boy before being consigned to run the brain of a chicken. Buzzy's is not an easy job; as the sign on the way to the theater warns, you are entering THE HOME OF THE FLYING ENDORPHINS. In the flick, Buzzy's 12-year-old wakes up late, dashes off without breakfast, meets the new girl in school, fights for her honor, gets called up before the principal, and, finally, returns home and has a much-needed snack. Buzzy attempts to coordinate a heart, operated by *Saturday Night Live*'s muscle team, Hans and Franz; a stomach, run by George Wendt, formerly of *Cheers,* in a sewer worker's overalls and rubber boots; and all the other body parts. Buzzy succeeds—but just barely. ☞ *Duration: 20 min. Crowds: Long lines, but they're quickly erased by the big theater, which seats 200 at a shot.* **Strategy:** *Go when everyone else is at Body Wars.* **Audience:** *All ages.* **Rating:** ★★★.

Fitness Fairground. This educational playground, which teaches both adults and children about good health, takes up much of Wonders of Life. You can pedal around the world on a stationary bicycle while watching an ever-changing view on video, and you can guess your stress level at an interactive computer terminal. *Goofy about Health,* an eight-minute multiscreen montage, follows Goofy's conversion from a foul-living "man-dog" to a fun-loving guy. The Sensory Funhouse provides great interactive fun for the little ones and their families. The Frontiers of Medicine, the only completely serious section of the pavilion, demonstrates leading-edge developments in medicine. ☞ *Duration: Up to you. Crowds: Shifting, but they don't affect your visit.* **Strategy:** *Hang loose and take turns while you're in the Fitness Fairground.* **Audience:** *All ages.* **Rating:** ★★.

Mission: SPACE

It took five years for Disney Imagineers, with the help of 25 experts from NASA, to design Mission: SPACE, the first ride ever to take guests "straight up" in a simulated rocket launch. The story transports you and co-riders to the year 2036 and the International Space Training Center, where you are an astronaut-in-training about to embark on your first launch. Before you board the four-person rocket capsule, you're assigned to a position: commander, navigator, pilot, or engineer. And at this point you're warned several times about the intensity of the ride and the risks for people with health concerns. Many

Fodor's Choice

people come off this ride feeling nauseated and disoriented from the high-speed spinning of the vehicle, which is the technology that makes you feel as if you're rocketing into space. But for those who can handle it, the sensation of lift-off is truly amazing. You'll feel the capsule tilt skyward and, on a screen that simulates a windshield, you'll see the clouds and even a flock of birds pass over you. Then you launch, a turbulent and heart-pounding experience that flattens you against your seat. Once you break into outer space, you'll even feel weightless. After landing, you exit your capsule into the Training Lab, where you can rejoin your little ones playing space-related games.

Parents should exercise caution when deciding whether or not to let their children ride. Even if your child meets the height requirement, she may not be old enough to enjoy the ride. In the capsule, you're instructed to keep your head back against the seat and to look straight ahead for the duration of the ride. (Closing your eyes or not looking straight ahead can bring on serious motion sickness.) Your role as a "crew member" also means you're supposed to hold onto a joy stick and push bottons at certain times. If you think your child can't or won't follow these instructions, keep her off the ride. Note that in the summer of 2005, a 4-year-old boy died while on Mission: SPACE. As we go to press, no evidence has been released to indicate that he had a pre-existing conditon and engineers ascertained that the ride did not malfunction.
☞ *Duration: 4 min. **Crowds:** Heavy, since this is Disney's most technologically advanced attraction and one of only a handful of thrill rides at Epcot. **Strategy:** Get there before 10 AM or use FASTPASS. Don't ride on a full stomach. **Audience:** Adults and children over 8. Pregnant women, adults over 55, and anyone with heart, back, neck, balance, blood presure, or motion sickness problems should not ride. Minimum height: 44" . **Rating:** ★★★.*

Test Track

This small-scale-with-big-thrills version of a General Motors vehicle proving ground takes you behind the scenes of automobile testing. The queue area showcases many of these tests in informative, action-packed exhibits—and they make the wait fun. On the ride, sporty convertible Test Track vehicles take you and five other passengers through seven different performance tests. In the Brake Test your ride vehicle makes two passes through a circular setup of traffic cones, and you learn how antilock brakes can make a wildly out-of-control skid become manageable. In the Environmental Chamber, the ride vehicle is exposed to extreme heat, bone-chilling cold, and a mist that simulates exposure to corrosive substances. After leaving these test chambers, vehicles accelerate quickly up a switchback "mountain road" in the Ride Handling Test. There's also a too-close-for-comfort view of a Barrier Test. The best part, the High-Speed Test, is last: your vehicle goes outside the Test Track building to negotiate a steeply banked loop at a speed of nearly 60 mph. As you leave the pavilion, kids can get a soaking in the Cool Wash, an interactive water area that lets them pretend they are in a car wash.
☞ *Duration: 5 min. **Crowds:** Heavy. **Strategy:** Go first thing in the morning and get a FASTPASS ticket, or you will wait—a long time. Note that*

the ride can't function on wet tracks, so don't head here right after a downpour. Audience: All but young children; the queue-area message will be lost on them, and the speeds and other effects may prove frightening. No pregnant women or guests wearing back, neck, or leg braces. Minimum height: 40". Rating: ★★★.

The Living Seas

Epcot is known for its fountains; the one outside the Living Seas, the first satellite pavilion on the western outer ring, flings surf in a never-ending wave against a rock garden beneath the stylized marquee. The pavilion itself is a favorite among children. Time and technology have caught up with the 5.7-million-gallon aquarium at the pavilion's core. Thrilling when it first opened, what was once revolutionary has now been equaled by top aquariums around the country. Still, the collection of sea life looks quite impressive when you circle the tank on the outside, even more so when you scuba dive within it on a guided tour or when you dine while admiring the sea life from the aquarium windows of the pavilion's Coral Reef restaurant. A seven-minute film introduces the ocean as the Earth's last frontier and touches on the mysteries that lie beneath. After a brief "hydrolator" ride to Sea Base Alpha in what appears to be an underwater elevator, you exit to Disney's version of the ocean floor and a model undersea research facility. Once you've explored Sea Base Alpha, you may want to meander around the glass-walled tank at your leisure on an upper level, pointing out barracudas, stingrays, parrot fish, sea turtles, and even sharks. In the wake of the Disney/Pixar hit film, *Finding Nemo,* Disney introduced character meet-and-greets with Nemo at this pavilion and also stocked the reef with more clown fish. The latest attraction additions feature "Nemo" animated characters Crush, the ancient sea turtle, and Dory, Nemo's forgetful sidekick, in real-time animated shows during which they "converse" with you in a small theater. The attraction uses voice-activated animation software and a behind-the-scenes actor to give Crush and Dory their conversational cues.

Sea Base Alpha. This typical Epcot playground in the guise of an underwater research facility is dedicated to specific subjects, such as ocean ecosystems, porpoises, and the endangered Florida manatee. Fully interactive, these contain films, touchy-feely sections, mini-aquariums, and video quizzes. Unfortunately, Sea Base Alpha is accessible only via "hydrolator", so access can be difficult when it's busy. ☞ *Duration: 30 min and up. Crowds: Large, all day long. Strategy: Stop in first thing in the morning, during lunch, or after 5. Audience: All ages. Rating:* ★★.

The Land

Shaped like an intergalactic greenhouse, the enormous, skylighted Land pavilion dedicates 6 acres and a host of different attractions to everyone's favorite topic: food. You can easily spend two hours exploring here, more if you take one of the guided greenhouse tours available throughout the day.

Soarin'. If you've ever wondered what it's like to fly, or at least hang glide, this is your chance to enjoy the sensation without actually taking the plunge. Opened in 2005, Soarin' is based on the popular attraction Soarin' Over California at Disney's California Adventure in Anaheim. This latest Epcot adventure uses motion-based technology to literally lift you in your seat 40 feet into the air within a giant projection-screen dome. As you soar above the Golden Gate Bridge, Napa Valley, Yosemite, and other wonders of California, you feel the wind and smell fragrant orange blossoms. The accompanying orchestral musical score created by Jerry Goldsmith (*Mulan, Star Trek*) builds on the thrill, and the crispness and definition of the film, projected at twice the rate of a typical motion picture, adds realism. ☞ *Crowds: Heavy due to attraction's newness.* **Strategy:** *Go early, grab a FASTPASS, or split up and use the single fliers line.* **Audience:** *Adults and children 40 inches or taller.* ★★★.

Living with the Land. Piloted by an informative, overalls-clad guide, your canopied boat cruises through three biomes—rain forest, desert, and prairie ecological communities—and into an experimental greenhouse that demonstrates how food sources may be grown in the future, not only on the planet but also in outer space. Shrimp, sunshine bass, tilapia, eels, catfish, and alligators are raised in controlled aquacells, and tomatoes, peppers, and squash thrive in the Desert Farm area through a system of drip irrigation that delivers just the right amount of water and nutrients to their roots. Gardeners are usually interested in the section on integrated pest management, which relies on "good" insects like ladybugs to control more harmful predators. Many of the growing areas are actual experiments-in-progress, in which Disney and the U.S. Department of Agriculture have joined forces to produce, say, a sweeter pineapple or a faster-growing pepper. Interestingly, although the plants and fish in the greenhouse are all quite real—and are regularly harvested for use in the Land's restaurants—those in the biomes are artful fakes, manufactured by Disney elves out of flexible, lightweight plastic. The grass is made out of glass fibers that have been implanted in rubber mats. ☞ *Duration: 14 min.* **Crowds:** *Moderate, all day.* **Strategy:** *The line moves fairly quickly, so go anytime. Use FASTPASS in the case of peak season crowds.* **Audience:** *Teens and adults.* **Rating:** ★★★.

The Circle of Life. Featuring three stars of *The Lion King*—Simba the lion, Timon the meerkat, and Pumbaa the waddling warthog—this film delivers a powerful message about protecting the world's environment for all living things. Part animation, part *National Geographic*–like film using spectacular 70-mm live-action footage, *Circle of Life* tells a fable about a "Hakuna Matata Lakeside Village" that Timon and Pumbaa are developing by clearing the African savanna. Simba cautions about mistreating the land by telling a story of a creature who occasionally forgets that everything is connected in the great Circle of Life. "That creature," he says, "is man." The lilting accompaniment, of course, is Tim Rice and Elton John's popular song, and the narration is provided by James Earl Jones. ☞ *Duration: 20 min.* **Crowds:** *Moderate to large, all day.* **Strategy:** *Hit this first in the Land.* **Audience:** *Enlightening for children and adults; a nap opportunity for toddlers.* **Rating:** ★★.

15 ROMANTIC THINGS TO DO AT WALT DISNEY WORLD

NOT EVERYTHING AT DISNEY WORLD involves children. Get a babysitter (available for a fee through Guest Services) and enjoy some private time, just the two of you.

1. Have dinner at the very grand Victoria & Albert's restaurant in the Grand Floridian. Remember to make a reservation three months in advance.

2. Have dinner at the California Grill and watch the Magic Kingdom fireworks.

3. Rent a boat for a cruise on the Seven Seas Lagoon or the waterways leading to it. Bring champagne and glasses.

4. Take a nighttime whirl on Cinderella's Golden Carrousel in Fantasyland. Sparkling lights make it magical.

5. Have your picture taken and grab a kiss in the heart-shape gazebo in the back of Minnie's Country House.

6. Plan a day of pampering at the Grand Floridian Spa.

7. Buy a faux diamond ring at the Emporium on Main Street in the Magic Kingdom. Propose to your sweetheart at your favorite spot in the World.

8. Have a caricature drawn of the two of you at the Downtown Disney Marketplace.

9. Sit by the fountain in front of Epcot's France pavilion and have some wine or a pastry and coffee.

10. Have a drink at the cozy Yachtsman's Crew bar in the Yacht Club hotel.

11. Take a walk on the BoardWalk. Watch IllumiNations from the bridge to the Yacht and Beach Club. Then boogie at the Atlantic Dance Hall.

12. Tie the knot all over again at the Wedding Pavilion. Invite Mickey and Minnie to the reception.

13. Rent a hot-air balloon for a magical tour of Walt Disney World.

14. Every night is New Year's Eve at Pleasure Island. Declare your love amid confetti and fireworks.

15. Enjoy a British lager outside at Epcot's Rose & Crown Pub—a perfect IllumiNations viewing spot. Book ahead and ask for a table with a view.

need a
break?

Talk about a self-contained ecosystem: the Land pavilion grows its own produce, which is cooked and delivered to your table at **Sunshine Seasons.** The restaurant embodies Disney's new "fast casual" service concept. You order at a counter then sit at a table in a more upscale environment than in usual fast-food places. The eatery's **Asian shop** offers chicken or tofu noodle bowls and spicy beef and vegetable stir-fries. A **sandwich shop** delivers grilled veggie Cubans, Italian paninis with sun-dried tomato mayo, and turkey muffalettas. The **salad shop** wows with roasted beet, goat cheese, and seared tuna among other options, over mixed greens. Wood-fired grills and rotisseries sizzle with chicken, beef, and salmon, and the bakery is a sure bet for fresh pastries and hand-dipped ice cream. To avoid the crowds, plan to eat at non-peak times—after 2 for lunch and before 5 or after 7 for dinner.

Imagination!

The theme here is the imagination and the fun that can be had when you let it loose. The leaping fountains outside make the point, as does the big attraction here, the 3-D film *Honey, I Shrunk the Audience.* The Journey into Imagination with Figment ride can be capped by a stroll through Image Works, a sort of interactive fun house devoted to music and art.

Fodor'sChoice

Honey, I Shrunk the Audience. Don't miss this 3-D adventure about the futuristic "shrinking" technologies demonstrated in the hit films that starred Rick Moranis. Moranis reprises his role as Dr. Wayne Szalinski, who's about to receive the Inventor of the Year Award from the Imagination Institute. While Dr. Szalinski is demonstrating his latest shrinking machine, though, things go really, really wrong. Be prepared to laugh and scream your head off, courtesy of the special in-theater effects and 3-D film technology that are used ingeniously, from start to finish, to dramatize a hoot of a story. ☞ *Duration: 14 min. Crowds: Large theater capacity should mean a relatively short wait, but the film's popularity can make for big crowds. Strategy: Go first thing in the morning or just before closing, or utilize the FASTPASS scheme. Audience: All but easily frightened children. For most, the humor quotient outweighs the few scary moments. Rating:* ★★★.

Journey into Imagination with Figment. If this isn't your first trip to Disney, you may remember Figment, the fun-loving dragon and original host of the Journey to Imagination ride. When this attraction was updated for Disney's millennium celebration, Figment stepped out of his star-ring role, to the dismay of many. So Disney returned Figment to celebrity status and teamed him with Dr. Nigel Channing, the presenter of Dr. Szalinski's award in *Honey, I Shrunk the Audience.* The pair take you on a sensory adventure designed to engage your imagination through sound, illusion, gravity, dimension, and color. After the ride, you can check out Image Works, where several interactive displays allow you to further stretch your imagination. ☞ *Duration: 8 min. Crowds: Although the ride is the newest at Epcot, lines move fairly quickly here.*

*Strategy: Ride while waiting for your Honey, I Shrunk the Audience FAST-PASS appointment. **Audience:** School-age children and adults. Preschoolers may be frightened by the brief period of darkness and the scanner at the end of the ride. **Rating:** ★★.*

World Showcase

Nowhere but at Epcot can you explore a little corner of 11 countries in one day. As you stroll the 1⅓ mi around the 40-acre World Showcase Lagoon, you circumnavigate the globe according to Disney by experiencing the native food, entertainment, culture, and arts and crafts at pavilions representing 11 different countries in Europe, Asia, North Africa, and the Americas. The pavilion employees are from the countries they represent—Disney hires them to live and work for up to a year as part of its international college program.

Instead of rides, you have breathtaking films at the Canada, China, and France pavilions; several art exhibitions; and the chance to chat in the native language of the friendly foreign staff members. Each pavilion also has a designated Kidcot Fun Stop, open daily from 11 AM or noon until around 8 or 9 PM, where youngsters can try their hands at crafts projects—they might make a Moroccan fez or a Norwegian troll, for instance. Live entertainment is an integral part of the pavilions' presentations, and some of your finest moments here will be watching incredibly talented Dragon Legend Chinese acrobats, singing along with a terrific band of Fab Four impersonators in the U.K. pavilion, or marveling at Imaginum, outside the Italy pavilion. Once known as the Living Statues, the group stuns passersby when its members suddenly change position and interact playfully with guests without breaking their statuesque demeanor. Dining is another favorite pastime at Epcot, and the World Showcase offers tempting tastes of the authentic cuisines of the countries that have pavilions.

The focal point of World Showcase is the American Adventure, directly opposite Spaceship Earth on the far side of the lagoon. The pavilions of other countries fan out from both sides, encircling the lagoon. Counterclockwise from World Showcase Plaza as you enter from Future World are Canada, the United Kingdom, France, Morocco, Japan, the American Adventure, Italy, Germany, China, Norway, and Mexico. The best times to visit are late April through June, during the Epcot International Flower & Garden Festival, and October through mid-November, during the Epcot International Food and Wine Festival.

groovy souvenirs

A World Showcase Passport ($9.95) is a wonderful way to keep a kid interested in this more adult area of Epcot. The passports, available at vendor carts, come with stickers and a badge, and children can present them to be stamped at each pavilion. The World Showcase is also a great place to look for foreign and unusual gifts—you might pick up silver jewelry in Mexico, a teapot in China, or a kimonoed doll in Japan.

Canada

"Oh, it's just our Canadian outdoors," said a typically modest native guide upon being asked the model for the striking rocky chasm and tumbling waterfall that represent just one of the high points of Canada. The beautiful formal gardens do have an antecedent: Butchart Gardens, in Victoria, British Columbia. And so does the Hôtel du Canada, a French Gothic mansion with spires, turrets, and a mansard roof; anyone who's ever stayed at Québec's Château Frontenac or Ottawa's Château Laurier will recognize the imposing style favored by architects of Canadian railroad hotels. Like the size of the Rocky Mountains, the scale of the structures seems immense; unlike the real thing, it's managed with a trick called forced perspective, which exaggerates the smallness of the distant parts to make the entire thing look gigantic. Another bit of design legerdemain: the World Showcase Rockies are made of chicken wire and painted concrete mounted on a movable platform similar to a parade float. Ah, wilderness!

Canada also contains shops selling maple syrup, lumberjack shirts, and other trapper paraphernalia. Its restaurant, Le Cellier Steakhouse, is a great place to stop for a relaxing lunch.

O Canada! That's just what you'll say after seeing this CircleVision film's stunning opening shot—footage of the Royal Canadian Mounted Police surrounding you as they circle the screen. From there, you whoosh over waterfalls, venture through Montréal and Toronto, sneak up on bears and bison, mush behind a husky-pulled dogsled, and land pluck in the middle of a hockey game. This is a standing-only theater, with lean rails. ☞ *Duration: 17 min. Crowds: Can be thick in late afternoon. Strategy: Go when World Showcase opens or in the evening. Audience: All ages, but no strollers permitted, and toddlers and small children can't see unless they're held aloft. Rating:* ★★★.

United Kingdom

Never has it been so easy to cross the English Channel. A pastiche of there-will-always-be-an-England architecture, the United Kingdom rambles between the elegant mansions lining a London square to the bustling, half-timber shops of a village high street to thatched-roof cottages from the countryside. (The thatch is made of plastic broom bristles in deference to local fire regulations.) And of course there's a pair of the familiar red phone booths that were once found all over the United Kingdom but are now on their way to being relics. The pavilion has no single major attraction. Instead, you can wander through shops selling tea and tea accessories, Welsh handicrafts, Royal Doulton figurines, and woolens and tartans from Pringle of Scotland. The Magic of Wales sells delicate British china and collectibles. Outside, the strolling World Showcase Players coax audience members into participating in their definitely low-brow versions of Shakespeare. There's also a lovely garden and park with benches in the back that's easy to miss—relax and kick back to the tunes of the British Invasion, a band known for its on-target Beatles performances. Kids love to run through the hedge maze as the parents travel back in time to "Yesterday."

need a break? Revive yourself with a pint of the best—although you'll be hard-put to decide between the offerings—at the **Rose & Crown Pub,** which also offers traditional afternoon tea on the outdoor terrace. The adjacent dining room serves more substantial fare (priority seating reservation required). The terrace outside is one of the best spots for watching IllumiNations; arrive early.

France

You don't need the scaled-down model of the Eiffel Tower to tell you that you've arrived in France, specifically Paris. There's the poignant accordion music wafting out of concealed speakers, the trim sycamores pruned in the French style to develop signature knots at the end of each branch, and the delicious aromas surrounding the Boulangerie Pâtisserie bake shop. This is the Paris of dreams, a Paris of the years just before World War I, when solid mansard-roof mansions were crowned with iron filigree, when the least brick was drenched in romanticism. Here's a replica of the conservatorylike Les Halles—the iron-and-glass barrel-roof market that no longer exists in the City of Light; there's an arching footbridge; and all around, of course, there are shops. You can inspect Limoges porcelain in the exquisite Plume et Palette; sample Guerlain perfume and cosmetics at La Signature; and acquire a bottle of Bouzy Rouge at Les Vins de France. If you plan to dine at the beautifully remodeled Les Chefs de France, late lunch is a good plan.

Impressions de France. The intimate Palais du Cinema, inspired by the royal theater at Fontainebleau, screens this homage to the glories of the country. Shown on five screens spanning 200-degrees in an air-conditioned, sit-down theater, the film takes you to vineyards at harvest time, Paris on Bastille Day, the Alps, Versailles, Normandy's Mont-St-Michel, and the stunning châteaux of the Loire Valley. The musical accompaniment also hits high notes and sweeps you away with familiar segments from Offenbach, Debussy, and Saint-Saëns, all woven together by long-time Disney musician Buddy Baker. ☞ *Duration: 18 min.* **Crowds:** *Considerable from World Showcase opening through late afternoon.* **Strategy:** *Come before noon or after dinner.* **Audience:** *Adults and children age 7 and up.* **Rating:** ★★★.

need a break? The frequent lines at **Boulangerie Pâtisserie,** a small Parisian-style sidewalk café, are worth the wait. Have a creamy café au lait and an éclair, napoleon, or some other French pastry while enjoying the fountains and floral displays.

Morocco

No magic carpet is required as you enter Morocco—just walk through the pointed arches of the Bab Boujouloud gate and you'll find yourself exploring the mysterious North African country of Morocco. The arches are ornamented with beautiful wood carvings and encrusted with intricate mosaics made of 9 tons of handmade, hand-cut tiles; 19 native artisans were sent to Epcot to install them and to create the dusty stucco walls that seem to have withstood centuries of sandstorms. Look closely and you'll see that every tile has a small crack or some other imperfection, and no tile depicts a living creature—in deference to the Islamic belief that only Allah creates perfection and life.

Koutoubia Minaret, a replica of the prayer tower in Marrakesh, acts as Morocco's landmark. Traditional winding alleyways, each corner bursting with carpets, brasses, leatherwork, and other North African craftsmanship, lead to a beautifully tiled fountain and lush gardens. The full-service restaurant, Marrakesh, is a highlight here if you enjoy eating couscous and roast lamb while distracted by a lithesome belly dancer. And one of the hottest fast-food spots on the Epcot dining scene is Tangierine Café, with tasty Mediterranean specialties and freshly baked Moroccan bread.

Japan

A brilliant vermilion torii gate, based on Hiroshima Bay's much-photographed Itsukushima Shrine, frames the World Showcase Lagoon and stands as the striking emblem of Disney's serene version of Japan. Disney horticulturists deserve a hand for creating an authentic landscape: 90% of the plants they used are native to Japan. Rocks, pebbled streams, pools, and carefully pruned trees and shrubs complete the meticulous picture. At sunset, or during a rainy dusk, the twisted branches of the corkscrew willows frame a perfect Japanese view of the five-story winged pagoda that is the heart of the pavilion. Based on the 8th-century Horyuji Temple in Nara, the brilliant blue pagoda has five levels, symbolizing the five elements of Buddhist belief—earth, water, fire, wind, and sky.

The peace is occasionally interrupted by authentic performances on drums and gongs. Other entertainment is provided by demonstrations of traditional Japanese crafts, such as kite-making and the snipping of brown rice toffee into intricate shapes. Mitsukoshi Department Store, an immense three-centuries-old retail firm known as Japan's Sears Roebuck, is a favorite among Epcot shoppers and carries everything from T-shirts to kimonos and row upon row of Japanese dolls. Diners are entertained by knife-juggling Japanese chefs at the Teppanyaki Dining Rooms.

American Adventure

In a Disney version of Philadelphia's Liberty Hall, the Imagineers prove that their kind of fantasy can beat reality hands down. The 110,000 bricks, made by hand from soft pink Georgia clay, sheathe the familiar structure, which acts as a beacon for those across Epcot's lagoon. The pavilion includes an all-American fast-food restaurant, a shop, lovely rose gardens, and an outdoor theater always booked with first-rate live entertainment.

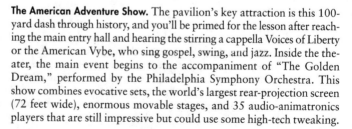

The American Adventure Show. The pavilion's key attraction is this 100-yard dash through history, and you'll be primed for the lesson after reaching the main entry hall and hearing the stirring a cappella Voices of Liberty or the American Vybe, who sing gospel, swing, and jazz. Inside the theater, the main event begins to the accompaniment of "The Golden Dream," performed by the Philadelphia Symphony Orchestra. This show combines evocative sets, the world's largest rear-projection screen (72 feet wide), enormous movable stages, and 35 audio-animatronics players that are still impressive but could use some high-tech tweaking.

Ben Franklin still climbs up the stairs, but his movements are more tentative when compared with newer-generation figures. Beginning with the arrival of the Pilgrims at Plymouth Rock and their grueling first winter, Ben Franklin and a wry, pipe-smoking Mark Twain narrate the episodes, both praiseworthy and shameful, that have shaped the American spirit. Disney detail is so painstaking that you never feel rushed, and, in fact, each speech and each scene seems polished like a little jewel. You feel the cold at Valley Forge and the triumph when Charles Lindbergh flies the Atlantic; you are moved by Nez Perce chief Joseph's forced abdication of Native American ancestral lands and by women's rights campaigner Susan B. Anthony's speech; you laugh with Will Rogers's aphorisms and learn about the pain of the Great Depression through an affecting radio broadcast by Franklin Delano Roosevelt. ☞ *Duration: 30 min. Crowds: Large, but the theater is huge, so you can almost always get into the next show. Strategy: Check the entertainment schedule and arrive 10 min before the Voices of Liberty or American Vybe are slated to perform. Grab a bench or a spot on the floor and enjoy the music before the show. Audience: All ages. Rating:* ★★★.

America Gardens Theater. On the edge of the lagoon, directly opposite Disney's magnificent bit of colonial fakery, is this venue for concerts and shows—some of the "Yankee Doodle Dandy" variety and some that are hot tickets themed to such Epcot events as the "Flower Power" concerts with '60s pop legends during the late-April-through-June International Flower & Garden Festival and "Eat to the Beat!" concerts during the October-through-mid-November Epcot International Food and Wine Festival. This is also the setting for the annual yuletide Candlelight Processional—a not-to-be-missed event if you're at WDW during the holidays. The special Candlelight Dinner Package (available through Disney's dining reservations hotline) includes dinner in a select World Showcase restaurant, and preferred seating for the moving performance. ☞ *Crowds: Large during holiday performances and celebrity concerts. Strategy: Check the entertainment schedule and arrive 30 min to 1 hr ahead of time for holiday and celebrity performances. Audience: Varies with performance.*

| need a break? | What else would you order at the counter-service **Liberty Inn** but burgers, apple pie, and other all-American fare? If the weather's cool enough, you can relax at an outdoor table and watch the world go by. On a warm summer evening, this is the place to get an ice-cream sundae before IllumiNations starts. |

Italy

In WDW's Italy, the star is the architecture: reproductions of Venice's Piazza San Marco and Doge's Palace, accurate right down to the gold leaf on the ringlets of the angel perched 100 feet atop the Campanile; the seawall stained with age, with barbershop-stripe poles to which two gondolas are tethered; and the Romanesque columns, Byzantine mosaics, Gothic arches, and stone walls that have all been carefully "antiqued" to look old. Mediterranean plants such as grapevines, kumquat, and olive trees add verisimilitude. Inside, shops sell Venetian beads and

ILLUSIONS OF GRANDEUR

MUCH OF DISNEY WORLD'S breathtaking majesty comes from its architecture, and a little design trick called forced perspective, in which buildings appear taller than they actually are.

The best example of forced perspective is on Main Street in the Magic Kingdom. Look very carefully at the upper floors of the shops. Together, the second and third floors take up the same amount of space as the ground floor. The buildings start at normal scale at the base but then get imperceptibly smaller toward the top to simulate that cozy hometown feeling. Forced perspective is used in Cinderella's castle, too. Notice how it gets narrower toward the towers. This trick of the eye makes it look as if the spires are soaring into the clouds.

In the Animal Kingdom, architectural scale is suppressed to allow trees to overshadow the buildings. The aim is to relay a sense of humility in the face of nature's wonders. Building height is limited to just 30 feet, whereas trees can tower well above that. But the showcase of the park is the 145-foot Tree of Life, which looks like a skyscraper as it rises from the center of Animal Kingdom. The Tree of Life is a sculptural masterpiece, too. Its trunk is carved with the images of hundreds of animals, illustrating another important Disney design tenet: every structure must tell a story.

— Ellen Parlapiano

glasswork, leather purses and belts, olive oils, pastas, and Perugina cookies and chocolate kisses. At the always-hopping L'Originale Alfredo di Roma Ristorante, authentic fettuccine Alfredo and other Italian specialties provide a great carb high for all-day visitors who don't mind being serenaded while they dine.

Germany

Germany, a make-believe village that distills the best folk architecture from all over that country, is so jovial that you practically expect the Seven Dwarfs to come "heigh-ho"-ing out to meet you. Instead, you'll hear the hourly chimes from the specially designed glockenspiel on the clock tower, musical toots and tweets from multitudinous cuckoo clocks, folk tunes from the spinning dolls and plush lambs sold at Der Teddy-bär, and the satisfied grunts of hungry visitors chowing down on hearty German cooking. The Biergarten's wonderful buffet serves several sausage varieties, as well as sauerkraut, spaetzle and roasted potatoes, rotisserie chicken, and German breads. There are also shops aplenty, including Die Weihnachts Ecke (The Christmas Corner), which sells nutcrackers and other traditional Christmas ornaments; Süssigkeiten, for irresistible butter cookies and animal crackers; and Volkskunst, with a folk-crafts collection that includes cuckoo clocks ranging from hummingbird scale to the size of an eagle.

need a break? Bratwurst or goulash and cold beer from the **Sommerfest** cart, at the entrance of the Biergarten restaurant, makes a perfect quick and hearty lunch, while the soft pretzels and strudel are ever-popular snacks. There's not much seating, so you may have to eat on the run.

Saluting Africa–Outpost

It's not one of the 11 World Showcase pavilions, but as you stroll between Germany and China, you'll have to make a brief cultural shift when you encounter the Orisi Risi interactive drum circle, with its traditional African folklore performances. Village Traders sells African handicrafts and—you guessed it—souvenirs relating to *The Lion King.* Buy an ice cream or frozen yogurt at the Refreshment Outpost and enjoy the break at a table by the lagoon while the kids test their drumming skills on bongos or play beneath the cool mist set up to offer respite on hot, sunny days.

China

A shimmering red-and-gold, three-tier replica of Beijing's Temple of Heaven towers over a serene Chinese garden, an art gallery displaying treasures from the People's Republic, a spacious emporium devoted to Chinese goods, and two restaurants. The gardens, planted with a native Chinese tallow tree, water lilies, bamboo, and a 100-year-old weeping mulberry tree, are one of the most peaceful spots in the World Showcase. Piped-in traditional Chinese music flows gently over the peaceful hush of the gardens.

Reflections of China. Think of the Temple of Heaven as an especially fitting theater for a movie in which sensational panoramas of the land and people are dramatically portrayed on a 360-degree CircleVision screen. In 2003 the film was re-edited to include more contemporary scenes, including striking footage of Hong Kong, Shanghai, and Macao. This may be the best of the World Showcase films—the only drawback is that the theater has no chairs; lean rails are provided. ☞ *Duration: 19 min. Crowds: Steady from World Showcase opening through late afternoon, but the theater's high capacity means you can usually get into the next show. Strategy: Go anytime. Audience: All ages, but no strollers permitted, and small children have to be held aloft to see. Rating:* ★★★.

need a break? **Lotus Blossom Café** has covered outdoor tables and serves egg rolls, sweet-and-sour anything, and not-too-exotic stir-fried dishes that you can wash down with cold Tsing Tao beer. The ginger ice cream is refreshing on a hot day.

Norway

Among the rough-hewn timbers and sharply pitched roofs here—softened and brightened by bloom-stuffed window boxes and figured shutters—are lots of smiling young Norwegians, all eager to speak English and show off their country. The pavilion complex contains a 14th-century, fortresslike castle that mimics Oslo's Akershus, cobbled streets, rocky waterfalls, and a stave church modeled after one built in 1250, with wood dragons glaring from the eaves. The church houses an exhibit called "To the Ends of the Earth," which tells the story of two early-20th-century polar expeditions by using vintage artifacts. It all puts you in the mood for the pavilion's shops, which sell spears, shields, and other Viking necessities. At the restaurant, Akershus, you'll find hot and cold dishes on the traditional Norwegian *koldtbord* (buffet). The restaurant is the only one in the park where you can have breakfast, lunch, or dinner with Disney princesses, including Aurora, Belle, and Snow White. Book at least two or three months ahead, or check at Guest Relations for seats left by cancellations.

Maelstrom. In Norway's dandy boat ride, you pile into 16-passenger, dragon-headed longboats for a voyage through time that, despite its scary name and encounters with evil trolls, is actually more interesting than frightful. The journey begins in a 10th-century village, where a boat, much like the ones used by Eric the Red, is being readied for a Viking voyage. You glide steeply up through a mythical forest populated by trolls, who cause the boat to plunge backward down a mild waterfall, then cruise amid the grandeur of the Geiranger fjord, following which you experience a storm in the North Sea and, as the presence of oil rigs signals a return to the 20th century, end up in a peaceful coastal village. Disembarking, you proceed into a theater for a quick and delightful film about Norway's scenic wonders, culture, and people. ☞ *Duration: 10 min. Crowds: Steady, with slow-moving lines from late morning through early evening. Strategy: Grab a FASTPASS appointment so you can return after lunch or dinner. Audience: All ages. Rating:* ★★.

Age of the Viking Ship. Children adore this replica of a Viking ship, an interactive playground filled with ropes and climbing adventures from bow to stern. ☞ *Duration: As long as you want. Crowds: Not that bad. Strategy: Go anytime. Audience: Toddlers and elementary-school-age children. Rating:* ★★.

> **need a break?**
>
> You can order smoked salmon and other open-face sandwiches, plus Norwegian Ringnes beer at **Kringla Bakeri og Kafe.** The pastries here are worth the stop. Go early or late for speediest service and room to sit in the outdoor seating area.

Mexico

Housed in a spectacular Maya pyramid surrounded by dense tropical plantings and brilliant blossoms, Mexico contains the El Río del Tiempo boat ride, an exhibit of pre-Columbian art, a very popular restaurant, and, of course, a shopping plaza, where you can unload many, many pesos.

Modeled on the market in the town of Taxco, Plaza de los Amigos is well named: there are lots of friendly people—the women dressed in ruffled off-the-shoulder peasant blouses and bright skirts, the men in white shirts and dashing sashes—all eager to sell you trinkets from a cluster of canopied carts. The perimeter is rimmed with stores with tile roofs, wrought-iron balconies, and flower-filled window boxes. What to buy?

Brightly colored paper blossoms, sombreros, baskets, pottery, leather goods, and colorful papier-mâché piñatas, which Epcot imports by the truckload.

El Río del Tiempo. True to its name, this attraction takes you on a trip down the River of Time. Your journey from the jungles of the Yucatán to modern-day Mexico City is enlivened by video images of feathered Toltec dancers; by garish Spanish-colonial audio-animatronics dancing puppets; and by film clips of cliff divers in Acapulco, speed boats in Manzanillo, and snorkeling around Isla Mujeres. ☞ *Duration: 9 min. Crowds: Moderate, slow-moving lines from late morning through late afternoon. Strategy: Skip this one unless you have small children, who usually enjoy the novelty of a boat ride. Audience: All ages. Rating:* ★.

Epcot A to Z

To research prices, get advice from other travelers, and book travel arrangements, visit www.fodors.com.

BABY CARE
Epcot has a **Baby Care Center** as peaceful as the one in the Magic Kingdom; it's near the Odyssey Center in Future World. Furnished with rocking chairs, it has a low lighting level that makes it comfortable for nursing, and cast members have supplies such as formula, baby food, pacifiers, and disposable diapers for sale. Changing tables are available here, as well as in all women's rooms and some men's rooms. You can also buy disposable diapers near the park entrance at Baby Services. For stroller rentals ($7 single, $14 double; plus $1 refundable deposit), look for the special stands on the east side of the Entrance Plaza and at World Showcase's International Gateway.

CAMERAS & FILM
Disposable cameras and memory cards are widely available, and you can get film developed or find assistance with minor camera problems at the **Kodak Camera Center,** in the Entrance Plaza, and at **Cameras and Film,** at the Imagination! pavilion. For photos snapped by Disney photographers, get the new **Disney PhotoPass,** which allows you to keep track of digital photos of your group shot in the parks. Later you can view and purchase them online.

DISABILITIES & ACCESSIBILITY
Accessibility standards in this park are high. Many attractions and most restaurants and shops are fully wheelchair accessible. The "Guidebook for Guests with Disabilities" lays out services and facilities available and includes information about companion restrooms and how to acquire Braille or audio guides and sign-language interpretation schedules for Epcot attractions—call two weeks in advance if you want to arrange sign-language interpretation on a day not scheduled. Assistive listening devices require a $25 deposit to amplify sound in many of the theater shows. Closed-captioning is available on TV monitors at attractions that have preshows.

At Future World, to go on the **Spaceship Earth Ride,** you must be able to walk four steps and transfer to a vehicle; in the unusual case that emergency evacuation may be necessary, it's by way of stairs. Service animals should not be taken on this ride. Although much of the enchantment is in the visual details, the narration is interesting as well. The Epcot Discovery Center here is wheelchair accessible. **Innoventions** is completely wheelchair accessible. **Universe of Energy** is accessible to guests using standard wheelchairs and those who can transfer to them; especially because this is one of the attractions that has sound tracks amplified by rental personal translator units, it's slightly more interesting to those with hearing impairments than to those with visual impairments. **Wonders of Life,** including **Cranium Command,** *The Making of Me,* and *Goofy about Health,* is totally wheelchair accessible, with special seating sections for guests using wheelchairs. Guests with visual impairments may wish to skip *Goofy about Health.* To ride the turbulent **Body Wars,** you must transfer to a ride seat; if you lack upper-body strength, request extra shoulder restraints. Service animals are not allowed on this ride. At **Test Track,** one TV monitor in the preshow area is closed-captioned for people with hearing impairments. Visitors in wheelchairs are provided a special area where they can practice transferring into the ride vehicle before actually boarding the high-speed ride. **Mission: SPACE** also requires a transfer from wheelchair to seat and has an area where you can practice beforehand. In **Living Seas,** guests using wheelchairs typically bypass the three-minute ride—no loss—and move directly into the **Sea Base Alpha** and aquarium area, the best part of the pavilion. In **The Land,** *Circle of Life* and the greenhouse tour are completely wheelchair accessible. "Reflective captioning, " in which captions are displayed at the bottom of glass panes mounted on stands, is available at the *Circle of Life.* If you can read lips, you'll enjoy the greenhouse tour. As for the **Living with the Land** boat ride, those using an oversize wheelchair or a scooter must transfer to a Disney chair. And in the new **Soarin'** riders must transfer from their wheelchairs to the ride system. Boarding the **Journey into Imagination with Figment** ride requires guests to take three steps and step up into a ride vehicle. The theater that screens *Honey, I Shrunk the Audience* is completely accessible, although you must transfer to a theater seat to experience some of the special effects. The preshow area has one TV monitor that is closed-captioned. The hands-on activities of Image Works have always been wheelchair accessible and should continue to be; there's something to suit most tastes here. **Ice Station Cool** is not wheelchair accessible.

At World Showcase, most people stroll about, but there are also Friendship boats, which require those using oversize wheelchairs or scooters to transfer to Disney chairs; the **American Adventure, France, China,** and **Canada** are all wheelchair accessible; personal translator units amplify the sound tracks here. **Germany, Italy, Japan, Morocco,** and the **United Kingdom** all have live entertainment, most with strong aural as well as visual elements; the plaza areas where the shows are presented are wheelchair accessible. In **Norway** you must be able to step down into and up out of a boat to ride the Maelstrom, and an emergency evacuation requires the use of stairs; service animals are not allowed. In **Mex-**

ico the El Río del Tiempo boat ride is accessible to guests using wheelchairs, but those using a scooter or oversize chair must transfer to a Disney model.

🛈 **WDW Guest Information** ☎ 407/824–4321, 407/939–7807, or 407/827–5141 TTY.

ENTERTAINMENT   During IllumiNations, certain areas along the lagoon's edge at Showcase Plaza, Canada, and Germany are reserved for guests using wheelchairs. Arrive at least 45 minutes before showtime to stake out a spot.

RESTAURANTS & SHOPS   With a few exceptions, all are wheelchair accessible. In both the Garden Grill and Living Seas' Coral Reef restaurant, only one level is wheelchair accessible.

WHEELCHAIR RENTALS   Wheelchairs are available inside the Entrance Plaza on the left, to the right of the ticket booths at the Gift Stop, and at World Showcase's International Gateway. Standard models are available ($7; $1 deposit, refundable as a Disney dollar); you can also rent an electric scooter ($30; $10 deposit).

FIRST AID
The park's First Aid Center, staffed by registered nurses, is in the Odyssey Center in Future World.

GETTING AROUND
It's a big place; a local joke suggests that Epcot is an acronym for "Every Person Comes Out Tired." But still, the most efficient way to get around is to walk. Just to vary things, you can cruise across the lagoon in one of the air-conditioned, 65-foot water taxis that depart every 12 minutes from two World Showcase Plaza docks at the border of Future World. The boat closer to Mexico zips to a dock by the Germany pavilion; the other heads to Morocco. You may have to stand in line for your turn to board, however.

If you think the huge distances involved may be a problem, start out by renting a stroller or wheelchair.

GUIDED TOURS
Reserve up to six weeks in advance for a behind-the-scenes tour, led by a knowledgeable Disney cast member. Don't forget to ask about tour discounts; some companies, such as American Express, may offer them. Several tours give close-up views of the phenomenal detail involved in the planning and maintenance of Epcot. All tours are open only to those 16 years of age and over (proof of age is required).

The UnDISCOVERed Future World ($49, plus park admission), leaves at 9 AM Monday, Wednesday, and Friday from the Guest Relations lobby just inside Epcot's main entrance. The four-hour behind-the-scenes walking tour covers all Future World pavilions, some VIP lounges, and includes peeks at backstage areas such as the barge marina where Disney stores and maintains its IllumiNations show equipment. The three-hour **Hidden Treasures of World Showcase** ($59, plus park admission), beginning at 9 AM on Tuesday and Thursday, offers a look at the art, architecture, and traditions of the 11 nations represented. Take the three-hour **Gardens of the World Tour** ($59, plus park admission) to see the World Showcase's realistic replicas of exotic plantings up close and to get tips for adding landscape magic to your own garden. The tour runs on Tuesday and Thursday at 9 AM.

Ever since the Segway Human Transporters (featured at Innoventions) became a novelty, a number of Disney employees have used them for speedy transportation around the park's World Showcase. Curious guests can now take their own 2-hour Segway guided tour, called the **Around the World at Epcot Tour,** daily at 8:30 or 9:30 AM. Billed as "the world's first self-balancing, electric-powered personal transportation device, " the Segway takes only a brief training session to master. Once you've learned the moves and strapped on your helmet, you can cruise with the group from one World Showcase country to the next. The tour begins at Guest Relations for those 16 and older ($80, park admission required).

If you want to get into the swim—and you have scuba open-water adult certification and can prove it—try Living Seas' **Epcot Divequest** ($140, park admission not required or included). Discounts for military personnel and some certified divers may be available. Guests of divers who want to watch must pay admission. Under the supervision of one of the Living Seas' master divers you can spend 2½ hours underwater in the mammoth aquarium. The tours take place daily at either 4:30 or 5:30. **Dolphins in Depth** ($150, neither park admission nor diving certification required) is an experience that encourages interaction with your favorite water friends. Tour officials meet you at the entrance at 9:45, where you'll be escorted to the Living Seas pavilion. Tours run Monday through Friday and last about 3 hours; you'll still need to pay park admission if you want to remain after the tour.

The **Epcot Seas Aqua Tour** ($100, no park admission required or included), developed in 2003, is designed for nondivers who want to get in with the fish. You wear a flotation device and diving gear, but you remain at the surface. Anyone age 8 and older can join the tour, which is limited to 12 guests. The tour meets daily at 12:30 and runs about 2½ hours. ◼ **Guided Tours** ☎ 407/939-8687.

LOCKERS

Lockers ($5; $2 deposit) are to the west of Spaceship Earth, outside the Entrance Plaza, and in the Bus Information Center by the bus parking lot. If what you need to store won't fit into the larger lockers, go to Guest Relations in the Entrance Plaza or at Earth Station.

LOST THINGS & PEOPLE

If you're worried about your children getting lost, get name tags for them at either Guest Relations or the Baby Care Center. Instruct them to speak to someone with a Disney name tag if you become separated. And if you do, immediately report your loss to any cast member and try not to panic; the staff here is experienced at reuniting families, and there are lost-children logbooks at Earth Station and the Baby Care Center. Earth Station also has a computerized Message Center, where you can leave notes for your traveling companions in any of the parks. For Lost

& Found, go to the west edge of the Entrance Plaza. After one day, all articles are sent to the Main Lost & Found office.

Epcot Lost & Found ☎ 407/560–7500. **Main Lost & Found** ✉ Magic Kingdom, Transportation and Ticket Center ☎ 407/824–4245.

MONEY MATTERS

For cash and currency exchange, go to the Guest Relations window. There are ATMs to the left of the park's main entrance; at the Disney Vacation Club kiosk on the walkway between Future World and the World Showcase; and at the American Adventure pavilion near the rest rooms.

PACKAGE PICKUP

Ask shop clerks to forward any large purchase you make to Guest Relations in the Entrance Plaza, so that you won't have to carry it around all day. Allow three hours.

VISITOR INFORMATION

Guest Relations, in Innoventions East and at the park's main entrance, is the place to pick up schedules of live entertainment, park brochures, maps, and the like. Map racks are also at the park's International Gateway entrance between the U.K. and France pavilions, and most shops keep a stack handy. The **WDW Dine Telephones**—in the Guest Relations lobby at Innoventions East—can come in handy. Using the interactive kiosks, you can obtain detailed information about every pavilion, leave messages for companions, and get answers to almost all of your questions. International visitors also can pick up a map in French, German, Portuguese, Spanish, or Japanese.

DISNEY–MGM STUDIOS

When Michael Eisner opened Disney–MGM Studios in May 1989, he welcomed attendees to "the Hollywood that never was and always will be." Attending the lavish, Hollywood-style opening were celebrities that included Bette Midler, Warren Beatty, and other Tinseltown icons. Unlike the first movie theme park—Universal Studios in southern California—Disney–MGM Studios combined Disney detail with MGM's motion-picture legacy and Walt Disney's own animated film classics. The park was designed to be a trip back in time to Hollywood's heyday, when Hedda Hopper, not tabloids, spread celebrity gossip and when the girl off the bus from Ohio could be the next Judy Garland. The result blends a theme park with fully functioning movie and television production capabilities, breathtaking rides with insightful tours, and nostalgia with high-tech wonders.

The rosy-hued view of the moviemaking business is presented in a dreamy stage set from the 1930s and '40s, amid sleek Art Moderne buildings in pastel colors, funky diners, kitschy decorations, and sculptured gardens populated by roving actors playing, well, roving actors, as well as casting directors, gossip columnists, and other colorful characters. Thanks to a rich library of film scores, the park is permeated with music, all familiar, all uplifting, all evoking the magic of the movies, and all constantly streaming from the camouflaged loudspeakers at a volume just right for humming along. The park icon, a 122-foot-high Sorcerer Mickey Hat, towers over Hollywood Boulevard. Unfortunately, the whimsical landmark blocks the view of the park's Chinese Theater, a more nostalgic introduction to old-time Hollywood. Watching over all from the park's backlot is the Earful Tower, a 13-story water tower adorned with giant mouse ears.

The park is divided into sightseeing clusters. Hollywood Boulevard is the main artery to the heart of the park, where you find the glistening red-and-gold replica of Graumann's Chinese Theater. Encircling it in a roughly counterclockwise fashion are Sunset Boulevard, the Animation Courtyard, Mickey Avenue, the Streets of America area, and Echo Lake.

The entire park is small enough—about 154 acres, and with only about 20 major attractions, as opposed to the more than 40 in the Magic Kingdom—that you should be able to cover it in a day. On nonpeak days, you might even be able to repeat a favorite ride. And even when the lines seem to stretch clear to Epcot, a little careful planning will allow you to see everything on one ticket.

Numbers in the margin correspond to points of interest on the Disney–MGM Studios map.

Entertainment

The **Disney Stars and Motor Cars** parade wends its way up Hollywood Boulevard in true Tinseltown style with a motorcade of characters from the park's many attractions and Disney's many films perched and draped across customized classic cars. Animated stars include Mickey Mouse, Minnie Mouse, Ariel, Mulan, Woody, Buzz Lightyear, and other Disney film celebrities. Also on view are Kermit and Miss Piggy, Luke Skywalker, and even the huggable Bear from the Big Blue House. ☞ *Duration: 25 min. Crowds: Heavy. Strategy: Stake out your curb spot an hr early and hang on to it. Audience: All ages. Rating:* ★★.

Fantasmic!, the Studios' after-dark show wows audiences of thousands with its 25 minutes of special effects and Disney characters. The omnipresent Mickey, in his Sorcerer's Apprentice costume, plays the embodiment of Good in the struggle against forces of Evil, personified by Disney villains and villainesses such as Cruella DeVil, Scar, and Maleficent. In some of the show's best moments, animated clips of images of these famous bad guys alternate with clips of Disney nice guys (and dolls), projected onto screens made of water—high-tech fountains surging high in the air. Disney being Disney, it's Good that emerges triumphant, amid a veritable tidal wave of water effects and flames, explosions, and fireworks worthy of a Stallone shoot-'em-up. Show up early at the 6,500-seat Hollywood Hills Amphitheatre opposite the Twilight Zone Tower of Terror. If you sit near the lagoon, spray from the fountains may chill you on cool nights. ☞ *Duration: 25 min. Crowds: Heavy. Strategy: Arrive at least 1 hr early and sit toward the rear, near the entrance/exit. Consider the Fantasmic! dinner package, which includes reserved seating for the show. Audience: All ages. Rating:* ★★★.

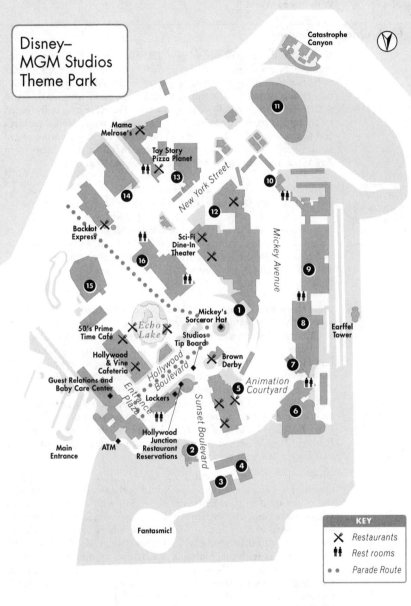

Disney–MGM Studios Theme Park

Catastrophe Canyon

Mama Melrose's

Toy Story Pizza Planet

New York Street

Backlot Express

Mickey Avenue

Sci-Fi Dine-In Theater

Mickey's Sorceror Hat

Studios Tip Board

50's Prime Time Café

Echo Lake

Brown Derby

Hollywood & Vine Cafeteria

Hollywood Boulevard

Animation Courtyard

Earffel Tower

Guest Relations and Baby Care Center

Entrance Plaza

Lockers

Sunset Boulevard

Main Entrance

ATM

Hollywood Junction Restaurant Reservations

Fantasmic!

KEY

✕ Restaurants

👫 Rest rooms

• • Parade Route

Hollywood Boulevard

With its palm trees, pastel buildings, and flashy neon, Hollywood Boulevard paints a rosy picture of Tinseltown in the 1930s. There's a sense of having walked right onto a movie set in the olden days, what with the art deco storefronts, strolling brass bands, and roving starlets and nefarious agents—actually costumed actors. These are frequently joined by characters from Disney movies new and old, who pose for pictures and sign autographs. *Beauty and the Beast*'s Belle is a favorite, as are Jafar, Princess Jasmine, and the Genie from *Aladdin,* the soldiers from *Toy Story,* and Lilo and Stitch from the film of the same name.

groovy
souvenirs

If you like to sift through antiques and novelty wares, make a stop at **Sid Cahuenga's One-of-a-Kind,** where you can find authentic Hollywood collectibles, curios, and autographed items that once belonged to celebrities. If you like antique or toy cars, sneak a peek at the pictures and automotive knickknacks in **Oscar's Classic Car Souvenirs & Super Service.** You'll find child-size character clothing at **L.A. Prop Cinema Storage,** at the corner of Sunset and Hollywood.

❶ Great Movie Ride. At the end of Hollywood Boulevard, just behind the Sorcerer Mickey Hat icon, are the fire-engine-red pagodas of a replica of Graumann's Chinese Theater, which houses this attraction. Outside the theater are the concrete handprints and footprints of such stars as Bob Hope, Liza Minnelli, and Sally Field. The line takes you through the lobby past such noteworthy artifacts as Dorothy's ruby slippers from *The Wizard of Oz,* a carousel horse from *Mary Poppins,* and the piano played by Sam in *Casablanca.* You then shuffle into the preshow area, an enormous screening room with continuously running clips from *Mary Poppins, Raiders of the Lost Ark, Singin' in the Rain, Fantasia, Footlight Parade,* and, of course, *Casablanca.* Once the great red doors swing open, it's your turn to ride.

Disney cast members dressed in 1920s newsboy costumes usher you onto open trams waiting against the backdrop of the Hollywood Hills, and you're off on a tour of cinematic climaxes—with a little help from audio-animatronics, scrim, smoke, and Disney magic. First comes the world of musical entertainment with, among others, Gene Kelly clutching that immortal lamppost as he begins "Singin' in the Rain" and Mary Poppins with her umbrella and her sooty admirers reprising "Chim-Chim-Cher-ee." Soon the lights dim, and your vehicle travels into a gangland shoot-out with James Cagney snarling in *Public Enemy.* A gangster hijacks your tram and whisks you off to a western showdown starring John Wayne.

Nothing like a little time warp to bring justice. With pipes streaming fog and alarms whooping, the tram meets some of the slimier characters from *Alien*—look up for truly scary stuff—and then eases into the

Best of the Park

Arrive well before the park opens. When it does, run, don't walk, right up Hollywood Boulevard, hang a right at Sunset Boulevard, and dash to the 13-story **Twilight Zone Tower of Terror.** You can make a FASTPASS appointment here, then go next door to ride **Rock 'n' Roller Coaster Starring Aerosmith.** After your Twilight Zone plunge, you may want to get a FASTPASS for a second go-round on your favorite of these two thrill rides. Make the **Great Movie Ride** at the Chinese Theater your next stop. If you're still waiting to return for your FASTPASS appointment at the Tower of Terror or Rock 'n' Roller Coaster, catch *Lights, Motors, Action!* **Extreme Stunt Show** or, if you have small children, *Playhouse Disney*—**Live on Stage!** When you've used your FASTPASS, head over to either *Who Wants to Be a Millionaire*—**Play It!,** or the **Indiana Jones Epic Stunt Spectacular!** You can get a FASTPASS to either stunt show if they're jammed.

For lunch, grab a sandwich or tabbouleh wrap on the run at the **ABC Commissary,** or do a sit-down meal at the **Sci-Fi Dine-In Theater,** where you can sit in a 1950s-era convertible and watch B-movie film clips. Then take in the **Magic of Disney Animation** before returning for your FASTPASS appointment with Indiana Jones or the stunt car drivers. Afterward, dash over to **Star Tours,** where you should take a FASTPASS timed ticket unless the line is very short. While you wait for your appointment, catch **Jim Henson's Muppet*Vision 3-D** or the **Disney Stars and Motor Cars** parade. If there's still time before your Star Tours return, check out **Sounds Dangerous Starring Drew Carey** or the **Disney–MGM Studios Backlot Tour.**

Keep your Star Tours appointment, and then let the kids scramble around on the *Honey, I Shrunk the Kids* **Movie Set Adventure,** or explore Sunset Boulevard, where the shops sell much of the same merchandise as those on Hollywood Boulevard but are less crowded. If there's time, try to catch a late performance of *Beauty and the Beast*—**Live on Stage!** Finally, line up for a grand finale to cap the night with fireworks, lasers, fountains, and the cast of popular Disney characters—**Fantasmic!** Remember to turn at the gate for one last look at the Earful Tower, its perky appendages outlined in gold lights.

On Rainy Days

If you must go on a rainy day, plan your day around the indoor attractions and make FASTPASS appointments back to back. Enjoy a relaxing lunch at the Brown Derby or a zany time in the '50s Prime Time Cafe, where a great cast of servers will help you forget all about the weather.

cobwebby, snake-ridden set of *Indiana Jones and the Temple of Doom,* where your hijacker attempts to steal an idol and gets his or her just desserts.

Each time you think you've witnessed the best scene, the tram moves into another set: Tarzan yodels and swings on a vine overhead; then Bogey bids Bergman goodbye with a "Here's looking at you, kid" in front of the plane to Lisbon. The finale has hundreds of robotic Munchkins cheerily enjoining you to "Follow the Yellow Brick Road," despite the cackling imprecations by the Wicked Witch of the West. Remember to check out Dorothy's tornado-tossed house—those on the right side of the tram can just spot the ruby slippers. The tram follows the Yellow Brick Road, and then there it is: the Emerald City. ☞ *Duration: 22 min. Crowds: Medium. If it's peak season and the inside lines start spilling out the door, expect at least a 25-min wait. Strategy: Go while waiting out a FAST-PASS appointment for another attraction. Audience: All but young children, for whom it may be too intense. Rating:* ★★★.

need a break? For a sweet burst of energy, snag a freshly baked chocolate-chip cookie and an espresso at **Starring Rolls Bakery,** near the Brown Derby. Or, if you're around for breakfast, try a croissant, turnover, or almost-authentic bagel.

Sunset Boulevard

This avenue pays tribute to famous Hollywood monuments, with facades derived from the Cathay Circle, the Beverly Wilshire Theatre, and other City of Angels landmarks.

As you turn onto Sunset Boulevard from Hollywood Boulevard, you'll run smack into Hollywood Junction Station, where reservations can be made for restaurants throughout the park. The nearby Legends of Hollywood brims with Pooh and Friends merchandise, and Once Upon a Time has character sketches, collectible figurines, home accessories, and other assorted gift items, as well as Pal Mickey.

❷ *Beauty and the Beast*—**Live on Stage!** This wildly popular stage show takes place at the Theater of the Stars, a re-creation of the famed Hollywood Bowl. The long-running production is a lively, colorful, and well-done condensation of the animated film. As you arrive or depart, it's fun to check out handprints and footprints set in concrete of the television celebrities who've visited Disney–MGM Studios. ☞ *Duration: 30 min. Crowds: Almost always. Strategy: Queue up at least 30 min prior to show time for good seats, especially with children. Performance days vary, so check ahead. Audience: All ages. Rating:* ★★★.

need a break? Grab lunch or a quick snack at one of the food stands along Sunset Boulevard. You can get a burger or chicken strips at **Rosie's All-American Cafe,** a slice of pizza from **Catalina Eddie's,** a fruit salad from the **Anaheim Produce Company,** or a turkey leg or hot dog at **Toluca Legs Turkey Company.**

When to Go

It's best to go to Disney–MGM Studios—like Epcot—early in the week, while most other people are rushing through Disney's Animal Kingdom and the Magic Kingdom.

Plan to arrive in the parking lot 30 minutes ahead of opening, so you can get to the entrance 15 minutes ahead.

When You're There

Pick up a guide map and "Times Guide" on your way into the park, and be sure to note where to meet the Disney characters if you have children in tow.

If you're interested in booking a Fantasmic! dinner package check in at Guest Relations as soon as you enter the park.

Check the map for the occasional TV and film celebrity visitors, and plan your day around the celebrity motorcade if it's a star you don't want to miss.

Set up a rendezvous point and time at the start of the day, just in case you and your companions get separated. Three excellent spots are by the giant Sorcerer Mickey Hat, at the statue of Miss Piggy near the Muppets attraction, and on Mickey Avenue by the large Coke bottle that sprays water.

FodorsChoice

❸ **Twilight Zone Tower of Terror.** Ominously overlooking Sunset Boulevard is a 13-story structure that was once the Hollywood Tower Hotel, now deserted. You take an eerie stroll through an overrun, mist-enshrouded garden and then into the dimly lighted lobby. In the dust-covered library a bolt of lightning suddenly zaps a television set to life. Rod Serling appears, recounting the story of the hotel's demise and inviting you to enter the Twilight Zone. Then, it's onward to the boiler room, where you climb aboard the hotel's giant elevator ride. As you head upward past seemingly empty hallways, ghostly former residents appear in front of you. The Fifth Dimension awaits, where you travel forward past recognizable scenes from the popular TV series. Suddenly—faster than you can say "Where's Rod Serling?"—the creaking vehicle plunges downward in a terrifying, 130-foot free-fall drop and then, before you can catch your breath, shoots quickly up, down, up, and down all over again. No use trying to guess how many stomach-churning ups and downs you'll experience—Disney's ride engineers have upped the ride's fright factor by programming random drop variations into the attraction. It's a different thrill every time. As you recover from your final plunge, Serling warns, "The next time you check into a deserted hotel on the dark side of Hollywood, make sure you know what vacancy you'll be filling, or you'll be a permanent member of . . . the Twilight Zone!" ☞ *Duration: 10 min.* **Crowds:** *Yes!* **Strategy:** *Get a FASTPASS reserved-time ticket.*

THE BIRTH OF WALT DISNEY WORLD

T'D BE A GREAT QUESTION for Regis to ask: Florida was founded by (a) Juan Ponce de León, (b) Millard Fillmore, (c) Sonny Bono, or (d) Walt Disney. For travelers who can't fathom Florida without Walt Disney World, the final answer is "d"—in Central Florida at least. The theme park's arrival spawned a multibillion-dollar tourism industry that begat a population boom that begat new roads, malls, and schools that begat a whole new culture.

So how did it happen? Why did Walt pin his hopes on forlorn Florida ranchlands 3,000 mi from Disneyland? In the 1950s, Walt barely had enough money to open his theme park in California, and lacking the funds to buy a buffer zone, he couldn't prevent cheap hotels and tourist traps from setting up shop next door. This time he wanted land. And lots of it. Beginning in the early 1960s, Walt embarked on a supersecret four-year project: he traveled the nation in search of a location with access to a major population center, good highways, a steady climate, and, most important, cheap and abundant land. Locations were narrowed down, and in the end Orlando was it.

In May 1965, major land transactions were being recorded a few miles southwest of Orlando. By late June, the Orlando Sentinel reported that more than 27,000 acres had been sold so far. In October, the paper revealed that Walt was the mastermind behind the purchases. Walt and his brother Roy hastily arranged a press conference. Once Walt described the $400 million project and the few thousand jobs it would create, Florida's government quickly gave him permission to establish the autonomous Reedy Creek Improvement District. With this, he could write his own zoning restrictions and plan his own roads, bridges, hotels—even a residential community for his employees.

Walt played a hands-on role in the planning of Disney World, but just over a year later, in December 1966, he died. As expected, his faithful brother Roy took control and spent the following five years supervising the construction of the Magic Kingdom. Fittingly, before the park opened on October 1, 1971, Roy changed the name of his brother's park to "Walt" Disney World. Roy passed away three months after the park's opening, but by then WDW was hitting its stride. For the next decade, it became part of Florida's landscape. Families that once saw Orlando merely as a whistle-stop on the way to Miami now made their vacation base at WDW.

Behind the scenes, however, a few cracks began to appear in the facade. In its first decade, growth was stagnant. By 1982, when Epcot opened, construction-cost overruns and low attendance created a 19% drop in profits. Meanwhile, the Disney Channel and Disney's film division were also sluggish. Eventually, in 1984, Michael Eisner came aboard as CEO and company chairman, along with Frank Wells as president and CFO. Their arrival got Disney out of the doldrums. Disney's unparalleled film catalog was brought out of storage with re-releases in theaters and on video. Jeffrey Katzenberg was put in charge of the Disney Studios, and with him came the release of "new classics" such as Aladdin, Beauty and the Beast, The Little Mermaid, and The Lion King.

In 1988 the Grand Floridian and Caribbean Beach resorts opened. The following year Disney–MGM Studios opened along with Typhoon Lagoon and

Pleasure Island. Five resort hotels opened in the early 1990s. By 1997 Blizzard Beach, Disney's Wide World of Sports, and Downtown Disney West Side had opened; and by 1998 Disney's Animal Kingdom had come to life. Also arriving in this decade of growth were the planned community of Celebration, the Disney cruise lines, the book-publishing arm of Hyperion, and the purchase of Miramax Films and ABC television.

Since the profitable mid-1990s, however, Disney has suffered its share of economic trouble and political unrest. Following a dip in earnings in 2002, and several box-office bombs (think: The Alamo), Roy E. Disney, Walt's nephew, resigned from his position as vice chairman of the board of directors to lead a movement to oust Michael Eisner from the company. When Eisner came up for re-election to the Disney board in early 2004, 43% of shareholders withheld their votes. Robert Iger is due to replace Eisner as CEO on October 1, 2005. Despite the turmoil at its parent company, Walt Disney World continues to grow and improve. A score of new shows and attractions opened in 2005, including Soarin' and the Lights, Motors, Action! Extreme Stunt Show. Expedition EVEREST is on the launch pad for 2006.

And it all started with a man who didn't have the cash to buy a little more land in Anaheim.

— Gary McKechnie

Otherwise, go early or wait until evening, when the crowds thin out. **Audience:** *Older children and adults. No pregnant women or guests with heart, back, or neck problems. Minimum height: 40″.* **Rating:** ★★★.

❹ Rock 'n' Roller Coaster Starring Aerosmith. Although this is an indoor roller coaster like Space Mountain in the Magic Kingdom, the similarity ends there. With its high-speed launch, multiple inversions, and loud rock music, it generates delighted screams from coaster junkies, though it's smooth enough and short enough that even the coaster-phobic have been known to enjoy it. The vehicles look like limos, and the track resembles the neck of an electric guitar that's been twisted; a hard-driving rock sound track by Aerosmith blasts from speakers mounted in each vehicle to accentuate the flips and turns. There's rock-and-roll memorabilia in the queue area, and Aerosmith stars in the preshow film. ☞ **Duration:** *preride 2 min, ride 1 min, 22 seconds.* **Crowds:** *Huge.* **Strategy:** *Ride early in the day, then pick up a FASTPASS to go again later, especially if you're visiting with older children or teens.* **Audience:** *Older children, teens, and adults. No guests with heart, back, or neck problems or motion sickness. Minimum height: 44″.* **Rating:** ★★★.

Fodor'sChoice

Animation Courtyard

As you exit Sunset Boulevard, veer right through the high-arched gateway to the Animation Courtyard. You're now at one end of Mickey Avenue, and straight ahead are the Magic of Disney Animation and *Voyage of the Little Mermaid*. At the far end of the avenue is the popular Disney–MGM Studios Backlot Tour.

❺ Playhouse Disney—Live on Stage! The former Soundstage Restaurant now holds one of the best Walt Disney World shows for children. *Playhouse Disney*—Live on Stage! uses a perky host on a larger-than-life "storybook stage" to present stars of several popular Disney Channel shows. Preschoolers and even toddlers can sing and dance in the aisles as Bear in the Big Blue House, Rolie Polie Olie, Pooh, and Stanley cha-cha-cha their way through positive life lessons. Who knew that personal grooming tips could be so much fun? ☞ **Duration:** *25 min.* **Crowds:** *Not a problem, but lines tend to be heavy in midafternoon.* **Strategy:** *Go first thing in the morning, when your child is most alert.* **Audience:** *Toddlers, preschoolers.* **Rating:** ★★★.

Fodor'sChoice
★❻ **The Magic of Disney Animation.** This tour through the Disney animation process is one of the park's most engaging attractions. More than any other backstage peek, this tour truly takes you inside the magic as you follow the many steps of 2-D animation, an art expected to be totally replaced in years to come by computer-generated films such as the Disney/Pixar blockbusters *Toy Story* and *Finding Nemo*. The animation studio was a satellite of Walt Disney's original California studio from 1988 through 2003. It was here that *Brother Bear, Lilo & Stitch,* and *Mulan* were produced, as were several Disney short films and portions of other popular Disney features.

You begin the tour in a small theater with a performance of *Drawn to Animation,* in which a real actor plays the role of an animator interacting with Mushu, the wisecracking animated character from *Mulan.* Mushu prances between two screens above the stage. In their very funny exchange, the two explain how an animated character evolves from original concept. The animators who actually created the spunky dragon appear on screen to help tell the story.

Next, you enter a creative zone where kiosks of computer touch screens invite you to add color to your favorite characters and even find out which Disney character is most like you (answer a brief quiz and you can't help but smile when you find your animated character double). Watch for popular Disney film characters, including *The Incredibles,* to appear in this area for autographs and photos.

The final stop is the Animation Academy, a delightful crash course in how to draw an animated character. Children and adults can sit side-by-side at a one of 38 backlit drafting tables as an artist gives easy-to-follow instructions on drawing a Disney character. Your sketch of Donald Duck (or the character du jour) is your souvenir. As you exit, check out the collection of drawings and cels, the clear celluloid sheets on which the characters were drawn for *Snow White, Fantasia,* and other Disney classics. Here, too, are the actual Academy Awards that Disney has won for its animated films. ☞ *Duration: About 30 min. Crowds: Steady all day. Strategy: Go in the morning or late afternoon, when you can get in with less waiting. Audience: All but toddlers, who may be unwilling to sit still for the Animation Academy. Rating:* ★★★.

❼ *Voyage of the Little Mermaid.* A boxy building on Mickey Avenue invites you to join Ariel, Sebastian, and the underwater gang in this stage show, which condenses the movie into a marathon presentation of the greatest hits. In an admirable effort at verisimilitude, a fine mist sprays the stage; if you're sitting in the front rows, expect to get spritzed. ☞ *Duration: 15 min. Crowds: Perpetual. Strategy: If you decide not to ride the Rock 'n' Roller Coaster, go first thing in the morning, putting the FASTPASS to good use. Otherwise, wait until the stroller brigade's exodus after 5. Audience: All ages, though small children may be frightened by the dark theater and the evil, larger-than-life Ursula. Rating:* ★★.

❽ *Walt Disney: One Man's Dream.* Next door to the Mermaid show, *One Man's Dream* is a photo, film, and audio tour through Walt's life. You get to peek at his Project X room, where many of his successes were born, and hear him tell much of his own story on tapes never before made public. If you qualify as a baby boomer, it's a real nostalgia trip to see Walt resurrected on film as his "Wonderful World of Color" intro splashes across the screen. And if you're into artifacts, there's plenty of Walt memorabilia to view as you absorb the history of this entertainment legend. ☞ *Duration: 20 min. Crowds: Heavy. Strategy: Get your FASTPASS appointment to see Who Wants to Be a Millionaire—Play It!, then see this attraction while waiting. Audience: Ages 10 and up. Rating:* ★★.

Mickey Avenue

Stroll down this street and you'll pass the soundstages that are used to produce some of today's television shows and motion pictures. On your left, there are several souvenir kiosks, as well as periodic street-side opportunities to mingle with character stars such as Buzz Lightyear, Woody, and pals Jessie and Bullseye from *Toy Story 2*. Check character schedules to be sure they're appearing.

❾ *Who Wants to Be a Millionaire—Play It!* Disney's popular live stage show on Soundstages 2 and 3 seats 600, all of whom have their own fastest-finger buttons and a chance at the hot seat next to the show's celebrity "Regis." Contestants don't vie for $1 million, but they do build points to get a shot at some parting prizes. Even kids can make it to the hot seat in this clever replica of the TV game show. Question categories range from Disney trivia (The animated TV series *Disney's Aladdin* stars all but which of the following characters: a. Aladdin, b. Jasmine, c. Iago, or d. Tarzan?) to geography (Havana is the capital of what country?). Everyone in the audience gets to play along with the contestant and accumulates points toward a potential shot at the hot seat. Instead of phoning a friend, you can phone a complete stranger (a theme-park visitor called to the phone by a Disney cast member stationed at one of two phones in the park). Disney pins, caps, and other prizes are awarded at graduated point levels, and big winners may earn a cruise aboard one of the Disney Cruise Line ships. ☞ *Duration: 30 min. Crowds: Heavy. Strategy: Line up while waiting for a FASTPASS appointment elsewhere. Audience: Ages 5 and up. Rating:* ★★★.

❿ **Disney–MGM Studios Backlot Tour.** The first stop on this tour, which you enter at the far end of Mickey Avenue, is an outdoor special-effects water tank, where audience members are recruited for an unforgettable (and very wet) video moment. Then it's time to queue up for the tram ride. As you walk through the line, you're also touring a huge prop warehouse, which stores everything you could possibly imagine, from chairs to traffic lights to newspaper stands.

Board the tram for a tour of the backlot's different departments: set design, costumes, props, lighting, and a standout movie set—Catastrophe Canyon. The tram's announcer swears that the film that's supposedly shooting in there is taking a break. But the next thing you know, the tram is bouncing up and down in a simulated earthquake, an oil tanker explodes in a mass of smoke and flame, and a water tower crashes to the ground, touching off a flash flood, which douses the tanker and threatens to drown the tram. As the tram pulls out, you see the backstage workings of the catastrophe: the canyon is actually a mammoth steel slide wrapped in copper-color concrete, and the 70,000 gallons of flood water—enough to fill 10 Olympic-size swimming pools—are recycled 100 times a day, or every 3½ minutes. You'll also ride past the Streets of America backlot, where San Francisco has a new presence and New York Street's brownstones, marble, brick, and stained glass are actually expertly painted facades of fiberglass and Styrofoam. Grips can slide the Empire State and Chrysler buildings out of the way anytime. ☞ *Duration: 35 min. Crowds: Steady through the afternoon, but lines seem to move quickly. Strategy: As you enter the tram, remember that people sitting on the left get wet. Go early; it closes at dusk. Audience: All but young children, who probably will be scared in Catastrophe Canyon. Rating:* ★★.

Streets of America

It's well worth touring the New York, San Francisco, and Chicago sets here on foot—as long as crews aren't filming—so that you can check out the windows of shops and apartments, the taxicabs, and other details.

⑪ *Lights, Motors, Action!* **Extreme Stunt Show.** In today's light-speed society, it makes sense that action films gross some of the highest figures at box offices around the world. And with the success of the high-octane vehicle stunt show at Disneyland Paris, it's only natural that Disney show designers would model this new stunt extravaganza after its action-packed counterpart. Here, Disney designers made it their mission to reveal the secrets behind Hollywood's greatest stunts, including heart-pounding car chases and explosions. The scene is a 177,000-square-foot Mediterranean village "movie set" inside a 5,000-seat, open-air theater. The premise? Filmmakers are producing a spy thriller on the set, and the director is organizing different out-of-sequence stunts. Heroes and villains perform high-speed spinouts, two-wheel driving, jumps, and high falls using various vehicles, including watercraft. Besides experiencing the thrill of seeing choreographed stunts live, you will learn how filmmakers combine shots of various stunts to create a completed scene, which plays on the stadium's mammoth video wall. Keep in mind that this show is pretty long, and you're sitting on a hard bench with no back the whole time. If you have small children or if you think you might want to leave during the show, sit toward the back. ☞ *Duration: 30 min. Crowds: Heavy due to attraction's newness. Strategy: You should be able to get into the theater even if you arrive close to show time. For the best seats, however, see it first, get a FASTPASS, or line up for the show while others are lining up for the parade. Audience: All, though babies and young children may be frightened by loud noises.* ★★.

⑫ *Honey, I Shrunk the Kids* **Movie Set Adventure.** Let your youngsters run free in this playground based on the movie, where there are scenes of Lilliputian kids in a larger-than-life world. They can slide down a gigantic blade of grass, crawl through caves, climb a mushroom mountain, inhale the scent of a humongous plant (which will then spit water back in their faces), and dodge sprinklers set in resilient flooring made of ground-up tires. All the requisite playground equipment is present: net climbs, ball crawls, caves, and slides. Because the area is enclosed, there's often a line to get in—but attraction hosts don't fudge on capacity limits, which maintains a comfort zone for those inside. ☞ *Duration: Up to you. Crowds: Steady. Strategy: Come after you've done several shows or attractions and your children need to cut loose. Audience: Children and those who love them. Rating:* ★★★.

❸ Jim Henson's Muppet*Vision 3-D. You don't have to be a Miss Piggyphile to get a kick out of this combination 3-D movie and musical revue, although all the Muppet characters make appearances, including Miss Piggy in roles that include the Statue of Liberty. In the waiting area, Muppet movie posters advertise the world's most glamorous porker in *Star Chores* and *To Have and Have More,* and Kermit the Frog in an Arnold Schwarzenegger parody, *Kürmit the Amphibian,* who's "so mean, he's green." When the theater was constructed, special effects were built into the walls; the 3-D effects are coordinated with other sensory stimulation so you're never sure what's coming off the screen and what's being shot out of vents in the ceiling and walls. ☞ **Duration:** *Clever 10-min preshow, 20-min show.* **Crowds:** *Moderate, but the theater is high-capacity, so if you get there 10 min early you can get in.* **Strategy:** *Arrive 10 min early or use FASTPASS. And don't worry—there are no bad seats.* **Audience:** *All ages.* **Rating:** ★★★.

Echo Lake

Segue from New York Street into Echo Lake, an idealized southern California. In the center is the cool, blue lake of the same name, an oasis fringed with trees and benches and ringed with landmarks: pink-and-aqua restaurants trimmed in chrome, presenting sassy waitresses and black-and-white television sets at the tables; the shipshape Min and Bill's Dockside Diner, which offers snacks; and Gertie, a dinosaur that dispenses ice cream, Disney souvenirs, and the occasional puff of smoke in true magic-dragon fashion. Look for Gertie's giant footprints in the sidewalk. (Gertie, by the way, was the first animated animal to show emotion—an inspiration to the pre-Mickey Walt.) Here, too, you'll find two of the park's longest-running attractions, the Indiana Jones Epic Stunt Spectacular! and Star Tours.

groovy souvenirs

Adventurous types should check out the genuine Indiana Jones bullwhips and fedoras sold at the **Indiana Jones Adventure Outpost,** next to the stunt amphitheater, and the Darth Vader and Wookie masks at **Tatooine Traders,** outside of Star Tours.

❹ Star Tours. Although the flight-simulator technology used for this ride was long ago surpassed on other thrill rides, most notably Universal Studios' *Back to the Future . . . The Ride,* this adventure (inspired by the *Star Wars* films) is still a pretty good trip. "May the force be with you," says the attendant on duty, "'cause I won't be!" Piloted by *Star Wars* characters R2D2 and C-3PO, the 40-passenger *StarSpeeder* that you board is supposed to take off on a routine flight to the moon of Endor. But with R2D2 at the helm, things quickly go awry: you shoot into deep space, dodge giant ice crystals and comet debris, innocently bumble into an intergalactic battle, and attempt to avoid laser-blasting fighters as you whiz through the canyons of some planetary city before coming to a heart-pounding halt. ☞ **Duration:** *5 min.* **Crowds:** *Lines swell periodically when the Indiana Jones Epic Stunt Spectacular! lets out.* **Strategy:** *To make sure you'll walk right on, go shortly before closing or first thing in the morning. Otherwise cruise on with the help of a FASTPASS timed*

*ticket. When you line up to enter the simulation chamber, keep to the far left to sit up front and closer to the screen for the most realistic sensations (the ride is rougher in back but the sensations of motion less exhilarating). **Audience:** Star Wars fans, children and adults. No pregnant women, children under 3, or guests with heart, back, neck, or motion sickness problems; children under 7 must be accompanied by an adult.* **Rating:** ★★★.

need a break?

If you have a sweet tooth, you should be sure to save room for some soft-serve Ice Cream of Extinction at **Gertie's,** the ice-cream bar and snack shop inside the big green dinosaur on the shore of Echo Lake. Nearby, **Min & Bill's Dockside Diner** is the spot for a stuffed pretzel or specialty shake. Step right up to the counter.

15 Indiana Jones Epic Stunt Spectacular! The rousing theme music from the Indiana Jones movies heralds action delivered by veteran stunt coordinator Glenn Randall, whose credits include *Raiders of the Lost Ark, Indiana Jones and the Temple of Doom, E.T.,* and *Jewel of the Nile.* Presented in a 2,200-seat amphitheater, the show starts with a series of near-death encounters in an ancient Maya temple. Clad in his signature fedora, Indy slides down a rope from the ceiling, dodges spears that shoot up from the floor, avoids getting chopped by booby-trapped idols, and snags a forbidden gemstone, setting off a gigantic boulder that threatens to render him two-dimensional.

Though it's hard to top that opener, Randall and his pals do just that with the help of 10 audience participants. "Okay, I need some rowdy people," the casting director calls. While the lucky few demonstrate their rowdiness, behind them the set crew casually wheels off the entire temple. Two people roll the boulder like a giant beach ball and replace it with a Cairo street, circa 1940. Then the nasty Ninja-Nazi stuntmen come out, and you start to think that this is one of those times when it's better to be in the audience. Eventually Indy comes sauntering down the "street" with his redoubtable girlfriend, Marian Ravenwood, portrayed by a Karen Allen look-alike. She is kidnapped and tossed into a truck while Indy fights his way free with bullwhip and gun, and bad guys tumble from every corner and cornice. Motorcycles buzz around; the street becomes a shambles; and, as a stunning climax, the truck carrying Marian flips and bursts into flame. The actors do a great job of explaining the stunts. You see how they're set up, watch the stars practice them in slow motion, and learn how cameras are camouflaged behind imitation rocks for trick shots. Only one stunt remains a secret: how do Indy and Marian escape the explosion? That's what keeps 'em coming back. ☞ *Duration: 30 min. Crowds: Large, but the theater's high capacity means that everyone who wants to get in usually does. Strategy: Go at night, when the idols' eyes glow red. If you sit up front, you can feel the heat when Marian's truck catches fire.* **Audience:** *All but young children.* **Rating:** ★★★.

16 Sounds Dangerous Starring Drew Carey. A multifaceted demonstration of the use of movie sound effects, this show uses many of the gadgets created by sound master Jimmy MacDonald, who became the voice of Mickey Mouse during the 1940s and invented some 20,000 sound effects during his 45 years at Walt Disney Studios. Most qualify as gizmos—a metal sheet that, when rattled, sounds like thunder; a box of sand for footsteps on gravel; and other noises made from nails, straw, mud, leather, and other ordinary components. The premise of the show is that you will help Drew Carey, who portrays an undercover cop, find out who smuggled the diamonds from the snow globe. Then you don headphones to listen to the many sounds that go into the production of a movie or television show. Because the entire show takes place in the dark, it's can be frightening for young children.

The Sounds Dangerous postshow is a treat consisting of hands-on exhibits called **SoundWorks.** There are buttons that go "boing" and knobs you push to alter your voice. Earie Encounters lets you imitate flying-saucer sounds from the 1956 film *Forbidden Planet.* At Movie Mimics you can try your chords at dubbing Mickey Mouse, Roger Rabbit, and other Disney heroes. ☞ *Duration: 30-min show; the rest is up to you. Crowds: Steady. Strategy: Arrive 15 min before show time. Audience: All but young, easily frightened children. Rating:* ★★.

Disney–MGM Studios A to Z

To research prices, get advice from other travelers, and book travel arrangements, visit www.fodors.com.

BABY CARE
At the small **Baby Care Center,** you'll find facilities for nursing as well as formula, baby food, pacifiers, and disposable diapers for sale. There are changing tables here and in all women's rooms and some men's rooms. You can also buy disposable diapers in the Guest Relations building. **Oscar's,** just inside the entrance turnstiles and to the right, is the place for stroller rentals ($7 single, $14 double; plus a $1 deposit refundable as a Disney dollar).

CAMERAS & FILM
Walk through the aperture-shape door of the **Darkroom** on Hollywood Boulevard, where you can buy film and disposable cameras and get minor camera repairs. This is also the place to pick up pictures you want quickly. You can drop your film off here for one-hour developing. If you're staying on-site, you can even have the pictures delivered to your hotel. Have your picture taken in front of the Chinese Theater, or with Mickey Mouse on Sunset Boulevard near the Brown Derby as an extra-special memento ($16.95 for an 8″×10″ photo).

DISABILITIES & ACCESSIBILITY
Almost everything in this park is wheelchair accessible.

ATTRACTIONS Studio attractions are wheelchair accessible, with certain restrictions on the Star Tours thrill ride and Twilight Zone Tower of Terror. Guests with hearing impairments can obtain closed-captioning devices for use in most of the attractions. You can reserve time with a sign-language interpreter by calling Guest Information at least two weeks in advance.

To board the **Great Movie Ride,** on Hollywood Boulevard, you must transfer to a Disney wheelchair if you use an oversize model or a scooter; the gunshot, explosion, and fire effects mean that service animals should not be taken on the rides.

To board Sunset Boulevard's **Twilight Zone Tower of Terror,** you must be able to walk unassisted to a seat on the ride and have full upper-body strength. The ride's free falls make it unsuitable for service animals. *Beauty and the Beast*—**Live on Stage!** at the Theater of the Stars is completely accessible to guests using wheelchairs. To ride the **Rock 'n' Roller Coaster Starring Aerosmith,** guests who use wheelchairs must transfer to a ride vehicle—an area in which to practice the transfer is available.

At Animation Courtyard, *Voyage of the Little Mermaid, Playhouse Disney*—**Live on Stage!,** and **The Magic of Disney Animation** are wheelchair accessible; all have preshow areas with TV monitors that are closed-captioned.

You can roll a wheelchair throughout the **Walt Disney: One Man's Dream** attraction, which features captioning in the theater. The **Disney–MGM Studios Backlot Tour** is wheelchair accessible, too. Guests with hearing impairments who lip-read should request a seat near the tour guide. The earthquake, fire, and water effects of the Catastrophe Canyon scene make the attraction inappropriate for some service animals. *Who Wants to Be a Millionaire*—**Play It!** is wheelchair accessible. The *Lights, Motors, Action!*—**Extreme Stunt Show** accommodates wheelchairs and offers an assistive listening device.

On New York Street, the *Honey, I Shrunk the Kids* **Movie Set Adventure** is barrier-free for most guests using wheelchairs, although the uneven surface may make maneuvering difficult. **Jim Henson's Muppet*Vision 3-D** is also completely wheelchair accessible. Those with hearing impairments may request a personal audio link that will amplify the sound here. A TV monitor in the preshow area is closed-captioned.

At Echo Lake, the **Indiana Jones Epic Stunt Spectacular!** is completely wheelchair accessible. Explosions and gunfire may make it inappropriate for service animals. **Star Tours,** a turbulent ride, is accessible by guests who can transfer to a ride seat; those lacking upper-body strength should request an extra shoulder restraint. Service animals should not ride. **Sounds Dangerous Starring Drew Carey** is completely wheelchair accessible. However, the entertainment value is derived from the different sound effects, so you may decide to skip this one if you have a hearing impairment.

🚩 **WDW Guest Information** ☎ 407/824–4321, 407/827–5141 TTY.

ENTERTAINMENT Most live entertainment locations are completely wheelchair accessible. Certain sections of parade routes are always reserved for guests with disabilities. Tapings of television shows are wheelchair accessible, but none of the soundstages currently have sign-language interpreters. The noise and explosions in **Fantasmic!** may frighten service animals.

All restaurants and shops are fully wheelchair accessible, but there are no braille menus or sign-language interpreters.

Oscar's Classic Car Souvenirs & Super Service, to the right in the Entrance Plaza, has standard chairs ($7; $1 deposit) as well as motor-powered chairs ($30; $10 deposit). No electric scooters are available in this park. If your rental needs replacing, ask a host or hostess.

FIRST AID
First Aid is in the Entrance Plaza adjoining Guest Relations.

GETTING AROUND
Inside this park, distances are short and walking is the optimal way to get around.

LOCKERS
Lockers are alongside Oscar's Classic Car Souvenirs, to the right of the Entrance Plaza after you pass through the turnstiles. The cost is $5, with a $2 refundable key deposit.

LOST THINGS & PEOPLE
If you're worried about your children getting lost, get name tags for them at Guest Relations, and instruct them to go to a Disney staffer, anyone wearing a name tag, if they can't find you. If the worst happens, ask any cast member before you panic; logbooks of lost children's names are kept at Guest Relations.

Guest Relations also has a computerized Message Center, where notes can be left for traveling companions at this and other parks. Report any lost or found articles at Guest Relations in the Entrance Plaza. Articles lost for more than one day should be sought at the Main Lost & Found office.

🚩 Disney-MGM Studios Lost & Found ☎ 407/560-7370. **Main Lost & Found** ✉ Magic Kingdom, Transportation and Ticket Center ☎ 407/824-4245.

MONEY MATTERS
There's an ATM near the Production Information Window, outside the park's Entrance Plaza. Currency exchange is available at the Guest Relations window.

PACKAGE PICKUP
Ask the shop clerk to forward any large purchase you make to Guest Relations, in the Entrance Plaza, so you won't have to carry it around all day. Allow three hours for it to get there.

VISITOR INFORMATION
The **Crossroads of the World** kiosk in the Entrance Plaza dispenses maps, entertainment schedules, brochures, and the like. Maps are available in French, German, Portuguese, Japanese, and Spanish, as well as English. Take specific questions to **Guest Relations,** inside the turnstiles on the left side of the Entrance Plaza.

The Production Information Window, also in the Entrance Plaza, is the place to find out what's being taped when and how to get into the audience.

At the corner where Hollywood Boulevard intersects with Sunset Boulevard is the **Studios Tip Board,** a large board with constantly updated information about attractions' wait times—reliable except for those moments when everyone follows the "See It Now!" advice and the line immediately triples. Studio staffers are on hand.

🎬 **Production Information Window** ☎ 407/560-4651.

DISNEY'S ANIMAL KINGDOM

Humankind's enduring love for animals is the inspiration for WDW's fourth theme park, Disney's Animal Kingdom. At 500 acres, the Animal Kingdom is the largest in area of all Disney theme parks worldwide and five times the size of the Magic Kingdom. The space gives Disney Imagineers plenty of scope for their creativity, and it allows for growth, an example of which is Expedition EVEREST. Slated to open in 2006, it's expected to be the park's biggest thrill attraction—a runaway train ride on a rugged mountain complete with icy ledges, dark caves, and a yeti legend.

Disney's Animal Kingdom park, opened in 1998, explores the stories of all animals—real, imaginary, and extinct. As you enter through the Oasis, exotic background music plays and you're surrounded by a green grotto, gentle waterfalls, and gardens alive with exotic birds, reptiles, and mammals. The Oasis opens early, so you can do a lot of critter-watching before its inhabitants settle down to snooze through the heat of the day.

At park opening (8 or 9 AM, depending on the season), Mickey, Minnie, and the gang arrive in a safari vehicle to lead the first guests into the heart of the park, where animals thrive in careful re-creations of natural landscapes in exotic lands ranging from Thailand and India to southern Africa. You'll also find rides, some of Disney's finest musical shows, eateries, and, of course, Disney characters—where else does the Lion King truly belong? Cast members come from all over the world, Kenya and South Africa as often as Kentucky and South Carolina. That's part of the charm of the place. All this is augmented by an earnest educational undercurrent that is meant to foster a renewed appreciation for the animal kingdom.

The park is laid out very much like its oldest sibling, the Magic Kingdom. The hub of this wheel is the spectacular Tree of Life in the middle of Discovery Island. Radiating from Discovery Island's hub are several spokes—the other "lands," each with a distinct personality. South of Discovery Island is Camp Minnie-Mickey, a character-greeting and show area.

Entertainment

Mickey's Jammin' Jungle Parade takes off at 4 PM daily on the pathway around Discovery Island with a "characters on safari" theme. Rafiki in his adventure Rover, Goofy in a safari jeep, and Mickey in his "Bon Voyage" caravan join other popular characters each day for the festive daytime fanfare. Adding to the pomp are a batch of oversized puppets—snakes, giraffes, frogs, tigers, monkeys, and others—created by famed designer Michael Curry, known for the puppet costumes of *The Lion King* on Broadway. Throw in some fanciful "party-animal" stilt walkers and animal rickshaws carrying VIPs or lucky park guests, and you've got another reason to strategize your day carefully. ☞ *Duration: 15 min. Crowds: Heavy. Strategy: Choose your spot along the parade route early, as this is one of Disney's most creative parades, and you should try not to miss it. Audience: All ages. Rating:* ★★★.

Numbers in the margin correspond to points of interest on the Disney's Animal Kingdom map.

The Oasis

This lush entrance garden makes you feel as if you've been plunked down in the middle of a rain forest. Cool mist, the aroma of flowers, and playful animals and colorful birds all enliven a miniature landscape of streams and grottoes, waterfalls, and glades fringed with banana leaves and jacaranda. On the finest Orlando mornings, when the mists shroud the landscape, it's the scene-setter for the rest of your day. It's also where you can take care of essentials before entering the park. Here you'll find stroller and wheelchair rentals, Guest Relations, an ATM, and the ticket booths.

groovy souvenirs

Before you pass through the turnstiles on your way into the Animal Kingdom, stop at the **Outpost Shop** for a must-have safari hat with Mouse ears. Once in Discovery Island, look for a Minnie Mouse headband with a safari-style bow at **Creature Comforts.**

Discovery Island

Primarily the site of the Tree of Life, this land is encircled by Discovery River, which isn't an actual attraction but can be viewed from a bridge in Harambe. The island's whimsical architecture, with wood carvings handmade in Bali, adds plenty of charm and a touch of fantasy to this park hub. The verdant **Discovery Island Trails** that lead to the Tree of Life provide habitats for kangaroos, lemurs, Galapagos tortoises, and other creatures you won't want to miss while here. It's hard to tear the kids from the glass panel in a cavelike observation area where you can see river otters frolic underwater and above. You'll find some great shops and some good counter-service eateries here, and the island is also the site of the daily Mickey's Jammin' Jungle Parade. Most of the visitor services that aren't in the Oasis are here, on the border with Harambe, including the Baby Care Center, First Aid Center, and Lost & Found.

Best of the Park

Whatever you do, arrive early. Get to the parking lot a half hour before the official park opening. Make a beeline for **Expedition EVEREST** (if it's open) or **Kilimanjaro Safaris** and make your FASTPASS appointment. Then, stroll through **Pangani Forest Exploration Trail** in Africa or the **Maharajah Jungle Trek** in Asia—if you choose the Africa option, take a brief break at **Kusafiri Coffee Shop & Bakery** for one of its huge hot iced-cinnamon rolls. By now, it should be time to return for your FASTPASS appointment. On the safari, it should still be early enough that the animals will be frisky, and you'll see more critters than you typically would on a real African safari. Next, head over to the **Tree of Life—*It's Tough to Be a Bug!*** Don't bother with the FASTPASS here unless the line wait is longer than 45 minutes. The queue meanders along paths that encircle the Tree of Life and allows relaxed viewing of the tree's animal carvings and animal habitats along the way.

Now zip over to **DINOSAUR** in DinoLand U.S.A. to pick up a timed FASTPASS ticket. Then try to grab a ride on **TriceraTop Spin** or **Primeval Whirl** before heading to **Restaurantosaurus** for a bite to eat. Kids love the food; parents, the music. Afterward, let the children explore the **Boneyard** while you digest. By now it should be time to return to DINOSAUR. Try to time your ride either before or just after the next performance of the *Tarzan Rocks!* stage show at the Theater in the Wild. Next head over to Asia, where you can make another FASTPASS appointment for the **Kali River Rapids.** Don't forget to check the entertainment schedule so you know when to find your spot for **Mickey's Jammin' Jungle Parade.** Take in the next **Flights of Wonder** show and then check your FASTPASS time and see if you can now get *very* wet on the thrilling Kali River Rapids. If you haven't already explored Asia, take a leisurely stroll along the **Maharajah Jungle Trek,** making sure to linger and watch the fascinating bats.

Do a half circle around Discovery Island and head on into Camp Minnie-Mickey, where you and the kids can have your pictures taken with—who else?—Mickey, Minnie, and several of their character friends. Then catch one of the two stage shows—the best is **Festival of the Lion King.** Later, shop in Discovery Island and have any bulky purchases sent to package pickup so you don't lug them around. If time allows, and especially if the kids are along, take the train to **Rafiki's Planet Watch.**

If the wait's not too long, have dinner at the **Rainforest Café**; the surroundings alone are worth the visit.

On Rainy Days

The animals love a cool, light rain, so don't avoid this park in wet weather unless you're feeling wimpy. You're going to get wet on Kali River Rapids anyway!

Fodor'sChoice

① **Tree of Life—*It's Tough to Be a Bug!*** A monument to all earth's creatures, the park's centerpiece is an imposing 14 stories high and 50 feet wide at its base. Its 100,000-plus leaves are several shades of green fabric, each carefully placed for a realistic effect. Carved into its thick trunk, gnarled roots, and soaring branches—some of which are supported by joints that allow them to sway in a strong wind—are nearly 350 intricate animal forms that include a baboon, a whale, a horse, the mighty lion, and even an ankylosaurus. Outside, paths tunnel underneath the roots as the fauna-encrusted trunk towers overhead. It's a rich and truly fascinating sight—the more you look the more you see. The path leads you inside the tree trunk to the star attraction of Discovery Island, where you get a bug's-eye view of life. The whimsical 3-D film adventure *It's Tough to Be a Bug!* is modeled vaguely on the animated film *A Bug's Life* from Disney and Pixar, the creators of *Toy Story*. Special film and theater effects spray you with "poison," zap you with a swatter, and even poke you with a stinger. It's all in good fun—and the surprise ending is too playful to give away. ☞ *Duration: 20 min for show; as long as you like at the Tree of Life.* **Crowds:** *Not usually a problem unless it's peak season.* **Strategy:** *This show is now a FASTPASS mainstay, so you can pick up your reservation after you've done the Kilimanjaro Safaris.* **Audience:** *All ages, but the theater is dark and some effects may frighten young children.* **Rating:** ★★★.

DinoLand U.S.A.

Just as it sounds, this is the place to come in contact with re-created prehistoric creatures, including the fear-inspiring carnosaurus and the gentle iguanadon. The landscaping includes live plants that have evolved over the last 65 million years. In collaboration with Chicago's Field Museum, Disney has added a complete, full-scale skeleton cast of Dino-Sue—also known as "Sue"—the 65-million-year-old Tyrannosaurus rex discovered near the Black Hills of South Dakota. After admiring "Sue," you can go on the thrilling DINOSAUR ride, amble along the Cretaceous Trail, play in the Boneyard, or take in the *Tarzan Rocks!* show at the Theater in the Wild. Kids will want to hitch a dino-ride on the TriceraTop Spin and on the Primeval Whirl family coaster, which has spinning "time machines." Check the "Times Guide" for "streetmosphere" appearances by zany comedic jugglers Smear, Splat, and Dip. There's no need to dig for souvenirs at Chester and Hester's Dinosaur Treasures gift shop—all you need is your wallet.

② **Boneyard.** Youngsters can slide, dig, bounce, slither, and stomp around this archaeological dig site–cum–playground, the finest play area in any of the four Disney parks. In addition to a huge sand pit where children can dig for mammoth bones, there are twisting short and long slides, climbing nets, caves, and a jeep to climb on. Stomp on the dino-footprints to make 'em roar. ☞ *Duration: Up to you and your children.* **Crowds:** *Can be heavy midmorning to early afternoon.* **Strategy:** *Let the kids burn off energy here while waiting for your FASTPASS appointment for DINOSAUR, or head over late in the day when kids need*

TIP SHEET

When to Go
Wednesday is probably the best day to go, but you can expect big crowds all week long and especially on weekends.

Arrive a half hour before park opening to get a jump on the crowds and to see the wild animals at their friskiest—as they were meant to be seen.

When You're There
Check the park's Tip Board for the latest information on lines just after crossing the bridge into Discovery Island.

Try to take a break in Discovery Island to enjoy the incredible architecture. The whimsical animal figures that adorn the shops and other buildings were carved by artisans in Bali specifically for this park.

Set up a rendezvous point and time at the start of the day, just in case you and your companions get separated. Some good places include the outdoor seating area of Tusker House restaurant in Africa, in front of DinoLand U.S.A.'s Boneyard, and at the turnstile of the *Festival of the Lion King* show.

---

a break to run free. **Audience:** *Toddlers, school-age children, and their families.* **Rating:** ★★★.

need a break?

Carnivores and omnivores alike will want to make tracks for **Dino Bite Snacks,** the perfect spot for cooling off with hand-dipped ice cream, sundaes, milk shakes, and floats.

3 **Cretaceous Trail.** Walk through a re-creation of a primeval forest containing some of the plant survivors from the dinosaur age, such as the monkey puzzle tree and ancient angiosperms. *Duration: Up to you. Crowds: Not a problem. Strategy: Stroll along here as you head toward Chester and Hester's for souvenirs or while you wait for the next Tarzan Rocks! show.* **Audience:** *All ages.* **Rating:** ★.

4 **DINOSAUR.** This wild adventure through time puts you face-to-face with huge dinosaurs that move and breathe with uncanny realism. When a carload of guests rouses a cantankerous carnotaurus from his Cretaceous slumber, it's show time. You travel back 65 million years on a fast-paced, twisting adventure and try to save the last living iguanodon as a massive asteroid hurtles toward Earth. Exciting audio-animatronics and special effects bring dinosaurs and the entire scene to life. *Duration: Not quite 4 min. Crowds: Can get heavy midmorning. Strategy: Go first thing in the morning or at the end of the day, or use the FASTPASS.* **Audience:** *All ages except very young children, preg-*

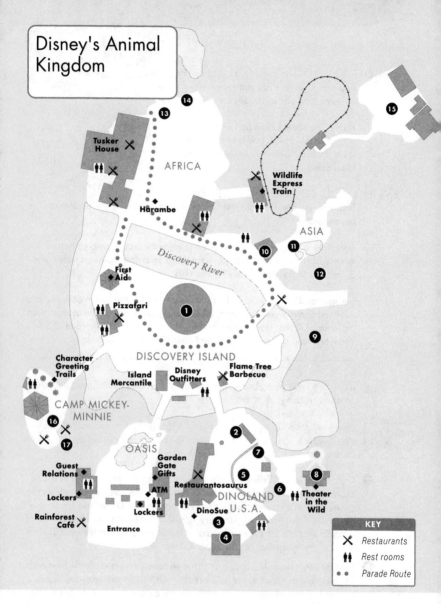

Disney's Animal Kingdom

Tusker House

AFRICA

Wildlife Express Train

Harambe

ASIA

Discovery River

First Aid

Pizzafari

DISCOVERY ISLAND

Character Greeting Trails

Island Mercantile

Disney Outfitters

Flame Tree Barbecue

CAMP MICKEY-MINNIE

OASIS

Garden Gate Gifts

ATM

Restaurantosaurus

DINOLAND U.S.A.

Theater in the Wild

Guest Relations

Lockers

DinoSue

Lockers

Rainforest Café

Entrance

KEY

✗	Restaurants
👫	Rest rooms
••	Parade Route

nant women, or guests with back, neck, or heart problems. *Minimum height: 40". Rating:* ★★★.

⑤ TriceraTop Spin. Until now, there wasn't a true "kiddie ride" anywhere at Disney's Animal Kingdom. TriceraTop Spin is designed for playful little dinophiles, who ought to get a kick out of whirling around this ride's giant spinning toy top and dodging incoming comets in their dino-mobiles. "Pop!" goes the top and out comes a grinning dinosaur as four passengers in each vehicle fly in a circle and maneuver up and down. ☞ *Duration: About 2 min. Crowds: Heavy due to the ride's relative newness. Strategy: Ride early while everyone else heads for the safari, or queue up while waiting for your FASTPASS appointment for DINOSAUR. Audience: Toddlers, school-age children and their families. Rating:* ★★.

⑥ Primeval Whirl. In a free-spinning, four-passenger vehicle, you head on a brief journey back in time on this outdoor open-air coaster, twisting, turning, and even venturing into the jaws of a dinosaur "skeleton." As you ride, crazy cartoon dinosaurs in shades of turquoise, orange, yellow, and purple pop up along the track bearing signs that warn "The End Is Near." More signs warn of "Meteors!" and suggest that you "Head for the Hills!"—coaster hills, that is. Halfway through the ride, your car seems to spin out of control and you take the next drop backward. The more weight there is in the vehicle, the more you spin. ☞ *Duration: About 2½ min. Crowds: Heavy demand due to the ride's relative newness. Strategy: Kids may want to ride twice, so take your first spin early, then get a FASTPASS to return later if the wait is longer than 20 min. Minimum height: 48". Rating:* ★★★.

⑦ Fossil Fun Games. A carnival-style midway in the middle of DinoLand U.S.A., this fun fair draws crowds with games like Whack a Packycephalosaur and the mallet-strength challenge, Dino-Whamma. The prehistoric fun comes at a price, however, and stone currency is not accepted. Prizes are mostly of the plush-character variety—you might win your sweetheart a stuffed Nala.

⑧ *Tarzan Rocks!* This live musical stage show, based on the animated film, includes live acrobatics, extreme stunts, and a rock performance that showcase the buff jungle dude and his toned jungle honey. Costumes are great and the action nonstop. Don't miss it unless your time is limited and you haven't yet seen the superior *Festival of the Lion King.* ☞ *Duration: 30 min. Crowds: Not a problem. Strategy: Arrive 15 min before show time and grab an ice-cream treat on the way—you can enjoy it in the theater as you wait for the curtain to rise. Audience: All ages. Rating:* ★★.

Asia

Meant to resemble a rural village somewhere in Asia, this land is full of remarkable rain-forest scenery and ruins. Groupings of trees grow from a crumbling tiger shrine and two massive towers, one representing Thailand, the other Nepal. The towers are the habitat for two families of gibbons, whose hooting fills the air at all hours of the day. While you're here, take a wild ride on Expedition EVEREST, stroll the Maharajah Jungle Trek, see the Flights of Wonder bird show, and raft the Kali River Rapids.

❾ Expedition EVEREST. This is the year Disney really turns up the thrill factor in the Animal Kingdom. Expedition EVEREST brings the park major real estate in the form of the imposing 200-foot-high Himalayan mountains. Legend holds that a fierce yeti guards the route to Mount Everest. Despite the threat, riders are invited to board a high-speed train into the mountains. You roll past lush bamboo forests, thundering waterfalls, and sparkling glacier fields as your train climbs higher and higher through snow-capped peaks. But the trip turns perilous when it seems that your train is suddenly out of control, barreling forward, then backward, around icy mountain ledges and through dark, snowy caverns. Will you find the yeti? Do you even want to? You'll have to take the plunge to find out. Since the coaster is supposed to be less intense than, say, Space Mountain, brave children as young as six can ride. ☞ *Crowds: Huge for this park's wildest thrill ride yet.* **Strategy:** *FAST-PASS.* **Audience:** *Anyone 44 inches or taller.*

❿ Flights of Wonder. This outdoor show area near the border with Africa is the place for spectacular demonstrations of skill by falcons, hawks, and other rare and fascinating birds, which swoop down over the audience. ☞ *Duration: 30 min. Crowds: Not a problem.* **Strategy:** *Arrive 15 min before show time and find a shaded seat beneath one of the awnings—the sun can be brutal.* **Audience:** *All.* **Rating:** ★★.

need a break?

For an Asian-style lunch, stop by the **Chakranadi Chicken Shop,** where the meals are healthful and tasty. There's chicken or vegetable stir-fry, fried rice, Thai beef, pot stickers, and other Asian specialties. To drink, you'll find beer and Chai tea.

⓫ Maharajah Jungle Trek. Get an up-close view of some unusual and interesting animals along this trail: a Komodo dragon perched on a rock; Malayan tapirs near the wooden footbridge; families of giant fruit bats that hang to munch fruit from wires and fly very close to the open and glass-protected viewing areas; and Bengal tigers in front of a maharajah's palace. The tigers have their own view (with no accessibility, of course) of a group of Asian deer and a herd of black buck, an antelope species. At the end of the trek, you walk through an aviary with a lotus pool. Disney interpreters, many from Asian countries, are on hand to answer any and all questions. ☞ *Duration: As long as you like.* **Crowds:** *Not bad because people are constantly moving.* **Strategy:** *Go anytime.* **Audience:** *All ages.* **Rating:** ★★★.

⓬ Kali River Rapids. Asia's thrilling adventure ride is to the Animal Kingdom what Splash Mountain is to Frontierland. Aboard a round raft that seats 12, you run the Chakranadi River. After passing through a huge bamboo tunnel filled with jasmine-scented mist, your raft climbs 40 feet upriver, lurches and spins through a series of sharp twists and turns, and then approaches an immense waterfall, which curtains a giant carved tiger face. Past rain forests and temple ruins, you find yourself face-to-face with the denuded slope of a logged-out woodland burning out of control. There are many more thrills, but why spill the beans? Be warned: you will get wet, and there's an 80% chance you will get so soaked you'll have to wring out your clothing in the nearest restroom afterward, so if you don't mind the extra baggage, plan ahead with a change of clothing and a plastic bag. ☞ *Duration: About 7 min. Crowds: Long lines all day. Strategy: Use your FASTPASS, or go during the parade. Audience: All but very young children and adults with heart, back, or neck problems or motion sickness. Minimum height: 38". Rating:* ★★★.

Africa

This largest of the lands is an area of forests and grasslands, predominantly an enclave for wildlife from the continent. The focus is on live animals at the key attractions. Harambe, on the northern bank of Discovery River, is Africa's starting point. Inspired by several East African coastal villages, this Disney town has so much detail that it's mind-boggling to try to soak it all up. Signs on the apparently peeling stucco walls of the buildings are faded, as if bleached by the sun, and everything has a hot, dusty look. For souvenirs with both Disney and African themes, browse through the Mombasa Marketplace and Ziwani Traders. Safari apparel, decorative articles for the home, and jewelry are on offer.

FodorsChoice **Kilimanjaro Safaris.** A giant Imagineered baobab tree is the starting point ★ ⑬ for this adventure into the up-country. Although re-creating an African safari in the United States (or even Florida, for that matter) may not be a new idea, this safari goes a step beyond merely allowing you to observe rhinos, hippos, antelope, wildebeests, giraffes, zebras, elephants, lions, and the like. There are illustrated game-spotting guides above the seats in the open-air safari vehicles, and as you lurch and bump over some 100 acres of savanna, forest, rivers, and rocky hills, you'll see most of these animals—sometimes so close you feel like you could reach out and touch them. It's easy to suspend disbelief here because the landscape is so effectively modeled and replenished by Disney horticulturists. This being a theme park, dangers lurk, in the form of ivory poachers, and it suddenly becomes your mission to save a group of elephants from would-be poachers. Even without the scripted peril, there's enough elephant excitement on the savanna to impress everyone. In the past few years, two baby elephants have been born—one, named Tufani, born May 22, 2003, is the fourth surviving elephant calf in North America resulting from artificial insemination. The second, Kianga, arrived July 6, 2004, as part of the park's breeding program coordinated by the American Zoo and Aquarium Association. You'll see the youngsters hanging out with the rest of the herd, and the park's animal team expects to see more elephant babies in the future. To get the most from your adventure, do this early in the day or in the late afternoon, when the animals are awake—humans aren't the only creatures that want to be napping inside on a hot Central Florida afternoon. ☞ *Duration: 20 min. Crowds: Heavy in the morning. Strategy: Arrive in the park first thing in the morning—it's worth the trouble—and come straight here using the FASTPASS if necessary. If you arrive at the park late morning, save this for the end* *of the day, when it isn't so hot. You'll probably see about the same number of animals as in early morning.* **Audience:** *All ages—parents can hold small tykes and explain the poacher fantasy.* **Rating:** ★★★.

need a break?

The tantalizing aroma of fresh-baked cinnamon buns leads to the **Kusafiri Coffee Shop & Bakery,** where, after just one look, you may give in to the urge. These buns are worth the banknotes, and they pair well with a cappuccino or espresso. Kids may opt for a giant cookie and milk.

⑭ Pangani Forest Exploration Trail. Calling this a nature walk doesn't really do it justice. A path winds through dense foliage, alongside streams, and past waterfalls. En route there are viewing points where you can stop and watch a beautiful rare okapi munching the vegetation, a family and a separate bachelor group of lowland gorillas, hippos (which you usually can see underwater), meerkats (a kind of mongoose), graceful gerenuk (an African antelope), exotic birds, and a bizarre colony of hairless mole rats. One habitat showcases colobus monkeys, mona monkeys, and an antelope species called the yellow-backed duiker. Native African interpreters are on hand at many viewing points to answer questions. ☞ **Duration:** *Up to you.* **Crowds:** *Heavy in the morning, but there's room for all, it seems.* **Strategy:** *Go while waiting for your safari FAST-PASS; try to avoid going at the hottest time of day, when the gorillas like to nap.* **Audience:** *All ages.* **Rating:** ★★★.

⑮ Rafiki's Planet Watch. Take the Wildlife Express steam train to this unique center of ecoawareness. Rafiki's, named for the wise baboon from *The Lion King,* is divided into three sections. At the Conservation Station, you can meet animal experts, enjoy interactive exhibits, learn about worldwide efforts to protect endangered species and their habitats, and find out ways to connect with conservation efforts in your own community. At the Habitat Habit! section, cotton-top tamarin monkeys play while you learn how to live with all earth's animals. And you don't have to be a kid to enjoy the Affection Section, where young children and adults who are giving their inner child free rein get face-to-face with goats and other small critters. ☞ **Duration:** *5-min ride (each way) the rest is up to you.* **Crowds:** *Can get heavy midmorning.* **Strategy:** *Go in late afternoon if you've hit all key attractions.* **Audience:** *All ages.* **Rating:** ★★.

Camp Minnie-Mickey

This Adirondack-style land is the setting for live performances at the Lion King Theater and Grandmother Willow's Grove, as well as a meet-and-greet area where Disney characters gather for picture-taking and autographs.

FodorśChoice

⑯ Festival of the Lion King. If you think you've seen enough *Lion King* to last a lifetime, you're wrong unless you've seen this show. In the air-conditioned theater-in-the-round, Disney presents a delightful tribal celebration of song, dance, and acrobatics that uses huge moving stages and floats. ☞ **Duration:** *30 min.* **Crowds:** *Not a problem.* **Strategy:** *Arrive 15 min before show time. If you have a child who might want to go on* *stage, sit in one of the front rows to increase his or her chance of getting chosen.* **Audience:** *All ages.* **Rating:** ★★★.

 ❶⑦ *Pocahontas and Her Forest Friends.* At Grandmother Willow's Grove, an actor portrays Pocahontas in this lesson on nature and how to preserve endangered species. Pocahontas works with an armadillo, a skunk, a boa constrictor, a red-tailed hawk, and other creatures. She also breaks out in song with "Just Around the River Bend." ☞ *Duration: 12 min. Crowds: Not a problem. Strategy: May not be performed every day in low season; check entertainment guide map and arrive 15 min before show time. Audience: All ages.* **Rating:** ★★.

Disney's Animal Kingdom A to Z

To research prices, get advice from other travelers, and book travel arrangements, visit www.fodors.com.

BABY CARE

The **Baby Care Center** is in Discovery Island. You can buy disposable diapers, formula, baby food, and pacifiers. For stroller rentals ($7 single, $14 double; plus $1 deposit), go to Garden Gate Gifts, in the Oasis.

CAMERAS & FILM

Disposable cameras are widely available, and you can buy film and memory cards at several shops throughout the park. If a Disney photographer takes a picture of you in the park, ask for a Disney PhotoPass—later, you can view and purchase the pictures online or at the park's Photo Center in the Oasis.

DISABILITIES & ACCESSIBILITY

All restaurants, shops, and attractions are completely wheelchair accessible, including the theater-in-the-round at Camp Minnie-Mickey and the Tree of Life theater showing *It's Tough to Be a Bug!*, which are also accessible to electric scooters. However, to fully experience all the bug movie's special effects, guests who use wheelchairs should transfer to one of the auditorium seats. Check the "Guidebook for Guests with Disabilities" for information about closed-captioning boxes for the monitor-equipped attractions such as the Tree of Life and how to get a sign-language interpretation schedule. Scripts and story lines for all attractions are available, and sign-language interpreters can be booked with two weeks notice. Assistive listening devices ($25 refundable deposit) amplify sound in theaters.

In DinoLand U.S.A., you must transfer from your wheelchair to board the **DINOSAUR** thrill ride. Note that you will be jostled quite a bit on this twisting, turning, bumpy ride. **Primeval Whirl** requires a transfer, but **TriceraTop Spin** is wheelchair accessible. To board **Kali River Rapids** in Asia, you'll need to make transfer from your wheelchair to one of the ride rafts. If you're like most of the passengers who get soaked on this water ride, you will be soggy for hours unless you have a change of clothing handy. In Africa, you can roll your wheelchair on board the Wildlife Express train to **Rafiki's Planet Watch,** where you'll need it to traverse the path from the train stop to the station. The **Kilimanjaro Safaris** attraction is also wheelchair accessible. Service animals are allowed in most areas of the park; however, some areas are off-limits, including the Affection Section petting-zoo area of Rafiki's Planet Watch, the aviaries of **Pangani Forest Exploration Trail** and **Maharajah Jungle Trek,** and both the DINOSAUR and Kali River Rapids rides. Braille guides are available at Guest Relations, and Assistive Listening Devices (ALDs) are operating at most attractions—check with Guest Relations as you enter the park to pick up ALDs ($25 deposit), audiotape guides ($25 deposit), and braille guides ($25 deposit).

WHEELCHAIR RENTALS
Garden Gate Gifts, in the Oasis, rents wheelchairs ($7; $1 deposit) and electric scooters ($30; $10 deposit).
🚹 **WDW Information** ☎ 407/824–4321, 407/827–5141 TTY.

FIRST AID
The park's First Aid Center, staffed by registered nurses, is in Discovery Island.

GETTING AROUND
You get around mostly on foot here, although you must take a train to Rafiki's Planet Watch.

GUIDED TOURS
Backstage Safari takes an in-depth look at animal conservation every Monday, Wednesday, Thursday, and Friday 8:15–11:15, stopping at the animal hospital and other behind-the-scenes areas. It's a great way to learn about animal behaviors and how handlers care for the critters in captivity, but don't expect to see many animals on this tour. Book ahead; you can make reservations up to a year in advance. Those in your party must all be at least 16 years old to participate and the cost is $65 plus park admission.

Wild by Design offers participants 14 and older insights into the creation of Disney's Animal Kingdom every Thursday and Friday, from 8:30 to 11:30. The tour touches on the park's art, architecture, history, and agriculture, and reveals how stories of exotic lands are told at the park. You get a glimpse of behind-the-scenes buildings to see custodians taking care of the animals. A light continental breakfast is served as part of the $58 tour price; park admission is required as well.
🚹 **Backstage Safari and Wild by Design** ☎ 407/939–8687.

LOCKERS
Lockers are in Guest Relations ($5; $2 key deposit).

LOST THINGS & PEOPLE
If you're worried about your children getting lost, get name tags for them at Discovery Island. Instruct them to speak to someone with a Disney name tag if you become separated. If you do, immediately report your loss to any cast member. Lost-children logbooks are at Discovery Island, which is also the location of the Lost & Found. To retrieve lost articles after leaving the park, call Lost & Found on the

same day, or call Main Lost & Found if more than a day has passed
since you've lost the article.
🔢 **Lost & Found** ☎ 407/938-2785. **Main Lost & Found** ☎ 407/824-4245.

MONEY MATTERS
For cash and currency exchange, go to Guest Relations. There's an ATM
in the Oasis to the right of the Entrance Plaza as you go into the park.

PACKAGE PICKUP
You can have shop clerks forward any large purchases to Garden Gate
Gifts, on the right side of the Entrance Plaza in the Oasis, so that you won't
have to carry them around all day. Allow three hours for the journey.

VISITOR INFORMATION
Guest Relations in the Oasis is the place to pick up park maps and entertainment schedules and ask questions. Foreign visitors may want to
stop here to get maps in five other languages besides English: French,
German, Portuguese, Japanese, and Spanish.

TYPHOON LAGOON

According to Disney legend, Typhoon Lagoon was created when the
quaint, thatched-roof, lushly landscaped Placid Palms Resort was struck
by a cataclysmic storm. It left a different world in its wake: surfboards
sundered trees; once upright palms imitated the Leaning Tower of Pisa;
and part of the original lagoon was cut off, trapping thousands of tropical fish—and a few sharks. Nothing, however, topped the fate of *Miss
Tilly,* a shrimp boat from "Safen Sound, Florida," which was hurled high
in the air and became impaled on Mt. Mayday, a magical volcano that
periodically tries to dislodge *Miss Tilly* with huge geysers of water.

Ordinary folks, the legend continues, would have been crushed by such
devastation. But the resourceful residents of Placid Palms were made of
hardier stuff—and from the wreckage they created 56-acre Typhoon Lagoon, the self-proclaimed "world's ultimate water park."

Typhoon Lagoon offers a full day's worth of activities. You can bob along
in 5-foot waves in a surf lagoon the size of two football fields, speed
down water slides, bump through rapids, go snorkeling, and, for a mel-
low break, float in inner tubes along the 2,100-foot Castaway Creek,
rubberneck from specially constructed grandstands as human cannon-
balls are ejected from the storm slides, or merely hunker down in one
of the many hammocks or lounge chairs and read a book. A children's
area replicates adult rides on a smaller scale. It's Disney's version of a
day at the beach—complete with friendly Disney lifeguards. And for the
first time since the park opened, Disney has added a new thrill attraction: the Crush 'N' Gusher water coaster.

The layout is so simple that it's hard to get lost. The wave and swimming lagoon is at the center of the park; the waves break on the beaches
closest to the entrance and are born in Mt. Mayday at the other end of
the park. Castaway Creek encircles the lagoon. Anything requiring a

gravitational plunge—storm slides, speed slides, and raft trips down rapids—starts around the summit of Mt. Mayday. Shark Reef and Ketchakiddie Creek flank the head of the lagoon, to Mt. Mayday's right and left, respectively, as you enter the park.

Numbers in the margin correspond to points of interest on the Typhoon Lagoon map.

❶ Typhoon Lagoon Surf Pool. This is the heart of the park, a swimming area that spreads out over 2½ acres and contains almost 3 million gallons of clear, chlorinated water. It's scalloped by lots of little coves, bays, and inlets, all edged with white-sand beaches—spread over a base of white concrete, as body surfers soon discover when they try to slide into shore. Ouch! The main attraction is the waves. Twelve huge water-collection chambers hidden in Mt. Mayday dump their load with a resounding "whoosh" into trapdoors to create waves large enough for Typhoon Lagoon to host amateur and professional surfing championships. A piercing double hoot from *Miss Tilly* signals the start and finish of wave action: every 2 hours, for 1½ hours, 5-foot waves issue forth every 90 seconds; the next half hour is devoted to moderate bobbing waves. Even during the big-wave periods, however, the waters in Blustery Bay and Whitecap Cove are protected enough for timid swimmers. Surfers who don't want to risk a fickle ocean can surf here on certain days before the park opens (call ahead for the schedule). Instruction and surfboard are included in the $135 cost, and the surfing experience lasts for 2½ hours. Reserve your waves by calling ☎ 407/939–7529.

❷ Castaway Creek. This circular, 15-foot-wide, 3-foot-deep waterway is everyone's water fantasy come true. Snag an inner tube and float along the creek that winds the entire park, a wet version of the Magic Kingdom's Walt Disney World Railroad. You pass through a rain forest that showers you with mist and spray, you slide through caves and grottos, you float by overhanging trees and flowering bushes, and you get dumped on at the Water Works, whose "broken" pipes the Typhoon Lagooners never got around to fixing. The current flows a gentle 2½ feet per second; it takes about 30 minutes to make a full circuit. Along the way there are exits where you can hop out and dry off or do something else—and then pick up another inner tube and jump right back in.

❸ Shark Reef. If you felt like leaping onto the stage at the Studios' *Voyage of the Little Mermaid* or jumping into the tank at Epcot's Living Seas, make tracks for this 360,000-gallon snorkeling tank. The coral reef is artificial, but the 4,000 tropical fish—including black-and-white-striped sergeant majors, sargassum trigger fish, yellowtail damselfish, and amiable nurse and bonnet-head sharks—are quite real. So are the southern stingrays that congregate in the warmer, shallower water by the entrance. To prevent algae growth, Shark Reef is kept at a brisk 72°F, which is about 15 degrees cooler than the rest of Typhoon Lagoon. A sunken tanker divides the reef; its portholes give landlubbers access to the underwater scene and let them go nose-to-nose with snorkelers. Go first thing in the morning or at the end of the day if you want to spend more time. During spring and summer, adults and children ages 10 and over

Typhoon Lagoon

KEY
✗ Restaurants
♟ Rest rooms

Miss Tilly

Beach Area
Castaway Cove

Typhoon Tilly's

Typhoon Lagoon

Low Tide Lou's

Rain Forest

Rain Forest

Getaway Glen

Raft Rentals

Beach Area

Slurp's Up

High & Dry Towels

Castaway Creek

Singapore Sal's Saleable Salvage

Leaning Palms

First Aid

Entrance

can take a personal snorkeling lesson at $20 per half hour (plus an additional $15 per participant for each air tank). If your kids want to learn how to explore the depths of the ocean Disney style, sign them up at Guest Relations when you purchase your tickets.

❹ Crush 'N' Gusher. If flume rides, storm slides, and tube races aren't wild enough for your inner thrill-seeker, get ready to defy gravity on Disney's first water coaster. Designed to propel you uphill and down along a series of flumes, caverns, and spillways, this ride should satisfy the most enthusiastic daredevil. Keeping with park lore, Crush 'N' Gusher flows through what appears to be a rusted-out tropical fruit factory, weaving in and out of the wreckage and debris that once transported fruit through the plant's wash facilities. Three fruit spillways are aptly named Banana Blaster, Coconut Crusher and Pineapple Plunger. ☞ *Audience: Children under 48″ are not allowed on this ride. No pregnant women or guests with heart, back, or neck problems or other physical limitations.*

need a break?

When you need to regain your energy, head to **Leaning Palms,** to your left as you enter the park, for standard beach fare—burgers, dogs, chef salads, and, of course, ice cream and frozen yogurt. For adults, **Let's Go Slurpin'** is a beach shack on the edge of Typhoon Lagoon that dispenses frozen margaritas as well as wine and beer. **Typhoon Tilly's Galley & Grog Shop,** on the right just south of Shark Reef, pours mostly sugary, nonalcoholic grog but also serves Davy Jones lager.

❺ Humunga Kowabunga. There's little time to scream, but you'll hear just such vociferous reactions as the survivors emerge from the catch pool opposite Shark Reef. The basic question is: want to get scared out of your wits in three seconds flat—and like it enough to go back for more? The two side-by-side Humunga Kowabunga speed slides rightly deserve their acclaim among thrill lovers, as they drop more than 50 feet in a distance barely four times that amount. For nonmathematicians, that's very steep. Oh yes, and then you go through a cave. In the dark. The average speed is 30 mph; however, you can really fly if you lie flat on your back, cross your ankles, wrap your arms around your chest, and arch your back. Just remember to smile for the rubberneckers on the grandstand at the bottom. ☞ *Audience: Children under 48″ are not allowed on this ride. No pregnant women or guests with heart, back, or neck problems or other physical limitations.*

❻ Storm Slides. Each of these three body slides is about 300 feet long and snakes in and out of rock formations, through caves and tunnels, and under waterfalls, but each has a slightly different view and offers a twist. The one in the middle has the longest tunnel; the others' secrets you'll have to discover for yourself. Maximum speed is about 20 mph, and the trip takes about 30 seconds.

❼ Mt. Mayday. What goes down can also go up—and up and up and up and up. "It's like climbing Mt. Everest," wailed one teenager about a climb that seems a lot steeper than this 85-foot peak would warrant. However, it's Mt. Everest with hibiscus flowers, a rope bridge, stepping-stones set in plunging waters, and—remember that typhoon?—a broken canoe scattered over the rocks near the top. The view encompasses the entire park.

Lovers of white-water rafting will find Mayday Falls, Keelhaul Falls, and Gang Plank Falls at Mt. Mayday. These white-water raft rides in oversize inner tubes plunge down the mount's left side. Like the Storm Slides, they have caves, waterfalls, and intricate rock work, but with some extra elements.

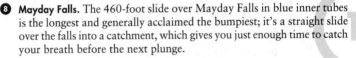

8 Mayday Falls. The 460-foot slide over Mayday Falls in blue inner tubes is the longest and generally acclaimed the bumpiest; it's a straight slide over the falls into a catchment, which gives you just enough time to catch your breath before the next plunge.

9 Keelhaul Falls. This spiraling, 400-foot ride in yellow inner tubes through raging rapids seems way faster than the purported 10 mph.

10 Gang Plank Falls. If you climb up Mt. Mayday for this ride, you'll go down in four-person, 6½-foot inflated rafts that descend crazily through 300 feet of rapids. This is a great ride for adventurous families to enjoy together—the rafts can hold five if some of the passengers are kids.

11 Ketchakiddie Creek. Typhoon Lagoon's children's area has slides, minirapids, squirting whales and seals, bouncing barrels, waterfalls, sprinklers, and all the other ingredients of a splash fiesta. The bubbling sand ponds, where youngsters can sit in what seems like an enormous whirlpool bath, are special favorites. ☞ *All adults must be accompanied by a child or children under 48″ and vice versa.*

12 Bay Slides. These scaled-down versions of the Storm Slides are geared toward younger kids.

Strategies for Your Visit to Typhoon Lagoon

There's really only one problem with Typhoon Lagoon—it's a crowd pleaser. The closing of River Country in 2002 has added to the number of waterlovers visiting Typhoon Lagoon, and the presence of Blizzard Beach has shown no signs of eroding its popularity. In summer and on weekends, the park often reaches its capacity of 7,200 people by midmorning.

If you must visit in summer, go for a few hours during late afternoon or when the weather clears up after a thundershower. Typically, rainstorms drive away the crowds. If you plan to make a whole day of it, avoid weekends—Typhoon Lagoon is big among locals as well as visitors. Arrive 30 minutes before opening time so you can park, buy tickets, rent towels, and snag inner tubes before the hordes descend. Set up camp and hit the slides, white-water rides, and Shark Reef first.

Women and girls should wear one-piece swimsuits unless they want to find their tops somewhere around their ears at the bottom of the water slide.

If you're visiting at a quiet time of year, go in the afternoon, when the water will have warmed up a bit.

There are plenty of lounge chairs and a number of hammocks but definitely not enough beach umbrellas. If you crave shade, commandeer a spot in the grassy area around Getaway Glen on the left side of the park just past the raft-rental concession. If you like moving about, people-watching, and having sand in your face, go front and center at the surf pool. For your own patch of sand and some peace and quiet, head for the coves and inlets on the left side of the lagoon.

Typhoon Lagoon A to Z

To research prices, get advice from other travelers, and book travel arrangements, visit www.fodors.com.

DISABILITIES & ACCESSIBILITY
The park gets high ratings in the accessibility department. All paths that connect the different areas of Typhoon Lagoon are wheelchair accessible. Those who use a wheelchair and who can transfer to a raft or inner tube can also float in **Typhoon Lagoon** and on **Castaway Creek.** Wheelchairs are available in the entrance turnstile area and are free with ID.

DRESSING ROOMS & LOCKERS
There are men's and women's thatched-roof dressing rooms and two sizes of full-day lockers ($5 and $7, plus $2 deposits for either) to the right of the entrance on your way into the park; a second, less-crowded set is near Typhoon Tilly's Galley & Grog Shop. The towels you can rent (for $1) at the stand to the right of the main entrance are a little skimpy; bring your own beach towel or buy one at Singapore Sal's if you like. The Typhoon Lagoon Imagineers thoughtfully placed rest rooms in every available nook and cranny. Most have showers and are much less crowded with clothes-changers than the main dressing rooms.

FIRST AID
The small First-Aid Stand, run by a registered nurse, is on your left as you enter the park, not far from the Leaning Palms food stand.

LOST THINGS & PEOPLE
Ask about your misplaced people and things at the Guest Relations window near the entrance turnstiles, to your left as you enter the park. Lost children are taken to High and Dry Towels.

PICNICKING
Picnicking is permitted, but you won't be allowed to bring in a cooler too large for one person to carry. Tables are set up at Getaway Glen and Castaway Cove, near Shark Reef. Bring a box lunch from your hotel or pick up provisions from the Goodings supermarket at the Crossroads shopping center (off SR 535), and you'll eat well without having to line up with the masses. Although you can find alcoholic beverages at Typhoon Lagoon, don't bring along your own or you'll be walking them back to the car. Glass containers are also prohibited.

SUPPLIES

The **rental-rafts concession,** the building with the boat sticking through the roof to the left of the entrance, past the Leaning Palms food concession, offers free inner tubes. You need to pick them up only for the lagoon; they're provided for Castaway Creek and all the white-water rides. You can borrow snorkels and masks at **Shark Reef.** Free life vests are available with a $25 refundable deposit at **High and Dry Towels.** Be sure to carry along your room key, credit card, car keys, or other form of ID (driver's licenses and passports are not accepted) to leave as collateral. You may not bring your own equipment into Typhoon Lagoon.

Singapore Sal's, to the right of the main entrance (on the way into the park), is the place to buy sunscreen, hats, sunglasses, and other beach paraphernalia.

VISITOR INFORMATION

The staff at the **Guest Relations** window outside the entrance turnstiles, to your left, can answer many questions; a chalkboard inside gives water temperature and surfing information. During off-season, which encompasses October through April, the park closes for several weeks for routine maintenance and refurbishment. Call WDW Information or check the disneyworld.com web site for days of operation.

🚹 **WDW Guest Information** ☎ 407/824-4321 ⊕ www.disneyworld.com.

BLIZZARD BEACH

With its oxymoronic name, Blizzard Beach promises the seemingly impossible—a seaside playground with an alpine theme. As with its older cousin, Typhoon Lagoon, the Disney Imagineers have created an entire legend to explain the park's origin: after a freak winter storm dropped snow over the western side of Walt Disney World, entrepreneurs decided to create Florida's first downhill ski resort. Saunalike temperatures soon returned. But just as the resort's operators were ready to close up shop, they spotted a playful alligator sliding down the "liquid ice" slopes. The realization that the melting snow had created the tallest, fastest, and most exhilarating water-filled ski and toboggan runs in the world gave birth to the ski resort–water park.

Disney Imagineers have gone all out here to create the paradox of a ski resort in the midst of a tropical lagoon. Lots of verbal puns and sight gags play with the snow-in-Florida motif. The park's centerpiece is Mt. Gushmore, with its 120-foot-high Summit Plummet, as well as other toboggan and water-sled runs with names such as Teamboat Springs, a white-water raft ride; Toboggan Racer; Slush Gusher; and Runoff Rapids. Between Mt. Gushmore's base and its summit, swim-skiers can also ride a chairlift converted from ski-resort to beach-resort use—with umbrellas and snow skis on their undersides. Devoted water-slide enthusiasts generally prefer Blizzard Beach to the other water parks.

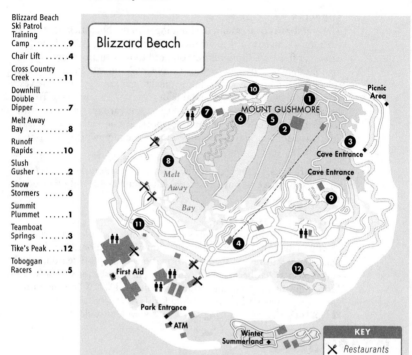

Numbers in the margin correspond to points of interest on the Blizzard Beach map.

Fodor'sChoice **Summit Plummet.** This is Mt. Gushmore's big gun, which Disney bills as
★ ❶ "the world's tallest, fastest free-fall speed slide." From Summit Plummet's "ski jump" tower, it's a wild 55-mph plunge straight down to a splash landing at the base of the mountain. It looks almost like a straight vertical drop. If you're watching from the beach below, you can't hear the yells of the participants, but rest assured—they're screaming their heads off. ☞ *Minimum height: 48″.*

❷ **Slush Gusher.** This speed slide, which drops through a snow-banked mountain gully, is shorter and less severe than Summit Plummet but a real thriller nonetheless. ☞ *Minimum height: 48″.*

❸ **Teamboat Springs.** Six-passenger rafts zip along in the world's longest family white-water raft ride. Since its original construction, it has doubled its speed of departure onto its twisting, 1,200-foot channel of rushing waterfalls. This is great for families—a good place for kids too big for Tike's Peak to test more grown-up waters.

4 **Chair Lift.** If you're waterlogged, take a ride from the beachfront base of Mt. Gushmore up over its face and on to the summit—and back down again.

5 **Toboggan Racers.** On this ride you slither down an eight-lane water slide over Mt. Gushmore's "snowy" slopes.

6 **Snow Stormers.** No water park would be complete without a fancy water slide, and Blizzard Beach has one—actually three flumes that descend from the top of Mt. Gushmore along a switchback course of ski-type slalom gates.

7 **Downhill Double Dipper.** These side-by-side racing slides are where future Olympic hopefuls 48 inches and taller can compete against one another.

need a break?

Lottawatta Lodge—a North American ski lodge with a Caribbean accent—is the park's main emporium of fast food. Lines are long at peak feeding times.

The **Warming Hut** has Disney's famous smoked turkey legs, salads, hot dogs, and ice cream. Hot dogs, snow cones, and ice cream are on the menu at **Avalunch. Frostbite Freddie's** and **Polar Pub** on the main beach both sell frozen drinks and spirits.

8 **Melt Away Bay.** The park's main pool is a 1-acre oasis that's constantly fed by "melting snow" waterfalls. The man-made waves are positively oceanlike. If you're not a strong swimmer, stay away from the far end of the pool, where the waves originate. You can get temporarily stuck in a pocket even if your head is still above water.

9 **Blizzard Beach Ski Patrol Training Camp.** The preteens in your crowd may want to spend most of their time on the T-bar drop, bungee-cord slides, and culvert slides here. In addition, there's a chance to take on Mogul Mania, a wide-open area where you can jump from one slippery mogul to the next. The moguls really look more like baby icebergs bobbing in a swimming pool.

10 **Runoff Rapids.** You have to steel your nerves to climb into an inner tube for these three twisting, turning flumes—even one that's in the dark. But once you're in, it's way more fun than scary.

11 **Cross Country Creek.** Just grab an inner tube, hop on, and circle the entire park on this creek during a leisurely 45-minute float. Along the way, you'll get doused with frigid water in an ice cave—wonderful on a steamy Florida day.

12 **Tike's Peak.** Disney is never one to leave the little ones out of the fun, and this junior-size version of Blizzard Beach, set slightly apart from the rest of the park, has scaled-down elements of Mt. Gushmore.

Strategies for Your Visit to Blizzard Beach

Blizzard Beach is just as popular as Typhoon Lagoon—it's a toss-up as to which is more crowded. Your best bet is to get here early, before the gates fling open. Expect long lines at the Summit Plummet and other major attractions. If you go in summer, try to arrive in late afternoon, just after the daily thunderstorm. The air will be hot and humid, but you'll be cool as a cucumber because the hordes will have departed for indoor pursuits. If thrill rides aren't your top priority, though, there's always plenty of room in the wave pool at Melt Away Bay. A relaxing inner-tube ride on Cross Country Creek is a cool alternative as well.

Blizzard Beach A to Z

To research prices, get advice from other travelers, and book travel arrangements, visit www.fodors.com.

DISABILITIES & ACCESSIBILITY
Most paths are flat and level. If you use a wheelchair, you'll also be able to float in **Cross Country Creek,** provided you can transfer to a large inner tube. Other guests with limited mobility might also be able to use the inner tubes at some of the park's tamer slides. A limited number of wheelchairs are available near the park entrance and are free if you leave an ID.

DRESSING ROOMS & LOCKERS
Dressing rooms are in the Village area, just inside the main entrance. There are showers and rest rooms here as well. Lockers are strategically located near the entrance, next to Snowless Joe's Rentals and near Tike's Peak, the children's area (more convenient if you have little swim-skiers in tow). At Snowless Joe's it costs $5 to rent a small locker, $7 for a large one; plus a $2 deposit required. Only small lockers are available at Tike's Peak. Rest rooms are conveniently located throughout the park; there are facilities in the Village area near the entrance, in Lottawatta Lodge, at the Ski Patrol Training Camp, and just past the Melt Away Bay beach area. Towels are available for rent at Snowless Joe's ($1), but they're tiny. If you care, buy a proper beach towel in the Beach Haus or bring your own.

FIRST AID
The First-Aid Stand, overseen by a registered nurse, is in the Village, between Lottawatta Lodge and the Beach Haus.

LOST THINGS & PEOPLE
Start your visit by naming a specific meeting place and time. Instruct your youngsters to let any lifeguard know if they get lost. If they do get lost, don't panic: head for Snowless Joe's, local lost-children central.

PICNICKING
Glass containers and bringing in your own alcoholic beverages are not allowed, but picnicking is, and several areas are good, most notably the terrace outside Lottawatta Lodge and its environs. Coolers must be small enough for one person to handle; otherwise, you won't be able to take them into the park.

GROUPS IN WALT DISNEY WORLD

WHETHER YOU'RE TRAVELING with relatives, friends, coworkers, club members, or any other kind of group, getting everyone to agree on what to do can be tricky. Preschoolers may be content on Dumbo, but thrill-seekers will want faster-paced rides. And grandparents might rather play golf than traipse around a water park. Likewise, when it comes to meals, everyone's preferences and dietary concerns may not coincide. And those doing the planning may find themselves also doing the mediating. That's where Disney's Magical Gatherings program comes in. Designed to help groups travel well together, the program, which is accessible online and over the phone, offers lots of free planning tips, plus a planner that can help you decide what to do together and when to split up.

Start by visiting Disney's Magical Gatherings Web site at ⊕ www. disneyworld.com/magicalgatherings. With its private chat rooms, your companions can "meet" virtually to discuss the trip. You can create polls to find out about your group's common interests and use the "My Favorites" feature to list everyone's can't-miss attractions. The "Group Favorites" button tabulates popular choices, so you can draft an itinerary that suits everyone.

Additionally, specially trained vacation planners can help you book a special tour, dinner reservation, or even a photo shoot just for your group. For example, if you have eight or more people in your group and are staying at a WDW resort, you can sign up for one of Disney's four Grand Gatherings. The **Good Morning Gathering** ($24.99; $11.99 ages 3 to 9) at Tony's Town Square Restaurant in the Magic Kingdom is an interactive sit-down breakfast hosted by a cast of colorful characters. You get to sing, dance, and play group games with Goofy, Pluto, and Chip and Dale, and you even meet privately with Mickey Mouse himself. The **Safari Celebration Dinner** ($59.99; $19.99 ages 3 to 9) in the Animal Kingdom begins with a guided safari through the park's jungles and rolling savanna. Afterward, you head to Tusker House Restaurant for a family-style dinner and show with African singers, drummers, story-tellers, and live animals. Timon, of The Lion King, and Turk, of Tarzan, make special appearances.

At the **International Storybook Dinner** ($59.99; $19.99 ages 3 to 9) in Epcot's Odyssey Restaurant, you dine on international cuisine in a fairy-tale setting. A costumed "magical bookmark" tells the story of Alice in Wonderland, and Alice actually pops out of the book to say hello in person. After dinner you are led outside to a private viewing area where you can watch the IllumiNations nighttime spectacular. For a cruise and an after-dinner treat, meet at the Contemporary resort for the **Magical Fireworks Voyage** ($32.99 $14.99 ages 3 to 9), which includes a dessert buffet. Captain Hook and Mr. Smee playfully capture your crew and usher you onto a boat commandeered by Patch the Pirate. But don't worry about walking the plank—you'll be too busy singing seafaring songs and playing trivia games as you cruise the Seven Seas Lagoon. You get to watch the Electrical Water Pageant and the Wishes fireworks extravaganza from the boat. On the way back to shore, Patch regales you with tales of Peter Pan, who'll be waiting at the dock to sign autographs and pose for pictures.

Book your gathering at least 90 days prior to your visit by calling ☎ 407/934-7639.

SUPPLIES

Personal flotation devices, better known as life jackets, are available free to children and adults at **Snowless Joe's** (leave your ID and a $25 deposit with an attendant until you return them). You can't rent inner tubes here: they're provided at the rides.

Sunglasses, sunscreen, bathing suits, waterproof disposable cameras, and other sundries are available at the **Beach Haus,** along with Blizzard Beach logo merchandise. Check out the ski equipment hanging from the ceiling. The **Sled Cart,** a kiosk-style shop, sells souvenirs, suntan lotion, and water toys.

VISITOR INFORMATION

Disney staffers at the Guest Relations window, to the left of the ticket booth as you enter the park, can answer most of your questions. Each year, the park closes for several weeks during the fall or winter months for routine maintenance and refurbishment. For the park's days of operation, call or check the disneyworld.com web site.

🚩 **Blizzard Beach** ☎ 407/824–4321 ⊕ www.disneyworld.com.

AND THERE'S MORE

DisneyQuest

This five-story interactive indoor theme park in Downtown Disney West Side is a virtual kingdom of attractions and adventures in a single building. Here Disney stories and characters come to life in a bold, interactive way—you not only partake of the magic, you're immersed in it. It's a wonderful, unique place to cool off on a hot summer day or to sit out an afternoon thunderstorm. To avoid crowds, arrive when it opens, usually at 11:30 AM, but some days earlier (call to verify). Its location in the middle of an entertainment and shopping complex ensures crowds after dark. Plan to stay for at least four hours or longer to get the most of your one-time admission—The Cheesecake Factory Express restaurant is inside so you can have lunch or dinner and then get back to the virtual fun. Be warned: your kids won't want to leave. Bring along some aspirin just in case you develop a case of virtual overload.

You begin your journey at the Ventureport after exiting the elevator, here known as the Cybrolator. The Ventureport serves as a crossroads within the complex, and from there you can go on to enter any one of four distinct entertainment environments, or "zones": the Explore Zone, the Score Zone, the Create Zone, and the Replay Zone. One price gains you admission to the building and allows you entrance to all of the attractions, excluding prize play games.

The Explore Zone

In this virtual adventureland, you're immersed in exotic and ancient locales. You can fly through the streets of Agrabah with the help of a virtual-reality helmet on a hunt to release the genie on Aladdin's Magic Carpet Ride. Then take a Virtual Jungle Cruise down the roiling rapids of a prehistoric world and paddle (yes, *really* paddle) to adventure in the midst of volcanoes, carnivorous dinosaurs, and other Cretaceous threats. End your stay in this zone at Pirates of the Caribbean: Battle for Buccaneer Gold, where you and the gang must brave the high seas from the helm of your ship, sinking pirate ships and acquiring treasure.

The Score Zone

The Score Zone is where you can match wits and game-playing skills against the best. Battling supervillains takes more physical energy than you'd think as you fly, headset firmly intact, through a 3-D comic world in Ride the Comix. Escape evil aliens and rescue stranded colonists with your crew during Invasion! An Alien Encounter. Or hip-check your friends in a life-size Mighty Ducks Pinball Slam game.

The Create Zone

Let your creative juices flow in this studio of expression and invention. You can learn the secrets of Disney animation at the Animation Academy, where magic overload led one man who attended to propose to his girl-friend—she said yes! Create your own twisted masterpiece at Sid's Create-A-Toy, based on the popular animated film *Toy Story*. Make yourself over, and then morph your image to keep 'em laughing at the Magic Mirror. Or, at Living Easels, create a *living* painting on a giant electronic screen. All of the above creative ventures are quite popular with the elementary-school crowd. The real thrills await at Cyberspace Mountain, where you can design your own roller coaster on a computer screen, then climb aboard a 360-degree pitch-and-roll simulator for the ride of your dreams. At Songmaker, produce your own hit in a sound booth equipped with a computer and audio system that helps incorporate all kinds of sounds into your recording (DisneyQuest claims there are 2 billion possible combinations of songs, lyrics, and musical styles). You can buy what you've created at the Create Zone counter.

The Replay Zone

The classic "prize play" machines are here, with futuristic twists. Play SkeeBall and Whack A Alien for 50¢ a pop by purchasing "play cards" of $5, $10, or $20, and earn tickets that are redeemable for prizes. Or sit with a partner in an asteroid cannon–equipped bumper car and blast others to make their cars do a 360-degree spin in Buzz Lightyear's As-troBlaster. Cash in your winnings for candy, stuffed animals, mugs, T-shirts, and other prizes at the Midway on the Moon.

> **need a break?**

At **Food Quest and Wonderland Café** you'll find varied soups, salads, sandwiches, pastas, pizza, and some of the best wraps around at this terrific eatery operated by the Cheesecake Factory Express. Desserts are worth the indulgence—cheesecake with strawberries, ice-cream treats, and chocolate pastries will rev you up for more virtual game play. Surf Disney's limited-access Web at your table—there's a computer terminal in many of the booths. You don't need a reservation to eat here, but you do need to pay the price of admission.

DisneyQuest A to Z

To research prices, get advice from other travelers, and book travel arrangements, visit www.fodors.com.

ADMISSION   Tickets to DisneyQuest cost $34 for adults and $28 for children ages three to nine, not including sales tax.

DISABILITIES &   DisneyQuest attractions all are wheelchair accessible, but most require
ACCESSIBILITY   transfer from wheelchair to the attraction itself, including the virtual thrill ride Cyberspace Mountain. You can, however, wheel right on to Pirates of the Caribbean: Battle for Buccaneer Gold, Aladdin's Magic Carpet Ride, and Mighty Ducks Pinball Slam. Wheelchairs can be rented ($7 plus $20 deposit) at the Downtown Disney Guest Services locations at Downtown Disney West Side or Marketplace. Electronic wheelchairs cost $30 per day and require a major credit card. If you have your own wheelchair, it would pay to bring it along. Guide dogs are permitted in all areas but are unable to ride several attractions.

VISITOR   Strollers are *not* permitted at DisneyQuest, which really doesn't provide
INFORMATION   much for very small children, though baby-changing stations are in both men's and women's rest rooms.

As you enter the building, children will pass a height check and if they're at least 51″ tall receive a wristband that allows access to all rides. The four attractions that have height requirements are Cyberspace Mountain (51″), Buzz Lightyear's Astro Blaster (51″), Mighty Ducks Pinball Slam (48″), and Pirates of the Caribbean: Battle for Buccaneer Gold (35″).

The Lost & Found is at the **Guest Services** window, film can be purchased at the Emporium, and cash is available at ATMs inside the House of Blues merchandise shop not far from the DisneyQuest entrance and inside Wetzel's Pretzels near the bridge to Pleasure Island.

Lost children are first walked through the building accompanied by a security guard. If that method is not successful, then the children are taken to the manager's office to wait for their mom or dad.

Downtown Disney

Downtown Disney is really three entertainment areas in one, with attractions, theaters, nightclubs, shopping, and dining. First, there's **West Side** with Cirque du Soleil and its breathtaking "La Nouba" performances five evenings a week; DisneyQuest; and the plush AMC movie theaters. The West Side's terrific lineup of shops and boutiques includes Guitar Gallery, Virgin Megastore, and the wonderful Hoypoloi fine art and jewelry gallery. For food and entertainment, consider a meal at the House of Blues, Wolfgang Puck Café, Bongos Cuban Café, or Planet Hollywood.

Then, there's **Pleasure Island,** which is primarily an evening entertainment complex geared toward adults (those under 18 are admitted if accompanied by an adult). The admission cost of $21.95 gets you into all the clubs. You'll find destinations like the improv Comedy Warehouse and the richly decorated Adventurer's Club. At Motion, a DJ spins hip-hop. Other clubs play rock and roll, disco, and alternative—serious dancers shouldn't miss Mannequins, with its turntable dance floor, dramatic lighting, and sleek mannequin displays. Dancers who just want to have fun should squeeze onto the dance floor at 8Trax, where pop artists of the

'70s are featured in a lava-lamp, disco-ball setting. On the "street" outside, video displays, carnival games, and a midnight every-night-is-New-Year's-Eve fireworks show make this party central. Photo ID is required for the wristband that lets you purchase alcoholic drinks.

Finally, there's the **Marketplace,** which has some of the wildest shops and restaurants in Walt Disney World. Whatever you haven't found in the theme parks you'll probably find here. If you have kids, and even if you don't, you should visit World of Disney, the largest Disney-character store on the planet; and Once Upon a Toy, which has the latest theme-park editions of games and toys (check out the "it's a small world" Play-Doh set and Haunted Mansion CLUE), plus play castles, trains, plush critters, and even mini-monorail sets. The Lego Imagination Center sells LEGO sets of all sizes, and there's a free outdoor LEGO building area with benches where parents can rest and watch. Disney's Wonderful World of Memories has scrapbooking and photo-album supplies, and a kiddie train ride pleases little passengers throughout the day.

Disney's BoardWalk

If you have fond memories of strolling along an Atlantic coast boardwalk, hearing the bumpity-bump of bicycle tires on the boards, smelling fresh-baked pizza pies, and watching lovers stroll hand-in-hand, you're in for a heaping dose of nostalgia at Disney's BoardWalk in the Epcot resort area. Even if you've never known such pleasures, it's worth a visit here to experience what you've missed. Much smaller than Downtown Disney, BoardWalk spans a portion of lakefront at the BoardWalk Inn and Villas and offers good restaurants, a sports bar, a dance hall, a piano bar, and sporadic outdoor performances.

The Flying Fish Café is known for first-rate dining and serves up signature entrées that include a potato-wrapped Florida red snapper. Spoodles is a fun family experience, with Mediterranean specialties and even a take-out pizza window. Sports fans flock to ESPN Club, where even the bathrooms have TV monitors. You can rent a bicycle for two or a cycling surrey if you want to work off some vacation calories.

A DJ runs the party nightly at the Atlantic Dance hall, with its spacious dance floor and waterfront balcony. At Jellyrolls, you can sing along with dueling pianos (there's a $7 cover charge after 7 PM). Boardwalk is the perfect place for low-key fun—you can play a few carnival games, duck into an art gallery or boutique, and enjoy a free view from the Crescent Lake bridge of IllumiNations at nearby Epcot.

Disney's Wide World of Sports

In the mid 1990s, seizing on the public's seemingly endless fascination with sports, Disney officials built an all-purpose, international sports complex—Disney's Wide World of Sports. Although the facilities aren't designed to provide a day's worth of entertainment, there are plenty of fun events and activities here for the sports enthusiast in your group.

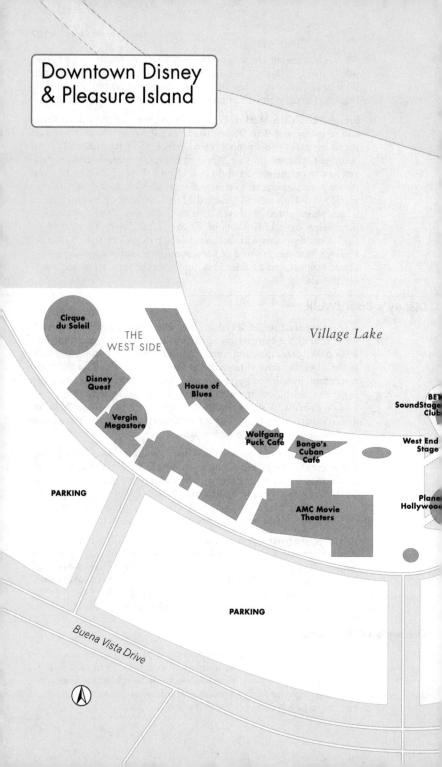

Downtown Disney
& Pleasure Island

Village Lake

Cirque
du Soleil

THE
WEST SIDE

Disney
Quest

House of
Blues

Vergin
Megastore

Wolfgang
Puck Café

Bongo's
Cuban
Café

BET
SoundStage
Club

West End
Stage

PARKING

AMC Movie
Theaters

Plane
Hollywood

PARKING

Buena Vista Drive

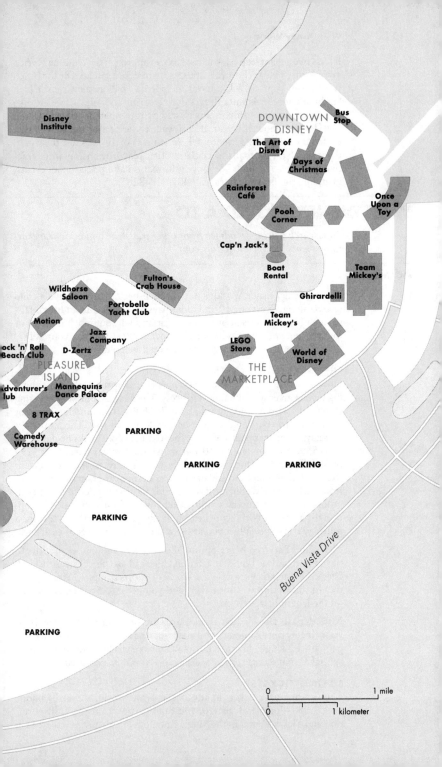

It feels like a giant leap back in time as you approach the old-time Florida architecture that anchors this 200-acre manicured spread. For the bench warmers in your crowd, options include baseball at the Cracker Jack Stadium with the Atlanta Braves during spring training. There are also dozens of championship events hosted by the Amateur Athletic Union (AAU) throughout the year. If you want to be part of the action, sign up for the Sports Experience, where athletes of all ages test their mettle at baseball, football, soccer, and other play stations on an interactive sports playground. For more information and prices on all events, including the Braves games, call 407/828–3267.

WALT DISNEY WORLD A TO Z

To research prices, get advice from other travelers, and book travel arrangements, visit www.fodors.com.

Admission

Visiting Walt Disney World is not cheap, especially if you have a child or two along. Everyone 10 and older pays adult price. In addition, Disney changes its prices about once a year and without much notice. For that reason, you may save yourself a few bucks if you buy your WDW tickets as soon as you know for sure you'll be going.

THE TICKETING SYSTEM

Once you've decided to take the plunge, Disney fortunately makes buying tickets an easy and painless process. The **Magic Your Way** ticketing system, debuted in 2005, is all about flexibility. You can literally tailor your ticket to your interests and desired length of stay. The more days you stay, the greater your savings on per-day ticket prices. A one-day ticket costs $59.75 for anyone age 10 and up, while a five-day ticket costs $193 or $38.60 per day. Once you decide how many days to stay, you'll want to decide what options to add on. The **Park Hopper** option lets you move from park to park within the day and adds $35 to the price of your ticket, no matter how many days your ticket covers. So it's an expensive option for a one- or two-day ticket, but it can be well worth the cost for a four-day trip, especially if you know what you want to see at each park.

The **Water Parks & More** option allows a certain number of visits to the minor parks: Typhoon Lagoon, Blizzard Beach, Pleasure Island, DisneyQuest and Disney's Wide World of Sports complex. You pay $45 to add this option to your ticket, and you get 2 to 5 visits, depending on the length of your stay.

Note that all Disney admission passes are nontransferable. The ID is your fingerprint. Although you slide your pass through the reader like people with single-day tickets, you also have to slip your finger into a special V-shape fingerprint reader before you'll be admitted.

BUYING TICKETS

You can buy park tickets in advance at disneyworld.com or by phone at 407/934–7638. In Orlando, you can buy tickets at the Transportation and Ticket Center in the Magic Kingdom (also known as the TTC);

Magic Your Way Price Chart

TICKET OPTIONS

	10-DAY	7-DAY	6-DAY	5-DAY	4-DAY	3-DAY	2-DAY	1-DAY
BASE TICKET								
Ages 10-up	$208	$199	$196	$193	$185	$171	$119	$59.75
Ages 3-9	$167	$160	$157	$155	$148	$137	$96	$48

Base Ticket *admits guest to one of the four major theme parks per day's use. Park choices are: Magic Kingdom, Epcot, Disney-MGM Studios, Disney's Animal Kingdom.*

ADD: Park Hopper	$35	$35	$35	$35	$35	$35	$35	$35

Park Hopper option entitles guest to visit more than one theme park per day's use. Park choices are any combination of Magic Kingdom, Epcot, Disney-MGM Studios, Disney's Animal Kingdom.

ADD: Water Parks & More	$45 5 visits	$45 5 visits	$45 4 visits	$45 3 visits	$45 3 visits	$45 2 visits	$45 2 visits	$45 2 visits

Water Parks & More option entitles guest to a specified number of visits (from 2 to 5) to a choice of entertainment and recreation venues. Choices are Blizzard Beach, Typhoon Lagoon, DisneyQuest, Pleasure Island, and Wide World of Sports.

ADD: No expiration	$100	$55	$45	$35	$15	$10	$10	n/a

No expiration means that unused admissions on a ticket may be used any time in the future. Without this option, tickets expire 14 days after first use.

MINOR PARKS AND ATTRACTIONS

TICKET	AGES 10-UP	AGES 3-9
Typhoon Lagoon or Blizzard Beach 1-Day 1-Park	$34	$28
DisneyQuest 1-Day	$34	$28
Disney's Wide World of Sports	$10.05	$7.48
Cirque du Soleil's La Nouba	$59-$87	$44-$65
Pleasure Island 1-Night Multi-Club Ticket	$20.95	$20.95

Admission to Pleasure Island clubs is restricted to guests 18 or older unless accompanied by an adult 21 or older. For some clubs all guests must be 21 or older.

* All prices are subject to Florida sales tax.

at ticket booths in front of the other theme-park entrances; in all on-site resorts if you're a registered guest; at the Walt Disney World kiosk on the second floor of the main terminal at Orlando International Airport; and at various hotels and other sites around Orlando. American Express, Visa, and MasterCard are accepted, as are cash, personal checks with ID, and traveler's checks.

DISCOUNTS

If you are or have been a member of the U.S. or foreign military, you're eligible for discount tickets, and you can stay at the on-site Shades of Green Resort for a fraction of what it costs to stay at other Disney resorts.

⚑ **Shades of Green Resort** ☎ 407/824-1403 ⊕ www.shadesofgreen.org

HAND STAMPS

If you want to leave any Disney park and return on the same day, be sure to have your hand stamped on the way out. You'll need both your ticket and the hand stamp to be readmitted.

⚑ **Orlando Convention & Visitors' Bureau** ⊠ 8723 International Dr. ☎ 407/363-5871. **Ticket Mail Order Dept. Walt Disney World** ✉ Box 10000, Lake Buena Vista, FL 32830 ⊕ www.disneyworld.com.

Arriving & Departing by Car

Walt Disney World has five exits off I–4. For the Magic Kingdom, Disney–MGM Studios, Disney's Animal Kingdom, Fort Wilderness, and the rest of the Magic Kingdom resort area, take the one marked **Magic Kingdom–U.S. 192 (Exit 64B)**. From here, it's a 4-mi drive along Disney's main entrance road to the toll gate, and another mile to the parking area; during peak vacation periods, be prepared for serious bumper-to-bumper traffic both on I–4 nearing the U.S. 192 exit and on U.S. 192 itself. A less-congested route to the theme parks and other WDW venues is via the exit marked **Epcot/Downtown Disney (Exit 67)**, 4 mi west of Exit 64.

Exit 65 will take you directly to Disney's Animal Kingdom and Wide World of Sports as well as the Animal Kingdom resort area via the Osceola Parkway.

For access to Downtown Disney (including the Marketplace, DisneyQuest, Pleasure Island, and West Side), as well as to Typhoon Lagoon, the Crossroads Shopping Center, and the establishments on Hotel Plaza Boulevard, get off at **Route 535–Lake Buena Vista (Exit 68)**.

The exit marked **Epcot–Downtown Disney (Exit 67)** is the one to use if you're bound for those destinations or for hotels in the Epcot and Downtown Disney resort areas; you can also get to Typhoon Lagoon and the Studios from here.

CAR CARE

The gas islands at the **Disney Car Care Center** near the Magic Kingdom are open daily until 90 minutes after the Magic Kingdom closes. You can also gas up on Buena Vista Drive near Disney's BoardWalk and in the Downtown Disney area across from Pleasure Island. In past years, prices here were always more than 20¢ higher per gallon than off-property; since Hess Express took over the three stations the rates have been in sync with (and sometimes even lower than) rates in other parts of town.

PARKING

Every theme park has a parking lot—and all are huge. Sections of the Magic Kingdom lot are named for Disney characters; Epcot's highlights modes of exploration; those at the Studios are named Stage, Music, Film, and Dance; and the Animal Kingdom's sound like Beanie Baby names—Unicorn, Butterfly, and so on. Although in theory Goofy 45 is unforgettable, by the end of the day, you'll be so goofy with eating and shopping and riding that you'll swear that you parked in Sleepy. When you board the tram, write down your location and keep it in a pocket. Trams make frequent trips between the parking area and the parks' turnstile areas. No valet parking is available for Walt Disney World theme parks.

Although valet parking is available at Downtown Disney, the congestion there is sometimes such that it may be faster to park in Siberia and walk. (Hint: Arrive at Downtown Disney early in the evening—around 6 PM—and you'll get a much closer parking space; you'll also avoid long restaurant lines.) At Disney's BoardWalk, you park in the hotel lot, where valets are available as well.

FEES For each major theme-park lot, admission is $8 for cars, $9 for RVs and campers, and free to those staying at Walt Disney World resorts who have their room card with them. Save your receipt; if you want to visit another park the same day, you won't have to pay to park twice. Parking is always free at Typhoon Lagoon, Blizzard Beach, Downtown Disney, and Disney's BoardWalk. You can valet park at BoardWalk for $7.

Dining

Priority-seating reservations are essential for most full-service restaurants. *See* Chapter 5 for descriptions of all Walt Disney World dining options.

Fresh fruits, salads, steamed vegetables, and low-fat foods are more widely available than you might expect. If you have special dietary requirements such as no sodium, kosher, or others—arrange meals 24 hours in advance by calling the Disney Reservation Center or ask for a listing of restaurants prepared to serve special-order meals without notice. Disney's new Balanced Menu Choices include creative vegetarian dishes, no-sugar-added offerings (including lemonade), and even reduced-portion options for indulgences like popcorn, ice cream, and french fries. Kids can choose veggies and dip, turkey wrap "pinwheels," and chicken nuggets, plus fruit or applesauce.
🗂 **Disney Reservation Center** ☎ 407/939-3463.

BEER, WINE & SPIRITS

The Magic Kingdom's no-liquor policy, a Walt Disney tradition that seems almost quaint in this day and age, does not extend to the rest of Walt Disney World, and in fact, most restaurants and watering holes, particularly those in the on-site hotels, mix elaborate fantasy drinks based on fruit juices or flavored with liqueurs.

Disabilities & Accessibility

Attractions in all the Disney parks typically have both a visual element that makes them appealing without sound and an audio element that conveys the charm even without the visuals; many are accessible by guests using wheelchairs, and most are accessible by guests with some mobility. Guide dogs and service animals are permitted, unless a ride or special effect could spook or traumatize the animal.

At many rides and attractions, guests with mobility, hearing, and visual disabilities use accessible entrances; to find out where to enter or ask specific questions, see any host or hostess.

WDW's "Guidebook for Guests with Disabilities" details many specific challenges and identifies the special entrances. In addition, story notes, scripts, and song lyrics are available at attractions—just ask an attractions host, who will provide a binder with the information you need. Ask for the "Guidebook for Guests with Disabilities" and other aids at the main visitor information desks in every park. There, you can also get **cassette tapes and portable players** that provide audio narration for most attractions (no charge, but refundable deposit required), as well as **wireless handheld captioning devices.** There are also **wheelchair rentals** in every park, and services that include American Sign Language interpretation.

Entertainment

Live entertainment adds texture to visits to the Disney theme parks and can often be a high point of the theme-park experience. Although the jokes may be occasionally silly, the humor broad, and the themes sometimes excessively wholesome, the level of professionalism is high and the energy of the performers unquestionable. Don't fail to pick up a "Times Guide & New Information" flyer on your way into the theme parks, and keep the schedules in mind as you make your way around.

The FASTPASS System

Imagine taking a trip to Disney and managing to avoid most of the lines. FASTPASS is your ticket to this terrific scenario, and it's included in regular park admission. You insert your theme-park ticket into a special FASTPASS turnstile. Out comes a FASTPASS ticket, printed with a one-hour window of time during which you can return to the attraction. In the meantime you're free to enjoy the other attractions in the park. At the appointed time you return to the attraction, head for the FASTPASS entrance, and proceed to the preshow or boarding area with little or no wait. It's important to note that once you've made one FASTPASS appointment you cannot make another until you're within the window of time for your first appointment.

Getting Around

Walt Disney World has its own free transportation system, including buses, trams, monorail trains, and boats, which can get you wherever you want to go. It's fairly simple once you get the hang of it.

In general, allow up to an hour to travel between sites on Disney property. If you use your own car to get around, you might save the time you would have spent waiting for buses or making several stops before you reach your destination. On the other hand, using Disney transportation will save you parking fees and the walk through the parking lot at day's end.

BY BOAT

Motor launches connect WDW destinations on waterways. Specifically, they operate from the Epcot resorts—except the Caribbean Beach—to the Studios and Epcot; between Bay Lake and the Magic Kingdom; and also between Fort Wilderness, the Wilderness Lodge, and the Polynesian, Contemporary, and Grand Floridian resorts. Launches from Old Key West, Saratoga Springs, and Port Orleans all travel to Downtown Disney, as well.

BY BUS

Buses provide direct service from every on-site resort to both major and minor theme parks, and express buses go directly between the major theme parks. You can go directly from or make connections at Downtown Disney, Epcot, and the Epcot resorts, including the Yacht and Beach Clubs, BoardWalk, the Caribbean Beach Resort, the Swan, and the Dolphin, as well as to Disney's Animal Kingdom and the Animal Kingdom resorts (the Animal Kingdom Lodge, the All-Star, and Coronado Springs resorts).

Buses to the Magic Kingdom all go straight to the turnstiles, allowing you to avoid the extra step of boarding a monorail or boat at the Ticket and Transportation Center (TTC) to get to the front of the Kingdom.

BY MONORAIL

The elevated monorail serves many important destinations. It has two loops: one linking the Magic Kingdom, TTC, and a handful of resorts (including the Contemporary, the Grand Floridian, and the Polynesian), the other looping from the TTC directly to Epcot. Before this monorail line pulls into the station, the elevated track passes through Future World—Epcot's northern half—and circles the giant silver geosphere housing the Spaceship Earth ride to give you a preview of what you'll see.

BY TRAM

Trams operate from the parking lot to the entrance of each theme park. If you parked fairly close in, though, you may save time, especially at park closing time, by walking.

Group Trips

Groups of eight or more can take advantage of Disney's new **Magical Gatherings** program by calling WDW Information at 407/824–4321 or using online vacation-planning tools at www.disneyworld.com/magicalgatherings. The program offers special group packages that include entertainment and meals tailored to your group's interest.

Guided Tours

For park-specific guided tours, *see* Guided Tours in the individual park A to Z sections, *above*.

For a personal tour of Walt Disney World by the main mouse himself, consider buying a **Pal Mickey.** These 10-inch stuffed Mickey toys represent Disney's latest exploration of wireless technology and its many uses. Equipped with sensors and a soundtrack, Pal Mickey periodically tells you very useful bits of information as you tour the parks. For example, he can tell you the minimum-height restriction of a certain ride as you approach it, and he can remind you when to take your place before shows and parades. When he has a message to share, Mickey giggles and the toy vibrates. To hear the message, you just squeeze his hand. You can always ignore the giggle or turn the toy off if you don't want to hear a message. You can purchase Pal Mickey for $60. Of course, Pal Mickey won't talk anymore once you're outside Walt Disney World.

Disney offers customized **VIP Tour Services** for those who don't mind shelling out a minimum of $625 or more for a day to avoid planning and get good seats at parades and shows. VIP tours don't help you skip lines, but they do help you maximize your time. Tour guides create efficient schedules for your visit depending on your interests and lead you around the parks to the attractions you want to see. The charge is $125 per hour (or $95 an hour for Disney resort guests during non-peak times of the year), and there's a five-hour tour minimum. During holiday peaks, there's a six-hour minimum. You can book up to 90 days in advance; there's a two-hour charge if you don't cancel at least 48 hours in advance. Tour guides can lead groups of up to 10 people.

🔲 **Disney Special Activities** ☎ 407/560-4033

Hours

Operating hours for the Magic Kingdom, Epcot, the Studios, and Animal Kingdom vary throughout the year and change for school and legal holidays. In general, the longest days are during prime summer months and over the year-end holidays, when the Magic Kingdom may be open as late as 10 or 11, later on New Year's Eve; Epcot is open until 9 or 9:30 in the World Showcase area and at several Future World attractions, the Studios until 7 or 8:30. At other times, the Magic Kingdom closes around 7 or 8—but there are variations, so call ahead.

The Animal Kingdom typically opens at 9 and closes at 5, though during peak holiday seasons it may open at 8 and close at 7 or 8. Note that, in general, the Magic Kingdom, Epcot, and the Studios open at 9. (Epcot's World Showcase opens at 11). The parking lots open at least an hour before the parks do. If you arrive at the Magic Kingdom turnstiles before the official opening time, you can often breakfast in a restaurant on Main Street, which usually opens before the rest of the park, and be ready to dash to one of the popular attractions in other lands at Rope Drop, the Magic Kingdom's official opening time.

Hours at Typhoon Lagoon and Blizzard Beach are 9 or 10 to 5 daily (until 7—occasionally 10—in summer).

EXTRA MAGIC HOUR
The Extra Magic Hour program gives resort guests free early and late-night admission to certain parks on specified days—call ahead for information about each park's "magic hour" days to plan your early- and late-visit strategies.

Lost & Found

There are Lost & Found offices in the Magic Kingdom, at Epcot, in Disney–MGM Studios, and at Disney's Animal Kingdom. After one day, all items are sent to the Main Lost & Found office.

Disney's Animal Kingdom ☎ 407/824-2222. **Disney–MGM Studios Lost & Found** ☎ 407/560-3720. **Epcot Lost & Found** ☎ 407/560-7500. **Magic Kingdom Lost & Found** ✉ City Hall ☎ 407/824-4521. **Main Lost & Found** ✉ Magic Kingdom, Transportation and Ticket Center ☎ 407/824-4245.

Money Matters

The SunTrust branch in Lake Buena Vista is across the street from the Downtown Disney Marketplace (☎ 407/762-4786). Automatic teller machines are scattered throughout the Magic Kingdom, Epcot, the Studios, Animal Kingdom, and Downtown Disney. Currency exchange services are available at Guest Services in each major theme park.

Reservations

It's a good idea to make reservations (Disney calls it "priority" seating) early for restaurants in Walt Disney World, including the heavily booked Epcot restaurants. Tours and gold tee times require reservations, too.

Disney Reservation Center ☎ 407/939-3463. **Golf Reservations** ☎ 407/939-4653.

Strategies for Your Visit

- Make your dining reservations and purchase your park tickets before you leave home.

- Plan to arrive at the parks at least 30 minutes ahead of the published opening times, so that you can use the lockers, rent strollers, and otherwise take care of business before everyone else.

- If you stay at a Disney resort, you can gain early admission to the theme parks on certain days via the Extra Magic Hour program. A new twist on this popular perk allows resort guests to stay up to three hours later in certain parks on specified days. Check at your resort or call the WDW information line to find out about each park's Extra Magic Hour days—it's a great way to see high-demand attractions before the masses get there or after the crowds have departed.

- See the three-star attractions either first thing in the morning, at the end of the day, during a parade, or with a FASTPASS appointment.

- Even with FASTPASS, you may end up in a line or two. If you have children who aren't quite ready to amuse themselves by people-watching, pack handheld games and other lightweight diversions to keep boredom at bay and avoid stressful blow-ups.

- Eat in a restaurant that takes reservations, bring your own food (a big money- *and* time-saver), or have meals when everyone else is riding the rides and seeing the sights. Mealtime rush hours are from noon to 2 PM and again from 6 to 8 PM.

- Spend afternoons watching high-capacity sit-down shows or catching live entertainment—or leave the theme parks entirely for a swim in your hotel pool. Don't forget to have your hand stamped on the way out.

- When park-hopping, use your own car to save time. There can be 30-minute waits for park-provided bus transportation. Your parking pass is good at any of the theme parks.

- If you plan to take in Blizzard Beach or Typhoon Lagoon, go early in your visit (but not on a weekend). You may like it so much that you'll want to go again.

- If you have small children and a meal with the characters is in your plans, save it for the end of your trip, when your youngsters will have become accustomed to these large, sometimes startling figures.

- Familiarize yourself with all age and height restrictions. Ideally, you should measure young children ahead of time so they won't get excited about rides they're too short to experience.

- Call ahead to check on operating hours and parade times, which vary greatly throughout the year. While you're there, check the "Times Guide" flyers and Tip Boards in every park.

Visitor Information

For general WDW information, contact Guest Information or visit Guest Relations in any Disney resort. If you want to speak directly to someone at a specific Disney location, use the WDW Central Switchboard. To inquire about specific resort facilities or detailed park information, call the individual property via the switchboard. For accommodations and shows, call the Disney Reservation Center. One of the easiest ways to get Disney information is via the WDW Web site.
🔢 **Disney Reservation Center** ☎ 407/939-3463. **WDW Central Switchboard** ☎ 407/824-2222. **WDW Guest Information** ☎ 407/824-4321. **WDW Web site** ⊕ www.disneyworld.com.

Universal
Orlando

FODOR'S CHOICE

The Amazing Adventures of Spider-Man, *in Islands of Adventure*

Animal Planet Live!, *in Universal Studios*

Dudley Do-Right's Ripsaw Falls, *in Islands of Adventure*

Dueling Dragons, *in Islands of Adventure*

Eighth Voyage of Sindbad, *in Islands of Adventure*

Incredible Hulk Coaster, *in Islands of Adventure*

Universal Horror Make-Up Show, *in Universal Studios*

Updated by
Gary
McKechnie

UNIVERSAL AND DISNEY HAVE BEEN BATTLING for years to attract attention and park goers away from each other. From the outset it was a contest between Disney–MGM Studios and Universal to draw film fans and production crews. Disney opened earlier and had the lead, but Universal used the extra time to tweak old rides, design new ones, and within a few years it had hit its stride to out-dazzle Disney with Islands of Adventure. Then CityWalk was added to compete with Disney's Pleasure Island. When its three themed hotels opened in 1999, 2001, and 2002, Universal became a complete resort destination and a serious Disney competitor.

Borrowing a concept from Walt Disney World Resort, which encompasses theme parks and hotels, Universal Orlando Resort refers to the conglomeration of Universal Studios Florida (the original movie theme park), Islands of Adventure (the second theme park), CityWalk (the dining-shopping-nightclub complex), and three fabulous, themed, on-property hotels.

Halfway between Walt Disney World and downtown Orlando, and just off heavily trafficked International Drive, Universal is surprisingly secluded. You drive into one of two massive parking complexes (at 3.4 million square feet they're the largest on earth) and take moving walkways to the theme parks. Or, if you're staying at a Universal hotel, you can take a motor launch.

While Disney creates a fantasy world for people who love fairy tales, especially young children, Universal Orlando is geared toward older kids, adults, and anyone who enjoys pop culture. Movie and TV fans will love this place. But along with pop culture comes plenty of commercialism: cash-depleting distractions like rock-climbing walls, souvenir kiosks, and other such traces of tackiness. (To be fair, Disney is adding more of these things as well.) However, the commitment to creativity, presentation, and cutting-edge technology continues. New attractions like Revenge of the Mummy and *Fear Factor Live* already have a following. And when you want to forsake land-based action rides, you can head over to Wet 'n Wild (owned by Universal, but not a part of Universal Orlando Resort) for an afternoon of aquatic adrenaline and a place to cool off.

UNIVERSAL STUDIOS FLORIDA

Disney does an extraordinary job when it comes to showmanship, which may be why Universal Studios has taken advantage of its distinctly non-Disney heritage to add attitude to its presentations. Universal Studios performers aren't above tossing in sometimes risqué jokes and asides to get a cheap laugh.

Although this theme park has something for everyone, its primary appeal is to those who like loud, fast, high-energy attractions. If you want to calm down, there are quiet, shaded parks and a children's area where the adults can enjoy a respite while the kids are ripping through assorted playlands at 100 mph. There are some visitors, however, who miss the sort of connection that Disney forges with the public through its carefully developed history of singable songs and cuddly characters.

The park has 444 acres of stage sets, shops, reproductions of New York and San Francisco, and anonymous soundstages housing themed attractions, as well as genuine moviemaking paraphernalia. On the map, it's all neatly divided into six neighborhoods, which wrap themselves around a huge lagoon. The neighborhoods are **Production Central,** which spreads over the entire left side of the Plaza of the Stars; **New York,** with excellent street performances at 70 Delancey; the bicoastal **San Francisco/Amity; World Expo; Woody Woodpecker's KidZone;** and **Hollywood.**

Although the park looks easy to navigate on the map, a blitz tour through it can be difficult, since it involves a couple of long detours and some backtracking. If you need help, theme-park hosts are trained to provide more information than you thought you needed. Look to them for advice on moving around the park. Also keep in mind that some rides—and many restaurants—delay their openings until late morning, which may throw a kink in your perfectly laid plans. In fact, if you arrive when the gates open, it's kind of eerie walking around in a nearly deserted theme park where it's just you and the staff. To make sure you maximize your time and hit all the best rides, follow this chapter's Blitz Tour.

On busy days, when everything's working right, the **Universal Express** system (which predates Disney's FASTPASS) can reserve you a place in a virtual line to get you on more rides faster. They've also introduced **Universal Express PLUS,** a perk priced from $15 to $25 (depending on the season) that allows you to cut to the front of the line all day long without waiting for a previous Universal Express pass to expire. An important note: from using the Express system to staying at a Universal resort hotel to buying a VIP pass, do whatever you can to avoid waiting in line—it will improve your vacation considerably. If you're visiting Universal in the off-season (traditionally October, February, May and the weeks after Thanksgiving and before Christmas), keep in mind that some rides and restaurants are shuttered: they're sometimes marked with misleading RESERVED FOR SPECIAL EVENT signs to keep people away.

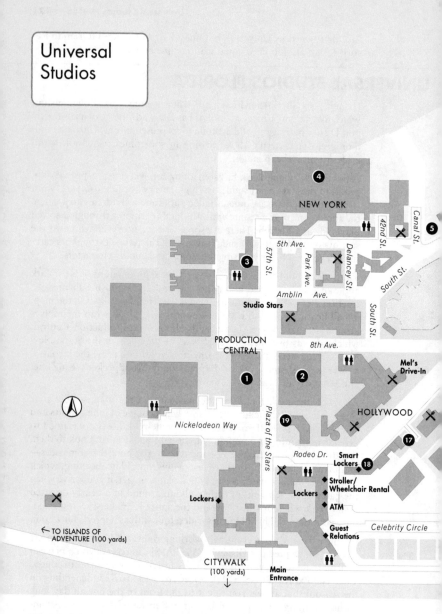

Universal
Studios

NEW YORK

42nd St.

Canal St.

5

5th Ave.

3

57th St.

Park Ave.

Delancey St.

South St.

Amblin Ave.

Studio Stars

South St.

**PRODUCTION
CENTRAL**

8th Ave.

1

2

Mel's
Drive-In

HOLLYWOOD

Nickelodeon Way

19

17

Rodeo Dr.

Smart
Lockers

18

Stroller/
Wheelchair Rental

Lockers ◆

Lockers ◆

ATM

◆

← TO ISLANDS OF
ADVENTURE (100 yards)

Guest
◆ Relations

Celebrity Circle

CITYWALK
(100 yards)
↓

**Main
Entrance**

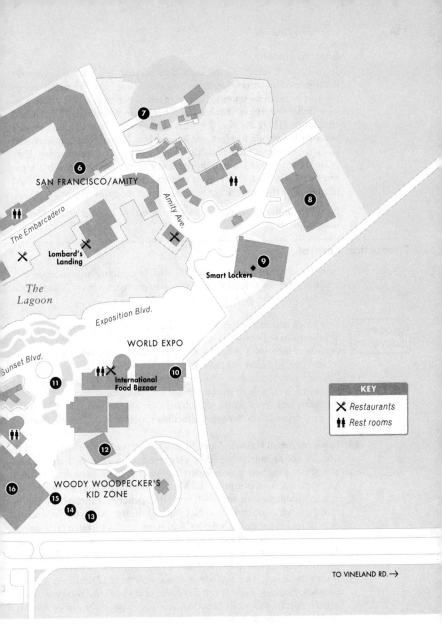

SAN FRANCISCO/AMITY

The Embarcadero

Lombard's
Landing

Amity Ave.

Smart Lockers

The
Lagoon

Exposition Blvd.

WORLD EXPO

Sunset Blvd.

International
Food Bazaar

WOODY WOODPECKER'S
KID ZONE

KEY
✕ Restaurants
👫 Rest rooms

TO VINELAND RD. →

Entertainment

If you're in Orlando at the right time of year, don't miss Universal's evening seasonal parties—most notably **Mardi Gras** (early February through early April), **Rock the Universe** (Christian music, September), the wildly popular **Halloween Horror Nights** (October), and **Grinchmas** (November/December). There are also CityWalk celebrations, including **Tony Hawk's Skate Bash, Orlando Beerfest,** and **Reggae Fest.** Except for Halloween and Rock the Universe, these festivals are included with park admission. They bring dazzling parades, live shows, and gastronomic delights. If a separate ticket is needed, then regular visitors are shooed out around 6 PM and need to have the event ticket to return when the gates reopen at 7 PM.

Numbers in the margin correspond to points of interest on the Universal Studios map.

Production Central

Composed of six huge warehouses with once-active soundstages, this area has plenty of attractions that appeal to pre-teens. Follow Nickelodeon Way left from the Plaza of the Stars.

 groovy souvenirs

Every ride and attraction has its affiliated theme shop, and it's important to remember that few attraction-specific souvenirs are sold outside of their own shop. So if you're struck by a movie- and ride-related pair of boxer shorts, seize the moment—and the shorts. Choice souvenirs include Universal Studios' trademark movie clipboard, available at the **Universal Studios Store,** on the Plaza of the Stars, and sepia prints of Richard Gere, Mel Gibson, and Marilyn Monroe from **Silver Screen Collectibles,** across from *Terminator 2.*

❶ **Jimmy Neutron's Nicktoon Blast.** Jimmy has arrived with a virtual-reality ride. The boy genius is joined by a large collection of Nickelodeon characters, including SpongeBob SquarePants and Rugrats, as he demonstrates his latest invention (the powerful Mark IV rocket). Things go awry when evil egg-shaped aliens make off with the rocket and threaten to dominate the world. Computer graphics and high-tech gizmos wow your senses as your rocket car dives, bounces, and skips its way through Nick-based cartoon settings. If your kids are regular Jimmy viewers or can sing SpongeBob's theme song, you have to do this ride. Be prepared: the show empties to a large gift shop selling Blues Clues, Dora the Explorer, Rugrats, Jimmy Neutron, and Sponge Bob souvenirs. ☞ *Duration: 8 mins. Crowds: Heaviest early in the day because it's near the entrance. Strategy: If you can talk your kids into waiting, come at the end of the day. Audience: All ages. Rating:* ★★★.

❷ **Shrek 4-D.** Mike Myers, Eddie Murphy, Cameron Diaz, and John Lithgow reprise their vocal roles as the swamp-dwelling ogre, Shrek; his faithful chatterbox companion, Donkey; Shrek's bride, Princess Fiona; and the vengeful Lord Farquaad in this animated 3-D saga. Grab your "Ogre-Vision" glasses and prepare for a tumultuous ride as Shrek tries to rescue Fiona from Lord Farquaad's ghost. If she won't be his wife in life, he figures she ought to be in death. The showdown puts you at the cen-

Best of the Park

If you want to attempt to see everything in one day, arrive early so that you can take care of business and see the top attractions before the park gets very crowded. Another way to increase your attraction quota is to ignore the faux Hollywood streets and the gift shops. During peak seasons, you can avoid long waits at major attractions with the highly recommended Universal Express and Express PLUS passes. These admit you to the attractions with little or no wait in line.

If you're one of the first people in the park and have plenty of early energy, circle the park twice to catch the A-list rides first, then pick up the B-list later. If you're dying to see **Shrek 4-D**, you'll need to hit it first (it's straight ahead on the right), and then backtrack and turn left to follow up with *Terminator 2 3-D*. Next, make tracks down the street to *Back to the Future . . . The Ride* while the lines are still at a minimum. As you continue counterclockwise, *Men in Black: Alien Attack* is next, followed by *Jaws, Earthquake—The Big One,* then the must-see *Revenge of the Mummy* attraction and, finally, back near the entrance to see *Twister . . . Ride It Out.*

You've just circled the park, and chances are the crowds have arrived. Based on your preferences, you can backtrack to pick up other entertaining attractions like **Jimmy Neutron's Nicktoon Blast, Animal Planet Live!,** and the **Universal Horror Make-Up Show.** The remaining rides and attractions are up to you. If the lines are short, all that remains are a tour of **Nickelodeon Studios,** the ride and show collection at *Woody Woodpecker's KidZone,* and **Lucy: A Tribute.** It's been a full day. Go get some rest.

On Rainy Days

Unless it's the week after Christmas, rainy days mean that the crowd will be noticeably thinner. Universal is one of the area's best bets in rainy weather—the park is fully operational, and there are many places to take shelter from downpours. Only a few street shows are canceled during bad weather.

---

ter of a 3-D movie adventure that includes a battle between fire-breathing dragons and a pretty scary plunge down a 1,000-foot deadly waterfall. Specially built theater seats and a few surprising sensory effects—mainly blasts of air and sprinkles of water—make the "4-D" part. Even with the show's capacity for 300, you'll probably have to wait in line an hour just to reach the preshow, which stars the Gingerbread Man and the Magic Mirror and is slightly entertaining, but at 13 to 15 minutes, lasts longer than the film itself. ☞ *Duration: 12 mins. Crowds: Will likely remain heavy as long as the movie remains popular. Strategy: Use a Universal Express pass if possible. Audience: All ages. Rating:* ★★.

Classic Monsters Cafe resembles a mad scientist's laboratory. The self-serve restaurant is open seasonally and offers wood-fired oven pizzas, pastas, chopped chef salads, four-cheese ravioli, and rotisserie chicken. Frankenstein's monster and other scary characters from vintage Universal films make the rounds of the tables as you eat. Be sure to check out the monster-meets-celebrity pictures at the entrance.

New York

This Universal take on the Big Apple recalls the original—right down to the cracked concrete and slightly stained cobblestones. Many of the sets you see are used in music videos and commercials. The **Blues Brothers Bluesmobile** regularly cruises the neighborhood, and musicians hop out to give scheduled performances at 70 Delancey. The show is surprisingly popular, with crowds congregating in the street for the live show.

❸ *Twister . . . Ride It Out.* This attraction accomplishes in two minutes what it took the highly contrived movie two long hours to do—and overall it's far more exciting. After enduring a slow line and a fairly boring lecture from the movie's stars about the destructive force of tornadoes, you're eventually ushered into a standing-room theater where a quiet country scene slowly transforms into a mighty scary make-believe windstorm. An ominous, five-story-high funnel cloud weaves in from the background to take center stage as 110 decibels of wind noise, crackling electrical lines, and shattered windows add to the confusion. A truck, signs, car, and cow are given frequent-flyer points as they sail across the stage; and even though you know you're in a building and more victims are waiting patiently outside, when the roof starts to fly away your first instinct is to head for the root cellar. Don't. Watch the whole thing and marvel at the special-effects masters who put this together—and tear it apart every few minutes. ☞ *Duration: 3 mins. Crowds: Expect very long lines. Strategy: You can use Universal Express here; otherwise, go first thing in the morning or at closing. Audience: All but young children, who may be frightened. Rating:* ★★.

❹ **Revenge of the Mummy.** Action, adventure, and horror—the staples of the *Mummy* movies—are in abundance in this spine-tingling thrill ride. First you enter the tomb of a pharaoh and walk through catacombs and past Egyptian artifacts before boarding a coaster car. Then you're taken into a haunted labyrinth, where you're given an opportunity to sell your soul for safety and riches. Opting against it, you're sent hurtling through underground passageways and Egyptian burial chambers on a $40 million ride that combines roller-coaster technology, pyrotechnics, and some super-scary skeletal warriors. Coaster junkies take note: you'll feel the 1.5 g-force as you fly uphill, and almost the entire ride takes place in the dark. ☞ *Duration: 3 mins. Crowds: Expect very long lines. Strategy: Use Universal Express or go first thing in the morning. Audience: All but young children, who may be frightened. Minimum Height: 48 ". Rating:* ★★★.

When to Go

Weekends are busiest here, with locals taking advantage of annual passes. Summers are usually crowded and hot and miserable all day, and the crowds return during spring break, the holidays, and special-event dates such as Halloween Horror Nights.

Hours change with the seasons, so call ahead or visit ⊕ www.universalorlando.com for current information.

Hit the Ground Running

If you aren't a resort guest, arrive in the parking lot 45 minutes early and head for the biggest attractions first.

Don't forget anything in your car. The parking garage is at least a half mile from both park entrances and a return round-trip will eat up valuable time.

If you're in a hurry to reach the park and don't feel you can stop for a bite, don't worry—there's a Starbucks, a Cinnabon, and other quick-bite eateries at CityWalk.

When entering the park, many people are attracted to the towering soundstages on the left. Head to the right, bypassing shops and restaurants, to avoid crowds, especially early in the day.

If you're overwhelmed by what to see and do, check with Guest Services, where Universal reps will create an itinerary for you, free of charge, based on your interests and available time.

When You're There

Set up a rendezvous point and time early in the day, just in case you and your companions get separated. Good places are in front of the Lucy Tribute near the entrance, by the stage area across from Mel's Drive-In, and by the seating area of Beetlejuice's Graveyard Revue.

Write down your parking location.

One of the best perks of riding solo, if you don't mind breaking up your group, is the advantage of going into the fast-moving Single Rider line.

Avoid backtracking if you're with small children. Universal is just too big. Expect kids to get wet at Fievel's Playland and absolutely drenched at Curious George Goes to Town—bring a bathing suit or change of clothing, and stash spare clothes in a nearby locker.

Head to the Front of the Line

Using a Universal Express pass is one of the best pieces of theme park intelligence you'll ever need to know. They're available during peak seasons to every guest at nearly every major ride and show. To obtain your free pass, go to a well-marked kiosk near the entrance of the ride, make a reservation for a time later in the day, go out and enjoy a meal or other lesser attraction, and then return at the time stamped on your pass for priority admission to the ride. To be fair, you'll have to use the first pass before you're able to get, or use, a second one.

The Universal Express PLUS pass is the for-profit version of the non-PLUS pass, and it offers the added bonus of front-of-line service without having to make an appointment. The pass is good for one express entrance at each ride all day. PLUS passes cost $25 in peak season and $15 in non-peak season.

Even better than the passes are the privileges you receive by staying at a Universal resort hotel. As a resort guest, your room key lets you bypass the crowds and go directly to the head of the line.

Another way to save time, if you don't mind breaking up your group, is to get into the Single Riders Line available at some attractions. The line moves quickly, as single riders fill up spaces left by uneven party numbers.

San Francisco/Amity

This area combines two sets. One part is the wharves and warehouses of San Francisco's Embarcadero and Fisherman's Wharf districts, with cable-car tracks and the distinctive redbrick Ghirardelli chocolate factory; the other is the New England fishing village terrorized in *Jaws*.

Shaiken's Souvenirs, on the Embarcadero, sells supercool Blues Brothers sunglasses and hats, among other movie apparel and accessories.

❺ Beetlejuice's Graveyard Revue. Whew! This is *some* show. In an amphitheater, a Transylvanian castle is the backdrop for Beetlejuice, who takes the stage and warms up the audience with his snappy lines, rude remarks, and sarcastic attitude. Then for some reason, which is hard or useless to remember, he introduces the stars of the show: Frankenstein's monster and his bride, the Werewolf, and Dracula. Thus begins a stage show never before seen on this planet. At some point, the monsters doff their traditional costumes in favor of glitzy and hip threads and sing the greatest hits of such diverse artists as Ricky Martin, Santana, Gloria Gaynor, and the Village People. Upping the weirdness factor, two Solid Gold–style dancers add sex appeal to the production. Despite a sense of pity for the performers (which once included *NSync's Joey Fatone and comedian Wayne Brady), this may be the only place you could see Frankenstein pretending to play an electric guitar and shout "Are you ready to rock, Orlando?" Don't be fooled by imitators. ☞ *Duration: 25 mins. Crowds: Steady, but high capacity of amphitheater means no waiting. Strategy: You can use Universal Express here; otherwise, go*

when ride lines are at capacity or after dark on hot days. **Audience:** *Older children and adults.* **Rating:** ★★.

 Earthquake—The Big One. Unless you volunteer as an extra, the preshow for onlookers can be a little slow. After Charlton Heston appears in a documentary about the 1973 movie and pre-selected volunteers participate in the making of a short disaster scene, you board a train and take a brief ride into a darkened San Francisco subway tunnel. This is where the heebie-jeebies kick in very, very quickly. The idea is that you've been cast as an extra for the "final scene," and when the train parks within the subterranean station, a few lights flash, the ground starts to shake, and suddenly you're smack dab in the middle of a two-minute, 8.3 Richter scale tremor that includes trembling earth, collapsing ceilings, blackouts, explosions, fire, and a massive underground flood coming from every angle. Don't miss it—unless you're claustrophobic or fear loud noises and crumbling buildings. In that case, *Earthquake* might put you over the edge. ☞ *Duration: 20 mins. Crowds: Heavy.* **Strategy:** *You can use Universal Express here; otherwise, go early or late.* **Audience:** *All but young children. No pregnant women or guests with heart, back, or neck problems or motion sickness. Minimum height: Without adult, 40".* **Rating:** ★★.

need a break? If you plan to have a full-service dinner in the evening, a quick burger may be all you need to make it through the day. **Richter's Burger Co.** lets you drop in and create your own burger or grilled chicken sandwich. Pretty quick, pretty convenient, and there are seats inside and out.

Jaws. This popular ride around a 7-acre lagoon has a fairly fast-moving line, but if it slows down you can always watch WJWS, a fake TV station airing joke commercials for products like used recreational vehicles and candied blowfish. You can guess what happens when you board your boat for a placid cruise around the bay. That's right. A 32-foot killer shark zeroes in at 20 mph, looking for a bite of your boat. Even though you know the shark is out there, things can still get pretty frightening with surprise attacks, explosions, and the teeth-grinding sounds on the side of your boat. And don't think you're safe just because you've reached the boathouse. The special effects on this ride really shine, especially the heat and fire from electrical explosions that could singe the eyebrows off Andy Rooney. Try it after dark for an extra thrill, and then cancel the following day's trip to the beach. ☞ *Duration: 7 mins. Crowds: Lines stay fairly long most of the day, but nothing like those at Shrek 4-D.* **Strategy:** *You can use Universal Express here; otherwise, go early or after dark for an even more terrifying experience—you can't see the attack as well, but can certainly hear and feel it.* **Audience:** *All but young children, who will be frightened. No pregnant women or guests with heart, back, or neck problems or motion sickness.* **Rating:** ★★★.

Fear Factor Live. If you can't get enough of watching people grasping for fame by eating worms, being sealed up in a roach-filled box, or wetting their pants as they're suspended from a helicopter, well, you can witness, and even participate in, stunts like this live at Universal's newest show, which opened in June 2005. The show is a perfect example of the type of collaboration that's possible between NBC and Universal (the two companies merged in 2004). If you dare to compete, sign up at the audience-participation desk near the park entrance. Of course, there are plenty of restrictions: you must be 18 or older, 5′ to 6′2″ tall, 110 to 220 lbs., and in good health. Apply as early as possible, as slots for the six daily shows are expected to fill quickly. If you're in the audience, you can still get in on the action by blasting contestants with water and air. Just don't blast your own dad—he'll be trying to win prizes like the Fear Factor Unleashed game for Xbox. ☞ *Duration: 25 min. Crowds: Expect large crowds as with all new attractions, though the 2,000-seat amphitheater means you should be able to get in close to showtime. Strategy: For a premium seat, arrive 30 minutes in advance or use Universal Express. Audience: All ages, though small children may not be entertained. Rating:* ★★★.

World Expo

The far corner of the park contains two of Universal Studios' most popular attractions, *Back to the Future . . .* **The Ride,** and *Men in Black:* **Alien Attack.** These two make this the section to see for major thrills.

❾ *Men in Black:* **Alien Attack.** This star attraction is billed as the world's first "ride-through video game." The preshow provides the story line: to earn membership into MIB, you and your colleagues have to round up aliens who escaped when their shuttle crashed on Earth. A laser gun is mounted on your futuristic car, but unfortunately, since the gun's red laser dot is just a pinpoint, it's hard to see where you've shot; so you go through the attraction not knowing if you're successfully hitting targets. Basically, you're on a trip through dark New York streets, firing blindly at aliens to rack up points. And they can fire back at you, sending your car spinning out of control. Be prepared to stomach the ending, when your car ends up swallowed by a 30-foot-high bug. Depending on your score, the ride ends with one of 35 endings, ranging from a hero's welcome to a loser's farewell. All in all, it's pretty exciting if a bit confusing, and you can compare scores with your friends at the end. ☞ *Duration: 4½ mins. Crowds: Up to an hour in busy season. Strategy: You can use Universal Express here; otherwise, go first thing in the morning. Hint: solo riders can take a faster line so if you don't mind splitting up for a few minutes, you'll save a lot of time. Audience: Older children and adults. The spinning nature of the cars may cause dizziness, so use caution: no guests with heart, back, or neck problems or motion sickness. Rating:* ★★★.

❿ *Back to the Future . . .* **The Ride.** At heart, this is just a motion simulator ride, but more than a decade after opening it remains one of the park's most popular—albeit nausea-inducing—experiences. Following a long wait and a preshow video that explains how Biff has swiped one of Doc Brown's time-travel vehicles, you get into a cramped eight-passenger De-Lorean, and take off to track down Biff and save the future. A series of realistic past, present, and future scenes projected onto a seven-story, one-of-a-kind Omnimax screen whooshes past you, making you feel completely disoriented. Having no sense of perspective (or seat belts) makes this the rocking, rolling, pitching, and yawing equivalent of a hyperactive paint mixer. It is scary, jarring, and jolting. If you like your rides shaken, not stirred, this one will be worth the wait—and the queasy feeling that will follow you around afterward. ☞ *Duration: 5 mins. Crowds: Peak times between 11 and 3; and slightly less crowded first thing in the morning, when Twister siphons off the crowds.* **Strategy:** *You can use Universal Express here; otherwise, dash over when the gates open, or about a half hour afterward, or go later at night.* **Audience:** *Older children and adults. No pregnant women or guests with heart, back, or neck problems or motion sickness. Minimum height: 40″.* **Rating:** ★★★.

need a break? The **International Food Bazaar,** near *Back to the Future,* is an efficient, multiethnic food court serving Italian (pizza, lasagna), American (fried chicken, meat loaf), Greek (gyros), and Chinese (orange chicken, stir-fried beef) dishes at affordable prices—usually $7 to $9. The Italian Caesar and Greek salads are especially welcome on a muggy day.

Woody Woodpecker's KidZone

Universal Studios caters to preschoolers with this compilation of rides, attractions, shows, and places for kids to get sprayed, splashed, and soaked. It's a great place for children to burn off their energy and give parents a break after nearly circling the park.

⓫ Animal Planet Live! Animal shows are usually fun, and this one is better than most. An arkful of animals are the stars here, and the tricks (or *behaviors*) they perform are loosely based on shows from the cable network: *Emergency Vets, Planet's Funniest Animals,* and *The Jeff Corwin Experience.* A raccoon opens the show, and Lassie makes a brief appearance, followed by an audience-participation segment in the clever, funny, and cute Dog Decathlon. Next, Gizmo the parrot from *Ace Ventura: Pet Detective* arrives to fly in front of a wind machine and blue screen, the televised image showing him soaring across a desert, a forest, and then in outer space. In the grand finale Bailey the orangutan does some impressions (how an ape does Ricky Martin is a mystery), then there's an overpoweringly adorable chimpanzee and, finally, a brief peek at a boa constrictor. If your family loves animals, then this is an entertaining show that shouldn't be missed. ☞ *Duration: 20 mins. Crowds: Can get crowded in peak times.* **Strategy:** *You can use Universal Express here; otherwise, go early for a good seat.* **Audience:** *All ages.* **Rating:** ★★★.

⓬ A Day in the Park with Barney. If you can't get enough of the big purple dinosaur, here he is again. After a long preshow starring a goofy, kid-friendly emcee, parents tote their preschoolers into a pleasant theater-in-the-round filled with brilliantly colored trees, clouds, and stars. Within minutes, the kids will go crazy as their beloved TV playmate (and Baby Bop) dance and sing though clap-along, sing-along monster classics including "Mr. Knickerbocker," "If You're Happy and You Know

BACKSTAGE AT UNIVERSAL

ODDS ARE that while you're midway through a 100-foot spiral and g-forces are pushing your forehead through your feet, you won't be thinking about the technological soup of rotors, generators, and gears it took to get you there. But every time you board a ride at Universal Studios or Islands of Adventure, what you experience is just the tip of a high-tech iceberg. Lasers, 3-D imaging, holograms, pulleys, motors, hydraulics, and supercharged power supplies are working like mad to ensure that, for a few minutes at least, you really think Poseidon is sparking lightning bolts or Spider-Man has joined you on a trip through New York.

Think of what your day would be like minus all this mechanical acumen. The Incredible Hulk Coaster, for instance, would be just a lump of metal and plastic. But add four massive motors spinning fast enough to generate power to 220 smaller motors, and you're whipping up enough force to throw this 32,000-pound vehicle (a mass equal to eight Mercedes-Benz cars) up a 150-foot track at a 30-degree incline, to rocket you from 0 to 40 mph in less than two seconds. If you want to experience a similar sensation, climb into an F-16 fighter jet and take it for a spin.

Less intense, but equally tricky, was creating a way to project a movie image onto a sheet of flowing water. At Poseidon's Fury, the 30-yard-wide water screen flows in a steady sheet so guests can watch Poseidon on what may be the world's largest plasma screen.

At The Amazing Adventures of Spider-Man, 3-D effects, sensory drops, and virtual reality will fool you into believing you're actually being subjected to an assault of flaming pumpkins, careening garbage trucks, electric bolts, anti-gravity guns, swirling fog, frigid water, and an incredibly intense 400-feet, white-knuckle, scream-like-a-baby sensory drop.

The volume of air that rushes through Twister . . . Ride It Out could fill more than four full-size airborne blimps in ONE MINUTE. Its 110-decibel sound system uses 54 speakers cranking out 42,000 watts; enough wattage to power five average homes.

At Back to the Future . . . The Ride, the elaborate, hand-designed and painted miniatures took two years to make and cost as much as a feature film. Twenty computers conduct 5,000 different cues to create the special ride and movie effects.

In E.T. Adventure, there are 4,400 illuminated stars in the sky, 3,340 miniature city buildings, 250 cars on the street, and 140 street lights in the city. The ride utilizes 284 miles of electrical wiring, 250 miles of fiber optics, 68 show control computers, and 2,500 separate commands from those computers.

Earthquake—The Big One registers 8.3 on the Richter scale, releasing a slab of falling roadway that weighs 45,000 pounds. Nearly 65,000 gallons of water are released and recycled every six minutes.

Jaws's seven-acre lagoon contains five million gallons of water, 2,000 mi of wire, and 10,000 cubic yards of concrete reinforced with 7,500 tons of steel. The 32-foot steel and fiberglass shark weighs three tons and swims at 20 feet per second.

Each time you step inside a Universal attraction, there are more high-tech happenings going on behind the scenes . . . or right before your eyes.

It," and (of course) "I Love You." Following the very pleasing and thought-ful show and a chance to meet Barney up close, you'll exit to a fairly elaborate play area featuring hands-on activities—a water harp, wood-pipe xylophone, and musical rocks—that propel the already excited kids to even greater heights. ☞ *Duration: 20 mins. Crowds: Room for all. Strategy: You can use Universal Express here; otherwise, arrive 10–15 mins early on crowded days for a good seat—up close and in the cen-ter. Audience: Young children. Rating:* ★★.

⑬ Curious George Goes to Town. The celebrated simian visits the Man with the Yellow Hat in a no-line, no-waiting, small-scale water park. The main town square has brightly colored building facades, and the plaza is an interactive aqua play area that adults avoid but kids are drawn to like fish to water. Yes, there's water, water everywhere, especially atop the clock tower, which periodically dumps a mighty huge 500 gallons down a roof and straight onto a screaming passel of preschoolers. Kids love the levers, valves, pumps, and hoses that gush at the rate of 200 gallons per minute, letting them get sprayed, spritzed, splashed, and splattered. At the head of the square, footprints lead to a dry play area, with a rope climb and a ball cage where youngsters can frolic among thousands of foam balls. Parents can get into the act, sit it out on nearby benches, or take a few minutes to buy souvenir towels to dry off their waterlogged kids. ☞ *Duration: As long as you like. Crowds: Heavy in midmorn-ing. Strategy: Go in late afternoon or early evening. Audience: Toddlers through preteens and their parents. Rating:* ★★★.

⑭ Fievel's Playland. Another Spielberg movie spin-off, this one from the animated film *An American Tail*, this playground's larger-than-life props and sets are designed to make everyone feel mouse-size. Boots, cans, and other ordinary objects disguise tunnel slides, water play areas, ball crawls, and a gigantic net-climb equipped with tubes, ladders, and rope bridges. A harmonica slide plays music when you slide along the open-ings, and a 200-foot water slide gives kids (and a parent if so desired) a chance to swoop down in Fievel's signature sardine can. It should keep the kids entertained for hours. The downside? You might have to build one of these for your backyard when you get home. ☞ *Duration: Up to your preschooler. Crowds: Not significant, although waits do develop for the water slide. Strategy: On hot days, go after supper. Audience: Toddlers, preschoolers, and their parents. Rating:* ★★.

⑮ Woody Woodpecker's Nuthouse Coaster. Unlike the maniacal coasters that put you through zero-G rolls and inversions, this low-speed, mild-thrill version (top speed 22 mph) makes it a safe bet for younger kids and action-phobic adults. (It's the same off-the-shelf design used on Is-lands of Adventure's Flying Unicorn and Goofy's Barnstormer at the Magic Kingdom.) The coaster races (a relative term) through a struc-ture that looks like a gadget-filled factory; the coaster's cars look like shipping crates—some labeled "mixed nuts," others "salted nuts," and some tagged "certifiably nuts." Woody's Nuthouse has several ups and downs to reward you for the wait, and children generally love the low-level introduction to thrill rides. ☞ *Duration: 1½ mins. Crowds: Heavy in midmorning and early afternoon, when the under-2 set is out in*

force. Strategy: Go at park closing, when most little ones have gone home. Audience: Young children and their parents. Rating: ★★★.

16 **E.T. Adventure.** Steven Spielberg puts one of his most beloved creations on display in this attraction adjacent to Fievel's Playland. With E.T. imploring "Home, home," you board bicycles mounted on a movable platform and fly 3 million light years from Earth (in reality just a few hundred yards), past a phalanx of policemen and FBI agents to reach E.T.'s home planet. Here the music follows the mood, and the strange sounds in E.T.'s world are as colorful as the characters, which climb on vines, play xylophones, and swing on branches in an alien Burning Man festival. Listen in at the end when E.T. offers you a personalized good-bye. ☞ *Duration: 5 mins. Crowds: Sometimes not bad, but can be heavy during busy seasons. Strategy: You can use Universal Express here; otherwise, go early. Audience: All ages. No guests with heart, back, or neck problems or motion sickness. Rating:* ★★★.

Hollywood

Angling off to the right of Plaza of the Stars, Rodeo Drive forms the backbone of Hollywood.

groovy souvenirs

Stop by the **Brown Derby Hat Shop** for the perfect topper, from red-and-white *Cat In The Hat* stovepipes to felt fedoras to bush hats from *Jurassic Park*.

17 **Universal Horror Make-Up Show.** On display in the entertaining preshow area are masks, props, rubber skeletons from the film *Scorpion King*— all great backdrops for a family photo. Beyond this, the real fun kicks off in the theater when a host brings out a "special-effects expert" to

Fodor'sChoice

describe what goes into (and what oozes out of) some of the creepiest movie effects. Corn syrup and food coloring make for a dandy blood substitute, for example. Despite the potentially frightening topic, the subject is handled with an extraordinary amount of dead-on humor. As movie secrets are betrayed, actors add in one-liners with comedy-club timing. Throw in some knives, guns, loose limbs, and a surprise ending, and you've got yourself a recipe for edge-of-your-seat fun. ☞ *Duration: 25 mins. Crowds: Not daunting. Strategy: You can use Universal Express here; otherwise, go in the afternoon or evening. Audience: All but young children, who may be frightened; older children eat up the blood-and-guts stories. Rating:* ★★★.

18 *Terminator 2* **3-D.** California's governor said he'd be back, and he is, along with the popular film's other main characters, including a buff Linda Hamilton and a taller Edward Furlong, a.k.a. young John Connor. Directed by James *Titanic* Cameron, who also directed the first two Terminator movies, the 12-minute show is—frame for frame—one of the most expensive live-action films ever produced. The attraction begins when you enter the headquarters of the futuristic consortium, Cyberdyne, and a "community relations and media control" hostess greets your group and introduces their latest line of law-enforcing robots. Things go awry (of course), and the Schwarzenegger film, combined with icy fog, live actors, gunfights, and a chilling grand finale, keep the pace moving at 100 mph—although the 3-D effects seem few and far between. Kids may be scared silly and require some parental counseling, but if you can handle a few surprises, don't miss this one. ☞ *Duration: 21 minutes, with preshow. Crowds: Always. Strategy: You can use Universal Express here; otherwise, go first thing in the morning. Audience: All but very young children, who may be frightened. Rating:* ★★★.

need a break?

Schwab's Pharmacy is a re-creation of the legendary drugstore where—studio publicists claim—Lana Turner was discovered. What you'll discover is a quick stop where you can order ice cream as well as hand-carved turkey and ham sandwiches.

🔟 **Lucy: A Tribute.** If you smile when you recall Lucy stomping grapes, practicing ballet, gobbling chocolates, or wailing when Ricky won't let her be in the show, then you need to stop here. This minimuseum (and major gift shop) pays tribute to Lucille Ball through scripts, props, costumes, awards, and clips from the comedian's estate. A challenging trivia quiz game has you trying to get Lucy, Ricky, Fred, and Ethel across country to Hollywood. It's a nice place to take a break and spend time with one of the funniest women of television. ☞ *Duration: About 15 mins. Crowds: Seldom a problem. Strategy: Save this for a peek on your way out or for a hot afternoon. Audience: Adults. Rating:* ★.

Universal Studios A to Z

To research prices, get advice from other travelers, and book travel arrangements, visit www.fodors.com.

BABY CARE
There are diaper-changing tables in both men's and women's rest rooms. Nursing facilities are at two Health Services (a.k.a. First Aid) centers. One is across from Beetlejuice's Show on Canal Street the other is by Guest Services, just inside Universal Studios' main entrance and to the right. No diapers are sold on the premises; instead, they're complimentary at Health Services. Several shops stock basic baby care items—wipes, etc.—but they are kept out of sight at the cash registers, so you just have to ask. Also, check the park maps: a baby bottle symbol lets you know which ones carry the items.

Strollers are for rent just inside the main entrance to the left, singles $10, doubles $16; no deposit required. No formula or baby food is sold in the park; the nearest sources are Kmart on Sand Lake Road, Walgreens on Kirkman Road, and Publix supermarkets on Sand Lake and Kirkman roads—each less than a half mile from Universal's gates.

CHILD SWAP
Many rides have Child Swap areas, so that one adult can watch a baby or toddler while the other enjoys the ride or show. The adults then change roles, and the former caretaker rides without having to wait in line all over again.

CAMERAS & FILM

Just inside the Universal Studios main entrance, at the **On Location** shop in the Front Lot, you can find nearly everything you need to make your vacation picture-perfect. The store sells disposable cameras from about $13 (no flash) to $17 (with flash), plus memory cards for digital cameras.

DISABILITIES & ACCESSIBILITY

At Universal, each attraction's sound track has appeal for those with visual impairments, and the sights interest those with hearing impairments.

In addition to being physically accommodating, the park has a professional staff that is quite helpful. At each park's Guest Services desk, you can pick up a "Studio Guide for Guests with Disabilities" (aka "Rider's Guide"), which contains information for guests who require specific needs on rides and offers details on interpreters, braille scripts, menus, and assisted devices. Walking areas for service animals are available at the Nickelodeon Courtyard and at *Men in Black* Alien Attack.

During orientation, all employees learn how to accommodate guests with disabilities, and you can occasionally spot staffers using wheelchairs. Additionally, power-assist buttons make it easier to get past heavy, hard-to-open doors; lap tables are provided for guests in shops; and already accessible bathroom facilities have such niceties as insulated under-sink pipes and companion rest rooms.

Many of the cobblestone streets have paved paths, and photo spots are arranged for wheelchair accessibility. Various attractions have been retrofitted so that most can be boarded directly in a standard wheelchair; those using oversize vehicles or scooters must transfer to a standard model available at the ride's entrance—or into the ride vehicle itself. All outdoor shows have special viewing areas for wheelchairs, and all restaurants are wheelchair accessible.

ATTRACTIONS **Animal Planet Live!,** the **Universal Horror Make-Up Show, Beetlejuice's Graveyard Revue,** *Twister* . . . **Ride It Out,** and *Terminator 2* **3-D** are all completely wheelchair-accessible, theater-style attractions. Good scripts and songs mean that even those with visual impairments can enjoy parts of all of these shows.

No motorized wheelchairs or electric convenience vehicles (ECVs) are permitted on any ride vehicle, at either park. To ride *E.T.* **Adventure** you must transfer to the ride vehicle or use a standard-size wheelchair. Service animals are not permitted. There is some sudden tilting and accelerating, but even those with most types of heart, back, or neck problems can ride in E.T.'s orbs (the spaceships) instead of the flying bicycles. Those who use wheelchairs must transfer to the ride vehicles to experience **Woody Woodpecker's Nuthouse Coaster,** but most of **Curious George Goes to Town** is barrier-free.

If you use a standard-size wheelchair or can transfer to one or to the ride vehicle directly, you can board *Earthquake*—**The Big One,** *Jaws,* and *Men in Black* directly. Service animals should not ride, and neither should you if you find turbulence a problem. Note that guests with visual impairments as well as those using wheelchairs should cross San Francisco/Amity with care. The cobblestones are rough on wheelchair and stroller wheels.

The **Nickelodeon Studios** presentation of Game Lab is also completely accessible to guests using wheelchairs and enjoyable for guests with other disabilities. If you lip-read, ask to stay up front.

One vehicle in **Jimmy Neutron's Nicktoon Blast** is equipped with an access door that allows for standard-size wheelchairs, and two vehicles in the back of the attraction have closed caption screens. **Shrek 4-D** has eight handicap-equipped seats. Assisted listening devices are available at Guest Services.

Lucy: A Tribute is wheelchair accessible, but the TV-show excerpts shown on overhead screens are not closed-captioned. *Back to the Future . . .* **The Ride** is not accessible to people who use wheelchairs, nor are service animals permitted.

SERVICES Many Universal Studios employees have had basic sign-language training; even some of the animated characters speak sign, but since many have only four fingers, it's an adapted version. Like Walt Disney World, Universal supplements the visuals with a special guidebook containing story lines and scripts for the main attractions. The **"Studio Guide for Guests with Disabilities"** pinpoints special entrances available for those with disabilities; these routes often bypass the main line. You can get this and various booklets at Guest Services, just inside the main entrance and to the right. There's an **outgoing TTY** (Text Type Y) series hearing-impaired system on the counter in Guest Services.

WHEELCHAIR RENTALS Manual wheelchairs ($12 per day) and electric scooters ($40 per day) can be rented just inside the main entrance and in San Francisco/Amity. Photo ID or a $50 deposit on a credit card is required for either. If the wheelchair breaks down, disappears, or otherwise needs replacing, speak to any shop attendant. It's a long, long way from the parking garage to the entrance. Consider renting a push wheelchair from the central concourse between the parking garages. You can upgrade to an ECV (electric convenience vehicle, or scooter) when you reach the park entrance. Quantities are limited, so it's recommended that you reserve in advance.

🖪 **Guest Services** ☏ 407/224-4233.

GUIDED TOURS

Universal has several variations on **VIP Tours,** which offer what's called "back-door admission" or, in plain English, the right to jump the line. It's the ultimate capitalist fantasy and worthwhile if you're in a hurry, if you're with a large group, if the day is crowded, and if you have the money to burn. The five-hour VIP tour costs $100 per person for one park and $125 for two parks, including park admission price. An eight-hour tour costs $1,400, and again includes park admission. Sales tax (6.5%) is extra. For $2,600, sign up for a two-day tour of both parks, which includes backstage access and discussions on the park's history, decorating, and landscaping. The tours also offer extras and upgrades such as priority restaurant seating, bilingual guides, gift bags, and valet parking. Best of all, the guides can answer practically any question you throw at them—they're masters of Universal trivia. For all VIP Tours, exclusive and nonexclusive, the maximum number of people is 15. Nonexclusive will place you with other guests, led by a VIP tour guide who knows the parks inside and out, and can speak to basically every detail of our property. The exclusive tour is the same, but the day is led by the guest, with the VIP guide assisting and providing access for the rides and attractions the guest wants to do.

🚩 VIP Tours ☎ 407/363-8295.

HEALTH SERVICES/FIRST AID

Universal Studios' First Aid centers are between New York and San Francisco (directly across from Beetlejuice's Graveyard Revue) and at the entrance between the bank and the Studio Audience Center.

HOURS

Universal Studios is open 365 days a year, from 9 to 7, with hours as late as 10 during summer and holiday periods.

LOCKERS

Locker rental charges are $7 for small lockers and $10 for large, family-sized ones per day. The high-priced lockers are clustered around the courtyard after you've cleared the turnstiles. If you time it right, you may not need one because Universal also has "Smart Lockers" at major thrill rides, which are free for up to 90 minutes. Consider these first.

LOST THINGS & PEOPLE

If you lose something, return to the last attraction or shop where you recall seeing it. If it's not there, head to Guest Services. If you lose a person, there's only one place to look: head directly to Guest Services near the main entrance.

MONEY MATTERS

There are two ATMs in each park, one of the first in the Studios being just inside the main entrances on the right and the second in San Francisco/Amity near Lombard's Landing. You can use traveler's checks like cash anywhere, and you can exchange foreign currency at Guest Services.

VISITOR INFORMATION

Visit **Guest Services,** in the Front Lot to the right after you pass through the turnstiles, for brochures and maps in French, Spanish, Portuguese, Japanese, and German, as well as English. The brochures also lay out the day's entertainment, tapings, and rare film shoots. If you have questions prior to visiting, call Universal's main line or Guest Services.

Studio Information Boards in front of Studio Stars and Mel's Drive-In restaurants provide up-to-the-minute ride and show operating information—including the length of lines at the major attractions.

🚩 Guest Services ☎ 407/224-6350. Universal Main Line ☎ 407/363-8000.

ISLANDS OF ADVENTURE

The creators of Islands of Adventure (IOA) brought theme-park attractions to a new level. From Marvel Super Hero Island and Toon Lagoon to Seuss Landing, Jurassic Park, and the Lost Continent, almost everything is impressive, and the shows, attractions, and at times the rides can even out-Disney Disney.

The park's five themed islands, connected by walkways, are arranged around a large central lagoon. The waterside is a good place to relax, either as a way to escape crowds or to recuperate from an adrenaline-surging coaster.

After passing the turnstiles, you've arrived at the Port of Entry plaza. This international bazaar brings together bits and pieces of architecture, land-scaping, music, and wares from many lands: you may see Dutch wind-mills, Indonesian pedicabs, African masks, and Egyptian figurines. But don't stop here. Head directly for the massive archway inscribed with the notice THE ADVENTURE BEGINS. You won't be disappointed.

Entertainment

Throughout the day there are character greetings and shows in each of the Islands. In Toon Lagoon, you may run into the **Toon Trolley,** which carries an assortment of Universal-related characters who disembark to sign autographs and pose for pictures. Adjacent to Ripsaw Falls, the Pandemonium Amphitheatre is usually dark, but does stage seasonal and/or special performances such as the skateboard and bicycle stunts of Extreme Adventures.

During the holidays, the **Grinchmas** celebration brings live shows and movie characters to Seuss Landing, and at Marvel Super Hero Island the **X-Men** make a guest appearance. During summer and holiday periods, when the park is open late, there's a big fireworks show that can be seen anywhere along the lagoon bordering the islands—the lagoon-side terrace of the Jurassic Park Discovery Center has a fairly unimpeded view.

Numbers in the margin correspond to points of interest on the Islands of Adventure map.

Marvel Super Hero Island

This island may return you to the halcyon days of yesteryear, when per-haps you were able to name every hero and villain in a Marvel comic book. The facades along Stanley Boulevard (named for Marvel's famed editor and co-creator Stan Lee) put you smack in the middle of these adventures, with cartoony colors and flourishes. Although the spiky, horrific tower of **Doctor Doom's Fearfall** makes it a focal point for the park, the **Amazing Adventures of Spider-Man** is the one to see. At various times Doctor Doom, Spider-Man, and the Incredible Hulk are available for photos, and sidewalk artists are on hand to paint your face like your favorite hero (or villain). Also dominating the scenery is the Hulk's own vivid-green coaster. Along with a hard-driving rock sound track, the screams emanating from Doctor Doom's and from the Hulk Coaster set the mood for this some-times pleasant, sometimes apocalyptic world.

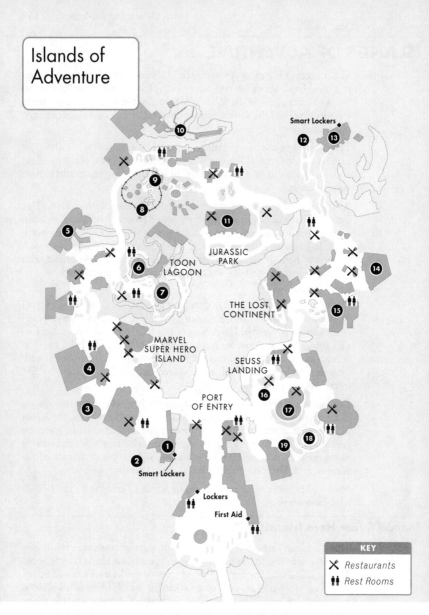

Islands of Adventure

Smart Lockers

JURASSIC PARK

TOON LAGOON

THE LOST CONTINENT

MARVEL SUPER HERO ISLAND

SEUSS LANDING

PORT OF ENTRY

Smart Lockers

Lockers

First Aid

Best of the Park

To see everything in Islands of Adventure, a full day is necessary, especially since the large number of thrill rides guarantees that long lines will greet you just about everywhere. To see the most without waiting, stay at a Universal resort hotel or arrive in the parking lot 45 minutes before the park's official opening. Also, take advantage of Universal Express ticketing.

This plan involves a lot of walking and retracing. It sounds crazy but it just . . . might . . . work. Unless you have preschoolers and need to see Seuss Landing first, take a left after the Port of Entry and head for the best and most popular attractions, starting the **Incredible Hulk Coaster** then the **Amazing Adventures of Spider-Man.** Then double back to Skip Toon Lagoon in favor of the **Jurassic Park River Adventure.** In the Lost Continent next door, do **Dueling Dragons.** If it's showtime, next catch the **Eighth Voyage of Sindbad.** On the way back to Toon Lagoon, let the kids see either the **Jurassic Park Discovery Center** or **Camp Jurassic,** or both.

At Toon Lagoon, see **Dudley Do-Right's Ripsaw Falls** before or after the drenching at **Popeye & Bluto's Bilge-Rat Barges.** By now, if you're in luck, the young Dr. Seuss fans and their families will have left the park, so it's time to hit Seuss Landing. Go to **Cat in the Hat** first, then on to **One Fish, Two Fish, Red Fish, Blue Fish.** Make a stop at the **Green Eggs and Ham Cafe** to see how those green eggs are made, even if you're not ready to chow down. **Caro-Seuss-el** lets you be a kid again. Before you exit, walk through *If I Ran the Zoo.* The unusual animals here are definitely worth a look.

The remaining attractions are worthwhile if you've happened to arrive on a slow day and finish ahead of time: **Doctor Doom's Fearfall** and **Storm Force Accelatron** in Marvel Super Hero Island, the **Triceratops Discovery Trail** and **Pteranodon Flyers** at Jurassic Park, and **The Flying Unicorn** and **Poseidon's Fury** in the Lost Continent.

On Rainy Days

Except during Christmas week, expect rainy days to be less crowded—even though the park is in full operation. (Coasters do run in the rain—although not in thunderstorms.) However, since most attractions are out in the open, you will get very wet.

FodorsChoice

① Incredible Hulk Coaster. If you follow a clockwise tour of IOA, this is the first ride that will catch your attention and probably the first you'll want to ride. The first third of the coaster is directly above the sidewalk and lagoon. You can watch as cars are spit out from a 150-foot catapult that propels them from 0 to 40 mph in less than two seconds. If that piques your interest, then enter the queue with walls illustrated with artwork that explains how the superheros and villains got their powers). After you get on the coaster, prepare yourself for flesh-pressing G-forces that match those of an F-16 fighter. Things are enjoyable in a rough sort of way, since you are instantly whipped into an upside-down, zero-G position 110 feet above the ground. That's when you go into the roller coaster's traditional first dive—straight down toward the lagoon below at some 60 mph. Racing along the track, you then spin through seven rollovers in all and plunge into two deep, foggy subterranean enclosures. And just when you think it's over, it's not. It just keeps rolling along way after you've exhausted your supply of screams and shrieks. Powerful. ☞ *Duration: 2¼ mins. Crowds: All the time. Strategy: You can use Universal Express here; otherwise, make a beeline either to this coaster or to Dueling Dragons as soon as you arrive in the park. The fog effects are most vivid first thing in the morning; darkness enhances the launch effect, since you can't see the light at the end of the tunnel. Front and rear seats give you almost entirely different experiences. The ride is fastest in the rear and has fine views, but is roughest on the sides; the front row, with its fabulous view of that green track racing into your face, is truly awesome— but you have to wait even longer for it. Audience: Coaster lovers. No pregnant women or guests with heart, back, or neck problems. Minimum height: 54". Rating:* ★★★.

❷ Storm Force Accelatron. This whirling ride is supposed to demonstrate the power of nature. Cartoon character Storm (of the X-Men) harnesses the power of weather to battle her archenemy Magneto (What?! *A story line?*) by having people like you board "Power Orbs." These containers convert human energy into electrical forces through the power of "cyclospin." Strip away the veneer, however, and what you've got is a mirror image of Disney World's twirling teacups. Definitely not a good idea if you get motion sickness or are prone to puking. ☞ *Duration: 2 mins. Crowds: Not a problem. Strategy: Go whenever—except after you've eaten. Audience: Older children and adults. No pregnant women or guests with heart, back, or neck problems. Minimum height: 54". Rating:* ★★.

❸ Doctor Doom's Fearfall. Although the 200-foot-tall towers look really, really scary, the ride is really just pretty scary. After being strapped into a chair, you're hoisted almost to the top and then dropped to earth—with a moment of weightlessness courtesy of the brief pause at the peak. The process is then repeated with a little more force, making your plunge a little faster. Check the line, estimate your desire to be shot into the air, and your need to see a panoramic view of the Orlando skyline and Universal's parks. Leave loose items in the bins provided; no one else can reach them while you're on your trip. ☞ *Duration: 1 min. Crowds: Can get crowded, but the line moves fast. Strategy: You can use Universal Express here; otherwise, go later in the day, when crowds are thinner, but not on a full stomach. Audience: Older children and adults. No pregnant women or guests with heart, back, or neck problems or motion sickness. Minimum height: 52". Rating:* ★.

TIP SHEET

When to Go Aside from spring break, summer vacation, and holidays—which inevitably pack the park—crowds vary depending on the day, the season, and the weather. As at Universal Studios, Monday through Wednesday are busy. Crowds thin on Thursday and Friday and build up again on weekends, when locals join in the fun.

Call a day or two before your visit to get official park hours, and arrive in the parking lot 45 minutes early. See the biggest attractions first.

When You're There Just in case you and your companions get separated, set up a rendezvous point and time at the start of the day. Don't pick an obvious and crowded location (such as the Jurassic Discovery Center), but a small restaurant or bridge between two islands.

Be sure to write down your parking location.

Have a filling snack around 10:30, lunch after 2, and dinner at 8 or later. Or lunch on the early side at a place that takes reservations, such as Thunder Falls Terrace or Mythos; then have dinner at 5. Be sure to make your reservations ahead of time or, at the very least, when you enter the park.

If you plan to ride Dueling Dragons or the Incredible Hulk Coaster, wear shoes that are strapped firmly onto your feet—no flip-flops or heel-less sandals. If you wear glasses, consider pocketing them or wearing a sports strap to keep them firmly against your head when you're flung upside down. Neither coaster is so rough that you are certain to lose your glasses, but better safe than sorry. You should also leave loose change in one of the (temporarily free) lockers.

Head to the Front of the Line Universal Express is available to all park guests at the more popular Islands of Adventure attractions. You check in at the ride entrance, are assigned a time, and then return later to bypass the line and ride within minutes. Pay extra ($15 to $25) for a Universal Express PLUS pass and you can go to the express line without having to make or wait for an appointment. Those staying at a Universal resort can avoid Universal Express altogether and need only to show their room key to get to the front of the line of any attraction. If attendance is unusually low, however, and lines are short, the Express system may be put on hold.

Fodor'sChoice

❹ The Amazing Adventures of Spider-Man. Even if you have never heard of Peter Parker or J. Jonah Jameson, the 4½ minutes spent in this building can make two hours standing in line worthwhile. Unlike any other ride at any theme park, this one combines moving vehicles, 3-D film, simulator technology, and special effects. Unless you use the Universal

Express pass, expect a winding and torturous walk in line through the *Daily Bugle*'s offices. You learn that members of the Sinister Syndicate (Doctor Octopus [a.k.a. Doc Oc], Electro, Hobgoblin, Hydro Man, and deadly Scream) have used their Doomsday Anti-Gravity Gun to steal the Statue of Liberty. None of this matters, really, since once you board your car and don your 3-D glasses, you are instantly swept up into a weird cartoon battle. When Spider-Man lands on your car, you feel the bump; when Electro runs overhead, you hear his footsteps following you. You feel the sizzle of electricity, a frigid spray of water from Hydro Man, and the heat from a flaming pumpkin tossed by the Hobgoblin. No matter how many times you visit this attraction, you cringe when Doc Oc breaks through a brick wall, raises your car to the top of a skyscraper, and then releases you for a 400-foot free fall to the pavement below. The bizarre angles and perspective at which scenes are shown are so disorienting, you really do feel as if you're swinging from a web. *Do not miss this one.* ☞ **Duration:** *4½ mins.* **Crowds:** *Usually inescapable unless you use Universal Express.* **Strategy:** *You can use Universal Express here; otherwise, go early in the day or at dusk. If you don't know much about Spider-Man's villains, check out the* WANTED *posters on the walls.* **Audience:** *All but timid young children; youngsters accustomed to action TV shows should be fine. No pregnant women or guests with heart, back, or neck problems. Minimum height: 40″; children under 48″ must be accompanied by an adult.* **Rating:** ★★★.

Toon Lagoon

As you leave Marvel's world, there's no water to separate it from Toon Lagoon, just a change of pavement color and texture, midway games along the walkway, and primary colors turning to purple and fuchsia. Toon Lagoon's main street, Comic Strip Lane, makes use of cartoon characters that are instantly recognizable to anyone—anyone born before 1942, that is. Pert little Betty Boop, gangling Olive Oyl, muscle-bound Popeye, Krazy Kat, Mark Trail, Flash Gordon, Pogo, and Alley Oop are all here, as are the relatively more contemporary Dudley Do-Right, Rocky, Bullwinkle, Beetle Bailey, Cathy, and Hagar the Horrible. Either way, the colorful backdrop and chirpy music are as cheerful as Jurassic Park next door is portentous. There are squirting fountains for kids, hidden alcoves, and elevated cartoon balloon captions to pose under for photos.

groovy souvenirs   Get your Betty Boop collectibles at the **Betty Boop Store.** Poncho collectors can get one at **Gasoline Alley,** along with clever blank books, and cartoon-character hats and wigs that recall Daisy Mae and others.

Fodor'sChoice

❺ Dudley Do-Right's Ripsaw Falls. Inspired by set-ups and a locale used on the popular 1960s animated pun-fest *Rocky and Bullwinkle,* this twisting, up-and-down flume ride is definitely wet and wild. You're supposed to help Dudley rescue Nell, his belle, from the evil and conniving Snidely Whiplash. By the time your mission is accomplished, you've dropped through the rooftop of a ramshackle dynamite shack and made an explosive dive 15 feet below water level into a 400,000-gallon lagoon, and you're not just damp—you're soaked to the skin. Actually, the final drop looks much scarier than it really is; the fact that the ride vehicles have no restraining devices at all is a clue to how low the danger quotient actually is here. You never know quite what's ahead—and you're definitely not expecting the big thrill when the time comes. If the weather is cold and you absolutely must stay dry, pick up a poncho at **Gasoline Alley**, opposite the entrance. ☞ *Crowds: Varies by season, but very heavy in the summer. Strategy: You can use Universal Express here; otherwise, go in late afternoon, when you're hot as can be, or at day's end, when you're ready to head back to your car. There's no seat where you can stay dry. Audience: All but the youngest children. No pregnant women or guests with heart, back, or neck problems. Minimum height: 44"; children under 48" must be accompanied by an adult. Rating:* ★★★.

need a break?

On Toon Lagoon, you can sample you-know-whats at **Blondie's Deli: Home of the Dagwood.** The jumbo sandwich that creates the restaurant's marquee is a hoot, and you can buy the real thing, by the inch, inside.

6 **Popeye & Bluto's Bilge-Rat Barges.** At times this river ride is quiet, but often it's a bumping, churning, twisting white-water raft ride that will drench you and your fellow travelers. As with every ride at IOA, there's a story line here, but the real attraction is getting soaked, splashed, sprayed, or deluged. The degree of wetness varies, since your circular raft's spinning may or may not place you beneath torrents of water flooding from a shore-line water tower or streaming from water guns from an adjacent play area. Warning: there are no lockers here—IOA expects you to stow your stuff in a "waterproof" holder in the center of the raft. But it's not waterproof, it's waterlogged, and your stuff *will* get wet. ☞ *Duration: 5 mins. Crowds: Heavy all day. Strategy: You can use Universal Express here; otherwise, go first thing in the morning or about 1 hr before closing. Audience: All but young children. No pregnant women or guests with heart, back, or neck problems or motion sickness. Minimum height: 48"; children under 48" must be accompanied by an adult. Rating:* ★★★.

7 **Me Ship, the *Olive*.** From bow to stern, dozens of participatory activities keep families busy as they climb around this boat moored on the edge of Toon Lagoon. Toddlers enjoy crawling in Swee' Pea's Playpen, and older children and their parents take aim at unsuspecting riders locked into the Bilge-Rat Barges. Primarily, this is designed for kids, with whistles, bells, and organs to trigger, as well as narrow tunnels to climb through and ladders to climb up. Check out the view of the park from the top of the ship. ☞ *Duration: As long as you wish. Crowds: Fairly heavy all day. Strategy: If you're with young children, go in the morning or around dinnertime. Audience: Young children. Rating:* ★★.

Jurassic Park

Walking through the arched gates of Jurassic Park brings a distinct change in mood. The music is stirring and slightly ominous, the vegetation tropical and junglelike. All this, plus the high-tension wires and warning signs, does a great job of re-creating the Jurassic Park of Steven Spielberg's blockbuster movie—and its insipid sequels. The half-fun, half-frightening **Jurassic Park River Adventure** is the island's standout attraction, bringing to life key segments of the movie's climax.

> groovy souvenirs

The **Dinostore,** on the pathway between Jurassic Park and the Lost Continent, has a *Tyrannosaurus rex* that looks as if he's hatching from an egg, and (yes, mom) educational dino toys, too.

8 Pteranodon Flyers. These gondolas are eye-catching and can't help but tempt you to stand in line for a lift. The problem is that the wide, wing-spanned chairs provide a very slow, very low-capacity ride that will eat up a lot of your park time. Do it only if you want a prehistoric-bird's-eye view of the *Jurassic Park* compound. ☞ *Duration: 2 mins. Crowds: Perpetual. Since the ride loads slowly, waits can take 1 hr or more.* **Strategy:** *Skip this on your first few visits.* **Audience:** *All ages. Adults must be accompanied by a child 36" to 56" tall.* **Rating:** ★.

9 Camp Jurassic. Remember when you were a kid content with just a swing set and monkey bars? Well, those toys of the past have been replaced by fantastic play areas like this, which are interwoven with the island's theme. Though the camp is primarily for kids, some adults join in, racing along footpaths through the forests, slithering down slides, clambering over swinging bridges and across boiling streams, scrambling up net climbs and rock formations, and exploring mysterious caves full of faux lava. Keep an eye open for the dinosaur footprints; when you jump on them, a dinosaur roars somewhere (different footprints are associated with different roars). Watch out for the watery cross fire nearby—or join in the shooting yourself. ☞ *Duration: As long as you want. Crowds: Sometimes more, sometimes less.* **Strategy:** *Go anytime.* **Audience:** *One and all.* **Rating:** ★★.

10 Jurassic Park River Adventure. You're about to take a peaceful cruise on a mysterious river past friendly, vegetarian dinosaurs. Of course, something has to go amiss or it wouldn't be much fun at all. A wrong turn is what it takes, and when you enter one of the research departments and see that it's overrun by spitting dinosaurs and razor-clawed raptors, things get plenty scary. This is all a buildup to the big finish: guarding the exit is a towering, roaring *T. Rex* with teeth the size of hams. By some strange quirk of fate, a convenient escape arrives via a tremendously steep and watery 85-foot plunge that will start you screaming. Smile! This is when the souvenir photos are shot. Thanks to high-capacity rafts, the line for this water ride moves fairly quickly. ☞ *Duration: 6 mins. Crowds: Huge all day long.* **Strategy:** *You can use Universal Express here; otherwise, go early or late.* **Audience:** *All but young children, who may be frightened. No pregnant women or guests with heart, back, or neck problems. Minimum height: 42".* **Rating:** ★★★.

11 Jurassic Park Discovery Center. If there's a scintilla of information your kids don't know about dinosaurs, they can learn it here. There are demonstration areas where a realistic raptor is being hatched and where you can see what you'd look like (or sound like) if you were a dino. In the Beasaurus area ("Be-a-Saurus"), you can look at the world from a dinosaur's point of view. There are numerous hands-on exhibits and a *Jeopardy!*-style quiz game where you can test your knowledge of dinosaur trivia. The casual restaurant upstairs is a nice place to take an air-conditioned break, and tables on the balcony overlook the lagoon. ☞ *Duration: As long as you like. **Crowds:** People mingle throughout, so that crowded feeling is almost extinct. **Strategy:** Go anytime. **Audience:** Older children and adults. **Rating:*** ★★.

need a break?

From **Thunder Falls Terrace,** which is open only in peak seasons, you can watch your fellow travelers make their harrowing plunge at the end of the Jurassic Park River Adventure. One terrace side, entirely glass, gives an optimal view. You can also sit outdoors next to the river's thundering waterfall.

Lost Continent

Ancient myths from around the world inspired this land. Just past a wooden bridge and huge mythical birds guarding the entrances, the trees are hung with weathered metal lanterns. From a distance comes the sound of booming thunder mixing with shimmering New Agey chimes and vaguely Celtic melodies. Farther along, things start to look like a sanitized version of a Renaissance Fair. Seers and fortune-tellers in a tent decorated with silken draperies and vintage Oriental carpets are on hand at **Mystics of the Seven Veils.** The gifted women read palms, tarot cards, and credit cards. In a courtyard outside the Sindbad show, a **Talking Fountain** offers flip responses to guest questions, such as "Is there a God?" Answer: "Yes. He's from Trenton and his name is Julio." Answers are followed by the fountain spraying unsuspecting guests.

groovy souvenirs

Puzzle-philes should check out **Tangles of Truth,** while Merlin wannabes can stock up on magic supplies at **Shop of Wonders.** The **Dragon's Keep** carries Celtic jewelry along with stuffed dragons, toy swords in various sizes and materials, and perfectly dreadful fake rats, mice, and body parts. **Treasures of Poseidon** is stocked with shells and baubles made from them, while a heavy drop hammer pounds out signs and symbols on classy medallions at the interesting **Coin Mint.**

⑫ Flying Unicorn. If you made the mistake of putting your kid on Dueling Dragons, the antidote may be this child-size roller coaster. Following a walk through a wizard's workshop, the low-key thrill ride places kids on the back of a unicorn for a very, very brief ride through a mythical forest. This is the park's equivalent of Universal Studios' Woody Woodpecker coaster. Kids lacking thrill-ride experience should enjoy this immensely. ☞ *Duration: Less than a minute. **Crowds:** Moderate, but since the ride is so brief, lines move quickly. You can use Universal Express here if the lines are heavy. **Audience:** Kids under 7, with adults riding along for moral support. **Minimum height: 36". Rating:*** ★★★.

❸ Dueling Dragons. Since the cars of this high-test roller coaster are suspended from the track, your feet will be flying off into the wild blue yonder as you whip through corkscrews and loops and are flung upside-down and around. The twin coasters are on separate tracks so the thrill is in the near misses, which makes front-row seats a prized commodity (there's a separate, much longer line if you just *have* to ride in the lead car). Coaster weights are checked by a computer, which programs the cars to have near-misses as close as 12 inches apart. Top speed on the ride ranges 55–60 mph, with the Fire Dragon (red) offering more inversions and the Ice Dragon (blue) providing more cornering. Either way, take advantage of the small lockers (free for 45 minutes) in which you can stash your stuff: wallets, glasses, change, and, perhaps, an air-sickness bag. (NO HURLING caps are sold in the adjacent gift shop.) ☞ *Duration: 2¼ mins.* **Crowds:** *Perpetual.* **Strategy:** *You can use Universal Express here; otherwise, ride after dark, when most visitors are going home; or go early. For the most exciting ride, go for the rear car of the Fire Dragon or the front car of the Ice Dragon; note that the queues for the front car of both coasters are much longer.* **Audience:** *Older children with roller-coaster experience and adults with cast-iron stomachs. No pregnant women or guests with heart, back, or neck problems. Minimum height: 54″.* **Rating:** ★★★.

need a break?   If you're ready to toast your conquest of mortal fear, head straight across the plaza to the **Enchanted Oak Tavern,** ingeniously sprawled inside the huge base of a gnarled old oak tree. Chow down on barbecued chicken and ribs or corn on the cob, although the surroundings surpass the food's quality. In the adjacent **Alchemy Bar,** order a glass of the park's own Dragon Scale Ale.

❹ Eighth Voyage of Sindbad. The story line of this stunt show is simple and satisfying: Sindbad and his sidekick arrive in search of treasure, get distracted by the beautiful princess, and are threatened by a sorceress. The good guy spends 25 nonstop minutes punching, climbing, kicking, diving, leaping, and Douglas Fairbanks–ing his way through the performance amid water explosions, flames, and pyrotechnics. Kids love the action, and women love Sindbad. The 1,700-seat theater can be a nice place to sit a spell and replenish your energy. ☞ *Duration: 25 mins.* **Crowds:** *Not a problem, due to size of the open-air auditorium.* **Strategy:** *You can use Universal Express here; otherwise, stake out seats about 15 mins prior to show time. Don't sit too close up front—you won't see the whole picture as well.* **Audience:** *Older children and adults.* **Rating:** ★★★.

❺ Poseidon's Fury. Following a short walk through cool ruins guarded by the Colossus of Rhodes, a young archaeologist arrives to take you on a trek to find Poseidon's trident. Although each chamber you enter on your walk looks interesting, the fact that very little happens in most of them can wear down the entertainment quotient. To reach the final chamber, you walk through a tunnel of water that suggests being sucked into a whirlpool—hard to describe, hard to forget. Then when the wall disappears, you are watching a 180-degree movie screen on which actors playing Poseidon and his archenemy appear. Soon, they are shouting at each other and pointing at each other and triggering a memorable fireworks and waterworks extravaganza where roughly 350,000 gallons of water, 200 flame effects, massive crashing waves, thick columns of water, and scorching fireballs begin erupting all around you. Although the first fifteen minutes don't offer much, the finale is loud, powerful, and hyperactive. Is it worth the time investment? That's up to you. ☞ *Duration: 20 mins. Crowds: Usually heavy. Strategy: You can use Universal Express here; otherwise, go at the end of the day. Stay to the left against the wall as you enter and position yourself opposite the podium in the center of the room. In each succeeding section of the presentation, get into the very first row, particularly if you aren't tall.* **Audience:** *Older children and adults.* **Rating:** ★★.

need a break?	Pick up soft drinks at **Oasis Coolers** or head for the **Frozen Desert**—and be sure to check out the gleaming mosaic sign, with its gilded tiles, as you wait for your chance to order a swirled fruit-and-ice-cream sundae. **Fire-Eater's Grill** serves grilled gyros, chicken fingers, hot dogs, and spicy chicken "stingers."

Seuss Landing

This 10-acre island is the perfect tribute to Theodor Seuss Geisel, putting into three dimensions what had for a long time been seen only on the printed page. While adults recall why Dr. Seuss was their favorite author, kids are introduced to the Cat, Things One and Two, Horton, the Lorax, and the Grinch.

Visually, this is the most exciting parcel of real estate in America. From the topiary sculptures to the jumbo red-and-white-striped hat near the entrance, the design is as whimsical as his books. Fencing is bent into curvy shapes, lampposts are lurching, and Seussian characters placed atop buildings seem to defy gravity. Everything, even the pavement, glows in lavenders, pinks, peaches, and oranges. Flowers in the planters echo the sherbet hues of the pavement.

From the main avenue, you can follow the webbed footprints to **Sneetch Beach,** where the Sneetches are frolicking in the lagoon alongside a strand littered with their beach things; the Seussonic boom box even has its own sound track, complete with commercials. Look carefully in the sand and you can see where the Sneetches jumped the fence to get to the beach, fell flat on their faces, and finally started dragging their radio rather than carrying it. Nearby is the **Zax Bypass**—two Zaxes facing off because neither one will budge. And keep an eye peeled for the characters—the grouchy Grinch, Thing One and Thing Two, and even the Cat himself.

groovy souvenirs	Stores such as **Cats, Hats & Things** and **Mulberry Store** stock wonderful Seussian souvenirs, from funny hats to Cat-top pencils and red-and-white-stripe coffee mugs. **Gertrude McFuzz's Fine-Feathered Finery** sells Seussian toppers. And when you're inspired to acquire a bit of two-dimensional Dr. Seuss, you can stop into **Dr. Seuss' All the Books You Can Read.** For a last-minute spree, the **Islands of Adventure Trading Company,** in the Port of Entry, stocks just about every kind of souvenir you saw elsewhere in the park.

⑯ If I Ran the Zoo. In this Seussian maze, kids can ditch the adults and have fun at their level. Here they encounter the trademarked fantasy creatures as they climb, jump, push buttons, and animate strange and wonderful animals. Park designers have learned that kids' basic needs include eating, sleeping, and getting splashed, so they've thoughtfully added interactive fountains. ☞ *Duration: Up to you and your young ones. Crowds: Probably heaviest early in the day.* **Strategy:** *If you can talk your kids into waiting, come at the end of your visit.* **Audience:** *Young children.* **Rating:** ★★★.

> need a
> break?

Would you eat ice cream on a boat? Would you drink juice with a goat? Taste vanilla on a cone? Sip some grape juice all alone? Then there are places you must stop. Stop at **Hop on Pop Ice Cream Shop.** What do you say after Moose Juice Goose Juice? Say, thank you, thank you, Dr. Seuss.

⑰ Caro-Seuss-el. The centerpiece of Seuss Landing could have come straight from the pages of a Seuss book. Ordinary horse-centered merry-go-rounds may seem passé now that Universal has created this menagerie: the cowfish from *McElligot's Pool*, the elephant birds from *Horton Hatches the Egg*, and the Birthday Katroo from *Happy Birthday to You!*—an ark of imaginary animals. The 54 mounts are interactive: the animals' eyes blink and their tails wag when you get on. It's a cliché, but there's a good chance you'll feel like a kid again when you hop aboard one of these fantastic creatures. ☞ *Crowds: Lines move pretty well, so don't be intimidated.* **Strategy:** *You can use Universal Express here; otherwise, make this a special end to your day.* **Audience:** *All ages. Children under 48" must be accompanied by an adult.* **Rating:** ★★★.

⑱ One Fish, Two Fish, Red Fish, Blue Fish. Dr. Seuss put elephants in trees and green eggs and ham on trains, so it doesn't seem far-fetched that fish can circle "squirting posts" to a Jamaican beat. After a rather lengthy wait, climb into your fish, and as it spins, you (or your child) control its up-and-down motion. The key is to follow the lyrics of the special song—if you go down when the song tells you to go up, you may be drenched courtesy of the aforementioned "squirting post." Mighty silly, mighty fun. ☞ *Crowds: Thick all day.* **Strategy:** *You can use Universal Express here; otherwise, go very early or at the end of your visit when the tykes have left, so you can be a kid at heart. Otherwise, skip on your first visit.* **Audience:** *Young children. Children under 48" must be accompanied by an adult.* **Rating:** ★★.

⑲ The Cat in the Hat. If you ever harbored a secret belief that a cat could actually come to your house to wreak havoc while your mom was out, then you get to live the experience here. After boarding a couch that soon spins, whirls, and rocks through the house, you roll past 18 scenes, 30 characters, and 130 effects that put you in the presence of the mischievous cat. He balances on a ball; hoists china on his umbrella; introduces Thing One and his wild sibling, Thing Two; and flies kites in the house while the voice of reason, the fish in the teapot,

sounds the warning about the impending return of the family matri-
arch. This ride promises high drama—and lots of family fun.
☞ *Crowds: Heavy.* **Strategy:** *You can use Universal Express here; other-*
wise, go early or near the end of the day, when the children go home.
Audience: *All ages. Children under 48″ must be accompanied by an*
adult. **Rating:** ★★★.

<table>
<tr><td>

**need a
break?**

</td><td>

Grab a quick bite inside the **Circus McGurkus** fast-food eatery. Check
out the walrus balancing on a whisker and the names on the booths:
Tum-tummied Swumm, Rolf from the Ocean of Olf, the Remarkable
Foon. Occasionally, a circus master–calliope player conducts a sing-
along with the diners below. If you prefer dining with large groups of
people, keep looking: the cavernous dining room seldom looks even
partially full.

</td></tr>
</table>

Islands of Adventure A to Z

To research prices, get advice from other travelers, and book travel ar-
rangements, visit www.fodors.com.

BABY CARE
There are diaper-changing tables in both men's and women's rest rooms,
and nursing areas in the women's rest rooms; stroller rentals ($10 per
day for singles, $16 for doubles) are at Guest Services in the Port of Entry.
Disposable diapers are available at no charge at Health Services, inside
Guest Services (don't be greedy; these freebies are for emergencies). Several shops here and at Universal Studios stock basic baby-care items—
diapers, wipes, etc.—but they are kept out of sight at the cash registers;
you just have to ask for them. Also, check the park maps: a baby bottle symbol lets you know which shops carry the items.

CHILD SWAP
All rides have Child Swap areas, so that one parent or adult party member can watch a baby or toddler while the other enjoys the ride or show.
The adults then do the Swap, and the former caretaker rides without
having to wait in line all over again.

CAMERAS & FILM
DeFotos is a camera shop in the Port of Entry on your right after the
turnstiles. They sell disposable cameras from about $13 (no flash) to
$17 (with flash).

DISABILITIES & ACCESSIBILITY
As at Universal Studios, Islands of Adventure has made an all-out effort not only to make the premises physically accessible for those with
disabilities but also to lift barriers created through the attitudes of
others. All employees attend workshops to remind them that people with
disabilities are people first. And you can occasionally spot staffers using
wheelchairs. Most attractions and all restaurants are wheelchair accessible. Ask for the comprehensive "Guests with Disabilities" guidebook
at Guest Services.

ATTRACTIONS   All attractions are completely accessible to guests who use wheelchairs with the exception of the **Incredible Hulk Coaster, Doctor Doom's Fear-fall,** and **Dueling Dragons,** for which you must transfer from your chair to ride. Ask an attendant for assistance or directions to wheelchair access.

SERVICES   Many employees have had basic sign-language training; even some of the animated characters speak sign, albeit sometimes an adapted version. You can pick up a "Guests with Disabilities" booklet at Guest Services, just inside the main entrance and to your right as you enter the park. There's also an **outgoing TTY** (Text Type Y) series hearing-impaired system on the counter in Guest Services.

WHEELCHAIR RENTALS   Manual wheelchairs ($12 per day) and electric scooters ($40 per day) can be rented at the Port of Entry to your left after the turnstiles. Photo ID or a $50 deposit on a credit card is required for either. If the wheelchair breaks down, disappears, or otherwise needs replacing, speak to any shop attendant. Since it's a long way between the parking garages and the park entrance, you may want to rent a push wheelchair at the garages and upgrade to an ECV (electric convenience vehicle) when you reach the park entrance. Quantities are limited, so it's recommended that you reserve in advance.
🛈 **Guest Services** ☎ 407/224–4233.

GUIDED TOURS

Like Universal Studios, Islands of Adventure has VIP tours, which offer what's called "back-door admission"—you go straight to the head of the line. It's worthwhile if you're in a hurry, if the day is crowded, and if you have the money. A five-hour VIP tour costs $100 per person for one park and $125 for two parks, including park admission price. An eight-hour tour for up to 15 people costs $1,400, again including park admission. Sales tax (6.5%) is extra. For $2,600, sign up for a two-day tour of both parks, which includes backstage access and discussions on the park's history, decorating, and landscaping.
🛈 **VIP Tours** ☎ 407/363–8295.

HEALTH SERVICES/FIRST AID

There are two First Aid Centers at Islands of Adventure: one at the front entrance inside Guest Services, and the main center near Sindbad's Village in the Lost Continent.

HOURS

Islands of Adventure is open 365 days a year, from 9 to 7, with hours extended to 10 during summer and holiday periods.

LOCKERS

The $7-a-day lockers are across from Guest Services at the entrance. There are also various Smart Lockers, which are free for the first 45 to 60 minutes (and $2 per hour afterward), scattered strategically throughout the park—notably at Dueling Dragons, the Incredible Hulk Coaster, and Jurassic Park River Adventure. Stash backpacks and cameras here while you're being drenched or going through the spin cycle.

LOST THINGS & PEOPLE

If you've misplaced something, return to the last attraction where you had it. If it's not there, head to Guest Services in the Port of Entry. If you lose your children or others, head directly to Guest Services.

MONEY MATTERS

There's an ATM outside the turnstiles to your right leading into the Port of Entry, as well as one near Dueling Dragons in the Lost Continent.

VISITOR INFORMATION

Guest Services is located just before the turnstiles on your right before you enter the park. Step through the turnstiles and you'll find a rack of brochures and maps in French, Spanish, Portuguese, Japanese, and German, as well as English. If you have questions prior to visiting, call Universal's main line or Guest Services.

Studio Information Boards are found at the Port of Entry in front of the Lagoon (where the circular walk around the park splits). The information boards are posted with up-to-the-minute ride and show operating information—including the length of lines at the major attractions.
🔢 Guest Services ☎ 407/224-6350. Universal Main Line ☎ 407/363-8000.

UNIVERSAL CITYWALK

CityWalk is Universal's answer to Downtown Disney. Like Disney, they've gathered themed retail stores and kiosks, restaurants, and nightclubs and placed them in one spot—here they're right at the entrance to both Universal Studios Florida and Islands of Adventure. CityWalk attracts a mix of conventioneers, vacationers, and what seems to be Orlando's entire youth market. You may be too anxious to stop on your way into the parks and too tired to linger on your way out, but at some point on your vacation you may drop by for a drink at Jimmy Buffett's Margaritaville, a meal at Emeril's, a concert at Hard Rock Live, or a souvenir from one of several gift stores. Visiting the stores and restaurants is free, as is parking after 6 PM. The only price you'll have to pay is a cover charge for the nightclubs, or you can invest in the more sensible $9.95 Party Pass for admission to all the clubs all night long. Pay $13 and you can add a movie to your evening out.

WET 'N WILD

The world's first water park, Wet 'n Wild, opened in 1977 and quickly became known as the place for thrilling water slides. Although it's now far from alone, Wet 'n Wild is still the nation's most popular water park, thanks to its ability to create more heart-stopping water slides, rides, and tubing adventures than its competitors. There are a complete water playground for kids, numerous high-energy slides for adults, a lazy river ride, and some quiet sandy beaches on which you can stretch out and get a tan.

After skimming down a super-speedy water slide, it may be time for a break. You can bring a cooler or stop for lunch at one of several food courts and find a picnic spot at various pavilions near the lakeside beach, pools, and attractions. Pools are heated in cooler weather, and Wet 'n Wild is one of the few water parks in the country to be open year-round.

If you're not a strong swimmer, don't worry. Ride entrances are marked with warnings to let you know which ones are safe for you, there are plenty of low-key attractions available, and during peak season as many as 400 lifeguards are on duty daily.

Black Hole. One of the most popular attractions here, this two-person tube ride (solo travelers share a lift with a stranger) starts in the bright light of day and suddenly plunges into a curvaceous 500-foot-long pitch-black tube illuminated only by a guiding, glowing line. The lack of light makes the spinning, twisting, 1,000-gallon-a-minute torrent more fun, and you'll likely be screaming your head off as you zip into curves and up the enclosed watery banked turns. *Minimum height: 36", 48" without an adult.*

The Blast. Replacing Ragin' Rapids is this two-passenger ride that gets you and a friend bumping down twists and turns through explosive pipe bursts and drenching waterspouts leading up to a final waterfall plunge. *Minimum height: 36", 48" without an adult.*

Blue Niagara. For a real thrill head to the top of this giant, six-story-tall slide. Twin tubes wrap around each other like snakes. Inside is a rushing waterfall. Since the tubes are roughly horizontal, you have the luxury of keeping your eyes open and watching the action unfold as you're shot through the curves. With two tubes, the line usually moves fairly quickly. *Minimum height: 36", 48" without an adult.*

Bomb Bay. Lines move quickly here, but not because the capacity is great. It's because a lot of kids chicken out once they reach the top. If you challenge yourself to the ultimate free fall, here's what happens: you step inside a large enclosed cylinder mounted above a nearly vertical drop. The attendant looks through the glass door to make sure your arms and legs are crossed (thereby preventing wedgies), and then punches a button to release the trapdoor. Like a bomb dropping out of a plane, you free-fall for 76 feet and then skim down the long, steep slide. The force of the water on your feet, legs, and back can be substantial, rivaling the emotional toll it took to do it in the first place. *Minimum height: 36", 48" without an adult.*

Bubba Tub. Because up to four people can take this ride together, this is one of the park's most popular attractions. After scaling the platform, your group boards a huge waiting inner tube. From the top of the six-story slide it flows over the edge and starts an up-and-down, triple-dip, roller-coaster ride that splashes down into a watery pool. *Minimum height: 36", 48" without an adult.*

Bubble Up. After catching sight of this enormous, wet beach ball about 12 feet tall, many kids race right over to try to climb to the top and then slide back down. Surrounding the ball is a wading pool, a respite between attempts to scale the watery mountain.

Dress the Part

Be sensible when choosing your bathing suit. You can't wear cutoffs or anything that has rivets, metal buttons, or zippers.

If your bare feet aren't used to it, the rough and hot surface of the sidewalks and sandpaperlike pool bottoms can do a number on your soles. Bring a pair of wading slippers when you're walking around, but be ready to carry them as you're plunging down a slide.

Keep money, keys, and other valuables in a locker. They could get lost on the super slides. If you wear prescription sunglasses, you can bring them on the rides; just take them off and clutch them tightly before you take the plunge.

While You're There

Keep in mind that lines here are Disney-esque. Once you think you're almost there, you discover there's another level or two to go. Get ready to be patient.

Bring a towel, but leave it behind when you ride.

Wear high SPF sunblock, and remember that you can get a sunburn even on a cloudy day.

Eat a high-protein meal to keep your energy going. A day here involves nearly nonstop walking, swimming, and climbing.

Der Stuka. Adjacent to Bomb Bay is a steep slide that offers a similar thrill, but without the trap-door drop. *Der Stuka,* "steep hill" in German, is hard to beat for sheer exhilaration. After climbing the winding six-story platform, you sit down on a horizontal slide, nudge yourself forward a few inches, and then gravity takes over. You're hurtling down a slippery, 250-foot-long speed slide that will tax your back and test the security of your bathing suit. This one's a real scream. *Minimum height: 36", 48" without an adult.*

Disco H20. Here's something even the folks at Studio 54 never dreamed of: a four-person raft that floats into a swirling aquatic nightclub. Once the 70-foot-tall building, your raft goes into a spin cycle as you're bombarded with sparkling lights, disco balls, and the sounds of the 70s' greatest hits. You must be 36" in height or you'll piss off the bouncer. ✉ *Minimum height: 36", 48" without an adult.*

The Flyer. Another good ride for families, this four-person toboggan carries you into switchback curves and down suddenly steep drops. The turns are similar to those on a real toboggan run. *Minimum height: 36", 48" without an adult.*

Hydra Fighter. Attached by a bungee cord to several towers are several two-person seats—each with a fire hose mounted on the front. Sitting back-to-back, you and your partner alternate between firing the hoses. The springy cord you're on starts to hoist you up and then from side to side. The stronger the stream of water, the higher and faster you go in all directions (and the farther you fall). Try to avoid sharing a seat with a chubby guy—it kills the bounce. Between getting everyone situated, letting them ride, and getting them unloaded, this one can mean a long wait. *Minimum height: 36", 48" without an adult.*

Kids' Park. Designed for children under 48", Kids' Park is like a day at the beach. There's a kid-sized sand castle to play in, and a 5-foot-tall bucket that dumps 250 gallons of water every few minutes onto a seashell-decorated awning, where it splashes off to spray all and sundry. In the center is a pool surrounded by miniaturized versions of the more popular grown-up attractions and rides. Children overjoyed when they play with a garden hose will go absolutely nuts when they see that they can slide, splash, squirt, and swim on rides here. Tables and chairs go fast, with many families here for nearly their whole visit.

Knee Ski/Wakeboard. A molasses-slow line marks the entrance to this seasonal attraction. A moving cable with ski ropes attached encircles a large lake. After donning protective headgear and a life vest, you kneel on a knee board or try to balance yourself on a wakeboard, grab a ski rope, and are given the opportunity to circumnavigate the lake. The ½-mi ride includes five turns: roughly 75% of the riders wipe out after turn number one, and 90% are gone by turn two. Only the agile and athletic few make it the distance. Hint: if you wipe out before turn one, you get to go back and try again. *Minimum height: 36", 48" without an adult.*

Lazy River. Had enough? Then settle into an inner tube for a peaceful trip down a gently moving stream. Bask in the sun as you drift by colorful flowers and tropical greenery. It's a nice break when your body just can't handle any more 45-degree drops.

Mach 5. After grabbing a soft foam board, you scale a few steps and arrive at one of three water slides. Conventional wisdom says that Lane B is the best, but it's possible all three are the same. Riding on your belly, you zip through some great twists, feel the sensation of hitting the high banks, and then splash down in a flood of water. Mucho fun. *Minimum height: 36", 48" without an adult.*

The Storm. At the top of the tower, two tubes carry a torrent of water. Climb in the tube, shove off in the midst of a tidal wave, and the slow, curving arc takes you around and around until you reach a 30-foot diameter bowl. Now you spin around again like soap suds whirling around a sink drain. After angular momentum has had its fun, you drop through a hole in the bottom of the bowl into a small pool. After you get your bearings and find the surface, you may be tempted to climb up and do it again. *Minimum height: 36", 48" without an adult.*

Surf Lagoon. This 17,000-square-foot lagoon is as close to a beach as you'll get in the park, which explains why it's generally packed. Also known as the Wave Pool, it's just past the turnstiles. Every so often, the lagoon is buffeted by 4-feet-high waves, which elicit screams of delight from kids. Likewise, adults are thrilled to find that the money they spent on the kid's floats, surfboards, and inner tubes was worth it.

The Surge. The title overstates the thrill of this ride, although it borders on exhilarating. Up to five passengers can fit in this giant raft: once you've gone over the lip of the first drop, there's no turning back. The raft zips down five stories while twisting and turning through a series of steeply banked curves and beneath waterfalls. If you or your kids are too nervous for rides like Bomb Bay or the Black Hole, then this is probably a safe bet. *Minimum height: 36", 48" without an adult.*

The Wild One. Open seasonally (usually April through September), this is a large, two-person inner tube that's towed around the lake. The ease of staying afloat is countered by the challenge of hanging on when you cross the boat's wake. *Minimum height: 36", 48" without an adult.*

Strategies for Your Visit to Wet 'n Wild

Wet 'n Wild is a must-stop spot for families. It can be very crowded, especially when the weather is hot. Peak months are June through August; slower ones December through February. The park fills up as the day progresses. If you want to try to avoid the hordes, get here in the morning a half hour before opening hours, or come on a cloudy day. In summer, come before or after the daily afternoon thunderstorms.

On the surface, there doesn't seem to be much reason to go to this park when it's gray and drizzly, but as a Wet 'n Wild spokeswoman observes, "This is a water park. If you aren't coming here to get wet, why are you here?" OK. If you do come on a day that rains, it will likely be a quick summer afternoon shower that will close attractions and clear pools only until 30 minutes or so after the thunder and lightning pass. If it looks like a soggy, thorough, all-day rain, skip it.

Wet 'n Wild A to Z

To research prices, get advice from other travelers, and book travel arrangements, visit www.fodors.com.

ADMISSION
Admission with tax is $36.16 for adults and $29.77 for children ages three to nine. The price drops by ten bucks roughly three to four hours before the park closes. Since closing times vary, call in advance to find out when the discount begins. For information about the Orlando FlexTicket, a combination ticket for all of the Universal Studios parks, *see* Discounts *in* Universal Orlando A to Z.

DISABILITIES & ACCESSIBILITY
Slides are accessible via stairway towers, which must be climbed. Guests with limited mobility might be able to bob about on a raft in **Surf Lagoon**, which has added a lift in which swimmers can be lowered into the water. Another activity is the chance to tube down the **Lazy River**. Many of the paths are flat and easily accessible in a wheelchair; how-

ever, no rides accommodate people using wheelchairs. Wheelchairs are available for $5 with a $25 refundable deposit.

FACILITIES
Don't think the expenses stop with parking and admission. If you came without a towel, you can rent one for $2 with a $2 deposit. Mighty small lockers, $5 with a $2 deposit, are near the entrance and at handy locations throughout the park. Tubes for the Wave Pool cost $4 with a $2 deposit. To save you $2, a combination of all three goes for nine bucks and requires a $4 deposit.

There are dressing rooms (with lockers), showers, and rest rooms to the left just after the main entrance. Additional rest rooms are near the Bubble Up, First Aid, and the Surge.

HEALTH SERVICES/FIRST AID
The First Aid Stand is between Surf Grill and Pizza & Subs.

HOURS
Wet 'n Wild is open 365 days a year, from 10 to 5, with hours extending from 9 AM to 9 PM in the summer. Call for exact hours during holiday periods.

LOST THINGS & PEOPLE
If you plan to split up, be sure everyone knows where and when you plan to meet. Lifeguards look out for kids who might be lost. If they spot one, they'll take the child to Guest Services, which will page the parent or guardian. The Lost & Found is at Guest Services, to the left just after you walk through the entrance to Wet 'n Wild.

MONEY MATTERS
The single ATM is at the rental facility, which is just inside the entrance and slightly to the right as you enter the park.

PARKING
Parking is $7 for cars, $8 for RVs.

PICNICKING
You are welcome to picnic and to bring coolers with food into the park. However, glass containers and alcoholic beverages are not permitted. There are many picnic areas scattered around Wet 'n Wild, in both covered and open areas.

SUPPLIES
Personal flotation devices, also known as life jackets, are provided by the staff. If you are looking for sunscreen, sunglasses, bathing suits, camera film, and other necessities, stop in the **Breakers Beach Shop** near the park entrance.

VISITOR INFORMATION
Wet 'n Wild has a **Guest Services** desk to the left as you enter the park.
🛈 General Information **Wet 'n Wild** ☎ 407/351-3200 recorded information, 407/351-1800 park operations.

UNIVERSAL ORLANDO TIMESAVERS

UNIVERSAL ORLANDO *isn't nearly the size of the Walt Disney World resort, so navigating it is much easier. There are some ways to reduce wait time even further.*

If you want to get to the best rides faster, skip the gargantuan parking garage and follow the signs to valet parking. For $16—twice the price of regular parking— you'll be in a lot just a few steps from the entrance to CityWalk and have a head start in reaching Universal Studios and Islands of Adventure, as well.

If you're toting a baby around with you, check out the Child Swap areas. Although you won't be able to ride with your spouse, one parent can enter the attraction, take a spin, and then return to take care of the baby while the other parent rides without having to wait in line again.

When you stay at one of Universal's resort hotels (Portofino Bay, Hard Rock Hotel, Royal Pacific), you receive early admission to the parks, priority seating at some restaurants, and the option of an unlimited-access ticket.

Do what you can to get into Universal Orlando's theme parks early—as early as 8 AM. Seriously. Seeing the park with about 100 other people is far better than seeing it with thousands. You can do in a few hours what could otherwise take an entire day. Plus, it's cooler in the morning: you can always leave and come back later if you get tired.

UNIVERSAL ORLANDO A TO Z

To research prices, get advice from other travelers, and book travel arrangements, visit www.fodors.com.

Admission

One-day one-park tickets for Universal Studios or Islands of Adventure cost $63.64 for adults and $51.12 for children. For a one-day, two-park visit, the cost is $84.09 adults, $72.37 for children (tax included). A two-day, two-park ticket, which is a good option since it includes a bonus pass for a free third day and admission to CityWalk clubs, is $111.78 for an adult and $101.13 for children 3–9.

Universal Express passes are included in the price of admission. Guests of on-site resorts can use their hotel key cards to access express lines, while guests staying off-site must use their paper tickets to make reservations for express-line access. If you're staying off-site, consider purchasing the **Universal Express PLUS pass** for an extra $15 to $25. The PLUS pass gives you express-line access without having to make reservations. Hint: There are discount coupons for most theme parks in tourist-friendly flyers distributed around Orlando, and the money you save through them may offset the cost of the PLUS pass. Tickets do not have to be used on consecutive days, but must be used within seven days of your first visit. You can get tickets in advance by mail through Ticketmaster or by contacting Universal Orlando Vacations.

HAND STAMPS   If you want to leave the park and come back the same day, have your hand stamped when you leave, and show your hand and ticket when you return.

🛈 **Ticketmaster** ☎ 800/745–5000. **Universal Studios Vacations** ☎ 888/322–5537.

DISCOUNTS

If you buy tickets at the Orlando/Orange County Convention & Visitors Bureau, you save about $5 per adult ticket ($3 on children's prices). American Automobile Association members get 10% off, sometimes more, at AAA offices.

The **Orlando FlexTicket** is similar to Walt Disney World's pass system. The four-park version gets you into Universal Studios, Islands of Adventure, Wet 'n Wild, and SeaWorld for $191.64 adults, $155.43 children three to nine, including tax, and five-park versions allow you 14 consecutive days of unlimited admission to all of the above as well as Busch Gardens Tampa ($228.92 and $191.64 adults/kids, including tax). SeaWorld–Busch Gardens combination Value Tickets, which include one day at each park, cost $85.95 for adults and $72.95 for children three to nine, with tax included.

🛈 **Orlando/Orange County Convention & Visitors Bureau** ✉ 8723 International Dr. ☎ 407/363–5871.

Arriving & Departing by Car

Traveling east on I–4 (from WDW and the Tampa area), get off at Universal Boulevard (Exit 75A). Then take a left onto Universal Boulevard and follow the signs.

Traveling west on I–4 (from the Daytona and Jacksonville areas), take Universal Boulevard (Exit 74B). Turn right onto Hollywood Way and follow the signs.

CAR CARE

A Hess gas station is conveniently located at the Turkey Lake Road entrance. If you need a battery jump in the parking garage, raise your hood and speak to the nearest employee.

PARKING

Universal's single parking garage complex, which serves both theme parks and CityWalk, is one of the world's largest car parks. Because your vehicle is covered, it's not so sweltering at the end of the day even when it's hot. The cost is $9 for cars and motorcycles, $10 for campers. Valet parking is available for $16.

Visitor Information

🛈 **Universal Orlando** ✉ 1000 Universal Studios Plaza, Orlando 32819-7610 ☎ 407/363–8000 or 888/331–9108 ⊕ www.universalorlando.com

SeaWorld Orlando, Discovery Cove & Busch Gardens

FODOR'S CHOICE

Kraken, *in SeaWorld*

Myombe Reserve, *in Busch Gardens*

Pets Ahoy, *in SeaWorld*

Rhino Rally, *in Busch Gardens*

Shamu Rocks America, *in SeaWorld*

SheiKra, *in Busch Gardens*

Updated by
Gary
McKechnie

WHEN ANHEUSER-BUSCH OPENED a small hospitality center next to its Tampa brewery in 1959, the company couldn't have foreseen what the park would become. Over the next four and a half decades wildlife and roller coasters were added, Busch acquired SeaWorld, and then developed Discovery Cove. Less glitzy than Walt Disney World or Universal, Busch Gardens, SeaWorld, and Discovery Cove are definitely worth a visit for a low-key, relaxing theme-park experience.

For entertainment value and location, perhaps the best choice is Sea-World. Ten minutes from both Universal and Walt Disney World, it is designed for animal lovers and anyone who prefers more natural pleasures. The legendary pet- and dolphin-theme presentations, as well as high-energy circus stage shows and the addition of two thrill coasters make this park a must-see.

Discovery Cove is more of a laid-back oasis, where you can spend time in a lagoon with dolphins and their trainers. There's time to relax on the beach, snorkel at your leisure among multicolor fish, and get up close to tropical birds in the aviary. The admission price includes a free seven-day pass to either SeaWorld or Busch Gardens.

Busch Gardens Tampa Bay is roughly 90 minutes from Orlando. Once this just seemed a useful place to stash the brewing family's collection of exotic animals and birds while tending to the real business of making and selling beer. In the end, the call of the wild proved so strong that the brewery became a sidekick to the Africa-theme zoological and thrill-ride park. If you've already counted on a Gulf Coast beach excursion, then the Tampa park is worth a stop.

SEAWORLD ORLANDO

There's a whole lot more to SeaWorld than Shamu, the "stage name" used for its mammoth killer-whale mascots. Sure, you can be splashed by the whales, stroke a stingray, see manatees face-to-snout, learn to love an eel, and be spat at by a walrus. But as the world's largest marine adventure park, SeaWorld celebrates all the mammals, birds, fish, and reptiles that live in and near the ocean.

Although SeaWorld can't rival Disney World when it comes to park design and attention to detail, it does offer a somewhat gentler and less-hurried touring experience governed mostly by show schedules. Every attraction is designed to showcase the beauty of the marine world and demonstrate ways that humans can protect its waters and wildlife. And because there are more exhibits and shows than rides—believe it or not, there are only three rides in the entire park—you can go at your own pace without that hurry-up-and-wait feeling.

First-timers may be slightly confused by the lack of distinct "lands" here—SeaWorld's performance venues, attractions, and activities surround a 17-acre lake, and the artful landscaping, curving paths, and concealing greenery sometimes lead to wrong turns. But armed with a map that lists show times, it's easy to plan a chronological approach that flows easily from one show and attraction to the next and allows enough time for rest stops and meal breaks.

Numbers in the margin correspond to points of interest on the SeaWorld map.

❶ Dolphin Nursery. In a large pool, dolphin moms and babies (with birth dates posted on signs) play and leap and splash. You can't get close enough to pet or feed them, so you'll have to be content peering from several feet away and asking the host questions during a regular Q and A session. Here's a popular answer: No, you can't take one home. Hint: If you just *have* to touch a dolphin, head over to Dolphin Cove in the Key West section. ☞ *Crowds: Not a problem.* **Strategy:** *Go during a Shamu show so the kids can be up front.* **Audience:** *All ages.* **Rating:** ★★.

❷ Tropical Reef. A good place to get out of the sun or rain, this indoor walk-through attraction contains 30 small aquariums filled with weird, ugly, and/or beautiful tropical fish, eels, worms, and crustaceans. The fish lie camouflaged on the bottom, dig holes, glow in the dark, or float lazily and stare at you through the glass. Clear and concise printed descriptions reveal interesting facts about each tank's inhabitants, leading to comments such as, "Hey, cool, look at this one!" or "Hey, let's go get some sushi." ☞ *Crowds: Not usually a problem.* **Strategy:** *Go at the end of the day—because it's near the entrance, most people stop here on their way in.* **Audience:** *All ages.* **Rating:** ★★.

❸ Turtle Point. At this re-creation of a small beach and lagoon, many of the sea turtles basking in the sun or drifting in the water were rescued from predators or fishing nets. Injuries make it impossible for these lumbering beauties to return to the wild. A kiosk is filled with sea-turtle info, and an educator is usually on hand to answer questions. Well worth a brief look. ☞ *Crowds: Sporadically crowded, but generally enough space for all to get a good view.* **Strategy:** *Go anytime.* **Audience:** *All ages.* **Rating:** ★★.

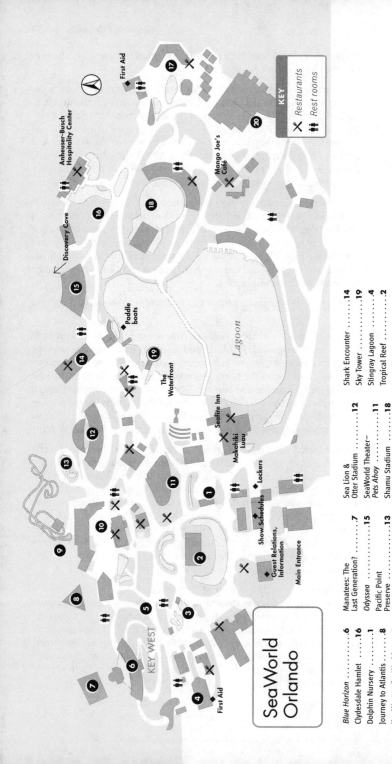

SeaWorld Orlando

KEY WEST

Main Entrance

Guest Relations, Information

Show Schedules

Lockers

Makahiki Luau

Seafire Inn

The Waterfront

Paddle boats

Lagoon

Discovery Cove

Anheuser-Busch Hospitality Center

Mango Joe's Café

First Aid

KEY

✕ *Restaurants*

⋔ *Rest rooms*

Best of the Park

Although there's room for all at the stadiums, the other attractions—especially Penguin Encounter and Key West at SeaWorld—can get unpleasantly crowded, and there may be lines at Wild Arctic, Shark Encounter, and Journey to Atlantis.

After passing the turnstiles, go straight ahead to the information desk for a park map and schedule of the day's shows. In this courtyard, take a moment to review show times and plan your day. With luck you can set up a clockwise tour of the park by seeing *Blue Horizons,* then visiting no-line attractions like **Turtle Point, Stingray Lagoon,** and **Dolphin Cove.** While you're in the neighborhood, allow time to see **Manatees.**

A few feet away are the park's two roller coasters, **Kraken** and **Journey to Atlantis.** Chances are there'll be a line, so you'll have to decide whether you want to stay or return once the crowds have thinned. **Penguin Encounter** is a good next stop, followed by a chance to visit and feed the sea lions at **Pacific Point Preserve.** Remember to keep track of the time so you can find a good seat at the **Sea Lion & Otter Stadium.** If you've built up an appetite by now, you may want to grab a quick bite at the **Smoky Creek Grill** or **Seafire Inn.**

Shark Encounter is the next upcoming popular attraction, followed by the stage show **Odyssea,** performed a few times a day. Next, stop by the arcades, games, and playground of **Shamu's Happy Harbor.** Check the show schedules again to take in a performance at **Shamu Stadium** and stick around afterward to visit the **Wild Arctic.**

You've now seen most of the attractions, and you'll likely have time to see the **Dolphin Nursery** and **Tropical Reef** before heading back to **Key West at Sea-World.** If your feet are still friendly, you may consider a cross-park hike back to **Shamu Stadium** for the *Shamu Rocks America* show.

On Rainy Days

Although SeaWorld gives the impression of open-air roominess, nearly a third of the attractions are actually indoors, and many others are shielded from the elements by canopies, cantilevered roofs, or tautly stretched tarpaulins. Rides that may close during a thunderstorm include Journey to Atlantis, Kraken, Sky Tower, Ski Show, Shamu's Happy Harbor, and the Paddle Boats. If you're unprepared for a cloudburst, pick up a poncho at one of the ubiquitous concession stands, and dive right in.

4 Stingray Lagoon. In a broad shallow pool, dozens of stingrays are close enough to touch, as evidenced by the many outstretched hands surrounding the rim. Smelts, silversides, shrimp, and squid are available for $4 a tray at nearby concession stands. The fishy treats are a delicacy for the rays, and when they flap up for lunch you can feed them and stroke their velvety skin. Even though they still have their stingers they won't hurt you; they just want food. This is one of the most rewarding experiences for everyone, and the animals are obligingly hungry all day. Look for the nursery pool with its baby rays. ☞ *Crowds: Can make it hard to get to the animals during busy seasons.* **Strategy:** *Walk by if it's crowded, but return before dusk, when the smelt concession stand closes.* **Audience:** *All ages.* **Rating:** ★★★.

5 Key West at SeaWorld. This laid-back 5-acre area is modeled after Key West, Florida's southernmost outpost, where the sunsets are spectacular and the mood is festive. There are no distinct "lands" within Sea-World, but Key West at SeaWorld comes close, containing individual tropical-style shows and attractions within its loosely defined borders. Along with an obvious Jimmy Buffett-y "island paradise" feel, a huge pool holds a few dozen Atlantic bottlenose dolphins that you can feed and pet. Fish trays cost $4. ☞ *Crowds: Can get thick but not overwhelming.* **Strategy:** *While on your way to or from a show, carve out some time to see the dolphins. If things are too crowded, go shopping until the crowds disperse.* **Audience:** *All ages.* **Rating:** ★★★.

6 Blue Horizon. This show blends avant garde costuming and acrobatics in the Cirque du Soleil style with a dolphin-and-trainer show. The premise is a young woman's discovery of the magic of dolphins. The first half of the program is designed to be ethereal and enchanting, but since the backstage is clearly visible and the "bird woman" flying in front of you is suspended by a thick steel cable, it's a little hard to believe in the fantasy. The second half of the show is better, relying on gymnastics and high dives, as well as several dolphins and trainers. There's no narration in this show—just a New Age musical accompaniment. ☞ *Duration: 30 min. Crowds: Heavy due to the attraction's newness.* **Strategy:** *Arrive 20 min early.* **Audience:** *All ages.* **Rating:** ★★.

7 Manatees: The Last Generation? If you don't have time to explore Florida's springs in search of manatees in the wild, then don't miss the chance to see this. The lumbering, whiskered manatees, which look like a cross between walruses and air bags, were brought here after near-fatal brushes with motorboats. Tramping down a clear tunnel beneath the naturalistic, 3½-acre lagoon, you enter Manatee Theater, where a film describes the lives of these gentle giants and the ways in which humans threaten the species' survival. In Manatee Habitat, a 300,000-gallon tank with a 126-foot seamless acrylic viewing panel, you can look in on the lettuce-chomping mammals as well as native fish, including tarpon, gar, and snook. Keep an eye out for mama manatees and their nursing calves. ☞ *Crowds: Since the area is fairly large, that "crowded" feeling is nonexistent.* **Strategy:** *Go during a Shamu show and not right after a dolphin show.* **Audience:** *All ages.* **Rating:** ★★★.

When to Go
Friday, Saturday, and Sunday are usually busier than the rest of the week, except during weeks that include Easter, July 4, and Christmas, when every day is equally busy.

As you get closer to the park, tune your car radio to 1540 AM for all the latest SeaWorld information.

Dress the Part
Wear comfortable sneakers—no heels or open sandals—since you may get your feet wet on the water rides.

Pack a bathing suit or dry clothes for yourself and your children, since sooner or later everyone is soaked. (The culprits: Shamu's Happy Harbor, the up-close rows in the Shamu show, and Journey to Atlantis.)

While You're There
If you prefer to take your own food, remove all plastic straws and lids before you arrive—they can harm fish and birds.

Budget ahead for food for the animals—feeding time is a major part of Sea-World charm. A small carton of fish costs $4.

Try to arrive early for Shamu shows, which generally fill to capacity on even the slowest days. Prepare to get wet in the "splash zone" down front.

---

groovy souvenirs

It's hard to pass up a plush Shamu—not least because the dolls are available all over the park. But if you're looking for a slightly less conventional souvenir, consider a soft manatee. You can buy either one at **Manatee Gifts.** Proceeds from the toys go to benefit a manatee preservation organization.

❽ Journey to Atlantis. SeaWorld's first entry in Florida's escalating "coaster wars" combines elements of a high-speed water ride and a roller coaster with lavish special effects. There are frequent twists, turns, and short, shallow dives but few hair-raising plunges except for the first, which sends you nearly 60 feet into the main harbor (plan on getting soaked to the skin), and the final drop, a 60-foot nosedive into S-shape, bobsledlike curves. Like most other attractions, this has a story line that doesn't really matter, but here it is: the lost continent of Atlantis has risen in the harbor of a quaint Greek fishing village, and you board a rickety Greek fishing boat to explore it. Once you're inside, an ominous current tugs at your boat, and an old fisherman offers a golden sea horse (actually Hermes—the messenger of the gods—in disguise!) to protect you from the evil Sirens. That's it. The wild, watery battle between Hermes and Allura (queen of the Sirens) is all a ploy to crank up effects using liquid crystal display technology, lasers, and holographic illusions. ☞ *Duration: 6 min. Crowds: Large. Strategy: Make a beeline here first thing in the morning or go about an hr before closing; going at night is definitely awesome, and the wait, if there is one, will be cooler. Audience: Older children and adults; definitely not for the faint of heart or for anyone with a fear of dark, enclosed spaces. Minimum height: 42". Rating:* ★★★.

❾ Kraken. Many people head straight for Kraken when the park opens, and as soon as you see its loops and dips, you'll know why. Until SheiKra opened at Busch Gardens, Kraken, at 149 feet, was the tallest coaster in Florida. And with floorless seats, seven inversions, and moments of weightlessness, it packs a serious punch. The theme of the coaster is a dragon chase—of course, Kraken's the dragon and you're the one being chased. Once you escape, look for the giant dragon eggs and the sign that warns you not to disturb them or risk Kraken's anger. *Duration: 6 min. Crowds: Expect lines. Strategy: Get to the park when it opens and head straight to Kraken; otherwise, hit it close to closing. Audience: Older children and adults. Minimum height: 54". Rating:* ★★★.

❿ Penguin Encounter. In a large white building between the Dolphin Stadium and the Sea Lion & Otter Stadium, 17 species of penguin scoot around a refrigerated re-creation of Antarctica. They're as cute as can be, waddling across icy promontories and plopping into frigid waters to display their aquatic skills. You watch an average day in their world through the thick see-through walls. A moving walkway rolls you past at a slow pace, but you can also step off to an area where you can stand and marvel at these tuxedo-clad creatures as they dive into 45°F (7°C) water and are showered with three tons of snow a day. Nearby, a similar viewing area for puffins and murres is nearly as entertaining. ☞ *Duration: Stay as long as you like. Crowds: Sometimes gridlocked despite the moving walkway nudging visitors past the glassed-in habitat. Strategy: Go while the dolphin and sea lion shows are on, and before you've gotten soaked at Journey to Atlantis, or you'll feel as icy as the penguins' environment. Audience: All ages. Rating:* ★★.

⓫ SeaWorld Theater—Pets Ahoy. Between Penguin Encounter and the Waterfront, SeaWorld Theater is the venue for the lively and highly entertaining *Pets Ahoy.* A dozen dogs, 18 cats, and an assortment of ducks, doves, parrots, and a pig (nearly all rescued from the local animal shelter) are the stars here. The animals perform a series of complex stunts, each more incredible than the last, until the hilarious finale. Stick around after the show and you'll have a chance to shake paws with the stars. ☞ *Duration: 20–25 min. Crowds: Can be substantial on busy days. Strategy: Gauge the crowds and get there early if necessary. Audience: All ages. Rating:* ★★★.

⓬ Sea Lion & Otter Stadium. Along with shows starring Shamu and the dolphins, the show here is one of the park's top crowd-pleasers. A multilevel pirate ship forms the set for *Clyde and Seamore Take Pirate Island,* a drama in which SeaWorld's celebrated sea lions, otters, and walruses prevail over pirate treachery. Get ready for plenty of audience interaction. Arrive 15 minutes early to catch the preshow—the mime is always a crowd favorite. ☞ *Duration: 40 min, including the 15-min preshow. Crowds: No problem. Strategy: Sit toward the center for the best view, and don't miss the beginning. Audience: All ages. Rating:* ★★★.

⑬ Pacific Point Preserve. A nonstop chorus of "aarrrps" and "yawps" coming from behind Clyde and Seamore's stadium will lead you to the 2½-acre home for California sea lions and harbor and fur seals. This naturalistic expanse of beaches, waves, and huge outcroppings of up-turned rock was designed to duplicate the rocky northern Pacific coast. You can stroll around the edge of the surf zone, a favorite hangout for fun-loving pinnipeds, and peep at their underwater activities through the Plexiglas wall at one side of the tank. Buy some smelts and watch the sea lions sing for their supper from close up. ☞ *Crowds: Not a problem. Strategy: Go anytime. Audience: All ages. Rating:* ★★★.

⑭ Shark Encounter. Within this large, innocuous white structure are some thoroughly creepy critters: eels, barracuda, sharks, and poisonous fish. Each animal is profiled via a video screen and educational posters. Then you walk through a series of four Plexiglas tubes, surrounded by tanks containing the world's largest collection of such animals—a half dozen species of shark alone in some 300,000 gallons of water. The entrance to the attraction has changed to make room for **Sharks Underwater Grill,** where diners can order fresh fish and Floribbean cuisine while watching their entrées' cousins. ☞ *Duration: Plan to spend 20 min. Crowds: Most significant when adjacent sea lion show gets out. Strategy: Go during the sea lion show. Audience: All ages. Rating:* ★★★.

⑮ *Odyssea.* Replacing the long-running and successful *Cirque de la Mer,* this show also stars Peruvian silent comic Cesar Aedo as an innocent spectator who's whisked into an underwater world where he witnesses the performances of sea creatures. With this storyline, the show can now present the type of circus acts you've probably seen several times before: a contortionist in a clam shell who can balance herself on one hand, gymnasts in a "kelp bed" twirling around on ropes, and trampoline artists dressed as penguins. Kind of odd. What you likely haven't seen is the giant, accordionlike, tubular worm that, well, you just have to see it. All in all, *Odyssea* is fun and free entertainment, although it's not quite as good as the previous show. ☞ *Duration: 30 min. Crowds: Heavy, but the auditorium seats more than 1,000 so you won't feel packed in. Strategy: Arrive at least fifteen minutes before curtain for a wide choice of seats. You'll be rewarded with an entertaining pre-show. Audience: All ages. Rating:* ★★★.

⑯ Clydesdale Hamlet. At its core, this is a walk around the stable where the hulking Clydesdale horses are kept, and a look at the clean corral where they get a chance to romp and play. A statue of a mighty stallion—which kids are encouraged to climb upon—makes a good theme-park photo opportunity. ☞ *Duration: You'll probably stay between 10 and 15 min. Crowds: Very light. Strategy: Go anytime. Audience: All ages. Rating:* ★.

need a break? Just far enough away from the Clydesdale stables, the light and airy **Anheuser-Busch Hospitality Center** combines cafeteria-style service with a bar serving Anheuser-Busch beverages (Michelob, Budweiser, O'Doul's) and soft drinks. Learn how to brew your own beer at the free half-hour A. B. Beer School, every hour. Hot tip: those 21 and over can also score two free beers here.

⓱ Shamu's Happy Harbor. If you want to take a break while your kids exhaust the last ounce of energy their little bodies contain, bring them here. This sprawling, towering, 3-acre outdoor play area has places to crawl, climb, explore, bounce, and get wet. There's also a four-story net climb and adjacent arcade with midway games. Youngsters go wild for the tent with an air-mattress floor, pipes to crawl through, and "ball rooms," one for toddlers and one for grade-schoolers, with thousands of plastic balls to wade through. With big sailing ships to explore and water to play in and around, Happy Harbor is spacious and airy. ☞ *Crowds: Often a challenge.* **Strategy:** *Don't go first thing in morning or you'll never drag your child away; but if you go midafternoon or toward dusk, expect plenty of hubbub. Bring a towel to dry them off.* **Audience:** *Toddlers through grade-schoolers.* **Rating:** ★★★.

⓲ Shamu Stadium. This is the place. Within this stadium is Shamu, SeaWorld's orca mascot, starring in the *Shamu Adventure,* which is hands down the most popular show in the park. The preshow, including video footage of orcas in the wild and a bald eagle in flight, introduces several daily performances of the whales' fantastic flips, jumps, and other acrobatic antics. In the funkier nighttime *Shamu Rocks America,* the famous orca jumps to music and the patriotic show is not to be missed. Wherever you sit, arrive early to get the seat of your choice. Careful: in the "splash zone," Shamu uses his weight and massive fluke to flood the front rows, which kids seem to think is the best thing going. ☞ *Duration: 30 min.* **Crowds:** *Sometimes a problem.* **Strategy:** *Go 45 min early for early-afternoon show. Close-up encounters through the Plexiglas walls are not to be missed, so trot on down.* **Audience:** *All ages.* **Rating:** ★★★.

FodorsChoice

need a break? Backstage at Shamu Stadium, **Dine With Shamu** includes a buffet meal (salads, pastas, seafood, beef, chicken, and desserts) and the chance to watch training sessions and talk to trainers in an exclusive area. A separate children's buffet is available. About 200 guests can be accommodated per seating, at $32 per adult and $18 per child age 3–9. Reservations can be made at the information counter at the park entrance or by calling ☎ 407/327–2420 or ☎ 800/327–2420.

⓳ Sky Tower. The focal point of the park is this 400-foot-tall tower, the main mast for a revolving double-decker platform. During the six-minute rotating round-trip up and down, you'll get the inside scoop on the park's history, its attractions, and surrounding sights. There's a separate $3 admission for this one. ☞ *Crowds: Fairly light.* **Strategy:** *Look for a line and go if there's none.* **Audience:** *All ages.* **Rating:** ★★.

❷⓪ Wild Arctic. Inside this pseudo–ice station, you embark on one of SeaWorld's three rides, a flight-simulator helicopter ride leading to rooms with interactive, educational displays. If your stomach can handle the rolls and pitches of a virtual helicopter, it makes for scary, enjoyable, queasy fun. Afterward, there are above- and below-water viewing stations where you can watch beluga whales blowing bubble rings, polar bears paddling around with their toys, and groaning walruses trying to hoist themselves onto a thick shelf of ice. ☞ *Crowds: Expect a wait during peak seasons.* **Strategy:** *Go early, late, or during a Shamu show. You can skip the simulated helicopter ride if you just want to see the mammals.* **Audience:** *All ages. Minimum height for motion option: 42".* **Rating:** ★★★.

need a break? A boardwalk leads from Shamu Stadium across the lagoon to the **Waterfront,** lined with shops, eateries, kiosks, and street performers. Although there are scheduled performances, chances are you'll just wander through the area en route to another attraction and catch some strolling musicians. The restaurants have entertainment, too, like at **Voyagers Wood Fired Pizzas** where chefs Dominick and Luigi flip jokes along with pizzas. Shops offer an impressive amount of exotic goods and include the **Tropica Trading Company,** with gifts from Bali, Indonesia, Italy, and South America; and **Allura's Treasure Trove,** a toy shop where you can design your own porcelain dolls. In summer and on holidays, the Waterfront is the base for a fireworks show.

SeaWorld Orlando A to Z

To research prices, get advice from other travelers, and book travel arrangements, visit www.fodors.com.

ADMISSION

TICKETS   At this writing, regular one-day tickets to SeaWorld cost $59.75 for adults, and $48 for children ages 3 to 9, not including tax. For a 10% discount and permission to bypass the admission line at the park, you can purchase and print out your tickets online at ⊕ www.seaworld.com.

DISCOUNTS   SeaWorld sometimes offers, but doesn't publicize, what they call their "2nd Day Free" passes. These are complimentary, nontransferable tickets valid for seven days and good for a second day's admission to the park. The passes are handed out near the exit to customers leaving the park. Make sure your entire party is together when arranging the following day's admission. Standard discounts are available for senior citizens, AAA members, military personnel, and guests with disabilities.

The Orlando FlexTicket, which covers SeaWorld, other Busch parks, and the Universal parks, is similar to Walt Disney World's pass system. The base price of a four-park ticket, which allows you up to 14 consecutive days of unlimited admission to Universal Orlando, Wet 'n Wild, and SeaWorld is $184.95 for adults, and $150.95 for children 3–9. The five-park ticket gets you in to all of the above as well as Busch Gardens and costs $224.95 for adults and $189.95 for children respectively. Sea-

World–Busch Gardens combination Value Tickets, for one day at each park, cost $95.98 for adults and $86.39 for children 3–9. None of these prices include sales tax.

🇫 **Orlando Flex Ticket** ☎ 800/224-3838 ⊕ www.orlandoflexticket.com

ARRIVING & DEPARTING BY CAR

SeaWorld is just off the intersection of I–4 and the Beeline Expressway, 10 minutes south of downtown Orlando and 15 minutes from Orlando International Airport. Of all the Central Florida theme parks, it's the easiest to find. If you're heading west on I–4 (toward Disney), take Exit 72 onto the Beeline Expressway (a.k.a. Highway 528) and take the first exit onto International Drive and follow signs a short distance to the parking lot. Heading east, take Exit 71.

PARKING   Parking costs $7 per car, $8 for an RV or camper. Preferred parking, which costs $10, allows you to park in the six rows closest to the front gate.

BABY CARE

Diaper-changing tables are in or near most women's rest rooms and in the men's rest room at the front entrance, near Shamu's Emporium. You can buy diapers at machines in all changing areas and at Shamu's Emporium. A special area for nursing is alongside the women's rest room at Friends of the Wild gift shop, equidistant from SeaWorld Theater, Penguin Encounter, and Sea Lion & Otter Stadium.

Gerber baby food is sold by request at most restaurants (for yourself you may want to order a more substantial entrée), as well as the Children's Store. For more infant items you'll have to leave the park for a short drive to a nearby supermarket or drugstore. Ask for directions to Publix or Walgreen's on International Drive, the CVS Pharmacy on Central Florida Parkway, or Kmart on Turkey Lake Road. Strollers can be rented at the Information Center for $10 for a single, $17 for a double, with a $2 refundable deposit.

CAMERAS & FILM

Memory cards for digital cameras, as well as disposable 35mm and APS (advanced photo system) cameras and film, are for sale on the premises.

DISABILITIES & ACCESSIBILITY

ATTRACTIONS   With wide sidewalks and gentle inclines to the seats at shows, SeaWorld may be Florida's most accessible theme park. The **Dolphin Stadium, Sea Lion & Otter Stadium, SeaWorld Theater,** and **Shamu Stadium** all provide reserved seating areas that are accessible and have entry via sloping ramps. The stadium shows usually fill to capacity, so plan to arrive 30–45 minutes before each show, 45–60 minutes in peak seasons.

At Shamu Stadium, the reserved seating area is inside the splash zone, so if you don't want to get soaking wet, get a host or hostess to recommend another place to sit.

Penguin Encounter, Shark Encounter, Tropical Reef, and **Journey to Atlantis** are all wheelchair accessible. To ride the moving-sidewalk viewing areas in Penguin Encounter, Shark Encounter, and Journey to Atlantis, you must transfer to a standard wheelchair, available in the boarding area, if you do not already use one. Tropical Reef and Penguin Encounter have minimal entertainment value for guests with visual impairments, but being hearing impaired does not detract from the enjoyment. To ride **Kraken** you must transfer to the ride vehicles.

Shamu's Happy Harbor has some activities that are accessible to children using wheelchairs, including many of the games in the midway. Most of the other attractions are geared toward those who can climb, crawl, or slide.

RESTAURANTS & Restaurants are accessible, but drinking straws are not provided here
SHOPS out of concern for the safety of the animals. Shops are level, but many are so packed with merchandise that maneuvering in a wheelchair can be a challenge.

SERVICES There are outgoing TTY (Text Type Y) hearing-impaired systems in the lobby of Guest Services and across from the Dolphin Stadium. Sign-language interpreters for guided tours are available with advance notice.

WHEELCHAIR Both standard ($8) and electric wheelchairs ($32) are available at Sea-
RENTALS World.

GUIDED TOURS

Following the lead of Disney and Universal, SeaWorld has created many backstage tours. The shortest is the $6.95 **Let's Talk Training** course held at Sea Lion & Otter Stadium Monday through Thursday. For an all-too-brief 25 minutes, you're shown how SeaWorld's animals are taught to perform.

There are three hour-long educational tours to choose from, including **Polar Expedition,** which gives you a backstage and upclose view of polar bears and penguins and beluga whales and goes behind the scenes at SeaWorld's Penguin Research Facility. **Predators** teaches about the care of the animals at Shark Encounter and includes a behind-the-scenes tour at Shamu Stadium. It ends with a backstage peek in the shark food preparation room as well as a chance to touch a live shark. **To The Rescue** takes a look at animal rescue, rehabilitation, and release efforts for manatees and turtles, with the tours going to the quarantine area and lab and surgery facilities and a chance to hand-feed exotic birds in a free-flight aviary. A dollar of your fee goes to help the SeaWorld and Busch Gardens Conservation Fund. All tours cost $8.95 for adults and $7.95 for children, and leave every 30 minutes until 3 PM. Register at the guided-tour center to the left of the Guest Relations information center at the park entrance.

For an in-depth SeaWorld experience (as well as a chance to cut in line), the six-hour **Adventure Express** is the ultimate tour and includes lunch and reserved seating at shows. An educator is assigned to your group to answer questions, and the group is limited to 16 people. The cost is $89 per adult and $79 for children, on top of park admission. There's free fish to feed the animals, backstage access to the penguins, and instant admission to Kraken, Journey to Atlantis, and Wild Arctic. You can make reservations in person at the guided-tour center or by phone.

Unlike other theme parks, SeaWorld has created a variety of programs that—for a price—will get animal lovers up close and personal with their favorite creatures. Reservations for the programs can be made at ☎ 800/432–1178 (press 5), online at ⊕ www.seaworld.com, or at the guided-tour center inside the park's entrance.

The **Marine Mammal Keeper Experience** is an eight-hour class at which you work side by side with a SeaWorld caretaker, helping to care for the manatees, dolphins, walruses, beluga whales, and seals. At the Manatee Rehab Center, you may even have the chance to bottle-feed a baby manatee. If you have $399 worth of animal love in your heart and are prepared to start the loving at 6:30 AM, then this one's for you. The price includes lunch and a seven-day admission to the park as well as a souvenir photo and T-shirt.

Sharks Deep Dive is based on the real-life shark dives adventurers do in exotic locations. Here guests 10 and older will don a SeaWorld wet-suit and either snorkel or scuba dive in an authentic shark cage for about a half hour as it is drawn through a 125-foot-long underwater habitat teeming with an array of more than 50 sharks, including sand tigers, sand bars, Atlantic and Pacific black tips, nurse, and sawfish, as well as hundreds of tropical fish. It costs $150 to scuba (you'll need proof of certification) or $125 to snorkel—but the price also includes two-day park admission, a commemorative T-shirt, and a shark information booklet.

Your kids should be tickled to know that SeaWorld's education department also offers more than 200 summer camp programs, including sleepovers and educational adventures for kids. They're not the the the only ones having fun—there are also Adventure Camp opportunities for the whole family.

🎟 Fees & Schedules **Guided Tour Center** ☎ 800/432–1178 or 800/406–2244. **Summer Camp Programs** ☎ 407/363–2380 **Education Reservation Office** ☎ 407/363–2398.

HEALTH SERVICES/FIRST AID
First Aid Centers, staffed by registered nurses, are behind Stingray Lagoon and near Shamu's Happy Harbor. In case of an emergency ask any SeaWorld employee to contact Security.

HOURS
SeaWorld opens daily at 9 AM, but closing hours vary between 6 and 7 PM, and, during the holidays, as late as 11 PM. To be safe, call in advance for park hours.

LOCKERS
Coin-operated lockers are available inside the main entrance and to the right as you enter, next to Shamu's Emporium. There are also lockers throughout the park and, conveniently, by the wild coaster, Kraken. The cost ranges between $1 and $1.50, depending on size.

LOST THINGS & PEOPLE
All employees who see lost-looking children take them to the information center, where you can also go to report lost children. A parkwide

paging system also helps reunite parents with kids. The center operates as the park's Lost & Found, too.

MONEY MATTERS

An ATM linked to various bank and credit-card networks is at the exit gate, but five others are around the park—mostly near shops, restaurants, and rest rooms. Foreign currency can be exchanged at the Special Services window at the main gate (daily 10–3).

PACKAGE PICKUP

Purchases made anywhere in the park can be sent to Package Pickup, in Shamu's Emporium, on request. Allow an hour for your purchases to make it there.

PET CARE CENTER

A pet care center near the main entrance accommodates dogs, cats, hamsters, and whatever other creatures you may have brought. Dogs must be walked at least once during the day. If you have a cat, bring a litter box. For meals, you're expected to bring food for your pet, but SeaWorld will spring for the water. The cost is $6.

VISITOR INFORMATION

The **Main Information Center** is just inside the park, near the entrance. A large board nearby lists all show times.

🚩 Tourist Information **SeaWorld Orlando** ✉ 7007 SeaWorld Dr., Orlando 32821 ☎ 407/351–3600 or 800/327–2424 ⊕ www.seaworld.com.

DISCOVERY COVE

Moving away from the traditional theme-park format, SeaWorld took a chance when it opened Discovery Cove, a 32-acre limited-admission park that's a re-creation of a Caribbean island, complete with coral reefs, sandy beaches, margaritas, and dolphins.

Here's how it works: after entering a huge thatch-roof tiki building, you register and are given a reserved time to swim with the dolphins, the highlight of your Discovery Cove day. You're issued a photo ID that allows you to charge drinks during the day, and that's all you need to worry about. With your admission, everything else is included—lockers, food, mask, fins, snorkel, wetsuit, swim vest, and towels.

Once inside, you are confronted with rocky lagoons surrounded by lush landscaping, intricate coral reefs, and underwater ruins. The pool where snorkeling lessons are taught has cascading waterfalls, and white beaches are fringed with thatched huts, cabanas, and hammocks. Exciting encounters with animal species from the Bahamas, Tahiti, and Micronesia are part of the experience. A free-flight aviary aflutter with exotic birds can be reached by way of a quiet walkway or by swimming beneath a waterfall.

Although $249 per person may seem steep, if you consider that a dolphin swim in the Florida Keys runs approximately $150 and that your admission includes a complimentary pass to SeaWorld *or* Busch Gardens, it starts to look like a bargain. Here's an alphabetical listing of what you'll see.

Aviary. The entrance to this 12,000-square-foot birdhouse is a kick. To get here you can walk in from the beach or, better yet, swim into it from the river that snakes through the park by going under a waterfall. You arrive in a small-bird sanctuary populated with darting hummingbirds, tiny finches, and honeycreepers. In the large-bird sanctuary, you get up close to perched and wandering toucans, red-legged seriem, and other colorful and exotic birds. Look for attendants who have carts filled with free fruit and birdfeed that you can use to attract the birds. Don't be frightened if one leaps onto your shoulder, and get ready to snap a photo. ☞ *Rating:* ★★★.

Beaches. Lined with swaying palms, tropical foliage, and quaint thatched huts, this is where you claim your own private spot in the sand, with shady umbrellas, hammocks, lounges, or beach chairs. Since the park's biggest-selling feature is limited guest capacity, the most seductive aspect is staking out your private stretch of sand and leaving the real world behind. For the most privacy, head to the far west end of Discovery Cove. A few cabanas and tents are available on a first-come, first-served basis, and towels and beach chairs are plentiful. ☞ *Rating:* ★★.

Coral Reef. Snorkelers follow butterfly fish, angelfish, parrotfish, and a few dozen other species through this authentic-looking coral reef. The brighter the day, the more brilliant the colors. Stingrays sail slowly and gracefully past as you float above. Some of the fish may come within touching distance, but when you reach out to them they scatter in nanoseconds. Also inside the coral reef is an artificial shipwreck where panels of Plexiglas in the hull reveal a pool filled with barracudas and sharks. Since it's hard to see the glass underwater, you'll get the heebie-jeebies when you see them face to face. ☞ *Rating:* ★★★.

Dolphin Lagoon. Before you get too excited about Discovery Cove's top attraction, remember that your "swim" with the dolphins is supervised and restricted to what's safe for both you and the dolphins. Your image of frolicking with the dolphins is probably mistaken. But despite the limitations, the attraction offers you the truly unique chance to touch, feed, play with, and even kiss a bottlenose dolphin, one of the most social and communicative marine animals.

Before you can get into the lagoon, you have to sit through a somewhat tedious 15-minute orientation with the rest of your group, i.e., the people with whom you will be sharing your dolphin. The orientation consists of an off-topic film about the SeaWorld companies and their animals, plus a few words from a dolphin trainer. Afterward, you proceed to the lagoon where you enter the surprisingly chilly water for roughly 25 minutes of "interaction" with one of 25 dolphins. You spend most of the time crouched down in knee-deep water, and a flotation vest is required, so even small children and nonswimmers can take part. Discovery Cove trainers teach you about dolphin behavior, and you discover the hand signals used to communicate with them. Your dolphin may roll over so you can touch his or her belly, and, at your signal,

Before You Go
Make reservations three to four months in advance for peak seasons. Admission slots for June start selling out in March.

The masks Discovery Cove provides don't accommodate glasses, so wear contacts if you can. Otherwise, try to get one of the limited number of prescription masks available at Tropical Gifts, which can be used for the day with a deposit of $75.

Don't bother to pack your own wetsuit or fins. Wetsuits and vests are available here, and fins, which annoy the fish, are discouraged.

When You're There
You can leave your keys, money, and other personal belongings in your locker all day. The plastic passes you are given upon entering the park are all you need to pick up your meals and (nonalcoholic) drinks.

If it becomes an all-day thunder and lightning rainstorm on your reserved day, attempts will be made to reschedule your visit when you're in town. If not, you have to settle for a refund.

---

leap into the air. Near the end of the session, you have a chance to swim out to deeper water, catch hold of the dolphin's fin and have him or her pull you back to shore. At some point, you pose for pictures, which you'll be corraled and cajoled into buying immediately after leaving the water. ☞ *Duration: 45–60 min. Audience: Anyone age 6 and older. Rating:* ★★★.

Ray Lagoon. This is where you can wade and play with dozens of southern and cow-nosed rays. Don't be afraid—they've had their barbs removed. Often, several rays get together and make continuous loops of the pool, so if you stay in one spot they'll continue to glide past you. ☞ *Rating:* ★★.

Tropical River. The Tropical River meanders its way throughout most of Discovery Cove. River swimmers float lazily through different environments—a sunny beach; a dense, tropical rain forest; an Amazon-like river; a tropical fishing village; an underwater cave; and the aviary. The only drawback here is that the bottom of the river is like the bottom of a pool and the redundancy of the scenery along the way makes it a little boring after a while. ☞ *Rating:* ★.

Discovery Cove A to Z

To research prices, get advice from other travelers, and book travel arrangements, visit www.fodors.com.

ADMISSION

If you're committed to visiting Discovery Cove, make reservations well in advance—attendance is limited to about 1,000 people a day. Tickets are $249 per person with the dolphin swim, with prices dropping to $149 if you choose to forsake the dolphin. Either fee includes unlimited access to all beach and snorkeling areas and the free-flight aviary; a full meal; use of a mask, snorkel, swim vest, towel, locker, and other amenities; parking; and a pass for seven days of unlimited, come-and-go-as-you-please admission to SeaWorld Orlando or Busch Gardens in Tampa.

DISABILITIES & ACCESSIBILITY

Wheelchairs with wide, baloonlike tires that roll over the sand are available. Call to request one in advance so that they have one waiting for you at the reception.

GUIDED TOURS

Discovery Cove's **Trainer for a Day** program allows up to 12 guests a day to work side by side and behind the scenes with animal experts and interact with dolphins, birds, sloths, anteaters, sharks, rays, and tropical fish. Whether they have an in-water training experience with a dolphin, pamper a pygmy falcon, feed tropical fish, or play with an anteater, participants have the hands-on opportunity to train and care for these unique animals. You'll receive a reserved dolphin swim, an enhanced dolphin interaction and training encounter, and a chance to feed and take care of exotic birds in the aviary. Plus, you have behind-the-scenes access for feedings in the coral reef, small-mammal playtime and training, animal food preparation and record review, and behavioral training class. You'll walk away with a lot of memories as well as a souvenir shirt, dolphin book, and waterproof camera. Be sure about this one. It costs $419 (plus 6.5% sales tax), but it does include the regular admission price.

HOURS

Discovery Cove is open daily from 9 to 5:30, with extended hours in summer and on some holidays. Allow a full day to see all attractions.

RESERVATIONS

Reservations for Discovery Cove can be made by calling ☎ 877/434–7268, daily 9–8. Additional information can be found at ⊕ www.discoverycove.com.

BUSCH GARDENS

After you've endured an overdose of urban density, you can drive through Tampa to reach an exotic thrill ride–adventure park–botanical garden. Busch Gardens manages to be the land-based equivalent of Sea-World—it's quiet and calming, but it's also entertaining, intriguing, and wild.

The dozen areas are loosely themed to recall turn-of-the-20th-century Africa. Scattered throughout are rides (including some thrilling roller coasters), water attractions, a sky ride, and shops galore. And throughout the park are some stunning animals to admire and learn about.

The main entrance takes you through Morocco. Walking counterclockwise from the main entrance along the winding paths, you encounter Myombe Reserve, Nairobi, Timbuktu, Congo, Stanleyville, Land of the Dragons, and the Bird Gardens. Take a sharp right from Myombe Reserve and Nairobi to get to the Crown Colony, Egypt, Edge of Africa, and the Serengeti Plain. Although it's not as easy to navigate as the "hub-and-wheel" design of Disney's Magic Kingdom, each area has its own distinctive architectural style as well as regional music pumped through carefully camouflaged loudspeakers.

Despite the proliferation of rides, animals are the cornerstone of Busch Gardens' appeal. More than 2,000 birds, mammals, and reptiles inhabit its 335 acres; the aviary houses some 600 rare birds; and about 500 African big-game animals roam uncaged on the 65-acre Serengeti Plain.

Aside from steam trains and the sky ride, there's no mass transit here. Exploring these far-flung lands requires strong legs and a comfortable pair of walking shoes. There's little of the crowd and bustle of the Disney parks here, however, so relax and enjoy the beauty of nature spiced up by an occasional adrenaline-pumping adventure.

Numbers in the margin correspond to points of interest on the Busch Gardens map.

Morocco

Busch Gardens' main entrance leads you through the gates of a tiled and turreted Moroccan fort and into a land of swirling colors, striped awnings, and exotic music. Before you go too far, be sure to pick up a park map. On the back of the map you'll find a handy listing of park information, entertainment and show times, tours, animal exhibits, and dining.

Morocco itself contains two eateries, the Zagora Café and Sultan's Sweets, and there are numerous souvenir stands arranged in a replica of an open-air *souk,* or marketplace. To the left are lockers as well as the open-air Marrakesh Theater stage for the *Moroccan Roll* musical revue. Throughout this area, Middle Eastern music fills the air, brightly colored wool tassels droop overhead, brass urns glimmer, bangles shimmer, veils waft in the wind, and mouthwatering smells float from the bakery.

❶ **Sultan's Tent.** From the entrance, the path to the right rolls past the shops and bazaars until, adjacent to the Zagora Café, you'll find a raised platform hung with colorful striped curtains. Different musical performances are offered at various times throughout the day. Just to the right, a lagoon is filled with some mighty hefty alligators. ☞ *Crowds: Not a problem.* **Strategy:** *Pause to take in the surroundings before entering.* **Audience:** *All ages.* **Rating:** ★.

❷ **Moroccan Palace Theater.** The stage show *KaTonga* (which means "gathering place") brings a bit of Broadway to northern Africa. The premise of the show follows aspiring storytellers as they try to master their craft with fanciful tales of animal folklore. As they recount their stories, en-

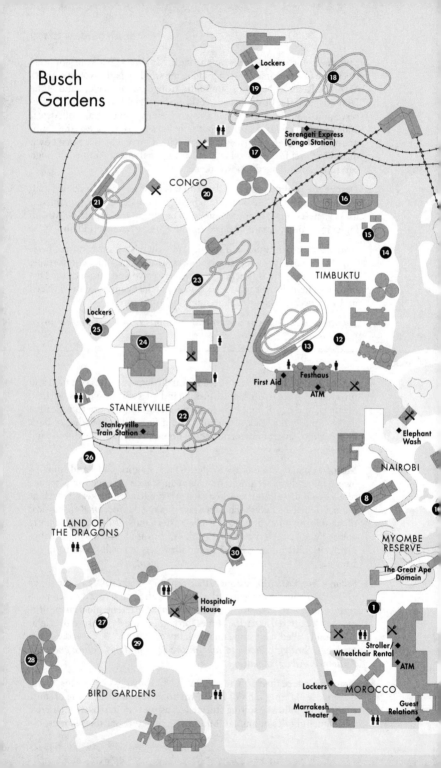

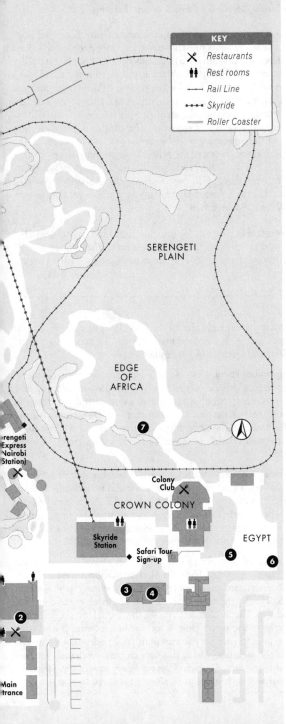

KEY

✕ Restaurants
🚻 Rest rooms
⊷ Rail Line
••• Skyride
═══ Roller Coaster

ergetic acrobats in colorful costumes and larger-than-life animal puppets dance to the heavy beats of African music. Among the show's characters, a monkey named Whirly learns confidence, Kipopo the caterpillar finds inner beauty, Rok Rok the bullfrog is taught to respect and listen to others, and an African crowned crane named Kilinda helps animals and people reach a common understanding. Among the show's collaborators was Broadway legend Michael Curry, best known for his Tony-award–winning work on *The Lion King*. The theater is gorgeous, and the creativity of the presentation will immerse you in the beauty of the African jungle and the mesmerizing power of a flooding river. ☞ *Duration: 35 min. Crowd: Sizable, but there's always enough room. Strategy: Shows 4 times daily, 6 in high season; check schedules posted outside. Arrive 30 min before show time if you'd like to get a good seat. Audience: All ages.* **Rating:** ★★.

Marrakesh Market is the stop for inexpensive bracelets, moderately priced brass, and exorbitantly priced Moroccan leather, not to mention a rainbow of gauze veils in which to swathe your own little Salome.

Crown Colony

Crown Colony, at the far right side of the park, is an upscale restaurant and not an area per se, but it does mark the confluence of Egypt, the Skyride Station, and a stable of Clydesdale horses.

❸ **Show Jumping Hall of Fame.** One of the Busch daughters is a successful equestrian, hence this permanent exhibit devoted to jumping and racing horses. Pictures, trophies, saddles, and decorations help tell the story of famous equestrians and their horses. ☞ *Duration: As long as you like. Crowds: Seldom a problem. Strategy: Skip it the first time, unless you have time to kill at the end of the day. Audience: All ages.* **Rating:** ★★.

❹ **Clydesdale Hamlet.** The usual batch of oversize beasts galumphs around a corral and stables; a particularly patient horse is periodically led out for photographs, much to the delight of kids and their parents. If your daughter is obsessed with *National Velvet*, and most other things equine, take her to the Show Jumping Hall of Fame next door. ☞ *Crowds: Very light. Strategy: Go anytime. Audience: All ages.* **Rating:** ★.

Skyride. This elevated tour places you five stories above Timbuktu and the Serengeti Plain. Departing from the Skyride Station across from the Crown Colony restaurant, you travel to the Congo station (which places you close to Kumba), where you can step off and back on to continue on for a round-trip. The Skyride lets you see the animals on the Serengeti Plain and hippos in the water from a lofty vantage point. It also provides aerial reconnaissance so you can plan your pedestrian approach to the park. If the weather is bad, this service may be closed. ☞ *Duration: Round-trip 7 min. Crowds: Can get heavy in midday. Strategy: Ride in the morning or toward park closing time. Audience: All ages.* **Rating:** ★★★.

Best of the Park

Figuring out the most efficient way to visit Busch Gardens is only slightly less complicated than planning a safari. Pick up a list of shows at the entrance gate and loosely schedule your day around them; they make welcome breaks in a full day on your feet. Must-see shows feature the birds, elephants, and Ka-Tonga. If you're a coaster enthusiast, after passing right on through Morocco head directly for **Gwazi** then **SheiKra**. If not, then head for the **Myombe Reserve.** Upon exiting you'll

be in Nairobi, where you should make tracks for **Rhino Rally,** which will get real crowded real quick. Then head to **R. L. Stine's Haunted Lighthouse 4-D** nearby. Afterward, you can breeze through the **Elephant Display, Animal Nursery,** and **Curiosity Caverns** en route to Egypt and **Montu.** After the coaster, stop by **Tut's Tomb** before taking a well-deserved break at the British Colonial–theme Crown Colony restaurant.

You've now covered about half the park, and you can take a round-trip **Skyride** or walk through the **Edge of Africa** before hoofing it over to the Congo. Ride the **Congo River Rapids, Kumba,** the **Tanganyika Tidal Wave,** and, if you wish, the slower **Stanley Falls Log Flume Ride.** Now that you're soaked to the bone, head through the **Land of the Dragons** (stopping if you have kids) and then to the **Lory Landing** aviary. If your timing is right, you can step right up for the performance at the **Bird Show Theater.** Follow the path to the free beer at the **Hospitality House.** If you skipped **Gwazi** earlier, head back toward Morocco and catch it now and then take in the last ice-show performance of the day at the **Moroccan Palace Theater.** It's a nice way to end your visit, and you can hit the Moroccan souk on your way out.

On Rainy Days

The Skyride may close temporarily because of lightning or high winds, but otherwise inclement weather generally means business as usual in the park. However, you will get wet, and because the animals seek shelter (as you probably will want to), your experience may not be as rich as it would be when the sun is out.

Egypt

Dominating this section of the park is the awesome roller coaster known as Montu. There are also plenty of shops, midway games to take your money, and an interesting tour through a replica of the tomb of King Tutankhamen ("Tut" to his friends).

 Tut's Tomb. The entrance (adjacent to a wide-open bazaar) may be hard to spot, but this re-creation of Howard Carter's 1922 discovery and excavation of the boy king's tomb is dead on. As in the real thing, the ceilings are low and confining, and an outer chamber contains perfect replicas of the beautiful objects and golden animals buried with Tut. When you enter the actual tomb, the outer sarcophagus is raised so you can view the mummy and iconic golden mask. Exit into the gift shop and buy some reproductions of the objects you just saw. ☞ *Duration: 10 min.* *Crowds: Lines are almost nonexistent.* *Strategy: Go anytime.* *Audience: Everyone.* *Rating:* ★★.

❻ Montu. Arriving at Montu is like walking onto the set of *Cleopatra.* The towering walls are carved with the likenesses of Egyptian pharoahs and animals. The snaking 4,000-foot-long roller coaster is a gut-wrenching thrill ride. As is true of its cousin Kumba, the mere sound and sheer size of Montu are intimidating, but take the chance if you want to brag about it later. ☞ *Duration: 3 min.* *Crowds: Lines can get long on busy days.* *Strategy: Go early in the morning or late in the day. Most of the time, settle in for a wait that will be worth it.* *Audience: Older children and adults. No guests with motion sickness or heart, neck, or back problems. Minimum height: 54".* *Rating:* ★★★.

Edge of Africa

On the southern edge of the Serengeti Plain, this 15-acre walk-through area showcases hippos, ring-tailed lemurs, crocodiles, and various species of fish. In addition, there are an African village, supposedly vacated by a Masai tribe that had been overtaken by lions and hyenas, and a safari encampment with giraffes and zebras, as well as habitats for meerkats (a kind of African mongoose) and vultures.

❼ Edge of Africa. Set off on a self-guided tour down a winding path and you'll reach caves where lions rest behind (hopefully) unbreakable glass. Throughout the area, you are quite close to lions, giraffes, hyenas, impalas, antelope, and ring-tailed lemurs. A real treat is stopping by the submerged acrylic windows to watch lumbering multi-ton hippos race gently underwater—a very odd, dreamlike vision. Animal lovers may want to invest in the half-hour-long Edge of Africa **Serengeti Safari,** which puts you and up to 19 others on the veldt in an open-air flatbed truck. During this up-close and personal encounter the guides are very informative, fielding as many questions as you want to ask. The highlight of the trip is getting to feed the animals yourself. The giraffes and ostriches are ready for food—and you should be ready for a perfect photo, especially when an 18-foot-tall giraffe reaches down to nibble leaves from your hand. Hint: Try to go on the first tour of the day, when it's cooler and the animals are still moving. ☞ *Tour times and cost: Departures vary from 2 to 6 times daily based on season. Call for frequency. Cost is $29.99; reservations are required.* *Duration: Safari tour 30 min.* *Crowds: Heavy. Tours depart from the Edge of Africa Gift Shop by the Skyride. You can shop here or walk around the plaza while awaiting your tour.* *Strategy: The earlier the better.* *Audience: Children under 5 are not admitted on the Safari Tour.* *Rating:* ★★★.

Serengeti Plain

This is one of the must-sees at Busch Gardens: 500 animals running free on 65 acres that are supposed to re-create their natural habitats (which

When to Go

Credit a huge number of local annual pass holders for making Friday through Saturday the most crowded times at the park. In summertime, however, it's hot enough that even the local crowd lightens up.

Because animals nap through most of the day, the bulk of the action occurs first thing in the morning and in late afternoon. Arrive early and try to see them during the first hour if possible.

Dress the Part

Know how to spot a theme-park novice? Look at their shoes. High heels and cowboy boots are signs of first-timers. Don't make that mistake here. At 350 acres, the park is more than three times the size of the Magic Kingdom.

Busch Gardens charges $5 for ponchos for water rides and 25¢ to give others riding the water rides a quick squirt. Water rides will get you wet—very wet—and you'll get quite cold on winter and overcast days.

If you carry a backpack, get ready to pay $1 to stow it in a locker each time you go on a coaster. There are lockers adjacent to the Moroccan Palace Theater at the entrance, as well as lockers outside most flume rides and coasters.

While You're There

As soon as you arrive in the park, set up a specific rendezvous location and time in case you and your companions get separated. Good spots to meet are in front of the Moroccan Palace Theater, at the entrance to any of the train stations, by the Clydesdale Hamlet, at the Edge of Africa Welcome Center, or at a park bench in Land of the Dragons.

A large sign at the entrance lists each day's performance schedule, which is also printed on a handout. Show times are also posted next to the individual stages and theaters.

If you want to snap loved ones in midride, look for photo-staging spots at Congo River Rapids, Kumba, and the Tanganyika Tidal Wave.

---

turn out to look remarkably similar to Florida pastureland). Still, they're not confined by cages. Residents of the grasslands include zebras, impalas, giraffes, ostriches, gazelles, kudus (a heftier impala), and white rhinos. In addition to the Safari Tour, there are a couple of other ways to see this area: the Serengeti Express railroad, which skirts the edge of the Serengeti; and the Skyride, which offers an aerial view.

Myombe Reserve: The Great Ape Domain

The entrance to this luxuriant walk-through rain forest (opposite the Moroccan Palace Theater) is easily overlooked, but should not be missed. The park's most-heralded animal attraction houses an extended family of chimpanzees and another family of Western lowland gorillas. The gorillas are magnificent, as you'd expect, and the opportunity to see them in a somewhat natural setting through a wide viewing area is thrilling.

Guides make scheduled appearances to disperse gorilla lore, including the fact that gorillas rest 40% of the day and feed another 30%, and that they enjoy a treat of termite mound tops that they snap off and eat. Plaques and educational signage also help you understand these animals. The gorillas seem to like the soft hay near the wide bay windows, so chances are you'll have plenty of time to share face time with these stunning creatures. The chimps, which often stay in the tall grass and in caves, can be harder to see. When you do catch a glimpse, it will always be entertaining. ☞ *Duration:* As long as you like. *Crowds:* Not significant. *Strategy:* Visit either first thing in the morning or late in the afternoon; both are close to feeding time, when both gorillas and chimps are more active. *Audience:* All ages. *Rating:* ★★★.

groovy souvenirs

There are three must-have stuffed animals on the Central Florida theme-park circuit, and two of them are at **J. R.'s Gorilla Hut,** just outside Myombe Reserve—cuddly gorillas and delightfully long-limbed chimpanzees whose Velcro palms attach in an everlasting hug. SeaWorld's killer-whales are the third.

Nairobi

Myombe's rain-forested path leads you to Nairobi, with its animal nursery, elephant display, and the Nairobi train station—a gingerbread clapboard structure. Nairobi also contains the highly entertaining Rhino Rally.

❽ Nairobi Field Station. The animal experts at Busch Gardens would prefer that the mothers care for their young, but when they can't, the tiny baby birds, reptiles, and animals are brought here. You can't go inside, but through the windows you'll see convalescing animals wrapped in nests of blankets. With more than 2,000 animals and birds in the park, the patient list changes daily—from newborns to injured animals. Just watch the featherless infant cockatoos and the cuteness factor is off the charts. ☞ *Duration:* As long as you like. *Crowds:* Not a problem. *Strategy:* Visit anytime. *Audience:* All ages. *Rating:* ★★.

❾ Elephant Display. A big attraction in Nairobi is this open enclosure where roughly a dozen elephants walk and sway and graze. There's a swimming pool where elephants snort, swim, and clean off before tossing dust on their backs to prevent sunburn. If you like watching elephants, this is the place to do it. ☞ *Duration:* As long as you like. *Crowds:* Never too crowded. *Strategy:* Go anytime. *Audience:* All ages. *Rating:* ★★.

⑩ **Curiosity Caverns.** This walk-through exhibit takes you through caves filled with snakes and bats and rats. In small but comfortable environments are a green tree python, rat snakes, a boa constrictor, and a reticulated python that has no trouble reaching a branch 10 feet off the ground. The lighting here is dark and mysterious: all the better for watching the fruit bats and vampire bats hanging from branches and stalactites. It may be more than just the coolness of the cave giving you chills. ☞ *Duration: Up to you. Crowds: Light, and it moves smoothly. Audience: All ages. Strategy: Go anytime. Rating:* ★★★.

Fodor's Choice

⑪ **Rhino Rally.** Even on very slow days it can take a long time to earn a seat in one of the 17-passenger Land Rovers that zip across the rugged terrain. Similar to Disney's Jungle Cruise, this attraction stars fast-talking drivers and lots of bad gags. A guest is chosen to be each expedition's race rally navigator; he or she helps direct the driver up steep hills and into deep rivers, bringing the truck very close to white rhinos, antelope, crocodiles, Cape buffalo, warthogs, and other exotic animals. The thrills and laughs don't stop at the water's edge, since the scary grand finale finds your vehicle entering a raging and turbulent river. Aside from the wait, this is a perfect ride. ☞ *Duration: 8 min. Crowds: Significant. Strategy: Very early or very late. Audience: All ages, but may be scary for younger kids. Rating:* ★★★.

Serengeti Express. The Kenya Kanteen outdoor café is a good place to watch and listen for the arrival of this faithful copy of an East African steam locomotive. It arrives here at the Nairobi Train Station. With room for 400, the train will likely have a seat for you. The train chugs around the Serengeti Plain and then circumnavigates the park in a 2½-mi journey, with a stop in Stanleyville. If you're taking pictures, try to sit on the left side of the benches: it's closer to the Serengeti Plain. ☞ *Duration: 20 min roundtrip; it's about 10 min to the Congo Train Station and another 5–6 min to Stanleyville. Crowds: Steady, but you almost always find a seat. Strategy: Since it comes only every 20 min, watch the mother elephants dunking the little ones in the elephant pool until you hear the whistle; then dash for the station. Audience: All ages. Rating:* ★★.

Timbuktu

Outside Timbuktu are the gates of a towering white mud fort. Inside is a collection of kid-size rides, arcades, and midway games.

⑫ **Sandstorm.** Why ride this spinning and pitching and revolving machine? Because it's the "number one ride for making guests throw up," says a Busch Gardens staffer. It doesn't look all that menacing, but the constant rotation of both your seat and the arm to which it's attached does the trick. ☞ *Duration: 2½ min. Crowds: Not a problem. Strategy: Go anytime. Audience: Older children and adults. No guests with motion sickness or heart, neck, or back problems. Rating:* ★★.

⑬ **Scorpion.** Compared with Montu and Kumba, this looming 1,805-foot steel roller coaster looks like child's play. But the beast is twisted into a gigantic 360-degree hoop with a 65-foot drop and reaches a maximum speed of 50 mph. Far scarier than it looks. ☞ *Duration: 2 min. Crowds:*

Lines can build at midday in busy periods. Strategy: Go early or late. Audience: Older children and adults. No guests with motion sickness or heart, neck, or back problems. Minimum height: 42″. Rating: ★★.

⑭ Phoenix. Similar to the pendulumlike pirate ships at traveling fairs, this towering structure offers increasingly elevated crescent swings back and forth, higher and higher, until the whole thing swoops sickeningly over the top. Nevertheless, it's far more gentle than most thrill rides. The only queasy feeling you may get is when you're hanging upside down at the top of the arc. Bon voyage! ☞ *Duration: 2 min. Crowds: Lines can build at midday in busy periods. Strategy: Go early or late. Audience: Older children and adults. No guests with motion sickness or heart, neck, or back problems. Minimum height: 48″. Rating:* ★★.

⑮ Cheetah Chase. This five-story, moderately thrilling family-style coaster offers a nice alternative to the hair-raising high-tech coasters and the small child-size versions. Several drops and a few hairpin turns is what you'll get. Nearby, you can pay a few bucks to win a cheap prize at a dozen midway games. Rhino Rings, fishing with a magnet, popping a frog onto a lily pad, swatting multiple King Tuts . . . it's all here, a cash-sucking profusion of chance. ☞ *Crowds: Can get heavy in midafternoon. Strategy: Do the ride in early morning. Audience: All ages. Rating:* ★★.

⑯ R. L. Stine's Haunted Lighthouse. Following the wake of "4-D" shows (3-D films plus sensory effects), like Disney's *It's Tough to be a Bug* and Universal's *Shrek 4-D,* Busch Gardens opened this 25-minute feature written exclusively for the attraction by the children's horror author. Aside from a poor script, a weird and implausible storyline, and wooden child actors who prove the value of Haley Joel Osment, the show can be fun for first-time viewers. The story starts with a century-old shipwreck and segues to veteran actor Christopher Lloyd as Cap'n Jack sharing seafaring tales with two young friends. These real kids eventually find themselves face to face with ghost kids who live in the lighthouse. There are several places where the 4-D kicks in with mild surprises that involve air, water, and creepy tingling sensations. Since it's new, you could see it once, but, unless you have kids, probably not a second time. ☞ *Duration: 25 min. Crowds: The theater holds several hundred people so lines are fairly tolerable. Strategy: Go early or late. Audience: Kids to adults, although some pre-K children may find it a little intense. Rating:* ★★.

Congo

Unlike the open, dusty plains of the Serengeti and Nairobi, Congo and Stanleyville next door are delightfully shaded by lush plantings and lofty, leafy trees, under whose branches nestle African fetish statues and piles of expedition-supply boxes.

A few huts scattered throughout contain snakes in wire boxes and inquisitive parrots perched in cages. Keepers are on hand to explain their behavior and hold them for you to stroke. One end of the Skyride and a stop on the Serengeti Express can also be found here. Hysterical shrieks often emanate from the area's several thrill rides, reminding you that the visitors, if not the natives, are perpetually restless.

⑰ Ubanga-Banga Bumper Cars. Aptly named, this popular attraction has a carnival allure, and young kids, along with big kids who have never grown up, love them. If it's been years since you've sat behind the wheel of a bumper car, you may be surprised that they're not quite as fast as the ones you recall from your youth—but they're still immensely fun. ☞ *Duration: About 4 min. Crowds: Never significant enough to cause a wait except in midafternoon during busy periods. Strategy: Go anytime, but don't wait if there's a line. Audience: Older children and adults. Rating:* ★★.

⑱ Kumba. The counterpart to Egypt's Montu, this is nearly 4,000 feet of twisting turquoise steel. The cars speed up to 60 mph as they race through three popular coaster maneuvers: a "diving loop" that plunges you from 110 feet; a camelback, with a 360-degree spiral and three seconds of weightlessness; and the world's largest loop, with a height of 108 feet. That's in addition to spirals, cobra rolls, and a corkscrew in the dark. When it's all over, you'll be holding your spinning head and walking away on wobbly knees. If you like coasters, don't miss this. ☞ *Duration: 3 min. Crowds: Often heavy. Strategy: Go as soon as the park opens. Audience: Older children and adults. No guests with motion sickness or heart, neck, or back problems. Minimum height: 54". Rating:* ★★★.

⑲ Congo River Rapids. People who love the pitching and plunging and soaking of water rides rate this as one of the best. Twelve people sit in an inner tube–like raft and set sail for a bumper-car ride on a stream. As you go bumping and bucketing through nearly ¼ mi of rapids and waterfalls and then through a dark cave, watch for surges of splashing water from the river, as well as the sadistic observers firing water cannons from the banks. The adjacent gift shop sells $5 ponchos that should keep you relatively dry. ☞ *Duration: 5 min. Crowds: There's usually a line. Strategy: Go early to avoid waits and have the best time. Audience: Older children and adults. No guests with motion sickness or heart, neck, or back problems. Children under 42" must be accompanied by an adult. Rating:* ★★★.

⑳ Claw Island (Bengal tigers). Somehow all the hoopla at the park doesn't seem to bother the lazy Bengal tigers. There are several observation points from the sidewalks and courtyards that encircle the island and moat. If you want to see the cats when they're most active, come in early morning or late afternoon. The shady benches overlooking the island are a pleasant place to recuperate before hitting the next ride. ☞ *Crowds: Nonexistent. Strategy: Go in the early morning, when the animals are awake. Audience: All ages. Rating:* ★★★.

㉑ Python. When this ride premiered in the late 1970s, it was a cutting-edge coaster. Today you'll be amazed that it only lasts just over a minute and is absent of the series of twists newer coasters offer. Passengers are hurled through two hoops at 50 mph on the 1,250-foot track of this steel roller coaster. Thrilling, but it takes a backseat to its wilder siblings. This may be a good test coaster for kids. ☞ *Duration: 70 seconds. Crowds: Significant only in busy seasons. Strategy: Go early or*

late during holiday periods. **Audience:** *Older children and adults. No guests with motion sickness or heart, neck, or back problems. Children must be accompanied by an adult. Minimum height: 48".* **Rating:** ★★.

Stanleyville

Named for a city in the Democratic Republic of Congo now known as Kisangani, this area is very much akin to the Congo in flavor. Here, too, you're surrounded by lush tropical vegetation native to that part of Africa. Since Stanleyville was revamped in 2005 when the SheiKra roller coaster opened, it now also looks like a recently unearthed city from a lost civilization.

FodorsChoice

㉒ SheiKra. The nation's only "dive coaster" is certain to thrill thrillseekers. Within the jungle ruins of an ancient civilization, you board a 24-passenger coaster that's the tallest (200 feet) in Florida, and then set off on a three-minute heart massage that begins with a 20-story ascent that leads to a 70-mph rocket shot straight down. This is followed by an Immelman turn (a fast roll) that leads to another terrific plunge of 138 feet into an underground tunnel, concluding the ride with a watery finale. Needless to say, you might want to watch it go round a few times before lining up. ☞ **Duration:** *3 min.* **Crowds:** *Significant, with lines even on average days.* **Strategy:** *Ride early in the morning or in the evening.* **Audience:** *Older children and adults. Minimum height: 54".* **Rating:** ★★★.

㉓ Stanley Falls Log Flume Ride. Although somewhat dated, the Log Flume is still very popular because of its 40-foot drop. The creaking creek ride is a little slow, but at least you're certain to get wet. ☞ **Duration:** *3½ min.* **Crowds:** *Significant, with lines even on average days.* **Strategy:** *Ride early in the morning or in the evening.* **Audience:** *Older children and adults. Minimum height: 42".* **Rating:** ★★.

㉔ Stanleyville Theater. This show venue changes its acts every one to six months to keep things current. Busch Gardens' talent scouts have gone as far as China, France, and Morocco to recruit first-class shows, which often consist of acrobats, jugglers, and other circus-style acts. A listing of the current performance is displayed at the entrance and on park brochures. Not only is the open-air theater a cool place to retreat, the beauty of these shows will remind you that Busch's best offerings aren't always from a tap or on a track. ☞ **Duration:** *30 min.* **Crowds:** *Theater can get crowded.* **Strategy:** *Arrive at least 15–20 min prior to show time.* **Audience:** *All ages.* **Rating:** ★★★.

㉕ Tanganyika Tidal Wave. Amazingly, the first *five minutes* of this ride reveals little. You drift along in the boat with just some scraggly plants and a few huts to look at, biding your time until you reach the first—and only—plunge. The attraction for most is the chance to get wet, and there are two ways to get covered in water here. During the ride itself, a 55-foot drop sends you into a splash pool where you will definitely get soaked. You can get even more drenched by standing at the viewing bridge at the bottom of the drop, where a recording of Tchaikovsky's *1812 Overture* heralds the next wave. Either huddle behind the Plexiglas shelter on the bridge or skitter off—fast. ☞ **Duration:** *6 min.*

Crowds: Significant, with lines even on average days. **Strategy:** *Ride early in the morning or in the evening.* **Audience:** *Older children and adults. Minimum height: 42".* **Rating:** ★★.

Land of the Dragons

This cluster of kid-size attractions is one of the best children's areas in any theme park. Rope climbs and bouncing walkways fill the three-story Tree House at the center, and there are miniature carousels, Ferris wheels, and cars that preschoolers can "drive." Several times daily, conservation specialists arrive to tell animal stories, sometimes bringing live animals as props. It's wonderfully colorful and cheerful, and some local season-ticket holders are known to spend hours here. ☞ *Crowds: Can peak when parents need a break.* **Strategy:** *Wait until later in the day, or you may never get your youngsters away; or go at midday for a respite from the heat.* **Audience:** *Young children.* **Rating:** ★★★.

Bird Gardens

Following the path from Stanleyville onto the bridge and over the train tracks brings you here. Bird Gardens has a sterling children's playground and more than 1,800 exotic birds from 350 species. The flock of vivid Caribbean flamingos is one of the largest in captivity; the hundred or so birds, which also includes a paler breed from Chile, are fed beta-carotene supplements to maintain their color.

26 **Lory Landing.** The multicolor birds from Indonesia and the South Pacific fly freely beneath two sprawling live oaks just over the ramp from Stanleyville. For $1 you can feed the lories Lorikeet Nectar, a juice mixed just for them. Most birds will land on a shoulder or outstretched hand to take a sip. A trainer is usually on hand to answer questions. ☞ *Duration: As long as you like. Crowds: Not a problem.* **Strategy:** *Go in the morning, when the birds will be hungriest.* **Audience:** *All ages.* **Rating:** ★★★.

27 **Flamingo Island.** Whether they're strutting, preening, standing on one leg, or bobbing for food, the sight of around 100 flamingos en masse is striking. ☞ *Duration: As long as you like. Crowds: Not a problem.* **Strategy:** *Go early or late to see birds at their most active.* **Audience:** *All ages.* **Rating:** ★★.

28 **Aviary.** Nearly 200 species of birds, including macaws and egrets, flutter freely among the trees and walk along the ground of this lushly landscaped walk-through cage. ☞ *Duration: As long as you like.* **Crowds:** *Not a problem.* **Strategy:** *Go early or late to see birds at their most active.* **Audience:** *All ages.* **Rating:** ★★.

29 **Bird Show Theatre.** *Wild Wings of Africa,* performed at this open amphitheater just behind Flamingo Island, brings together macaws, condors, and eagles. Bird enthusiasts rate this show as one of the best, due to the interesting stunts and the variety of birds on display. You can have your photo taken with one of the squawking stars at the adjacent posing area just after each show. ☞ *Duration: 30 min. Crowds: Sometimes* *significant during holiday periods.* **Strategy:** *Arrive 15 min before show time in busy seasons.* **Audience:** *All ages.* **Rating:** ★★.

30 Gwazi. Even up close, this wooden roller coaster looks like a shaky stack of toothpicks. The clattering of the cars on the rails and the clanking of the chains on the gears makes this a nostalgic thrill. Your confidence is tested early and often: Gwazi goes much faster and falls far longer than you'd expect from an "old-fashioned" ride. Two trains on separate tracks depart from the station in unison and then hurtle toward each other in an apparent head-on collision no fewer than six times. Although the cars' individual speeds are roughly 50 mph, staffers love to point out that the "fly-by" speed makes it seem more like 100. Add to this a 90-foot drop, and there's every reason to scream your lungs out. Modeled after Coney Island's Cyclone, Gwazi attracts those who know the original, as well as families drawn by the lack of inversions. ☞ **Crowds:** *Expect heavy lines all day: its location near the entrance helps keep it busy.* **Strategy:** *Ride early or late. Leave your possessions with a non-rider or in lockers at the bottom of the ride.* **Audience:** *Older children and adults. No guests with motion sickness or heart, neck, or back problems. Minimum height: 48".* **Rating:** ★★★.

Busch Gardens A to Z

To research prices, get advice from other travelers, and book travel arrangements, visit www.fodors.com.

ADMISSION

TICKETS At this writing, adults pay $55.95 and children three to nine pay $45.95, including tax. It's possible you won't see everything during your visit, so you may want to take advantage of the $10.95 next-day admission offer. Those tickets, which need to be purchased on the first day of your visit, are on sale at Guest Services near the entrance. If you think you might qualify, remember that Busch Gardens offers discounts to guests with disabilities, senior citizens, military personnel, and AAA members. To save time in line, you can buy and print tickets online at ⊕ www. buschgardens.com to purchase tickets.

Realizing that an international slate of visitors may not always find Florida's weather conducive to touring the park, Busch Gardens makes a very generous offer with its **Rain Guarantee.** If you seriously think that it's too hot, cold, muggy, humid, rainy, or whatever, go to Guest Relations near the entrance to see whether they'll credit you for a free return visit. This applies whether it's the beginning or the end of the day.

DISCOUNTS Special pricing and discounts appear and disappear with great frequency. Before buying a one-day ticket, check for current offers posted at the entrance. The combination Busch Gardens–SeaWorld value tickets let you spend one day in each park any time until the end of the year. The price without tax is $94.95 for adults and $84.95 for children ages three to nine. If you arrive between January and April, ask about the Fun Card: for the cost of a full-price one-day admission, you receive free admission to the park for a full year.

The Orlando FlexTicket is good for 14 days of unlimited admission to Busch Gardens, Universal Orlando parks, Wet 'n Wild, and SeaWorld, but only in its five-park version. The cost without tax is $224.95 for adults and $189.95 for children ages three to nine. For more information and configurations about these discount options, check online at ⊕ www.orlandoflexticket.com.

ARRIVING & DEPARTING BY CAR

Busch Gardens is at the corner of Busch Boulevard and 40th Street, 8 mi northeast of downtown Tampa, 2 mi east of I–275, and 2 mi west of I–75. It will take you an hour and 15 minutes to drive the 81 mi from Orlando on I–4. From Orlando, travel west on I–4, then north on I–75 to Fowler Avenue (Exit 265). This is also the exit for the University of South Florida. Bear left on the exit ramp, and it will lead you onto Fowler Avenue. Head west on Fowler Avenue to McKinley Avenue. (McKinley Avenue is the first light past the main entrance to the university.) Turn left on McKinley. Go south on McKinley to parking and the main entrance to the park. If you're already in Tampa and taking the much easier I–275, look for Busch Boulevard at Exit 33 and follow it east 2 mi to the park.

CAR CARE If you have car trouble, raise your hood and the parking patrol will assist you.

PARKING The cost for parking is $7 for motorcycles and cars, and $11 for trucks and campers. For $11, motorcycles and cars can buy preferred parking closer to the front gates.

BABY CARE

Nursing facilities and diaper-changing tables are in Land of the Dragons; only the women's rest rooms also have changing tables. Stroller rentals are available at Stroller and Wheelchair Rental in Morocco ($11 for singles, $15 for doubles—and they resemble safari trucks!).

Disposable diapers are sold at Stroller and Wheelchair Rental. Baby food and formula are sold at the Food Lion on 50th Street and Busch Boulevard. Go down a little farther, to 56th Street, to find a Kmart (on Busch Boulevard itself) as well as a Publix and a Kash 'N' Karry, which are on 56th Street, left off Busch Boulevard.

CAMERAS & FILM

Disposable cameras are for sale at **Safari Foto,** near the main entrance, as well as at other stores throughout the park.

DISABILITIES & ACCESSIBILITY

To many wheelchair users, the Busch Gardens experience is represented less by the wild rides than by the animals, which are on display at almost every turn. However, almost all the rides are accessible by guests who can transfer into the ride vehicles.

ATTRACTIONS All attractions are wheelchair accessible in Morocco, Myombe Reserve, and Nairobi. To play in Land of the Dragons, children must be able to leave their wheelchairs, although there's an adjoining wheelchair-accessible playground to the side.

You must leave your wheelchair to board vehicles at **Montu** in Egypt; **Congo River Rapids, Ubanga-Banga Bumper Cars,** and **Python** in Congo; **Stanley Falls** and **Tanganyika Tidal Wave** in Stanleyville; **Cheetah Chase, Phoenix, Sandstorm,** and **Scorpion** in Timbuktu; and **Gwazi** in Bird Gardens. For these, you must also be able to hold lap bars or railings, as well as sit upright and absorb sudden and dramatic movements.

Transferring out of a wheelchair is also required for the **Congo kiddie rides,** including the bumper cars.

RESTAURANTS & SHOPS
All shops and restaurants that you'll encounter in Busch Gardens are wheelchair accessible.

SERVICES
The park publishes a leaflet describing each attraction's accessibility. It's available at Guest Relations.

WHEELCHAIR RENTALS
At **Stroller and Wheelchair Rental** in Morocco, you can rent standard chairs ($9), and motorized wheelchairs ($32). If your rented wheelchair disappears and needs replacing, ask for a replacement in any gift shop.

GUIDED TOURS

The **Serengeti Safari** leaves Edge of Africa five times a day—the first tour leaving at 11:15—on a 30-minute tour of the Serengeti Plain. Excursions are available on a first-come, first-served basis, so reservations are strongly recommended ($29.99). The animals are more active earlier in the day. Inquire about availability at the Adventure Tour Center at the park entrance, or at the Edge of Africa gift shop across from the Crown Colony Restaurant.

Serengeti Safari ☎ 813/984-4043 or 813/984-4073

HEALTH SERVICES/FIRST AID

If you need urgent medical assistance, see a host or hostess. Otherwise, the primary First Aid location is in Timbuktu, with a second location at the Skyride Station in Crown Colony.

HOURS

The park is open daily from 10 to 6, except in summer and some holidays, when hours are extended.

LOCKERS

Lockers are available in the Moroccan village; in Stanleyville, near the Tanganyika Tidal Wave; and in the Congo, at the Kumba and Congo River Rapids rides. The cost is $1. There are change machines near the lockers.

LOST THINGS & PEOPLE

Guest Relations, at the main entrance, handles Lost & Found. For lost companions, go to Security or speak to any of the security personnel, who wear white shirts, badges, and hats.

MONEY MATTERS

There are three ATMs—one just outside the main entrance, another in Timbuktu, and a third at the Zagora Cafe. For currency exchange, go to the Guest Relations window near the main entrance in Morocco.

PACKAGE PICKUP

If you'd rather not lug your purchases around all day, have them sent from any store in the park to **Sahara Traders,** in the Moroccan village area near the entrance. You can pick them up on your way out. The service is free; allow an hour for delivery.

VISITOR INFORMATION

On-site park information is available at **Guest Relations,** near the main entrance, in Morocco. Here you can find out if there are any tapings of *Jack Hanna's Animal Adventures* in the park that day.

🚩 Tourist Information **Busch Gardens** ✇ Box 9158, Tampa 33674 ☎ 813/987–5082 or 888/800–5447 ⊕ www.buschgardens.com.

Away from the Theme Parks

FODOR'S CHOICE

Historic Bok Sanctuary, *in Lake Wales*

Charles Hosmer Morse Museum, *in Winter Park*

Green Meadows Farm, *in Kissimmee*

Orlando Science Center, *in downtown Orlando*

Wekiwa Springs State Park, *in Apopka*

Updated by
Jennie Hess

WHEN YOU'RE READY TO PUT SOME DISTANCE between you and Mickey, you'll find that Orlando and the surrounding Central Florida area offer much more than theme parks. Nature buffs like to escape to the Ocala National Forest or the Audubon Center for Birds of Prey, just north of Orlando in Maitland. Art devotees head for Winter Park and the newly renovated Rollins College's Cornell Fine Arts Museum or the Charles Hosmer Morse Museum of American Art and its stunning collection of Tiffany glass. New Agers flock to the town of Cassadaga, where more than half the residents are psychics, mediums, and healers. Attraction lovers seek out the additional rides and shows, such as WonderWorks and the Orlando Science Center. Indeed, you can discover an abundance of sights that are equally enjoyable and often less crowded and less expensive than those at the theme parks.

Take this opportunity to explore one or more of the many attractions throughout Central Florida. But don't make the mistake of darting into a museum in one neighborhood and beelining it to a great park in another or you could spend all your time in the car. These towns are spread out over quite a wide area, so check the map before you start.

Just to the southeast of Walt Disney World is the sprawling town of Kissimmee, which has a few sights of its own. Another group of things to do is clustered to the northeast of WDW, on International Drive, halfway to Orlando. Downtown Orlando has a combination of skyscrapers, quiet parks and gardens, museums, theaters, coffeehouses, art exhibits, shops, and restaurants. Northeast of downtown is Winter Park, a quiet college town with old oak trees, several fine museums, a delightful scenic pontoon-boat tour, sidewalk cafés, and boutique shopping. Just north is Maitland, where there's a bird sanctuary and an art center.

Farther afield lie local and state parks, zoos, lakes, and the Ocala National Forest. So choose what you like, and linger for a while.

Numbers in the margin correspond to points of interest on the Away from the Theme Parks map.

ORLANDO & ENVIRONS

Kissimmee

10 mi southeast of WDW; take I–4 Exit 64A.

Although Kissimmee is primarily known as the gateway to Walt Disney World, its non-WDW attractions just might tickle your fancy.

★ ☾ ❶ Long before Walt Disney World, there was **Gatorland.** This campy attraction near the Orlando-Kissimmee border on U.S. 441 has endured since 1949 without much change, despite competition from the major parks. Through the monstrous aqua gator-jaw doorway await thrills and chills in the form of thousands of alligators and crocodiles swimming and basking in the Florida sun. There's also a small petting zoo, an aviary, and a water playground called Lily's Pad for younger children. A free train ride provides an overview of the park, taking you through an alligator breeding marsh and a natural swamp setting where you can spot gators, birds, and turtles. A three-story observation tower overlooks the breeding marsh, swamped with gator grunts, especially come sundown during mating season.

For a glimpse of 37 giant rare and deadly crocodiles, check out the exhibit called **Jungle Crocs of the World.** To see eager gators leaping out of the water to catch their food, see the **Gator Jumparoo Show.** The most thrilling is the first one in the morning, when the gators are hungriest. There's also a **Gator Wrestlin' Show,** and although there's no doubt who's going to win the match, it's still fun to see the handlers take on those tough guys with the beady eyes. In the educational **Up Close Encounters–Snake Show,** 30 to 40 rattlesnakes fill a pit around the show's host. This is a real Florida experience, and you leave knowing the difference between a gator and a croc. ✉ *14501 S. Orange Blossom Trail, between Orlando and Kissimmee* ☎ *407/855–5496 or 800/393–5297* ⊕ *www. gatorland.com* ☞ *$21.25 adults, $10.60 children 3–12; discount coupons online* ☾ *Daily 9–5.*

☾ ❷ Friendly farmhands keep things moving on the two-hour guided tour of **Green Meadows Farm**—a 40-acre property with almost 300 animals.
FodorśChoice There's little chance to get bored and no waiting in line, because tours
★ are always starting. Everyone can milk the fat mama cow, and chickens and geese are turned loose in their yard to run and squawk while city slickers try to catch them. Children take a quick pony ride, and everyone gets jostled about on the old-fashioned hayride. Youngsters come away saying, "I milked a cow, caught a chicken, petted a pig, and fed a goat." Take U.S. 192 for 3 mi east of I–4 to South Poinciana Boulevard; turn right and drive 5 mi. ✉ *1368 S. Poinciana Blvd.* ☎ *407/846–0770* ⊕ *www.greenmeadowsfarm.com* ☞ *$18; discount coupons online* ☾ *Daily 9:30–5:30; last tour begins at 4* PM.

☾ ❸ **Water Mania** has all the requisite rides and slides without Walt Disney World's aesthetics. However, it's the only water park around to have **Wipe Out,** a surfing simulator, where you grab a body board and ride

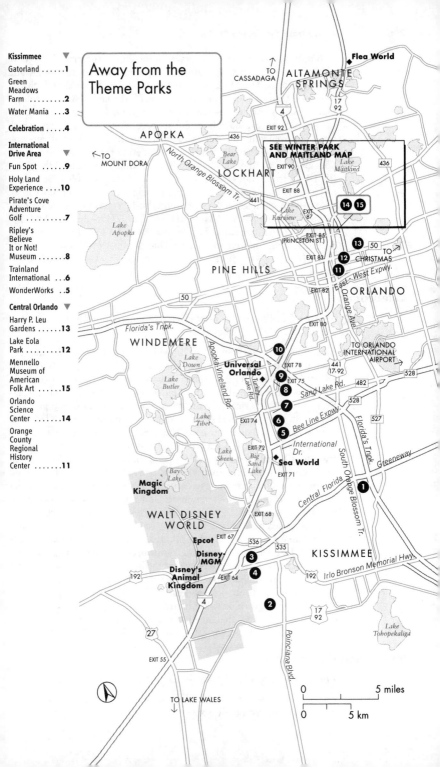

Away from the Theme Parks

SEE WINTER PARK AND MAITLAND MAP

TO CASSADAGA

Flea World

ALTAMONTE SPRINGS

EXIT 92

APOPKA

436

TO MOUNT DORA

North Orange Blossom Tr.

Bear Lake

LOCKHART

EXIT 90

Lake Maitland

436

EXIT 88

441

EXIT 87

Lake Fairview

14 15

Lake Apopka

EXIT 85 (PRINCETON ST.)

13 50

TO CHRISTMAS

EXIT 83

12

PINE HILLS

11

East - West Expwy.

EXIT 82

ORLANDO

50

EXIT 80

Florida's Tnpk.

WINDEMERE

Apopka Vineland Rd.

Lake Down

TO ORLANDO INTERNATIONAL AIRPORT

Lake Butler

10

EXIT 78

441 17.92

528

Universal Orlando

9

EXIT 75

Turkey Lake Rd.

Sand Lake Rd.

482

528

Lake Tibet

8

7

EXIT 74

Bee Line Expwy.

527

6

Lake Sheen

5

EXIT 72

International Dr.

Big Sand Lake

Sea World

EXIT 71

Florida's Tnpk.

Greeneway

Bay Lake

Magic Kingdom

1

South Orange Blossom Tr.

WALT DISNEY WORLD

EXIT 68

Central Florida Pkwy.

Epcot

EXIT 67

536

535

KISSIMMEE

Disney-MGM

3

Disney's Animal Kingdom

4

EXIT 64

192

Irlo Bronson Memorial Hwy.

192

4

2

17 92

27

Poinciana Blvd.

Lake Tohopekaliga

EXIT 55

N

0   5 miles

0   5 km

TO LAKE WALES

a continuous wave form. The giant Pirate Ship in the **Pirate's Lagoon,** one of two children's play areas, is equipped with water slides and water cannons. The **Abyss** is an enclosed tube slide through which you twist and turn on a one- or two-person raft through 380 feet of deep-blue darkness. At this 36-acre park there are also a sandy beach, go-carts, a picnic area, snack bars, gift shops, and periodic concerts, which can be enjoyed while floating in an inner tube. Its 18-hole miniature golf course won't win any local prizes, considering the competition, but it does give you another way to pass the time while you're out of the water. It's 1½ mi from Walt Disney World, about ¼ mi east of I–4. Be sure to call for exact opening and closing times, which can vary due to weather. Also call for unadvertised special rates during certain off-season times. ✉ *6073 W. Irlo Bronson Memorial Hwy.* ☎ *407/396–2626 or 800/527–3092* ⊕ *www.watermania-florida.com* 🖅 *$28.84 adults, $22.42 ages 3–9, discount coupons online; parking $6* ☉ *Mid-Mar.–early Sept., daily 10–5; rest of Sept., weekdays 11–5, weekends 10–5; Oct., Thurs.–Sun. 11–5.*

Celebration

❹ *6 mi south of Epcot; take I–4 to Exit 64A and follow the "Celebration" signs.*

This Disney-created community, in which every blade of grass in every lawn is just right, looks like something out of *The Stepford Wives,* the 1975 film remade in 2004. But Celebration, which draws on vernacular architecture from all over the United States and was based on ideas from some of America's top architects and planners, offers a great retreat from the theme parks and from the garish reality of the U.S. 192 tourist strip just 1 mi to the east. The shell of it appears to be nearly as faux as Main Street, U.S.A., but as the town evolves, you see signs that real life is being lived here—and a good life it is. Celebration is a real town, complete with its own hospital and school system. Houses and apartments, which are built to conform to a strict set of design guidelines, spread out from the compact and charming downtown area, which wraps around the edge of a lake. The town is so perfect it could be a movie set, and it's a delightful place to spend a morning or afternoon. Sidewalks are built for strolling, restaurants have outdoor seating with lake views, and inviting shops beckon. After a walk around the lake, take your youngsters over to the huge interactive fountain and have fun getting sopping wet. Starting the Friday after Thanksgiving Day and continuing through New Year's Eve, honest-to-goodness snow sprinkles softly down over Main Street every night on the hour from 6 to 9, to the absolute delight of children of all ages. Search ⊕ www.celebrationfl.com for event listings or call 407/566–2200.

International Drive Area

7 mi northeast of WDW; take I–4 Exit 74 or 75 unless otherwise noted.

A short drive northeast of WDW are a number of attractions that children adore; unfortunately, some may put wear and tear on parents.

Just up the street, the Ripley's Believe It or Not! building seems to be sinking into the ground, but true to Orlando tradition, the newer attraction, **WonderWorks**, one-ups the competition: it's sinking into the ground at a precarious angle and upside down. If the strange sight of a topsy-turvy facade complete with upended palm trees and simulated FedEx box doesn't catch your attention, the swirling "dust" and piped-out creaking sounds will. Inside, the upside-down theme continues only as far as the lobby. After that, it's a playground of 100 interactive experiences, some incorporating virtual reality. Some are educational (similar to those at a science museum) and others just pure entertainment. Experience an earthquake or a hurricane, swim with sharks, play laser tag in the largest laser-tag arcade-arena in the world, design and ride your own awesome roller coaster, lie on a bed of real nails, create a 3-D impression of your entire body on the Wonder Wall, or even play basketball with a 7-foot opponent. ⊠ *9067 International Dr.* ☎ *407/352–8655* ⊕ *www.wonderworksonline.com* ⊠ *$17.95 adults, $12.95 children 4–12; packages include laser tag and Outta Control Magic (dinner) Show; see online coupons* ⊘ *Daily 9 AM–midnight.*

Trainland International is just what the conductor ordered for the train enthusiast young or old. The museum has one of the nation's largest indoor G-gauge layouts (with tiny tracks only 1¾ inches wide), and you can see scale-model Aristocraft, LGB, USA, and Bachman locomotives pulling 14 continuously operating trains through a vast wonderland of spaces: forests, farmland, cities, and mountainous wilderness. It's quite a sight to watch the trains barely miss one another as they emerge from one of the 32 underground tunnels, cross one of the 24 bridges, or round a curve and switch onto a new track. You can join in an indoor-outdoor scavenger hunt to look for things hidden in the scenery; winners are entered in a monthly random drawing to receive a model train set or a $100 gift certificate to the store. Don't leave without hopping on the diesel train that takes you for a ride through the outdoor gardens. ⊠ *8990 International Dr.* ☎ *407/ 363–9002* ⊠ *$5.95 adults, $4.95 children 3–12. Train ride $3 for adults, $2 for children* ⊘ *Sun.–Thurs. 10 AM–7 PM, Fri.–Sat. 10 AM–8 PM.*

You can play the crème de la crème of miniature golf at the two **Pirate's Cove Adventure Golf** locations. Each site has two 18-hole courses that wind around artificial mountains, through caves, and into lush foliage. The beginner's course is called Captain Kidd's Adventure; a more difficult game can be played on Blackbeard's Challenge. The courses are opposite Mercado Mediterranean Village and in the Crossroads of Lake Buena Vista shopping plaza. ⊠ *8501 International Dr.* ☎ *407/352–7378* ⊕ *www.pirates-cove.net* ⊠ *Crossroads Center, I–4 Exit 68* ☎ *407/ 827–1242* ⊠ *$8.95 adults, $7.95 children 4–12* ⊘ *Daily 9 AM–11:30 PM on I-Drive and 9 AM–11 PM at Crossroads.*

Ripley's Believe It or Not! Museum challenges the imagination. A 10-foot-square section of the Berlin Wall. A pain and torture chamber. A Rolls-Royce constructed entirely of matchsticks. A 26′ × 20′ portrait of van Gogh made from 3,000 postcards. These and almost 200 other oddities speak for themselves in this museum-cum-attraction in the heart of tourist territory on International Drive. The building itself is designed to appear as if it's sliding into one of Florida's notorious sinkholes. Give yourself an hour or two to soak up the weirdness here, but remember, this is a looking, not touching, experience, which may drive antsy youngsters—and their parents—crazy. The museum is ¼ mi south of Sand Lake Road. ⊠ *8201 International Dr.* ☎ *407/363–4418 or 800/998–4418* ⊕ *www.ripleysorlando.com* ⬚ *$16.95 adults, $11.95 children 4–12* ☉ *Daily 9 AM–1 AM; last admission at midnight.*

☾ ❾ **Fun Spot.** Four go-cart tracks offer a variety of driving experiences for children and adults. Though drivers must be at least 8 years old and meet height requirements, parents can drive smaller children in two-seater cars on several of the tracks, including the Conquest Track. Park rides range from twirling toddler Teacups to the dizzying Paratrooper and an old-fashioned Revolver Ferris Wheel. Inside the arcade, traditional Whack a Mole and Spider Stompin' challenges get as much attention as the interactive high-tech video games. From Exit 75A, turn left onto International Dr. then left on Grand National to Del Verde Way. ⊠ *5551 Del Verde Way, I-4 to Exit 75A* ☎ *407/363–3867* ⊕ *www.fun-spot.com* ⬚ *$29.95 adults, $9.95 children 2–6; arcade tokens 25¢ each or $25 for 120* ☉ *Weekdays noon–11 PM, weekends 10 AM–midnight.*

❿ The **Holy Land Experience,** the project of a Baptist minister who was raised Jewish, is a 14-acre Christian theme park modeled after the ancient city of Jerusalem as it is imagined to have appeared between 1450 BC and AD 66. You can visit a first-century street market and bargain with the vendors (played by actors), and see the Qumran Caves and the Holy Temple. Shofars, menorahs, and gifts imported from Israel are for sale; Goliath Burgers feed the hungry. There are no rides. ⊠ *4655 Vineland Rd., I–4 east to Exit 78, turn left onto Conroy Rd. and then right onto Vineland Rd.* ☎ *407/367–2065 or 866/872–4659* ⊕ *www.theholylandexperience.com* ⬚ *$29.99 adults, $19.99 children 6–12; parking $3* ☉ *Weekdays 10–5, Sat. 9–6, Sun. noon–6; hrs vary seasonally.*

Central Orlando

15 mi northeast of WDW; take I–4 Exit 82C or 83A eastbound, or Exit 85 for Loch Haven Park sights.

Downtown Orlando is a dynamic area with high-rises, sports venues, interesting museums, restaurants, and nightspots. Numerous parks and lakes provide pleasant relief from the tall office buildings. A few steps away from downtown's tourist centers are delightful residential neighborhoods with brick-paved streets and live oaks dripping with Spanish moss.

☾ ⓫ The **Orange County Regional History Center** takes you on a journey back in time to discover how Florida's Paleo-Indians hunted and fished the land; what the Sunshine State was like when Spaniards first arrived in the New World; and how life in Florida was different when citrus was king. Visit a cracker cabin from the late 1800s, complete with Spanish moss–stuffed mattresses, mosquito netting over the beds, and a room where game was preserved pre-refrigeration. Seminole Indian displays include interactive screens, and tin-can tourist camps of the early 1900s preview Florida's destiny as a future vacation mecca. ⊠ *65 E. Central*

Blvd. ☎ *407/836–8500 or 800/965–2030* ⊕ *www.thehistorycenter.org* ⊒ *$7 adults, $3.50 children 3–12* ⊙ *Mon.–Sat. 10–5, Sun. noon–5.*

♻ ⑫ In the heart of downtown is **Lake Eola Park,** with its signature fountain in the center. The park represents an inner-city victory over decay. Established in 1892, the now family-friendly park experienced a series of ups and downs that left it very run-down by the late 1970s. With the support of determined citizens, the park gradually underwent a renovation that restored the fountain and added a wide walkway around the lake. Now families with young children use the well-lighted playground in the evening and downtown residents toss bread to the ducks, swans, and birds and walk their dogs late at night in safety. The **Walt Disney Amphitheater,** perched on the lake, is a dramatic site for the annual Shakespeare Festival (April and May) as well as for weekend concerts and other events.

Don't resist the park's biggest draw, a ride in a swan-shape pedal boat. Two adults or one adult and two children can fit comfortably into the boats. Children under 10 must be accompanied by an adult. If you want to splurge, book a GondEola—a ride in an authentic 32-foot Venetian gondola, where dinner or gourmet snacks and beverages are served while a gondolier sings or plays your favorite tunes.

Several good restaurants along the water provide lake-view and patio dining. The view at dusk, as the fountain lights up in all its colors and the sun sets behind Orlando's ever-growing skyline, is spectacular. ✉ *Robinson St. and Rosalind Ave., Downtown Orlando* ☎ *407/246–2827 park, 407/658–4226 swan boats and GondEola* ⊕ *www.gondeola.com* ⊒ *Swan boat rental $10 per half hr; GondEola packages $45–$150 per couple* ⊙ *Park daily 6 AM–midnight; swan boats daily 10 AM–8 PM; GondEola 5 PM–midnight.*

❶❸ The **Harry P. Leu Gardens,** a few miles outside of downtown on the former lakefront estate of a citrus entrepreneur, are a quiet respite from the artificial world of the theme parks. On the grounds' 50 acres is a collection of historical blooms, many varieties of which were established before 1900. You can see ancient oaks, a 50-foot floral clock, and one of the largest camellia collections in eastern North America (in bloom October–March). **Mary Jane's Rose Garden,** named after Leu's wife, is filled with more than 1,000 bushes; it's the largest formal rose garden south of Atlanta. The simple 19th-century **Leu House Museum,** once the Leu family home, preserves the furnishings and appointments of a well-to-do, turn-of-the-20th-century Florida family. ✉ *1920 N. Forest Ave. North-Central Orlando* ☎ *407/246–2620* ⊕ *www.leugardens.org* ⊒ *$5 adults, $1 children kindergarten–12th grade; free Mon. 9–noon* ⊙ *Garden daily 9–5; guided house tours Aug.–June, daily on the hr and half hr 10–3:30.*

♻ ⑭
Fodor'sChoice
★

With all the high-tech glitz and imagined worlds of the theme parks, is it worth visiting the reality-based **Orlando Science Center**? Absolutely. The action-packed, 207,000-square-foot, four-level building is the perfect antidote to long lines and overwhelming gimmickry. Multiple themed display halls house exciting hands-on exhibits covering mechanics; electricity and magnetism; math; health and fitness; nature; the solar system; and light, lasers, and optics. Walk through an enormous open mouth (literally) and take a journey through the human body (figuratively). Raise a suspended VW bug with the help of a lever, and learn about physics while you're showing off (you don't need to tell the children it's educational if you don't want to). New exhibits are added periodically; one of the most recent, **Touch the Sky,** reveals the wonders of aviation aboard a flight simulator, in a wind tunnel, and on a control-tower tour. The **Dr. Phillips CineDome,** a movie theater with a giant eight-story screen, offers large-format IWERKS films (Ub Iwerks was an associate of Walt Disney's in the early days), as well as planetarium programs. In addition, the **Darden Adventure Theater** is home to the center's in-house performance troupe, the Einstein Players. On Friday and Saturday night, you can peer through Florida's largest publicly accessible refractor telescope to view the planets and many of their moons, plus other galaxies and nebulas. ⊠ *777 E. Princeton St.* ☎ *407/514–2000 or 888/672–4386* ⊕ *www.osc.org* ⊠ *$14.95 adults, $9.95 children 3–11; after 6 Fri. and Sat. $9.95 adults and $4.95 children; parking $3.50; tickets include all exhibits, films, and planetarium shows* ⊙ *Memorial Day–mid-Aug., Mon.–Thurs. 9–5, Fri. and Sat. 9–9, Sun. noon–5; mid-Aug.–Memorial Day, Tues.–Thurs. 9–5, Fri. and Sat. 9–9, Sun. noon–5.*

⑮ The **Mennello Museum of American Folk Art** is one of the few museums in the United States, and the only one in Florida, devoted to folk art. It contains the nation's most extensive permanent collection of Earl Cunningham paintings as well as works by many other self-taught artists. At the museum shop you can purchase folk art books, toys, and unusual gifts. ⊠ *900 E. Princeton St.* ☎ *407/246–4278* ⊕ *www.mennellomuseum. com* ⊠ *$4 adults, $1 students, children under 12 free* ⊙ *Tues.–Sat. 10:30–4:30, Sun. noon–4:30.*

Winter Park

20 mi northeast of WDW; take I–4 Exit 87 and head east 3 mi on Fairbanks Ave.

This peaceful, upscale community may be just north of the hustle and bustle of Orlando, but it feels miles away. You can spend a pleasant day here shopping, eating, visiting museums, and taking in the scenery along Park Avenue. When you want a rest, look for a bench in the shady Central Park. Away from the avenue, stroll beneath the moss-covered trees that form a canopy over brick streets, and cruise the area's lakes on pontoon boats to see wildlife and the old estates that surround canal-linked lakes.

★ In the center of town is **Park Avenue,** an inviting brick street with chic boutiques, sidewalk cafés, restaurants, and hidden alleyways that lead to peaceful nooks and crannies with even more restaurants and shops. Park Avenue is a shopper's heaven.

⑯ **Central Park** has lovely green lawns, a rose garden, a fountain, a gazebo, and stage that is often the setting for concerts. On the southwest corner, the Winter Park Farmer's Market lures locals and visitors each Saturday morning. If you don't want to browse in the shops across the street, a walk through the park is a delightful alternative. ⊠ *Park Ave.* ⊙ *Sunrise–sunset.*

WINTER PARK: A POCKET OF OLD FLORIDA CHARM

I F YOU TAKE A SEAT on a bench near the rose garden in Central Park and listen as the Amtrak passenger train rolls by the west end of the park, it's not hard to imagine how Winter Park looked and sounded in the late-19th century.

The town's name reflects its early role as a warm-weather haven for northerners. From the late 1880s until the early 1930s, each winter hundreds of vacationers from northern states like New York and Pennsylvania would travel to Florida by rail to escape the harsh weather. For many, Winter Park was the final destination. Here visitors would relax amid the orange groves and stroll along Park Avenue, which attracts window shoppers and tea drinkers to this day. The lovely, 8-square-mi village retains its charm with brick-paved streets, historic buildings, and well-maintained lakes and parkland. Even the town's bucolic 9-hole golf course is on the National Register of Historic Places.

For the quintessential Winter Park experience, spend a few hours taking in the sights on Park Avenue. Serious shoppers can spend hours dipping into the small boutiques and chain stores that line the avenue. But save at least an hour or two for the **Charles Hosmer Morse Museum of American Art,** which has the largest collection of artwork by Louis Comfort Tiffany. This is where you'll find such treasures as the Tiffany Chapel and dozens of Tiffany's beautiful stained-glass windows, lamps, and pieces of jewelry. Many of the works were rescued from Tiffany's Long Island estate, Laurelton Hall, after a 1957 fire destroyed much of the property. The museum also contains collections of American decorative art from the mid-19th to the early 20th centuries and American paintings from the same period.

Another fine museum is on the Rollins College campus. The **Cornell Fine Arts Museum** has a collection of 6,000 art objects, including 19th- and 20th-century American and European paintings and sculptures. North of the college on Osceola Avenue is the **Albin Polasek Museum and Sculpture Gardens,** where you can get a guided tour of the former home of the prolific Czech-American sculptor Albin Polasek (1879–1965). On-property examples of Polasek's works include statues in several mediums.

Perhaps one of the loveliest ways to visit the village is on the **Scenic Boat Tour** (⊕ www.scenicboattours.com), in operation since 1938. The 18-passenger pontoon boat cruises 12 mi of Winter Park waterways, including three lakes and oak- and cypress-shaded canals built in the 1800s as a transportation system for the logging industry. A well-schooled skipper shares stories about the moguls who built their mansions along the shore. You can spot countless ducks and wading birds, including egrets, blue herons, and the enigmatic "snakebird," or anhinga—often seen drying its wings while perched on shore or diving beneath the lake surface for dinner. You may even glimpse an alligator or see an osprey or bald eagle soar overhead.

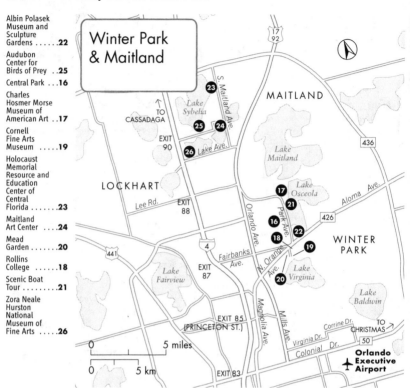

The world's most comprehensive collection of the work of Louis Comfort Tiffany, including immense stained-glass windows, lamps, watercolors, and desk sets, is at the **Charles Hosmer Morse Museum of American Art.** The museum's constant draws include exhibits on the Tiffany Long Island mansion, Laurelton Hall, and the 1,082-square-foot Tiffany Chapel, originally built for the 1893 world's fair in Chicago. It took craftsmen 2½ years to painstakingly reassemble the chapel here. Also displayed at the museum are collections of paintings by 19th- and 20th-century American artists, and jewelry and pottery, including a fine display of Rookwood vases. ⊠ *445 N. Park Ave.* ☎ *407/645–5311* ⊕ *www.morsemuseum. org* ⊠ *$3 adults, $1 students, children under 12 free; Sept.–May, Fri. free 4–8* ⊙ *Tues.–Sat. 9:30–4, Sun. 1–4; Sept.–May, Fri. until 8.*

Rollins College, a private liberal arts school, is in the heart of Winter Park's downtown. Among the school's alums was the late Mister (Fred) Rogers—yes, this was once his neighborhood. Anthony Perkins also attended. The grounds include the **Knowles Memorial Chapel,** built in 1932, and the **Annie Russell Theatre,** a 1931 building that's often the venue for quality local theatrical productions. ⊠ *1000 Holt Ave.* ☎ *407/ 646–2000, 407/646–2145 theater box office* ⊕ *www.rollins.edu.*

⑲ On the Rollins College campus, the newly renovated **Cornell Fine Arts Museum** houses the oldest collection of art in Florida, its first paintings acquired in 1896. More than 6,000 objects are on display, including 19th- and 20th-century American and European paintings, decorative arts, and sculpture. Artists represented include William Merritt Chase, Childe Hassam, and Louis Comfort Tiffany. In addition, special exhibitions are scheduled throughout the year. Outside the museum, a small but charming garden overlooks Lake Virginia. ⊠ *Rollins College, end of Holt Ave.* ☎ *407/646–2526* ⊕ *www.rollins.edu/cfam* ⊠ *Free* ⊙ *Tues.–Fri. 10–5, weekends 1–5.*

⑳ The 55 acres in the unusual park, **Mead Garden,** have been intentionally left to grow as a natural preserve. Walkers and runners are attracted to the trails that wind around the creek, and a boardwalk provides a better view of the delicate wetlands. ⊠ *1300 S. Denning Ave.* ☎ *407/599–3334* ⊠ *Free* ⊙ *Daily 8–sunset.*

★ **㉑** From the dock at the end of Morse Avenue you can depart for the **Scenic Boat Tour,** a Winter Park tradition that's been in continuous operation for more than 60 years. The relaxing, narrated one-hour pontoon boat tour, which leaves hourly, cruises by 12 mi of Winter Park's opulent lakeside estates and travels through narrow canals and across three lakes. ⊠ *312 E. Morse Blvd.* ☎ *407/644–4056* ⊕ *www.scenicboattours.com* ⊠ *$8 adults, $4 children 2–11* ⊙ *Daily 10–4.*

㉒ Stroll along on a guided tour through lush gardens showcasing the graceful sculptures created by internationally known sculptor Albin Polasek (1879–1965) at the **Albin Polasek Museum and Sculpture Gardens.** The late artist's home, studio, galleries, and private chapel are centered on 3 acres of exquisitely tended lawns, colorful flower beds, and tropical foliage. Paths and walkways lead past classical life-size, figurative sculptures and whimsical mythological pieces. Inside the museum are works by Hawthorne, Chase, Mucha, and Saint-Gaudens. ⊠ *633 Osceola Ave.* ☎ *407/647–6294* ⊕ *www.polasek.org* ⊠ *$5 adults, $3 students ages 13 and up with student ID, children under 12 free* ⊙ *Sept.–June, Tues.–Sat. 10–4, Sun. 1–4.*

Maitland

25 mi northeast of WDW; take I–4 Exit 90A, then Maitland Blvd. east, and turn right (south) on Maitland Ave.

An Orlando suburb with an interesting mix, Maitland is home to both the Florida Save the Manatee Society and one of Central Florida's larger office parks. A number of spectacular homes grace the shores of this town's various lakes, and there's a bird sanctuary and an art center there as well.

㉓ The **Holocaust Memorial Resource and Education Center of Central Florida** chronicles major events of the Holocaust. Exhibits are arranged in chronological order and include a large number of photographs and audiovisual presentations. The museum also contains a library and archives. ⊠ *851 N. Maitland Ave.* ☎ *407/628–0555* ⊕ *www.holocaustedu.org* ⊠ *Free, but donations welcome* ⊙ *Mon.–Thurs. 9–4, Fri. 9–1, Sun. 1–4.*

㉔ It's local lore that the historic **Maitland Art Center,** near Lake Sybelia, is inhabited by the spirit of its architect-painter founder, André Smith. He began constructing his studio retreat in 1937, and the grounds and 23 buildings themselves are works of art. The seemingly infinite reliefs and other details on all the structures reflect Smith's fascination with Maya and Aztec motifs and further account for the mystical aura. An outdoor chapel is a favorite spot for weddings, and romantic gardens blend harmoniously with the natural surroundings. Inside, galleries display an extensive collection of Smith's work as well as changing exhibits by local, regional, and national artists. Take Maitland Avenue ¾ mi south of Maitland Boulevard; turn right on Packwood Avenue. ⊠ *231 W. Packwood Ave.* ☎ *407/539–2181* ⊕ *www.maitlandartcenter.org* 🖅 *Donations welcome* ⊘ *Weekdays 9–5:30, weekends noon–4:30.*

More than 20 bird species, including hawks, eagles, owls, falcons, and vultures, make their home at the **Audubon Center for Birds of Prey.** This wildlife rehabilitation center has viewing windows into its medical exam labs, a self-guided conservation tour with interactive exhibits, and walkways through the wetlands. Visitors can call ahead for a free private tour. There's an earnestness to this working facility on Lake Sybelia in Maitland, which takes in more than 600 injured wild birds of prey each year. Fewer than half the birds are able to return to the wild; permanently injured birds continue to live at the center and can be seen in the aviaries along the pathways and sitting on outdoor perches. The center also tracks eagles and occasionally sets up a closed-circuit monitor to observe a nest, so visitors can watch a genuine nature show. From Maitland Avenue, turn right on U.S. 17–92, right on Kennedy Boulevard, and right on Audubon Way. ⊠ *1101 Audubon Way* ☎ *407/644–0190* ⊕ *www.audubonofflorida. org* 🖅 *$5 adults, $4 children 3–12* ⊘ *Tues.–Sun. 10–4.*

The **Zora Neale Hurston National Museum of Fine Arts** showcases creative works by artists of African descent. The museum holds five six-week-long exhibits each year, with one reserved for promising up-and-coming artists. The museum is named after former local resident Zora Neale Hurston (1891–1960), a writer, folklorist, and anthropologist best known for her novel *Their Eyes Were Watching God.* ⊠ *227 E. Kennedy Blvd., Eatonville* ☎ *407/647–3307* ⊕ *www.zorafestival.com* 🖅 *Donations accepted; $5 for groups of four or more* ⊘ *Weekdays 9–4, Sun. 2–5.*

SIDE TRIPS FROM ORLANDO

When you feel like venturing farther afield, hop in your car and within an hour or two you can be where you can celebrate Christmas year-round, canoe down a river, meet with a psychic, feed farm animals at a small zoo, or walk in a beautiful park. The areas below are arranged in a roughly clockwise fashion starting northwest of Orlando.

Apopka

13 mi northwest of Orlando and 28 mi north of WDW.

Orange groves used to cover this part of Florida, but housing developments continue to replace one grove after another. East of Apopka is a state park with pristine waterways and scenic drives through longleaf-pine forests.

Where the tannin-stained Wekiva River meets the crystal-clear Wekiwa headspring, there's a curious and visible exchange—like strong tea infusing water. Wekiva is a Creek Indian word meaning "flowing water"; wekiwa means "spring of water." **Wekiwa Springs State Park** sprawls around this area on 6,400 acres. The parkland is well suited to camping, hiking, and picnicking; the spring to swimming; and the river to canoeing and fishing. Canoe trips can range from a simple hour-long paddle around the lagoon to observe a colony of water turtles to a full-day excursion through the less-congested parts of the river that haven't changed much since the area was inhabited by the Timacuan Indians. Take I–4 Exit 94 (Longwood) and turn left on Route 434. Go 1¼ mi to Wekiwa Springs Road; turn right and go 4½ mi to the entrance, on the right. ⊠ *1800 Wekiva Circle* ☎ *407/884–2008* ⊕ *www.myflorida.com* 🖭 *$3–$5 per vehicle* ☉ *Daily 8–sunset.*

groovy souvenirs

As you drive northwest on U.S. 441, you head into aptly named **Lake County,** an area renowned for its pristine water and excellent fishing. Watch the flat countryside, thick with scrub pines, take on a gentle roll through citrus groves and pastures surrounded by live oaks.

Mount Dora

35 mi northwest of Orlando and 50 mi north of WDW; take U.S. 441 (Orange Blossom Trail in Orlando) north or take I–4 to Exit 92, then Rte. 436 west to U.S. 441, and follow the signs.

The unspoiled Lake Harris chain of lakes surrounds remote Mount Dora, an artsy valley community with a slow and easy pace, a rich history, New England–style charm, and excellent antiquing. Although the town's population is only about 10,000, there's plenty of excitement here, especially in fall and winter. The first weekend in February is the annual Mount Dora Art Festival, which opens Central Florida's spring art-fair season. Attracting more than 250,000 people over a three-day period, it's one of the region's major outdoor events. During the year there's a sailing regatta (April), a bicycle festival (October), a crafts fair (October), and many other happenings. Mount Dora draws large crowds during monthly (third-weekend, except Dec.) antique fairs and thrice-yearly antique "extravaganzas" (third weekends of Jan., Feb. and Nov.) at popular **Renninger's Twin Markets**, an antique center plus farmer's and flea market.

Take a walk down **Donnelly Street.** The yellow Queen Anne–style mansion is **Donnelly House** (⊠ 515 Donnelly St.), an 1893 architectural gem. Notice the details on the leaded-glass windows. Built in the 1920s, what was once known as the Dora Hotel is now **The Renaissance** (⊠ 413 Donnelly St.), a shopping arcade with restaurants and an Icelandic pub.

If you walk along **5th Avenue** you'll pass a number of charming restaurants and gift and antiques shops. At **Uncle Al's Time Capsule** (⊠ 140 E. 4th Ave. ☎ 352/383–1958), you can sift through some terrific Hollywood memorabilia and collectibles.

The **5th Avenue Café & Market** (⊠ 116 E. 5th Ave. ☎ 352/383–0090) is the perfect spot for breakfast, lunch, or a romantic dinner. Sunday brunch is served from 10 to 3, and menu offerings include organic specialties, homemade soups, fresh fish, and seasonal fruits and veggies. For waterfront dining, check out **Pisces Rising** (⊠ 239 W. 4th Ave. ☎ 352/385–2669), an upscale seafood and steak house with a deck overlooking the lake.

☾ **Gilbert Park** has a public dock and boat-launching ramp, a playground, and a large picnic pavilion with grills. ⊠ *Tremain St. and Liberty Ave.* ☉ *Daily 7:30–1 hr after sunset.*

A stroll around the lakefront grounds of the **Lakeside Inn** (⊠ 100 N. Alexander St. ☎ 352/383–4104), a country inn built in 1883, makes you feel as if you've stepped out of the pages of *The Great Gatsby*; there's even a croquet court.

A historic train depot serves as the offices of the **Mount Dora Chamber of Commerce.** Stop in and pick up a self-guided tour map that tells you everything you need to know—from historic landmarks to restaurants. Don't forget to ask about the trolley tour schedule. ⊠ *341 Alexander St., at 3rd Ave.* ☎ *352/383–2165* ⊕ *www.mountdora.com* ☉ *Weekdays 9–5, Sat. 10–4; after hrs, maps on display at kiosk.*

☾ The **Mount Dora & Lake Eustis Railway** offers scenic train excursions. The Friday- and Saturday-night Orange Blossom Dinner Train is a 30-mi round-trip lasting 2½ hours and including a four-course dinner, while the Herbie Express is a 9-mile, 90-minute trip in a 1942 locomotive-driven coach. The ride takes you along the shore of Lake Dora, past orange groves and into the town of Tavares and back. ⊠ *Alexander St. and 3rd Ave.* ☎ *352/383–8878* ⊕ *www.mtdorarailway.com* ⊠ *Dinner Train, $50; Herbie Express, $10 adults, $7 children 12 and under* ☉ *Dinner train, daily; Herbie Express, seasonally.*

Palm Island Park, on the shores of Lake Dora adjacent to Gilbert Park and within walking distance of downtown, gives nature lovers a close-up view of Florida's wildlife and flora. Take a stroll along the boardwalks and watch out for herons, raccoons, otters, and even an alligator or two. You also see pond cypress, bald cypress, and many varieties of palm. Fishing in the lake is permitted, and well-placed picnic tables offer pleasant spots to enjoy a meal. ⊠ *1 Liberty Ave.* ☉ *Daily 7:30–1 hr after sunset.*

Ocala National Forest

☾ *60 mi northwest of WDW; take I–4 east to Exit 92, and head west on Rte. 436 to U.S. 441, which you take north to Rte. 19 north.*

Between the Oklawaha and the St. Johns rivers lies the 366,000-acre Ocala National Forest. Clear streams wind through tall stands of pine or hardwoods. This spot is known for its canoeing, hiking, swimming, and camping, and for its invigorating springs. Here you can walk beneath tall pine trees and canoe down meandering streams and across placid lakes. Stop in at the **Ocala National Forest Visitor Center** (⊠ 45621 Rte. 19, Altoona ☎ 352/669–7495) for general park information. The center is open daily 9–5.

There are a number of developed recreation sites in the forest, including **Alexander Springs** (☎ 352/669–3522). This park is favored by the locals in the summer for its cold, fresh water. After hiking down to its small beach, swim out, preferably with a snorkel and fins, to the steep drop-off at the head of the spring, where the water rushes out from rock formations below. It's not unusual to see alligators sitting on the bank opposite the sandy beach—remember that they're still wild, can move very fast, and should not be provoked. Notice that the natives leave the water before sundown—feeding time! To get to Alexander Springs from the Ocala National Forest Visitor Center at Altoona, go north on Route 19 and turn right on Route 445. The entrance is on the left, and there's a $4 entrance fee.

Cassadaga

35 mi northeast of Orlando and 50 mi northeast of WDW; take I–4 to Exit 114 (Cassadaga and Lake Helen), turn left on Rte. 472, then right on Martin Luther King Parkway, then right again on Cassadaga Road (Rte. 4139), and continue 1½ mi.

This tiny town is headquarters of the **Southern Cassadaga Spiritualist Camp Meeting Association**, now on the National Register of Historic Places. More than half of this community's 350 residents are psychics, mediums, and healers, which makes it the nation's largest such community. At the **Bookstore & Information Center** (✉ Andrew Jackson Davis Bldg., 1112 Stevens St. ☎ 386/228–2880 ⊕ www.cassadaga.org) in the center of town pick up the brochure describing the town's history and its philosophy of spiritualism. The pamphlet also lists certified mediums and their locations; you can book a full hour of consultation or opt for a mini 15-minute meeting. It's suggested that the best way to find a medium who's right for you is to walk or drive through this rustic, five-block by five-block neighborhood and see if you can find a house that's giving off the right energy. Then call ahead to schedule an appointment.

Church services are held at **Colby Memorial Temple**, and visitors are welcome. Spiritualist services are nonsensational, meditative gatherings, with the most unconventional aspect being the "message" portion, during which certified mediums deliver specific messages to attendees from spirits in the beyond. ✉ *1112 Stevens St.* ☎ *386/228–3171* ⊗ *Services Sun. 10:30–11:45 AM and 12:30–1:30 PM, and Wed. 7:30–9 PM.*

This community rich in spirit doesn't offer much to the material world, except the modest **Cassadaga Spiritualist Camp Bookstore and Information Center.** People here are friendly and wholesome and accustomed to curiosity seekers, but they do request respect. ✉ *1112 Stevens St.* ☎ *386/228–2880* ⊗ *Mon.–Sat. 10–5, Sun. 11:30–5.*

Sanford

22 mi north of Orlando and 37 mi northeast of WDW; take I–4 to Exit 104.

This growing community on the shores of Lake Monroe has attracted a number of Orlandoans seeking a respite from the burgeoning urban sprawl. A small collection of antiques stores, secondhand shops, and galleries, some in buildings dating from the 1880s, can be found along 1st Street.

C A visit to the **Central Florida Zoological Park** is likely to disappoint if you're expecting a grand metro zoo. However, this is a respectable display representing more than 100 species of animals, tucked under pine trees, and, like the city of Orlando, it continues to grow. The most popular animals are the kangaroos, elephants, tortoises, snakes, and insects. The zoo is becoming specialized in exotic cats, too, including servals, caracals, and cheetahs, and there's an aviary that houses American bald eagles that have been grounded owing to injury. Children love the **Animal Adventure,** which has domestic and farm animals to pet and feed. Take I–4 Exit 104, and drive 1 mi east on U.S. 17–92 to the entrance, on the right. ✉ *3755 N. W. U.S. 17–92* ☎ *407/323–4450* ⊕ *www.centralfloridazoo.org* 💲 *$8.75 adults, $4.75 children 3–12; Thurs. 9–10 half price* ☉ *Daily 9–5.*

Christmas

33 mi northeast from WDW; 18 mi east of Orlando on Rte. 50 (Colonial Dr.).

There really is a Santa Claus in this tiny hamlet. Locals zipping to the beach or en route to Kennedy Space Center, on the coast near Cocoa Beach, can miss this town if they blink. But they flock here during December to have their holiday missives postmarked at the local post office. The headquarters of the Tosohatchee State Preserve, with more than 28,000 acres of woodlands, are also here.

C If the children have been cooped up in the car for a while, the **Fort Christmas Historical Park, Fort, and Museum** is a great place for them to let off steam. There's a large play area and picnic spot, plus a restored 1837 fort, built as a supply depot and to house soldiers during the Second Seminole War. Inside the fort is a museum that details Florida pioneer life in the mid-19th century. There are also seven pioneer homes that have been restored and are furnished in the style of the early 1800s as well as a sugarcane mill. During the week the fort is often brimming with local schoolchildren, who visit on Florida-history field trips. ✉ *2 mi north of Rte. 50 on Rte. 420, Ft. Christmas Rd.* ☎ *407/568–4149* ⊕ *www.parks. orangecountyfl.net* 💲 *Free* ☉ *Park daily 8–8; in winter 8–6, Fort and Museum Tues.–Sat. 10–5, Sun. 1–5; call for guided-tour schedule.*

C Hop on a boat and take a thrilling ride through a real Florida swamp teeming with alligators. At **Jungle Adventures** pontoon boats bring you face-to-face with these slithery reptiles in their natural habitat. At daily wildlife shows you can see the rare and endangered Florida panther, the Florida black bear, alligators, and various snakes. There are also daily alligator feeding demonstrations. ✉ *26205 E. Rte. 50, 17 mi east of Orlando* ☎ *407/568–2885 or 877/424–2867* ⊕ *www.jungleadventures.com* 💲 *$17.50 adults, $8.50 children 3–11; online coupon* ☉ *Daily 9:30–5:30.*

The **Orlando Wetlands Park** showcases the first large-scale man-made wetlands in Florida to be created and maintained with highly treated, reclaimed water, and it provides a habitat for native wildlife. Created in 1987, the park is home to more than 170 species of birds, plus otters, foxes, deer, turtles, snakes, and alligators. You may also stumble upon two Seminole Indian huts, known as *chickees*, set up in the park. There are a 2-mi bird viewing trail, many shorter trails that lead to good bird- and wildlife-viewing places, and a lake. More than 18 mi of trails are open for hiking and biking, but the woodland trails are off-limits for bikes. Don't expect to find a snack bar or crowds of people here. Unlike most other Central Florida attractions, this one is basically a showcase for nature. Pavilions and grills are available for picnicking. From Route 50, go 2⅓ mi north on Route 420 (Ft. Christmas Road), turn east on Wheeler Road, and drive 1½ mi east. ⊠ *25155 Wheeler Rd.* ☎ *407/568–1706* ⊕ *www.cityoforlando.net* 🖼 *Free* ☉ *Jan. 21–Sept. 30, daily sunrise–sunset.*

Lake Wales

57 mi southwest of Orlando; 42 mi southwest of WDW.

If after several days at the theme parks you find that you're in need of a back-to-nature fix, head south along U.S. 27. Along the way you see what's left of Central Florida's citrus groves (quite a lot of them remain) as well as a few RV parks, but the big bonus is getting away from the congestion of the city. If you just can't bear a day without a theme park, stop in at nearby Cypress Gardens.

Fodor'sChoice   **Historic Bok Sanctuary,** known for years as Bok Tower Gardens, is an ap-
★   pealing sanctuary of plants, flowers, trees, and wildlife that's overlooked by most visitors, but it's definitely worth a trip. Shady paths meander through pine forests in this peaceful world of silvery moats, mocking-birds and swans, blooming thickets, and hidden sundials. You'll be able to boast that you stood on the highest measured point on Florida's peninsula, a colossal 298 feet above sea level. The majestic, 200-foot Bok Tower is constructed of coquina—from seashells—and pink, white, and gray marble, and it was refreshed for the sanctuary's 75th anniversary celebration in February 2004. The tower houses a carillon with 57 bronze bells that ring out each day at 3 PM during a 45-minute live recital, which may include early American folk songs, Appalachian tunes, Irish ballads, or Latin hymns. The bells are also featured in recordings every half hour after 10 AM, and sometimes even moonlight recitals.

The landscape was designed in 1928 by Frederick Law Olmsted Jr., son of the planner of New York's Central Park. The grounds include the 20-room, Mediterranean-style **Pinewood Estate,** built in 1930. Take I–4 to Exit 55, and head south on U.S. 27 for about 23 mi. Proceed past Eagle Ridge Mall, then turn left after two traffic lights onto Mountain Lake Cut Off Road and follow signs. ⊠ *1151 Tower Blvd., Lake Wales* ☎ *863/676–1408* ⊕ *www.boktower.org* 🖼 *$8 adults, $3 children 5–12, free Sat. 8–9; Pinewood Estate general tour $5 adults, $3 children 5–12; holiday tour $15 adults, $8 children 5–12* ☉ *Daily 8–6; Pinewood Estate tours late Jan.–Oct., Mon.–Sat. 11:30 and 1:30 PM, Sun. 1:30 PM, holiday tours late Nov.–early Jan., Mon.–Sat. 10–5, Sun. 1–5.*

Where to Eat

FODOR'S CHOICE

Boma, *in Walt Disney World*

Cinderella's Royal Table, *in Walt Disney World*

Jiko, *in Walt Disney World*

Le Coq au Vin, *in South-Central Orlando*

Les Chefs de France, *in Walt Disney World*

Seasons 52, *on Sand Lake Road*

Victoria and Albert's, *in Walt Disney World*

Revised by
Rowland
Stiteler

FOOD IN THE PARKS RANGES FROM FAST TO FABULOUS. Hamburgers, chicken fingers, and fries dominate at most of the counter-service places, but fresh sandwiches, salads, and fruit are always available, too. Of course, the full-service restaurants offer the best selection, from the Hollywood Brown Derby's signature Cobb salad to steak at Le Cellier. Priority-seating reservations are generally essential for restaurant meals, especially at dinner. Without reservations, you may find yourself having a burger (again) for dinner, or having to leave Walt Disney World, which some people prefer to do anyway.

While some of Orlando's top restaurants—Victoria and Albert's, the California Grill, Bice, and Emeril's, for example—are in Walt Disney World or Universal, many others are outside the parks. Sand Lake Road, International Drive, and Celebration all have excellent restaurants, such as Seasons 52 and Bonefish Grill, that are perfect for a refreshing and romantic dinner in the real world.

WALT DISNEY WORLD AREA

Meals with Disney Characters

At these breakfasts, brunches, and dinners staged in hotel and theme-park restaurants all over Walt Disney World, kids can snuggle up to all the best-loved Disney characters. Sometimes the food is served buffet style; sometimes it's served to you banquet style. The cast of characters, times, and prices changes frequently (although locations of performances remain fairly constant), so be sure to call ahead.

Reservations are always available and often required; some meals can fill up more than 60 days in advance. However, you can also book by phone on the same day you plan to dine, and it never hurts to double-check the character lineup before you leave for the meal. If you have your heart set on a specific meal, make your reservations when you book your trip—up to six months in advance. Smoking is not permitted.

Breakfast

Main Street, U.S.A.'s **Crystal Palace Buffet** (☎ 407/939–3463 ☜ $17.99 adults, $9.99 children ages 3–11) has breakfast with Winnie the Pooh and friends daily from 8 AM to 10:30 AM.

At Disney's Beach Club, characters are on hand at the **Cape May Café** (☎ 407/939–3463 ☜ $17.99 adults, $9.99 children ages 3–11) from 7:30 to 11 daily. At the Contemporary Resort, **Chef Mickey's** (☎ 407/939–3463 ☜ $17.99 adults, $9.99 children ages 3–11) has a no-holds-barred buffet from 7 to 11:15 daily. The Polynesian Resort's **'Ohana** (☎ 407/939–3463 ☜ $17.99 adults, $9.99 children ages 3–11) serves breakfast with Mickey and his friends daily from 7:30 to 11. At the Wyndham Palace Resort & Spa you can drop in Sunday from 8 to 11 for a character meal at the **Watercress Restaurant** (☎ 407/827–2727 ☜ $21.95 adults, $12.95 children under age 9).

BY RESERVATION ONLY The Princess Storybook Breakfasts with Snow White, Sleeping Beauty, and at least three other princesses are held at Epcot Center in **Restaurant Akershus** (☎ 407/939–3463 ☜ $21.99 adults, $11.99 children ages 3–11) in the Norway Pavilion from 8:30 to 10:30 daily. Donald Duck and his friends at Donald's Breakfastosaurus 8:10 to 10 daily at the **Restaurantosaurus** (☎ 407/939–3463 ☜ $17.99 adults, $9.99 children ages 3–11), in Disney's Animal Kingdom. Mary Poppins presides at **1900 Park Fare Restaurant** (☎ 407/824–2383 ☜ $17.99 adults, $10.99 children ages 3–11) in the Grand Floridian from 7:30 to 11:30 daily. Cinderella herself hosts Magic Kingdom breakfasts from 8:05 to 10 daily at **Cinderella's Royal Table** (☎ 407/939–3463 ☜ $21.99 adults, $11.99 children ages 3–11). This breakfast is extremely popular. Book 90 days in advance to be assured seating.

Fodor'sChoice ★

Lunch

Winnie the Pooh, Tigger, and Eeyore come to the **Crystal Palace Buffet** (☎ 407/939–3463 ☜ $19.99 adults, $10.99 children ages 3–11) on Main Street U.S.A. from 11:10 to 2:30. Mickey, Pluto, and Chip 'n' Dale are on hand from 12 to 3:50 at the **Garden Grill** (☎ 407/939–3463 ☜ $20.99 adults, $10.99 children ages 3–11) in The Land pavilion at Epcot.

The Princess Storybook Lunches with Snow White, Sleeping Beauty, and at least three other princesses are held at Epcot in **Restaurant Akershus** (☎ 407/939–3463 ☜ $23.99 adults, $12.99 children ages 3–11) in the Norway Pavilion from 11:40 AM to 2:50 PM.

Afternoon Snacks

For the **Alice In Wonderland Tea Party** (☎ 407/939–3463 ☜ $28.17) at the Grand Floridian Resort, Alice and other Wonderland characters preside over afternoon tea on weekdays from 1:30 to 2:30. With the cast's help, children can bake their own cupcakes and then eat them at the tea party. Open only to children ages 3 to 10; all participants must be potty-trained. The **Garden Grill ice cream social** (☎ 407/939–3463 ☜ $6.99), at the Land in Epcot, has seatings at 3, 3:10, and 3:20. Mickey comes around to visit and it's usually not crowded.

KNOW-HOW

Dress Because tourism is king around Orlando, casual dress is the rule. Very few restaurants require jackets or other dress-up attire for men, and many that once did are lightening up. Except in the priciest establishments, you can wear very casual clothing. In the reviews, dress is mentioned only when men are required to wear a jacket.

Reservations All WDW restaurants and most restaurants elsewhere in greater Orlando take "priority seating" reservations. A priority-seating reservation is like a FASTPASS to a meal. You don't get your table right away, but you should get the next one that becomes available. Say you make your reservation for 7 PM. Once you arrive, the hostess will give you a round plastic buzzer that looks sort of like a hockey puck. Then you can walk around, get a drink at the bar, or just wait nearby until the buzzer vibrates and flashes red. That means your table is ready and you can go back to the hostess stand to be seated. You will most likely be seated within 15 minutes of your arrival.

For restaurant reservations within Walt Disney World, call 407/939–3463 or 407/560–7277. And, although you can't make reservations online at ⊕ www.disneyworld.com, you can certainly get plenty of information, like the hours, price range, and specialties of all Disney eateries. For Universal Orlando reservations, call 407/224–9255.

In reviews, reservations are mentioned only when they're essential or not accepted. Unless otherwise noted, the restaurants listed are open daily for lunch and dinner.

	WHAT IT COSTS				
	$$$$	**$$$**	**$$**	**$**	**¢**
AT DINNER	over $30	$22–$30	$15–$21	$8–$14	under $8

Prices are per person for a main course.

Timing When you're touring the theme parks, you can save a lot of time by eating in the off-hours. Lines at the counter-service places can get very long between 12 and 2, and waiting in line for food can get more frustrating than waiting in line for a ride. Try eating lunch at 11 and dinner at 5, or lunch at 2:30 and dinner at 9.

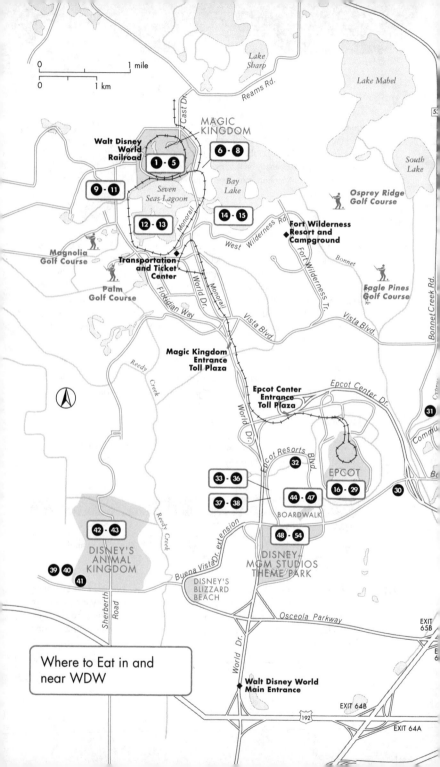

Where to Eat in and near WDW

Dinner

All character dinners require reservations. Minnie Mouse and friends (which in this case does not include Mickey) get patriotic during their evening appearance at the Liberty Square **Liberty Tree Tavern** (☎ 407/939–3463 ✆ $22.99 adults, $10.99 children ages 3–11). A "revolutionary" feast of smoked pork, turkey, carved beef, and all the trimmings is served nightly from 4 PM to 8:40 PM. Farmer Mickey appears at Future World's **Garden Grill** (☎ 407/939–3463 ✆ $22.99 adults, $10.99 children ages 3–11) from 4 to 8 daily. Winnie the Pooh and friends appear at a nightly buffet from 4 to 8:45 at the **Crystal Palace Buffet** (☎ 407/939–3463 ✆ $22.99 adults, $10.99 children ages 3–11) on Main Street, U.S.A.

Every night at 8 (7 in winter), near Fort Wilderness's Meadow Trading Post, there is a **Character Campfire** (☎ 407/824–2727) with a free sing-along. There are usually around five characters there, with Chip 'n' Dale frequent attendees.

Cinderella's Gala Feast is held at the Grand Floridian's **1900 Park Fare** (☎ 407/939–3463 ✆ $27.99 adults, $12.99 children ages 3–11), for a buffet served from 4:30 to 8:20 daily. The Contemporary Resort hosts a wildly popular dinner starring the head honcho himself at **Chef Mickey's** (☎ 407/939–3463 ✆ $26.99 adults, $11.99 children ages 3–11), from 5 to 9:15 daily. At the Walt Disney World Swan, you can dine with *Lion King* characters Monday and Friday from 5:30 to 10 at **Gulliver's Grill** (☎ 407/934–1609). Gulliver's hosts Goofy and Pluto the other five nights of the week. Meals are à la carte—an adult dinner runs $18 to $30 and a child's meal $4 to $10. The same restaurant is called Garden Grove during breakfast and lunch.

The Princess Storybook Dinner with Snow White, Sleeping Beauty, and at least three other princesses are held at Epcot Center in **Restaurant Akershus** (☎ 407/939–3463 ✆ $27.99 adults, $12.99 children ages 3–11) in the Norway Pavilion from 4:20 PM to 8:40 PM.

Magic Kingdom

Dining options in the Magic Kingdom are mainly counter-service, and every land has its share of fast-food places selling burgers, hot dogs, grilled-chicken sandwiches, and salads. The walkways are peppered with carts dispensing popcorn, ice-cream bars, lemonade, bottled water, and soda.

For a meal in one of the full-service restaurants in the Kingdom, you must make priority-seating reservations. You can make them at the restaurants on the day you want to eat or through the **Disney Reservations Center** (☎ 407/939–3463).

American/Casual

$$$ ✕ **Cinderella's Royal Table.** Cinderella, her sisters, and other Disney
Fodor'sChoice princesses appear at breakfast time at this eatery in the castle's old
★ mead hall; book reservations 60 days in advance to be sure to see them. The menu for grown-ups includes entrées like prime rib with mashed potatoes, and roasted chicken breast on bread pudding with spinach, garlic, and red-onion marmalade. If your kids don't feel up to anything

as square as a balanced meal, there are cheeseburgers, chicken tenders, or cheese-dog rolls for $4.99 a pop. For dessert, try the strawberry short-cake or a fruit smoothie in a Cinderella glass. An early character breakfast here is a mighty special treat for the entire family—and a good way to get a jump on the Rope Drop stampede. Frozen smoothies are served in Cinderella collector's mugs for $8 each. ⊠ *Cinderella Castle* ☎ *407/939–3463* ⚓ *Reservations essential* ▭ *AE, MC, V.*

$$$ ✕ **Liberty Tree Tavern.** This "tavern" is dry, but it's a prime spot on the parade route, so you can catch a good meal while you wait. Colonial-period comfort food like roast turkey, smoked pork ribs, and beef brisket is a mainstay here, and you can sample all of the choices at the $21.99, prix-fixe, family-style dinners. Lunch prices are à la carte, with the least-expensive sandwich for adults—an 8-ounce bacon cheeseburger—going for $10.29. If you want something really hearty, go for the New England pot roast, cooked in a wine and mushroom sauce and served with mashed potatoes. Kids can eat macaroni and cheese, hot dogs, hamburgers, or chicken strips for $5. The restaurant is decorated in lovely Williamsburg colors, with Early American–style antiques and lots of brightly polished brass. ⊠ *Liberty Sq.* ☎ *407/824–6461* ▭ *AE, MC, V.*

$$–$$$ ✕ **Crystal Palace.** Named for the big glass atrium surrounding the restaurant, the Crystal Palace is a great escape in summer, when the air-conditioning is turned to near meat-locker level. The buffet-style meal includes upscale and surprisingly good fare, including prime rib, peel-and-eat shrimp, soups, pastas, fresh-baked breads, and ice-cream sundaes, all part of a one-price package (dinner price is $21.99 for adults). There's also a kids-only buffet with what youngsters consider the basic food groups: macaroni and cheese, pizza, and chocolate chip cookies for $9.99 per child. The Crystal Palace is huge but charming with numerous nooks and crannies, comfortable banquettes, cozy cast-iron tables, and abundant sunlight. It's also one of the few places in the Magic Kingdom that serve breakfast. Winnie the Pooh and his pals from the Hundred Acre Wood visit at breakfast, lunch, and dinner. ⊠ *At the Hub end of Main St. facing Cinderella Castle* ☎ *407/939–3463* ▭ *AE, MC, V.*

¢–$ ✕ **Cosmic Ray's Starlight Cafe.** Kosher burgers, rotisserie chicken, barbecued ribs, cheese steak sandwiches, hot dogs, and chicken strips, all served with potato croquettes, are available at the counter of this fast-food outlet in Tomorrowland. Robotic Las Vegas–style lounge singer Sonny E. Clipse croons for the crowds. ⊠ *Tomorrowland* ☎ *407/503–3463* ▭ *AE, MC, V.*

Italian

$$–$$$ ✕ **Tony's Town Square Restaurant.** Inspired by the animated classic *Lady and the Tramp,* Tony's offers everything from spaghetti and meatballs to wood-oven pizza and a very decent pork osso buco. There's no wine list, but you can get the smoothie of the day in a *Lady and the Tramp* collector's mug for $8. A more tempting dessert is the excellent tiramisu. The restaurant's recommended breakfast fare includes a tasty Italian frittata and a bacon, egg, and cheese calzone. If you can't get a table right away, you can watch *Lady and the Tramp* in the waiting area. ⊠ *Main St., U.S.A., Liberty Sq.* ☎ *407/939–3463* ▭ *AE, MC, V.*

Magic Kingdom Resort Area

Restaurants are in the Contemporary, Polynesian, and Grand Floridian hotels, and the rustic Wilderness Lodge.

American/Casual

$$$ ✕ **Chef Mickey's.** This is the holy shrine for character meals, with Mickey, Minnie, and Goofy always around for breakfast and dinner, so it's not really the best spot to read the *New York Times* in solitude. Folks come here for entertainment and comfort food. The dinner buffet includes prime rib, baked ham, and changing specials like beef tips with mushrooms or baked cod with tarragon butter. The Parmesan mashed potatoes have been a popular menu item for years, but you can also get more unusual offerings like broccoli with black olives and feta. The all-you-can-eat dessert bar has sundaes and chocolate cake. ⊠ *Contemporary Resort* ☎ *407/939–3463* ⊟ *AE, MC, V.*

$$–$$$ ✕ **Whispering Canyon Cafe.** No whispering goes on here. The servers, dressed as cowboys and cowgirls, deliver corny jokes and other talk designed to keep things jovial at this family-style restaurant, where huge stacks of pancakes and big servings of spare ribs are the orders of the day. The all-you-can-eat breakfast platter puts eggs, sausage, biscuits, and tasty waffles in front of you for $9.69. For dinner, the $22 all-you-can-eat skillet with pork ribs and roasted chicken is the best deal for big eaters. It includes pork ribs, pulled pork, roast chicken, beef stew, and sides like roasted red potatoes and corn on the cob. Kids love the "Worms in the Dirt" dessert, a concoction of chocolate cake and chocolate pudding, with gummy worms mixed in. ⊠ *Wilderness Lodge* ☎ *407/939–3463* ⊟ *AE, MC, V.*

Contemporary

$$$$ ✕ **Victoria and Albert's.** At this Disney fantasy, the servers work in man-
Fodor'sChoice woman pairs, reciting specials in tandem. It's one of the plushest fine-
★ dining experiences in Florida: a regal meal in a lavish, Victorian-style room. The seven-course, prix-fixe menu ($95; wine is an additional $50) changes daily. Appetizer choices might include Iranian caviar, veal sweetbreads, or artichokes in a mushroom sauce; entrées may be Kobe beef with celery-root purée or veal tenderloin with cauliflower-and-potato purée. For most of the year, there are two seatings, at 5:45 and 9. In July and August, however, there's generally just one seating—at 6:30. The chef's table dinner event is $115 to $162 (with wine pairing) per person. Make your reservations 90 days in advance. ⊠ *Grand Floridian* ☎ *407/939–3463* ⌕ *Reservations essential* ⌂ *Jacket required* ⊟ *AE, MC, V* ☉ *No lunch.*

$$$–$$$$ ✕ **Citricos.** Although the name implies that you might be eating lots of local citrus-flavored specialties, you won't find them here, aside from drinks like a "Citropolitan" martini, infused with lemon and lime liqueur, and an orange chocolate mousse for dessert. Standout entrées include grilled pork tenderloin with celery-root mash, baby carrots, and red wine sauce; and roasted free-range chicken with vegetable quinoa and tomato-cilantro sauce. The wine list, one of Disney's most extensive, includes vintages from around the world. ⊠ *Grand Floridian* ☎ *407/939–3463* ⊟ *AE, MC, V.*

★ **$$–$$$$** ✕ **California Grill.** The view of the surrounding Disney parks from this rooftop restaurant is as stunning as the food, and you can watch the nightly Magic Kingdom fireworks from the patio. Start with the brick-oven flatbread with grilled duck sausage or the *unagi* (eel) sushi. For a main course, try the oak-fired beef filet with three-cheese potato gratin and tamarind barbecue sauce. Good dessert choices include the orange crepes with Grand Marnier custard, raspberries, and blackberry coulis; and the butterscotch, orange, and vanilla crème brûlée. ⊠ *Contemporary Resort* ☎ *407/939–3463* ▭ *AE, MC, V.*

★ **$$$** ✕ **Artist Point.** If you're not a guest at the Wilderness Lodge, a meal here is worth it just to see the giant totem poles and huge rock fireplace in the lobby. The specialty is cedar-plank salmon and mashed potatoes with roasted fennel and truffle butter (worth its $28 price tag). Another good option: grilled buffalo sirloin with sweet potato–hazelnut gratin and sweet-onion jam. For dessert, try the wild berry cobbler or the flourless chocolate–whiskey cake with pecans and raspberry sorbet. There's a good northwestern U.S. wine list, and wine pairings for the meal cost $18 to $23 per person. ⊠ *Wilderness Lodge* ☎ *407/939–3463* ⚑ *Reservations essential* ▭ *AE, MC, V.*

$–$$$ ✕ **Kona Cafe.** Desserts get a lot of emphasis at this eclectic restaurant, with choices like caramel-banana crème brûlée and apple brown Betty. Best of the entrées are macadamia-crusted mahi mahi and pan-Asian pasta (noodles, chicken, and vegetables stir-fried and served in a sauce of ginger, lemon grass, and soy sauce). The blackened mahi mahi sandwich, with an Asian tartar sauce, makes an outstanding lunch. If you want a cocktail, the Lapu Lapu, made with rum, orange juice, and chunks of pineapple, makes for soothing liquid solace at the end of a long day on your feet. As the name of the place hints, coffee is a specialty, too. ⊠ *Polynesian Resort* ☎ *407/939–3463* ▭ *AE, MC, V.*

Polynesian

$$$ ✕ **'Ohana.** The only option here is an all-you-can-eat prix-fixe meal ($24.99 for adults, $10.99 for kids) of shrimp, or grilled pork, beef, or turkey sliced directly onto your plate from mammoth skewers. The chef performs in front of an 18-foot fire pit, grilling the meats as flames shoot up to sear in the flavors and entertain the diners. Special desserts include the coconut snowball and the mandarin orange sponge cake. For the adults, there's a Bloody Mary made with touch of hot wasabi mustard. ⊠ *Polynesian Resort* ☎ *407/939–3463* ▭ *AE, MC, V.*

Seafood

$$$–$$$$ ✕ **Narcoosee's.** The dining room here overlooks the Seven Seas Lagoon and is a great place to catch the Electric Water Pageant at night. Grilled salmon and pan-roasted American red snapper are popular entrées, as is the traditional surf n' turf centerpiece: Maine lobster and a tender filet mignon. Good nonseafood choices include grilled pork tenderloin, and seared scallops with spinach-striped cheese tortellini. For dessert, don't miss the strawberry shortcake (made with fresh, Florida-grown strawberries) and the key lime crème brûlée. ⊠ *Grand Floridian Resort* ☎ *407/939–3463* ▭ *AE, MC, V.*

Steak

$–$$$ ✕ **Concourse Steak House.** If you've always liked that trademark monorail that runs from the Magic Kingdom into the Contemporary Resort, you might want to have a meal here. You can watch the monorail breeze by overhead as you dine. And don't worry, the place isn't as noisy as it might seem. Beef selections include a well-prepared Kansas City strip and a succulent prime rib. Among the other entrées are herb-crusted salmon and penne with pesto, a vegetarian option to which you can add shrimp, chicken, or sirloin steak, if you like. For dessert, try the New York cheesecake and Grand Marnier mousse combo, a relative bargain at $6. ⊠ *Contemporary Resort* ☎ 407/939–3463 ▭ *AE, MC, V.*

Epcot

Epcot's World Showcase offers some of the finest dining in Orlando. Every pavilion has at least one and often two or even three eateries. Where there's a choice, it's between a relatively expensive full-service restaurant and a more affordable, ethnic fast-food spot, plus carts and shops selling snacks ranging from French pastries to Japanese ices—whatever's appropriate to the pavilion.

Lunch and dinner priority-seating reservations are essential at the full-service restaurants; you can make them up to 60 days in advance by calling ☎ 407/939–3463 or going in person to Guest Relations at the park (only on the day of the meal) or to the restaurants themselves when they open for lunch, usually at noon. No matter how you book, show up a bit early to be sure of getting your table. You can pay with cash; charge with American Express, MasterCard, or Visa; or, if you're a guest at a hotel on Disney property, charge the tab to your room.

Dress is informal—no one expects you to go all the way back to your hotel to tidy up. And if you have unruly youngsters in tow, you probably won't be alone. Kosher and vegetarian meals are available on request.

American

$$–$$$ ✕ **Garden Grill.** Solid family-style lunch or dinner fare is served here as the restaurant revolves, giving you an ever-changing view of each biome on the Living with the Land boat ride. The restaurant offers an all-you-can-eat buffet ($21 for adults at lunch, $23 at dinner; $11 for children 3–11 at both meals). Typical choices include rotisserie pork, catfish sticks, chicken strips, and macaroni and cheese. Besides the Princess breakfast in Norway, this is the only Epcot restaurant that has Disney character meet-and-greets during meals. ⊠ *The Land* ▭ *AE, MC, V.*

American/Casual

¢–$ ✕ **Sunshine Seasons.** Talk about a self-contained ecosystem: The Land pavilion where you'll find this restaurant grows its own produce. You order at a counter, then sit at a table and wait for your fresh-made food to be delivered. Try the Asian shop's chicken noodle soup bowls or spicy vegetable stir-fries. There are also creative salads, wrap sandwiches, and lasagna and other kinds of pasta. Meat eaters can go for the rotisserie chicken or beef, and if you have room for dessert, head for the bakery or hand-dipped ice cream counter. The food is healthy, tasty, and reasonably priced, making Sunshine Seasons one of the most popular Epcot eateries. To avoid the crowds, plan to eat at non-peak times—after 2 for lunch and before 5 or after 7 for dinner. ⊠ *The Land* ▭ *AE, MC, V.*

Canadian

$$–$$$ ✕ **Le Cellier.** With the best Canadian wine cellar in the state, this charming eatery with stone arches and dark-wood paneling has a good selection of Canadian beer as well. Aged beef is king, although many steaks appear only on the dinner menu. If you are a carnivore, go for the herb-crusted prime rib. Even though the menu changes periodically (gone are the buffalo steaks, alas), they've always got the maple-ginger-glazed Canadian salmon. For a light meal, try the Prince Edward Island mussels. Dessert salutes to the land up north include a crème brûlée made with maple sugar and the Canadian Club chocolate cake. ⊠ *Canada* ▭ *AE, MC, V.*

Chinese

$–$$$$ ✕ **Nine Dragons Restaurant.** Though a showcase for all regions of Chinese cooking, including Szechuan and Hunan, the majority of the menu is Cantonese, from an excellent *moo goo gai pan* (a stir-fried chicken and vegetable dish) and sweet-and-sour pork to lobster. Other good choices are the "Imperial Pine Cone Fish"—a crispy whole (deboned) snapper topped with sweet-and-sour sauce, and the Cantonese roast duckling. For a really memorable experience, try the three-course Peking duck dinner for two, which includes a duck-broth soup with cabbage, tasty fried duck skin rolled in pancakes, and stir-fried shredded duck with Chinese vegetables. The red-bean ice cream is a great finale to your meal. The distinctive building has a curved, yellow-tile roof with ornate carvings inspired by the Forbidden City. ⊠ *China* ▭ *AE, MC, V.*

English

$–$$ ✕ **Rose & Crown.** If you are an Anglophile and you love a good, thick beer, this is the place to soak up both the suds and the British street culture. "Wenches" serve up traditional English fare—fish-and-chips, meat pies, Yorkshire pudding, and the ever-popular "bangers and mash"—sausage over mashed potatoes. A good and somewhat eclectic choice is the English pie sampler, which includes chicken and leek pie, pork pie, and cottage pie (with ground beef, mashed potatoes, and cheese), plus a side of green beans. Vegetarians will even find an offering of curried veggies and tofu on the menu. For dessert, try the sticky toffee pudding with rum-butter sauce. If you are not driving soon after the meal, try the Imperial Ale sampler, which includes five 6-ounce glasses for $9.35. The terrace has a splendid view of IllumiNations. ⊠ *United Kingdom* ▭ *AE, MC, V.*

French

★ $$$$ ✕ **Bistro de Paris.** The great secret in the France pavilion—and, indeed, in all of Epcot—is the Bistro de Paris, upstairs from Les Chefs de France. The sophisticated menu changes regularly and reflects the cutting edge of French cooking; representative dishes include pan-seared lobster, roasted rack of venison with black-pepper sauce, and seared scallops with truffle-potato purée. Escargots, as an appetizer, are a relative bargain at

$10. Save room for the Grand Marnier flambéed crepes. Come late, ask for a window seat, and plan to linger to watch the nightly Epcot light show, which usually starts around 9 PM. Moderately priced French wines are available by the bottle and the glass. ⊠ *France* 🖃 *AE, MC, V.*

$$–$$$$
Fodor'sChoice
★
✕ **Les Chefs de France.** What some consider the best restaurant at Disney was created by three of France's most famous chefs: Paul Bocuse, Gaston Lenôtre, and Roger Vergé. Classic escargots, a good starter, are prepared in a casserole with garlic butter; you might follow up with duck à l'orange or chicken Cordon Bleu, and end with crepes *au chocolat.* The nearby Boulangerie Pâtisserie, run by the same team, offers tarts, croissants, eclairs, napoleons, and more to go. ⊠ *France* 🖃 *AE, MC, V.*

German

$$
✕ **Biergarten.** Oktoberfest runs 365 days a year here. The cheerful, sometimes raucous, crowds are what you would expect in a place with an oompah band. Waitresses in Bavarian garb serve *breseln,* hot German pretzels, which are made fresh daily on the premises. The menu and level of frivolity are the same at lunch and dinner. For a single price ($19.99 for adults, $7.99 for kids ages 3–11), mountains of sauerbraten, bratwurst, chicken schnitzel, apple strudel, and Black Forest cake await you at the all-you-can-eat buffet. And if you aren't feeling too Teutonic, there's also rotisserie chicken and roast pork. Patrons pound pitchers of all kinds of beer and wine on the long communal tables—even when the yodelers, singers, and dancers aren't egging them on. ⊠ *Germany* 🖃 *AE, MC, V.*

Italian

★ $$–$$$$
✕ **L'Originale Alfredo di Roma Ristorante.** Waiters skip around singing arias, a show in itself. Their voices and the restaurant's namesake dish, made with mountains of imported Italian butter, account for its popularity. The classic dish—fettuccine with cream, butter, and loads of freshly grated Parmesan cheese—was invented by Alfredo de Lelio. (Disney and de Lelio's descendants both had a hand in creating this restaurant). Besides the excellent pastas, try the chef's tip of the hat to Florida—roasted grouper with a lemon, butter, and white wine sauce—or the tender, slow-roasted chicken served with polenta. The minestrone is excellent, and if you can't pass up the fettuccine Alfredo, it's available as an appetizer for $9.95. Dessert offerings include a good tiramisu and an even better cannoli. ⊠ *Italy* 🖃 *AE, MC, V.*

Japanese

$$–$$$$
✕ **Mitsukoshi.** Three restaurants are enclosed in this complex, which overlooks tranquil gardens. **Yakitori House,** a gussied-up fast-food stand in a small pavilion, is modeled after a teahouse in Kyoto's Katsura Summer Palace. At the **Tempura Kiku,** diners watch the chefs prepare sushi, sashimi, and tempura (batter-dipped deep-fried shrimp, scallops, and vegetables). In the five **Teppanyaki** dining rooms, chefs frenetically chop vegetables, meat, and fish and stir-fry them at the grills set into the communal tables. The **Matsu No Ma Lounge,** more serene than the restaurants, has a great view of the World Showcase Lagoon. It also offers one of Epcot's

great bargains: a 12-piece sushi platter for $21.25. Grown-ups might also go for the sake martini. ⊠ *Japan* ⊟ *AE, MC, V.*

Mexican

$$–$$$ ✕ **San Angel Inn.** In the dark, grottolike main dining room, a deep purple, dimly lit mural of a night scene in Central Mexico seems to envelop the diners. San Angel is a popular respite for the weary, especially when the humidity outside makes Central Florida feel like equatorial Africa. At dinner, guitar and marimba music fills the air. Start with the *queso fundido* (melted cheese and Mexican chorizo sausage served with soft tortillas) and then try the authentic *mole poblano* (chicken simmered in a rich sauce of chilies, green tomatoes, ground tortillas, cocoa, cumin, and 11 other spices) or the *puntas de filete* (tender beef tips sautéed with onions and poblano chili strips, and accompanied by rice and refried beans). For dessert, the flan is served with a piña colada sauce and topped with a fresh strawberry. ⊠ *Mexico* ⊟ *AE, MC, V.*

Moroccan

$$–$$$ ✕ **Marrakesh.** Chef Abrache Lahcen of Morocco presents the best cooking of his homeland in this ornate eatery, which looks like something from the set of *Casablanca*. Your appetizer might be *harira* soup, with tomatoes, lentils, and lamb—by custom served during Ramadan; then move on to the chicken, lamb, or vegetable couscous, Morocco's national dish. A good way to try a bit of everything is the Marrakesh Feast ($27.75 per person), which includes chicken bastilla and beef *brewat* (minced beef in a layered pastry dusted with cinnamon and powdered sugar), plus vegetable couscous and assorted Moroccan pastries; or better still, upgrade to the Royal Feast ($30 per person), which includes everything in the Marrakesh Feast, plus crepes for dessert. ⊠ *Morocco* ⊟ *AE, MC, V.*

Scandinavian

★ **$$** ✕ **Restaurant Akershus.** The Norwegian buffet at this restaurant is as extensive as you'll find on this side of the Atlantic. Appetizers usually include herring, prepared several ways, and cold seafood, including *gravlax* (cured salmon served with mustard sauce) or *fiskepudding* (a seafood mousse served with herb dressing). For your main course, you might try some hot sausages, lamb, veal, venison stew, or grilled Atlantic salmon. The à la carte desserts include raspberry tarts, bread pudding, and chocolate mousse with strawberry sauce. Akershus hosts a princess breakfast with Belle, Jasmine, Sleeping Beauty, and Snow White but *not* Cinderella. Call 407/939–3463 for reservations. ⊠ *Norway* ⊟ *AE, MC, V.*

Seafood

$$–$$$$ ✕ **Coral Reef Restaurant.** One of this restaurant's walls is made entirely of glass and looks directly into the 6-million-gallon Living Seas aquarium. And with a three-tiered seating area, everyone will have a good view. Edible attractions include salmon stuffed with basil; Ahi tuna lightly grilled; and Dublin mussels and clams steamed in a Harp beer broth. Crab fritters with spicy marinara sauce make a great appetizer. You might finish off with Kahlua tiramisu in raspberry sauce. ⊠ *The Living Seas* ⊟ *AE, MC, V.*

Epcot Resort Area

The hotels and nightlife complexes clustered around Epcot, Disney's BoardWalk, and the Yacht and Beach Club hold many good restaurants.

American/Casual

$–$$$ ✕ **Big River Grille & Brewing Co.** Strange but good brews, like Pale Rocket Red Ale and Gadzooks Pilsner, abound here. You can dine inside among the giant copper brewing tanks, or sip your suds outside on the lake-view patio. The menu emphasizes meat, with baby-back ribs, barbecue pork, and a house-special flame-grilled meat loaf made with ground beef and Italian sausage. The cheddar cheese–mashed potatoes are a perfect accompaniment. There's also a worthwhile grilled Atlantic salmon fillet with dill butter. ⊠ *Disney's BoardWalk* ☎ *407/560–0253* 🖃 *AE, MC, V.*

$$ ✕ **Shutters at Old Port Royale.** American cuisine inspired by the flavors of the Caribbean is the theme at this bright and breezy restaurant. Shutters lets you have your spicy jerk chicken and your almond-raspberry cheesecake, too. The wide-ranging bill of fare pays homage to the islands with offerings like jerk chicken quesadilla and Red Stripe beer from Jamaica. At the same time, there's a host of classic American offerings, such as smoked prime rib, grilled sirloin steak, mashed potatoes, and chocolate-hazelnut cake. ⊠ *Caribbean Beach Resort* ☎ *407/939–3463* 🖃 *AE, D, DC, MC, V.*

$–$$ ✕ **ESPN Sports Club.** Not only can you watch sports on big-screen TV here, but you can also periodically see ESPN programs being taped in the club itself and be part of the audience of sports radio talk shows. Food ranges from an outstanding half-pound burger to a 10-ounce sirloin and grilled chicken and shrimp in penne pasta, topped with marinara sauce. If you want an appetizer, try the Macho Nachos, crispy corn tortilla chips piled high with spicy ground beef, shredded cheddar cheese, salsa, sour cream, and sliced jalapeños. The apple brown Betty, with a granola-streusel topping, is a satisfying dessert. This place is open quite late by Disney standards—until 2 AM on Friday and Saturday. ⊠ *Disney's BoardWalk* ☎ *407/939–5100* 🖃 *AE, MC, V.*

¢ ✕ **Tubbi's Buffeteria.** This buffet in the Walt Disney World Dolphin would be forgettable were it not for its hours and reasonable prices— Tubbi's serves up inexpensive hot food around the clock. You can find lots of kids' favorites here, like pizza, hot dogs, hamburgers, and grilled-cheese sandwiches, plus a supply of nonfood necessities like laundry detergent and disposable diapers. Breakfast, including a worthy omelet, is served from 6 to 11:30 AM. And for the parents, there's a selection of imported bottled beer. ⊠ *Walt Disney World Dolphin* ☎ *407/934–4000* 🖃 *AE, MC, V.*

Contemporary

$$$–$$$$ ✕ **bluezoo.** Celebrity chef Todd English, the creator of the Olives restaurants, opened this cutting-edge seafood eatery in late 2003. The sleek, modern interior resembles an underwater dining hall, with blue walls and carpeting, aluminum fish suspended from the ceiling, and bubble-like lighting fixtures. The menu is creative and pricey, with entrées like whole crispy-fried sea bass with chili bean sauce. If you don't care for fish, alternatives include chicken with lemon risotto, and roast beef with potatoes, asparagus, and fried onion rings. The coconut–cream crème brulée is supremely satisfying. ☒ *Walt Disney World Dolphin* ☎ 407/934–1111 ▤ *AE, D, DC, MC, V* ☉ *No lunch.*

$–$$$$ ✕ **Gulliver's Grill at Garden Grove.** The legend is that this eatery was founded by Peter Miles Gulliver, a direct descendant of the Jonathan Swift character. Eat among tall palms and lush greenery inside a giant greenhouse. The menu includes something for everyone—pizza, burgers, and peanut butter and jelly sandwiches for the kids; and fresh Florida grouper, filet mignon, and old-fashioned meat loaf for adults. Catch the *Legend of the Lion King* characters on Monday and Friday, and Goofy and Pluto the rest of the week. ☒ *Walt Disney World Swan* ☎ 407/934–3000 ⋈ *Reservations essential* ▤ *AE, D, DC, MC, V* ☉ *No lunch.*

Italian

$–$$$$ ✕ **Palio.** You can find some of the classic upscale Italian dishes here, like osso buco with white-wine vegetable sauce; chicken cacciatore in a great tangy tomato sauce; and risotto with lobster, shrimp, baby clams, basil, garlic, tomato, and green onions. The wood-fired oven produces good pizza, too. A standout dessert is the crème brûlée filled with chunks of pistachio brownie. Strolling minstrels are on hand to entertain. ☒ *Walt Disney World Swan* ☎ 407/934–3000 ▤ *AE, MC, V.*

Japanese

$$–$$$ ✕ **Kimonos.** Knife-wielding sushi chefs prepare world-class sushi and sashimi but also excellent beef teriyaki and other Japanese treats good for a full dinner or just a snack. One of the best bets here is the sushi-sashimi combination, which gives you a generous amount of both for the price. Popular rolls include the California roll (crab, avocado, and cucumber), Mexican roll (shrimp tempura), and the bagel roll (smoked salmon, cream cheese, and scallion). ☒ *Walt Disney World Swan* ☎ 407/934–3000 ▤ *AE, D, DC, MC, V* ☉ *No lunch.*

Mediterranean

$$–$$$ ✕ **Spoodles.** The international tapas-style menu here draws on the best foods of the Mediterranean, from tuna with sun-dried tomato couscous to Italian fettuccine with rich Parmesan cream sauce. Oak-fired flatbreads with such toppings as roasted peppers make stellar appetizers. For an unusual entrée, try the Spanish peppers stuffed with roasted vegetables and chickpeas, and served with almond pilaf, spicy onion-and-tomato relish, and manchego cheese. For dessert, try the cheesecake with banana slices or go for a sampler from the dessert tower. There's also a walk-up pizza window if you prefer to stroll the boardwalk. ☒ *Disney's BoardWalk* ☎ 407/939–3463 ▤ *AE, MC, V.*

Seafood

$$–$$$ ✕ **Flying Fish.** One of Disney's better restaurants, this fish house's best dishes include potato-wrapped red snapper, and pork chop with blue cheese–potato gratin. The "peeky toe" crab cakes with ancho-chili rémoulade are an appetizer that never leaves the frequently changing menu—try them and you will see why. Save room for the banana napoleon. ☒ *Disney's BoardWalk* ☎ 407/939–2359 ▤ *AE, MC, V.*

Steak

$$$–$$$$ ✕ **Shula's Steak House.** The hardwood floors, dark-wood paneling, and pictures of former Miami Dolphins coach Don Shula make this restaurant resemble an annex of the NFL Hall of Fame. Among the best selections are the porterhouse and prime rib. Finish the 48-ounce porterhouse and you get a football with your picture on it, but it's not an easy task to eat three pounds of red meat at one sitting unless you are a polar bear. The least expensive steak is still hefty at 20 ounces and $31. If you're not a carnivore, go for the Norwegian salmon, the Florida snapper, or the huge (up to 4 pounds) Maine lobster. Save room for the chocolate soufflé for two. ⊠ *Walt Disney World Dolphin* ☎ *407/934–1362* 🖃 *AE, D, DC, MC, V* ☉ *No lunch.*

$$–$$$$ ✕ **Yachtsman Steak House.** Aged beef, the attraction at this steak house in the ultrapolished Yacht and Beach Club, can be seen mellowing in the glassed-in butcher shop near the entryway. The slow-roasted prime rib is superb, but so is the surf and turf: an 8-ounce filet mignon and a 6-ounce lobster tail. For dessert, try the chocolate layer cake with wine-marinated cherries. ⊠ *Yacht and Beach Club* ☎ *407/939–3463* 🖃 *AE, MC, V* ☉ *No lunch.*

Disney–MGM Studios

The Studios tend to offer more casual American cuisine than the other parks. In other words, it's cheeseburger city. However, there are some good, imaginative offerings, too. Where else but here can you watch '50s sitcoms nonstop while you devour veal-and-shiitake-mushroom meat loaf? Waits can be long. To make priority-seating reservations, call 407/939–3463 up to 90 days in advance, or stop in person at the restaurant or first thing in the morning at Hollywood Junction Restaurant Reservations. There are three ways to book dinner packages that include the *Fantasmic!* after-dark show: by phone, in person at a Disney hotel, at the park's Guest Relations, and at Hollywood Junction.

American

$–$$ ✕ **'50s Prime Time Café.** Who says you can't go home again? If you grew up in middle America in the 1950s, just step inside. While *I Love Lucy* and *The Donna Reed Show* play on a television screen, you can feast on meat loaf, pot roast, or fried chicken, all served on a Formica tabletop. At $13, the meat loaf is one of the best inexpensive dinners in any Orlando theme park. Follow it up with chocolate cake or a thick milk shake—available in chocolate, strawberry, vanilla, even peanut butter and jelly. If you're not feeling totally wholesome, go for Dad's Electric Lemonade (rum, vodka, blue curaçao, sweet-and-sour mix, and Sprite). Just like Mother, the menu admonishes, "Don't put your elbows on the table!" ⊠ *Echo Lake, Disney–MGM Studios* ☎ *407/939–3463* 🖃 *AE, MC, V.*

American/Casual

$–$$ ✕ **Hollywood & Vine.** This restaurant is designed for those who like lots of food and lots of choices. You can have everything from frittatas to fried rice at the same meal. Even though the buffet ($20 for adults; $10 for children ages 3–11) is all-you-can-eat at a relatively low price, it does offer some upscale entrées like oven-roasted prime rib, sage-rubbed rotisserie turkey, or penne with shrimp and scallops. There are plenty of kids' favorites, such as mac and cheese, hot dogs, and fried chicken. Minnie, Goofy, Pluto, and Chip 'n' Dale put in appearances at breakfast and lunch character meals. There's a Hollywood theme to the place; characters and servers are just hoping to be discovered by some passing Hollywood agent. Priority seating reservations are a must. ✉ *Echo Lake, Disney–MGM Studios* ☎ 407/939–3463 ▤ *AE, MC, V.*

$–$$ ✕ **Sci-Fi Dine-In Theater Restaurant.** If you don't mind zombies leering at you while you consume chef salads, barbecue pork sandwiches, charbroiled sirloin, and Milky-Way-Out Milk Shakes, then head to this enclosed faux drive-in, where you can sit in a fake candy-color '50s convertible and watch trailers from classics like *Attack of the Fifty-Foot Woman* and *Teenagers from Outer Space.* The menu is not limited to choices like the $11 cheeseburger, however; for something different, try the slow-roasted barbecue ribs, the pan-fried catfish, or the 10-ounce charbroiled sirloin steak. The milk shakes are delicious. ✉ *Echo Lake, Disney–MGM Studios* ☎ 407/939–3463 ▤ *AE, MC, V.*

Contemporary

$–$$ ✕ **Hollywood Brown Derby.** At this reproduction of the famous 1940s Hollywood restaurant, the walls are lined with movie-star caricatures, just like in Tinseltown, and the staff are in black tie. The house specialty is the Cobb salad, which by legend was invented by Brown Derby founder Robert Cobb; the salad consists of lettuce enlivened by loads of tomato, bacon, turkey, blue cheese, chopped egg, and avocado, all tossed tableside. And the butter comes in molds shaped like Mickey Mouse heads. Other menu choices include sesame-seared tuna with whipped potatoes; and spiced, pan-roasted pork tenderloin with white-cheddar grits. For dessert, try the Brown Derby grapefruit cake, with layers of cream cheese icing. If you request the *Fantasmic!* dinner package, make a reservation for no later than two hours before the start of the show. ✉ *Hollywood Blvd., Disney–MGM Studios* ☎ 407/939–3463 ▤ *AE, MC, V.*

Fast Food

¢–$ ✕ **ABC Commissary.** This place has a refreshingly different fast-food menu that includes tabbouleh wraps, beef fajitas, and fish-and-chips, plus standard kid fare like chicken nuggets, and macaroni and cheese. Indoor seating offers great respite from the heat in summer. ✉ *Echo Lake, Disney–MGM Studios* ▤ *AE, MC, V.*

¢–$ ✕ **Studio Catering Company.** With a creative and inexpensive menu, plus a convenient location near the Disney–MGM Studios Backlot Tour exit, this snack stop gets plenty of crowds at lunchtime. You'll find grilled chicken and chilled ham wraps, tantalizing flatbreads piled with steak gyro, Tandoori chicken, and lamb with baba ghanoush fillings. ✉ *Streets of America, Disney–MGM Studios* ▤ *AE, MC, V.*

Italian

$$ ✕ **Mama Melrose's Ristorante Italiano.** To replace the energy you've no doubt depleted by miles of theme-park walking, you can load up on carbs at this casual Italian restaurant that looks like an old warehouse. Wood-fired flatbreads with hearty toppings such as chicken and Italian cheeses make great starters before the arrival of such main courses as eggplant

Parmesan and grilled salmon with sun-dried tomato pesto. The sangria, available by the carafe for $16.50, flows generously. Cappuccino crème brûlée is the way to go for dessert. Kids' choices include a good burger and a $5 pizza. Ask for the *Fantasmic!* dinner package if you want priority seating for the show. ⊠ *Street of America, Disney–MGM Studios* ☎ *407/939–3463* ▤ *AE, MC, V.*

Disney's Animal Kingdom

African

$$$–$$$$
Fodor'sChoice
★

✕ **Jiko.** The specialty here is African-style cooking, such as steamed golden bass with spicy Chaka-Laka sauce and mealie corn pap. The menu changes periodically but typically includes such entrées as roasted chicken with mashed potatoes, and pomegranate-glaze quails stuffed with saffron basmati rice. For dessert, try a non-African treat: baklava—the honey-soaked treat is the best on the menu. ⊠ *Disney's Animal Kingdom Lodge* ☎ *407/939–3463* ⚇ *Reservations essential* ▤ *AE, D, MC, V.*

American/Casual

★ **$–$$**
✕ **Rainforest Café.** You don't have to pay park admission to dine at the Rainforest Café, the only full-service eatery in the Animal Kingdom area, with entrances both inside the park and at the gate. Since the Café resembles the one in Downtown Disney Marketplace, complete with the long lines for lunch and dinner, go early or late. If you can, make reservations by phone ahead of time. Choices include chicken-fried steak with country gravy and Nile Shrimp Enbrochette (broiled jumbo shrimp stuffed with crabmeat, jalapeño, four cheeses, and wrapped in bacon). The coconut bread pudding with apricot filling and whipped cream is great. Breakfast, from steak and eggs to excellent French toast, is served beginning at 7:30. ⊠ *Disney's Animal Kingdom* ☎ *407/938–9100 or 407/939–3463* ▤ *AE, D, DC, MC, V.*

Contemporary

$$–$$$
Fodor'sChoice
★

✕ **Boma.** Boma takes Western-style ingredients and prepares them with an African twist. The dozen or so walk-up cooking stations have such entrées as spit-roasted pork, spiced roast chicken, pepper steak, and banana leaf–wrapped sea bass or salmon. The zebra bones dessert is just chocolate mousse covered with white chocolate and striped with dark chocolate. All meals are prix fixe ($24 for adults; $10 for children ages 3 to 11). The South African wine list is outstanding. Priority seating reservations are essential if you are not a guest at the hotel. ⊠ *Disney's Animal Kingdom Lodge* ☎ *407/939–3463* ⚇ *Reservations essential* ▤ *AE, D, DC, MC, V* ☉ *No lunch.*

Fast Food

¢–$
✕ **Flame Tree Barbecue.** At this counter-service, outdoor eatery you can dig into ribs, brisket, and pulled pork with several sauce choices. There are also great vegetarian wraps. The tables, set beneath intricately carved wood pavilions, make great spots for a picnic and they're not usually crowded. ⊠ *Discovery Island, Animal Kingdom* ▤ *AE, MC, V.*

¢–$
✕ **Tusker House.** This counter-service restaurant offers tasty and healthy fare like rotisserie chicken, and a big garden salad served with focaccia

bread on the side, along with the standard WDW kids' fast-food fare. Breakfast fare includes eggs, ham, biscuits and gravy and lighter options like fruit cups and cereal. ⊠ *Harambe, Animal Kingdom* ⊟ *AE, MC, V.*

Downtown Disney

Downtown Disney has three sections: the Marketplace, a small shopping-and-dining area; Pleasure Island, a nightlife complex with a hefty admission after dark; and, close by, Disney's West Side, another group of hipper-than-hip entertainment, dining, and shopping spots. The edge of Disney property is about a block away.

American/Casual

$–$$$ ✕ **Planet Hollywood.** Patrons still flock to see the movie memorabilia assembled by celebrity owners Schwarzenegger, Stallone, Willis, and restaurateur Robert Earl. The wait has been abated by a system that allows you to sign in, take a number, and get an assigned time window to return and eat. The place covers 20,000 square feet if you count the indoor waterfall. On offer are sandwiches and tasty burgers as well as grilled specialties including steak, salmon, ribs, and pork chops. You can also indulge in unusual pastas and salads. Among the better offerings are the Texas tostadas and shrimp Alfredo. ⊠ *Downtown Disney West Side, at entrance to Pleasure Island* ☎ *407/827–7827* ⚱ *Reservations not accepted* ⊟ *AE, D, DC, MC, V.*

$$ ✕ **Olivia's Café.** This is like a meal at Grandma's—provided she lives south of the Mason-Dixon line. The menu ranges from fried shrimp, grilled grouper, and crab cakes to fried chicken with mashed potatoes and gravy. One meat option stands out—the slow-roasted prime rib. For dessert try the white-chocolate key lime cheesecake. The indoor palms and rough wood walls resemble those of an old Key West house, but the inside is just pleasant, not that special. The outdoor seating, which overlooks a waterway, is attractive any time that midsummer's heat is not bearing down. ⊠ *Old Key West Resort* ☎ *407/939–3463* ⊟ *AE, D, DC, MC, V.*

★ **$–$$** ✕ **Rainforest Café.** People start queuing up a half hour before the 10:30 AM opening of this 30,000-square-foot jungle fantasy in Downtown Disney's Marketplace, drawn as much by the gimmicks (man-made rainstorms, volcano eruptions) as the menu. But the food, a mix of American fare with imaginative names, is nevertheless worthwhile. Top choices include "Eyes of the Ocelot," a nice meat loaf topped with sautéed mushrooms; and "Mojo Bones," tender ribs with barbecue sauce. Best dessert: "Tortoise" Pie—actually chocolate espresso ice cream and Oreo cookies. ⊠ *Downtown Disney Marketplace* ☎ *407/827–8500 or 407/939–3463* ⊟ *AE, D, DC, MC, V.*

Contemporary

$$–$$$$ ✕ **Wolfgang Puck.** There are lots of choices here, from wood-oven pizza at the informal Puck Express to five-course meals in the upstairs formal dining room, where there's also a sushi bar and an informal café. At Express try the barbecue chicken pizza or spinach and mushroom pizza. The dining room always offers inspired pastas with sauces sublimely laced with chunks of lobster, salmon, or chicken; and a Puck trademark—Wiener schnitzel. Special five-course prix-fixe dinners ($100 with wine, $65 without) require 24-hour notice. ⊠ *Downtown Disney West Side* ☎ *407/938–9653* ⊟ *AE, MC, V.*

Cuban

$$–$$$ ✕ **Bongos Cuban Café.** Singer Gloria Estefan's Cuban eatery is inside a two-story building shaped like a pineapple. Hot-pressed Cuban sandwiches, black-bean soup, deep-fried plantain chips, and beans and rice are mainstays on the menu for the lunch crowd. One of the best entrées is "La Habana": lobster, shrimp, scallops, calamari, clams, and mussels in a piquant creole sauce. Other worthwhile offerings include *masitas de puerco* (pork chunks served with grilled onions) and the shrimp enchilada. There's live Latin music on Friday and Saturday. ⊠ *Downtown Disney West Side* ☎ *407/828–0999* ⚑ *Reservations not accepted* ⊟ *AE, D, DC, MC, V.*

Italian

$$–$$$$ ✕ **Portobello Yacht Club.** The northern Italian cuisine here is uniformly good. The *spaghettini alla Portobello* (with scallops, clams, and Alaskan king crab) is outstanding; other fine options include the charcoal-grilled rack of lamb served with creamy risotto cake, and the *rigatoni alla Calabrese,* with sausage, mushrooms, tomatoes, and black olives. There's always a fresh-catch special, as well as tasty wood-oven pizza. ⊠ *Pleasure Island* ☎ *407/934–8888* ⊟ *AE, MC, V.*

Seafood

$$–$$$$ ✕ **Fulton's Crab House.** Set in a faux riverboat docked in a lagoon between Pleasure Island and the Marketplace, this fish house offers fine, if expensive, dining. The signature seafood is flown in daily. Dungeness crab from the Pacific coast, Alaskan king crab, Florida stone crab: it's all fresh. Start with the crab and lobster bisque, then try one of the many combination entrées like the gulf shrimp and Dungeness crab cake platter. The sublime cappuccino ice cream cake is $13, but one order is easily enough for two. ⊠ *Downtown Disney Marketplace* ☎ *407/934–2628* ⊟ *AE, MC, V.*

LAKE BUENA VISTA

The community of Lake Buena Vista stretches north of Downtown Disney and southeast to the other side of I–4, off Exit 68. This is where most off-site visitors to Disney World stay, and there are some good mealtime options.

Continental

$$$–$$$$ ✕ **Arthur's 27.** The haute cuisine here comes with a world-class view from the 27th floor of the Wyndham Palace Resort, overlooking all of Disney World. The menu changes often but typically includes dishes like sugarcane-seared pork tenderloin and truffle-stuffed veal chop. There are also more exotic choices, such as buffalo medallions and roasted capon. Best dessert is the stellar Grand Marnier soufflé. There are also prix-fixe options: $68 for five courses, $62 for four. ⊠ *Wyndham Palace Re-*

sort & Spa, 1900 Buena Vista Dr., I–4 Exit 68, Lake Buena Vista ☎ *407/827–3450* ⚓ *Reservations essential* ☰ *AE, D, DC, MC, V.*

French

$$$–$$$$ ✕ **La Coquina.** This restaurant, just outside Disney property, bills itself as French with an Asian influence, and if you sample the veal tenderloin with sake-glazed prawns, you'll approve of its methods. Come for Sunday brunch, when the generous selection of goodies makes the price ($49.95 adults, $24.95 kids) almost seem like a bargain. In an unusual touch, during brunch your waiter takes you into the kitchen, where you pick out what you want and watch the chef cook it to order. For a closer look at the chef in action, ask the manager about sitting at the special chef's table in the kitchen. ⊠ *Hyatt Regency Grand Cypress, 1 Grand Cypress Blvd.* ☎ *407/239–1234* ☰ *AE, D, DC, MC, V.*

Seafood

$–$$$ ✕ **Landry's Seafood House.** Set in a fake warehouse building—popular architecture in Central Florida—this branch of a nationwide chain delivers good seafood at reasonable prices. The food is first-rate, especially Cajun dishes like the fresh-caught fish Pontchartrain, a broiled fish with slightly spicy seasoning and a creamy white-wine sauce that's topped with a lump of crabmeat. For starters, try the seafood gumbo or the fried calamari. Combination platters abound, including a $15 one that includes crab fingers, fried oysters, shrimp, and a catfish filet. ⊠ *8800 Vineland Ave., Rte. 535, Lake Buena Vista* ☎ *407/827–6466* ☰ *AE, D, DC, MC, V.*

Tex-Mex

$–$$ ✕ **Chevy's.** True, the ersatz cantina motif here looks like that of every other Mexican place in every suburb you've ever seen. But the food is a shocker: it's quite good. Try the hot tamales, or the shrimp and crab enchiladas topped with pesto-cream sauce. The menu, making use of some gringo creativity, includes chicken with Dijon mustard wrapped in a tortilla, and a huge burrito made with pork and beef barbecue. If you're up for a mucho grande feast from the grill, try the *plato gordo,* which is heaped with Baja-style ribs (grilled with a tangy sauce), grilled chicken breast, seasoned jumbo shrimp, skirt steak, and grilled garden fresh vegetables. For dessert, look for the good flan and cream pies. ⊠ *12547 Rte. 535, Lake Buena Vista* ☎ *407/827–1052* ⊠ *2809 W. Vine St., Kissimmee* ☎ *407/847–2244* ☰ *AE, MC, V.*

UNIVERSAL ORLANDO AREA

With more than a dozen restaurants and the world's largest Hard Rock Cafe, Universal Orlando's CityWalk is a culinary force. At Islands of Adventure, each of the six lands has between two and six eateries—not all of them strictly burgers-and-fries affairs. Universal has done a good job of providing information and access to these eateries, with a special **reservation and information line** (☎ 407/224–9255 ⊕ www.universalorlando. com) and a Web site that includes menus for many of the restaurants.

To get to Universal, take I–4 Exit 75A from eastbound lanes, Exit 74B when you're westbound.

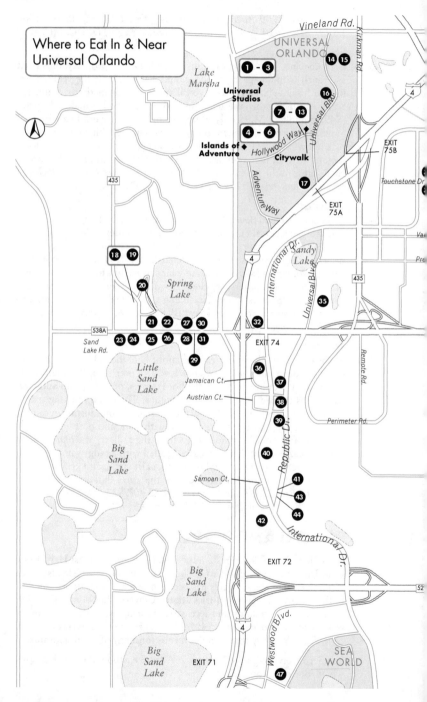

Where to Eat In & Near Universal Orlando

Meals with Universal Characters

Universal Studios offers meals with its characters, specifically Scooby-Doo, Woody Woodpecker, and Curious George, although the line up is not nearly as extensive as what is offered at Disney World.

Breakfast

You can catch the Dr. Seuss characters, including the Cat in the Hat, Sam I Am, and Thing One and Thing Two, for breakfast at the **Confisco Grille** (☎ 407/363–8000), at the entrance to Islands of Adventure, from 9 to 10:30. The meal costs $15.95 for adults and $9.95 for children.

Dinner

Character dinners at Universal take place at the three on-property hotels, and are by reservation only. Characters appearing at these restaurants vary, so please call the restaurant in advance to see which of the following will be appearing: Shaggy, Scooby-Doo, Woody Woodpecker, or Curious George. Reservations can be made at the **character meal reservation line** (☎ 407/503–3463).

Character dinners at **Islands Dining Room** (☎ 407/503–3430), in the Royal Pacific Resort, take place Monday, Tuesday, and Saturday from 6:30 to 9:30. Children age 12 and under eat from the buffet ($3.99), while adults order from a menu ($15–$25), except on Saturday, when the buffet is open to everyone and costs $24.50 for adults. Dinners at **Trattoria del Porto** (☎ 407/503–1430), in the Portofino Bay Hotel, take place on Friday from 6:30 and cost $24.50 for adults and $12.50 for children 12 and under. **The Kitchen** (☎ 407/503–2430) at the Hard Rock Hotel hosts character dinners Saturday from 6:30 to 9:30. Menu entrées range from $15 to $21.

Universal Studios

Most restaurants are on Plaza of the Stars and Hollywood Boulevard. Several accept "priority seating," which is not a reservation but an arrival time. You'll receive the first available seat after that particular time. You can make arrangements up to 30 days in advance by calling or dropping by Guest Services when you arrive or heading over to the restaurant in person.

Seafood

$$–$$$ ✕ **Lombard's Landing.** Fresh grilled or fried fish, fried shrimp, and steamed clams and mussels are the specialty at this restaurant designed to resemble a Fisherman's Wharf warehouse from 19th-century San Francisco. You can also get a steak, pasta, hamburgers, chicken, and salad. ⊠ *San Francisco/Amity, Universal Studios* ☎ *407/224–6400* 🖃 *AE, D, MC, V.*

Irish

$–$$ ✕ **Finnegan's Bar & Grill.** In an Irish pub that would look just right in downtown New York during the Ellis Island era, Finnegan's offers classic Irish comfort food like shepherd's pie, Irish stew, and fish-and-chips, plus Guinness, Harp, and Bass on tap. If shepherd's pie isn't your thing, there are also steaks, burgers, and a darn good Celtic chicken salad. Irish folk music, sometimes live, completes the theme. ✉ *Production Central, Universal Studios* ☎ *407/363–8757* ▤ *AE, D, MC, V.*

American

$–$$ ✕ **Mel's Drive-In.** At the corner of Hollywood Boulevard and 8th Avenue—which turns into Sunset Boulevard along the bottom shore of the lagoon—is (no reservations), a flashy '50s eatery with a menu and decorative muscle cars straight out of *American Graffiti*. For burgers and fries, this is one of the best choices in the park, and it comes complete with a roving doo-wop group. You're on vacation—go ahead and have that extra-thick shake. Mel's is also a great place to meet, in case you decide to go your separate ways in the park. ✉ *Hollywood Boulevard, Universal Studios* ☎ *407/363–8757* ⌲ *No reservations* ▤ *AE, D, MC, V.*

Islands of Adventure

Islands of Adventure, where it's as easy to get a glass of merlot and a croissant as it is to get a burger and fries, offers a few culinary adventures as well. There are only a couple of full-service, sit-down restaurants in the park, but the offerings at several of the cafeteria-style eateries are pretty creative and tasty, too.

American

$–$$ ✕ **Confisco Grille.** You could walk right past this Mediterranean eatery, but if you want a good meal and sit-down service, don't pass by too quickly. The menu changes often, but typical entrées include pan-seared pork medallions with roasted garlic and red peppers, baked cod with spinach and mashed potatoes, and Thai noodles with chicken, shrimp, tofu, and bean sprouts. Save room for desserts like chocolate-banana bread pudding or crème brûlée. You can catch the Dr. Seuss characters here at breakfast. ✉ *6000 Universal Blvd., Port of Entry, Islands of Adventure* ☎ *407/224–9255* ▤ *AE, D, MC, V* ☉ *No lunch.*

American/Casual

¢–$ ✕ **Green Eggs and Ham Cafe.** This Dr. Seuss–inspired spot is the only place in Orlando where the eggs are intentionally green. The eggs (tinted with food coloring) are in an egg and ham sandwich, the most popular item at this walk-up, outdoor eatery, which looks like a hallucinatory McDonald's. There's also a fairly tasty "green" garden salad, as well as some other conventional fare, including a normal cheeseburger, fries, and "frings," a type of onion ring. ✉ *6000 Universal Blvd., Seuss Landing, Islands of Adventure* ☎ *407/224–9255* ▤ *AE, D, MC, V.*

Contemporary

$–$$ ✕ **Mythos.** The name sounds Greek, but the dishes are eclectic. The menu, which changes frequently, usually includes standouts like meat loaf, roast pork tenderloin, and assorted kinds of wood-fired pizzas. Among the creative desserts is a fine pumpkin cheesecake. But the building itself is enough to grab your attention. It looks like a giant rock formation from the outside and a huge cave (albeit one with plush upholstered seating) from the inside. Mythos also has a waterfront view of the big lagoon in the center of the theme park. ⊠ *6000 Universal Blvd., Lost Continent, Islands of Adventure* ☎ *407/224–9255* ▭ *AE, D, MC, V.*

CityWalk

American/Casual

$–$$ ✕ **Hard Rock Cafe Orlando.** Built to resemble Rome's Colosseum, this 800-seat restaurant is the largest of the 100-odd Hard Rocks in the world, but getting a seat at lunch can still require a long wait. The music is always loud and the walls are filled with rock memorabilia. Appetizers range from spring rolls to boneless chicken tenders. The most popular menu item is still the $8.49 burger, with the baby-back ribs and the homemade-style meat loaf both strong contenders. If you don't eat meat, try the pasta with roast vegetables and pesto. The best dessert is the $5 chocolate-chip cookie (it's big), which is covered with ice cream. ⊠ *6000 Universal Blvd., CityWalk* ☎ *407/224–3663 or 407/351–7625* ⌦ *Reservations not accepted* ▭ *AE, D, DC, MC, V.*

$–$$ ✕ **Jimmy Buffett's Margaritaville.** Parrot-heads can probably name the top two menu items before they even walk in the door. You've got your cheeseburger, featured in the song "Cheeseburger in Paradise," and, of course, your Ultimate Margarita. The rest of the menu is an eclectic mix of quesadillas, chowder, crab cakes, jambalaya, jerk salmon, and a pretty decent steak. Worthy dessert choices include the Last Mango in Paradise cheesecake, the key lime pie, and a tasty chocolate-banana bread pudding. ⊠ *6000 Universal Blvd., CityWalk* ☎ *407/224–2155* ▭ *AE, D, MC, V.*

$–$$ ✕ **NASCAR Café Orlando.** If you are a racing fanatic, this is your place. If the memorabilia on the walls is not enough for you, a couple of actual race cars hang from the ceiling. The food is better than you might think: highlights include a good chicken-mushroom soup, fried chicken over smashed potatoes, barbecue ribs, and the Thunder Road burger with melted pimento cheese and sautéed onions. Aside from the white-chocolate cheesecake, desserts are largely forgettable. ⊠ *6000 Universal Blvd., CityWalk* ☎ *407/224–3663* ▭ *AE, D, MC, V.*

$–$$ ✕ **NBA City.** The NBA memorabilia and video games are great, but the food is actually the real draw here. Best appetizers include sweet-and-spicy smoked wings, and pecan-crusted chicken tenders with orange marmalade sauce. For an entrée, try the lemon chicken served with garlic risotto. The brick-oven pizzas include a BLT variety. Finish off with the pecan tart made with Vermont maple syrup and topped with fresh cream. The big-screen TVs, which naturally broadcast nonstop basketball action, probably won't surprise you, but the relatively quiet bar upstairs, with elegant blond-wood furniture, probably will. ⊠ *6000 Universal Blvd., CityWalk* ☎ *407/363–5919* ▭ *AE, D, MC, V.*

Contemporary

★ **$$–$$$$** ✕ **Emeril's.** The popular eatery is a culinary shrine to Emeril Lagasse, the famous Food Network chef who occasionally appears here. The menu changes frequently, but you can always count on New Orleans treats like andouille sausage, shrimp, and red beans appearing in some form or fashion. Entrées may include chili-glazed chicken with a black bean–avocado tart, and roast quail with andouille-cornbread stuffing. The wood-baked pizza, topped with exotic mushrooms, is stellar. Save room for Emeril's ice-cream parfait—banana-daiquiri ice cream topped with hot fudge, caramel sauce, walnuts, and a double chocolate fudge cookie. ☒ *6000 Universal Blvd., CityWalk* ☎ *407/224–2424* ⌖ *Reservations essential* ▤ *AE, D, MC, V.*

Italian

$–$$ ✕ **Pastamoré.** Since it doesn't have name appeal like its neighbor Emeril's, Pastamoré is something of a CityWalk sleeper. But this could be the best uncrowded restaurant at Universal, with wood-fired pizza, fresh pastas, and Italian beer and wines. Especially notable are the huge Italian sandwiches, with ingredients like marinated chicken, peppers, and sun-dried tomatoes, as well as a good tiramisu. In an unusual touch, you can also come here for Italian breakfast breads—the place opens at 8 AM. The breakfast pizza, topped with sausage and eggs, will make you glad you didn't opt for a McMuffin. ☒ *6000 Universal Blvd., CityWalk* ☎ *407/224–3663* ▤ *AE, D, MC, V.*

Latin

$$–$$$ ✕ **The Latin Quarter.** This grottolike restaurant and club, with domed ceilings and stone walls, is one of those jumping-by-night, dormant-by-day spots, but the food is good all the time. Cuisines from 21 Latin nations are on the menu, as is a wide selection of South American beers. Good entrée choices include *churrasco* (skirt steak), *puerco asado* (roast pork), cumin-rubbed grilled chicken, guava-spiced spare ribs, and an outstanding fried snapper with tomato salsa. Most main dishes come with black beans and rice. Best bets for dessert: the crepes and the mango and guava cheesecakes. ☒ *6000 Universal Blvd., CityWalk* ☎ *407/224–3663* ▤ *AE, D, MC, V.*

Hard Rock Hotel

Steak

$$–$$$$ ✕ **The Palm.** With its dark-wood interior and hundreds of framed celebrity caricatures, this restaurant resembles its famed New York City namesake. Steaks are the reason to dine here, but most are available only at dinner. The steak fillet cooked on a hot stone is a specialty, as is the Double Steak, a 36-ounce New York strip for two (or one extreme carnivore). There are several veal dishes on the menu, along with a 3-pound Maine lobster, and linguine with clam sauce. ☒ *1000 Universal Studios Plaza, Universal Orlando* ☎ *407/503–7256* ▤ *AE, D, DC, MC, V* ⊘ *No lunch weekends.*

Portofino Bay Hotel

Italian

$$$–$$$$ ✕ **Bice.** In 2004 trendy, pricey Bice replaced the hotel's former top-billed restaurant, Delfino Riviera. Bice (pronounced "*beach*-ay") is an Italian nickname for Beatrice, as in Beatrice Ruggeri, who founded the original Milan locaton of this family restaurant in 1926. But the word "family" does not carry the connotation "mom and pop" at Bice, where white starched tablecloths set the stage for sophisticated cuisine. The restaurant retains its frescoed ceilings, marble floors, and, of course, picture windows overlooking great views of the man-made bay just outside. This restaurant is expensive, but some of the entrées that seem worth it are the one-pound veal chop with polenta ($42) and the veal Milanese ($38). While you're running up your tab, you may as well also try the tasty lentil soup with black truffle fondue ($12). Desserts, ranging from tiramisu to chocolate soufflé with vanilla ice cream and honey, are delicious. ⊠ *5601 Universal Blvd., Universal Orlando* ☎ *407/503–1415* ▤ *AE, D, DC, MC, V* ☻ *No lunch.*

$$–$$$ ✕ **Mama Della's.** The premise here is that Mama Della is a middle-age Italian housewife who has opened up her home as a restaurant. "Mama" is always on hand (there are several of them, working in shifts), strolling among the tables and making small talk. The food, which is served family style, is no fantasy—it's excellent. The menu has Italian traditions like chicken cacciatore, veal parmigiana, and spaghetti with sirloin meatballs or bolognese sauce, and all of the pastas are made in-house. Tiramisu and Italian chocolate torte are sure bets for dessert. ⊠ *5601 Universal Blvd., Universal Orlando* ☎ *407/503–1000* ▤ *AE, D, DC, MC, V* ☻ *Closed Mon. No lunch.*

Royal Pacific Resort

Pan-Asian

★ $$–$$$$ ✕ **Tchoup Chop.** With its cathedral ceiling, the inside of this restaurant looks almost churchlike, and the food at Emeril Lagasse's Pacific-influenced restaurant is certainly righteous. Following the theme of the Royal Pacific Resort, the decorators included a tiki bar with lots of bamboo, a couple of indoor waterfalls, and a long pool with porcelain lily pads running the length of the dining room. The menu combines Lagasse's own New Orleans–style cuisine with an Asian theme. Entrées include grilled pork chops with ginger-roasted sweet potatoes, and a Hawaiian-style dinner plate with Kiawe smoked ribs, Kahua pork and noodle sauté, and teriyaki grilled chicken. For dessert try the bittersweet chocolate layer cake with banana sauce or the frozen coconut served with white-chocolate fudge, cashew brittle, sweet cream, and a giant strawberry. ⊠ *6300 Hollywood Way, Universal Orlando* ☎ *407/503–2467* ⚏ *Reservations essential* ▤ *AE, D, DC, MC, V.*

KISSIMMEE

Although Orlando is the focus of most theme-park visitors, Kissimmee is actually closer to Walt Disney World. To visit the area, follow I–4 to Exit 64A. Allow about 15 or 20 minutes to travel from WDW, or about 30 minutes from I-Drive.

Contemporary

$$$–$$$$ ✕ **The Venetian Room.** Inside the Caribe Royale Resort, one of Orlando's bigger convention hotels, this place was doubtless designed for execs on expense accounts. But the serene, luxurious, and romantic atmosphere makes it a great place for dinner with your spouse or significant other. The architecture alone is enough to lure you in. It's designed to look like Renaissance Venice: the entryway has a giant copper dome over the door and the dining room has dark-wood furniture, crystal chandeliers, and carpets that could grace a European palace. A tad cliché but tasty just as well is the pan-seared foie gras starter. You can follow that with farm-raised squab or beef tenderloin with black truffle sauce, then perhaps a Grand Marnier soufflé or the Venetian Room chocolate sampler (mousse, cake, and truffles). ⊠ *Caribe Royale Resort, 8101 World Center Dr., I-Drive Area* ☎ *407/238–8060* ▱ *AE, D, DC, MC, V* ☺ *No lunch.*

Italian

$–$$ ✕ **Romano's Macaroni Grill.** You may have a branch of this prolific chain in your hometown, and the three popular Orlando locations deliver a known quantity—good but not great cuisine. It's friendly, it's casual, and it's comfortable. The scaloppine, made with chicken instead of the traditional veal, is topped with artichokes and capers and served with angel-hair pasta. Mama's Trio includes lasagna, chicken cannelloni, and chicken parmigiana. House wines are brought to the table in gallon bottles—you serve yourself and then report how many glasses you had. Your kids can pass the time doodling with crayons on the white-paper table covering. ⊠ *5320 W. Irlo Bronson Memorial Hwy., Kissimmee* ☎ *407/396–6155* ⊠ *884 W. Rte. 436, Altamonte Springs* ☎ *407/682–2577* ⊠ *12148 S. Apopka–Vineland Rd., Lake Buena Vista* ☎ *407/239–6676* ▱ *AE, D, DC, MC, V.*

Steak

$$$–$$$$ ✕ **Old Hickory Steak House.** If paying $40 for a steak (and an extra $7 for a side of fries) then dining inside a barn seems a bit surreal, remember that this is Orlando. The barn, like many of the unusual eateries in the Orlando area, is a faux building, a movie-set kind of edifice designed for effect. Dine on the deck adjacent to the barn and you will overlook the hotel's faux Everglades, where electronic alligators cavort with fiberglass frogs. The experience is designed to entertain, and it does; the food at the steak house is worth the roughly $50 a person you'll spend for dinner if you eschew alcohol. You could really get into the groove by indulging in the tenderloin of alligator lasagna. Otherwise, there's Angus beef and American buffalo. ⊠ *Gaylord Palms Resort, 6000 W. Osceola Pkwy., I–4 Exit 65, Kissimmee* ☎ *407/586–0000* ▱ *AE, DC, MC, V* ☺ *No lunch.*

CELEBRATION

If this small town with Victorian-style homes and perfectly manicured lawns reminds you a bit of Main Street, U.S.A., in the Magic Kingdom, it should. The utopian residential community was created by Disney, with all the Disney attention to detail. Every view of every street is warm and pleasant, though the best are out the windows of the town's four restaurants, all of which face a pastoral (if man-made) lake. There's even an interactive fountain in the small park near the lake, giving kids a great place to splash. To get here take I–4 to Exit 64A and follow the "Celebration" signs.

American/Casual

$–$$$$ ✕ **Celebration Town Tavern.** This New England–cuisine eatery has a split personality. Half is the casual Celebration Town Tavern, with sandwiches and less expensive fare; the other half is the slightly more formal Bostonian, with dishes like prime rib and fresh, two-pound Maine lobster. Both halves are open for lunch and dinner, and you can order the larger-portioned entrées from the Bostonian menu in the Tavern. You'll find standouts such as Manhattan and New England clam chowder, lobster quesadilla, as well as a good selection of sandwiches at the Tavern, although you can choose from heaping platters of fried Ipswich clams, fried oysters, or Florida stone crabs served in season (spring) at the Bostonian. There are great New England crab cakes and, of course, Boston cream pie. ✉ *721 Front St., Celebration* ☎ *407/566–2526* ▭ *AE, D, MC, V.*

$–$$ ✕ **Market Street Café.** The menu at this informal diner resembling a 1950s classic ranges from the house-special baked-potato omelet (served until 4:30 PM) to chicken Alfredo and prime rib. One appetizer, the cheese quesadilla, is large enough to make a meal. Standout entrées include the pot roast and meat loaf. In addition to a hearty version of the quintessential American hamburger, there's also a salmon burger and a veggie burger for the cholesterol-wary. The excellent house-made potato chips come with a blue cheese sauce. ✉ *701 Front St., Celebration* ☎ *407/566–1144* ⚑ *Reservations not accepted* ▭ *AE, D, MC, V.*

¢–$ ✕ **Herman's.** The old-fashioned ice-cream parlor motif of this place goes well with the Victorian-era small-town style of Celebration, and like all the eateries in this pleasant little burg, Herman's faces a small lake in the town's center. The truffle brownie stacker—a fudge brownie topped with vanilla ice cream, caramel, chocolate sauce, and fresh raspberries and blueberries—is worth the visit in itself. The sandwich menu is pretty sophisticated, too. The Italian *panini* are made with garlic focaccia and pesto sauce, and piled high with options like Italian sausage, roast beef, or sliced turkey. A mango, tomato, and cucumber salad with Dijon vinaigrette is a good choice for calorie-watchers. ✉ *671 Front St., Suite 140, Celebration* ☎ *407/566–1300* ▭ *AE, MC, V.*

Italian

$–$$$ ✕ **Café d' Antonio.** The wood-burning oven and grill are worked pretty hard here, and the mountains of hardwood used in the open kitchen flavor the best of the menu—the pizza, the grilled fish and chicken, the steaks and chops, even the lasagna. Standouts include lasagna Bolognese, shrimp wrapped in pancetta, and duck roasted with figs. For dessert, try the hazelnut chocolate cake or the ricotta cheesecake. Italian vintages dominate the wine list. As at the rest of Celebration's restaurants, there's an awning-covered terrace overlooking the lagoon. ✉ *691 Front St., Celebration* ☎ *407/566–2233* ▭ *AE, D, MC, V.*

Japanese

$–$$ ✕ **Seito Celebration.** Operated by the Seils, the Japanese family that owns Seito Sushi in downtown Orlando, this quiet and casual eatery offers the same excellent sushi as its sister location. You can dine on your favorite rolls while overlooking the lake in the center of Celebration.

Non-sushi entrées like salmon teriyaki and New York strip steak are also available. While cold tofu may sound like a health-food freak's revenge, it's actually a great appetizer here, served with ginger, scallions, and soy sauce. The bananas fried in tempura batter make an excellent dessert. ⊠ *671 Front St., Suite 100, Celebration* ☎ *407/566–1889* ⊟ *AE, D, DC, MC, V.*

Latin

$$–$$$ ✕ **Columbia Restaurant.** Celebration's branch of this statewide, family-owned Latin chain is generally as good as the original in Tampa. Start with tapas like Cuban caviar (which is actually black-bean dip with Cuban crackers) and ribs with guava barbecue sauce. Then zero in on the paella—either *à la Valenciana,* with clams, shrimp, scallops, chicken, pork, and calamari mixed into tasty yellow rice; or the all-seafood *marinara,* which also includes lobster. A good lighter dish is the Atlantic *merluza,* a delicate white fish rolled in bread crumbs, then grilled and topped with lemon butter, parsley, and diced eggs. Desserts include key lime pie and a good Cuban flan. ⊠ *649 Front St., Celebration* ☎ *407/ 566–1505* ⊟ *AE, D, DC, MC, V.*

ORLANDO METRO AREA

International Drive

A number of restaurants are scattered among the hotels that line manicured International Drive. Many are branches of chains, from fast-food spots to theme coffee shops and up. The food is sometimes quite good. To get to the area, take I-4 Exit 72 or 74A. Count on it taking about a half hour from the Kissimmee area or from WDW property.

American/Casual

$–$$$ ✕ **B-Line Diner.** As you might expect from its hotel location, this slick, 1950s-style diner with red-vinyl counter seats is not exactly cheap, but the salads, sandwiches, and griddle foods are tops. The greatest combo ever—a thick, juicy burger served with fries and a wonderful milk shake—is done beautifully. You can also get pork chops, strip steak, and fried snapper. Desserts range from hazelnut-orange cake to coconut cream pie to banana splits. It's open 24 hours. ⊠ *Peabody Orlando, 9801 International Dr., I-Drive Area* ☎ *407/352–4000* ⊟ *AE, D, DC, MC, V.*

$–$$$ ✕ **Dan Marino's Town Tavern.** Part of a Florida sports bar chain begun by the Miami Dolphins quarterback, the Tavern mixes burgers and steaks with some sophisticated surprises, including seared tuna, and filet mignon in mushroom–merlot sauce over mashed potatoes. ⊠ *Pointe*Orlando, 9101 International Dr., I-Drive Area* ☎ *407/363–1013* ⊟ *AE, MC.*

$–$$ ✕ **Murray Brothers Caddyshack.** No national restaurant chain, especially one that seeks to draw clientele with a high-profile celebrity name, would miss having a location in Orlando, on International Drive if possible, and Murray Brothers Caddyshack has done both. The entertainment level in this place is not quite like being an extra in a Bill Murray movie, but the good news is that the food essentially makes up for the fact that this is basically just a big sports bar with lots of televisions. Best bets here include the ribs and pork chops, both slow-cooked in a tangy Kentucky bourbon sauce and served with your choice of garlic mashed potatoes, a baked potato, or fries, plus creamed spinach. Good desserts include the hot fudge sundae and the Belgian waffle piled high with vanilla ice cream. If you hit the place in late afternoon or early evening, it won't be especially noisy. Don't plan to eat too late—the bar is open until midnight but the kitchen closes at 10 PM. ⊠ *Festival Bay shopping center, 5250 International Dr., I-Drive Area* ☎ *407/351–3848* ▤ *AE, D, MC, V.*

Caribbean

$–$$$ ✕ **Bahama Breeze.** Even though the lineage is corporate, the menu here is creative and tasty. The big outdoor dining area, casual style, and the Caribbean cooking draw a crowd: so be prepared for a wait. Meanwhile, you can sip piña coladas and other West Indian delights on a big wooden porch. The food is worth the wait. Start with fried coconut-covered prawns, and move on to the West Indies ribs with guava glaze. Homemade key lime pie is the perfect finish. ⊠ *8849 International Dr., I-Drive Area* ☎ *407/248–2499* ⊠ *8735 Vineland Ave., I–4 Exit 68, I-Drive Area* ☎ *407/938–9010* ⌂ *Reservations not accepted* ▤ *AE, D, DC, MC.*

Chinese

$–$$$$ ✕ **Ming Court.** A walled courtyard and serene pond make you forget you're on International Drive. The extensive menu includes simple chicken Szechuan, jumbo shrimp with honey-glaze walnuts, and aged filet mignon grilled in a spicy Szechuan sauce. The flourless chocolate cake, certainly not Asian, has been a popular standard for years. Ming Court is within walking distance of the Orange County Convention Center and can be quite busy at lunchtime. ⊠ *9188 International Dr., I-Drive Area* ☎ *407/351–9988* ▤ *AE, D, DC, MC, V.*

Contemporary

★ $$$$ ✕ **Norman's.** Chef-entrepreneur Norman Van Aken brings impressive credentials to the restaurant that bears his name, as one might expect from the headline eatery in the first and only Ritz-Carlton in Orlando. Van Aken's culinary roots go back to the Florida Keys, where he is credited with creating "Floribbean" cuisine, a blend that is part Key West, part Havana, part Kingston, Jamaica. In the '90s, Van Aken became a star in Miami with his Coral Gables restaurant. The Orlando operation is a formal restaurant with marble floors, starched tablecloths, waiters in black-tie, and a creative, if expensive, prix-fixe menu. The offerings change frequently, but typical dishes include mango-glazed barbecue duck stuffed into a green chili-studded pancake, and roast pork Havana with mole sauce and Haitian-style golden grits. For dessert, try the "New World banana split," with macadamia nut–brittle ice cream and rum-flambéed banana. The least expensive dinner option is a three-course, prix-fixe meal for $55 per person. ⊠ *Ritz-Carlton Grande Lakes, 4000 Central Florida Pkwy., I-Drive Area* ☎ *407/393–4333* ▤ *AE, D, DC, MC, V* ◷ *No lunch.*

¢–$ ✕ **Café Tu Tu Tango.** The food here is served tapas-style—everything is appetizer-sized. The eclectic menu is fitting for a restaurant on International Drive. If you want a compendium of cuisines at one go, try the black-bean soup with cilantro sour cream, grilled baby lamb chops with curried apple chutney, coconut-curry mussels, and the Barcelona stir fry (a mix of shrimp, calamari, chicken, andouille sausage, mushrooms, peppers, and garlic). The restaurant is supposedly a crazy artist's loft; artists paint at easels while diners sip drinks like Matisse Margaritas. Although nothing costs more than $8, it's not hard to spend $50 for lunch for two. ⊠ *8625 International Dr., I-Drive Area* ☎ *407/248–2222* ♺ *Reservations not accepted* ▭ *AE, D, DC, MC, V.*

Fast Food
¢ ✕ **McDonald's.** Once the world's largest McDonald's (now there's a bigger one in Moscow), this one still has the largest PlayPlace and the billboard out front proclaims just that. Perfect for Orlando, this McDonald's definitely has more frills than your usual roadside double arches. The '50s-style dining room has a rock 'n' roll theme, and there's an arcade where you can win prizes. Plus you can shop for discount attraction tickets, hotel rooms, McDonald's collector plates and pins, and even socks, since they're required in the huge indoor playground. Try out the new Bistro Gourmet menu, which includes healthier fare than burgers, such as panini sandwiches, wraps, and tossed pastas. ⊠ *6875 W. Sand Lake Rd., I-Drive Area* ☎ *407/351–2185* ♺ *Reservations not accepted* ▭ *AE, DC, MC, V.*

Italian
$$–$$$$ ✕ **Capriccio's.** From the marble-top tables in this Italian restaurant you can view the open kitchen and the wood-burning pizza ovens, which turn out whole-wheat-flour pies ranging from pizza *salsiccia*, with pepperoni and Italian sausage, to pizza *formaggio* (with Gorgonzola, pecorino, Parmesan, mozzarella, and garlic cream). For dessert, sample the imported-from-Italy ladyfingers with amaretto sauce. ⊠ *Peabody Orlando, 9801 International Dr., I-Drive Area* ☎ *407/352–4000* ▭ *AE, DC, MC, V* ⊘ *Closed Mon.*

$$–$$$ ✕ **Bergamo's.** If you like Broadway show tunes with your spaghetti and opera with your osso buco, then head here for the booming voices as well as the good food, both of which are provided by servers in satin vests. Management does not rely on the entertainment alone to fill seats: the food is very worthwhile. Try the linguine *pescatore* (fisherman's linguine), with lobster, shrimp, crab meat and mussels; or the classic osso buco with risotto Milanese. And while the idea of a mango-basil cheesecake dessert sounds a tad strange, you'll probably love it, too. ⊠ *8445 International Dr., I–4 Exit 74A, I-Drive Area* ☎ *407/352–3805* ▭ *AE, D, DC, MC, V* ⊘ *No lunch.*

Japanese
$$–$$$$ ✕ **Ran-Getsu.** The surroundings are a Disney-style version of Asia, but the food is fresh and carefully prepared, much of it table-side. Unless you're alone, you can have your meal Japanese-style at the low tables overlooking a carp-filled pond and decorative gardens. You might start

REFUELING AROUND ORLANDO

FOR THOSE TIMES *when you're out and about in Orlando and all you want is a quick bite, consider these local and national chains. They seem to crop up on every shopping strip and in every mall in the metro area. Most have several formica-topped tables where you can sit for lunch before heading back out to the shops and attractions.*

Amigo's. *Tex-Mex restaurants come and go in Central Florida, but this local chain run by a family of transplanted Texans is consistently in the top tier. Go for the Santa Fe dinner, which includes tamales, enchiladas, chiles rellenos, and wonderful refried beans. The dinner's so big, it almost takes a burro to bring it to your table. Lighter fare includes spinach enchiladas.*

California Pizza Kitchen: *There's usually a line at the Mall at Millenia location, but the wait is worth it. The specialty is individual-size pizza, served on a plate with toppings ranging from Jamaican jerk chicken to spicy Italian peppers. You can also get fettucine with garlic-cream sauce, and Santa Fe chicken topped with sour cream, salsa, and guacamole.*

Don Pablo's: *Chicken enchiladas and beef fajitas are on the bill of fare at this Tex-Mex outpost. The I-Drive location is in a big, barnlike building.*

Johnny Rockets: *Burgers and chili dogs are served in a vibrant, '50s-diner-style environment here.*
There are branches at the Mall at Millenia, on International Drive, and in Winter Park.

Moe's: *The nomenclature is a little ridiculous here. Burritos with names like "Joey Bag of Donuts," seem geared to make you laugh, but once you taste them, your mouth will be happy to just chew. This is good, fast, fresh Mex for the road.*

Panera Bread: *Fresh-baked pastries, bagels, and espresso drinks are the mainstays here, although you can grab a hearty and inexpensive meal like smoked-chicken panini on onion focaccia and still have change left from a $10 bill. Of the 10 locations in the metro area, Lake Eola and Mall at Millenia are standouts.*

TooJay's Gourmet Deli: *This kosher deli and versatile family dining spot has classic sandwiches like turkey Reubens, and corned beef and pastrami smeared with chopped liver, plus hot comfort food like pot roast, matzo ball soup, meat-loaf melt, and brisket with onions and horseradish. Don't miss the rugalach, traditional Jewish cookies that have fruit or chocolate rolled into the dough.*

Wolfgang Puck Express: *At Puck's pricey café, a meal is an event. But at the two Downtown Disney express walk-up windows, a meal is poetry in motion. Grab a wood-oven pizza or soup and salad, and you're out of there in 10 minutes.*

with creamy, spicy shrimp and scallops served gratin style, and continue with the *shabu-shabu* (thinly sliced beef and vegetables cooked tableside in a simmering broth), or the *kushiyaki* (grilled skewers of shrimp, beef, chicken, and scallops). If you feel adventurous, try the deep-fried alligator tail glazed in a ginger-soy sauce. ⊠ *8400 International Dr., I-Drive Area* ☎ *407/345–0044* ▭ *AE, DC, MC, V* ☺ *No lunch.*

Seafood

$$$–$$$$ ✕ **Atlantis.** A harpist plays in this dining room, which is decorated with frescoes, dark-wood paneling, and plush green carpet. The waiters even bring out the entrées on silver-dome trays. Go for one of the various lobster dishes or the grilled fish, such as yellowfin tuna and salmon. There are also worthy red-meat dishes, including roast loin of lamb, and the obligatory surf-and-turf combo—in this case a sirloin served with lobster and pesto sauce. Desserts include some fine soufflés, which must be ordered 30 minutes in advance. ⊠ *Renaissance Orlando Resort, 6677 Sea Harbor Dr., I-Drive Area* ☎ *407/351–5555* ⊟ *AE, MC, V* ☉ *No lunch.*

Steak

★ **$$$$** ✕ **Texas de Brazil.** The chain that brought this restaurant to Orlando is from Texas, but the concept is straight out of Rio, where the *churrascarias* (barbecue restaurants) offer you the option of eating yourself into oblivion. Just as it is in Rio, here you'll find a card on your table, red on one side and green on the other. As long as you leave the green side up, an endless cavalcade of waiters will bring expertly grilled and roasted beefsteak, pork, chicken, and sausage. Buffet stations offer sides like garlic mashed potatoes, baked potatoes, black beans and rice, a wide assortment of salads, and decadent desserts such as Brazilian papaya cream. The fixed-price meal costs $39. For an additional cost you can choose from more than 400 wines. Children 12 and under eat for half price, and kids under six eat free. You can dine outdoors or in, where the restaurant has bright red walls, dark furniture, and white tablecloths. ⊠ *5259 International Dr., I-Drive Area* ☎ *407/355–0355* ⊟ *AE, D, DC, MC, V* ☉ *No lunch.*

★ **$$–$$$$** ✕ **Vito's Chop House.** There's a reason why they keep the blinds closed most of the time: it's for the wines' sake. The dining room doubles as the cellar, with hundreds of bottles stacked in every nook and cranny. The steaks and the wood-grilled pork chops are superb. A popular entrée is the roast chicken cacciatore, and a second house favorite is the fried lobster tails on linguini with marinara sauce. Worthwhile desserts include grilled peach di Vito, an excellent key lime pie, and Italian wedding cake. Finish your meal by enjoying a fine cigar along with a glass of aged cognac, armagnac, or grappa in the lounge. ⊠ *8633 International Dr., I-Drive Area* ☎ *407/354–2467* ⌧ *Reservations essential* ⊟ *AE, D, DC, MC, V* ☉ *No lunch.*

Thai

$–$$ ✕ **Siam Orchid.** One of Orlando's more elegant Asian restaurants occupies a gorgeous structure a bit off International Drive. Waitresses, who wear costumes from Thailand, serve authentic fare such as Siam wings, a chicken wing stuffed to look like a drumstick, and *pla rad prik,* a whole, deep-fried fish covered with a sauce flavored with red chilies, bell peppers, and garlic. Pad thai dishes come in a variety of choices: beef, pork, seafood, and vegetable. If you like it spicy, remember to say "Thai hot," but be sure you mean it. ⊠ *7575 Universal Blvd., I-Drive Area* ☎ *407/351–0821* ⊟ *AE, DC, MC, V.*

Sand Lake Road

This is the part of the city nearest the main Disney tourism area, a mere five minutes or so northeast of International Drive or Universal Orlando. Because the neighborhood has many expensive homes, with high incomes to match, it's where you'll find some of the city's more upscale stores and restaurants. Over the past few years one of the most significant dining sectors in Orlando has sprung up along Sand Lake Road, Exit 74A, just about a mile west of crowded International Drive, where the quality of the average restaurant is not up to par with the eateries on Sand Lake.

American

$$–$$$ ✕ **Woodstone Grill & Wine Bar.** Live jazz and blues music fills the night at this strip-mall bar, but don't worry—the food and drink here aren't second-rate warm-up acts. They're headliners in their own right. Standout entrées include the roast duck flambéed in orange liqueur and the lobster-stuffed ravioli with saffron cream sauce. The wine list here is extensive, with offerings from Napa Valley to New Zealand. The crowd tends to dress up, but coats and ties are not required. Wood tables and ceramic tile floors give the place a rustic, elegant look. ⊠ 7563 *W. Sand Lake Rd., Sand Lake Rd. Area* ☎ 407/351–1227 ▤ *AE, D, DC, MC, V.*

Contemporary

$$–$$$$ ✕ **Chatham's Place.** In Florida, grouper is about as ubiquitous as Coca-Cola, but to discover its full potential, try the rendition here: it's sautéed in pecan butter and flavored with cayenne. Other good entrées include the spicy chicken, and the filet mignon served with a peppercorn and cognac sauce. The most popular appetizer is the Maryland-style crab cakes, but the New Orleans–style shrimp brochette is also noteworthy. The chef does wonders with desserts like pecan–macadamia nut pie. Take I–4 Exit 74A. ⊠ 7575 *Dr. Phillips Blvd., Sand Lake Rd. Area* ☎ 407/ 345–2992 ▤ *AE, D, DC, MC, V.*

$$–$$$ ✕ **The Melting Pot.** This fondue restaurant keeps you busy while you eat—you'll be doing part of the cooking. Diners dip morsels ranging from lobster tails to sirloin slices into flavorful broths and oils in stainless steel pots built into the center of the table. The lineup also includes the traditional cheese fondues and chocolate fondues for dessert. You can even order s'mores. ⊠ *Fountains Plaza, 7549 W. Sand Lake Rd., I–4 Exit 74A, Sand Lake Rd. Area* ☎ 407/903–1100 ▤ *AE, D, DC, MC, V.*

$–$$$
Fodor'sChoice ✕ **Seasons 52.** Parts of the menu change every week of the year at this
★ innovative restaurant, which began with the concept of serving different foods at different times, depending on what's in season. Meals here tend to be light, healthy, and very flavorful. You might have sesame pork chops with chilled asparagus and citrus-soy dressing, grilled scallops, and steamed mussels in orange-ginger sauce over pearl pasta, or salmon cooked on a cedar plank and accompanied by grilled vegetables. An impressive wine list complements the long and colorful menu. Another health-conscious concept adopted at Seasons 52 is the "mini indulgence" dessert: classics like chocolate cake, butterscotch pudding, and rocky

road ice cream served in portions designed not to bust your daily calorie budget. Although the cuisine is haute, the prices are modest—not bad for a snazzy, urbane, dark-wood-walled bistro and wine bar. ⊠ *7700 Sand Lake Rd., Sand Lake Rd. Area* ☎ *407/354–5212* ▭ *AE, D, DC, MC, V* ⊘ *No lunch*.

Hawaiian

$$-$$$ ✗ **Roy's.** Chef Roy Yamaguchi has more or less perfected his own cuisine type—Hawaiian fusion, replete with lots of tropical fruit–based sauces and lots of imagination. The menu changes daily, but typical dishes include treats like hickory-smoked and grilled ostrich loin, and macadamia nut–crusted bass with Thai curry-peanut sauce. Frequently served desserts include macadamia-nut tart and coconut-crusted, fried cheesecake. If your tastes prefer to remain on the mainland, go for classics like a wood-fired, homemade-style meat loaf and warm apple crumb pie with vanilla-bean ice cream. ⊠ *7760 W. Sand Lake Rd., I–4 Exit 74A, Sand Lake Rd. Area* ☎ *407/352–4844* ▭ *AE, D, DC, MC, V.*

Italian

$$-$$$$ ✗ **Christini's.** Locals, visitors, and Disney execs gladly pay the price at Christini's, one of the city's best places for northern Italian. Owner Chris Christini is on hand nightly to make sure that everything is perfect. Try the veal piccata or the fettuccine *alla Christini,* the house specialty fettuccine Alfredo. The multicourse dinner often takes a couple of hours or more, but if you like Italian minstrels at your table, this place should please you. Take I–4 Exit 74A. ⊠ *Dr. Phillips Marketplace, 7600 Dr. Phillips Blvd., Sand Lake Rd. Area* ☎ *407/345–8770* ▭ *AE, D, DC, MC, V.*

$$-$$$ ✗ **Antonio's.** This pleasant trattoria has great service, welcoming surroundings, and a good chef with both the skill and the authority to give the place individuality. Tasty creations include jumbo shrimp sautéed with garlic and rosemary and served with a light tomato sauce; *frutti di mare,* with shrimp, scallops, clams, and mussels; and chicken breast sautéed with mushrooms and baby peas in tomato sauce. Daily specials of fish (like Florida grouper) and red meat are always available. ⊠ *Fountains Plaza, 7559 W. Sand Lake Rd., I–4 Exit 74A, Sand Lake Rd. Area* ☎ *407/363–9191* ▭ *AE, D, DC, MC, V* ⊘ *Closed Sun. No lunch Sat.*

$-$$$ ✗ **Timpano Italian Chophouse.** In this celebration of the America of the '50s and '60s, you may feel transported to Vegas when you hear the piano player and vocalist—and sometimes the waiters—belt out Sinatra and Wayne Newton chestnuts. American beef definitely gets its due here, but that doesn't cancel out any of the Italian flair. Along with the 18-ounce New York strip and the 16-ounce center-cut pork chops, there are credible versions of veal piccata with tomatoes, capers, and artichokes; and grilled grouper with black and white beans. Other Italian touches include a good minestrone soup; sides of pasta are available with any main course. ⊠ *7488 W. Sand Lake Rd., I–4 Exit 75A, Sand Lake Rd. Area* ☎ *407/248–0429* ▭ *AE, D, DC, MC, V.*

Latin

$$-$$$$ ✗ **Samba Room.** Although owned by the same company that operates the TGI Friday's chain, this big, vibrant restaurant is a good version of an "authentic" Latin experience. You may agree once you've heard the bongos and tasted the paella. To sample the extensive menu, go for the *bocaditas* (small plates) offerings, which include mango barbecued ribs with plantain fries and grilled mussels with a coconut sour-orange sauce. A standout on the main course menu is the Argentinean-style skirt steak. For dessert, try the coconut crème brûlée and the green-apple and banana cobbler. ☒ *7468 W. Sand Lake Rd., I–4 Exit 75A, Sand Lake Rd. Area* ☏ *407/226–0550* ▭ *AE, D, MC, V.*

Mexican

¢ ✕ **Moe's.** Based on the names chosen for the menu entries, the Moe in this equation could almost be the guy who cavorted on film with Larry and Curly. There's an "Ugly Naked Guy" taco, and other offerings are called "The Other Lewinsky" and "Joey Bag of Donuts." But the food is more sublime than the nomenclature. The Ugly Naked Guy, for instance, is a vegetarian taco with guacamole and a side of red beans for $2.29. And the Joey Bag of Donuts is a marinated steak with beans and rice for $4.95. Moe's is a great fast-food alternative with most meals costing well south of $10. ☒ *7541D W. Sand Lake Rd., I–4 Exit 74A, Sand Lake Rd. Area* ☏ *407/264–9903* ☒ *847 S. Orlando Ave., Winter Park* ☏ *407/629–4500* ⌖ *Reservations not accepted* ▭ *AE, D, MC, V.*

Middle Eastern

$$–$$$ ✕ **Cedar's Restaurant.** Set in a small strip shopping center that's become part of a restaurant row, this family-owned Lebanese eatery includes Middle Eastern standards like shish kebab, falafel, and hummus as well as tasty daily specials. One of the best of the latter is the fish *tajine,* grilled fish in a sauce of sesame paste, sautéed onions, pine nuts, and cilantro. You may also want to try sautéed or grilled quail with a cilantro and garlic sauce. A tad more formal than the average Orlando-area Middle Eastern restaurant, Cedar's has tables with white linen tablecloths and diners who tend to go for resort casual attire. ☒ *7732 W. Sand Lake Rd., I–4 Exit 74A, Sand Lake Rd. Area* ☏ *407/351–6000* ▭ *AE, D, DC, MC, V.*

Seafood

$–$$$$ ✕ **MoonFish.** The big waterfall on the sign on the front of the building will grab your attention, but once you get inside, you'll find the gimmickry gives way to solid cuisine served in a serene space with dark-wood paneling and white cloths on the tables. Specialties range from grilled Caribbean green back lobster tail to Alaskan red king crab, and Florida stone crab in season (spring). The restaurant also specializes in aged beef, which you can view in a big refrigerator cabinet as you walk in the door. There's also a raw bar with oysters and a sushi bar with the usual selections, including yellowtail tuna, octopus, squid, and eel. ☒ *7525 W. Sand Lake Rd., I–4 Exit 74A, Sand Lake Rd. Area* ☏ *407/ 363–7262* ▭ *AE, D, DC, MC, V.*

★ $–$$ ✕ **Bonefish Grill.** After polishing its culinary act in the Tampa Bay area, this Florida-based seafood chain has moved into the Orlando market with a casually elegant eatery that offers standout dishes like grouper piccata, rock shrimp fettucine diablo, and a house specialty, Lily's fire-roasted chicken topped with goat cheese, spinach, artichokes, and a lemon-basil sauce. Meat lovers may prefer the boneless pork chops topped with fontina cheese. For the record, there's no bonefish on the menu. It's an inedible gamefish, caught for sport in the Florida Keys. ⊠ *7830 Sand Lake Rd., I–4 Exit 74A, Sand Lake Rd. Area* ☎ *407/355–7707* ▱ *AE, D, DC, MC, V* ☺ *No lunch.*

Steak

$$–$$$$ ✕ **Morton's of Chicago.** Center stage in the kitchen is a huge broiler, kept at 900°F to sear in the flavor of the porterhouses, sirloins, T-bones, and other cuts of aged beef. Morton's looks like a sophisticated private club, and youngsters with mouse caps are not common among the clientele. It's not unusual for checks to hit $65 a head, but if beef is your passion, this is the place. A good, fruity dessert is the raspberry soufflé. The wine list has about 500 vintages from around the world. Take I–4 Exit 74A. ⊠ *Dr. Phillips Marketplace, 7600 Dr. Phillips Blvd., Suite 132, Sand Lake Rd. Area* ☎ *407/248–3485* ▱ *AE, DC, MC, V.*

Orlando International Airport

Eclectic

$$–$$$ ✕ **Hemisphere.** The view competes with the food on the ninth floor of the Hyatt Regency Orlando International hotel. Although Hemisphere overlooks a major runway, you don't get any jet noise, just a nice air show. Entrées change frequently, but often include selections such as miso-glazed sea bass on soba noodles, tamarind barbecue glazed filet mignon with fingerling potatoes, and grilled swordfish with truffle-scented mashed potatoes. Desserts change daily, but there's always a good tiramisu. ⊠ *Hyatt Regency, Orlando International Airport* ☎ *407/825–1234 Ext. 1900* ▱ *AE, DC, MC, V* ☺ *No lunch.*

Central Orlando

The center of Orlando shows what the town as a whole was like before it became a big theme park. Quiet streets are lined with huge oaks covered with Spanish moss. Museums and galleries are along main thoroughfares, as are dozens of tiny lakes, where herons, egrets, and, yes, alligators, peacefully coexist with human city dwellers. This is quintessential urban Florida.

The restaurants in this area, a good half hour from the Disney tourism area via I–4, tend to have more of their own sense of character and style than the eateries going full tilt for your dollars in Kissimmee or on International Drive.

American/Casual

¢–$ ✕ **JW's Southern Fixins.** There's nothing fancy about this humble diner, whose red-and-white plastic tablecloths appear to have belonged to the last three restaurants that occupied this little building. But if you believe in the nobility of simple food well-prepared, this place will look like a palace to you. The best bet is the plate of slow-roasted pork ribs, although JW's excellent version of the quintessential American meat loaf is definitely a competitor for top spot. There is no set menu. It's writ-

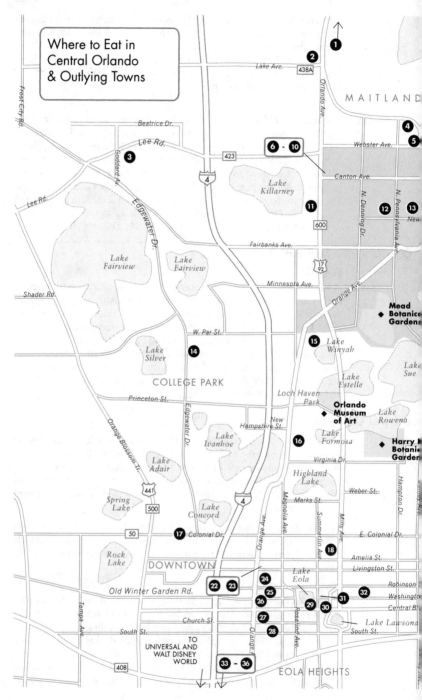

Where to Eat in
Central Orlando
& Outlying Towns

ten daily on a blackboard, but you can count on collard greens and black-eyed peas. No alcoholic beverages are served, but there's a fabulous pumpkin pie. ⊠ *900 W. Colonial Dr., Central Orlando* ☎ *407/236–9411* ▭ *AE, D, DC, MC, V* ☺ *Closed Sun.*

Contemporary

★ **$$$–$$$$** ✕ **Manuel's on the 28th.** Restaurants with great views don't always have much more than that to offer, but this lofty spot on the 28th floor is also a culinary landmark. The menu changes regularly, but there's always a representative sampling of fish, Angus beef, pork, and duck. Dinner offerings may include sea scallops covered in macadamia nuts, Black Angus filet mignon, and even wild boar loin marinated in coconut milk. For an appetizer, try the smoked confit of duck with *boursin* (a creamy white cheese). For dessert, try the baked apples wrapped in pastry, beggar's-purse style, and topped with caramel sauce. ⊠ *Bank of America bldg., 390 N. Orange Ave., Suite 2800, Downtown Orlando* ☎ *407/246–6580* ▭ *AE, D, DC, MC, V* ☺ *Closed Sun. and Mon. No lunch.*

$–$$$$ ✕ **HUE.** On the ground floor of a condo high-rise on the edge of Lake Eola, this place takes its name from a self-created acronym: Hip Urban Environment. While it may not be quite as cool as its press clippings, the food is both good and eclectic, with offerings ranging from succulent duck tostados with black beans, jack cheese, and salsa to crispy oysters with garlic mayo to wood-grilled New York strip steak with a red wine demi-glace. Unfortunately, the large outdoor dining area overlooks the street and not the lake. ⊠ *629 E. Central Blvd., Thornton Park* ☎ *407/849–1800* ⌔ *Reservations not accepted* ▭ *AE, D, DC, MC, V.*

$$–$$$ ✕ **The Boheme Restaurant.** The company that operates Manuel's on the 28th also runs the Boheme. No panorama here, but the food is every bit as adventurous. As a prelude, try the escargots with mushrooms stuffed into a puffed pastry. For a main course, try the corn-fed Angus beef. At breakfast, the French toast with a triple sec–strawberry glaze is an excellent way to awaken your palate. The Sunday brunch here is a worthwhile experience: you can get prime rib and sushi as well as omelets. ⊠ *Westin Grand Bohemian, 325 S. Orange Ave., Downtown Orlando* ☎ *407/313–9000* ⌔ *Reservations essential* ▭ *AE, D, DC, MC, V.*

$$–$$$ ✕ **Rocco's of Thornton Park.** Every Southern city needs an eatery that serves fried green tomatoes. At Rocco's, a chic little bistro near the street fountain in Thornton Park, the dish takes a Continental turn, with the addition of lump blue crab meat, spicy ragout, capers, and calmata olives. There are plenty of other good options, too, like grilled lobster tail with sautéed vegetables, roast pork chops with ginger demi-glace, and crispy fried chicken with a Creole mustard sauce. In winter and spring, stop in for the Sunday brunch with all-you-can eat pancakes in half a dozen varieties for $15. Rocco's is also a great place for a late-night meal, serving the full menu until 1 AM Thursday though Saturday, plus a killer vodka cocktail called the Key Lime Pie. ⊠ *900 E. Washington Ave., Thornton Park* ☎ *407/246–0255* ▭ *AE, D, DC, MC, V.*

$–$$$ ✕ **Harvey's Bistro.** A loyal business crowd peoples this clubby café at lunch. It also attracts a nighttime following by staying open until 11 on weekends. The menu has a good mix of bistro and comfort foods. The smoked duck and spinach pizza is a top starter. Pasta favorites include chicken Stroganoff, duck and shrimp in Asian peanut sauce on linguine, and salmon with lobster Alfredo sauce. If you're a red-meat fan, rejoice. Harvey's has a good pot roast, a pan-seared tenderloin, and meat loaf baked in parchment. ⊠ *Bank of America bldg., 390 N. Orange Ave., Downtown Orlando* ☎ *407/246–6560* ▭ *AE, D, DC, MC, V* ☺ *Closed Sun. No lunch Sat.*

¢–$ ✕ **The Globe.** During the six months of the year when Orlando has the humidity and temperature of midsummer in New York, the sidewalk cafés here are a test for one's stamina. But during the other six months, when the weather is absolute gold, places like the Globe come into their own. On downtown Orlando's block-long Wall Street (formerly lined with stock brokerages), the Globe is a lovely place to people-watch over lunch. Settle down under big umbrellas and ponder the eclectic menu. Standouts include the crab-cake sandwich and an Asian-style noodle bowl with roast pork, chicken, shrimp, and veggies. The bread pudding with rum-butter sauce is to die for. ⊠ *27 Wall St. Plaza, Downtown Orlando* ☎ *407/849–9904.* ▭ *AE, D, DC, MC, V.*

¢–$ ✕ **Johnny's Fillin' Station.** In a building that once housed a filling station, this burger joint and sports bar is a monument to the fact that good eating can sometimes be had in extremely humble surroundings. Orlando residents rave about the hamburgers, which are straight-forward half-pound burgers infused with what the management calls a "family recipe." Generous portions of onions, tomatoes, and other ingredients you can request—like grilled mushrooms and peppers—make these burgers wonderfully sloppy. Make sure to grab extra napkins. The burgers are the best thing on the menu, but other options include chicken wings, cheese steak sandwiches, and fish and chips. This place is also a sports bar and can get pretty loud and crowded. ⊠ *2631 Ferncreek Ave., Central Orlando* ☎ *407/894–6900* ▭ *D, MC, V.*

Cuban

$–$$$ ✕ **Numero Uno.** To the followers of this long-popular Latin restaurant, the name is accurate. Downtowners have been filling the place at lunch for years. It bills itself as "the home of paella," and that's probably the best choice. If you have a good appetite and you either called to order ahead or can spare the 75-minute wait, then try the *boliche* (a tender pork roast stuffed with chorizo in a tomato-base sauce) with a side order of plantains. Otherwise, you can go for traditional Cuban fare like shredded flank steak or *arroz con pollo* (rice with chicken). Finish with the *tres leches* (three-milk cake), made with regular, evaporated, and sweetened-condensed milk. Take I–4 Exit 81A or 81B. ⊠ *2499 S. Orange Ave., South-Central Orlando* ☎ *407/841–3840* ▭ *AE, D, DC, MC, V.*

French

$$–$$$$ ✕ **Le Coq au Vin.** Chef-owner Louis Perrotte is something of a culinary
Fodor'sChoice god in Orlando, but he doesn't let it go to his head. He operates a mod-
★ est little kitchen in a small house in south Orlando. Perrotte's homey eatery is usually filled with locals who appreciate the lovely traditional French fare: bronzed grouper with toasted pecans; Long Island duck with green peppercorns; and braised chicken with red wine, mushrooms, and bacon. The menu changes seasonally to insure the freshest ingredients

for house specialties. But the house namesake dish is always available and always excellent. For dessert, try the Grand Marnier soufflé. ✉ *4800 S. Orange Ave., South-Central Orlando* ☎ *407/851–6980* ▤ *AE, DC, MC, V* ☯ *Closed Mon.*

Greek

$–$$ ✕ **The Athenian.** This unpretentious little place serves up some great Greek cooking at reasonable prices. Don't miss the classic *moussaka* (eggplant, potatoes, and meat sauce, topped with sour cream). For a cross section of Hellenic cookery, go for the Athenian combo, with *dolmades* (stuffed grape leaves), moussaka, gyro, and *tsatsiki* (yogurt-based) sauce, all for $13, or try the octopus and *spanakopita* (spinach pie) combo for the same price. The sidewalk café section is pleasant. ✉ *2918 N. Orange Ave., Central Orlando* ☎ *407/898–2151* ▤ *AE, D, DC, MC, V.*

Italian

$–$$ ✕ **Tiramisu Cafe.** As the name implies, this is a great place to pop in for a quick Italian dessert and a cup of cappuccino. But this small bistro on the edge of Lake Ivanhoe in Orlando's antiques and gallery district offers a lot more, including a sidewalk seating area and some great light Italian cooking. Focaccia pizzas—individual servings on crusts of Italian flatbread—are among the better choices, as are the Italian soups, smoked and grilled fish selections, and focaccia sandwiches, especially the smoked salmon with capers and onions. Take I–4 Exit 84. ✉ *1600 N. Orange Ave., at N. E. Ivanhoe Blvd. Northern Orlando* ☎ *407/228–0303* ▤ *AE, MC, V* ☯ *Closed Sun.*

★ **¢–$** ✕ **Alfonso's Pizza & More.** This is a strong contender for the best pizza in Orlando (in the non–wood-fired oven division). Since it's just across the street from a high school, things get frenzied at lunch. The hand-tossed pizza's toppings range from pepperoni to pineapple—but the calzones and some of the pasta dishes, such as fettuccine Alfredo, are quite worthy as well. There are also subs and salads for lighter fare. The secret to the superior pizza is simple: the dough and all the sauces are made from scratch daily. Take I–4 Exit 84 to the College Park neighborhood area. ✉ *3231 Edgewater Dr., College Park* ☎ *407/872–7324* ▤ *MC, V.*

★ **¢–$** ✕ **Anthony's Pizzeria.** This neighborhood spot in Thornton Park is well known to locals for its deep-dish pizza, but the pasta is worthy in its own right—and correctly priced for those on a budget. Try the sausage and peppers in marinara sauce with your choice of spaghetti, ziti, or linguine. If you're in a hurry, go for pizza by the slice, ranging from $1.65 for plain cheese to $3.95 for a slice of the stuffed pizza with ham, salami, pepperoni, peppers, onions, provolone, and mozzarella. ✉ *100 N. Summerlin Ave., Thornton Park* ☎ *407/648–0009* ▤ *MC, V.*

¢–$ ✕ **NYPD Pizza.** A solid establishment in business since 1996, NYPD is a good fast-food alternative to a chain restaurant. Walk in for a slice of brick-oven, hand-tossed pizza and you're back on the road in five minutes with a wholly satisfying lunch. Standouts include the simple pesto pizza, with olive oil and garlic, and the barbecue-chicken pizza. Lasagna and chicken parmigiana are also available. Coney Island–style potato knishes make good snacks. Dessert standouts include a credible cannoli and, of course, New York cheesecake. Hardwood floors and brick walls make this place feel old-fashioned, and live music at night keeps things interesting. ⊠ *373 N. Orange Ave., Downtown Orlando* ☎ *407/872–6973* ▭ *AE, D, MC, V* ☾ *Closed Sun.* ⊠ *2589 S. Hiawassee Rd., MetroWest* ☎ *407/293–8880* ▭ *AE, D, MC, V.*

Japanese

$$–$$$$ ✕ **Amura.** A quiet respite from the vibrant—and loud—bars around it, Amura, Japanese for "Asian village," is comfortable and sophisticated. The sushi menu has about 40 choices, from *aoyagi* (round clams) to yellowtail tuna. For a taste of everything, try the Tokyo special plate—with chicken teriyaki, ginger pork, salmon teriyaki, California roll, and tempura-fried veggies. The Mexican roll, with avocado, shrimp, and jalapeño peppers, makes for an unusual appetizer. The Sand Lake Road location has a big, performance-style dining room, where the tables all surround grills and the chef cooks while you watch. The original downtown location has a quieter, more family-like atmosphere. ⊠ *7786 W. Sand Lake Rd., I-4 Exit 74A, Sand Lake Rd. Area* ☎ *407/370–0007* ▭ *AE, D, DC, MC, V* ☾ *No lunch Sun.*

$$–$$$ ✕ **Shari Sushi Lounge.** Resplendent with chrome and glass, this trendy eatery has more of the atmosphere of a fast-lane singles bar than of an Asian oasis, but the dishes from the kitchen—fresh sushi and daily fresh fish entrées—acquit the place well as a legit dining establishment. Start with the *tako* (not taco) salad, with octopus, cucumber, enoki mushrooms, mandarin oranges, and spicy kim chee sauce. ⊠ *621 E. Central, Thornton Park* ☎ *407/420–9420* ▭ *AE, D, DC, MC, V.*

Mexican

¢–$ ✕ **Baja Burrito Kitchen.** Because of the excellent fish tacos as well as a specialty called the LA Burrito (grilled chicken or steak, plus guacamole and jack cheese), Baja Burrito calls itself a "Cal-Mex" palace. However, the mainstays of the menu—like a huge $6 burrito filled with chicken or steak, pinto beans, guacamole, and sour cream—will be familiar to denizens of the American heartland. It's not fancy, but it won't drain your wallet. ⊠ *2716 E. Colonial Dr., near Fashion Sq. Mall, Central Orlando* ☎ *407/895–6112* ⊠ *931 N. State Rd. 434, Altamonte Springs* ☎ *407/788–2252* ⚑ *Reservations not accepted* ▭ *AE, D, MC, V.*

¢–$ ✕ **Tijuana Flats.** At this fine little downtown cantina you'll find a wild, weird assortment of bottled hot sauces from around the world. You can buy a bottle of Blair's Sudden Death or Sgt. Pepper's Tejas Tears for $7, or simply opt for the fiery house brand, free with your meal. The best menu options are plate-covering chimichangas; lime-marinated steak burritos with cheddar and jack cheese; and chipotle sauce–splashed corn tortillas loaded with meat, beans, and cheese. Mexican beers and $7.50 pitchers of Dos Equis flow freely. The sidewalk seating area faces the Orange County Historical Center and a pleasant little park. ⊠ *50 E. Central Blvd., Downtown Orlando* ☎ *407/839–0007* ▭ *AE, D, DC, MC, V.*

Seafood

$$–$$$ ✕ **Straub's Fine Seafood.** With offerings like escargots for $6—less than the price of a burger in Kissimmee—Straub's proves that the farther you drive from Disney, the less you pay. Owner Robert Straub, a fishmonger of many years, prepares a fine mesquite-grilled Atlantic salmon with béarnaise on the side. He fillets all his own fish and won't serve anything he can't get fresh. The Captain's Platter, with lobster and mesquite-grilled shrimp, is a great choice. The menu states the calorie count and fat content of every fish item, but for the coconut-banana cream pie you just don't want to know. ⊠ *5101 E. Colonial Dr., near Orlando Executive Airport, Central Orlando* ☎ *407/273–9330* ✉ *512 E. Altamonte Dr., Altamonte Springs* ☎ *407/831–2250* ▭ *AE, D, DC, MC, V.*

Steak

$$–$$$$ ✕ **Del Frisco.** Locals like this quiet, uncomplicated steak house, which delivers carefully prepared, corn-fed beef and attentive service. When your steak arrives, the waiter asks you to cut into it and check that it was cooked as you ordered it. The menu is simple: T-bones, porterhouses, filet mignon, and such seafood as Maine lobster, Alaskan crab, and a good lobster bisque. Bread is baked daily at the restaurant, and the bread pudding, with a Jack Daniels sauce, is worth a try. There's a piano bar next to the dining room. ⊠ *729 Lee Rd., North-Central Orlando* ☎ *407/645–4443* ▭ *AE, D, DC, MC, V* ☉ *Closed Sun. No lunch.*

$$–$$$ ✕ **Linda's La Cantina.** Beef is serious business here. As the menu says, management "cannot be responsible for steaks cooked medium-well and well done." Despite that stuffy-sounding caveat, this down-home steak house has been a favorite among locals since the Eisenhower administration. The menu is short and to the point, including about a dozen steaks and just enough ancillary items to fill up a page. Among the best is the La Cantina large T-bone—more beef than most can handle, for $22. With every entrée you get a heaping order of spaghetti (which isn't particularly noteworthy) or a baked potato. The chicken, veal, or eggplant Parmesan topped with marinara sauce is good for nonsteak lovers. ⊠ *4721 E. Colonial Dr., near Orlando Executive Airport, Central Orlando* ☎ *407/894–4491* ▭ *AE, D, MC, V.*

Vietnamese

★ ¢–$ ✕ **Little Saigon.** This local favorite is one of the best of Orlando's ethnic restaurants. Sample the summer rolls (spring-roll filling in a soft wrapper) with peanut sauce, or excellent Vietnamese crepes, filled with shredded pork and noodles. Then move on to the grilled pork and egg, served atop rice noodles, or the traditional soup filled with noodles, rice, vegetables, and your choice of either chicken or seafood; ask to have extra meat in the soup if you're hungry, and be sure they bring you the mint and bean sprouts to sprinkle in. ⊠ *1106 E. Colonial Dr., South-Central Orlando* ☎ *407/423–8539* ▭ *MC, V* ☞ *Beer and wine only.*

OUTLYING TOWNS

Winter Park

Winter Park is a charming suburb on the northern end of Orlando, 25 minutes from Disney. It's affluent, understated, and sophisticated—and can be pleasurable when you need a break from the theme parks. To get into the area, follow I–4 to Exit 87.

American/Casual

$ ✕ **Briarpatch Restaurant & Ice Cream Parlor.** With a faux country store facade, this small eatery makes quite a contrast to its neighbors—upscale stores such as Gucci. But it makes a great place to catch a hearty and inexpensive meal before shopping 'til you drop. Standouts include pesto-crusted salmon with bowtie pasta and old fashioned liver and onions with mashed potatoes. Good breakfast choices include Belgian waffles and raisin-bread French toast and freshly made scones. About 30 flavors of ice cream are available to help cool off on those long strolls down Park Avenue. ⊠ *252 Park Ave. N, Winter Park* ☎ *407/628–8651* ⚉ *Reservations not accepted* ▤ *AE, D, DC, MC, V.*

Chinese

$–$$ ✕ **P. F. Chang's.** Two huge, faux-stone, Ming dynasty–style statues of horses stand guard outside this Chinese restaurant, which is a bit like a California wine bar. There's a lengthy wine list, for instance, and very un-Asian desserts such as chocolate macadamia-nut pie and fruit tarts. You might start with shrimp dumplings, fried or steamed, and continue with orange chicken or perhaps crispy catfish in Szechuan sauce. The Mall at Millenia location has an outdoor dining area. ⊠ *423 N. Orlando Ave., U.S. 17–92, Winter Park* ☎ *407/622–0188* ⊠ *4200 Conroy Rd., Mall at Millenia* ☎ *407/345–2888* ▤ *AE, MC, V.*

Contemporary

$–$$$ ✕ **Cheesecake Factory.** You can select from more than 3 dozen varieties of the namesake treat, from chocolate Oreo mudslide cheesecake to southern pecan cheesecake. If you just don't like cheesecake, try the excellent apple dumplings. But this big restaurant also offers many full-meal options, from cajun jambalaya pasta to to chicken marsala to wood-oven pizza to herb-crusted fillet of salmon. Great appetizers include avocado and sun-dried tomato egg rolls, and bruschetta topped with chopped tomato, garlic, basil, and olive oil. ⊠ *520 N. Orlando Ave., Winter Park* ☎ *407/644–4220* ⊠ *4200 Conroy Rd., Mall at Millenia* ☎ *407/226–0333* ⚉ *Reservations not accepted* ▤ *AE, D, DC, MC, V.*

$–$$$ ✕ **Houston's.** This Atlanta-based chain seized a prime spot on big Lake Killarney, with a spectacular view. As you watch the egrets and herons on the lake, you can savor some meaty fare. The fancy wood-grilled burger acquits itself well, but there's nothing like the steaks, wood-grilled or pan-seared to your specifications. The grilled fish entrées, such as tuna and salmon, offer tasty alternatives. On the lighter side, the Club Salad with chicken, bacon, avocados and croutons (definitely pick the blue-cheese dressing) could easily feed two. Of the excellent soups, the New Orleans–style red beans and rice is the best. The patio makes a great place for a drink around sunset. ⊠ *215 S. Orlando Ave., U.S. 17–92, Winter Park* ☎ *407/740–4005* ⚉ *Reservations not accepted* ▤ *AE, MC, V.*

$–$$ ✕ **Dexter's.** The good wine list and imaginative menu tend to attract quite a crowd of locals. Dexter's has its own wine label and publishes a monthly newsletter about wine. Two of the best entrées here are the chicken tortilla pie—a stack of puffy, fried tortillas layered with chicken and cheese—and the mesquite-grilled chicken quesadilla with fire-roasted poblano peppers. There's often live music on Thursday night. The East Washington location is in gentrified Thornton Park, just east of downtown Orlando; you may be the only out-of-towner here. ⊠ *558 W. New England Ave., Winter Park* ☎ *407/629–1150* ⊠ *808 E. Washington St., Thornton Park* ☎ *407/648–2777* ⌁ *Reservations not accepted* ▤ *AE, D, DC, MC, V.*

Continental

$$–$$$ ✕ **Chef Justin's Park Plaza Gardens.** Sitting at the sidewalk café and bar is like sitting on the main street of the quintessential American small town. But the locals know the real gem is hidden inside—an atrium with live ficus trees, a brick floor, and brick walls that give the place a Vieux Carré feel. Chef Justin Plank's menu combines the best of French and Italian cuisine with an American twist. You might have onion soup or a turkey and Brie croissant sandwich for lunch, and baked grouper or herbed pork tenderloin for dinner. ⊠ *319 Park Ave. S, Winter Park* ☎ *407/ 645–2475* ▤ *AE, D, DC, MC, V.*

Italian

$$–$$$ ✕ **Brio Tuscan Grille.** Head to this trendy restaurant for wood-grilled pizzas and oak-grilled steaks, lamb chops, veal scaloppine, and even lobster. Try the strip steak topped with Gorgonzola, or the grilled chicken topped with Parmesan and sautéed spinach. A good appetizer choice is the *brio bruschetta,* a wood-baked flatbread covered with shrimp scampi, mozzarella, and roasted peppers. The dining room's Italian archways are elegant, but the sidewalk tables are also a good option. ⊠ *480 N. Orlando Ave., Winter Park* ☎ *407/622–5611* ⊠ *4200 Conroy Rd., Mall at Millenia* ☎ *407/351–8909* ▤ *AE, MC, V.*

¢–$$ ✕ **Pannullo's.** The view of the tidy little downtown park across the street rivals the quality of the Italian cuisine when you dine in the sidewalk seating section. But when the rain or the heat drives you indoors, you've still got the consistently great cooking at this place, which includes an excellent chicken or veal piccata and a compelling cheese tortellini. Pizza-by-the-slice starts at $2.25 if you are in a hurry or on a budget. ⊠ *216 Park Ave. S, Winter Park* ☎ *407/629–7270* ▤ *AE, D, DC, MC, V.*

Japanese

$–$$$ ✕ **Seito Sushi.** Tucked into a corner of Winter Park Village, this pleasant eatery combines two great elements: sushi and sidewalk dining. Order a Japanese beer (or some hot sake) and sample the raw fish offerings, including the signature Seito roll, composed of tuna, whitefish, salmon, and crabmeat in a cucumber skin. Another favorite roll is the lobster Katsu, with deep-fried lobster topped with snow crab and avocado. There's also plenty of inspired cooked cuisine, including sea bass with Asian rice, an excellent salmon teriyaki, and even a good New York strip steak. Top off your meal with some red-bean ice cream or fried bananas. ⊠ *510 N. Orlando Ave., Winter Park* ☎ *407/644–5050* ▤ *AE, MC, V.*

Seafood

$$–$$$$ ✕ **Black Fin.** The interior of this fish-focused restaurant feels like an old mansion, even though Black Fin is inside a modern shopping complex.

Representative offerings include shrimp linguini, grilled striped bass with peach-mango chutney, broiled Caribbean lobster, Alaskan king crab, and a lobster and filet mignon combo. Don't overlook the large selection of fresh oyster appetizers prepared on the half shell, including Florentine, broussard, or spicy hot. Save room for the chocolate-Kahlua mousse cake. ⊠ *460 N. Orlando Ave., Winter Park* ☎ *407/691–4653* ⊟ *AE, D, DC, MC, V.*

Maitland

Not quite as far from Disney as the northernmost Orlando suburbs, this town, 25 minutes from Disney and 5 mi north of downtown Orlando, is still more like reality than you can find on I-Drive. And like most Orlando residential areas, it's dotted with serene lakes shaded by stately oaks and has worthwhile shopping and dining as well. To get into the area, follow I–4 to Exit 90.

Italian

$$–$$$$ ✕ **Antonio's La Fiamma.** The wood-burning grill and oven do more than give the place a delightful smell. They're used to turn out great grilled fish dishes, delicious pizzas, and homemade bread. Try the scallops served with a puree of white beans and tomato, or the equally compelling veal chop with mushrooms and baked goat cheese. For a quick bite, the deli-style version downstairs has many of the same menu items. ⊠ *611 S. Orlando Ave., U.S. 17–92, Maitland* ☎ *407/645–5523* ⊟ *AE, MC, V* ☺ *Closed Sun.*

Longwood

A northern suburb 45 minutes from Disney, Longwood is a long way from the tourism treadmill. The community has some worthy restaurants as well. To get into the area, follow I–4 to Exit 94.

Italian

★ **$$–$$$$** ✕ **Enzo's on the Lake.** This is one of Orlando's foodies' favorite restaurants, even though it's on a tacky stretch of highway filled with used-car lots. Enzo Perlini, the Roman charmer who owns the place, has turned a rather ordinary lakefront house into an Italian villa. It's worth the trip, about 45 minutes from WDW, to sample the antipasti. Mussels in the shell, with a broth of tomatoes, olive oil, and garlic, make a great appetizer. The fettuccine with lobster and shrimp in saffron salsa is very popular, as is the grilled veal chop served in a mushroom and white wine sauce. ⊠ *1130 S. U.S. 17–92, Longwood* ☎ *407/834–9872* ⊟ *AE, DC, MC, V* ☺ *Closed Sun.*

Lake Wales

A tiny hamlet about an hour southwest of Walt Disney World, Lake Wales offers no particular reason to visit except for its lush orange groves, a calming attraction (Cypress Gardens), and one outstanding restaurant. To get into the area, follow I–4 to Exit 55 and U.S. 27 south.

Continental

$$$$ ✕ **Chalet Suzanne.** If you are on your way south, or are visiting Bok Tower Gardens, consider making time for a good meal at this family-owned country inn. Many devotees come for the traditional dinner—all lunch and dinner meals are prix-fixe affairs—or for a sophisticated breakfast of eggs Benedict or Swedish pancakes with lingonberries. The best meal, if you are on a budget, is lunch. For dinner, try the lump crab cake with herb butter. The house chicken Suzanne (baked and carefully basted) is tender and worth the dinner price of $59, but it's just as tasty at lunch for $32. ⊠ *3800 Chalet Suzanne La., I–4 Exit 55, Lake Wales* 🕿 *863/ 676–6011* ▭ *AE, DC, MC, V.*

Where to Stay

6

FODOR'S CHOICE

BoardWalk Inn and Villas, *in Walt Disney World*

Gaylord Palms Resort, *in Kissimmee*

Grand Floridian Resort & Spa, *in Walt Disney World*

Hyatt Regency Grand Cypress Resort, *near Lake Buena Vista*

Reunion Resort & Club of Orlando, *near Celebration*

Ritz-Carlton Orlando Grande Lakes, *in Southwestern Orlando*

Royal Pacific Resort, *in Universal Studios*

Wilderness Lodge, *in Walt Disney World*

Yacht and Beach Club Resorts, *in Walt Disney World*

Updated by
Rowland
Stiteler

ONCE UPON A TIME, SIMPLY BEING in the midst of the world's largest concentration of theme parks was enough of a selling point to make most Orlando hotels thrive. But somewhere along the way, as the room inventory topped 120,000 (more hotel rooms than New York City or Los Angeles), the competition became so intense that hotels needed to become attractions in themselves. Hoteliers learned that you've got to have a bit of showbiz to bring 'em in, so the choices here are anything but ordinary. Orlando may not be Las Vegas, but its hotels are definitely big, fancy, and, in some cases, leaning toward gaudy.

The idea in Orlando is for a hotel to entertain you as much as provide lodging. The Gaylord Palms Resort, with a 4-acre glass-covered atrium, has its own version of the Everglades inside, plus a re-creation of old St. Augustine, a mini Key West, and a 60-foot sailboat that houses a bar on an indoor waterway. Besides showy lobbies, restaurants, and pool areas, most of the larger hotels also have their own in-house children's clubs, many of which provide clown shows, magic shows, and other forms of live entertainment. It's as if the owners expect you to never leave the hotel during your entire vacation.

Most of the bigger, glitzier hotels have room rates commensurate with their huge construction and maintenance budgets—it's not unusual in this market for the cost of building a hotel to come in at $350,000 or more per guest room. But many other hotels maintain moderate and inexpensive rates. Because of the sheer number of properties in the Orlando area, you will find choices in every price range. One trend is the proliferation of all-suites properties, many with in-room kitchens and relatively low rates. And Disney has its own low-budget hotels, too—the All-Star resorts and the Pop Century Resort. With budget properties popping up along International Drive and even in Walt Disney World, the small, cheap motels along U.S. 192 in Kissimmee are less of a good deal than they were 20 years ago. You no longer save much money by taking the 5-mi daily commute to the Kissimmee motel strip.

AH HA!

When considering where to stay, give careful thought to the kind of vacation you want, what you want to see during your visit, and how long your trip will last. If you're traveling with children, ask if they stay free with you and if the hotel has children's programs. Finally, don't overlook time spent in transit; if you're not staying at a property in or within 5 mi of Walt Disney World, you may use up a few hours a day sitting in traffic.

One rule of thumb in selecting a hotel—assuming you plan far enough in advance—is to request a brochure or check out the hotel's Web site. If there are lots of pictures of, say, Walt Disney World and no pictures of the hotel, chances are that the hotel is bare-bones. Places that don't renovate regularly often try to use proximity to Disney as their sole selling point.

Staying in WDW

If you stay in WDW, you can put aside your car keys, because Disney buses and monorails are efficient enough to make it possible to visit one park in the morning and another after lunch with a Park Hopper pass. You have the freedom to return to your hotel for R&R when the crowds are thickest, and if it turns out that half the family wants to spend the afternoon in Epcot and the other half wants to float around Typhoon Lagoon, it's not a problem.

Rooms in the more expensive Disney-owned properties are large enough to accommodate up to five, and villas sleep six or seven. All rooms have cable TV with the Disney Channel and a daily events channel.

If you're an on-site guest at a Disney hotel, you are guaranteed entry to parks even when they have reached capacity, as the Magic Kingdom, Disney–MGM Studios, Blizzard Beach, and Typhoon Lagoon sometimes do. And depending on the time of year, the parks often open an hour earlier just for Disney hotel guests. There are other conveniences, too. You can charge most meals and purchases throughout WDW to your hotel room. And if you golf, keep in mind that Disney guests get first choice of tee times at the golf courses and can reserve them up to 30 days in advance.

Staying Around Orlando

The hotels closest to WDW are clustered in a few principal areas: along International Drive; in the U.S. 192 area and Kissimmee; and in the Downtown Disney–Lake Buena Vista area, just off I–4 Exit 68. Nearly every hotel in these areas provides frequent transportation to and from WDW. In addition, there are some noteworthy, if far-flung, options in the suburbs and in the Greater Orlando area. If you're willing to make the commute, you'll probably save a bundle. Whereas the Hilton near Downtown Disney charges upwards of $200 a night in season, another Hilton about 45 minutes away in Altamonte Springs has rates that start at $140. Other costs, such as gas and restaurants, are also lower in the northeast suburbs. One suburban caveat: traffic on I–4 in Orlando experiences typical freeway gridlock during morning (7–9) and evening (4–6) rush hours.

Reservations

Reserve your hotel several months in advance—as much as a year ahead if you want to snag the best rooms during high season. All on-site accommodations owned by Disney may be booked through the **WDW Central Reservations Office** (🏠 Box 10100, Suite 300, Lake Buena Vista 32830 ☎ 407/934–7639 ⊕ www.disneyworld.com). People with disabilities can call **WDW Special Request Reservations** (☎ 407/939–7807) to get information or book rooms at any of the on-site Disney properties. Rooms at most non-Disney chain hotels can be reserved by calling either the hotel itself or the toll-free number for the entire chain. When you book a room, be sure to mention whether you have a disability or are traveling with children and whether you prefer a certain type of bed or have any other concerns. You may need to pay a deposit for your first night's stay within three weeks of making your reservation. At many hotels you can get a refund if you cancel at least five days before your scheduled arrival. However, individual hotel policies vary, and some properties may require up to 15 days' notice for a full refund. Check before booking.

If neither the WDW Central Reservations Office nor the off-site hotels have space on your preferred dates, look into packages from American Express, Delta, or other operators, which have been allotted whole blocks of rooms. In addition, because there are always cancellations, it's worth trying at the last minute; for same-day bookings, call the property directly. Packages, including airfare, cruises, car rentals, and hotels both on and off Disney property, can be arranged through your travel agent or **Walt Disney Travel Co.** (✉ 7100 Municipal Dr., Orlando 32819 ☎ 407/828–3232 ⊕ www.disneyworld.com).

Prices

The lodgings we list are the top selections of their type in each category. Rates are lowest from early January to mid-February, from late-April to mid-June, and from mid-August to the third week in December. Always call several places—availability and special deals can often drive room rates at a $$$$ hotel down into the $$ range—and don't forget to ask if you're eligible for a discount. Many hotels offer special rates for members of, for example, the American Automobile Association (AAA) or the American Association of Retired Persons (AARP). Don't overlook the savings to be gained from preparing your own breakfast and maybe a few other meals as well, which you can do if you choose a room or suite with a kitchenette or kitchen. In listings, we always name the facilities that are available, but we don't specify whether they cost extra.

WHAT IT COSTS				
$$$$	**$$$**	**$$**	**$**	**¢**
FOR 2 PEOPLE over $220	$160–$220	$110–$159	$80–$109	under $80

Price categories reflect the range between the least and most expensive standard double rooms in nonholiday high season, based on the European Plan (with no meals) unless otherwise noted. City and state taxes (10%–12%) are extra.

So, your first big decision when it comes to your vacation will probably be whether to stay within WDW or outside the property. Clearly, Disney is a major player in the Orlando hotel market, with more than 28,000 rooms, about a quarter of all hotel rooms in the metro area. If you're coming to Orlando for only a few days and are interested solely in the Magic Kingdom, Epcot, and other Disney attractions, then hotels in Walt Disney World—whether or not they're actually owned by Disney—are definitely the most convenient. The on-site hotels were built with families in mind. Older children can use the transportation system on their own without inviting trouble. (Disney property is quite safe, day or night.) And younger children get a thrill from knowing that they're actually staying in Walt Disney World.

If you're planning to visit attractions other than WDW, then staying off-site holds a number of advantages. You enjoy more peace and quiet and may have easier access to Orlando, SeaWorld, and Universal Studios, and you're likely to save money. To help you find your perfect room, we've reviewed hundreds of offerings throughout the main hotel hubs both in and surrounding Walt Disney World.

THE DISNEY RESORTS

Disney-operated hotels are fantasies unto themselves. Each is immaculately designed according to a theme (quaint New England, the relaxed culture of the Polynesian Islands, an African safari village, etc.) and each offers the same perks: free transportation from the airport and to the parks, the option to charge all your purchases to your room, special guest-only park visiting times, and much more. If you stay on site, you'll have better access to the parks and you'll be more immersed in the Disney experience.

Magic Kingdom Resort Area

Take I–4 Exit 62, 64B, or 65.

The ritzy hotels near the Magic Kingdom all lie on the monorail route and are only minutes away from the park. Fort Wilderness Resort and Campground, with RV and tent sites, is a bit farther southeast of the Magic Kingdom, and access to the parks is by bus.

$$$$ 🏨 **Contemporary Resort.** Looking like an intergalactic docking bay, this 15-story, flat-topped pyramid bustles from dawn to after midnight. Upper floors of the main tower (where rooms are more expensive) offer a great view of all the day and night activities in and around the Magic Kingdom. The best reason to stay? Location, location, location. The monorail runs through the tower lobby, so it takes just minutes to get to the Magic Kingdom and Epcot. Restaurants here include the character-meal palace Chef Mickey's, the laid-back Concourse Steak House, and the top-floor and top-rated California Grill. There is a concierge level with its own private club, but be prepared to pay $400 per night for a room. ☎ 407/824–1000 🖷 407/824–3539 ⬦ *1,013 rooms, 25 suites* ⬦ *3 restaurants, snack bar, room service, in-room safes, some refrigerators, cable TV, in-room broadband, golf privileges, 6 tennis courts, 3*

DISNEY MAGICAL EXPRESS

THE NEWEST PERK FOR DISNEY HOTEL GUESTS, *introduced in May 2005, offers an easy answer to that bothersome question, "What do I do for ground transportation?" If you're focusing your trip on WDW and staying at a Disney hotel, you don't need to rent a car, and you don't even have to think about finding a shuttle or taxi. Or picking up your luggage. With Disney Magical Express, once you get off your plane at Orlando International Airport, you're met by a Disney representative who leads you to a coach that takes you directly to your hotel. Your luggage is retrieved and delivered separately and usually arrives at your hotel room an hour or two after you do. (So if you need anything from your bags right away, carry it with you.)*

When you're ready to leave, the process works in reverse. You get your boarding pass and check your bags at the hotel. Then you go to the airport and go directly to your gate, skipping check-in. You won't see your bags until you're in your hometown airport. Best of all, the service is free. The one catch is that you must travel on one of the participating airlines: American, Continental, Delta or Song, United or Ted.

pools, wading pool, health club, hair salon, 2 hot tubs, massage, beach, boating, marina, waterskiing, basketball, volleyball, 2 lobby lounges, video game room, shops, babysitting, children's programs (ages 4–12), playground, laundry facilities, laundry service, concierge, concierge floor, business services, convention center, meeting rooms, no-smoking rooms ▭ *AE, D, DC, MC, V.*

$$$$ 🏠 **Fort Wilderness Resort Cabins.** If you're seeking a calm spot amid the theme-park storm, you need go no farther than these 700 acres of scrubby pine, tiny streams, and peaceful canals on the shore of subtropical Bay Lake, about a mile from the Wilderness Lodge. This is about as relaxed as it gets in Walt Disney World. Sports facilities abound, bike trails are popular, and there's a marina where you can rent a sailboat. The larger cabins can accommodate four grown-ups and two youngsters; the bedroom has a double bed and a bunk bed, and the living room has a double sleeper sofa or Murphy bed. Each cabin has a fully equipped kitchen, and daily housekeeping is provided. ☎ 407/824–2900 🖷 407/824–3508 🛏 *408 cabins* ⌂ *Cafeteria, grocery, snack bar, kitchens, microwaves, cable TV, 2 tennis courts, 2 pools, beach, boating, bicycles, basketball, horseback riding, volleyball, babysitting, playground, laundry facilities, no-smoking rooms* ▭ *AE, D, DC, MC, V.*

$$$$ Grand Floridian Resort & Spa. This Victorian-style property on the shores
Fodor'sChoice of the Seven Seas Lagoon has a red gabled roof, delicate gingerbread,
★ rambling verandas, and brick chimneys. Rooms have ornate hardwood
furniture and fancy-print carpeting. Add a dinner or two at Victoria and
Albert's, or Cítricos, and you'll probably spend more in a weekend here
than on an average mortgage payment, but you'll have the memory of
the best that Disney offers. The Grand Floridian is what Disney considers its flagship resort—no other has better amenities or higher rates.
Yet you won't look out of place walking through the lobby in flip flops.
☎ 407/824–3000 📠 407/824–3186 🛏 *900 rooms, 90 suites* 🍴 *5
restaurants, snack bar, room service, in-room safes, cable TV, in-room
broadband, golf privileges, 2 tennis courts, 3 pools, wading pool, health
club, hair salon, massage, spa, beach, boating, marina, waterskiing, croquet, shuffleboard, volleyball, 4 lounges, video game room, babysitting,
children's programs (ages 4–12), playground, laundry facilities, laundry service, concierge, concierge floor, business services, convention
center, meeting rooms, no-smoking rooms* ▭ *AE, D, DC, MC, V.*

$$$$ Polynesian Resort. If it weren't for the kids in Mickey Mouse caps, you
might think you were in Fiji. A three-story tropical atrium fills the lobby.
Orchids bloom alongside coconut palms and banana trees, and water cascades from volcanic-rock fountains. A mainstay here is the evening luau
(Wednesday through Sunday), in which Polynesian dancers perform before a feast with Hawaiian-style roast pork. Rooms sleep five, since they
all have two queen-size beds and a daybed. Lagoon-view rooms—which
overlook the Electrical Water Pageant—are the most peaceful and the priciest. Most rooms have a balcony or patio. If you stay on a concierge floor,
you have access to a lounge with free continental breakfast, midday snacks,
and evening hors d'oeuvres, cordials, and dessert, although the concierge rooms will cost about $100 more per night than standard rooms.
☎ 407/824–2000 📠 407/824–3174 🛏 *853 rooms, 5 suites* 🍴 *4 restaurants, snack bar, room service, in-room safes, cable TV, in-room broadband, golf privileges, 2 pools, wading pool, health club, hair salon,
massage, beach, boating, volleyball, bar, lobby lounge, video game room,
babysitting, children's programs (ages 4–12), playground, laundry facilities,
laundry service, concierge, concierge floors, business services, no-smoking rooms* ▭ *AE, D, DC, MC, V.*

$$$–$$$$ Wilderness Lodge. The architects outdid themselves with this seven-
Fodor'sChoice story hotel modeled after the majestic turn-of-the-20th-century lodges
★ of the American Northwest. The five-story lobby, supported by tow-
ering tree trunks, has an 82-foot-high, three-sided fireplace made of
rocks from the Grand Canyon and lit by enormous tepee-shape chan-
deliers. Two 55-foot-tall hand-carved totem poles complete the illu-
sion. Rooms have leather chairs, patchwork quilts, and cowboy art.
Each has a balcony or a patio. The hotel's showstopper is its Fire Rock
Geyser, a faux Old Faithful, near the large pool, which begins as an
artificially heated hot spring in the lobby. ☎ 407/824–3200 📠 407/
824–3232 🛏 *728 rooms, 31 suites* 🍴 *3 restaurants, some room ser-
vice, cable TV with movies, in-room broadband, pool, wading pool,
2 hot tubs, beach, boating, bicycles, 2 lobby lounges, video game
room, babysitting, children's programs (ages 4–12), laundry facilities,*

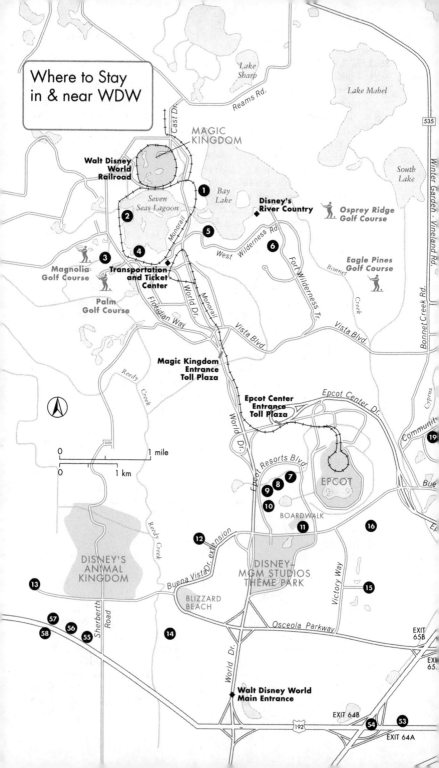

Where to Stay in & near WDW

Lake Sharp

Lake Mabel

Reams Rd.

535

MAGIC KINGDOM

East Dr.

Walt Disney World Railroad

Seven Seas Lagoon

Bay Lake

①

South Lake

②

⑤

Disney's River Country

Osprey Ridge Golf Course

④

③

West Wilderness Rd.

⑥

Eagle Pines Golf Course

Magnolia Golf Course

Transportation and Ticket Center

Monorail

World Dr.

Fort Wilderness Tr.

Bonnet Creek

Bonnet Creek Rd.

Palm Golf Course

Floridian Way

Vista Blvd.

Vista Blvd.

Reedy Creek

Magic Kingdom Entrance Toll Plaza

Epcot Center Dr.

Epcot Center Entrance Toll Plaza

World Dr.

Community

19

N

0   1 mile
0   1 km

Epcot Resorts Blvd.

EPCOT

⑦

⑨ ⑧

⑩

BOARDWALK

⑪

⑯

Reedy Creek

DISNEY'S ANIMAL KINGDOM

⑫

Buena Vista Dr. extension

DISNEY-MGM STUDIOS THEME PARK

Victory Way

⑬

BLIZZARD BEACH

⑮

Sherberth Road

⑤⑦

⑤⑥

⑤⑧

⑤⑤

⑭

Osceola Parkway

EXIT 65B

EXIT 65

World Dr.

Walt Disney World Main Entrance

EXIT 64B

⑤④

⑤③

192

EXIT 64A

laundry service, concierge, concierge floor, business services, no-smoking rooms ☰ *AE, D, DC, MC, V.*

🔥 **Fort Wilderness Resort Campground.** Bringing a tent or RV is one of the cheapest ways to stay on WDW property, especially considering that sites accommodate up to 10. Tent sites with water and electricity are real bargains. RV sites cost more but are equipped with electric, water, and sewage hookups as well as outdoor charcoal grills and picnic tables. Campground guests have full use of the recreational facilities and services available to Fort Wilderness cabin guests, such as horseback riding and tennis. The campgrounds are the only place in WDW where your pet can stay with you for a $5 daily fee. ☎ *407/824–2900* 🖷 *407/824–3508* 🛏 *788 campsites (695 with full hookups, 90 partial hookups)* ▥ *$38–$89* ♿ *Grills, 2 pools, playground, flush toilets, full hookups, dump station, drinking water, guest laundry, showers, picnic tables, food service, electricity, public telephone* ☰ *AE, D, DC, MC, V.*

Epcot Resort Area

Take I–4 Exit 64B or 65.

From the Epcot resorts you can walk or take a boat to the International Gateway entrance to Epcot, or you can take the shuttle from your hotel or drive to the Future World (front) entrance.

$$$$ 🏨 **Beach Club Villas.** Everything you could ever want in a vacation home, each villa has a separate living room, kitchen, and one or two bedrooms, except the studios, which are more like hotel rooms. Interiors are soft yellow and green with white iron bedsteads. Private balconies on the upper levels or porches at street level ensure that you can enjoy your morning cup of coffee in the sun with a view of the lake. The villas are marketed as time-share properties for Disney Vacation Club members, but available rooms are also rented on a per-night basis. You'll have access to all the facilities of the adjacent Yacht and Beach Club resorts, including Stormalong Bay. ☎ *407/934–8000* 🖷 *407/934–3850* 🛏 *205 villas* ♿ *Restaurant, snack bar, room service, in-room safes, cable TV with movies, in-room broadband, golf privileges, miniature golf, 2 tennis courts, 3 pools, gym, health club, hair salon, massage, sauna, beach, boating, fishing, croquet, volleyball, 3 lobby lounges, video game room, babysitting, laundry service, concierge, business services, convention center, no-smoking rooms* ☰ *AE, D, DC, MC, V.*

$$$$
Fodor'sChoice
★ **BoardWalk Inn and Villas.** A beautiful re-creation of Victorian-era Atlantic City, WDW's smallest deluxe hotel is the crowning jewel of the BoardWalk complex. WDW's architectural master, Robert A. M. Stern, designed this inn to mimic 19th-century New England building styles. Rooms have floral-print bedspreads and blue-and-white painted furniture. A 200-foot water slide in the form of a classic wooden roller coaster cascades into the pool area. And there's plenty to do at the Board-Walk entertainment area on the lake: you can ride surrey bikes, watch a game at the ESPN Sports Club, or dine in some of Disney's better restaurants. Rooms overlooking Crescent Lake and the boardwalk cost the most and are the noisiest. ☎ *407/939–5100 inn, 407/939–6200 villas* 🖷 *407/939–5150* 🛏 *370 rooms, 19 suites, 526 villas* ♿ *4 restaurants,*

room service, in-room safes, in-room broadband, golf privileges, miniature golf, tennis court, pool, gym, health club, fishing, croquet, lobby lounge, nightclub, video game room, babysitting, children's programs (ages 4–12), laundry facilities, laundry service, concierge, business services, convention center, no-smoking rooms ▤ *AE, D, DC, MC, V.*

$$$$
Fodor'sChoice
★
▦ **Yacht and Beach Club Resorts.** Straight out of a Cape Cod summer, these properties on Seven Seas Lagoon are coastal-style inns on a grand Disney scale. The five-story Yacht Club has hardwood floors, a lobby full of gleaming brass and polished leather, an oyster-gray clapboard facade, and evergreen landscaping; there's even a lighthouse on its pier. Rooms have floral-print bedspreads and a small ship's wheel on the headboard. At the Beach Club, a croquet lawn and cabana-dotted white-sand beach set the scene. Stormalong Bay, a 3-acre water park with water slides and whirlpools, is part of this Club. ☎ *407/934–8000 Beach Club, 407/934–7000 Yacht Club* 🖷 *407/934–3850 Beach Club, 407/934–3450 Yacht Club* 🛏 *1,213 rooms, 112 suites* ⚐ *4 restaurants, snack bar, room service, in-room safes, cable TV with movies, in-room broadband, golf privileges, 2 tennis courts, 3 pools, gym, health club, hair salon, massage, sauna, beach, boating, bicycles, croquet, volleyball, 3 lobby lounges, video game room, babysitting, children's programs (ages 4–12), laundry service, concierge, business services, convention center, no-smoking rooms* ▤ *AE, D, DC, MC, V.*

★ $$–$$$
▦ **Caribbean Beach Resort.** Awash in dizzying Caribbean colors, this hotel complex was the first of Disney's moderately priced accommodations. Six palm-studded "villages" share 45-acre Barefoot Bay and its white-sand beach. A promenade circles the lake and bridges over it connect to a 1-acre path-crossed play and picnic area called Parrot Cay. You can rent boats for a tour on the lake, or rent bikes for a ride around the property. The Old Port Royale complex, decorated with pirates' cannons, tropical birds, and statues, has a food court, tropical lounge, and pool with waterfalls and a big water slide. Rooms are done in soft pastel colors like turquoise and peach, with white wood furniture. ☎ *407/934–3400* 🖷 *407/934–3288* 🛏 *2,112 rooms* ⚐ *Restaurant, food court, room service, in-room safes, cable TV with movies, in-room broadband, golf privileges, 7 pools, wading pool, hot tub, beach, boating, bicycles, lobby lounge, video game room, babysitting, playground, laundry facilities, laundry service, no-smoking rooms* ▤ *AE, D, DC, MC, V.*

$$–$$$
▦ **Coronado Springs Resort.** This moderately priced hotel on yet another Disney-made lake serves two constituencies. Because of its on-property convention center and exhibit hall, it's Disney's most popular convention hotel. But lots of conventioneers bring the kids these days, and the resort is also popular with families on vacation, who come for its casual southwestern architecture; its wonderful, lively, Mexican-style Pepper Market food court; and its elaborate swimming pool complex, which has a Mayan pyramid with a big water slide. There's a full-service health club, but if you like jogging, walking, or biking you're in the right place—a sidewalk circles the property's 15-acre lake. ☎ *407/939–1000* 🖷 *407/939–1001* 🛏 *1,967 rooms* ⚐ *2 restaurants, food court, room service, in-room safes, cable TV with movies, in-room broadband, golf privileges, 4 pools, health club, hair salon, boating, bicycles, bar,*

video game room, babysitting, playground, laundry service, business services, convention center, no-smoking rooms ▱ *AE, D, DC, MC, V.*

Animal Kingdom Resort Area

Take I–4 Exit 64B.

In the park's southwest corner, Disney's third resort area comprises the fabulous Africa-theme Animal Kingdom Lodge, plus two budget-priced hotel complexes: All-Star Village, not far from U.S. 192, and the Pop Century Resort, on Osceola Parkway.

★ $$$–$$$$ 🖼 **Animal Kingdom Lodge.** Giraffes, zebras, and other African wildlife roam three 11-acre savannas separated by wings of this grand hotel. The atrium lobby exudes African style, from the inlaid carvings on the hardwood floors to the massive faux-thatched roof almost 100 feet above. Cultural ambassadors, natives of Africa, give talks about their homelands, the animals, and the artwork on display; in the evening, they tell folk stories around the fire circle on the Arusha Rock terrace. All of the somewhat tentlike rooms (with drapes descending from the ceiling) have a bit of African art, including carved headboards and watercolors, pen-and-ink drawings, or original African prints. Most rooms have balconies overlooking the private wildlife reserve. And don't miss the chance to try some authentic African cooking at one of the resort's two restaurants. ☎ *407/934–7639* 🖷 *407/934–7629* ▱ *1,293 rooms* ♧ *3 restaurants, in-room safes, cable TV with movies, in-room broadband, golf privileges, 2 pools, health club, spa, bar, lobby lounge, babysitting, children's programs (ages 4–12), playground, laundry facilities, laundry service, business services, no-smoking rooms* ▱ *AE, D, DC, MC, V.*

¢–$$ 🖼 **All-Star Sports, All-Star Music, and All-Star Movies Resorts.** If you want to immerse yourself in a kids-are-king atmosphere throughout your visit, these mega-resorts, in which virtually every guest room seems to house an entire family, are the place to be. In the Sports resort, Goofy is the pitcher in the baseball-diamond pool; in the Music resort you'll walk by giant bongos; and in the Movies resort, huge characters like *Toy Story*'s Buzz Lightyear frame each building. Each room has two double beds, a closet rod, an armoire, and a desk. The All-Star resorts are as economically priced as most any hotel in Orlando, and kids love being right next door to Blizzard Beach. The food courts sell standard fast food, and you can even have pizza delivered to your room. Don't take a room near the food courts or pools if a little noise bothers you. ☎ *407/939–5000 Sports, 407/939–6000 Music, 407/939–7000 Movies* 🖷 *407/939–7333 Sports, 407/939–7222 Music, 407/939–7111 Movies* ▱ *1,920 rooms at each* ♧ *3 food courts, room service, in-room safes, cable TV with movies, in-room broadband, golf privileges, 6 pools, 3 bars, video game rooms, babysitting, playground, laundry facilities, laundry service, Internet, no-smoking rooms* ▱ *AE, D, DC, MC, V.*

¢–$$ 🖼 **Pop Century Resort.** Following the success of the moderately priced, gargantuan All-Star resorts, Disney opened this budget-hotel megaplex in late 2003. Three-story-tall juke boxes, bowling pins, and Duncan yo-yos, a giant-size Big Wheel tricycle and Rubik's Cube, and various other pop-culture icons are scattered about the grounds. Brightly colored rooms are functional for families, with two double beds or one king. A big food court, cafeteria-style eatery, and room-delivery pizza service offer reasonably priced food. ☎ 407/934–7639 ⇥ *2,880 rooms* ⬧ *Food court, room service, in-room safes, cable TV with movies, in-room broadband, golf privileges, 2 pools, health club, hair salon, bar, video game room, babysitting, playground, laundry service, no-smoking rooms* ▱ *AE, D, DC, MC, V.*

Downtown Disney Resort Area

Take I–4 Exit 64B or 68.

The Downtown Disney–Lake Buena Vista resort area, east of Epcot, has two midprice resorts with an Old South theme, plus the upscale Old Key West Resort. From here shuttles are available to all of the parks.

$$$$ ▦ **Old Key West Resort.** A red-and-white lighthouse helps you find your way through this marina-style resort. Freestanding villas resemble turn-of-the-20th-century Key West houses, with white clapboard siding and private balconies that overlook the waterways winding through the grounds. The one-, two-, or three-bedroom houses have whirlpools in the master bedrooms, full-size kitchens, full-size washers and dryers, and outdoor patios. The 2,265-square-foot three-bedroom grand villas accommodate up to 12 adults—so grab some friends. The resort is part of the Disney Vacation Club network, but rooms are rented to anyone when they're available. ☎ 407/827–7700 ⊟ 407/827–7710 ⇥ *761 units* ⬧ *Restaurant, snack bar, in-room safes, microwaves, cable TV with movies, in-room broadband, golf privileges, 3 tennis courts, 4 pools, health club, 4 hot tubs, spa, boating, bicycles, basketball, shuffleboard, lobby lounge, video game room, babysitting, playground, laundry facilities, laundry service, no-smoking rooms* ▱ *AE, D, DC, MC, V.*

$$$$ ▦ **Saratoga Springs Resort.** Opened in 2004, Saratoga Springs is the newest Disney resort and also the largest Disney Vacation Club property ever, with 552 units on 16 acres. A cluster of three- and four-story, residential-style buildings, decorated in and out to look like the 19th-century resorts of upstate New York, overlook a giant pool with man-made hot springs surrounded by faux boulders. Standard rooms include microwaves and refrigerators, while suites have full kitchens. Three-bedroom family suites, occupying two levels, have dining rooms, living rooms, and four bathrooms. Dark wood, early American-style furniture. and overstuffed couches give the rooms a homey, rural New England look. You walk to Downtown Disney in 10 minutes or take the ferry boat, which docks near Fulton's Crab House. ☎ 407/934–7639 ⇥ *552 units* ⬧ *Restaurant, snack bar, in-room safes, microwaves, cable TV with movies, in-room broadband, golf privileges, 2 tennis courts, 2 pools, health club, 4 hot tubs, spa, boating, bicycles, basketball, shuffleboard, lobby lounge, theater, video game room, business services, no-smoking rooms* ▱ *AE, D, DC, MC, V.*

$$–$$$ ▦ **Port Orleans Resort–French Quarter.** This vision of New Orleans has ornate row houses with vine-covered balconies, clustered around squares planted with magnolias. Lamp-lighted sidewalks are named for French

Quarter thoroughfares. As part of a massive renovation begun in 2004, French Quarter rooms have all-new furniture, carpeting, fabrics, and wallpaper. In the food court, the New Orleans theme continues with specialties such as jambalaya and beignets. Doubloon Lagoon, one of Disney's most exotic pools, includes a clever "sea serpent" water slide that swallows swimmers and then spits them into the water. Note that waterview rooms, from which you can see either the lagoon or the Sassagoula River, cost $15 to $25 more per night than standard rooms. ☎ *407/934–5000* 🖷 *407/934–5353* 🖳 *1,008 rooms* ⌂ *Restaurant, food court, inroom safes, cable TV with video games, in-room broadband, golf privileges, pool, wading pool, hot tub, boating, bicycles, croquet, lobby lounge, babysitting, laundry facilities, laundry service, no-smoking rooms* ☰ *AE, D, DC, MC, V.*

$$–$$$ 🏨 **Port Orleans Resort–Riverside.** Disney's Imagineers drew inspiration from the Old South for this sprawling resort. Buildings look like plantation-style mansions and rustic bayou dwellings. Rooms accommodate up to four in two double beds. Elegantly decorated, they have wooden armoires, quilted bedspreads, and gleaming brass faucets; a few rooms have king-size beds. The registration area looks like a steamboat interior, and the 3½-acre, old-fashioned swimming-hole complex called Ol' Man Island has a pool with slides, rope swings, and a nearby play area. ☎ *407/934–6000* 🖷 *407/934–5777* 🖳 *2,048 rooms* ⌂ *Restaurant, snack bar, in-room safes, cable TV with movies, in-room broadband, golf privileges, 6 pools, health club, boating, bicycles, lobby lounge, video game room, babysitting, playground, laundry facilities, laundry service, no-smoking rooms* ☰ *AE, D, DC, MC, V.*

OTHER HOTELS IN & NEAR WDW

Although not operated by the Disney organization, the Swan and the Dolphin just outside Epcot, Shades of Green near the Magic Kingdom, and the hotels along Hotel Plaza Boulevard near Downtown Disney call themselves "official" Walt Disney World hotels. While the Swan, Dolphin, and Shades of Green have the special privileges of on-site Disney hotels, such as free transportation to and from the parks and early park entry, the Downtown Disney resorts have their own systems to shuttle hotel guests to the parks.

Magic Kingdom Resort Area

¢–$ 🏨 **Shades of Green.** Operated by the U.S. Armed Forces Recreation Center, the resort is available only to vacationing active-duty and retired personnel from the armed forces, as well as reserves, National Guard, active civilian employees of the Department of Defense, widows or widowers of service members, disabled veterans, and medal of honor recipients. Rates vary with your rank, but are significantly lower than rates at Disney hotels open to the general public. The resort was completely renovated in 2004—you'll find a Tuscan-style restaurant, a ballroom for weddings and other events, 11 new family suites that sleep up to eight adults each, and two swimming pools surrounded by expansive decks and lush, tropical foliage. ✉ *1950 W. Magnolia Palm Dr., Lake Buena Vista 32830-2789* ☎ *407/824–3600 or 888/593–2242* 🖷 *407/824–3665* ⊕ *www.shadesofgreen.org* ⌨ *586 rooms, 11 suites* ⑂ *4 restaurants, room service, in-room safes, refrigerators, cable TV with movies and video games, in-room broadband, golf privileges, 2 outdoor tennis courts, 2 pools, wading pool, health club, 2 bars, babysitting, children's programs (ages 4–12), laundry facilities, laundry service, no-smoking rooms* ▭ *AE, D, MC, V.*

Epcot Resort Area

Take I–4 Exit 64B or 65.

★ **$$$$** 🖳 **Walt Disney World Dolphin.** World-renowned architect Michael Graves designed the neighboring Dolphin and Swan hotels. Outside, a pair of 56-foot-tall sea creatures bookend the 25-story glass pyramid of a building. The fabric-draped lobby inside resembles a giant sultan's tent. All rooms have either two queen beds or one king and bright, beach-inspired bedspreads and drapes. The pillow-top mattresses, down comforters, and multitude of overstuffed pillows make the beds here some of the most comfortable resting places in the kingdom. Extensive children's programs include Camp Dolphin summer camp and the five-hour Dolphin Dinner Club. BlueZoo, the on-site restaurant by celebrity chef Todd English, is the trendiest eatery in the place, but the kids may prefer Tubbi's Buffeteria, where you can get mac and cheese 24 hours a day. ✉ *1500 Epcot Resorts Blvd., Lake Buena Vista 32830-2653* ☎ *407/934–4000 or 800/227–1500* 🖷 *407/934–4884* ⊕ *www. swandolphin.com* ⌨ *1,509 rooms, 136 suites* ⑂ *9 restaurants, cafeteria, room service, in-room safes, cable TV with movies and video games, in-room broadband, golf privileges, 4 tennis courts, 5 pools, wading pool, gym, massage, spa, beach, boating, volleyball, 3 lobby lounges, video game room, shop, babysitting, children's programs (ages 4–12), concierge, concierge floor, business services, convention center, no-smoking rooms* ▭ *AE, D, DC, MC, V.*

$$$$ 🖳 **Walt Disney World Swan.** Facing the Dolphin across Crescent Lake, the Swan is another example of the postmodern "Learning from Las Vegas" school of entertainment architecture characteristic of Michael Graves. Two 46-foot swans grace the rooftop of this coral-and-aquamarine hotel, and the massive main lobby is decorated with a playful mix of tropical imagery. Guest rooms are quirkily decorated with floral and geometric patterns, pineapples painted on furniture, and exotic bird-shape lamps. Every room has two queen beds or one king, two phone lines (one data port), and a coffeemaker; some have balconies. ✉ *1200 Epcot Resorts Blvd., Lake Buena Vista 32830* ☎ *407/934–3000 or 800/ 248–7926* 🖷 *407/934–4499* ⊕ *www.swandolphin.com* ⌨ *756 rooms, 55 suites* ⑂ *6 restaurants, room service, in-room safes, cable TV with movies and video games, in-room broadband, golf privileges, 4 tennis courts, 5 pools, gym, massage, spa, beach, boating, volleyball, 2 lobby lounges, video game room, babysitting, children's programs (ages 4–12), playground, concierge, concierge floor, business services, convention center, no-smoking rooms* ▭ *AE, D, DC, MC, V.*

Downtown Disney Resort Area

Take I–4 Exit 68.

A number of non-Disney-owned resorts are clustered on Disney property not far from Downtown Disney, and several more sprawling, high-quality resorts are just outside the park's northernmost entrance. Several of these hotels market themselves as "official" Disney hotels, meaning that they have special agreements with Disney that allow them to offers their guests such perks as early park admission. The hotels on Hotel Plaza Boulevard are within walking distance of Downtown Disney Marketplace, though most offer shuttle service anyway.

★ **$$$$** 🏨 **Wyndham Palace Resort & Spa in the WDW Resort.** This luxury hotel gets kudos as much for its on-site charms (such as a huge health spa) as for its location—100 yards from the Wolfgang Puck's in Downtown Disney. All rooms have patios or balconies, most of which have great views of Downtown Disney. As a guest, you also receive free transportation to all Disney parks, the chance to sign up for Disney character meals, and access to Disney golf courses. The Top of the Palace, the club-bar on the 27th floor, offers a champagne toast to guests every evening at sunset to accompany the wonderful view of the sun sinking into the Disney complex. Book reservations early if you want a meal at the rooftop restaurant, Arthur's 27. ⊠ *1900 Buena Vista Dr., Downtown Disney 32830* ☎ *407/827–2727 or 877/999–3223* 🖶 *407/827–6034* ⊕ *www.wyndham. com* 🛏 *1,014 rooms, 209 suites* ♿ *4 restaurants, patisserie, snack bar, room service, in-room safes, cable TV with movies, in-room broadband, tennis courts, 3 pools, health club, hot tub, massage, spa, 4 lounges, video game room, babysitting, children's programs (ages 4–12), playground, laundry facilities, laundry service, concierge, business services, convention center, no-smoking rooms* ⊟ *AE, D, DC, MC, V.*

$$$–$$$$ 🏨 **Hilton in the WDW Resort.** An ingeniously designed waterfall tumbles off the covered entrance and into a stone fountain surrounded by palm trees. Although not huge, rooms are upbeat, cozy, and contemporary, and many on the upper floors have great views of Downtown Disney, which is just a short walk away. The hotel offers two good eateries: Finn's Grill, specializing in Florida seafood, and a Benihana Steakhouse and Sushi Bar. Hotel guests can enter Disney parks one hour before they open. ⊠ *1751 Hotel Plaza Blvd., Downtown Disney 32830* ☎ *407/827–4000, 800/782–4414 reservations* 🖶 *407/827–6369* ⊕ *www.hilton. com* 🛏 *814 rooms, 27 suites* ♿ *7 restaurants, room service, in-room safes, cable TV with movies, in-room broadband, 3 pools, health club, outdoor hot tub, lobby lounge, babysitting, children's programs (ages 3–12), laundry facilities, laundry service, business services, meeting rooms, no-smoking rooms* ⊟ *AE, DC, MC.*

$$–$$$ 🏨 **DoubleTree Guest Suites in the WDW Resort.** The lavender-and-pink exterior looks strange, but the interior is another story. Comfortable one- and two-bedroom suites are decorated in tasteful hues, with blue carpeting and orange drapes and bedspreads. Each bedroom has either a king bed or two doubles. Units come with three TVs, including one in the bathroom, and a wet bar, microwave, refrigerator and coffeemaker.

The smallish lobby has a charming feature—a small aviary with birds from South America and Africa. There's a special "registration desk" for kids, where they can get coloring books and balloons. ✉ *2305 Hotel Plaza Blvd., Downtown Disney 32830* ☎ *407/934–1000 or 800/ 222–8733* 🖷 *407/934–1015* ⊕ *www.doubletreeguestsuites.com* ➲ *229 units* ♿ *Restaurant, room service, in-room safes, microwaves, refrigerators, cable TV with movies, in-room broadband, golf privileges, 2 tennis courts, pool, wading pool, gym, hot tub, 2 bars, laundry facilities, laundry service, business services, meeting rooms, no-smoking rooms* ▭ *AE, DC, MC, V.*

$–$$ 🖵 **Best Western Lake Buena Vista.** This 18-story property has an attractive mural of Florida wildlife and landscapes gracing the lobby, though the view of a junglelike wetland out the windows of the atrium restaurant is more compelling. Most rooms have private, furnished balconies with spectacular views of nightly Disney firework shows. Disney shuttles are available, but you can walk to Downtown Disney in 10 minutes or less. With standard rooms as cheap as $99 a night in high season, the hotel offers one of the best bargains on Hotel Row. ✉ *2000 Hotel Plaza Blvd., Downtown Disney 32830* ☎ *407/828–2424 or 800/ 348–3765* 🖷 *407/828–8933* ⊕ *www.orlandoresorthotel.com* ➲ *325 rooms* ♿ *Restaurant, snack bar, room service, cable TV with movies, in-room broadband, pool, wading pool, lobby lounge, playground, laundry facilities, laundry service, business services, meeting rooms, no-smoking rooms* ▭ *AE, D, DC, MC, V.*

$–$$ 🖵 **Grosvenor Resort.** This pink high-rise (the name is pronounced *Grove-*ner) across from Downtown Disney is nondescript on the outside but quite pleasant on the inside. Blond-wood furniture and rose carpeting make the rooms homey, and those in the tower have a great view of Downtown Disney. Public areas are decorated in an easygoing Caribbean style. One of the restaurants, Baskervilles, hosts a Disney character breakfast three days a week and a Saturday murder-mystery dinner show. A free shuttle takes you to all Disney theme parks. ✉ *1850 Hotel Plaza Blvd., Downtown Disney 32830* ☎ *407/828–4444 or 800/624– 4109* 🖷 *407/828–8192* ⊕ *www.grosvenorresort.com* ➲ *626 rooms, 5 suites* ♿ *3 restaurants, room service, in-room safes, refrigerators, cable TV with movies, in-room VCRs, in-room broadband, 2 tennis courts, 2 pools, wading pool, hot tub, basketball, volleyball, lobby lounge, video game room, babysitting, playground, laundry service, business services, meeting rooms, no-smoking rooms* ▭ *AE, DC, MC, V.*

Lake Buena Vista Area

Many people choose to stay in one of the resorts a bit farther northeast of Downtown Disney because, though equally grand, they tend to be less expensive than those right on Hotel Plaza Boulevard. If you're willing to take a five-minute drive or shuttle ride, you might save as much as 35% off your room tab.

Perennially popular with families are the all-suites properties, many with in-room kitchens, just east of Lake Buena Vista Drive. Furthermore, the 1,100-room Marriott Village at Lake Buena Vista, across I–4 from

SPAS THAT PAMPER WITH PANACHE

ONCE UPON A TIME something crucial was missing in Central Florida's vacation kingdom. There were castles and thrill rides, performing whales and golf meccas, but there were no standout spas, no havens of respite for the millions who trekked their feet flat and rubbed their shoulders raw lugging backpacks from one attraction to the next.

Now weary travelers can rejoice. It's a spa-world after all in Central Florida. Several pampering palaces at first-rate resorts can add blessed balance to your visit. Some of the finest spas have seized upon Florida's reputation as a citrus production center and will baste and massage you with essences of lemon, lime, orange, and grapefruit. Others import exotic treatments from Bali, Japan, and France. Each spa offers signature treatments, in addition to the usual massages, facials, and pedicures, performed by experienced therapists and aestheticians from all over the world. You can even find leg-relief treatments for exhausted park hoppers. All resort spas offer bottled water, teas, and fresh-fruit snacks, and with any treatment you'll have access to saunas, steam rooms, whirlpools, and fitness facilities.

The **Wyndham Palace Resort & Spa** has one of the most popular rejuvenation centers in the area, attracting visitors and locals with intimate, beautiful surroundings, reasonable prices, and light lunches in the courtyard. Here you might try the ultrarelaxing, skin-smoothing Golden Door Pineapple Body Scrub (50 minutes, $99), which exfoliates your skin then softens it with oils and moisturizers. It's like being transported to your own tropical island. To extend the feeling, add on the Tranquility Facial (50 minutes, $99), which also comes with a paraffin hand-and-foot treatment. Take your beautified body to Downtown Disney afterward for shopping, lunch or dinner—it's just across the street.

Further fruit-enhanced fantasies can be realized at the truly lavish **Ritz-Carlton Spa Orlando, Grande Lakes,** where the two-hour Tuscan Citrus Cure ($320) is one of several signature treatments. You retire to a special suite for a lemon-crush scrub and lime shower that preps you for a tailored aromatherapy massage. From there, you climb into the suite's tub for a soothing milk soak—you can control the jets to suit your mood. Your therapist completes the treatment with a sweet-orange moisturizing body wrap, and before emerging from your cocoon you're treated to a neck or scalp massage. The Ritz has the newest, largest spa in town, with 42 treatment rooms in a 40,000-square-foot facility. It also has the highest prices. But if you want to indulge in the royal lifestyle, this is the place to do it.

A stone's throw from the theme parks is the 20,000-square-foot **Canyon Ranch SpaClub at Gaylord Palms.** Here the Canyon Ranch Stone Massage (80 minutes, $185) paves the path to nirvana. Smooth volcanic stones of several sizes are heated to a temperature between 115° and 124°. After applying oil to the stones, your therapist works them along your body using either Swedish, deep tissue, shiatsu, or Reiki techniques. If you've already experienced a traditional massage, this is a wonderfully soothing alternative. Another signature Canyon Ranch service is the 100-minute Euphoria conditioning massage and body treatment ($250). The Gaylord Palms is one of the area's most elaborate resorts, so plan to have lunch or explore the Everglades–Key West–St. Augustine—themed atrium to wrap up the experience.

A Balinese paradise in landlocked Central Florida? It's right there at Universal Orlando's Portofino Bay Hotel, where the **Mandara Spa** delivers the signature Mandara Four Hand Massage (50 minutes, $100), in which two therapists massage you simultaneously, and the Balinese Massage (50 minutes, $90), involving acupressure and Swedish techniques. Depending on your skin's condition, you may also receive a mini milk bath, and a wrap with eucalyptus and lavender oils designed to relieve tension, all as part of the treatment.

Almost as soon as you enter Disney's **Grand Floridian Spa & Health Club** you can feel the stress melt away. Established in 1997, the Grand's spa has kept up its flawless reputation with its signature treatments, such as the Citrus Zest Therapies (75 minutes, $180), in which a soothing dose of grapefruit body oil is used in an aromatherapy massage, followed by reflexology. Families can enjoy the experience together—there's a couples treatment room, and there's a menu of facials, manicures, and pedicures for kids. Arrive early for complimentary use of the fitness center and a soak in the hot tub.

Healing spring waters of turn-of-the-20th-century Saratoga, New York, inspired the theme for **The Spa at Disney's Saratoga Springs**—it's the perfect place to sink into the luxury of a hydro-massage or emerge with the glow from a maple-enhanced body treatment. The Mineral Springs Hydro-Massage (45 minutes, $105) uses herbs to detoxify and awaken your skin. The Maple Sugar Body Polish (50 minutes, $120) deep-cleans and exfoliates to boost circulation and hydrate your skin. Heated stones do the work during the Adirondack Stone Therapy Massage (80 minutes, $175)—you'll be utterly relaxed. Kids' treatments include first facials, manicures,

and pedicures. You can order a flavorful, nourishing lunch from nearby Artist's Palette.

Even if golf isn't a passion, you'll want to swing by **The Spa at Omni Orlando ChampionsGate Resort,** just south of Walt Disney World, for its tropical-inspired treatments. Pineapple- and coconut-infused wraps envelop the weary body and let you drift off to Fiji or some other palm-studded isle. Sip on cranberry–hibiscus or green-passion tea as you relax in a plush robe before your treatment. If the Florida sun has dried out your skin, order the Aspara Essential Oil Wrap (50 minutes, $99)—you'll be swaddled in a warm cocoon of the herbal remedies while you enjoy a head and foot massage. It's a great headache reliever. The spa's classic Swedish Massage (name your touch for 50 minutes, $92) is a value-packed therapy and great theme-park recovery strategy. Take advantage of the salon to prep for a night on the town.

Most spas can book treatments on short notice, but your best bet is to call ahead and reserve the indulgence you don't want to miss.

— Jennie Hess

Downtown Disney, has made a splash in hotel-laden Orlando with its utter comprehensiveness. The gated, secure village has three hotels, a multirestaurant complex, a video-rental store, a 24-hour convenience store, and a Hertz rental-car station. There's also an on-property Disney booking station, staffed by a Disney employee who can answer questions and make suggestions.

$$$$
Fodor's Choice
★

Hyatt Regency Grand Cypress Resort. On 1,500 acres just outside Disney's north entrance, this spectacular resort has a private lake; three golf courses; and miles of tropical nature trails for bicycling, horseback riding, and jogging. The huge, 800,000-gallon pool has a 45-foot water slide and is fed by 12 waterfalls. Tropical birds and plants and Chinese sculptures fill the 18-story atrium. The hotel's fine dining room La Coquina, offers one of the best Sunday brunches in the Orlando area. Accommodations are divided between the hotel and the **Villas of Grand Cypress** (⊠ 1 N. Jacaranda Dr., Lake Buena Vista Area 32836 ☎ 407/239–1234 or 800/835–7377), with 200 villas. Although pricey, the resort provides tremendous value. All rooms are decorated with tasteful rattan furniture and have a private balcony overlooking either the Lake Buena Vista area or the pool. Villas have fireplaces and whirlpool baths. ⊠ 1 Grand Cypress Blvd., Lake Buena Vista Area 32836 ☎ 407/239–1234 or 800/233–1234 🖷 407/239–3800 ⊕ www.hyattgrandcypress. com ⇨ 750 rooms ♿ 5 restaurants, room service, in-room safes, cable TV with movies, in-room broadband, 9-hole golf course, 2 18-hole golf courses, 12 tennis courts, 2 pools, health club, 3 hot tubs, massage, spa, boating, bicycles, horseback riding, 4 lobby lounges, babysitting, children's programs (ages 5–12), laundry service, business services, convention center, meeting rooms, no-smoking rooms ▤ AE, D, DC, MC, V.

$$$$
Orlando World Center Marriott. At 2,000 rooms, this is one of the largest hotels in Orlando, and one very popular with conventions. All rooms have patios or balconies, and the lineup of amenities and facilities seems endless—there's even on-site photo processing. Upscale villas—the Royal Palms, Imperial Palms, and Sabal Palms—are available for daily and weekly rentals. The hotel's Hawk's Landing Steakhouse and Grille is among the better beef-centric restaurants in the Disney area. Golf at the 6,800-yard championship Hawk's Landing golf course becomes a bargain for guests—a golf package including one round costs about $20 more than the standard rate for a deluxe room, depending on the season. ⊠ 8701 World Center Dr., I–4 Exit 65, Lake Buena Vista Area 32821 ☎ 407/239–4200 or 800/228–9290 🖷 407/238–8777 ⊕ www. marriottworldcenter.com ⇨ 2,000 rooms, 98 suites, 259 villas ♿ 7 restaurants, ice-cream parlor, room service, cable TV with movies, in-room broadband, 18-hole golf course, 4 pools (1 indoor), wading pool, health club, hair salon, 4 hot tubs, 2 lobby lounges, babysitting, children's programs (ages 4–12), laundry facilities, laundry service, business services, convention center, no-smoking rooms ▤ AE, D, DC, MC, V.

$$$–$$$$
Nickelodeon Family Suites by Holiday Inn. After a $20 million renovation, this hotel—the first in a new chain formed by partners Nickelodeon and Holiday Inn—opened in early 2005. The Nick theme extends everywhere, from the suites, where separate kids rooms have bunk beds and SpongeBob wall murals, to the two giant pools built up

like water parks. Kids will look forward to wake-up calls from Nickelodeon stars, character breakfasts, and live entertainment. You can choose between one, two- and three-bedroom suites, with or without full kitchens. ⊠ *14500 Continental Gateway, I–4 Exit 67, Lake Buena Vista Area 32821* ☎ *407/387–5437 or 877/387–5437* 🖷 *407/387–1490* ⊕ *www.nickhotels.com* ⌨ *800 suites ♢ 3 restaurants, ice-cream parlor, room service, in-room safes, some kitchens, microwave, refrigerator, cable TV with movies, in-room broadband, 2 pools, health club, hair salon, 2 hot tubs, 2 lobby lounges, babysitting, children's programs (ages 4–12), laundry facilities, laundry service, business services, no-smoking rooms* ☰ *AE, D, DC, MC, V.*

$$$ 🖭 **Caribe Royale All-Suites Resort & Convention Center.** This big pink palace of a hotel, with flowing palm trees and massive, man-made waterfalls, wouldn't look out of place in Vegas. Huge ballrooms attract corporate conferences, but there are key family-friendly ingredients, too: free transportation to Walt Disney World (10 minutes away), and a huge children's recreation area, including a big pool with a 65-foot water slide. All suites have a spacious living room with a pull-out sofa bed, a kitchenette, and one or more private bedrooms. ⊠ *8101 World Center Dr., Lake Buena Vista Area 32821* ☎ *407/238–8000 or 800/823–8300* 🖷 *407/238–8088* ⊕ *www.cariberoyale.com* ⌨ *1,218 suites, 120 villas ♢ 4 restaurants, room service, microwaves, refrigerators, cable TV with movies, in-room broadband, 2 tennis courts, pool, wading pool, lobby lounge, laundry facilities, laundry service, concierge, business services, convention center, no-smoking rooms* ☰ *AE, D, DC, MC, V* ⦿ *BP.*

$$$ 🖭 **Celebrity Resorts at Lake Buena Vista.** The large, comfortable, one- to three-bedroom suites here can sleep 4 to 10 people. Add full kitchens, dining and living areas, and washer-dryer sets, and you have excellent accommodations for families who want more space and amenities for their money. The Spanish-style architecture gives way to tastefully furnished interiors, although doors between rooms in the same suite are a little thin. Master bedrooms have floor-to-ceiling mirrors on two walls, and whirlpool tubs in the bathrooms. A small playground and a large, attractive outdoor pool are surrounded by pretty landscaping, and Downtown Disney is just a mile away. ⊠ *8451 Palm Pkwy., Lake Buena Vista 32836* ☎ *407/238–1700* 🖷 *407/238–0255* ⊕ *www. celebrityresorts.com/lbv* ⌨ *66 suites ♢ Restaurant, in-room safes, some in-room hot tubs, some kitchens, cable TV, in-room broadband, tennis court, 4 pools, wading pool, gym, hot tub, basketball, racquetball, video game room, shop, children's programs (ages 4–12), playground, laundry facilities, laundry service, no-smoking rooms* ☰ *AE, D, MC, V* ⦿ *EP.*

$$–$$$ 🖭 **Embassy Suites Hotel Lake Buena Vista.** Some locals are shocked by the wild turquoise, pink, and peach facade (clearly visible from I–4, it's something of a local landmark), but the Embassy Suites resort is an attractive option for other reasons. It's just 1 mi from Downtown Disney, 3 mi from SeaWorld, and 7 mi from Universal Orlando. Each suite has a separate living room and two TVs. The central atrium lobby, loaded with tropical vegetation and soothed by the sounds of a rushing fountain, is

a great place to enjoy the complimentary cooked-to-order breakfast and evening cocktails. Pet-friendly suites are available for guests with pets 25 lbs. or less. ⊠ *8100 Lake Ave., Lake Buena Vista 32836* ☎ *407/ 239–1144, 800/257–8483, or 800/362–2779* 🖷 *407/239–1718* ⊕ *www. embassysuitesorlando.com* ⏎ *333 suites △ 2 restaurants, room service, in-room safes, microwaves, refrigerators, cable TV with movies, in- room broadband, tennis court, indoor-outdoor pool, wading pool, gym, hot tub, basketball, shuffleboard, volleyball, lobby lounge, babysitting, children's programs (ages 4–12), playground, business services, meet- ing room, no-smoking rooms* 🖃 *AE, D, DC, MC, V* ⏰ *BP.*

$$–$$$ 🖼 **Sheraton Safari Hotel.** This little piece of Nairobi in the hotel district adjacent to Downtown Disney is a bona fide success. From the pool's jungle motif to the bamboo enclosures around the lobby pay phones, this place is a trip. Although there are some leopard skin–print furni- ture coverings and wild-animal portraits on the walls, the guests are rel- atively sedate. Suites include kitchenettes with microwaves, and six deluxe suites have full kitchens. Watch your kids slide down the giant water slide in the pool area while you sip drinks at the poolside Zanz- ibar. ⊠ *12205 Apopka Vineland Rd., Lake Buena Vista Area 32836* ☎ *407/239–0444 or 800/423–3297* 🖷 *407/239–4566* ⊕ *www. sheratonsafari.com* ⏎ *489 rooms, 96 suites △ 2 restaurants, room service, in-room safes, some kitchenettes, some microwaves, some re- frigerators, cable TV with movies, in-room broadband, pool, health club, hot tub, lobby lounge, business services, meeting room, no-smoking rooms* 🖃 *AE, D, DC, MC, V.*

$$–$$$ 🖼 **Sheraton Vistana Resort.** Consider this peaceful resort, just across I–4 from Downtown Disney, if you're traveling with a large family or group of friends. The spacious, tastefully decorated villas and town houses come in one- and two-bedroom versions with a living room, full kitchen, and washer and dryer. Tennis players take note: there are clay and all-weather courts, free for guests to use, and private or semiprivate lessons are avail- able for a fee. Plus, with seven outdoor heated swimming pools, five kid- die pools, and eight outdoor hot tubs, you can spend the whole day just soaking up the sun. ⊠ *8800 Vistana Center Dr., Lake Buena Vista 32821* ☎ *407/239–3100 or 800/208–0003* 🖷 *407/239–3111* ⊕ *www. starwoodvo.com* ⏎ *1,700 units △ 2 restaurants, grocery, in-room safes, kitchens, microwaves, refrigerators, cable TV with movies, in-room broadband, miniature golf, 13 tennis courts, 7 pools, 5 wading pools, health club, 8 hot tubs, massage, basketball, shuffleboard, lobby lounge, babysitting, children's programs (ages 4–12), concierge, business services, meeting rooms, no-smoking rooms* 🖃 *AE, D, DC, MC, V.*

$$ 🖼 **Buena Vista Suites.** In this all-suites property you get a bedroom, a separate living room with a fold-out sofa bed, two TVs, two phones, and a small kitchen area with a coffeemaker, sink, microwave, and re- frigerator. King suites have a single king bed and a whirlpool bath. The hotel serves a complimentary full-breakfast buffet daily and provides complimentary shuttle transportation to the Walt Disney World theme parks. ⊠ *8203 World Center Dr., Lake Buena Vista Area 32821* ☎ *407/ 239–8588 or 800/537–7737* 🖷 *407/239–1401* ⊕ *www.buenavistasuites. com* ⏎ *280 suites △ Restaurant, room service, in-room safes, mi-*

crowaves, refrigerators, cable TV with movies, in-room broadband, 2 tennis courts, pool, wading pool, gym, hot tub, laundry facilities, car rental, no-smoking rooms ▤ AE, D, DC, MC, V ▢ BP.

$$ ▣ **Homewood Suites Lake Buena Vista.** The suites here are pleasant if not enormous, and both the prices and location make this a great home base for a family vacation. Each suite has a full kitchen, complete with dishes. Downtown Disney Marketplace is about 1 mi away, and at least a dozen other restaurants and a Publix supermarket are ½ mi away. The suites sleep up to six if you fold out the couch-bed in the living room. In addition to a daily free, hot buffet breakfast, snacks are laid out for a "social hour" Monday through Thursday 5–7 PM. ✉ 8200 Palm Pkwy., Lake Buena Vista 32836 ☎ 407/465–8200 or 800/225–5466 📠 407/465–0200 ⊕ www.homewoodsuiteslbv.com ▭ 123 suites ⚹ In-room safes, kitchens, microwaves, refrigerators, cable TV with movies, in-room broadband, pool, gym, hot tub, business services, no-smoking rooms ▤ AE, D, DC, MC, V ▢ CP.

$$ ▣ **Marriott Residence Inn.** Billing itself as a Caribbean-style oasis, with lush palms and an outdoor waterfall near the swimming pool, this all-suites hotel's most compelling features are a bit more pragmatic: every room has a full kitchen with a stove and dishwasher, and there's an on-site convenience store. (A supermarket is a few blocks down Palm Parkway.) Pleasant suites include a separate living room/kitchen and bedrooms. Two-bedroom suites have two bathrooms. The recreation area has both a kids' pool and a putting green. ✉ 11450 Marbella Palms Ct., Lake Buena Vista 32836 ☎ 407/465–0075 📠 407/465–0050 ⊕ www.residenceinnlbv.com ▭ 210 suites ⚹ In-room safes, kitchenettes, microwaves, refrigerators, cable TV with movies, in-room broadband, putting green, pool, wading pool, gym, hot tub, basketball, playground, laundry facilities, laundry service, business services, meeting rooms, no-smoking rooms ▤ AE, D, DC, MC, V.

$–$$ ▣ **Marriott Village at Little Lake Bryan.** The private, gated Marriott Village, comprising three separate hotels, offers extra security and a sense of community at reasonable prices. The **Courtyard** welcomes families and business travelers with large, standard rooms decorated with yellow and green floral patterns and blond-wood furniture, plus 3,000 square feet of meeting space. Each room has a coffeemaker and Web TV, and the indoor-outdoor pool area has a bar with seating in the pool. At **SpringHill Suites,** accommodations have kitchenettes, separate sleeping and dining areas, and Sony Playstations. The **Fairfield Inn** is the least expensive of the three, but rooms are just as bright and pleasant as in the other two, if not quite as amenity-laden. Complimentary continental breakfast is available at all three hotels, and the Village Marketplace has several chain restaurants, including a Pizza Hut and TCBY Yogurt. Best of all, there's a Disney planning center on site where you can buy theme-park tickets. ✉ 8623 Vineland Ave., Lake Buena Vista Area 32821 ☎ 407/938–9001 or 877/682–8552 📠 407/938–9002 ⊕ www.marriottvillage.com ▭ 700 rooms, 400 suites ⚹ 8 restaurants, room service, in-room safes, some in-room hot tubs, microwaves, refrigerators, cable TV with movies and video games, in-room broadband, 3 pools, 3 wading pools, gym, hot tubs, 3 bars, children's programs (ages 4–12), *laundry facilities, laundry service, business services, meeting rooms, no-smoking rooms* ⊟ *AE, D, DC, MC, V* ⏀ *CP.*

★ **$–$$** ▦ **PerriHouse Bed & Breakfast Inn.** An eight-room bed-and-breakfast inside a serene bird sanctuary is a unique lodging experience in fast-lane Orlando. The PerriHouse offers you a chance to split your time between sightseeing and spending quiet moments bird-watching: the 16-acre sanctuary has observation paths, a pond, a feeding station, and a small birdhouse museum. About 200 trees and more than 1,500 bushes have been planted, making it attractive to bobwhites, downy woodpeckers, red-tail hawks, and the occasional bald eagle. The inn is a private and romantic getaway, with four-poster and canopy beds and some fireplaces. The inn books some interesting adventures for its guests, ranging from bass fishing trips to sessions at an Orlando skydiving simulator. ⊠ *10417 Vista Oak Ct., Lake Buena Vista 32836* ☎ *407/876–4830 or 800/780–4830* ⊟ *407/876–0241* ⊕ *www.perrihouse.com* ⋈ *8 rooms* ⟋ *In-room safes, cable TV, in-room broadband, golf privileges, pool, hot tub* ⊟ *AE, D, DC, MC, V* ⏀ *CP.*

$–$$ ▦ **Riu Orlando Hotel.** What looks like a brown-brick office building from the outside has a look that's anything but institutional inside, with homey guest rooms and an atrium restaurant. After traipsing through theme parks and malls, what you may want most is to lounge around a living room just the way you do at home. The rooms in this six-story complex let you do just that, with big, comfy fold-out couches and big-screen TVs. Rooms also have coffeemakers, hair dryers, irons, and ironing boards. ⊠ *8688 Palm Pkwy., Lake Buena Vista Area 32836* ☎ *407/239–8500 or 888/222–9963* ⊟ *407/239–8591* ⊕ *www.riu.com* ⋈ *167 rooms* ⟋ *Restaurant, room service, in-room safes, room TVs with video games, in-room broadband, pool, hot tub, lobby lounge, business services, meeting rooms, no-smoking rooms* ⊟ *AE, D, DC, MC, V.*

$ ▦ **Country Inn & Suites by Carlson.** The signature lobby fireplace looks a little ridiculous in an Orlando hotel, but the in-room amenities and the proximity to Downtown Disney (½ mi away) make this place a good bet for either families or couples. For $120 you can book what the hotel calls a one-bedroom "Country Kids Suite," with two beds, two TVs (one of which is hooked up for video games), a refrigerator, and a microwave. There's no full-service restaurant, but the hotel is next door to two restaurants and within walking distance of a dozen others. Shuttle service to the Disney parks is provided. ⊠ *12191 S. Apopka Vineland Rd., Lake Buena Vista Area 32836* ☎ *407/239–1115 or 800/456–4000* ⊟ *407/239–8882* ⊕ *www.countryinns.com* ⋈ *170 rooms, 50 suites* ⟋ *In-room safes, microwaves, refrigerators, cable TV with movies, in-room broadband, pool, wading pool, gym, hot tub, laundry facilities, no-smoking rooms* ⊟ *AE, D, DC, MC, V* ⏀ *CP.*

¢–$ ▦ **Hawthorn Suites Resort Lake Buena Vista.** The free breakfast bar becomes just a bar during the social hour from Monday through Thursday, 5 to 7 PM, but if you'd rather go out, Downtown Disney is just 1 mi away. Every suite at the Hawthorn has a separate bedroom and a full kitchen, including a dishwasher, a two-burner stovetop, a microwave, and a refrigerator, so you can even stay in and cook. High-speed internet access is available in the lobby only. ⊠ *8303 Palm Pkwy., Lake*

Buena Vista 32836 ☎ *407/597–5000 or 800/936–9417* 🖷 *407/597–6000* ⊕ *www.hawthornsuiteslbv.com* ⚑ *120 suites* ♿ *In-room safes, kitchens, microwaves, refrigerators, cable TV, in-room broadband, pool, wading pool, exercise equipment, hot tub, basketball, bar, playground, laundry facilities, business services, meeting room, no-smoking rooms* ▤ *AE, D, DC, MC, V* ⚑ *CP.*

¢–$ 🖼 **Holiday Inn SunSpree Lake Buena Vista.** This family-oriented hotel has a children's registration desk, and there's usually a costumed clown to hand out balloons. Off the lobby you'll find the CyberArcade; a small theater where clowns perform weekends at 7 PM; and a buffet restaurant where kids accompanied by adults eat free at their own little picnic tables. Families love the Kidsuites, playhouse-style rooms within a larger room. ✉ *13351 Rte. 535, Lake Buena Vista 32821* ☎ *407/239–4500 or 800/366–6299* 🖷 *407/239–7713* ⊕ *www.kidsuites.com* ⚑ *507 rooms* ♿ *Restaurant, grocery, in-room safes, microwaves, refrigerators, cable TV with movies and video games, in-room broadband, pool, wading pool, gym, 2 hot tubs, basketball, Ping-Pong, bar, lobby lounge, theater, video game room, children's programs (ages 4–12), playground, laundry facilities, laundry service, business services, no-smoking rooms* ▤ *AE, D, DC, MC, V.*

KISSIMMEE

Take I–4 Exit 64A, unless otherwise noted.

If you're looking for anything remotely quaint, charming, or sophisticated, move on. With a few exceptions (namely, the flashy Gaylord Palms Resort), the U.S. 192 strip—a.k.a. the Irlo Bronson Memorial Highway—is a neon-and-plastic strip crammed with bargain-basement motels, cheap restaurants, fast-food spots, nickel-and-dime attractions, overpriced gas stations, and minimarts where a small bottle of aspirin costs $8. In past years, when Disney was in its infancy, this was the best place to find affordable rooms. But now that budget hotels have cropped up all along International Drive, you can often find better rooms closer to the theme parks by passing the Kissimmee motel strip and heading a few exits north.

There are exceptions, however—a few big-name companies like Marriott have excellent lodging on or near U.S. 192, and some of the older hotels have maintained decent standards and kept their prices very interesting. You can find clean, simple rooms in Kissimmee for $40 to $80 a night, depending on facilities and proximity to Walt Disney World.

One Kissimmee caveat: beware of the word "maingate" in many hotel names. It's a good 6 mi from Kissimmee's "maingate" hotel area to the Walt Disney World entrance. The "maingate west" area, however, is about 2 mi from the park. Of course, the greater the distance from Walt Disney World, the lower the room rates. A few additional minutes' drive may save you a significant amount of money, so shop around. And if you wait until arrival to find a place, don't be bashful about asking to see the rooms. It's a buyer's market.

$$$$ 🏨 **Gaylord Palms Resort.** Built in the style of a grand turn-of-the-20th-
Fodor'sChoice century Florida mansion, this resort is meant to awe. Inside its enor-
★ mous atrium, covered by a 4-acre glass roof, are re-creations of such
Florida landmarks as the Everglades, Key West, and old St. Augustine.
The five dramatic atrium restaurants include Sunset Sam's Fish Camp,
perched on a 60-foot fishing boat docked on the hotel's indoor ocean,
and the Old Hickory Steak House in an old warehouse overlooking the
alligator-ridden Everglades. Rooms carry on the Florida themes with colorful, tropical decorations. With extensive children's programs, two pool
areas, and a huge Canyon Ranch spa, the hotel connives to make you
never want to leave. The newest guest room amenity is Gaylord iCon-
nect, a computer system, complete with a 15-inch flat-screen monitor,
that connects you to the Internet plus a hotel network for booking dinner and activity reservations. ⊠ *6000 Osceola Pkwy., I–4 Exit 65,
Kissimmee 34746* ☎ *407/586–0000* 🖷 *407/586–1999* ⊕ *www.
gaylordpalms.com* 🖛 *1,406 rooms, 86 suites* ⚲ *4 restaurants, in-room
safes, cable TV with movies, in-room broadband, golf privileges, 2
pools, gym, hot tub, massage, spa, 2 bars, lobby lounge, children's programs (ages 4–12), laundry service, business services, convention center, meeting rooms, no-smoking rooms* ⊟ *AE, D, DC, MC, V.*

$$$$ 🏨 **Omni Orlando Resort at ChampionsGate.** Omni took over a 1,200-acre
golf club with two Greg Norman–designed courses and a David Led-
better academy to create this huge Mediterranean-style hotel complex,
which opened in late 2004. With a 70,000-square-foot conference center, the resort definitely attracts conventions and corporate meetings. But
there's kid appeal, too, in the form of an 850-foot-long, lazy-river-style
swimming pool and excellent children's programs. And the hotel is a
10-minute drive from the gates of Disney World. Rooms are attractive
if not distinctive, with earth-tone walls, gold carpets and drapes, and
marble vanity tops in the bathrooms. Weary golfers, park goers, and business travelers can rejuvenate at the European-style spa. ⊠ *1500 Masters Blvd., I–4 Exit 58, ChampionsGate, FL (Kissimmee Area) 33896*
☎ *407/390–6664 or 800/843–6664* 🖷 *407/390–6676* ⊕ *www.
omnihotels.com* 🖛 *730 rooms, 32 suites* ⚲ *5 restaurants, 3 bars, room
service, cable TV with movies, in-room broadband, 2 pools, wading pool,
2 18-hole golf courses, 2 tennis courts, hair salon, health club, hot tub,
spa, lobby lounge, babysitting, children's programs (ages 0–12), laundry facilities, laundry service, business services, convention center, no-
smoking rooms* ⊟ *AE, D, DC, MC, V.*

$$$$ 🏨 **Reunion Resort & Club of Orlando.** A spacious luxurious villa overlooking
Fodor'sChoice an expansive and perfectly groomed golf course makes an excellent get-
★ away from the theme parks. The Reunion Resort, opened in 2004, is
set on 28,000 acres of former orange grove land, far from the hustle
and bustle of I–4, and yet only 12 minutes from Walt Disney World.
Besides the tranquillity of the property, you have access to three private
world-caliber golf courses, designed by Tom Watson, Arnold Palmer, and
Jack Nicklaus. The resort was developed mainly as an exclusive residential and vacation-home complex, but its condo-style villas are also
available on a per-night basis. Villas that sleep four people start at $235
a night and include full kitchens. Activities include walking and horse-

back riding on the resort's meandering trails. ⊠ *1000 Reunion Way, Reunion 34747* ☎ *407/396–3200* ⊕ *www.reunionresort.com* ⤸ *60 units* ⚮ *Restaurant, room service, in-room safes, cable TV, in-room broadband, 3 18-hole golf courses, pool, health club, spa, bicycles, bar, shops, babysitting, children's programs (ages 4–12), laundry facilities, laundry service, no-smoking rooms* ▭ *AE, D, DC, MC, V.*

$$–$$$ ▦ **Celebration Hotel.** Like everything in the fantasy-driven, Disney-created town of Celebration, this 115-room hotel borrows from the best of the 19th and 21st centuries. The lobby resembles those of grand Victorian-era hotels, with hardwood floors and decorative millwork on the walls and ceilings. Rooms may look as if they date from the early 1900s, but each has a 25-inch TV, two phone lines, high-speed Internet access port, and a six-channel stereo sound system. Even though it's less than 1 mi south of the U.S. 192 tourist strip in Kissimmee, the hotel's surroundings are serene. The entire hotel is non-smoking. ⊠ *700 Bloom St., Celebration 34747* ☎ *407/566–6000 or 888/499–3800* 🖷 *407/ 566–1844* ⊕ *www.celebrationhotel.com* ⤸ *115 rooms* ⚮ *2 restaurants, cable TV with movies, in-room broadband, golf privileges, pool, health club, hot tub, lobby lounge, laundry service, no-smoking rooms* ▭ *AE, D, DC, MC, V.*

$–$$ ▦ **DoubleTree Resort Villas at Orlando Maingate.** The red-tile-and-stucco villas and palm-studded grounds are attractive, but the brochure stretches a point when it says the resort has the charm of a small village in the Spanish region of Andalusia. Nevertheless, the spacious accommodations are noteworthy. Each of the one-, two-, or three-bedroom units has a living and dining area, a full kitchen complete with utensils, and two TVs; the three-bedroom villa has 1,200 square feet of living space and sleeps up to eight comfortably. A wonderful small touch: the "welcome" chocolate-chip cookies. ⊠ *4787 W. Irlo Bronson Hwy., Kissimmee 34746* ☎ *407/397–0555 or 800/222–8733* 🖷 *407/397–0553* ⊕ *www.doubletree.com* ⤸ *150 villas* ⚮ *Restaurant, grocery, room service, in-room safes, cable TV with movies, in-room broadband, tennis court, pool, wading pool, health club, hot tub, lobby lounge, laundry facilities, no-smoking rooms* ▭ *AE, D, DC, MC, V.*

$–$$ ▦ **Magical Memories Villas.** Despite the name, this resort is not affiliated with Disney, but you will probably feel the magic anyway when you get your bill. Two-bedroom villas with full kitchens start at $89 a night here. Three- and four-bedroom villas are also available. Although the furnishings are pretty standard, the villas are spacious and bright, with large windows and pastel pink walls. All the suites include a washer and dryer, and a set of linens. Daily housekeeping is extra. ⊠ *5075 U.S. 192 W, Kissimmee 34746* ☎ *407/390–8200 or 800/736–0402* 🖷 *407/390–0718* ⊕ *www.magicalmemories.com* ⤸ *140 villas* ⚮ *Kitchens, microwaves, refrigerators, cable TV, in-room VCRs, in-room broadband, tennis court, pool, gym, hot tub, billiards, volleyball, video game room, laundry facilities, some pets allowed (fee), no-smoking rooms* ▭ *D, MC, V.*

★ **$–$$** ▦ **Radisson Resort Parkway.** This bright, spacious Radisson may offer the best deal in the neighborhood: an attractive location amid 1½ acres of lush tropical foliage, with good facilities and competitive prices. The focal point of the resort is its giant pool, complete with waterfalls, waterslide, and whirlpools. A free shuttle makes 10-minute trips to Disney. Children age 10 and younger eat for free in the hotel restaurants, when accompanied by an adult who orders a meal. Other on-site refueling options include Starbucks, Krispy Kreme, and Pizza Hut. Generously proportioned rooms are decorated with blond-wood furniture and vibrant, multicolor bedspreads and curtains. Rooms with the best view and light face the pool, which has a 40-foot water slide and wide, gentle waterfall. Off the lobby is a lively sports bar with an 11′ × 6′ TV. ⊠ *2900 Parkway Blvd., Kissimmee 34746* ☎ *407/396–7000 or 800/ 634–4774* 🖷 *407/396–6792* ⊕ *www.radissonparkway.com* 🛏 *712 rooms, 8 suites* ⚏ *2 restaurants, snack bar, cable TV with movies, in-room broadband, 2 tennis courts, 2 pools, wading pool, gym, 2 hot tubs, sauna, volleyball, lobby lounge, sports bar, laundry facilities, laundry service, business services, meeting rooms, no-smoking rooms* ▤ *AE, D, DC, MC, V.*

$–$$ ▦ **AmeriSuites Lake Buena Vista South.** A stay here gets you into the adjacent Caribbean-themed outdoor recreation complex for free. The complex includes an 18-hole miniature golf course and three outdoor pools, one with a waterslide. Complimentary continental breakfast is served daily, and there's free scheduled shuttle service to WDW, Universal Studios, SeaWorld, Wet 'n Wild, and the Lake Buena Vista Factory Stores. The brightly colored, tropical-style suites have separate bedrooms and living rooms with kitchenettes and king-size sofa beds. ⊠ *4991 Calypso Cay Way, Kissimmee 34746* ☎ *407/997–1300 or 800/833–1516* 🖷 *407/997–1301* ⊕ *www.amerisuites.com* 🛏 *151 suites* ⚏ *In-room safes, kitchenettes, microwaves, refrigerators, cable TV with movies, in-room broadband, pool, gym, laundry service, meeting rooms, no-smoking rooms* ▤ *AE, D, DC, MC, V* ⧖ *BP.*

¢–$$ ▦ **Celebrity Resorts Kissimmee.** A collection of villas a few blocks south of U.S. 192, this resort puts you far enough from the highway to avoid the clutter of the tourist strip, but close enough to conveniently reach its shops and restaurants. And it's about 4 mi from the Walt Disney World entrance. As at the Celebrity Resort in Lake Buena Vista, accommodations here range from standard hotel rooms to two-bedroom deluxe suites that can sleep up to 10 people. Suites have living rooms with sofa beds and separate dining areas. Each kitchen is equipped with a refrigerator, oven, microwave, dishwasher, and coffeemaker, plus dishes and utensils, and a washer and dryer. ⊠ *2800 N. Poinciana Blvd., Kissimmee 34746* ☎ *407/997–5000 or 800/423–8604* 🖷 *407/997–5225* ⊕ *www. celebrityresorts.com* 🛏 *311 suites* ⚏ *Restaurant, room service, in-room safes, some kitchens, microwaves, refrigerators, cable TV, in-room broadband, tennis court, 4 pools, wading pool, gym, hot tub, basketball, racquetball, video game room, babysitting, children's programs (4–12), laundry facilities, laundry service, no-smoking rooms* ▤ *AE, D, MC, V.*

¢–$$ ▦ **Holiday Inn Maingate West.** This six-story, classic Holiday Inn has large standard rooms with two double beds. Kidsuites have queen beds for the adults, full kitchens, and an extra room for the kids, with bunk beds, a TV and VCR, a CD player, Nintendo 64, and board games. You can grab a free shuttle to Disney World. Another bonus, the hotel accepts pets for a $25 fee, plus a $50 refundable deposit. ⊠ *7601 Black Lake Rd., 2 mi west of I–4, Kissimmee 34747* ☎ *407/396–1100 or 800/365–6935* 🖷 *407/396–0689* ⊕ *www.enjoyfloridahotels.com* 🛏 *295 rooms, 30 suites* ⚘ *Restaurant, room service, in-room safes, microwaves, refrigerators, cable TV with movies, in-room broadband, pool, wading pool, gym, volleyball, lobby lounge, laundry facilities, laundry service, some pets allowed (fee), business services, no-smoking rooms* ▤ *AE, D, DC, MC, V.*

¢–$ 🖭 **La Quinta Inn Lakeside.** Fifteen two-story, balconied buildings make up this 27-acre hotel complex. A small man-made lake offers pedal boating, and four outdoor tennis courts are available on a first-come, first-serve basis. Rooms come with two double beds or one king. Children's activities involve arts and crafts, movies, or miniature golf in a comfortable play area. Kids under 10 eat free at breakfast with at least one paying adult. There's free scheduled transportation to the local theme parks. ⊠ *7769 W. Irlo Bronson Memorial Hwy., 2 mi west of I–4, Kissimmee 34747* ☎ *407/396–2222 or 800/848–0801* 🖷 *407/239–2650* ⊕ *www.laquintainnlakeside.com* 🛏 *651 rooms* ⚘ *2 restaurants, room service, in-room safes, refrigerators, cable TV with movies, miniature golf, 4 tennis courts, 3 pools, wading pool, gym, boating, fishing, lobby lounge, children's programs (ages 4–12), playground, laundry facilities, laundry service, no-smoking rooms* ▤ *AE, D, DC, MC, V.*

¢–$ 🖭 **Seralago Hotel & Suites Main Gate East.** Formerly a Holiday Inn, this hotel was updated with new pink and blue interiors when it became a Seralogo Hotel in 2004. Kidsuites include a special room, designed to look like a fort from the Wild West, for kids, with bunk beds, TVs, and video games. All rooms have kitchenettes, with refrigerators and microwaves, and VCRs. The hotel is within walking distance of the Old Town shopping and entertainment complex, and 3 mi from WDW. Free scheduled transportation to Disney World's four theme parks is available. ⊠ *5678 W. Irlo Bronson Memorial Hwy., Kissimmee 34746* ☎ *407/396–4488, 800/366–5437, or 800/465–4329* 🖷 *407/396–1296* ⊕ *www.orlandofamilyfunhotel.com* 🛏 *614 rooms, 110 suites* ⚘ *Restaurant, food court, grocery, room service, kitchenettes, cable TV with video games, in-room VCRs, 2 tennis courts, 2 pools, wading pool, 2 hot tubs, basketball, volleyball, bar, video game room, children's programs (ages 3–12), playground, dry cleaning, laundry facilities, meeting rooms, no-smoking rooms* ▤ *AE, D, DC, MC, V.*

UNIVERSAL ORLANDO AREA

Take I–4 Exit 74B or 75A, unless otherwise noted.

Universal Orlando's on-site hotels, all managed by Loews Hotels, were built in a little luxury enclave that has everything you need, so you never have to leave Universal property. In minutes you can walk from any hotel to CityWalk, Universal's dining and entertainment district, or take a ferry that cruises the adjacent man-made river. If you need something as mundane as a new toothbrush, there's plenty of shopping just across the street from Universal on Kirkman Road.

A significant perk for staying at one of these properties is that your hotel key lets you go directly to the head of the line for most Universal Orlando attractions. Other special services at some hotels include a "Did You Forget?" closet that offers everything from kid's strollers to dog leashes to computer accessories.

If the on-property Universal hotels are a bit pricey for your budget, don't worry, a burgeoning hotel district with almost a dozen name-brand hotels has sprung up across Kirkman Road, offering convenient accommodations and some room rates less than $50 a night. While these off-property hotels don't offer perks like head-of-the-line privileges inside the park, you'll probably be smiling when you see your hotel bill.

$$$$ 🏨 **Hard Rock Hotel.** Although it's not quite as plush as Portofino Bay, the price tag isn't quite as high either, and you still get the perk of using your hotel key card to bypass the lines at attractions. Inside the California mission–style building you'll find lots of rock-music memorabilia, including the slip Madonna wore in her "Like a Prayer" video. Rooms have black-and-white photos of pop icons and serious sound systems with CD players. Stay in a suite and you'll get a big-screen TV and a wet bar. Kid-friendly suites have a small extra room for children. The Kitchen, one of the hotel's restaurants, occasionally hosts visiting musicians cooking their favorite meals at the Chef's Table. ⊠ *5800 Universal Blvd., Universal Studios 32819* 🕾 *407/503–7625 or 800/232–7827* 🖷 *407/503–7655* ⊕ *www.universalorlando.com* ⇨ *621 rooms, 29 suites* ⚹ *3 restaurants, room service, in-room safes, refrigerators, cable TV with movies, in-room VCRs, in-room broadband, 2 pools, health club, 3 bars, video game room, babysitting, children's programs (ages 4–14), laundry service, business services, meeting rooms, some pets allowed, no-smoking rooms* ⊟ *AE, D, DC, MC, V.*

$$$$ 🏨 **Portofino Bay Hotel.** The charm and romance of Portofino, Italy, are conjured up at this lovely luxury resort. The illusion is so faultless, right down to the cobblestone streets, that you might find it hard to believe that the different-colored row houses lining the "bay" are a facade. You can walk or ride the ferry from the hotel to Universal Studios and Islands of Adventure, and use your hotel key card to bypass lines at attractions. Large, plush rooms here are done in cream and white, with down comforters and high-quality wood furnishings. There are two Italian restaurants, Mama Della's and Delfino Riviera, and gelato machines surround the massive pool. The Feast of St. Gennaro (the patron saint of Naples) is held here in September, as well as monthly Italian wine tastings. ⊠ *5601 Universal Blvd., Universal Studios 32819* 🕾 *407/503–1000 or 800/232–7827* 🖷 *407/224–5311* ⊕ *www.universalorlando.com* ⇨ *699 rooms, 51 suites* ⚹ *3 restaurants, pizzeria, room service, in-room fax, in-room safes, cable TV with movies, in-room VCRs, in-room broadband, 3 pools, health club, massage, spa, boccie, bar, babysitting, children's programs (ages 4–14), playground, laundry service, business services* ⊟ *AE, D, DC, MC, V.*

$$$–$$$$ 🏨 **Royal Pacific Resort.** The hotel entrance—a footbridge across a tropical stream—sets the tone for the South Pacific theme of this hotel, which FodorśChoice is on 53 acres planted with tropical shrubs and trees, most of them
★

palms. The resort's focal point is a 12,000-square-foot, lagoon-style swimming pool, which has a small beach and an interactive water play area. Indonesian wood carvings decorate the walls everywhere, even in the rooms; and Emeril Lagasse's newest Orlando restaurant, Tchoup Chop, brings in crowds. Use your hotel key card to skip lines at the Universal theme parks. ⊠ *6300 Hollywood Way, Universal Studios 32819* ☎ *407/503–3000 or 800/232–7827* 🖷 *407/503–3010* ⊕ *www. universalorlando.com* ⮑ *1,000 rooms, 113 suites* ♴ *3 restaurants, room service, in-room safes, minibars, cable TV with movies, in-room VCRs, in-room broadband, putting green, pool, wading pool, health club, hot tub, massage, sauna, steam room, 2 bars, lobby lounge, children's programs (ages 4–14), laundry facilities, laundry service, concierge floor, business services, convention center, some pets allowed, no-smoking rooms* ▭ *AE, DC, MC, V.*

$$–$$$ 🏨 **DoubleTree Hotel at the Entrance to Universal Orlando.** When it opened in the mid-1970s, this was the largest convention hotel between Miami and Atlanta. It's still a hotbed of business-trippers, but it also attracts plenty of pleasure-seekers, since it's right at the Universal Orlando entrance. Don't worry about noisy conventioneers—the meeting and convention facilities are completely isolated from the guest towers. If you happen to be at the hotel on business, the hotel has a teleconferencing center from which you can originate live video links with points all over the world. In early 2005 the hotel started a $14 million renovation program to refurbish all guest rooms. ⊠ *5780 Major Blvd., I–4 Exit 75B, Universal Studios Area 32819* ☎ *407/351–1000* 🖷 *407/363–0106* ⊕ *www.orlandoradissonhotel.com* ⮑ *742 rooms, 15 suites* ♴ *Restaurant, room service, in-room safes, cable TV, in-room broadband, golf privileges, pool, wading pool, gym, hot tub, lobby lounge, babysitting, playground, dry cleaning, laundry facilities, business services, convention center, meeting rooms, no-smoking rooms* ▭ *AE, D, DC, MC.*

$–$$ 🏨 **Holiday Inn Hotel & Suites Orlando/Universal.** Staying at this hotel directly across the street from Universal Orlando could eliminate your need for a rental car if Universal, SeaWorld, Wet 'n Wild, and International Drive are your only planned vacation stops. There's a shuttle to all four, though you can easily walk to Universal. Rooms come with coffeemakers, hair dryers, irons, and ironing boards; one- and two-bedroom suites also have refrigerators, microwaves, dishwashers, and tableware. Suites cost about $20 more per night than the standard guest rooms. ⊠ *5905 S. Kirkman Rd., I–4 Exit 75B, Universal Studios Area 32819* ☎ *407/351– 3333 or 800/327–1364* 🖷 *407/351–3527* ⊕ *www.hiuniversal.com* ⮑ *390 rooms, 120 suites* ♴ *Restaurant, room service, in-room safes, some microwaves, some refrigerators, cable TV with movies, in-room broadband, pool, health club, lounge, babysitting, laundry service, business services, meeting rooms, some pets allowed, no-smoking rooms* ▭ *AE, D, DC, MC, V.*

$ 🏨 **Sleep Inn & Suites Universal Orlando.** This 11-story, 196-room hotel is the largest in the Sleep Inn chain. Rooms have two double beds or one king, and suites add full kitchens and a sofa that folds out into a double bed. In every room, baths have large, walk-in showers. Free bus service is available to Universal's entrance (only two blocks away), Sea-

Where to Stay in & near
Universal Orlando

World, and Wet 'n Wild. Restaurants and shopping are also within walking distance. Suites, which run about $10 more than the standard rooms, offer refrigerators and microwaves. ⊠ *5605 Major Blvd., Universal Studios Area 32819* ☎ *407/363–1333* 🖷 *407/363–4510* ⊕ *www. choicehotels.com* ↵ *196 rooms, 40 suites* ⚹ *In-room safes, kitchens, microwaves, refrigerators, cable TV with movies and video games, in-room broadband, pool, gym, video game room, laundry facilities, laundry service, business services, meeting rooms, no-smoking rooms* ▤ *AE, D, DC, MC, V* 🍽 *CP.*

★ ¢–$ 🏨 **Studio PLUS Orlando/Universal Studios.** This is no luxury resort, but the rooms are spacious, tidy, and pleasant. What's more, every suite has a full kitchen, so you can save money on meals if you enjoy cooking. Each suite also has a work table with data ports on the phones, a queen-size bed, and a sofa that folds out into a double bed. Two blocks from Universal, the hotel is in a central neighborhood replete with shopping and dining choices. ⊠ *5610 Vineland Rd., Universal Studios Area 32819* ☎ *407/370–4428 or 800/398–7829* 🖷 *407/370–9456* ⊕ *www. studioplus.com* ↵ *84 suites* ⚹ *Kitchens, microwaves, refrigerators, cable TV, in-room broadband, pool, gym, laundry facilities, no-smoking rooms* ▤ *AE, D, DC, MC, V.*

¢ 🏨 **Suburban Extended Stay America Orlando/Universal Studios.** The brick exterior with Victorian-style architectural touches makes the place look like a dorm at a small-town college, but the amenities inside are far more extensive than what you probably had at your alma mater. Each efficiency studio has a full kitchen, complete with microwave, stovetop, refrigerator, dishes, and dishwasher. There's no on-site gym, but a Bally's fitness center is a short walk away, and the neighborhood has lots of entertainment and dining options. Take Exit 75B off I–4. ⊠ *5615 Major Blvd., Universal Studios Area 32819* ☎ *407/313–2000 or 800/951–7829* 🖷 *407/313–2010* ⊕ *www.suburbanhotels.com* ↵ *150 suites* ⚹ *In-room safes, cable TV, in-room broadband, pool, playground, laundry facilities, business services, no-smoking rooms* ▤ *AE, D, DC, MC, V.*

ORLANDO METRO AREA

International Drive

Take I–4 Exit 72, 74A, or 75A, unless otherwise noted.

The sprawl of newish hotels, restaurants, shopping malls, and dozens of small attractions known as International Drive—"I-Drive" to locals—makes a convenient base for visits to Walt Disney World, Universal, and other attractions in the Orlando area. Parallel to I–4, this four-lane boulevard stretches from Universal Orlando in the north all the way to Kissimmee in the south. Each part of I-Drive has its own personality. The southern end is classier, and south of SeaWorld there's still, amazingly, quite a lot of wide-open space just waiting for new hotels and restaurants to open up. The concentration of cheaper restaurants, fast-food joints, and T-shirt shops increases as you go north; Universal Orlando is in this area, but remains a self-contained enclave.

I-Drive's popularity makes it a crowded place to drive in any season. Try to avoid the morning (7–9 AM) and evening (4–6 PM) rush hours. If you're planning a day visiting I-Drive attractions, consider riding the I-Ride Trolley, which travels the length of I-Drive from Florida's Turnpike to the outlet center on Vineland Avenue, stopping at Wet 'n Wild and SeaWorld.

★ $$$$ 🏨 **JW Marriott Orlando Grande Lakes.** With more than 70,000 square feet of meeting space, this hotel caters to a convention clientele. But because the hotel is part of a lush resort that includes a European-style spa and a Greg Norman–designed golf course, it also is an appealing place for tourists with a flexible budget. Rooms, at 420 square feet, are on the large side, and most have balconies that overlook the resort's huge pool complex. Wander down a long connector hallway to the adjoining Ritz-Carlton, where you can use your room charge card in the restaurants and shops. ✉ *4040 Central Florida Pkwy., I-Drive Area 32837* 📞 *407/206–2300 or 800/576–5750* 📠 *407/393–4001* 🌐 *www.grandelakes. com* 🛏 *1,000 rooms, 57 suites* ♿ *4 restaurants, room service, cable TV with movies, in-room broadband, 18-hole golf course, pool, health club, outdoor hot tubs, spa, 2 bars, lobby lounge, laundry service, concierge, concierge floor, business services, meeting rooms, no-smoking rooms* ▭ *AE, D, DC, MC, V.*

★ $$$$ 🏨 **Peabody Orlando.** Every day at 11 AM the celebrated Peabody ducks exit a private elevator and waddle across the lobby to the marble fountain where they pass the day, basking in their fame. At 5 they repeat the ritual in reverse. Built by the owners of the landmark Peabody Hotel in Memphis, this 27-story structure looks like three high-rise offices from afar, but don't be put off by the austerity. The interior is handsome and impressive, with gilt and marble halls. A concierge in the lobby can answer your questions about attractions as well as arts and cultural events in and around Orlando. Some of the oversize upper-floor rooms have panoramic views of WDW. You can leave your cares behind at the spa or health club. ✉ *9801 International Dr., I-Drive Area 32819* 📞 *407/352–4000 or 800/732–2639* 📠 *407/354–1424* 🌐 *www.peabodyorlando. com* 🛏 *891 rooms* ♿ *3 restaurants, room service, in-room safes, cable TV with movies, in-room broadband, golf privileges, 4 tennis courts, pool, wading pool, health club, hot tub, massage, spa, 2 lobby lounges, babysitting, concierge, business services, convention center, no-smoking rooms* ▭ *AE, D, DC, MC, V.*

$$$$ 🏨 **Ritz-Carlton Orlando Grande Lakes.** The first and only Ritz-Carlton in
Fodor's Choice Orlando, this hotel is a particularly extravagant link in the luxury chain.
★ Service is exemplary, from the fully attended porte cochere entrance to the 18-hole golf course and 40-room spa. Rooms and suites have elegant wood furnishings, down comforters, decadent marble bathrooms (with separate showers and bathtubs), and large balconies. A lovely, Roman-style pool area has fountains and a hot tub. Make reservations for dinner at Norman's when you reserve your room. An enclosed hallway connects the Ritz-Carlton to the nearby JW Marriott Hotel, where you'll find more restaurants and a kid-friendly water park. ✉ *4012 Central Florida Pkwy., I-Drive Area 32837* 📞 *407/206–2400 or 800/576–*

5760 🖷 407/206–2401 ⊕ www.grandelakes.com ⤳ 520 rooms, 64 suites ♨ 4 restaurants, room service, cable TV with movies, in-room broadband, 18-hole golf course, pool, health club, outdoor hot tubs, spa, 2 bars, lobby lounge, children's programs (ages 4–12), laundry service, concierge, concierge floor, business services, meeting rooms, no-smoking rooms ▭ AE, D, DC, MC, V.

$$$–$$$$ 🏨 **Marriott's Cypress Harbour Resort.** This big, elaborate vacation club and resort is a destination unto itself, with waterways, boating, swimming, golf, and other amenities designed to make you want to spend your time on the property. The two-bedroom, two-bathroom villas sleep up to eight people and include washer and dryer sets. An on-property market has groceries, liquor, cigars, and video rentals. There's also a Pizza Hut Express and Edy's ice cream. ⊠ 11251 Harbour Villa Rd., I-Drive Area, 32821 ☎ 407/238–1300 or 800/845–5279 🖷 407/238–1083 ⊕ www.vacationclub.com ⤳ 510 villas ♨ 2 restaurants, in-room safes, cable TV, in-room broadband, golf privileges, 2 tennis courts, 3 pools, wading pool, gym, 6 hot tubs, beach, boating, fishing, shuffleboard, volleyball, lounge, video game room, babysitting, children's programs (ages 4–12), playground, laundry facilities, laundry service, concierge, business services, no-smoking rooms ▭ AE, D, DC, MC, V.

$$$ 🏨 **Embassy Suites Hotel International Drive South.** This all-suites hotel has an expansive Mediterranean-style lobby with marble floors, pillars, hanging lamps, and old-fashioned ceiling fans. The atrium is alive with tropical gardens full of fountains and palm trees. Elsewhere, ceramic tile walkways and brick arches complement the tropical mood. The hotel offers a good number of little extras, like a health club with a fine steam room, free shuttle service to all four Disney parks and Universal Orlando, and a free hot breakfast and nightly beverages. ⊠ 8978 International Dr., I-Drive Area 32819 ☎ 407/352–1400 or 800/433–7275 🖷 407/363–1120 ⊕ www.embassysuitesorlando.com ⤳ 244 suites ♨ Restaurant, in-room safes, cable TV with movies, in-room broadband, 2 pools (1 indoor), health club, hot tub, sauna, steam room, lobby lounge, business services, meeting rooms, no-smoking rooms ▭ AE, D, DC, MC, V ⎟⎦ BP.

$$$ 🏨 **Renaissance Orlando Resort at SeaWorld.** The hotel's 10-story atrium is full of waterfalls, goldfish ponds, and palm trees; as you shoot skyward in sleek glass elevators, look for the exotic birds—on loan from SeaWorld across the street—twittering in the large, hand-carved, gilded Venetian aviary. Rooms have more floor space than the average Central Florida hotel, plus nice touches like high-speed Internet connections, speakers, and two-line phones. Atlantis, the formal restaurant, is something of an undiscovered gem, serving Mediterranean cuisine. ⊠ 6677 Sea Harbor Dr., I-Drive Area 32821 ☎ 407/351–5555 or 800/468–3571 🖷 407/351–4618 ⊕ www.renaissancehotels.com ⤳ 778 rooms ♨ 4 restaurants, room service, cable TV with movies, in-room broadband, golf privileges, 4 tennis courts, pool, wading pool, health club, hair salon, hot tub, massage, sauna, volleyball, 3 lounges, babysitting, laundry service, concierge, business services, convention center, no-smoking rooms ▭ AE, D, DC, MC, V.

$$$ 🏨 **Rosen Centre Hotel.** This 24-story palace is adjacent to the Orange County Convention Center and within easy walking distance of some of International Drive's newer attractions, like the Pointe*Orlando shopping and entertainment center and Ripley's Believe It or Not! There's a massive pool area surrounded by tropical vegetation and a couple of good restaurants, including the Everglades Room and Cafe Gauguin, where you can admire a big Gauguin-inspired mural while you eat. Universal Orlando ticket and shuttle services are available here. In 2004 all Rosen conference hotels started a service called BAGS, also used by Disney properties. With BAGS, you can get a boarding pass for your flight and check in your luggage at the hotel, thus eliminating airport check-in at Orlando International. ⊠ *9840 International Dr., I-Drive Area 32819* ☎ *407/996–9840 or 800/204–7234* 🖷 *407/996–3169* ⊕ *www.rosencentre.com* ⟿ *1,334 rooms, 80 suites* ⚹ *3 restaurants, pizzeria, room service, pool, health club, hot tub, massage, 2 bars, lobby lounge, laundry service, business services, convention center, no-smoking rooms* ▤ *AE, D, DC, MC, V.*

$$–$$$ 🏨 **Embassy Suites International Drive/Jamaican Court.** The concept of an all-suites hotel that serves a free buffet breakfast and complimentary cocktails, pioneered by the Embassy Suites chain, has proved very popular in Orlando. This particular hotel has a central atrium with a lounge where a player piano sets the mood. Each suite has a bedroom and separate living room with a wet bar, pullout sofa, and two TVs—all at a better price than for many single rooms in the area. Two-room suites can sleep six. ⊠ *8250 Jamaican Ct., I-Drive Area 32819* ☎ *407/345–8250 or 800/ 327–9797* 🖷 *407/352–1463* ⊕ *www.orlandoembassysuites.com* ⟿ *246 suites* ⚹ *Room service, in-room safes, refrigerators, cable TV with movies, in-room broadband, indoor-outdoor pool, gym, hot tub, sauna, steam room, lobby lounge, babysitting, business services, meeting rooms, car rental, no-smoking rooms* ▤ *AE, D, DC, MC, V* ⧒ *BP.*

$$–$$$ 🏨 **Sheraton World Resort.** On 28 acres just south of the Orange County Convention Center, this 17-story hotel welcomes families as well as conventioneers. It's roughly midway between the airport and WDW, less than a mile from SeaWorld, and a five-minute shuttle ride from Universal Orlando. ⊠ *10100 International Dr., I-Drive Area 32821* ☎ *407/352– 1100 or 800/327–0363* 🖷 *407/352–3679* ⊕ *www.sheratonworld.com* ⟿ *1,102 rooms, 68 suites* ⚹ *3 restaurants, room service, in-room safes, cable TV with movies, in-room broadband, miniature golf, 3 pools, health club, hot tub, massage, lobby lounge, laundry service, business services, convention center, meeting rooms, car rental, no-smoking rooms* ▤ *AE, D, DC, MC, V.*

$$–$$$ 🏨 **Wyndham Orlando Resort.** Two-story villas, palm trees, and romantic lagoons make this resort look like a Caribbean getaway. You'll find a children's entertainment center and an upscale shopping court. The two-story villas are comfortable, if not necessarily candidates for *Architectural Digest.* But you can't beat the prime location—you could almost throw a baseball from the hotel's driveway and have it land inside the Universal Orlando complex. If you choose the Family Fun Suites option, the youngsters get a separate room with bunk beds. This is one of the few hotels in Orlando that allows pets (with a $50, nonrefundable fee). ✉ *8001 International Dr., I-Drive Area 32819* ☎ *407/351–2420 or 800/996–3426* 🖷 *407/351–5016* ⊕ *www.wyndham.com* ➹ *1,064 rooms* ⚓ *3 restaurants, room service, in-room safes, refrigerators, cable TV with movies, in-room broadband, 4 tennis courts, 3 pools, health club, hot tub, lobby lounge, shops, laundry service, business services, convention center, car rental, some pets allowed (fee), no-smoking rooms* ▭ *AE, D, DC, MC, V.*

$$ 🏨 **Sheraton Studio City.** Atop this Sheraton is a giant silver globe suitable for Times Square on New Year's Eve. But the interior has a Hollywood theme, with movie posters and black-and-white art deco touches throughout the public spaces and rooms, most of which have two queen beds. The 21st floor has 15 extra-large rooms with floor-to-ceiling windows. Free shuttles go to the major theme parks and shopping malls. ✉ *5905 International Dr., I-Drive Area 32819* ☎ *407/351–2100 or 800/ 327–1366* 🖷 *407/345–5249* ⊕ *www.sheratonstudiocity.com* ➹ *302 rooms* ⚓ *Restaurant, room service, in-room safes, cable TV with movies and video games, in-room broadband, pool, wading pool, hair salon, hot tub, bar, lobby lounge, video game room, laundry service, concierge, business services, meeting rooms, no-smoking rooms* ▭ *AE, D, DC, MC, V.*

$$ 🏨 **Staybridge Suites International Drive.** The one- and two-bedroom units at this all-suites hotel sleep four to eight people and are a great option for families. Each has a separate living room and kitchen with simple but up-to-date furnishings. Lush landscaping makes the place seem secluded even though it's on International Drive. ✉ *8480 International Dr., I–4 Exit 74A, I-Drive Area 32819* ☎ *407/352–2400 or 800/238–8000* 🖷 *407/ 352–4631* ⊕ *www.lbvorlando.staybridge.com* ➹ *146 suites* ⚓ *Grocery, in-room safes, kitchens, microwaves, refrigerators, cable TV with movies, in-room broadband, pool, wading pool, gym, hot tub, lobby lounge, video game room, laundry facilities, laundry service, business services, meeting rooms, no-smoking rooms* ▭ *AE, D, DC, MC, V* ⁙⊙⁙ *CP.*

$–$$ 🏨 **Enclave Suites at Orlando.** With three 10-story buildings surrounding a private lake, an office, restaurant, and recreation area, this all-suites lodging is less a hotel than a condominium complex. Here what you would spend for a normal room in a fancy hotel gets you a complete apartment with a living room, a full kitchen, two bedrooms, and small terraces with a view of a nearby lake. KidsQuarter suites, which can accommodate six people, have small children's rooms with bunk beds and Shamu murals. There's free transportation to SeaWorld, Wet 'n Wild, and Universal Orlando, but Wet 'n Wild is an easy walk. A free hot breakfast buffet is served daily. ✉ *6165 Carrier Dr., I-Drive Area 32819* ☎ *407/ 351–1155 or 800/457–0077* 🖷 *407/351–2001* ⊕ *www.enclavesuites. com* ➹ *321 suites* ⚓ *Food court, grocery, pizzeria, snack bar, in-room safes, kitchens, microwaves, refrigerators, cable TV with movies, in-room broadband, tennis court, 3 pools (1 indoor), 2 wading pools, gym, hot tub, playground, laundry facilities, laundry service, meeting rooms, no-smoking rooms* ▭ *AE, D, DC, MC, V.*

$–$$ 🏨 **La Quinta Inn & Suites Orlando Convention Center.** A half mile south of the Orange County Convention Center, this family-oriented hotel is in the heart of the more upscale part of International Drive. The hotel has the added convenience of a front entrance on Universal Boulevard, the relatively undiscovered thoroughfare a block east of I-Drive. Despite the proximity to the tourist strip, things are still serene here. The king rooms and suites have refrigerators and microwaves; and, although there's no restaurant, the hotel provides a complimentary continental breakfast daily, and there are a half-dozen eateries nearby. ⊠ *8504 Universal Blvd., I–4 Exit 74A, I-Drive Area 32819* ☎ *407/345–1365* 🖶 *407/345–5586* ⊕ *www.orlandolaquinta.com* 🛏 *170 rooms, 15 suites ♦ In-room safes, some microwaves, some refrigerators, room TVs with movies, in-room broadband, pool, gym, outdoor hot tub, bar, video game room, laundry facilities, laundry service, business services, meeting rooms, some pets allowed, no-smoking rooms* ☐ *AE, D, DC, MC, V.*

$–$$ 🏨 **Marriott Residence Inn SeaWorld International Center.** The longish name hints at all the markets the hotel is attempting to tap. SeaWorld, International Drive, and the Orange County Convention Center, all within a 2-mile radius, are served by hotel shuttles. Even the least expensive suites can sleep five people. A complimentary breakfast is served daily, and several nearby restaurants will deliver your order to your room. The recreation area around the pool is like a summer camp, with a basketball court, playground equipment, picnic tables, and gas grills. Get a firm grip on directions if you are driving. The hotel is adjacent to I–4, but it's 2 mi from the interstate via two expressways, including Beeline Expressway. ⊠ *11000 Westwood Blvd., I–4 Exit 72, I-Drive Area 32821* ☎ *407/313–3600 800/331–3131* 🖶 *407/313–3611* ⊕ *www.residenceinnseaworld.com* 🛏 *350 suites ♦ Pizzeria, in-room safes, kitchens, cable TV with movies, in-room broadband, pool, wading pool, gym, outdoor hot tub, basketball, bar, playground, laundry facilities, laundry service, business services, meeting rooms, no-smoking rooms* ☐ *AE, D, DC, MC, V* ○◎ *BP.*

$–$$ 🏨 **Parc Corniche Condominium Suite Hotel.** A good bet for golf enthusiasts, the suites-only resort is framed by a Joe Lee–designed course. Each of the one- and two-bedroom suites, which are full of pastels and tropical patterns, has a kitchen complete with dishes and a dishwasher, plus a patio or balcony with golf-course views. The largest accommodations, with two bedrooms and two baths, can sleep up to six. A complimentary Continental breakfast is served daily, and SeaWorld is only a few blocks away. ⊠ *6300 Parc Corniche Dr., I-Drive Area 32821* ☎ *407/239–7100 or 800/446–2721* 🖶 *407/239–8501* ⊕ *www.parccorniche.com* 🛏 *210 suites ♦ Restaurant, picnic area, room service, cable TV with movies, 18-hole golf course, pool, wading pool, hot tub, babysitting, playground, laundry facilities, laundry service, business services, no-smoking rooms* ☐ *AE, D, DC, MC, V* ○◎ *BP.*

$–$$ 🏨 **Rosen Plaza Hotel.** Harris Rosen, the largest independent hotel owner in the Orlando market, loves to offer bargains, and you can find one here. This is essentially a convention hotel, although leisure travelers like the prime location and the long list of amenities. Rooms, which were redecorated in 2004, are larger than most standard hotel rooms, with two queen-size beds. Two upscale restaurants, Jack's Place and Café Matisse, offer great steaks and a great buffet, respectively, but the best food option is the pizza at Rossini's. You can also grab quick eats at the reasonably priced 24-hour deli. With the BAGS service, you can get your airline boarding pass and check your bags in the hotel lobby, so you can go straight to your gate at Orlando International. ⊠ *9700 International Dr., I-Drive Area 32819* ☎ *407/996–9700 or 800/627–8258* 🖶 *407/996–9119* ⊕ *www.rosenplaza.com* ⊅ *810 rooms* ⚲ *2 restaurants, coffee shop, ice-cream parlor, pizzeria, room service, in-room safes, cable TV, in-room broadband, pool, hot tub, bar, lobby lounge, nightclub, video game room, babysitting, laundry facilities, laundry service, business services, meeting rooms, no-smoking rooms* ▤ *AE, D, DC, MC, V.*

$–$$ 🏨 **Sierra Suites Hotel.** The two Orlando locations of this all-suites hotel chain are designed for the business traveler: personal voice mail, two phone lines, speakerphone, and a good-size work table in each room. But the benefit for families is that you get a lot for your money. There's a full kitchen, including dishwasher, cookware, and silverware—everything you need to avoid restaurant tabs for as long as you like. The earth-tone color scheme is warm if not memorable, and the suites have two queen- or one king-size bed, plus a sofa bed. Although neither Sierra has a restaurant, lots of eateries are within walking distance of both. ⊠ *8750 Universal Blvd., I–4 Exit 74A, I-Drive Area 32819* ☎ *407/903–1500 or 800/474–3772* 🖶 *407/903–1555* ⊕ *www.sierrasuites. com* ⊅ *137 suites* ⚲ *In-room safes, kitchens, cable TV with movies, pool, gym, outdoor hot tub, laundry facilities, laundry service, business services, no-smoking rooms* ⊠ *8100 Palm Pkwy., I–4 Exit 68, 32836* ☎ *407/239–4300 or 800/474–3772* 🖶 *407/239–4446* ⊅ *125 suites* ⚲ *In-room safes, kitchens, cable TV with movies, pool, gym, outdoor hot tub, laundry facilities, laundry service, no-smoking rooms* ▤ *AE, D, DC, MC, V.*

$–$$ 🏨 **The DoubleTree Castle.** You won't really think you're in a castle at this midprice hotel, although the tall gold-and-silver spires, medieval-style mosaics, arched doorways, and U.K. tourists may make you feel like reading Harry Potter. Take your book to either the rooftop terrace or the inviting courtyard, which has a big, round swimming pool. Rooms have gold-framed mirrors and black-velvet headboards. Café Tu Tu Tango, one of the better restaurants in this part of Orlando, has a zesty, small-dish, multicultural menu. ⊠ *8629 International Dr., I-Drive Area 32819* ☎ *407/345–1511 or 800/952–2785* 🖶 *407/248–8181* ⊕ *www.doubletreecastle. com* ⊅ *216 rooms* ⚲ *2 restaurants, room service, in-room safes, minibars, refrigerators, cable TV with movies, in-room broadband, pool, gym, hot tub, lobby lounge, video game room, laundry service, business services, no-smoking rooms* ▤ *AE, D, DC, MC, V.*

$ 🏨 **Inn of America.** This no-frills, three-story hotel offers basic but well-kept rooms at an excellent price. It's squeezed between International Drive and I–4, within a few minutes' drive of all the major attractions. Although it doesn't have the amenities of top-of-the-line hotels, there are nice perks such as complimentary Continental breakfast in the dining room, free local phone calls, and in-room wireless high-speed Internet. There's an outdoor heated pool and a YMCA nearby. ⊠ *8342 Jamaican Ct., I-Drive Area 32819* ☎ *407/363–1944* 🖶 *407/363–4844* ⊕ *www.innofamerica. com* ⊅ *134 rooms* ⚲ *In-room safes, room TVs with movies, in-room* *broadband, pool, business services, no-smoking rooms* ☒ *AE, D, DC, MC, V* ⦿ *CP.*

¢–$ ⊞ **Holiday Inn Hotel & Suites–Orlando Convention Center.** A bright yellow facade fronted by palm trees welcomes you to this six-story, family-friendly hotel. Furnishings are simple, but rooms are large, with either two queen beds or one king. The hotel is one block from the Mercado shopping and dining complex at the heart of International Drive, and it's within walking distance of two-thirds of the attractions on I-Drive. Shuttles run to Universal Orlando, SeaWorld, and Wet 'n Wild, all within 2 miles. ☒ *8214 Universal Blvd., I–4 Exit 74A, I-Drive Area 32819* ☎ *407/581–9001* 🖷 *407/581–9002* ⊕ *www.holidayinnconvention.com* ⇖ *115 rooms, 35 suites* ☖ *Restaurant, in-room safes, some kitchens, microwaves, refrigerators, cable TV with movies, in-room broadband, 2 pools, gym, outdoor hot tub, bar, video game room, laundry facilities, laundry service, business services, meeting rooms, no-smoking rooms* ☒ *AE, D, DC, MC, V.*

¢–$ ⊞ **Travelodge Orlando Convention Center.** If you don't want a room with just the bare essentials yet don't have the budget for luxury, this three-story motel is a find. The rooms are comfy if not spectacular; all have two double beds. Children 17 and under stay free in their parents' room (with a maximum of four people per room). The hotel is ¼ mi from SeaWorld. Free scheduled transportation is provided to SeaWorld, Universal Studios, and Disney World. ☒ *6263 Westwood Blvd., I-Drive Area 32821* ☎ *407/345–8000 or 800/346–1551* 🖷 *407/345–1508* ⊕ *www.travelodge.com* ⇖ *144 rooms* ☖ *Restaurant, in-room safes, room TVs with movies, in-room broadband, 2 pools, exercise equipment, bar, video game room, laundry facilities, laundry service, business services, no-smoking rooms* ☒ *AE, DC, MC, V.*

¢ ⊞ **Studio PLUS Orlando Convention Center.** Tucked behind a pine forest, this small, all-suites property feels remote, but SeaWorld, the Orange County Convention Center, and Pointe*Orlando are all within a 1-mi drive. Amenities are minimal, and the pool area is smallish, but this is a great place to save on your vacation budget. Weekly rates start as low as $255. ☒ *6443 Westwood Blvd., I–4 Exit 72, I-Drive Area 32821* ☎ *407/351–1982 or 800/398–7829* 🖷 *407/351–1719* ⊕ *www.extstay.com* ⇖ *113 suites* ☖ *In-room safes, kitchens, cable TV, in-room broadband, pool, exercise equipment, laundry facilities, business services, no-smoking rooms* ☒ *AE, D, DC, MC, V.*

Downtown Orlando

Downtown Orlando, north of Walt Disney World and the International Drive area, is a thriving business district. To get there take Exit 83B off I–4 westbound, Exit 84 off I–4 eastbound.

$$$–$$$$ ⊞ **Westin Grand Bohemian.** This European-style property is downtown Orlando's only luxury hotel. Opposite city hall, the Grand Bohemian showcases more than 100 pieces of art—including an Imperial Grand Bösendorfer piano, one of only two in the world, which sits in a posh ground-floor lounge. Rooms have dark-wood furnishings with brushed-silver accents. Tall headboards are upholstered in iridescent fabrics. Off

Where to Stay in
Central Orlando
& Outlying Towns

the main lobby are a Starbucks and an art gallery. ✉ *325 S. Orange
Ave., Downtown Orlando 32801* ☎ *407/313–9000 or 866/663–0024*
🖷 *407/313–9001* ⊕ *www.grandbohemianhotel.com* 🖙 *250 rooms,
36 suites* ♿ *Restaurant, room service, cable TV with movies, in-room
broadband, pool, gym, massage, bar, concierge, concierge floor, business services, meeting rooms, parking (fee), no-smoking rooms* ⊟ *AE,
D, DC, MC, V.*

★ **$$–$$$** 🏨 **The Courtyard at Lake Lucerne.** This group of four B&Bs, all next door
to each other, is almost under an expressway bridge at the southwestern edge of downtown. The beautifully restored Victorian houses surround a lush, palm-lined courtyard. There's no noise from the expressway,
and as you sit on the porch of one of the mansions it's easy to imagine
yourself back in the time when citrus ruled and the few tourists who
came to the area arrived at the old railroad station on Church Street,
six blocks away. Rooms have hardwood floors, Persian rugs, and antique furniture. ✉ *211 N. Lucerne Circle E, Downtown Orlando 32801*
☎ *407/648–5188* 🖷 *407/246–1368* ⊕ *www.orlandohistoricinn.com*
🖙 *15 rooms, 15 suites* ♿ *Cable TV, in-room broadband, meeting
room, no-smoking rooms* ⊟ *MC, V* ⭐ *CP.*

★ **$$–$$$** 🏨 **Eō Inn & Urban Spa.** The entrance to this boutique hotel is at the rear
of the building, behind Panera Bread, the bakery and restaurant that

occupies the ground floor. Consequently, this charming three-story hotel in a 1923 building is somewhat of an undiscovered gem. The spa, which offers many services from Swedish massage to beauty treatments, does a brisk business on its own, but hotel guests can always get an appointment. Rooms have black-and-white photographs on the walls and thick down comforters on the beds, as well as high-speed Internet connections. Best of all, Lake Eola, with its 1-mi walking path, is across the street—treat yourself to a king suite overlooking the lake. Thornton Park restaurants and night spots are within easy walking distance. ⊠ *227 N. Eola Dr., off E. Robinson St., Thornton Park 32801* ☎ *407/ 481–8485 or 888/481–8488* 🖷 *407/481–8495* ⊕ *www.eoinn.com* ⇨ *17 rooms* ⚫ *In-room safes, cable TV with movies, in-room broadband, outdoor hot tubs, massage, sauna, spa, laundry service, business services, no-smoking rooms* ▤ *AE, D, DC, MC, V.*

$$ 🏨 **Embassy Suites Orlando Downtown.** Although designed for business travelers, this downtown all-suites property has nice touches for vacationers, too. All suites have two TVs—one in each room. Many suites overlook nearby Lake Eola, and the hotel is a short walk from a half-dozen sidewalk cafés. The seven-story indoor atrium gives the hotel a classy touch. ⊠ *191 E. Pine St., Downtown Orlando 32801* ☎ *407/841–1000 or 800/609–3339* 🖷 *407/841–0010* ⊕ *www. embassyorlandodowntown.com* ⇨ *167 suites* ⚫ *Restaurant, in-room safes, microwaves, refrigerators, cable TV with movies, in-room broadband, pool, gym, outdoor hot tub, lobby lounge, laundry service, business services, meeting rooms, no-smoking rooms* ▤ *AE, D, DC, MC, V* ⏏❙ *BP.*

Orlando International Airport

The area around the airport, especially the neighborhood just north of the Beeline Expressway, has become hotel city over the past few years, with virtually every big-name hotel you can think of, including plenty of family-style choices, such as suites with kitchens. All the hotels listed include free airport shuttle service.

$$$–$$$$ 🏨 **Hyatt Regency Orlando International Airport.** If you have to catch an early morning flight, this hotel inside the main terminal complex is a good option. Counting the time you spend waiting for the elevator, your room is just a five-minute walk from the nearest airline ticket counter. Rooms have views of either the runways or a 10-story-tall terminal atrium, and the terminal-side rooms all have balconies. Hemisphere, the hotel's upscale restaurant on the 9th floor, offers a seasonal "worldly eclectic" menu and a spectacular view of the airport runways. An in-house health club and swimming pool provide places to unwind. ⊠ *9300 Airport Blvd., Orlando International Airport 32827* ☎ *407/825–1234 or 800/233– 1234* 🖷 *407/856–1672* ⊕ *www.orlandoairport.hyatt.com* ⇨ *446 rooms* ⚫ *2 restaurants, room service, cable TV with movies, in-room broadband, pool, health club, hot tub, laundry service, business services, meeting rooms, no-smoking rooms* ▤ *AE, D, DC, MC, V.*

$$ 🏨 **The Florida Mall Hotel.** About 5 mi from the airport gates, this hotel is between Orlando International and International Drive. And if you like to shop in nontourist-driven stores, there's a real bonus here: the hotel is connected to one of Orlando's biggest shopping centers, the up-scale Florida Mall, with seven major department stores and 250 spe-cialty shops. The hotel feels quite upscale, too, with polished marble floors, fountains in the lobby, and a good in-house restaurant, Le Jardin. Rooms, renovated in 2004, have either two queen beds or a king and a fold-out sofa; microwaves and refrigerators are available for a small fee. ✉ *1500 Sand Lake Rd., at S. Orange Blossom Trail, Orlando International Airport 32809* ☎ *407/859–1500 or 800/588–4656* 📠 *407/816–5193* ⊕ *www.thefloridamallhotel.com* ➮ *510 rooms* � *Restaurant, room service, cable TV, in-room broadband, pool, health club, hot tub, laundry service, business services, meeting rooms, no-smoking rooms* ▤ *AE, D, DC, MC, V.*

¢–$ 🏨 **AmeriSuites Orlando Airport Northeast and Northwest.** These two ho-tels (one on each side of State Road 436, north of the airport) offer suites with separate bedrooms and living room–kitchen areas. With red car-peting, gold drapes, an overstuffed couch and lounge chair, and of course, a coffeemaker, the living area has the warm feeling of the quintessential American home. The best factor is that you can pay for a suite and get change back from a $100 bill, even in high season. ✉ *7500 Augusta National Dr., Orlando International Airport 32822* ☎ *407/240–3939* 📠 *407/240–3920* ⊕ *www.amerisuites.com* ➮ *128 suites* � *In-room safes, microwaves, refrigerators, cable TV with movies, in-room broadband, pool, gym, hot tub, laundry facilities, laundry ser-vice, meeting rooms, no-smoking rooms* ✉ *5435 Forbes Pl., Orlando International Airport 32822* ☎ *407/816–7800 or 800/833–1516* 📠 *407/816–0050* ⊕ *www.amerisuites.com* ➮ *135 suites* � *In-room safes, microwaves, refrigerators, cable TV with movies, in-room broadband, pool, gym, hot tub, laundry facilities, laundry service, business services, meeting rooms, no-smoking rooms* ▤ *AE, D, DC, MC, V* ⑩ *BP.*

OUTLYING TOWNS

Travel farther afield and you can get more comforts and facilities for the money, and maybe even some genuine Orlando charm—of the cozy country-inn variety.

Altamonte Springs

Take I–4 Exit 92.

Staying among the suburban developments, office parks, and shopping malls of Altamonte Springs may not be as glamorous as dwelling with the Disney characters, but accommodations in this suburb, a 45-minute drive from the theme parks, cost on average about 35% less than com-parable lodgings elsewhere in the Orlando area. If you have a yen to visit Daytona Beach, you can get there in about 45 minutes, too. In ad-dition, the area is convenient to Enzo's on the Lake, one of Orlando's best restaurants, as well as to the jumbo Altamonte Mall. One warn-ing: much of the metro-area population lives in this northeastern sec-tor and works in central Orlando. I–4 rush hours can be a big problem.

$–$$ 🏨 **Hilton Orlando/Altamonte Springs.** Although the emphasis at this eight-story, concrete-and-glass tower is on the business traveler, the hotel's quiet elegance is a plus for everyone who stays here. The comfortable rooms are decorated with dark-green florals and prints. This hotel also has two floors of one- and two-bedroom suites and individual rooms with concierge service. Executive-level guests enjoy a free continental breakfast and another great bonus—free milk and cookies at the end of each day. ✉ *350 S. Northlake Blvd., 32715* ☎ *407/830–1985 or 800/445–8667* 🖷 *407/331–2911* ⊕ *www.hilton.com* 🛏 *322 rooms, 5 suites* ⚲ *Restaurant, room service, in-room safes, cable TV with movies, in-room broadband, pool, gym, outdoor hot tub, lobby lounge, laundry facilities, laundry service, concierge, concierge floor, business services, meeting rooms, no-smoking rooms* ▭ *AE, D, DC, MC, V* ⧈*CP.*

Davenport

Take I–4 Exit 55.

The beauty of Davenport is that virtually no one in Orlando has ever heard of it, even though it's only 13 mi southwest of Walt Disney World's main gate. The relative obscurity of this town makes it a bargain oasis. If you don't mind the absence of nightlife and entertainment, you'll save 30% or more at Davenport hotels, which surround I–4 at Exit 55 and Baseball City, the big stadium complex there, compared with the same hotel chains on International Drive. Both areas are about the same distance from WDW but in opposite directions.

¢–$$ 🏨 **Holiday Inn Express.** Large burgundy-accented rooms and suites at this tidy hotel have irons, ironing boards, hair dryers, and coffeemakers. There's no on-site restaurant, but a free continental breakfast buffet is set up in a small dining area near the lobby, and several chain restaurants are nearby. All rooms include microwaves and refrigerators. ✉ *43824 U.S. 27 N, 33837* ☎ *863/424–2120 or 800/225–3351* 🖷 *863/424–5317* ⊕ *www.hiexpress.com* 🛏 *104 rooms* ⚲ *Some microwaves, some refrigerators, cable TV, in-room broadband, pool, outdoor hot tub, laundry facilities, business services, meeting room, no-smoking rooms* ▭ *AE, D, DC, MC, V* ⧈*EP.*

$ 🏨 **Hampton Inn Orlando Maingate South.** They've taken some poetic (or marketing) license with the name here. For the record, the hotel is 27 mi from Walt Disney World's main entrance. Disney's south entrance is just 13 mi away, however, and the hotel offers good bargains and access to attractions west of Orlando, like Cypress Gardens and Fantasy of Flight. Rooms are bright and pleasant—some come with DVD players—and you get a free hot breakfast and local phone calls. ✉ *44117 U.S. 27 N, 33897* ☎ *407/345–1112 or 800/426–7866* 🖷 *407/352–6591* ⊕ *www. hamptoninn.com* 🛏 *83 rooms* ⚲ *Cable TV, in-room broadband, pool, exercise equipment, outdoor hot tub, laundry facilities, meeting room, business services, no-smoking rooms* ▭ *AE, D, DC, MC, V* ⧈*CP.*

¢–$ 🏨 **Best Western Maingate South.** The hotel is nothing extraordinary, but offers a nice palm-lined courtyard with a swimming pool and outdoor hot tub. The guest rooms, with pink and blue floral-pattern bedspreads and blue carpets, are pleasant if not palatial. There's no restaurant, but a Bob Evans Family Restaurant is just across the parking lot, and there's a free continental breakfast in a small dining area adjacent to the lobby. There's a free shuttle bus to Walt Disney World, plus shuttles to SeaWorld and Universal Orlando for a small fee. The hotel does allow pets less than 20 pounds with $10.00 nonrefundable charge per pet, per night. ⊠ *2425 Frontage Rd., 33837* ☎ *863/424–2596 or 800/424–1880* 🖷 *863/420–8717* ⊕ *www.bestwestern.com* 🖘 *113 rooms* ⟷ *Cable TV, in-room broadband, pool, outdoor hot tub, laundry facilities, some pets allowed (fee), business services, no-smoking rooms* ▤ *AE, D, DC, MC, V* ¡◎¡ *CP.*

Lake Mary

Take I–4 Exit 98C.

You may choose Lake Mary for the same reason the American Automobile Association moved its national headquarters here—it's close to Orlando but just far enough away from the theme park areas to be removed from the crowds. If you love the outdoors you'll appreciate Lake Mary's proximity to the Orlando area's most treasured natural resource, Wekiva Springs State Park. Daytona Beach is an easy one-hour drive away.

$–$$ ▦ **Hilton Garden Inn Lake Mary.** About 20 minutes north of downtown Orlando, this hotel is a great place to stay if you're driving into town late at night and want to avoid the heavy traffic on I–4. Free HBO, kitchenettes, and hot tubs in the suites are a few of this hotel's extras. If you don't want to cook, you can take your youngsters to the nearest Chuck E. Cheese's, about a mile away off Rinehart Road. Lake Mary is the quintessential upscale suburb, and you'll find plenty of shops and restaurants in the area. Wekiva Springs State Park is a 20-minute drive away. ⊠ *705 Currency Circle, 32746* ☎ *407/531–9900 or 800/445–8667* 🖷 *407/531–1144* ⊕ *www.hilton.com* 🖘 *123 rooms* ⟷ *Grocery, in-room safes, some in-room hot tubs, microwaves, refrigerators, cable TV with movies, in-room broadband, pool, health club, outdoor hot tub, bar, laundry facilities, laundry service, business services, no-smoking rooms* ▤ *AE, D, DC, MC.*

$–$$ ▦ **Marriott Lake Mary.** This stylish 10-story hotel markets itself to business travelers, but its location on the north side of Lake Mary gives it a strategic location for tourists as well. It's roughly equidistant between Disney World and Daytona Beach, with each about 40 mi away. The hotel offers a European-style flair, with a chic continental eatery, Bistro 1501, on the ground floor. All rooms have work desks and high-speed Internet access. ⊠ *1501 International Pkwy., 32746* ☎ *407/995–1100 or 888/236–2427* 🖷 *407/995–1150* ⊕ *www.marriott.com* 🖘 *299 rooms, 5 suites* ⟷ *Restaurant, room service, in-room safes, cable TV with movies, in-room broadband, pool, gym, outdoor hot tub, bar, laundry facilities, laundry service, concierge, concierge floor, business services, no-smoking rooms* ▤ *AE, D, DC, MC, V.*

¢–$ ▦ **Homewood Suites.** Part of a Hilton-owned chain, this all-suites hotel targets business travelers, but offers some great amenities that benefit families. Each suite has two TVs and a full kitchen. If you don't care to cook, there's a free full breakfast every day. You are also welcome to complimentary drinks during an evening social hour Monday through Thursday. T.G.I. Friday's and several other chain eateries are within a five-minute walk. ⊠ *755 Currency Circle, 32746* ☎ *407/805–9111 or 800/225–5466* 🖨 *407/805–0236* ⊕ *www.homewood-suites.com* ⇨ *112 suites* ⬧ *In-room safes, cable TV with movies, in-room broadband, pool, gym, outdoor hot tub, bar, laundry facilities, laundry service, concierge, concierge floor, business services, no-smoking rooms* ⊟ *AE, D, DC, MC, V* ⦿ *BP.*

Lake Wales

Take I–4 Exit 55 and U.S. 27 S.

South of greater Orlando, this town is a good base for people visiting Bok Tower Gardens or for those on their way to or from South Florida. It's within about 45 minutes of the parks.

$$$–$$$$ 🏨 **Chalet Suzanne.** This quiet, family-owned country inn, a world away from the world of Disney, was constructed in the 1930s, and subsequent updates have not taken away its original architectural charm. The buildings and winding pathways recall a Swiss village, despite the pink and blue paint. Some of the lovely antiques-dotted guest rooms have original tile baths, whereas others have whirlpools. The best overlook a lake or garden. But perhaps the biggest treat is a meal in the inn's elegant restaurant, where a six-course dinner is the house specialty. ⊠ *3800 Chalet Suzanne La., 33859* ☎ *863/676–6011 or 800/433–6011* 🖨 *863/676–1814* ⊕ *www.chaletsuzanne.com* ⇨ *30 rooms* ⬧ *Restaurant, cable TV, pool, lake, badminton, croquet, volleyball, bar, no-smoking rooms* ⊟ *AE, D, DC, MC, V* ⦿ *BP.*

Winter Park

Take I–4 Exit 87 or 88.

Winter Park, a small college town and greater Orlando's poshest and best-established neighborhood, is full of chichi shops and restaurants. If its heart is the main thoroughfare of Park Avenue, then its soul must be Central Park, an inviting greensward dotted with huge trees hung with Spanish moss. It feels a million miles away from the tourist track, but it's just a short drive from the major attractions.

$$–$$$$ 🏨 **Park Plaza Hotel.** Small and intimate, this 1922 establishment feels almost like a private home. Best accommodations are front garden suites with a living room that opens onto a long balcony usually abloom with impatiens and bougainvillea. Balconies are so covered with shrubs and ferns that they are somewhat private, inspiring more than a few romantic interludes, a member of management confided. There's not much for kids here, but for adults a half-dozen sidewalk cafés and many more upscale boutiques and shops surround the hotel. Also, the Charles Hosmer Morse Museum of Art is within two blocks. Park Plaza Gardens, the restaurant downstairs, offers quiet atrium dining and excellent upscale cuisine. ⊠ *307 Park Ave. S, 32789* ☎ *407/647–1072 or 800/228–7220* 🖨 *407/647–4081* ⊕ *www.parkplazahotel.com* ⇨ *27 rooms* ⬧ *Restaurant, room service, cable TV, lobby lounge, laundry service, no-smoking rooms; no kids under 5* ⊟ *AE, DC, MC, V.*

ORLANDO HOTEL CHART

HOTEL NAME	Worth Noting	Cost	Rooms	Suites/Villas	Kitchens	Restaurants	Kid's Programs	playground	Pools	Spa	Golf
The Disney Resorts											
All-Star Resorts	budget and family-friendly	$77–$131	5760				yes		6		
★ Animal Kingdom Lodge	exotic African theme	$199–$620	1293			3	yes		2	yes	priv.
Beach Club Villas	serene luxury	$294–$1040		205		1			3		priv.
★ BoardWalk Inn and Villas	lively and compact	$294–$1970	370	526		4	yes		1		priv.
★ Caribbean Beach Resort	basic and moderately-priced	$134–$209	2112			1	yes		7		priv.
Contemporary Resort	convenient and modern	$244–$695	1013	25		3	yes		3		priv.
Coronado Springs Resort	huge convention resort	$134–$209	1967			2	yes		4		priv.
Fort Wilderness Resort Cabins	rustic; good for families	$234–$339	408	yes			yes		2		
Fort Wilderness Campground	cheapest way to stay on-site	$38–$89	788	yes			yes		2		
★ Grand Floridian Resort & Spa	Victorian luxury	$349–$870	900	90		5	yes		3	yes	priv.
Old Key West Resort	good for groups	$259–$1505		761		1	yes		4	yes	priv.
Polynesian Resort	tropical island theme	$304–$720	858	5		4	yes		2		priv.
Pop Century Resort	latest budget option	$77–$131	2880				yes		2		priv.
Port Orleans Resort–French Quarter	New Orleans charm	$134–$209	1008			1			1		priv.
Port Orleans Resort–Riverside	Old South style	$134–$209	2048			1	yes		6		priv.
Saratoga Springs Resort	newest condo-style resort	$259–$1505	552			1			2	yes	priv.
★ Wilderness Lodge	like a National Park lodge	$199–$490	728	31		3	yes		1		
★ Yacht and Beach Club Resorts	refined, upscale, sophisticated	$294–$680	1213	112		4	yes		3		priv.
Other Hotels in WDW											
Best Western Lake Buena Vista	high-rise with fab views	$99–$139	325			1	yes		1		
DoubleTree Guest Suites	simple yet cheerful	$134–$168	229			1	yes		1		priv.
Grosvenor Resort	plain but upbeat & affordable	$99–$119	626	5		3	yes		2		
Hilton in the WDW Resort	renov. in 2004; beautiful views	$189–$249	814	27		7	yes		3		
Shades of Green	military only	$95–$200	586	11		4	yes		2		priv.

Name	Description	Rates										
★ Walt Disney World Dolphin	colorful hotel near Epcot	$339–$454	1509	136		9	yes		yes	5	yes	priv.
Walt Disney World Swan	colorful hotel near Epcot	$339–$454	756	55		6	yes		yes	5	yes	priv.
★ Wyndham Palace Resort & Spa	great restaurants & amenities	$233–$259	1014	209		4	yes		yes	3	yes	

Lake Buena Vista (LBV) Area

Name	Description	Rates										
Buena Vista Suites	basic but roomy suites	$119–$149		280		1				1		
Caribe Royale All-Suites Resort	big pink palace; fabulous pool	$179–$199	1218	120		4				1		
Celebrity Resorts Lake Buena Vista	very large family suites	$190–$306		66	yes	1	yes		yes	4		
Country Inn & Suites by Carlson	inexpensive family suites	$79–$99	170	50		1				1		
Embassy Suites Resort LBV	pink & turquoise standby	$159–$184		333		2	yes		yes	1		
Hawthorn Suites Resort LBV	least expensive family suites	$79–$109		120	yes		yes		yes	1		
Holiday Inn SunSpree	very popular Kidsuites	$69–$102	507			1			yes	1		
Homewood Suites Lake Buena Vista	Hilton-run all-suites chain	$129–$159		123	yes		yes			1	yes	
★ Hyatt Regency Grand Cypress	gorgeous pool; nature trails	$269–$344	750	210	yes	5	yes	yes	yes	2		3 courses
Marriott Residence Inn	Caribbean-style oasis	$129–$154		400		8	yes		yes	3		
Marriott Village at Little Lake Bryan	private gated property	$93–$129	700	400	yes	8	yes		yes	3		
Nickelodeon Family Suites	kids love the Nick theme	$189–$265		800	yes	3	yes		yes	2		1 course
Orlando World Center Marriott	huge convention hotel	$239–$292	2000	357		7	yes		yes	4		priv.
★ PerriHouse Bed & Breakfast Inn	small B&B in nature preserve	$105–$150	8			1				1		
Riu Orlando Hotel	looks like an office park	$90–$120	167			1				1		
Sheraton Safari Hotel	fun jungle theme; large rooms	$129–$169	489	96	yes	2				1		
Sheraton Vistana Resort	sprawling all-suites retreat	$140–$189	0	1700	yes	2		yes		7		

Kissimmee

Name	Description	Rates										
AmeriSuites LBV South	budget vacation club	$89–$119		151	yes	2				1		
Celebration Hotel	grand Victorian-style hotel	$149–$199	115							1		priv.

HOTEL NAME	Worth Noting	Cost	Rooms	Suites/Villas	Kitchens	Restaurants	Kid's Programs	playground	Pools	Spa	Golf
Celebrity Resorts Kissimmee	large family suites	$74–$119	311		yes	1	yes		4		
DoubleTree Resort Villas	Spanish-style villa complex	$109–$134	150			1			1		
★ Gaylord Palms Resort	huge, flashy, FLA.-theme hotel	$269–$319	1406	86		4	yes		2	yes	priv.
Holiday Inn Maingate West	classic HI with Kidsuites	$79–$119	295	30		1			1		
La Quinta Inn Lakeside	27 lakeside acres	$79–$99	651			2	yes	yes	3		
Magical Memories Villas	sunny, colorful, affordable	$89–$119	140		yes		yes		1		
Omni Orlando Resort	deluxe hotel and golf resort	$224–$279	730	32		5	yes		2	yes	2 courses
★ Radisson Resort Parkway	pool with waterfalls & slide	$83–$119	712	8		2	yes		2		
★ Reunion Resort & Club of Orlando	ultra-luxurious golf retreat	$235–$299		60	1	1	yes		1	yes	3 courses
Seralago Hotel & Suites	Wild West-theme Kidsuites	$56–$85	614	110	yes	1	yes	yes	2		
In Universal Orlando											
Hard Rock Hotel	rock 'n' roll theme	$234–$274	621	29		3	yes		2		
Portofino Bay Hotel	Italian Riviera theme	$269–$324	699	51		3	yes	yes	3	yes	
★ Royal Pacific Resort	South Pacific theme	$204–$244	1000	113		3	yes		1		
Near Universal Orlando											
DoubleTree Hotel	renov. in 2005	$143–$179	742	15		1	yes	yes	2		priv.
Holiday Inn Hotel & Suites	simple but well located	$89–$119	390	120		1		yes	1		
Sleep Inn & Suites	basic rooms, good prices	$84–$109	196	40	yes			yes	1		
★ Studio PLUS	cheap suites with kitchens	$69–$83		84	yes				1		
Suburban Extended Stay America	attractive red-brick gem	$49–$69	150				yes	yes	1		
International Drive											
DoubleTree Castle	medieval castle theme	$99–$119	216			2		yes	1		
Embassy Suites I-Drive South	marble lobby	$179–$189		244	1				2		
Embassy Suites Jamaican Court	comfy two-room suites	$139–$179		246					1		
Enclave Suites	large condo complex	$99–$139	321		yes		yes		3		

Hotel	Description	Price									
Holiday Inn Hotel & Suites	bright-yellow, cheerful hotel	$79–$109	115	35	yes	1			2		
Inn of America	no-frills budget property	$89–$99	134						1		
★ JW Marriott Orlando Grande Lakes	business-traveler favorite	$249–$329	1000	57		4			1	yes	1 course
La Quinta Inn & Suites Orlando	off-the-beaten-path chain	$89–$129	170	15					1		
Marriott Residence Inn SeaWorld	grills & playground	$99–$139		350	yes			yes	1		
Marriott's Cypress Harbour Resort	lots of outdoor activities	$189–$249	510			2	yes	yes	3		priv.
Parc Corniche Condominium Suites	Joe Lee golf course	$89–$119	210			1		yes	1		1 course
★ Peabody Orlando	loveable ducks live here	$295–$325	891			3			1	yes	priv.
Renaissance Orlando at SeaWorld	10-story tropical atrium	$194–$209	778			4			1		priv.
☆ Ritz-Carlton Orlando Grande Lakes	excellent service; fit for royalty	$249–$339	520	64		4	yes		1	yes	1 course
Rosen Centre Hotel	gaudy convention hotel	$189–$219	1334	80		3			1		
Rosen Plaza Hotel	gaudy convention hotel	$99–$129	810			2			1		
Sheraton Studio City	Hollywood theme	$89–$119	302			1			1		
Sheraton World Resort	upscale with a tropical theme	$179–$208	1102	68	yes	3			3		
Sierra Suites Hotel	business-traveler favorite	$96–$129		262	yes				1		
Staybridge Suites International Drive	modern budget suites	$129–$149		146	yes				1		
Studio PLUS Orlando Convention Ctr.	budget suites near SeaWorld	$45–$55		113					1		
Travelodge Orlando Convention Ctr.	small rooms with balconies	$59–$99	144			1			2		
Wyndham Orlando Resort	Caribbean-style getaway	$156–$179	1064			3			3		

Downtown Orlando

Hotel	Description	Price									
★ Courtyard at Lake Lucerne	Victorian B&Bs	$115–$215	15	15							
Embassy Suites Orlando Downtown	up-to-date & well-located	$135–$159	167			1			1		
★ Eō Inn & Urban Spa	stylish boutique hotel	$129–$169	17							yes	
Westin Grand Bohemian	sumptuous rooms & artwork	$209–$299	250	36		1			1		

HOTEL NAME	Worth Noting	Cost	Rooms	Suites/Villas	Kitchens	Restaurants	Kid's Programs	playground	Pools	Spa	Golf
Orlando International Airport											
AmeriSuites Orlando Airport NE & NW	budget suites near airport	$65–$95		263					1		
Florida Mall Hotel	walk to the mall	$129–$149	510			1			1		
Hyatt Regency Orlando Intl. Airport	restaurant with a view	$199–$224	446			2			1		
Outlying Towns											
Best Western Maingate South	close to Davenport	$69–$99	113						1		
Chalet Suzanne	country inn with great meals	$169–$229	30			1			1		
Hampton Inn Maingate South	13 mi south of WDW	$99–$109	83						1		
Hilton Garden Inn Lake Mary	20 mi north of Orlando	$89–$119	123						1		
Hilton Orlando/Altamonte Springs	quiet elegance north of town	$109–$129	322	5		1			1		
Holiday Inn Express Disney South	15 mi south of WDW	$75–$129	104						1		
Homewood Suites Lake Mary	20 mi north of Orlando	$79–$99		112					1		
Marriott Lake Mary	20 mi north of Orlando	$109–$129	299	5		1			1		
Park Plaza Hotel Winter Park	1922 boutique hotel	$115–$225	27			1			1		

Shopping

7

FODOR'S CHOICE

Belz Factory Outlet World, *in the I-Drive Area*
Downtown Disney, *in Walt Disney World*
Florida Mall, *in the I-Drive Area*
Main Street, U.S.A., Magic Kingdom, *in Walt Disney World*
Mall at Millenia, *in the I-Drive Area*
World Showcase, Epcot, *in Walt Disney World*

Updated by
Alicia Rivas

FROM FAIRYTALE KINGDOMS TO OLD WEST–STYLE TRADING POSTS TO OUTLET MALLS, Walt Disney World and Orlando have a plethora of shopping opportunities. The colors are bright and energetic, the textures soft and cuddly, and the designs fresh and thoughtful. Before you board any roller coaster or giggle at any show, you will catch yourself window shopping and delighting in the thought of making a purchase. And when it comes time to do some serious shopping, you may have a hard time deciding what to buy with all the options available. Of course, your best bet is to wait a couple of days before you buy anything; survey the scene a little before spending all the money in your budget.

The one store not to miss is World of Disney in the Marketplace section of Downtown Disney. You could actually skip all of the stores in the theme parks and find everything you want at this store in an hour. And it may be a cliché, but there really is something for everyone, whether you're looking for a small inexpensive souvenir, such as the $3 princess pen, or a Disney collectible, like a Mickey watch or figurine.

WALT DISNEY WORLD

Even if you're not inclined to buy, the shops on Disney property are worth a look. Across the board, they are open, inviting, cleverly themed, and have beautiful displays. Of course, you could easily pick up $100 worth of goods before you've ventured even 10 feet into a store, but you're better off practicing some restraint. Enjoy the experience of just looking first. If you see something you like, think about it while you enjoy the rest of your day. You might see something even better in the next store. If you're still thinking of that beautiful stuffed Cheshire cat or Cinderella snow globe at the end of the day, you can always go back to get it. That way you don't weigh yourself down with purchases until you're ready to leave. If you're a Disney hotel guest, you never have to carry off your purchases—Disney stores will deliver your merchandise to your room for free.

Also, don't let the price tags scare you off. Small souvenirs (key chains, pens, small toys, etc.) for less than $10 are available in almost every store. Just be careful with souvenir-hungry kids. Many attractions exit directly into gift shops. Even if you put your kid on a strict budget, he may be overwhelmed by the mind-boggling choices at hand and be completely unable to make a selection. If you return home and realize that you've forgotten a critical souvenir, call WDW's Merchandise Mail Order service at 407/363–6200.

Magic Kingdom

Everywhere you turn in the Magic Kingdom there are shops and stalls urging you to take home a little piece of the magic.

Main Street, U.S.A.

Main Street, U.S.A., which serves as your gateway to the Magic Kingdom, is end to end with little shops selling clothing and memorabilia. Fodor'sChoice **The Chapeau** sells those classic monogrammed mouse ears. The hats won't ★ stay on all day, though, and they'll get squished in a backpack, so this is another good souvenir to get at the end of the day. Or buy a Disney baseball cap to protect you from the sun.

The **Main Street Market House** is a fun little shop for foodies looking to add a little Disney to their kitchen. It's also a great place to pick up some inexpensive keepsakes. Tubby little Mickey coffee mugs go for around $10, and Mickey's "Really Swell" coffee can be had for $7.50 per half-pound. Whimsical Goofy chef's aprons for $16 also make great gifts. For the kids, who always seem to cost more, there are Mickey waffle irons, and toasters that will toast the mighty mouse's image onto your bread.

Uptown Jewelers is a great spot for window shopping. Along with a dazzling display of jewelry, figurines, and collectible Disney lithographs, you can see Disney artists at work in the Watchmaker's corner. The artists sketch Disney characters and themes for the watch faces that are then built into Citizens watches. Ranging in price from $200–$350, these one-of-a-kind watches are exclusive to this store and cannot be purchased anywhere else.

Serious collectors of Disney memorabilia stop at **Main Street Gallery,** next to City Hall. Limited-edition sculptures, dolls, posters, and sometimes even park signs are available. You can buy a Pal Mickey plush toy stuffed with a receiver and audio device that plays sound tracks at various attractions—it's as if Mickey is giving you a personal guided tour of his kingdom.

The big daddy of all Magic Kingdom shops is the **Emporium.** This 17,000-square-foot store stocks thousands of Disney character products, from sunglasses to stuffed animals. Girls will be thrilled to see lots of princess items, including pillows and pajamas. One of the best souvenirs ever is a princess cameo ring encircled with feathers. At $2 each, the rings are a very inexpensive way to give your little princess a gem of her own. Although perpetually crowded and absolutely mobbed at closing time, the Emporium is, hands down, one of the best sources for souvenirs. Hang on to your kids in here; they're likely to wander away as they spot yet another trinket they have to have.

Adventureland

Just outside the Pirates of the Caribbean ride, the **Pirate's Bazaar** is a good place to shop for your next Halloween costume. The pirate hats, swords, and hooks-for-hands are a hit with everyone who has a bit of the scoundrel in them. And if you think you're too cool for a souvenir T-shirt, the Bazaar's hip and slightly Gothic shirts will make you reconsider. There are gritty, almost sinister skull-and-bones appliqués on biker vests, skull caps, and even beer koozies. Movie novelty collectors can buy any number of items with the logo from the *Pirates of the Caribbean* film.

Nearby, the **Agrabah Bazaar** has Aladdin-wear and the all-important Jasmine costume, as well as Moroccan-made carpets, carvings, and masks.

Frontierland

Emporia in Frontierland are generally referred to as "posts," as in the **Frontier Trading Post,** which is largely devoted to Disney collector pin trading. Large signs with advice for pin traders indicate that this place is a real trading post as well as a store.

The **Prairie Outpost & Supply,** sells sheriff badges, leatherwork, cowboy hats, and southwestern, Native American, and Mexican crafts. Yee-haw!

Popular among boys are the Davy Crockett coonskin hats and personalized sheriff badges at **Big Al's,** across from the Country Bear Jamboree.

The **Briar Patch,** next door to Splash Mountain, looks like the inside of a tree hollow, with big, snarled roots across the ceiling and a pair of old wooden rockers in front of the hearth. If you're lucky enough to grab one of the rockers, you can rest your feet a spell while your kids snuggle and cuddle the many plush toys in the shop.

History buffs can find presidential and Civil War memorabilia at Liberty Square's **Heritage House.**

Fantasyland

For the famous black Mouseketeer hats, head to **Sir Mickey's.**

After you ride the Many Adventures of Winnie the Pooh, you end up at **Pooh's Thotful Shop,** a small store devoted entirely to Pooh merchandise, although these items are also available in other Disney stores.

Tinker Bell's Treasures is pretty much princessland, with sparkly, shimmering dresses, hats, dolls, and jewelry. You can even take home your very own Cinderella Castle for a mere $55.

Toontown's **County Bounty** is a voluminous carnival-tentlike store centered around a giant, cylindrical Mr. Potato Head dispenser. For $18, you get a potato head, a box, and all the accessories you can stuff inside the box. Some of the pieces are classic Mr. Potato Head parts, others are all Disney. There are mouse ears, Goofy hats, Minnie Bows, and so on. With an estimated 40 different parts to choose from, this may be the most interactive purchase you ever make.

Inside Cinderella Castle, the **King's Gallery** sells items to help you furnish your own castle, like imported European clocks, chess sets, and tapestries.

Epcot

There are a few stores in Future World, but it's the World Showcase that has the really unique gifts.

World Showcase

Fodor's Choice ★ Each of the countries represented has at least one gift shop loaded with things reflective of the history and culture of that nation's homeland, and many of the items are authentic imported handicrafts.

If your shopping time is limited, check out the two shops at the entrance to World Showcase. **Disney Traders** sells Disney dolls dressed in various national costumes as well as the requisite T-shirts and sweatshirts. Also sold here—and at some scattered kiosks throughout the park—is a great keepsake for youngsters: a World Showcase Passport ($9.95). At each pavilion, children can present their passports to be stamped—it's a great way to keep their interest up in this more adult area of Epcot. At **Port of Entry,** you'll find lots of merchandise for kids, including clothing and art kits.

UNITED KINGDOM Anglophiles will find their hearts gladdened upon entering the cobblestoned village at the United Kingdom, where an English Pub sits on one side, and a collection of British, Irish, and Scottish shops beckon you on the other. Consider the possibilities of an English garden at the **Magic of Wales.** You can pick up gardening tools, flower pots, and lavender potpourri. Take your time exploring the **Crown & Crest,** which has impressive handcrafted chess, some featuring the characters from *Alice in Wonderland.* If you wish you still had that Beatles lunch box from childhood, you might be able to buy a replacement here. Or perhaps you'll marvel at the magnificent knight's swords that can be had for $285 to $525.

FRANCE In France, keep a nose out for Guerlain perfume and cosmetics at **La Signature.** Every princess needs a tiny Limoges porcelain box for her earrings; look for the perfect one in the exquisite **Plume et Palette.** At **Les Vins de France,** you can do some wine tasting and then pick up a bottle of your favorite.

MOROCCO Morroco has an open-air market like something out of an Indiana Jones movie. It's also a great place to pick up something really different, like a Morrocan tarboosh or fez for $8. If you're feeling really exotic, you can buy a belly dancing kit, complete with a scarf, hat, finger cymbals, and a CD for $110.

JAPAN Instead of another princess doll, consider the kimonoed dolls at **Mitsukoshi.** Or instead of another T-shirt, consider a silk kimono. Koi ponds, Taiko drummers, and an impressive Bonsai tree collection will help to bring a moment of serenity to your trip, that is until one of the kids catches a glimpse of the Japanese toys, collectibles, and candy artistry for sale here.

ITALY For chic Italian handbags, accessories, and collectibles, stop in at **Il Bel Cristallo.** Other gifts to look for include Venetian beads and glasswork, olive oils, pastas, and Perugia cookies and chocolate kisses (*baci*).

GERMANY In Germany, pay a visit to the **Weinkeller,** where you can sample German wines by the glass. There are plenty to choose from, including rare German Eis wines. For a good conversation piece, check out the nutcrackers at **Die Weinachts Ecke.**

SALUTING AFRICA OUTPOST At the **Village Traders,** wood carvers from Kenya whittle beautiful giraffes, elephants, and other animals while you watch. If you ask, the carvers may tell you stories about their homeland as they work. Each piece is unique, and some are a bit pricey, but you can buy an intricately carved wooden flute for $15. You'll find items from India and Australia for sale, too.

CHINA **Yong Feng Shangdian** is considered by some well-traveled guests to be the largest Chinese department store in the United States. It has exquisite desks, cabinets, and dining-room furniture featuring heavy lacquer and beautiful inlays. There are also handpainted figurines, hand-carved chess sets, traditional clothing, and colorful parasols upon which you can have your name painted in Chinese.

NORWAY You can find Norwegian pewter, leather goods, and colorful sweaters at the **Puffin's Roost.** Viking wannabes can check out the spears, shields, and helmets.

MEXICO For a fun and colorful gift for kids, consider the piñatas at **Plaza de los Amigos,** in Mexico. Other good souvenirs include brightly colored paper blossoms, sombreros, baskets, pottery, and leather goods.

Future World

Future World shopping won't tempt you to spend a lot of money unless you're heavily into the art of Disney animation. For the serious collector, the **Art of Disney** sells limited-edition figurines and cels (the sheets of celluloid on which cartoons are drawn). **Green Thumb Emporium,** in the Land pavilion, sells kitchen- and garden-related knickknacks—from hydroponic plants to vegetable refrigerator magnets. **Mouse Gear,** the biggest Disney apparel store at Epcot, has a very impressive selection of Disney and Epcot logo items. You can pick up sweats emblazoned with Disney characters exercising at **Well & Goods Limited** in the Wonders of Life. Racing and automobile enthusiasts will likely be a bit disappointed by **Inside Track** near the Test Track exit. It sells some racing merchandise and other car-related items, but with less of a selection than a racing hobbyist store.

Disney–MGM Studios

Hollywood Boulevard

Hollywood Boulevard is set up like Main Street U.S.A. in the Magic Kingdom—you can bypass the shops on your way in because you'll pass them again on the way out.

Of the shops here, **Sid Cahuenga's One-of-a-Kind,** an antiques and curios store, is the most interesting. With its bungalow style architecture and 1930s phonograph music playing in the background, this very cool little shop might trick you into thinking it's actually a vintage store. You can pick up autographed items, such as a $425 Indiana Jones publicity photo signed by Harrison Ford. If you're a die-hard Old Blue Eyes fan, you can buy an authentic Frank Sinatra–signed picture for $2,475. Sid's even sells clothes worn by your favorite soap star. A dress worn by Susan Lucci might set you back a couple of hundred bucks.

If you're in the market for something you can actually wear, pop in to **Keystone Clothiers.** This store is full of Mickey clothing that is clearly geared toward adults. The styles are hip and trendy, with some items capitalizing on popular vintage styles. Backpacks, for instance, sport vintage Mickey or vintage 1930s Sleeping Beauty artwork. For kid's clothing, go to **L.A. Prop Cinema Storage,** at the corner of Sunset and Hollywood.

Echo Lake
Almost as popular as the pirate swords and hats in the Magic Kingdom are the Indiana Jones bullwhips and fedoras sold at the **Indiana Jones Adventure Outpost,** next to the stunt amphitheater, and the Darth Vader and Wookie masks at **Tatooine Traders,** outside of Star Tours. Serious Star Wars collectors might also find the action figure that's been eluding them, as well as books and comics. It's a busy store that inspires browsing.

New York Street
The Writer's Stop offers one of the few decent cups of coffee to be had in Disney parks, as well as Earl Grey tea. If you happen to hit it right, you might get a book signed by a celebrity author, but the shop is small, the book selection is limited, and it's not conducive to hanging around. It is, however, a good place to pick up an autograph book. **It's a Wonderful Shop,** open seasonally, is where to pick up special Christmas decorations.

Animation Courtyard
Budding animators can hone their talents with Paint-a-Cel, a kit with two picture cels ready to be illustrated sold at the **Animation Gallery.**

Sunset Boulevard
If you have younger children, consider a stop at **Legends of Hollywood** on Sunset Boulevard—it's brimming with Pooh-theme kids' clothing, toys, and accessories. Making the most of villains in vogue, the **Beverly Sunset** has Disney's best bad guys: Cruella DeVil, Mufasa, and the Siamese cats from *Lady and the Tramp.* You can also pick up weird Tim Burton wear featuring characters from *The Nightmare Before Christmas.*

Disney's Animal Kingdom

Before you pass through the turnstiles on your way into the Animal Kingdom, stop at the **Outpost Shop** for a must-have safari hat with Mouse ears.

If you're traveling with small children, you won't escape Animal Kingdom without a visit to Dinoland U.S.A., where you'll find **Chester & Hester's Dinosaur Treasures.** This purposely tacky tourist outlet is the Animal Kingdom's premier toy store, with the toys mostly being of the prehistoric sort.

For African imports and animal items, as well as T-shirts, toys, and trinkets, check out the Harambe village shops. **Mombasa Marketplace and Ziwani Traders,** which you'll spot as you leave Kilimajaro Safaris, sells $10 Animal Kingdom over-the-shoulder water bottle holders, $19 colorful African sarongs, plush safari animals, and T-shirts with sparkly, leopard-print, Mickey silhouettes. Kids will be drawn to the unique African percussion and wind instruments—flutes cost just $2.50.

At **Creature Comforts** (before you cross from Discovery Island to Harambe), you can get a Minnie Mouse headband with a safari-style bow, sunglasses, prince and princess costumes, and great kiddie togs. **Island Mercantile,** to the left as you enter Discovery Island, has loads of little trinkets, like Mickey pens and key chains, plus cute, safari, Tigger and Pooh backpacks for $30, and Disney headgear for your dog.

Disney Outfitters, directly across from Island Mercantile and by the Tip Board, is another spot for finding some unique items. Kenana Knitter Critters are sized-for-stuffing stockings knit by Kenyan women who sign the tags. Made from soft, earth-tone yarns, each $30 stocking has an adorable animal head. You'll also find pottery with colorful safari scenes hand painted by artists in Zimbabwe. Prices range from $20 for a ramekin to $50 for a salt and pepper set.

Downtown Disney

FodorsChoice The largest concentration of stores on Disney property is found in
★ Downtown Disney. This three-in-one shopping and entertainment complex comprises the Marketplace, West Side, and Pleasure Island, which is known primarily for its clubs.

Marketplace
A lakefront outdoor mall with meandering sidewalks, hidden alcoves, jumping fountains that kids can splash around in, and absolutely fabulous toy stores, the Marketplace is a great place to spend a relaxing afternoon or evening, especially if you're looking for a way to give the kids a break from standing in line. There are plenty of spots to grab a bite, rest your feet, or enjoy a cup of coffee while taking in the pleasant water views and the hustle and bustle of excited tourists. The Marketplace is generally open from 9:30 AM to 11 PM. If you happen to run out of cash while you're shopping, you can apply for instant Disney credit at any register. How convenient.

LEGO Imagination Center. An impressive backdrop of large and elaborate LEGO sculptures and piles of colorful LEGO pieces wait for children and their parents to build toy kitties, cars, or cold fusion chambers. ☎407/828–0065.

Once Upon A Toy. A joint venture by Disney and Hasbro, this huge toy store is the kind of place childhood dreams are made of. There are tons of classic games redesigned with Disney themes. You'll find Princess Monopoly and the Pirates of the Caribbean Game of Life, just to name a couple. Overhead is a massive Tinker Toy creation and an oversized toy train making the rounds on a suspended track. Toys in the main room seem to be mostly for boys, but another room has a huge faux-candy castle and a My Little Pony Creation Station. You can test drive many of the toys and play with touch-screen computers. With so many things to do, this is one store that might let you escape without making a purchase. ☎ *407/934–7775.*

World of Disney. You might make it through Once Upon a Toy without pulling out your wallet, but you probably won't be so lucky at World of Disney. For Disney fans, this is *the* Disney superstore. It pushes you into sensory overload with nearly a half-million Disney items from Tinkerbell wings to Tigger hats. But if you have girls in your party, it's the Princess Room that will get you into the most trouble. Five-foot-tall likenesses of Cinderella and Sleeping Beauty stand watch over hoards of little misses scrambling to pick out just the right accessories. Besides princess dolls, clothes, shoes, and jewelry, you can buy a Belle (or Cinderella or Sleeping Beauty) wig to complete the look. Be warned, if you have a princess-obsessed child, the dazzling $55 princess dresses are going to be a must-have in her eyes, and people will be plucking them off the racks left and right of her. Of course there are things in the $10 to $30 range, including some cute pajamas, but it's hard to compare with those dresses. For grown-ups there are elegant watches, limited-edition artwork, and stylish furniture pieces with a Disney twist. ☎ *407/828–1451.*

Pin Traders. It's nice to know that you can visit the biggest and best location for pin collectors without paying park admission. The Marketplace location has not only the largest selection, it also sells many limited-edition pins that are hard to find elsewhere. There are enough pins lining the walls to make you go cross-eyed, but the employees in this shop know their inventory very well, so if you're looking for something in particular, be sure to ask. And if you're having trouble managing your collection, you can buy additional lanyards, pin bags, and cork boards, too. ☎ *407/828–1451.*

West Side

The West Side is generally a wide promenade bordered by an intriguing mix of shops and restaurants. There are also gift shops attached to **Cirque du Soleil, DisneyQuest,** the **House of Blues,** and **Planet Hollywood.**

Guitar Gallery. This shop sells videos, music books, accessories, guitars, guitars, and more guitars, ranging in price from $89 to $20,000. Keep an eye open for the guitar heroes who drop in prior to gigs at the neighboring House of Blues. If you miss your favorite musician, the clerks have had the stars sign oversize guitar picks, which they display throughout the store. ☎ *407/827–0118.*

Magic Masters. This small shop is arguably the most popular one here. As the magician on duty performs close-up card tricks and sleight of hand, an enraptured audience packs the shop for the free show. After the trick is finished, the sales pitch begins with a promise that (if you buy) they'll teach you how to do that particular feat of prestidigitation before you leave. ☎ *407/827–5900.*

Magnetron. As the name implies, this place sells magnets—some 20,000 of them. So what's the big attraction? Well, they light up, change color, glow in the dark, and come in every shape, size, color, and pop culture character (check out magneto-Elvis). ☎ *407/827–0108.*

Sosa Family Cigar Company. Cigars are kicking ash at this family-owned business. A fella's usually rolling stogies by hand in the front window and there's even a humidor room filled with see-gars. Smoking! ☎ *407/ 827–0114.*

Starabilia's. If you're comfortable paying a few hundred simoleons for a framed, autographed picture of the cast of your favorite '70s sitcom, stop by Starabilia's. Although prices for the memorabilia run high—shoppers have paid from $195 for a Pee-Wee Herman autograph to $250,000 for a Hofner bass signed by The Beatles—you can't lose any money window-shopping, and the turnover of goods means the inventory's always entertaining. ☎ *407/827–0104.*

Virgin Megastore. At 49,000 square feet, this enormous store has a selection as large as its prices. You can find better deals elsewhere, but not every record store has around 150,000 music titles, more than 300 listening stations, a full-service café, a 10,000-square-foot book department, clothing, accessories, and tens of thousands of DVD, software, and video titles. ☎ *407/828–0222.*

There are several smaller, yet still enjoyable, shops along the **West Side pedestrian mall.** If you need a boost of sugar, the **Candy Cauldron** is filled with chocolate, fudge, hard candy, and other similarly wholesome foods. **Celebrity Eyeworks** carries designer sunglasses as well as replicas of glasses worn by celebrities in popular (as well as forgettable) films of the last few decades. **Mickey's Groove** has hip lamps, posters, greeting cards, and souvenirs inspired by the rodent. **Hoypolloi** adds art to the mix, with beautifully creative sculptures in various mediums—glass, wood, clay, and metals.

UNIVERSAL ORLANDO

Universal Studios Florida

Every ride and attraction has its affiliated theme shop; in addition, Rodeo Drive and Hollywood Boulevard are pockmarked with money pits. It's important to remember that few attraction-specific souvenirs are sold outside of their own shop. So if you're struck by a movie- and ride-related pair of boxer shorts, seize the moment—and the shorts. Other choice souvenirs include Universal Studios' trademark movie clipboard, available at the **Universal Studio Store**; sepia prints of Richard Gere, Mel Gibson, and Marilyn Monroe from **Silver Screen Collectibles**; supercool Blues Brothers sunglasses from **Shaiken's Souvenirs**; plush animals, available at **Safari Outfitters, Ltd.** Stop by Hollywood's **Brown Derby** for the perfect topper, from fedoras to bush hats from *Jurassic Park*.

Islands of Adventure

From your own stuffed Cat in the Hat to a *Jurassic Park* dinosaur and a Blondie mug, you can find just about every pop culture icon in take-home form here. **Wossamotta U.** is a good source for Bullwinkle stuffed animals and clothing. The **Dinostore** in Jurassic Park has a *Tyrannosaurus rex* that looks as if he's hatching from an egg, and (yes, mom) educational dino toys, too. Watch for—or watch out for—the **Comics Shop**. Kids may not be able to leave without a Spider-Man toy.

Merlin wannabes should head for **Shop of Wonders** in the Lost Continent to stock on magic supplies. And poncho collectors can get one at **Gasoline Alley** in Toon Lagoon, along with clever blank books and cartoon-character hats and wigs that recall Daisy Mae and others. For a last-minute spree, the **Universal Studios Islands of Adventure Trading Company**, in the Port of Entry, stocks the park's most popular souvenirs.

CityWalk

To spice up the mix of CityWalk's entertainment and nightlife, Universal added stores geared to trendy teens and middle-age conventioneers who can't go back home without a little something. Most stores are tucked between buildings on your left and right when you exit the moving walkway that rolls in from the parking garages, and a few are hidden upstairs—watch for the large overhead signs. Hours vary but are generally 11 AM–11 PM, closing at midnight on weekends. CityWalk parking is free after 6 PM. You can call the shops directly or get complete theme-park, nightlife, and shopping information from **Universal Orlando** (☎ 407/363–8000 ⊕ www.citywalkorlando.com).

All Star Collectibles. Some sports collectors will buy anything signed, thrown, hit, or scratched by their favorite players. That's where All Star comes in. This place appeals to sports junkies with its one-of-a-kind objects and paraphernalia that professional autograph hounds hound athletes into signing. If you follow Florida sports, the state's college and professional teams are well represented. ☎ *407/224–2380*.

Cartooniversal. Small but packed with great products, Cartooniversal is the place to pick up your kid's favorite cartoon hero: Spider-Man, Spongebob, and the Cat and the Hat are everywhere. A big plush Scooby Doo goes for $29.95, and X-Men T-shirts go for $14.95. ☎ *407/224–2464*.

Cigarz. You have to duck down an alley to find this store, but the heavy aroma wafting from within might help to guide you. Just be careful not to walk into the giant Indian as you step through the doorway. Cigarz has a walk-in humidor, a full-length bar, and plenty of tables and ashtrays for enjoying your newly acquired stogie. Employees here take great pride in having hard-to-find smokes always in stock. Labels like OpusX, Ashton VSG, and Diamond Crown Maximus can be had for $9–$20 each, but you have to ask. Cigarz is open daily from 11 AM to 2 AM. ☎ *407/370–2999*.

Endangered Species. Designed to resemble a jungle, this store aims to raise awareness of endangered species, ecosystems, and cultures worldwide.

Some items, such as plush toys made by Aurora World Inc., clearly state on the tags that a portion of the proceeds are donated to conservation efforts. Periodically, artists, authors, and educators come in to discuss issues regarding the preservation of the planet. ☎ *407/224–2310.*

Fresh Produce Sportswear. Bright, colorful beach clothes for women are sold here. Everything is made from 100% cotton, and the styles are loose and relaxed. You won't find much for dad, but moms and daughters can pick up matching outfits. ☎ *407/363–9363.*

Glow! Teens and preteens are the main market for Glow! Illuminated exclusively by black lights, there are lots of glow-in-the-dark stickers, shirts, candleholders, and wall hangings. ☎ *407/224–2401.*

Jimmy Buffett's Margaritaville. If you absolutely *must* buy a Jimmy Buffett souvenir and can't make it to Key West, this is the next best thing. You can stock up on JB T-shirts, books, toy guitars, margarita glasses, sunglasses, picture frames, license plates, key chains, and theme hats (cheeseburger, parrot, and toucan). ☎ *407/224–2144.*

Quiet Flight. Florida has managed to turn a natural detriment (small waves) into an asset—Florida's Cocoa Beach is the "Small Wave Capital of the World." This explains Quiet Flight, which sells surfwear like Billabong, Quicksilver, and Oakley. You'll find plenty of clothes but no surf boards. You can, however, shop for a skateboard. Quiet Flight opens a little earlier than other CityWalk stores, so you can start shopping at 9 AM. ☎ *407/224–2126.*

Universal Studios Store. Although impressive in size, this store does not have all of the merchandise that's available in the individual park gift shops. Only the best-sellers are for sale here—T-shirts, stuffed animals, and limited-edition comic book artwork. What's exclusive to this store are the mini movie posters, featuring some of Universal Studios greatest monster movies, priced at $11.99. It's also one of the few places on the property selling Universal trading pins. While you're here, be sure to check the back of the store for clearance racks. ☎ *407/224–2207.*

SEAWORLD

Just as Disney offers all things Mickey, SeaWorld offers all things Shamu. If the classic plush Shamu toy isn't your thing, then perhaps you'd like a handpainted Shamu martini glass from **Ocean Treasures** at The Waterfront, where you can also find some rather sophisticated black-and-white Shamu T-shirts as well as demure Shamu desk accessories for the office.

The Waterfront, a promenade lined with open-air restaurants and shops, resembles an international bazaar. You'll find wood carvings, handcrafted jewelry, and dinnerware painted with brilliant tropical flowers.

The sweet scents of tropical fruits lure you into the **Tropica Trading Company,** where you can design your own scent at the Fragrance Blending Bar. You can also pick up glasses hand-painted with tropical fish, and add to your resort-wear wardrobe while you're at it.

Allura's Treasure Trove has an enchanting assortment of mermaids and mermaid apparel. Plus, a corner of the store is devoted to Design a Doll, which allows you to select the face, eye color, hair color, and clothing you'd like for your own individual doll. The price for the basic doll is $29, and accessories cost between $3.99 and $43.99.

If you've promised your little one a stuffed toy, you might want to hold out until you've been through the **Wild Arctic gift shop,** which has an irresistible collection of soft, white, baby seals and fluffy polar bears. It's hard to walk past them without hugging at least one. You might also consider a soft manatee toy, available from **Manatee Gifts,** west of Dolphin Stadium. Proceeds from the toys go to benefit a manatee preservation organization.

During your visit, a park photographer may shoot a picture of you interacting with the animals. You can buy the souvenir photograph at **Keyhole Photo,** near Shamu's Emporium. You can also have your picture taken with one of the famous Budweiser Clydesdales at Clydesdale Hamlet. And if you're a real Anheuser-Busch enthusiast, then you might want to hit **Bud's Shop** near Turtle Point.

If you've left the park before realizing that you simply must have a Shamu slicker, visit **Shamu's Emporium,** just outside the entrance. Also, any purchase you make inside the park can be sent to Shamu's Emporium for pickup as you exit.

BUSCH GARDENS

There are three must-have stuffed animals on the Central Florida theme-park circuit, and two of them are here (SeaWorld's killer whales are the other). Cuddly gorillas are available at **J. R.'s Gorilla Hut,** just outside Myombe Reserve, along with a delightfully long-limbed chimpanzee whose Velcro palms attach in an everlasting hug. A must-stop for shoppers is the **Stanleyville Bazaar,** which carries African carvings and handicrafts, colorful clothing, and toys. In Morocco you can browse through jewelry, flowy veils, and leather goods at **Marrakesh Market.**

If you leave the park without purchasing that beautiful bird key ring and want to run back for one, ask about one of the 30-minute shopping passes, available for a deposit equaling the price of admission.

THE ORLANDO AREA

Factory Outlets

The International Drive area is filled with factory outlet stores, most on the northeast end. These outlets are clumped together in expansive malls or scattered along the drive, and much of the merchandise is ostensibly discounted 20%–75%. You can find just about anything, some of it top quality, but be advised: retailers have learned that they can fool shoppers into believing they must be getting a deal because they're at a stripped-down outlet store. Actually, prices may be the same as or higher than those at other locations.

Fodor'sChoice **Belz Factory Outlet World.** Two malls and four annexes make Belz the
★ area's largest collection of outlet stores. One of the best places to find
deals is Off 5th, the Saks Fifth Avenue Outlet. There are almost always sales under way, allowing you to pick up high-end labels at
sometimes ridiculous prices. Other notable stores include Maidenform,
Danskin, Jonathan Logan, Calvin Klein, Van Heusen, Burlington
Brands, Bugle Boy, Gap, OshKosh, Bally Shoes, Bass Shoes, DKNY,
Fossil, Big Dog, Guess?, Polo, Etienne Aigner, Tommy Hilfiger, and
Banister. Especially popular are the outlets for athletic shoes: Converse,
Reebok, Foot Locker, and Nike. There are also good buys in house-
wares and linens in such outlets as Pfaltzgraff, Corning/Revere, Mikasa,
and Fitz & Floyd. Don't worry about carting home breakable or cum-
bersome articles; these stores will ship your purchases anywhere in the
United States by UPS. Although the mall isn't fancy, it's clean and pleasant, attracting shoppers from South America, Japan, and across the
USA. Mall 2 offers a carousel for children and an adequate food
court. The information booth sells discount tickets to all the non-Disney theme parks. ⊠ *5401 W. Oak Ridge Rd., at northern tip of International Dr.* ☎ *407/354–0126 or 407/352–9611* ⊕ *www.belz.com*
⊘ *Mon.–Sat. 10–9, Sun. 10–6.*

Lake Buena Vista Factory Stores. Although there's scant curb appeal, this
is a nice gathering of standard outlet stores. The center is roughly 2 miles
south of I–4 and includes Reebok, Nine West, Big Dog, Sony, Liz Clai-
borne, Wrangler, Disney's Character Corner, American Tourister, Mu-
rano, Sony/JVC, Tommy Hilfiger, Ralph Lauren, Jockey, Casio, OshKosh,
Fossil, and the area's only Old Navy Outlet. Take Exit 68 at I–4.
⊠ *15591 State Rd. 535, 1 mi north of Hwy. 192* ☎ *407/238–9301*
⊕ *www.lbvfs.com* ⊘ *Mon.–Sat. 10–9, Sun. 10–6.*

Orlando Premium Outlet. This outlet capitalizes on its proximity to Disney (it's at the confluence of I–4, Highway 535, and International Drive).
It can be tricky to reach—you have to take I–4 Exit 68 at Highway 535,
head a few blocks east, and find the very subtle entrance to Little Lake
Bryan Road (it parallels I–4). Parking is plentiful, and the center's design makes this almost an open-air market, so walking can be pleasant
on a nice day. You'll find Nike, Adidas, Timberland, Polo, Giorgio Armani, Burberry, Tommy Hilfiger, Dockers, Reebok, Versace, Guess?,
Bebe, Mikasa, Max Mara, Nautica, Calvin Klein, and about 100 other
stores. This mall has pretty much the same stores as Belz, so if you've hit
one, you can skip the other. ⊠ *8200 Vineland Rd.* ☎ *407/238–7787*
⊕ *www.premiumoutlets.com* ⊘ *Mon.–Sat. 10–10, Sun. 10–9.*

★ **Outdoor World.** The very large and very nice megastore carries goods
and provisions for every aspect of outdoor life. In a sparkling 150,000-
square-foot Western-style lodge accented by antler door handles, fishing ponds, deer tracks in the concrete, and a massive stone fireplace,
the store packs in countless fishing boats, RVs, tents, rifles, deep-sea
fishing gear, freshwater fishing tackle, scuba equipment, fly-tying materials (classes are offered, too), a pro shop, outdoor clothing, Uncle
Buck's Cabin (a restaurant and snack bar), and a shooting gallery. If
you're an outdoor enthusiast, this is a must-see. ⊠ *5156 International*

Shopping in North Orlando

Dr. ☎ 407/563–5200 ⊕ www.basspro.com ☉ Mon.–Sat. 9 AM–10 PM, Sun. 10 AM–7 PM.

Sports Dominator. The huge, multilevel Sports Dominator could probably equip all the players of Major League Baseball and the NFL, NBA, and NHL combined. Each sport receives its own section, crowding the floor with soccer balls, golf clubs, catcher's mitts, jerseys, bows, and a few thousand more pieces of sports gear. The prices may not be lower than anywhere else, but the selection is a winner. ✉ 6464 International Dr. ☎ 407/354–2100 ⊕ www.sportsdominator.com ☉ Daily 9 AM–10 PM.

Flea Markets

Flea World. It's a long traffic-choked haul from the attractions area (about 30 mi northeast), but Flea World claims to be America's largest flea market under one roof. Merchants at more than 1,700 booths sell predominately new merchandise—everything from car tires, Ginsu knives, and pet tarantulas to gourmet coffee, biker clothes, darts, NASCAR souvenirs, rugs, books, incense, leather lingerie, and beaded evening gowns. It's also a great place to buy cheap Florida and Mickey Mouse T-shirts. In one building, 50 antiques and collectibles dealers cater to people who can pass up the combination digital ruler and egg timer

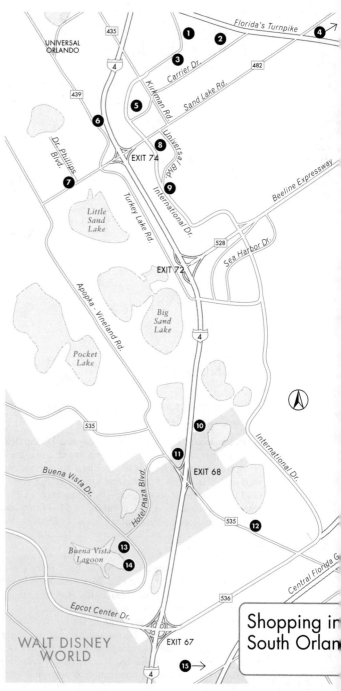

Shopping in
South Orlan

for some authentic good old junque and collectibles. A free newspaper, distributed at the parking lot entrance, provides a map and directory. Children are entertained at Fun World next door, which offers two unusual miniature golf courses, arcade games, go-carts, bumper cars, bumper boats, children's rides, and batting cages. Flea World is 3 mi east of I–4 Exit 98 on Lake Mary Boulevard, then 1 mi south on U.S. 17–92. ⊠ *U.S. 17–92, Sanford* ☎ *407/321–1792* ⊕ *www.fleaworld.com* ⊠ *Free* ⊙ *Fri.–Sun. 9–6.*

192 Flea Market Outlet. With 400 booths, this market is about a fourth the size of Sanford's Flea World, but it's much more convenient to the major Orlando attractions (about 10 mi away in Kissimmee) and is open daily. The all-new merchandise includes "tons of items": toys, luggage, sunglasses, jewelry, clothes, beach towels, sneakers, electronics, and the obligatory T-shirts. ⊠ *4301 W. Vine St., Hwy. 192, Kissimmee* ☎ *407/ 396–4555* ⊙ *Daily 9–6.*

★ **Renninger's Twin Markets.** In the charming town of Mount Dora (30 mi northwest of downtown Orlando), Renninger's may be Florida's largest gathering of antiques and collectibles dealers. At the top of the hill, 400 flea-market dealers sell household goods, garage-sale surplus, produce, baked goods, pets, and anything else you can think of. At the bottom of the hill, 200 antiques dealers set up shop to sell ephemera, old phonographs, deco fixtures, antique furniture, and other stuff Granny had in her attic. If you have the time, hit the flea market first, since that's where antiques dealers find many of their treasures. Both markets are open every weekend, but on the third weekend of the month the antiques market has a fair attracting about 500 dealers. The really big shows, however, are the three-day extravaganzas held on the third weekends of November, January, and February—these draw approximately 1,500 dealers. These events can be all-day affairs; otherwise, spend the morning at Renninger's and then move on to downtown Mount Dora in time for lunch. From I–4, take the Florida Turnpike north to Exit 267A to reach Highway 429 east and, 8 mi later, Highway 441 north to Mount Dora. Summers are very slow, the pace picks up from October through May. ⊠ *U.S. 441, Mount Dora* ☎ *352/383–8393* ⊕ *www.renningers.com* ⊠ *Markets and Antiques Fairs free; Extravaganzas $10 Fri., $5 Sat., $3 Sun.* ⊙ *Markets, weekends 9–5; Antiques Fairs, Mar.–Oct., 3rd weekend of month, 9–5; Extravaganzas Nov., Jan., and Feb., 3rd weekend of month, Fri. 10–5, weekends 9–5.*

Shopping Centers & Malls

International Drive Area, Orlando

Fodor'sChoice
★ **Florida Mall.** With 260-plus stores, this is easily the largest mall in Central Florida. Anchor stores and specialty shops include Nordstrom, Sears Roebuck, JCPenney, Dillard's, Saks Fifth Avenue, Restoration Hardware, J. Crew, Pottery Barn, Brooks Brothers, Cutter & Buck, Harry & David Gourmet Foods, and Swarovski. A 17-restaurant food court and four sit-down restaurants assure you won't go hungry. Stroller and wheelchair rentals are available, along with concierge services and, because the mall attracts crowds of Brazilian and Puerto Rican tourists,

foreign language assistance. The mall is minutes from the Orlando International Airport and 4½ mi east of I–4 and International Drive at the corner of Sand Lake Road and South Orange Blossom Trail. ⊠ *8001 S. Orange Blossom Trail* ☎ *407/851–6255* ⊕ *www.shopsimon.com* ☉ *Mon.–Sat. 10–9:30, Sun. 11–7.*

★ **Festival Bay.** Long awaited and much delayed, this mall opened in 2003 to much fanfare. Most of its stores, such as Shepler's Western Wear and Ron Jon Surf Shop, are new to the Orlando market. Taking a new approach to retailing, Festival Bay has an indoor miniature golf course called Putting Edge and a 55,000-square-foot Vans Skatepark, with ramps for skateboarders and in-line skaters. Shops include Steve & Barry's University Sportswear, Epoxy, Hilo Hattie, CoKooning, and Storyville. There's also a 20-screen Cinemark Theater. Festival Bay is adjacent to the Factory Outlet Mall. ⊠ *5250 International Dr., I-Drive Area* ☎ *407/351–7718* ⊕ *www.shopsimon.com* ☉ *Mon.–Sat. 10–10, Sun. 11–7.*

Fodor'sChoice **Mall at Millenia.** The best way to describe this mall is "high-end." Designers such as Gucci, Dior, Burberry, Chanel, Jimmy Choo, Hugo Boss, Cartier, and Tiffany have stores here. You'll also fine Anthropologie, Neiman Marcus, Bloomingdale's, Bang & Olufsen, and Orlando's only
★ Apple store. The **Millenia Gallery** (☎ 407/226–8701 ⊕ www.milleniagallery.com) treats window shoppers and serious art buyers to paintings by Picasso, pop art by Warhol, and hand-blown glass art by Chihuly. Beyond the gallery's three exhibit halls is a second-floor balcony displaying outdoor sculptures. A few minutes northwest of Universal, the mall is easy to reach via Exit 78 off I–4. ⊠ *4200 S. Conroy Rd.* ☎ *407/363–3555* ⊕ *www.mallatmillenia.com* ☉ *Mon.–Sat. 10–9:30, Sun. 11–7.*

Marketplace. Convenient for visitors staying on or near International Drive, the Marketplace (not to be confused with Disney's Marketplace) provides all the basic necessities in one spot. Stores include a pharmacy, post office, one-hour film processor, stationery store, bakery, dry cleaner, hair salon, optical shop, natural-food grocery, and 24-hour supermarket. Also in the Marketplace are three popular restaurants: Christini's, Enzo's, and the Phoenician. Take the I–4 Sand Lake Road exit (Exit 74AB) and head west. ⊠ *7600 Dr. Phillips Blvd.* ☎ *No phone* ☉ *Hrs vary.*

Mercado. This is a Mediterranean-style entertainment-retail center for bus tours and tourists meandering along International Drive. It's home to specialty shops and an international food court, and live entertainment is offered at various times throughout the day. That said, a dwindling number of shops makes this one a toss-up. ⊠ *8445 International Dr.* ☎ *407/345–9337* ⊕ *www.themercado.com* ☉ *Daily 10 AM–11 PM.*

Pointe*Orlando. Strategically located within walking distance of the Peabody Orlando and Orange County Convention Center, this is perhaps the most impressive retail center along the I-Drive corridor. In addition to WonderWorks and the enormous Muvico Pointe 21 theater, the massive complex houses more than 60 specialty shops, including A/X Armani Exchange, Abercrombie & Fitch, Foot Locker Superstore, Chico's, Denim Place, Gap, Tommy Hilfiger, Victoria's Secret, Dan

Marino's Town Tavern, Hooters, Monty's Conch Harbor, and Johnny Rockets. There are also a few dozen pushcart vendors selling hair ribbons, sunglasses, and other small items. Considering you have to pay to park ($2 for 15 minutes–2 hours, $5 daily), the nearby ATM is more than convenient. ⊠ *9101 International Dr.* ☎ *407/248–2838* ⊕ *www.pointeorlandofl.com* ⊘ *Sun.–Thurs. 10–10, Fri. and Sat. 10 AM–11 PM.*

Lake Buena Vista

Crossroads of Lake Buena Vista. Directly across from the main entrance to Walt Disney World, 11 restaurants and more than 25 shops cater primarily to tourists. Upscale and casual shops are geared to sun and surf, electronics, and children, but the necessities, such as the 24-hour **Gooding's supermarket** (☎ 407/827–1200), post office, bank, and cleaners, are also here. You can find the usual franchised restaurants as well as some local spots, such as the casual Pebbles. While you shop, your offspring can entertain themselves at Pirate's Cove Adventure Golf. To reach it, head out the Disney entrance/exit of Lake Buena Vista or take I–4 to Exit 68. ⊠ *12545–12551 Rte. 535* ⊘ *Stores daily 10–1; restaurant hrs vary.*

Northern Suburbs

Seminole Towne Center. This mall fills the shopping needs of Orlando's burgeoning northern suburbs. About 30 mi northeast of downtown Orlando, the mall is anchored by Dillard's, Sears Roebuck, JCPenney, Burdines, and Parisian, and contains more than 120 retailers. For something tropical, try A Shop Called Mango, owned by singer Jimmy Buffett. And just in case you missed something in the theme parks, there's a branch of the Disney Store here. Strollers and wheelchairs are available for rent. There's a pretty good food court, too. About five minutes east on Highway 46, downtown Sanford has a nice—if sporadic—mix of antiques shops. The mall is ¼ mi east of I–4 (Exit 101C) and south of Route 46. ⊠ *200 Towne Center Circle, Sanford* ☎ *407/323–2262* ⊕ *www.shopsimon.com* ⊘ *Mon.–Sat. 10–9, Sun. noon–6.*

Winter Park Village Marketplace. Just a few miles north of Orlando in fashionable Winter Park is this hopping spot, with a nice mix of shops and restaurants and a 20-screen movie theater. Evenings are particularly active with young professional types coming by for stores such as Borders, Pier One, Wolf Camera, Chamberlin's natural foods market, Owen Allen (creative furniture), Ann Taylor, Hallmark, and Kidz Quest, or to grab a bite at P. F. Chang's, Brio Tuscan Grille, or Johnny Rockets. From I–4, take Exit 88 (Lee Road) and head east 2 mi to Route 17–92, then turn right (south)—the Village is ¼ mi on your left. ⊠ *500 N. Orlando Ave., Winter Park* ⊕ *www.shopwinterparkvillage.com* ⊘ *Mon.–Sat. 10–9, Sun. noon–6.*

Shopping Districts

Orlando's Antiques Row

Orlando has a small antiques row north of downtown on **North Orange Avenue.** At present, some shops are battling increased rents and the incursion of medical offices flowing in from the nearby hospital. Still, there are enough vintage clothing stores, baseball card shops, and funky furniture and import stores to make it worth a visit if you're in the neighborhood or are en route to dinner on Winter Park's Park Avenue. Most are open Monday–Saturday 10–6, and some have Sunday hours of noon–6. Get off I–4 at Exit 85, take Princeton Street east to North Orange Avenue, and turn right.

Among the shops scattered in the few blocks south of Princeton are A&T Antiques, which prides itself on having the area's largest selection of antiques, although that matters only if you like European and country-pine furniture; Flo's Attic, specializing in furniture, pottery, china, and jewelry; and Washburn Imports, loaded with funky furniture and home decorations from faraway destinations. Prices are fair and the mix appears better than at many import stores. If you're wondering where old vinyl records have gone, they're at Rock 'n' Roll Heaven. Crammed with rare albums, 45s, rock paraphernalia, board games, and sheet music, the shop is a fun spot for the curious and a must-see for collectors. The Ehmen brothers are devoted to the genre and take pride in selling only mint-condition records. They also sell funkified dance discs in a side room.

> **need a break?** The **White Wolf Café** (⊠ 1829 N. Orange Ave. ☎ 407/895–5590) is a happening sidewalk eatery attracting weekend shoppers and evening locals. Specialties include a salad entrée with chicken, goat cheese, walnuts, and dried cranberries on a field of mixed greens.

On Ivanhoe Boulevard off North Orange is a group of shops that sell delightful (but pricey) antiques in a collection called **Ivanhoe Row.** The Fly Fisherman specializes in accoutrements for the angler, Swanson's Antiques carries a fine selection of 19th- and 20th-century furniture and bric-a-brac, and Fredlund Wildlife Gallery sells paintings and sculptures of animals. Other shops include the William Moseley Gallery (19th-century oil paintings), Tim's Wine Market, Jarboe (upscale women's fashions), and Christopher Jude (upscale men's clothing). After antiquing, cross the street and take a stroll in the beautiful park surrounding the lake.

Mount Dora

Founded by homesteaders in 1874, this charming little town has 19th-century stores, houses, and bed-and-breakfasts tucked into rolling hills that overlook Lake Dora. The New England–style village is recognized as the antiques capital of Florida, and is also called "Festival City" for its art, antiques, and crafts shows that take place nearly every weekend in fall, winter, and spring. There are dozens of crafts shops, boutiques, galleries, and antiques shops here—and more opening nearly every day.

The intersection of **5th Avenue and Donnelly Street** is the hub, and shops spread out from there in every direction. Among the standouts are Uncle Al's Time Capsule (collectibles and autographed celeb photos), Piglet's Pantry (fancy pet food and toys), Yesterday, Today and Tomorrow (surprisingly chic ladies' fashions), and Dickens-Reed (a cozy village bookstore and coffee shop).

When you're finished shopping, you can get a bite at any of Mount Dora's varied eating establishments, from the tea and scones at the Windsor

Rose Tea Room and crepes at Cecile's French Corner to the steaks at the Frosty Mug Icelandic Pub. Look for Shiraz bistro, which serves tasty urban cuisine—it's hidden upstairs in a retail complex. Mount Dora is west of U.S. 441 on Old U.S. 441 or Route 44B. Contact the **Chamber of Commerce** (☎ 352/383–2165 ⊕ www.mountdora.com) for more information.

Winter Park

★ Unquestionably one of the most inviting spots in Central Florida, **Park Avenue** in downtown Winter Park offers a full day of shopping and entertainment. The last couple of years have seen a mass exodus of the chain stores that came to dominate shopping on Park Avenue, leaving the street open to the return of boutique shopping. Most of these stores are privately owned and offer merchandise that cannot be easily found elsewhere.

On the north end of Park Avenue is the **Charles Hosmer Morse Museum of American Art,** of which the centerpiece is the work of Louis Comfort Tiffany. It's a great little museum with a fantastic shop selling lots of Tiffany-theme gifts and books. On the other side of the street is **Olive This Relish That,** a great shop for foodies who covet things like *fleur de sel* (fine French sea salt) and Riedel wine glasses. Across the street is **Shoooz,** which sells funky but functional Euro shoes. Just a short walk from there, **Jacobson's** is a chic clothing boutique.

Toward the south end of Park Avenue, you'll find **Peterbrooke Chocolatier,** which makes all of its chocolates on premises and almost always has something on hand to sample, such as its to-die-for chocolate-covered popcorn. Next door is **Red Marq,** a truly hip card shop that goes way beyond anything Hallmark has to offer. Across the street, **NFX Apothecary** sells indulgent soaps, lotions, and cosmetics. **Shoúture,** a high-end shoe boutique, stocks such designers as Hollywould, Constanca Basto, and Lily Holt. And if your feet are weary from shopping, don't worry, most Shoúture purchases will qualify you for a complimentary pedicure. **The Doggie Door** is an upscale pet boutique attracting customers from as far away as Europe with its designer pet totes, leashes, collars, and pet beds that can be custom upholstered to coordinate with your home décor. In spite of the name, it promotes itself as a multipet store, and sells upscale items for cat lovers as well.

For shoppers and nonshoppers alike part of the fun of Park Avenue is exploring the little nooks and crannies that divert you from the main drag. Tucked in an alley between Lyman and New England Avenues is **Palmano's,** a great little coffee bar that will sell you a hot cup of brew or a pound of its fresh roasted beans. It's also a great place to grab a glass of wine in the evening. Between Welbourne and Morse avenues, around the corner from Barnie's Coffee, you find **Greeneda Court.** A walk to the back reveals a delightful fountain and wrought-iron tables and chairs where you can sit and relax with a cappuccino from Barnie's. Of course the antiques store hidden there could keep you on your feet.

In the middle of the next block, tucked in behind the Rune Stone, a European toy store that adults enjoy as much as the kids, are the **Hidden**

Garden Shops, which house Pooh's Corner, a delightful children's bookstore specializing in hard-to-find titles. Also on Park Avenue are numerous art galleries, antique jewelry stores, a cigar shop, and a gentlemen's barber shop where you can treat yourself to a haircut and a shave.

The third weekend in March brings the **Winter Park Sidewalk Art Festival** (☎ 407/672–6390); more than 40 years after its debut it still attracts thousands of art aficionados and a few hundred of America's better artists. ⊠ *Park Ave. between Fairbanks and Canton Aves.* ⊙ *Most shops Mon.–Sat. 10–5, some also Sun. noon–5.*

Farmers' Market. If you know you want to hit Park Avenue while you're in Central Florida, you might try to schedule your visit on a Saturday. Then you can begin your day at the Winter Park Farmer's Market, which takes place every week at the city's old train depot, two blocks west of Park Avenue. It's a bustling, vibrant market with vendors selling a wide selection of farm-fresh produce, dazzling flowers, and prepared foods. On any given morning you may find a chef stirring a steaming pot of Irish oatmeal, or a woman selling authentic, handmade tamales. There are plenty of baked goods and hot coffee available, along with places to sit and enjoy your treats.

When you've finished your breakfast there, walk two blocks west to the city's fledgling **Craft Market.** Everything sold here is handcrafted, assuring that you'll find something truly unique—a clever purse made from a handsome cigar box; beaded jewelry; knit hats, scarves, and ponchos from Peru; and handsewn quilts. Some vendors accept credit cards, others cash only. You may also find that some prices are negotiable. ⊠ *New England and New York Aves.* ☎ *407/599–3358* ⊙ *Sat. 7 AM–1 PM.*

Sports & the Outdoors

8

FODOR'S CHOICE

Bob's Balloons, *near Lake Buena Vista*

Disney's Wide World of Sports Complex, *in Walt Disney World*

Grand Cypress Equestrian Center, *near Lake Buena Vista*

Osprey Ridge Golf Course, *in Walt Disney World*

Sky Venture, *off International Drive*

Wekiva River, *in Apopka*

Winter Summerland Miniature Golf Course, *in Walt Disney World*

Updated by
Rowland
Stiteler

THERE'S MORE TO AN ACTIVE ORLANDO experience than walking 10 mi a day in the theme parks. Northern travelers were flocking to central Florida's myriad lakes, streams, and golf resorts decades before there was a Disney World. There's nothing that can quite compare to an afternoon paddling down a Florida river, watching the alligators splash into the water and the snowy egrets glide among the palm trees.

You can find just about every outdoor sport in the Orlando area—unless it involves a ski lift. There are plenty of tennis courts and more than 130 golf courses, staffed by nearly three dozen PGA pros, in a 40-mi radius. Some of the world's best-known golfing champions—huge names such as Arnold Palmer and Tiger Woods—have homes in the Orlando area. Anglers soak up the Orlando sun on the dozens of small lakes, and the metropolitan area has as many big-league professional bass fishermen as big-league baseball stars and PGA golf luminaries.

As a professional sports town, Orlando holds a hot ticket. The Orlando Magic basketball team is big-time, and baseball fans have plenty of minor-league action to enjoy. The Southern Professional Hockey League franchise, the Florida Seals, has a rabid fan base, and the Walt Disney World Speedway is the home of the Indy 200 and the Richard Petty Driving Experience. At Disney's Wide World of Sports you can watch or you can play. The complex hosts participatory and tournament-type events in more than 25 individual and team sports, including basketball, softball, and track-and-field; and it serves as the spring-training home of the Atlanta Braves.

But not everything in Orlando is wholesome, Disney-style family fun. Wagering a wad of cash at the jai-alai fronton or the dog track is guaranteed to wipe the refrain from "It's a Small World" right out of your head. Most of the tracks and frontons now have closed-circuit TV links with major horse-racing tracks, so you can bet on the ponies and then watch the race on a big-screen TV. And even if you bet and lose steadily, you won't necessarily spend more than you would at most Disney attractions—that is, depending on how much you wager.

Auto Racing

★ **The Richard Petty Driving Experience** allows you to ride in or even drive a NASCAR-style stock car on a real racetrack. Depending on what you're willing to spend—prices range from $95 to $1,249—you can do everything from riding shotgun for three laps on the 1-mi track to taking driving lessons, culminating in your very own solo behind the wheel. The Richard Petty organization has a second Central Florida location at the Daytona International Speedway, but it involves riding in the car with an experienced race-car driver rather than driving a car yourself. ⊠ *Walt Disney World Speedway* ☎ *800/237–3889* ⊕ *www.1800bepetty.com.*

Ballooning

FodorśChoice ★

It's hard to imagine a more inspiring way to enjoy the beautiful Central Florida outdoors than with a hot-air balloon ride. **Bob's Balloons** offers one-hour rides over protected marsh land and will even fly over Disney World if wind and weather conditions are right. You meet in Lake Buena Vista at dawn, where Bob and his assistant, Mike, take you by van to the launch site. It takes about 15 minutes to get the balloon in the air and then you're off on an adventure that definitely surpasses Peter Pan's Flight in the Magic Kingdom. From the treetop view you'll see farm and forest land for miles, along with horses, deer, wild boar, cattle, and birds flying *below* you. Bob may take you as high as 1,000 feet, from which point you'll be able to see Disney's landmarks: the Expedition Everest mountain, the Epcot ball, and more. Several other balloons are likely to go up near you—there's a tight-knit community of ballooners in the Orlando area—so you'll view these colorful sky ornaments from a parallel level. There are seats in the basket, but you'll probably be too thrilled to sit down. Afterward, Bob and Mike treat you to a lovely champagne picnic brunch (minus coffee, so don't forget to have a cup before you leave). ☎ *407/466–6380 or 877/824–4606* ⊕ *www.bobsballoons.com* ⊠ *$165, $75 per child under 90 lbs.* ▭ *D, MC, V.*

Baseball

Watching a minor-league game or a major-league spring-training game in a small ballpark can take you back to a time when going to a game didn't mean bringing binoculars or watching the big screen to see what was happening. Minor-league teams play April through September, and spring training lasts only a few weeks, usually February through March. It can be a thrill to watch stars of the big leagues up close in spring-training games while you, and they, enjoy a spring break before getting back to work. Tickets to the minors usually run $5 to $8, and spring-training seats cost $12.50 to $20.50.

Major League Spring Training

For dates and more information about spring training, get a copy of the free *Florida Spring Training Guide.* For a copy, contact the **Florida Sports Foundation** (⊠ 2930 Kerry Forest Pkwy., Suite 101, Tallahassee 32309 ☎ 850/488–8347 ⊕ www.flasports.com), which publishes the guide each February.

The Atlanta Braves hold spring training and exhibition baseball games with other major-league teams during February and March. Tickets are $12.50 to $20.50, and are available through Ticketmaster or at the stadium box office. The Braves have an instructional training season for rookie prospects in September and October. It's not quite the same as watching the big-name pros play in the spring, but it's fun for die-hard baseball fans. ⊠ *Disney's Wide World of Sports Stadium, 700 W. Victory Way, Kissimmee* ☎ *407/939–4263, 407/839–3900 Ticketmaster* ⊕ *atlanta.braves.mlb.com.*

The Houston Astros (⊠ Osceola County Stadium, 631 Heritage Pkwy., Kissimmee 34744 ☎ 321/697–3200 ⊕ www.osceola.org) have spring training 18 mi south of Orlando. Ticket prices are $12 to $15.

Basketball

★ **The Orlando Magic** has driven the city to new heights of hoop fanaticism. Tickets, which run $10–$150, are so hard to get that your best bet for seeing a game might be a sports bar. ⊠ *TD Waterhouse Centre, 600 W. Amelia St., 2 blocks west of I–4 Exit 41, Downtown Orlando* ☎ *407/ 839–3900 Ticketmaster, 407/896–2442 season tickets* ⊕ *www.nba. com/magic.*

Biking

Walt Disney World

The most scenic biking in Orlando is on Walt Disney World property, along roads that take you past forests, lakes, golf courses, wooded campgrounds, and resort villas. Most rental locations have children's bikes with training wheels and bikes with baby seats, in addition to regular adult bikes. Disney's lawyers are always watching out for liability problems, so management asks that you wear helmets, which are free with all bike rentals.

Theoretically, bike rentals are only for those lodging on WDW property; in practice, rental outfits usually check IDs only in busy seasons. Bikes must be used, however, only in the area in which you rent them. You must be 18 or older to rent a bike at all Disney locations.

You can rent bikes for $8 per hour and surrey bikes for $18 (two seats) and $22 (four seats) per half hour at the **Barefoot Bay Marina** (☎ 407/ 934–2850), open daily from 10 to 5. Regular bikes at **Coronado Springs Resort** (☎ 407/939–1000), near Disney–MGM Studios, rent for $8 per hour or $22 per day, and surrey bikes rent for $17 (two seats) and $21 (four seats) per half hour. The surrey bikes look like old-fashioned carriages and are a great way to take your family on a sightseeing tour. The covered tops provide a rare commodity at Disney—shade. At **Fort Wilderness Bike Barn** (☎ 407/824–2742), bikes rent for $8 per hour and $21 per day. At the **BoardWalk Resort** (☎ 407/939–6486 surrey bikes), near Disney–MGM Studios, two types of bikes are available at two separate kiosks. Surrey bikes cost $18, $20, and $24 per half hour, depending on the size of the bike. Regular bicycles are $7 per hour.

Orlando Area

Thanks to the Orlando community's commitment to the nationwide Rails to Trails program, the city now has several bike trails, converted from former railroad lines, in both rural and urban surroundings. You can venture into the city of Winter Park and pick up a trail that starts at the mall, or travel into the backwoods through heavily vegetated landscape and by scenic lakes. The Clermont–Lake County region is out in the boonies, where orange groves provide great scenery, and some hills afford challenges. Information about Orlando bike trails can be obtained from the **Orlando City Transportation Planning Bureau** (☎ 407/246–2775 ⊕ www.cityoforlando.net) and www.floridagreenwaysandtrails.com.

★ The **West Orange Trail,** the longest bike trail in the Orlando area, runs some 20 mi through western Orlando and the neighboring towns of Winter Garden and Apopka. Highlights of the trail are the xeriscape–butterfly garden a mile east of the Oakland Outpost and views of Lake Apopka. You can access the trail at **Chapin's Station** (⊠ 501 Crown Point Cross Rd., Winter Garden 34787 ☎ 407/654–1108). **West Orange Trail Bikes & Blades** (⊠ 17914 State Rd. 438, Winter Garden ☎ 407/877–0600) rents bicycles and in-line skates.

A favorite of local bikers, joggers, and skaters, **the Cady Way Trail** connects eastern Orlando with the well-manicured enclave suburb of Winter Park. The pleasant trail is only 3½ mi long, with water fountains and shaded seating along the route. The best access point is the parking lot on the east side of the **Orlando Fashion Square Mall** (⊠ 3201 E. Colonial Dr., about 3 mi east of I–4 Exit 83B). You can also enter the trail at its east end, in **Cady Way Park** (⊠ 1300 S. Denning Ave.).

The paved **Cross Seminole Trail,** part of the Florida National Scenic Trail, is scheduled to become a link in a 30-mi bike path running through the northern suburbs and eventually connecting to the Cady Way trail. At this writing, 3.7 mi of the trail are open. From downtown Orlando, take the East–West Expressway toll road to Route 417 (the Central Florida Greeneway), also a toll road. Follow Route 417 north, then exit onto Route 434. Head west for about 750 feet. The trailhead is on the left.

Dog Racing

The Sanford Orlando Kennel Club has dog racing and betting, as well as South Florida horse racing simulcasts and betting. The season, which for years was November through April, has been extended to 12 months a year, so the club is open year-round. Races start at 7:30 PM Monday through Saturday and matinees on Monday, Wednesday, and Saturday at 12:30. Entry fees are $1 for general admission and $2 for the clubhouse (where you get better views) with a $4 minimum per person for food and drink. ⊠ *301 Dog Track Rd., Longwood* ☎ *407/831–1600* ⊕ *www.floridagreyhoundracing.com.*

Fishing

Central Florida freshwater lakes and rivers swarm with all kinds of fish, especially largemouth black bass but also perch, catfish, sunfish, and pike.

Licenses

To fish in most Florida waters (but not at Walt Disney World) anglers over 16 need a fishing license, available at bait-and-tackle shops, fishing camps, most sporting-goods stores, and Wal-Marts and Kmarts. Some of these locations may not sell saltwater licenses, or they may serve non-Florida residents only; call ahead to be on the safe side. Freshwater or saltwater licenses cost $16.50 for seven consecutive days and $31.50 for one year. For Florida residents under age 65, a freshwater or saltwater license is $13.50 each, or $23.50 for both. Information on obtaining fishing licenses is available from the **Florida Game & Fish Commission** (☎ 850/488–3641). Fishing on a private lake with the owner's permission—which is what anglers do at Disney World—does not require a Florida fishing license.

Walt Disney World

★ **Bay Lake Fishing Trips** (☎ 407/939–7529) offers two-hour fishing excursions on regularly stocked Bay Lake and Seven Seas Lagoon. Departing from the Fort Wilderness, Wilderness Lodge, Contemporary, Polynesian, and Grand Floridian resort marinas, trips include boat, equipment, and a guide for up to five anglers. These organized outings are the only way you're allowed to fish on the lakes, which are brimming with fish. The trips work on a catch-and-release program, though, so you can't take fish home. Reservations are required. Yacht and Beach Club guests and Boardwalk Hotel guests can book a similar fishing excursion on Crescent Lake for the same fee as the Bay Lake trip. The best thing about these excursions is that the boat captain is happy to bait your hook, unhook your catches, and snap pictures of you with your fish. Two-hour trips, which depart daily at 7, 10, and 1:30, cost $215 for the morning departures and $195 for the afternoon departure, plus $80 for each additional hour. Shinners (live bait) are available for $15 per dozen.

On **Captain Jack's Guided Bass Tours** (☎ 407/828–2204), bass specialists go along for the two-hour fishing expeditions on Lake Buena Vista. Anglers depart from the Downtown Disney Marketplace marina at 7, 10, and 1:30. Trips for groups of 2 to 5 people cost $215 for the morning departures and $195 for the afternoon departure. Per-person admission, available only for the 1:30 trip, is $80.

The Fort Wilderness Bike Barn (☎ 407/824–2742), open daily 8–6, rents poles and tackle for fishing in the canals around the Port Orleans–Riverside (formerly Dixie Landings) and Port Orleans resorts and at Fort Wilderness Resort and Campground. Fishing without a guide is permitted in these areas. A cane pole with tackle is $4 per hour and $8 per day; rod and reel with tackle is $5 per hour and $9.50 per day. You must be at least 18 to rent a rod and reel. Policy stipulates that rod users must be at least 12 years old, though this is not strictly enforced.

☾ **BoardWalk—Kids-Only Fishing Trips** (☎ 407/939–7529), for ages 6 to 12 are led by adult Disney staff members who drive the boats and serve as guides. One-hour excursions cost $30 per child and set out from the Boardwalk Community Hall Monday through Friday at 10 AM.

Ol' Man Island Fishing Hole (⊠ Port Orleans–Riverside ☎ 407/934–5409) has fishing off a dock. Catch-and-release is encouraged, but you can have your fish packed in ice to take home—you have to clean them yourself. Cane poles and bait are $4 per hour; a rod and reel is $8 per hour and can be shared by the whole family. You must rent your equipment here to use the dock. Two-hour excursions in a boat with a driver are $80 per person, and include rod, reel, and bait. The Fishing Hole is open daily 7–3, and reservations are required.

Sassagoula River Fishing Trips (⊠ Port Orleans–Riverside ☎ 407/939–7529) include guide, rod, bait, and soft drinks. Trips are two hours long, $80 per person, and leave daily at 7 AM and 10 AM and 1:30 PM. Cost for up to five anglers is $215 for the morning departures and $195 for the afternoon departures. You must reserve in advance.

Orlando Area

Top Central Florida fishing waters include Lake Kissimmee, the Butler and Conway chains of lakes, and Lake Tohopekaliga—a Native American name that means "Sleeping Tiger." (Locals call it Lake Toho.) The lake got its centuries-old name because it becomes incredibly rough during thunderstorms and has sent more than a few fishermen to a watery grave. Be careful in summer when you see storm clouds. Your best chance for trophy fish is between November and April on Toho or Kissimmee. For good creels, the best bet is usually the Butler area, which has the additional advantage of its scenery—lots of live oaks and cypresses, plus the occasional osprey or bald eagle. Toho and Kissimmee are also good for largemouth bass and crappie. The Butler chain yields largemouth, some pickerel, and the occasional huge catfish. Services range from equipment and boat rental to full-day trips with guides and guarantees. Like virtually all lakes in Florida, the big Orlando-area lakes are teeming with alligators, which you'll find totally harmless unless you engage in the unwise practice of swimming at night. Small pets are more vulnerable than humans, and should never be allowed to swim in Florida lakes or rivers.

FISHING CAMPS A number of excellent fishing camps in the form of lakeside campgrounds draw a more outdoorsy crowd than you'll find elsewhere in the area.

East Lake Fish Camp (⊠ 3705 Big Bass Rd., Kissimmee ☎ 407/348–2040), on East Lake Tohopekaliga, has a restaurant and country store, sells live bait and propane, and rents boats. You can also take a ride on an airboat. The camp has 286 RV sites that rent at $20 per night for two people. Simple, rustic cabins are $65 per night for two people and $5 per night for each additional person with a limit of five per cabin. Try to reserve one of the 24 cabins at least two weeks in advance in winter and spring.

Lake Toho Resort (⊠ 4715 Kissimmee Park Rd., St. Cloud ☎ 407/892–8795 ⊕ www.laketohoresort.com), on West Lake Tohopekaliga, has 200 RV sites. Most of the full hookups are booked year-round, but electrical and water hookups are usually available, as are live bait, food, and drinks. The RV sites are $22 per night and $250 per month, plus electricity.

Richardson's Fish Camp (✉ 1550 Scotty's Rd., Kissimmee ☎ 407/846–6540), on West Lake Tohopekaliga, has 11 cabins with kitchenettes, 16 RV sites, six tent sites, boat slips, and a bait shop. The RV sites are $25 per night, tent sites are about $20, and cabins are $44 for one bedroom, about $68 for two bedrooms, and $79 for three bedrooms.

GUIDES Guides fish out of the area's fishing camps, and you can usually make arrangements to hire them through the camp office. Rates vary, but for two people a good price is $150 for a half day and $225 for a full day. Many area guides are part-timers who fish on weekends or take a day off from their full-time job.

All Florida Fishing (✉ 4500 Joe Overstreet Rd., Kenansville 34739 ☎ 407/436–1966 or 800/347–4007 ⊕ www.all-florida-fishing.com) takes you on half- and full-day trips to go after the big bass that make the Kissimmee chain of lakes southeast of Disney ideal for sportfishing. Captain Rob Murchie also leads full-day saltwater fishing expeditions in the Indian River Lagoon and Atlantic, an hour's drive to the east, in pursuit of tarpon and other game fish. Half-day freshwater trips are $225; full-day trips are $325. Saltwater trips (full day only) are $350. Prices are for one to two people. A third participant can join the group for $50. You can buy your license and bait here.

Pro Bass Guide Service (✉ 398 Grove Ct., Winter Garden 34787 ☎ 407/877–9676 or 800/771–9676 ⊕ www.probassguideservice.com), run by Captain Paul Solomon, has been in business for more than 20 years and provides boat, tackle, transportation, soft drinks, and ice for bass fishing on local lakes. Live bait is available for an extra charge. Prices per person start at $260 for a half day and $300 for a full day. Each additional adult is $100.

Football

The Orlando Predators play in the indoor Arena Football League. Teams have only eight players, each of whom holds both offensive and defensive positions. Games are held May through August, and tickets are $6 to $100. Rarely available special season "Dream Seats" put you front row, midfield for $960–$1,200 per person. ✉ *TD Waterhouse Centre, 600 W. Amelia St., Orlando* ☎ *407/648–4444, 407/872–7362 season ticket information* ⊕ *www.orlandopredators.com.*

Golf

Sunny weather practically year-round makes Central Florida a golfer's haven, and there are about 130 golf courses within a 45-minute drive of Orlando International Airport. Most of Florida is extremely flat, but many of the courses listed here have man-made hills that make them more challenging. Many resort hotels let nonguests use their golf facilities. Some country clubs are affiliated with particular hotels, and their guests can play at preferred rates. If you're staying near a course you'd like to use, call and inquire. Because hotels have become so attuned to the popularity of golf, many that don't have golf courses nearby may still have golf privileges or discounts at courses around town. Check with your hotel about what it offers before you set out on your own.

In general, even public courses have dress codes—most courses would just as soon see you stark naked as wearing a tank top, for instance—so call to find out the specifics at each, and be sure to reserve tee times in advance. The yardages quoted are those from the blue tees. Greens fees usually vary by season, but the highest and lowest figures are provided, and virtually all include mandatory cart rental, except for the few 9-hole walking courses.

Golfpac (⊠ 483 Montgomery Pl., Altamonte Springs 32714 ☎ 407/ 260–2288 or 800/327–0878 ⊕ www.golfpactravel.com) packages golf vacations and prearranges tee times at more than 78 courses around Orlando. Rates vary based on hotel and course, and at least 60 to 90 days' advance notice is recommended to set up a vacation.

Walt Disney World
Where else would you find a sand trap shaped like the head of a well-known mouse? Walt Disney World has 99 holes of golf on five championship courses—all on the PGA Tour route—plus a 9-hole walking course. Eagle Pines and Osprey Ridge are the newcomers, flanking the Bonnet Creek Golf Club just east of Fort Wilderness. WDW's original courses, the Palm and the Magnolia, flank the Shades of Green Resort to the west and the Lake Buena Vista course near Downtown Disney's Marketplace. All courses are full-service facilities, and include a driving range, pro shop, locker room, snack bar–restaurant, and PGA-staffed teaching and training program. Disney provides a special perk to any guest at a WDW hotel who checks in specifically to play golf: free cab fare for you and your clubs between the hotel and the course you play. (It saves you from having to lug your clubs onto a hotel shuttle bus.) Ask at the front desk when you check into the hotel.

GREENS FEES There are lots of variables here, with prices ranging from $20 for a youngster 17 or under to play 9 holes at Oak Trail walking course, to an adult nonhotel guest paying $145 to play 18 holes at one of Disney's newer courses in peak season. Disney guests get a price break, with rates ranging from $79 for a Disney hotel guest playing Monday through Thursday at the Lake Buena Vista course to $145 for a day visitor playing the Osprey Ridge course. All have a twilight discount rate, $60–$80, which goes into effect at 2 PM from October 31 to January 14 and at 3 PM from April 1 to October 26. The 9-hole, par-36 Oak Trail course is best for those on a budget, with a year-round rate of $20 for golfers 17 and under and $38 golfers 18 and older. Rates at all courses except Oak Trail include an electric golf cart. No electric carts are allowed at Oak Trail, and a pull cart for your bag is $6. If you've got the stamina and desire to play the same course twice in the same day, you can do so for half price the second time around, but you can't reserve that option in advance, and this "Re-Play Option," as Disney calls it, is subject to availability. Note that golf rates change frequently, so double-check them when you reserve.

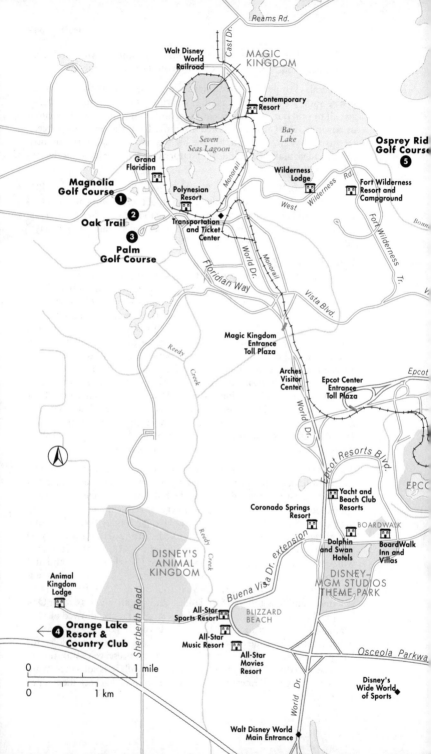

Reams Rd.

Cast Dr.

Walt Disney
World
Railroad

MAGIC
KINGDOM

Contemporary
Resort

Seven Seas Lagoon

Bay
Lake

Osprey Rid
Golf Course ⑤

Grand
Floridian

Magnolia
Golf Course ①

Wilderness
Lodge

West Wilderness Rd.

Fort Wilderness
Resort and
Campground

Oak Trail ②

Polynesian
Resort

Monorail

Fork Wilderness Tr.

Bonne

Palm
Golf Course ③

Transportation
and Ticket
Center

Floridian Way

World Dr.

Monorail

Vista Blvd.

V

Reedy Creek

Magic Kingdom
Entrance
Toll Plaza

Epcot

Arches
Visitor
Center

Epcot Center
Entrance
Toll Plaza

World Dr.

Epcot Resorts Blvd.

EPCO

Coronado Springs
Resort

Yacht and
Beach Club
Resorts

DISNEY'S
ANIMAL
KINGDOM

Buena Vista Dr. extension

BOARDWALK

Dolphin
and Swan
Hotels

BoardWalk
Inn and
Villas

Reedy Creek

Animal
Kingdom
Lodge

Sherberth Road

DISNEY–
MGM STUDIOS
THEME PARK

All-Star
Sports Resort

BLIZZARD
BEACH

Orange Lake ④
Resort &
Country Club

All-Star
Music Resort

All-Star
Movies
Resort

Osceola Parkwa

0   1 mile

0   1 km

World Dr.

Disney's
Wide World
of Sports

Walt Disney World
Main Entrance

FY

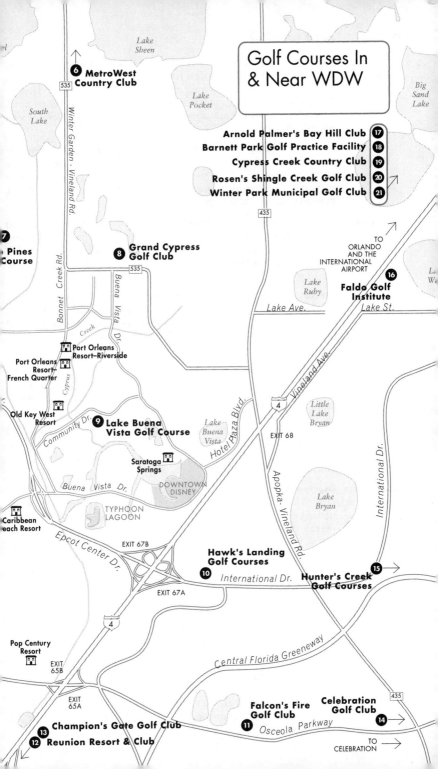

TEE TIMES & RESERVATIONS Tee times are available daily from 6:45 AM until dark. You can book them up to 90 days in advance if you're staying at a WDW-owned hotel, 30 days ahead if you're staying elsewhere from May through December, and four days in advance from January through April. For tee times and private lessons at any course, call **Walt Disney World Golf & Recreation Reservations** (☎ 407/939–4653).

GOLF INSTRUCTION One-on-one instruction from PGA-accredited professionals is available at any Disney course. Prices for private lessons vary; 30-minute lessons cost $50 for adults and $30 for youngsters 17 and under, while 90-minute playing lessons for adults cost $150. Call the **Walt Disney World Golf & Recreation Reservations** to book a lesson.

COURSES **Eagle Pines,** one of the newer Walt Disney World courses, was designed by golf-course architect Pete Dye. The dish-shape fairways and vast sand beds are lined with pines and punctuated by challenging bunkers. *Golf Digest* gave this course four and a half stars. ⊠ *Bonnet Creek Golf Club* ⛳ *18 holes, 6,772 yards, par 72, USGA rating 72.3.*

The Lake Buena Vista course winds among Downtown Disney–area town houses and villas. Greens are narrow, and hitting straight is important because errant balls risk ending up in someone's bedroom. Be prepared for the famous island green on the 7th. ⊠ *Lake Buena Vista Dr.* ⛳ *18 holes, 6,819 yards, par 72, USGA rating 72.7.*

The Magnolia, played by the pros in the Disney–Oldsmobile Golf Classic, is long but forgiving, with extra-wide fairways. More than 1,500 magnolia trees line the course. ⊠ *Shades of Green, 1950 W. Magnolia-Palm Dr.* ⛳ *18 holes, 7,190 yards, par 72, USGA rating 73.9.*

Oak Trail is a 9-hole, par-36 walking course, designed to be fun for the entire family. It was designed by Ron Garl and is noted for its small, undulating greens. ⊠ *Shades of Green, 1950 W. Magnolia-Palm Dr.* ⛳ *9 holes, 2,913 yards, par 36.*

Fodor's Choice ★ **Osprey Ridge,** sculpted from some of the still-forested portions of the huge WDW acreage, was transformed into a relaxing tour in the hands of designer Tom Fazio. However, tees and greens as much as 20 feet above the fairways keep competitive players from getting too comfortable. The course was rated four and a half stars by *Golf Digest*. Rental clubs require photo ID and a major credit card for refundable deposit of $500 per set. ⊠ *Bonnet Creek Golf Club, 3451 Golf View Dr.* ⛳ *18 holes, 7,101 yards, par 72, USGA rating 73.9.*

The Palm, one of WDW's original courses, has been confounding the pros as part of the annual Disney–Oldsmobile Golf Classic for years. It's not as long as the Magnolia, or as wide, but it has 9 water holes and 94 bunkers. ⊠ *Shades of Green, 1950 W. Magnolia-Palm Dr.* ⛳ *18 holes, 6,957 yards, par 72, USGA rating 73.*

Orlando Area

Greens fees at most non-Disney courses fluctuate with the season. A twilight discount applies after 2 PM in busy seasons and after 3 PM during the rest of the year; the discount is usually half off the normal rate. Because golf is so incredibly popular around Orlando, courses raise their rates regularly.

Arnold Palmer's Bay Hill Club & Lodge golf courses are open only to those who have been invited by a member or who book lodging at the club's 65-room hotel. But with double-occupancy rates for rooms overlooking the course running as low as $315 in summer, including a round of golf, many consider staying at the club an interesting prospect. The course is the site of the annual Bay Hill Invitational, and its par-72, 18th hole is considered one of the toughest on the PGA tour. ⊠ *9000 Bay Hill Rd., Orlando* ☎ *407/876–2429 or 888/422–9445* ⊕ *www.bayhill.com* ⏌ *18 holes, 7,207 yards, par 72, USGA rating 75.1; 9 holes, 3,409 yards, par 36* ☜ *Greens fees included in room rates; $189 single, $315 double* ⌨ *Restaurant, private lessons, club rental.*

Barnett Park Golf Practice Facility, besides having an attractive course, has a great asset: it's free. All a golfer has to do is show up to use the net-enclosed driving range (with 10 pads), the three chipping holes with grass and sand surroundings, and the 9-hole putting green. As a special bonus, children ages 7–13 can spend time with a pro at no charge from 3 to 4:30 PM on Wednesday. ⊠ *4801 W. Colonial Dr., Orlando* ☎ *407/836–6248* ☜ *Free.*

The Celebration Golf Club course—in addition to its great pedigree (it was designed by Robert Trent Jones Jr. and Sr.)—has the same thing going for it that the Disney-created town of Celebration, Florida, has: it's just 1 mi off the U.S. 192 tourist strip and a 10-minute drive from Walt Disney World, yet it is lovely and wooded, and as serene and bucolic as any spot in Florida. In addition to the 18-hole course, driving range, and 3-hole junior course, the club includes a quaint, tin-roof clubhouse with a pro shop and restaurant, flanked by a tall, wooden windmill that is a local landmark. The club has golf packages, which include lodging at the nearby Celebration Hotel. ⊠ *701 Golf Park Dr., Celebration* ☎ *407/566–4653* ⊕ *www.celebrationgolf.com* ⏌ *18 holes, 6,783 yards, par 72, USGA rating 73* ☜ *Greens fees $45–$130, depending on time of year, time of day you play, whether you're a Florida resident, and whether you're a Celebration resident; daily discount rates begin at 2 PM* ⌨ *Restaurant, pro shop, private lessons, club rental.*

★ **Champions Gate Golf Club,** which has the David Leadbetter Golf Academy on its property, has courses designed by Greg Norman. The club is less than 10 mi from Walt Disney World at Exit 24 on I-4. The two courses have distinct styles; the 7,406-yard International has the feel of the best British Isles courses, whereas the 7,048-yard National course is designed in the style of the better domestic courses, with a number of par-3 holes with unusual bunkers. ⊠ *1400 Masters Blvd., Champions Gate* ☎ *407/787–4653, 888/558–9301, 888/633–5323 Ext. 23 Leadbetter Academy* ⊕ *www.championsgategolf.com* ⏌ *International: 18 holes, 7,406 yards, par 72, USGA rating 73.7; National: 18 holes, 7,048 yards, par 72, USGA rating 72.0* ☜ *Greens fees $59–$140, depending on time of year and time of day you play. Golf lessons at Leadbetter Academy are $225 per hr and $1,750 per day* *for private lessons; group lessons are $195 for 3 hrs; a 3-day minischool is $900; a 3-day complete school is $3,000* ☞ *Pro shop, golf school, private lessons, club rental.*

Cypress Creek Country Club is a demanding course with 16 water holes and lots of trees. ⊠ *5353 Vineland Rd., Orlando* ☎ *407/351–2187* ⊕ *www.cypresscreekcc.com* 🏌 *18 holes, 7,014 yards, par 72, USGA rating 73.6* ⛳ *Greens fees $40–$55* ☞ *Tee times 7 days in advance. Restaurants, private lessons, club rental, putting green.*

Falcon's Fire Golf Club, designed by golf-course architect Rees Jones, has strategically placed fairway bunkers that demand accuracy off the tee. This club is just off the Irlo Bronson Highway and is one of the most convenient to the hotels in the so-called "Maingate" area. ⊠ *3200 Seralago Blvd., Kissimmee* ☎ *407/239–5445* ⊕ *www.falconsfire.com* 🏌 *18 holes, 6,901 yards, par 72, USGA rating 73.8* ⛳ *Greens fees $85–$130, $70 after 2* PM, *$40 after 4* PM ☞ *Tee times 8–60 days in advance. Restaurants, private and group lessons, club rental, lockers, driving range, putting green.*

Faldo Golf Institute by Marriott is the team effort of world-famous golf pro Nick Faldo and Marriott Corp. An extensive-curriculum golf school and 9-hole golf course occupy the grounds of the corporation's biggest time-share complex, Marriott's Grande Vista. Here you can do anything from taking a one-hour, $125 lesson with a Faldo-trained pro (although not with the great Faldo himself, of course) to immersing yourself in a three-day extravaganza ($795–$1,000) in which you learn more about golf technique than most nonfanatics would care to know. Private instruction starts at $125 per hour. Among the high-tech teaching methods at the school is the Faldo Swing Studio, in which instructors tape you doing your initial, unrefined swing; analyze the tape; and then teach you how to reform your physical skills the Faldo Way. The course, designed by Ron Garl, is geared to make you use every club in your bag—and perhaps a few you may elect to buy in the pro shop. As with virtually everything else in Florida, prices go up in peak seasonal months, but there's always a group discount at the Faldo Institute, even for groups as small as two people. ⊠ *Marriott Grande Vista, 12001 Avenida Verde, Orlando 32821* ☎ *407/903–6295* ⊕ *www.gofaldo.com* 🏌 *9 holes, 2,400 yards, par 32.*

Grand Cypress Golf Club, fashioned after a Scottish glen, is comprised of four nines: the North, South, East, and New courses. The North and South courses have fairways constructed on different levels, giving them added definition. The New Course was inspired by the Old Course at St. Andrews, and has deep bunkers, double greens, a snaking burn, and even an old stone bridge. ⊠ *1 N. Jacaranda, Orlando 32836* ☎ *407/239–1909 or 800/835–7377* ⊕ *www.grandcypress.com* 🏌 *North: 9 holes, 3,521 yards, par 36; South: 9 holes, 3,472 yards, par 36; East: 9 holes, 3,434 yards, par 36; New: 9 holes, 6,773 yards, par 72. USGA rating 72.* ⛳ *Greens fees $115–$180* ☞ *Tee times 7:30* AM–6 PM. *Restaurant, club rental, shoe rental, locker room, driving range, putting green, free valet parking.*

Hawk's Landing Golf Course, originally designed by Joe Lee, was extensively upgraded with a Robert E. Cupp III design in 2000. The course includes 16 water holes, lots of sand, and exotic landscaping. ⊠ *Orlando World Center Marriott, 8701 World Center Dr., Orlando 32821* ☎ *407/238–8660* ⊕ *www.golfhawkslanding.com* ⚑ *18 holes, 6,810 yards, par 72, USGA rating 73.2* ⛳ *Greens fees $65–$165* ☞ *Tee times 7 days in advance for public, 90 days in advance for World Center guests. Restaurants, private and group lessons, club and shoe rental.*

Hunter's Creek Golf Course, designed by Lloyd Clifton, has large greens and 14 water holes. ⊠ *14401 Sports Club Way, Orlando 32837* ☎ *407/240–4653* ⚑ *18 holes, 7,432 yards, par 72, USGA rating 76.1* ⛳ *Greens fees $40–$75* ☞ *Tee times 3 days in advance. Snack bar, private lessons, club rental.*

MetroWest Country Club has a rolling Robert Trent Jones Sr. course, with few trees but lots of sand. ⊠ *2100 S. Hiawassee Rd., Orlando 32835* ☎ *407/299–1099* ⊕ *www.metrowestgolf.com* ⚑ *18 holes, 7,051 yards, par 72, USGA rating 74.1* ⛳ *Greens fees $49–$69 residents, $59–$94 nonresidents* ☞ *Tee times 7 days in advance. Restaurant (lunch only), private and group lessons, club rental.*

The Orange Lake Resort & Country Club, about five minutes from Walt Disney World's main entrance, has three very similar 9-hole courses: the Orange, Lake, and Cypress. Distances aren't long, but fairways are very narrow, and there's a great deal of water, making the courses difficult. A fourth course, the 18-hole Legends, was designed by Arnold Palmer. Standard practice is to play two of the three 9-hole courses in combination for a single round of golf, or play Legends. ⊠ *8505 W. Irlo Bronson Memorial Hwy., Kissimmee 34747* ☎ *407/239–0000 or 800/877–6522* ⚑ *Lake/Orange: 18 holes, 6,531 yards, par 72, USGA rating 72.2; Orange/Cypress: 18 holes, 6,670 yards, par 72, USGA rating 72.6; Cypress/Lake: 18 holes, 6,571 yards, par 72, USGA rating 72.3; Legends: 18 holes, 7,074 yards, par 72, USGA rating 74.3* ⛳ *Greens fees $22–$90 for guests of the resort; $31–$135 nonguests* ☞ *Tee times 2 days in advance. Restaurant, private and group lessons, club rental, driving range, putting green.*

The private **Reunion Resort & Club of Orlando,** has three 18-hole, championship-quality courses: the Legacy, the Tradition, and the Independence, designed by golf legends Arnold Palmer, Jack Nicklaus, and Tom Watson, respectively. The courses' fairways have hills, ponds, and stands of mature palms, oaks, and pines. You'll also find a swimming pavilion, tennis courts, and a shopping and dining area called Main Street Village. You must be a guest of the resort to play here. ⊠ *1000 Reunion Way, Reunion 34747* ☎ *407/662–1000 or 888/300–2434* ⊕ *www.reunionresort.com* ⚑ *The Legacy: 18 holes, 7010 yards, par 72 par; The Tradition: 18 holes, 7255 yards, par 72 par; The Independence: 18 holes, 7257 yards, par 72 par* ⛳ *Greens fees $150* ☞ *Tee times 7–sunset. Restaurant, club rental, shoe rental, locker room, driving range, putting green.*

Rosen's Shingle Creek Golf Club, designed by David Harman, lies alongside a lovely creek, the headwaters of the Everglades. The course is challenging yet playable, with dense stands of oak and pine trees and interconnected waterways. The golf carts even have GPS yardage systems. Universal Studios and the Orange County Convention Center are within a few minutes' drive. ⊠ *9939 Universal Blvd., Orlando 32819* ☎ *407/996–9933 or 866/996–9933* 🖷 *407/996–9935* ⊕ *www.shinglecreekgolf.com* 🏌 *18 holes, 7,205 yards, par 72, USGA rating 69.8* ⛳ *Greens fees $89–$119, $49 after 3 PM* ☞ *Tee times 7–sunset. Restaurant, club rental, shoe rental, driving range, putting green.*

The Winter Park Municipal Golf Club, opened in 1914, is an inexpensive 9-hole course with a low-key approach (their five carts are reserved for players with disabilities, for instance). It has narrow fairways and a cozy clubhouse where you can buy everything from a 50¢ candy bar to a $200 golf bag. ⊠ *761 Old England Ave., Winter Park 32789* ☎ *407/623–3339* 🏌 *9 holes, 2,400 yards, par 35, USGA rating 64.5* ⛳ *Greens fees $10, or $16.25 to play the course twice* ☞ *Wed.–Thurs. 8:45–10 AM members only. Club rental, putting green.*

Health Clubs & Spas

Admission prices listed are per person per day, unless otherwise noted. For massage and most other special services, admission is free.

Walt Disney World

Although most of the Walt Disney World health clubs accept only guests of Walt Disney World hotels—and some accept only guests of that particular hotel—it's not difficult to find a hotel fitness center or spa that is open to the public. In fact, the number of hotels adding public spas grows each year. Because massage therapy schools are turning out hundreds of graduates every year in Orlando, competition has increased, and getting rubbed the right way has become more and more of a bargain. Some hotel spas have even (gasp!) lowered their rates (minimally) for an hour of massage.

The **Dolphin Health Club,** at the eye-catching hotel of the same name, has step and water aerobic classes, hand weights, treadmills, stationary bikes, personal training, massage, a sauna, and a hot tub. ⊠ *Walt Disney World Dolphin* ⊕ *www.swandolphin.com* ☎ *407/934–4264* ⛳ *Free for Dolphin guests, $11 nonguests. Swedish massage: $55 for 25 min, $80 for 50 min, and $135 for 75 min; deep massage: $55 for 25 min, $90 for 50 min, $140 for 80 min* ⊙ *Daily 6 AM–9 PM.*

The **Grand Floridian Spa & Health Club** has Cybex full-circuit strength and cardiovascular equipment, plus treadmills, stair steppers, free weights, personal training, saunas, steam rooms, and hot tubs. In addition to massage, facials, soothing soaks, manicures, and pedicures, the spa offers special massage rooms for couples and "My First" treatments for kids ages 4 to 12. ⊠ *Grand Floridian* ☎ *407/824–2332* ⛳ *$18 per day; $30 per person or $40 per family up to 5 members for length of stay. Massage: $60 for 25 min, $105 for 50 min, $150 for 80 min. Add aromatherapy to any massage for $15* ⊙ *Daily 6 AM–9 PM.*

The **La Vida Health Club** has the standard health-club options for Disney's mid-priced resorts, including massage. The club is in a separate building in the middle of the Coronado Springs Resort, so you can wear your bathrobe to it without having to flounce through lobbies. ⊠ *Coronado Springs Resort* ☎ *407/939–3030* ☜ *$15 per day; $25 per person or $45 per family for length of stay. Massage: $55 for 25 min, $80 for 50 min, $130 for 75 min* ☉ *Daily 6* AM*–9* PM.

Muscles and Bustles Health Club has Cybex equipment, circuit training, tanning, massage, and steam rooms. ⊠ *BoardWalk Inn and Villas* ☎ *407/939–2370* ☜ *$15 per day; $25 per person or $45 per family for length of stay. Massage: $55 for 25 min, $80 for 50 min, $130 for 75 min. Add aromatherapy or deep-tissue massage for $15* ☉ *Daily 6* AM*–9* PM.

The Olympiad Fitness Center, open to all Disney guests, has stair climbers, stationary bikes, cross-country ski machines, treadmills, hand weights, a dry sauna, and a tanning bed. Massages are available at the club or in your room. ⊠ *Contemporary Resort* ☎ *407/824–3410* ☜ *$15 per day; $25 per person or $45 per family for length of stay. Massage: $55 for 25 min, $80 for 50 min, $130 for 75 min; for in-room rate add $40 to all. Add aromatherapy to any massage for $15* ☉ *Daily 6* AM*–9* PM.

Ship Shape Health Club has state-of-the-art fitness, cardiovascular equipment, and free weights, plus massage, a sauna, a spa, and a steam room. All-day admission is free with the purchase of a massage. ⊠ *Yacht and Beach Club Resorts* ☎ *407/934–3256* ☜ *$15 per day; $25 per person or $45 per family for length of stay. Massage: $55 for 25 min, $80 for 55 min, $130 for 75 min. Add $15 to any massage for aromatherapy or deep tissue massage* ☉ *Daily 6* AM*–9* PM.

★ The **Wyndham Palace Resort & Spa Health Club** is the place to visit if you want to get your body treated with seaweed, mud, mustard, and other nourishing liquids and semisolids. The 10,200-square-foot Palace Spa offers more than 60 treatments and services, including a tranquillity facial and a pineapple body scrub. There's also a full-service beauty salon, an expansive fitness center, swimming pools, whirlpools, and saunas and steam rooms. ⊠ *1900 Buena Vista Dr., Downtown Disney* ☎ *407/827–2727* ☜ *$11 hotel guests; $20 nonguests, free with purchase of massage or spa treatment. Massage: $62 for 25 min, $85–$95 for 50 min, $130–$145 for 80 min* ☉ *Sun.–Fri. 9–7, Sat. 8* AM*–9* PM.

Zahanati Massage & Fitness Center offers facials, body treatments, and various massages. You can work out on state-of-the-art exercise equipment, make an appointment for a personal training session, and take advantage of amenities including dry saunas and steam rooms. ⊠ *Animal Kingdom Lodge* ☎ *407/938–4715 or 407/938–3000* ☜ *$15 per day; $25 per person or $45 per family for length of stay. Massage: $55 for 25 min, $80 for 50 min, $130 for 75 min* ☉ *6* AM*–9* PM.

Universal Orlando

The **Mandara Spa** was named for the mythical mountain Mandara Giri. A Sanskrit legend tells of a spring on the mountain from which flowed an "elixir of immortality and eternal youth." Naturally, treatments at this 11,000-square-foot facility are designed to make you feel refreshed and revitalized. There's also a full-service salon and a fitness center. ⊠ *Portofino Bay Hotel* ☎ *407/503–1000* ✆ *$12 hotel guests; $12 nonguests, free with purchase of massage or spa treatment. Massage: $85–$135 for 50 min* ⊙ *6 AM–10 PM.*

Orlando Area

To find out what's hot in exercise facilities when you visit, the best bet is to ask at your hotel, because clubs outside WDW come and go. The local YMCAs, however, are longtime favorites. Most have a single-visit fee of $10–$12, and you don't have to be a Y member. To find the YMCA nearest to where you're staying, phone the **Metropolitan YMCA office** (☎ 407/896–9220).

The **Central Florida YMCA** has Cybex machines, free weights, racquet-ball, a half-Olympic-size pool, two gyms, and aerobics classes. It's an older property, but the weight-room facilities have been revamped. For prospective members, the first two visits are free. ⊠ *433 N. Mills Ave., Orlando* ☎ *407/896–6901* ⊕ *www.centralfloridaymca.org* ✆ *$12; 5 free visits per month for YMCA members from outside Orlando* ⊙ *Weekdays 5 AM–9:30 PM, Sat. 8–6, Sun. noon–6.*

YMCA Aquatic Center is definitely more posh than the average Y. It has Cybex and Body Masters weight machines, racquetball, two swimming pools (one Olympic-size), and a diving well. Members can call ahead to reserve racquetball courts. ⊠ *8422 International Dr., Orlando* ☎ *407/363–1911* ⊕ *www.ymcaaquaticcenter.com* ✆ *$10; 3 free visits per month for YMCA members from outside Orlando* ⊙ *Weekdays 6 AM–9 PM, Sat. 8–5, Sun. noon–4.*

The **Celebration Fitness Centre & Day Spa**, operated in conjunction with the Celebration Health Florida Hospital, promotes healthy living through exercise and relaxation treatments, and caters especially to those with a medical need. You can take low- and high-impact aerobics, Pilates, tai chi, and spinning classes. There's a 25-meter lap pool, a warm-water exercise pool with an underwater treadmill, a basketball court, and cardio and weight machines. Body treatments include massages, sea-salt wraps, aromatherapy facials, microdermabrasion, waxing services, manicures, and pedicures. ⊠ *700 Bloom St., Celebration* ☎ *407/566–6000 or 407/303–4444* ⊕ *www.celebrationfitness.com* ✆ *$15 per day, free with purchase of massage or spa treatment. Massage: $45 for 25 min, $70 for 50 min, $100 for 80 min* ⊙ *Weekdays 8–8, weekends 8–6.*

★ The **Ritz-Carlton Spa at the Grande Lakes Orlando** has more than 40,000 square feet of space with 40 different treatment rooms, a 4,000-square-foot heated lap pool, a relaxation conservatory, a full-service salon, and a boutique. Florida's bounty of oranges, lemons, and grapefruits is used for beauty treatments. In addition to the usual pampering, you can take classes in South American salsa dancing, Russian ballet, Middle Eastern belly dancing, or Indian meditation. ⊠ *4012 Central Florida Pkwy, I-Drive Area* ☎ *407/206–2400* ✆ *$15 hotel guests; $25 nonguests, free* *with purchase of massage or spa treatment. Massage: $65 for 25 min, $100 for 50 min, $155 for 80 min ⊙ 8 AM–8 PM.*

Horseback Riding

Walt Disney World

🅲 **Fort Wilderness Resort and Campground** (⊠ Fort Wilderness Resort ☎ 407/824–2832) offers tame trail rides through backwoods. Children must be at least nine to ride, and adults must weigh less than 250 pounds. Trail rides are $32 for 45 minutes; hours of operation vary by season. You must check in 30 minutes prior to your ride, and reservations are essential. Both horseback riding and the campground are open to nonguests.

Orlando Area

Fodor'sChoice **Grand Cypress Equestrian Center** gives private lessons in hunt seat, jump-
★ ing, combined training, dressage, and Western riding. Supervised novice and advanced group trail rides are available daily 8:30 to 5. Trail rides are $45 per hour. Private lessons are $55 per half hour and $100 per hour. Call at least a week ahead for reservations in winter and spring. ⊠ *Hyatt Regency Grand Cypress Resort, 1 Equestrian Dr., Lake Buena Vista Area* ☎ *407/239–4608.*

🅲 **Horse World Riding Stables,** open daily 9 to 5, has basic and longer, more advanced nature-trail tours along beautifully wooded trails near Kissimmee. The stables area has picnic tables, farm animals you can pet, and a pond to fish in. Trail rides are $39 for basic, $48 for intermediate, and $69 for advanced. Trail rides for children 5 and under are $15, and the stables offer birthday party packages for kids, as well as hay rides for groups. Reservations a day in advance are recommended for the advanced trails. ⊠ *3705 S. Poinciana Blvd., Kissimmee* ☎ *407/847–4343* ⊕ *www.horseworldstables.com.*

Ice Hockey

The Florida Seals don't play in the top-notch National Hockey League, and they don't bring the likes of the Boston Bruins to town. But the Seals do compete in the feisty Southern Professional Hockey League, facing teams from Florida cities, like Jacksonville and St. Petersburg, and other cities, like Macon, Georgia, and Knoxville, Tennessee. Single-game seats go for $10–$25. All home games are played at the Silver SpursArena in Kissimmee. ⊠ *Silver Spurs Arena, 1875 Silver Spur La., Osceola Heritage Park* ☎ *321/939–2465* ⊕ *www.floridaseals.com.*

Jai Alai

Orlando-Seminole Jai-Alai (⊠ 6405 S. U.S. 17–92, Casselberry ☎ 407/331–6221), about 20 minutes north of Orlando off I–4 Exit 48, offers South Florida horse-racing simulcasts and betting in addition to jai alai at the fronton. Admission is $1, and $2–$5 for reserved seating. Simulcast races are Monday through Saturday noon–9 PM and Sunday noon–7:30 PM. Specific times vary, so call ahead for a schedule.

Miniature Golf

Fantasia Gardens (☎ 407/560–4870), near Disney-MGM Studios and the Swan and Dolphin resorts, recalls Disney's *Fantasia* with a huge statue of Mickey in his sorcerer's outfit directing dancing broomsticks. Music from the film plays over loud speakers. Games cost $10.70 for adults, $8.56 for children ages 3 to 9, and there's a 50% discount for the second consecutive round played.

Winter Summerland (☎ 407/560–7161) has everything from sand castles to snowbanks, and is allegedly where Santa and his elves spend their summer vacation. The course is close to Disney's Animal Kingdom and the Coronado Springs and All-Star resorts. Adults play for $10.70 and children ages 3 to 9 play for $8.56, including tax. A 50% discount applies to your second consecutive round.

FodorsChoice ★

Rock Climbing

The Aiguille Rock Climbing Center, has the only cliffs in the Orlando area—on 6,500 square feet of rock-studded walls. Climbers can reach a height of 45 feet, and different areas of the indoor, air-conditioned facility are set up to provide varying levels of challenges for varying skill levels. For safety, all climbers are tethered to a rope controlled by someone on the ground level. ⊠ *999 Charles St., Longwood* ☎ *407/332–1430* ⊕ *www.climborlando.com* ✉ *Day passes $15 adults, $10 children under 12; $6.50 equipment rental, which includes proper shoes and harness; $5.35 helmets; $30 per hr for rock climbing instruction, reservation required* ⊗ *Weekdays 10–10, Sat. 10 AM–11 PM, Sun. noon–7.*

Running

Walt Disney World

Walt Disney World has several scenic running trails. Pick up maps at any Disney resort. Early in the morning all the roads are fairly uncrowded and make for good running. The roads that snake through Downtown Disney resorts are pleasant, as are the cart paths on the golf courses.

At the **Caribbean Beach Resort** (☎ 407/934–3400), there's a 1½-mi running promenade around Barefoot Bay. **Fort Wilderness Campground** (☎ 407/824–2900) has a 2⅓-mi running course with woods, as well as numerous exercise stations along the way.

Orlando Area

Orlando has two excellent bike trails, the West Orange Trail and the Cady Way Trail, which are also good for running. Rural Orlando has some unbelievable hiking trails with long, densely wooded, nonrocky stretches that are tremendous for running, and often you can run for a half hour and not see any other living being—except wild game.

Turkey Lake Park, about 4 mi from Disney, has a 3-mi biking trail that's popular with runners. Several wooded hiking trails also make for a good run. The park closes at 5 PM, and fees are $4 per car. ⊠ *3401 S. Hiawassee Rd., Orlando* ☎ *407/299–5581.*

The Rollins College area, in Winter Park, has paths along the shady streets and around the lakes, where you can breathe in fresh air and the aroma of old money.

The Orlando Runners Club meets every Sunday at 7 AM in Central Park (corner of Park Avenue and Welbourne Boulevard) for 6-, 10-, and 11-mi jaunts. The club also has a weekly Wednesday night run through downtown Orlando. The Track Shack, a sporting goods store open weekdays 10–7 and Saturdays 10–5, has details. *C/o Track Shack ⊠ 1104 N. Mills Ave.* ☎ *407/898–1313 ⊕ www.orlandorunnersclub.org.*

The Tosohatchee State Reserve runs through a huge pine forest and around the edges of a virgin cypress swamp. You can spot deer, all sorts of wildfowl—including an occasional eagle—and possibly some wild hogs or black bear along the miles of wilderness trails. The park's entrance fee is $2 per car. ⊠ *3365 Taylor Creek Rd., Christmas* ☎ *407/568–5893.*

Orlando Wilderness Park, managed by the Orlando Parks and Recreation Department, is off U.S. 50, just north of the town of Christmas. The park is a conservation success story. The 4-mi walking-jogging-biking trail circles a wetlands area that's actually used to clean Orlando wastewater. Don't worry, there's no foul smell—but there are fowl, plenty of them. Bird-watchers consider this one of the best spots in the state. An additional 5-mi trail that links up to the primary trail takes you to the banks of the St. Johns River. Park admission is free. ⊠ *Wheeler Rd. at State Rd. 420, Christmas* ☎ *407/246–2288.*

Skateboarding

♻ **Vans Skatepark**—for those hip enough to know that a bowl is not something from which you consume soup but a giant, concrete skate course—is a 61,000-square-foot skatepark with a great indoor bowl. The park has a 31,000-square-foot plywood indoor street course, an 11,000-square-foot concrete indoor street course, a snack bar, and a viewing area. Skaters must be over 18 or have a parent or guardian sign a release form. Mandatory protective gear is for rent here. Two hours of skating costs $12 for nonmembers on weekdays and $15 on weekends. ⊠ *5220 International Dr., Orlando* ☎ *407/351–3881 ⊕ www.vans.com.*

Sky Diving & Parasailing

Sammy Duvall's Water Sports Centre (⊠ Disney's Contemporary Resort ☎ 407/939–0754) offers parasailing on Bay Lake in addition to water sports. Flights, $85 per outing, reach a height of 450 feet and last 7–10 minutes. Individual participants must weigh at least 100 pounds, but youngsters may go aloft accompanied by an adult. Tandem flights are $135.

Fodor'sChoice ★ **Sky Venture,** a 120-mph vertical-lift wind tunnel, allows you to experience everything sky divers enjoy, all within an air blast that reaches only 12 feet. The experience starts with sky-diving instruction, after which you suit up and hit the wind tunnel, where you soar like a bird under the watchful eye of your instructor. While you are "falling" on the wind stream, you even experience what divers called "ground rush," because you are surrounded by a video depiction of a real sky dive. The experience is so realistic that sky-diving clubs come to Sky Venture to hone their skills. Famous people who have tried this include George Bush Sr. There's no minimum (or maximum) age requirement, but you must be 250 pounds or less and at least 4 feet tall. You can purchase a video of your jump for $16. ⊠ *6805 Visitors Circle, I-Drive Area Orlando* ☎ *407/903–1150* ⊕ *www.skyventure.com* ✉ *$38.50 per jump for adults, $33.50 for children 12 and under; $600 per hr, $330 per ½ hr* ⊙ *Weekdays 2–midnight, weekends noon–midnight.*

Soccer

Disney's Wide World of Sports Complex (☎ 407/828–3267 ⊕ www. disneyworldsports.com), among its cornucopia of events, presents soccer matches and tournaments, including the annual Disney Soccer Showcase, an October match that attracts men's and women's teams from around the world.

Tennis

Walt Disney World

You can play tennis at any number of Disney hotels, and you may find the courts a pleasant respite from the milling throngs in the parks. All have lights and are open 7 AM to 8 PM, unless otherwise noted, and most have lockers and rental rackets for $3 to $5 a day. There seems to be a long-term plan to move from hard courts to clay. Most courts are open to all players—court staff can opt to turn away nonguests when things get busy, but that doesn't often happen. Disney offers group and individual tennis lessons at all of its tennis complexes.

The Contemporary Resort, with its sprawl of six HydroGrid courts, is the center of Disney's tennis program. It has two backboards and an automatic ball machine. Reservations are available up to 24 hours in advance, and there's an arrange-a-game service. ☎ *407/939–7529 reservations* ✉ *Free; lessons $50 per hr or $30 per half hr for individual and $40 per hr for group of two* ⊙ *Daily 7–7.*

Fort Wilderness Resort and Campground has two tennis courts in the middle of a field. They're popular with youngsters, and if you hate players who are too free about letting their balls stray to their neighbors' court, this is not the place for you. There are no court reservations and instruction is not available. ⊠ *3520 N. Fort Wilderness Trail* ☎ *407/824–2742* ✉ *Free* ⊙ *Daily 8–6.*

The Grand Floridian has two Har-Tru clay courts that attract a somewhat serious-minded tennis crowd. Court reservations are available up to 24 hours in advance. ☎ *407/939–7529* ✉ *Free* ⊙ *Daily 8–8.*

The Yacht and Beach Club Resorts have two blacktop tennis courts. Court reservations are not required. Equipment is available at the towel window at no charge. ☎ *407/939–7529* ✉ *Free* ⊙ *Daily 7 AM–10 PM.*

Orlando Area

Lake Cane Tennis Center has 17 lighted hard courts. Six pros provide private and group lessons. ⊠ *5108 Turkey Lake Rd., Orlando* ☎ *407/352–4913* ✆ *$3 per hr weekdays during day, $5 per hr weekends and weekday evenings after 5, $40 per hr and $21 per ½ hr private lessons* ⊙ *Weekdays 8 AM–10 PM, weekends 7 AM–8:30 PM.*

Orange Lake Country Club has, in addition to its golf courses, seven lighted, all-weather hard tennis courts. It's five minutes from Walt Disney World's main entrance. Court reservations are necessary. ⊠ *8505 W. Irlo Bronson Memorial Hwy., Kissimmee* ☎ *407/239–0000 or 800/877–6522* ✆ *Free for guests, $5 per hr nonguests, $60 per hr for private lessons, $10 per ½ hr for group clinics, $2 per hr and $5 per day racket rental* ⊙ *Daily dawn–11 PM.*

The Orlando Tennis Center has 16 lighted tennis courts (11 Har-Tru and five asphalt), four outdoor racquetball courts, and three teaching tennis pros. Call in advance for court availability. Normal rates are slightly cheaper for Orlando residents with proper ID. ⊠ *649 W. Livingston St., Orlando* ☎ *407/246–2162* ✆ *$6 per 1½ hr for tennis on Har-Tru and $4 per 1½ hr on asphalt, $2 per hr for racquetball, $40 per hr and $20 per ½ hr for private lessons, $7 group lessons* ⊙ *Weekdays 8 AM–10 PM, weekends 8–3.*

Walt Disney World Sports

Fodor'sChoice **Disney's Wide World of Sports Complex** is proof that Disney doesn't do
★ anything unless it does it in a big way. The huge complex contains a 7,500-seat baseball stadium—housed in a giant stucco structure that from the outside looks like a Moroccan palace—a 5,000-seat field house, and a number of fan-oriented commercial ventures such as the Official All-Star Cafe and shops that sell clothing and other items sanctioned by Major League Baseball, the NBA, and the NFL. During spring training, the perennially great Atlanta Braves play here, and the minor-league Orlando Rays have games during the regular season. But that's just the tip of the iceberg. The complex hosts all manner of individual and team competitions, including big-ticket tennis tournaments. In all, some 30 spectator sports are represented among the annual events presented, including Harlem Globetrotters basketball games, baseball fantasy camps held in conjunction with the Braves at the beginning of spring training each year, and track events ranging from the Walt Disney World Marathon to dozens of annual Amateur Athletic Union (AAU) championships. The complex has softball, basketball, and other games for group events ranging from family reunions to corporate picnics. ⊠ *Osceola Pkwy.* ☎ *407/828–3267 events information* ⊕ *dwws.disney.go.com/wideworldofsports.*

A key source for sports information on all things Disney is the **Sports Information and Reservations Hotline** (☎ 407/939–7529 ⊕ www.disneyworld.disney.go.com).

Water Sports

Walt Disney World

Boating is big at Disney, and it has the largest fleet of for-rent pleasure craft in the nation. There are marinas at the Caribbean Beach Resort, Contemporary Resort, Downtown Disney Marketplace, Fort Wilderness Resort and Campground, Grand Floridian, Old Key West Resort, Polynesian Resort, Port Orleans Resort, Port Orleans–Riverside Resort, and the Wilderness Lodge. The Yacht and Beach Club Resorts rent Sunfish sailboats, catamarans, motor-powered pontoon boats, pedal boats, and tiny two-passenger Water Sprites—a hit with children—for use on Bay Lake and the adjoining Seven Seas Lagoon, Club Lake, Lake Buena Vista, or Buena Vista Lagoon. Most hotels rent Water Sprites, but you should check each hotel's rental roster. The Polynesian Resort marina rents outrigger canoes. Fort Wilderness rents canoes for paddling along the placid canals in the area. And you can sail and waterski on Bay Lake and the Seven Seas Lagoon; stop at the Fort Wilderness, Contemporary, Polynesian, or Grand Floridian marina to rent sailboats or sign up for waterskiing. Call 407/939–0754 for parasailing, waterskiing, and Jet Skis reservations.

Sammy Duvall's Water Sports Centre (⊠ Disney's Contemporary Resort ☎ 407/939–0754) offers waterskiing, wakeboarding (like waterskiing on a small surf board; usually done on your knees), and parasailing on Bay Lake. Boat and equipment rental is included with waterskiing (maximum of five people) and wakeboarding (maximum of four people), as are the services of an expert instructor. Each is $140 per hour, plus tax.

Orlando Area

Alexander Creek and Juniper Creek offer wonderful wilderness canoeing, with abundant wildlife and moss-draped oaks and bald cypresses canopying the clean, clear waters. Some of these runs are quite rough—lots of ducking under brush and maneuvering around trees. You must pack out what you pack in. On Alexander Creek, **Alexander Springs Canoe Rental** (⊠ 49525 Rte. 445, Altoona ☎ 352/669–3522) rents canoes for $10.50 for two hours, $17 for 4 hours, or $26 per day—with $20 cash deposit and ID—plus a $3 per person park entrance fee. All canoes must be returned to the beach by 3:30. **Juniper Springs Canoe Rental** (⊠ 2670 E. Hwy. 40, Silver Springs ☎ 352/625–2808) has canoes on Juniper Creek. The cost is $28 for a 7-mi trip of approximately four hours—with $20 cash deposit and ID. Rentals are available daily 8–noon. ⊠ *Ocala National Forest, just north of the greater Orlando area.*

The St. Johns River winds through pine and cypress woods and past pastures where cows graze placidly, skirting the occasional housing development. There's good bird- and wildlife-watching around the river; herons, ibis, storks, and sometimes bald eagles can be spotted, along with alligators and manatees. It's a favored local boating spot, for everything from a day of waterskiing to a weeklong trip in a houseboat. Rentals are available in Deland (west of I–4 via U.S. 44). For St. Johns River excursions, **Hontoon Landing Resort and Marina** (⊠ 2317 River Ridge Rd., Deland ☎ 386/734–2474, 800/248–2474 in Florida ⊕ www.

hontoon.com) rents luxury houseboats for use on St. Johns River—$595 to $1,295 for a day, $850 to $1,875 for a weekend, and $1,195 to $2,795 for a week. Pontoon boats that hold up to 10 people cost $100 to $135 daily. For $55 a day, you can rent a 16 foot fishing boat. Bargain month is January—when it's cold by Florida standards but simply pleasant if you're from up north—with houseboat rentals dropping as low as $925 for a four-day, midweek rental.

Fodor'sChoice
★

Wekiva River, a great waterway for nature lovers, runs through 6,397-acre **Wekiva Springs State Park** (⊠ 1800 Wekiva Circle, I–4 Exit 94, Apopka ☎ 407/884–2008 ⊕ www.dep.state.fl.us/parks) into the St. Johns River. Bordered by cypress marshlands, its clear, spring-fed waters showcase Florida wildlife, including otters, raccoons, alligators, bobcats, deer, turtles, and numerous birds. Canoes and camp sites can be rented near the southern entrance of the park in Apopka. Canoes are available for $17 for a half-day and $26 for a full day. The park has 60 camp sites, some of which are "canoe sites," in that they can only be reached via the river itself, while others are "trail sites," meaning you must hike a good bit of the park's 13.5-mi hiking trail to reach them. Most sites, however, are for the less hardy among us—you can drive right up to them. Sites go for $18.86 a night with electric hook-ups or $16.73 with no electricity.

After Dark

9

FODOR'S CHOICE

Cirque du Soleil–*La Nouba, in Downtown Disney*

Comedy Warehouse, *on Pleasure Island*

House of Blues, *in Downtown Disney*

IllumiNations, *at Epcot*

SpectroMagic, *in the Magic Kingdom*

Updated by
Gary
McKechnie

FOR SOME, ORLANDO IS simply a factory town, and the factories just happen to be theme parks. To others, it's a backwater burg that lacks sophistication and culture. Then there are the preteen girls who see it as the breeding ground for bubblegum boy groups like *NSync and the Backstreet Boys. But just about everyone agrees that Orlando is an entertainment capital, and as such is obligated to provide evening diversions to everyone who visits.

About 43 million visitors come to Orlando each year, and many are adults traveling without children. This is why, after years of denial, Disney heeded the command of the profits and built Pleasure Island and later West Side, now both part of the Downtown Disney entertainment complex. In response, Universal Orlando opened CityWalk to siphon off from Disney what Disney had siphoned off from downtown Orlando, which is now struggling to find its footing amid the increased competition.

If you're here for at least two nights and don't mind losing some sleep, reserve one evening for Downtown Disney and the next for CityWalk. They are both well worth seeing. If you want a one-night blowout, however, head to Disney—believe it or not! By virtue of Disney's status as essentially a separate governmental entity—kind of like a Native American reservation—clubs on Disney property tend to stay open later than bars elsewhere. While most bars in Orange County close around 1 AM, Disney clubs usually stay open until 2. Keep in mind that as of 2003, smoking is banned in all Florida restaurants and bars that serve food. If you want to smoke inside, you'll have to find a drinks-only bar.

WALT DISNEY WORLD

When you enter the fiefdom known as Walt Disney World, you're likely to see as many watering holes as cartoon characters. After beating your feet around a theme park all day, there are lounges, bars, speakeasies, pubs, sports bars, and microbreweries where you can settle down with a soothing libation. Your choice of nightlife can be found at various Disney shopping and entertainment complexes—from the casual down-by-the-shore BoardWalk to the much larger multi-area Downtown Disney, which comprises the Marketplace, Pleasure Island, and West Side. Everywhere you look, jazz trios, bluesmen, DJs, and rockers are tuning up and turning on their amps after dinner's done. Plus, two long-running dinner shows provide an evening of song, dance, and dining, all for a single price.

Don't assume that all after-dark activities center solely around adult bars and expensive shows. A wealth of free shows are performed at Epcot's pavilions and stages at the Magic Kingdom and Disney–MGM Studios. Even if you head back to your hotel for an afternoon nap or swim, you can always return to a theme park to catch the fireworks show. Get information on WDW nightlife from the Walt Disney World information hotline (☎ 407/824–2222 or 407/824–4500) or check online at ⊕ www. waltdisneyworld.com. Disney nightspots accept American Express, MasterCard, and Visa. And cash. Lots of it.

Disney's BoardWalk

At the turn of the 20th century, Americans escaping the cities for the Atlantic seaside spent their days on breeze-swept boardwalks above the strand, where early thrill rides kept company with band concerts and other activities. Here, across Crescent Lake from Disney's Yacht and Beach Club Resorts, WDW has created its own version of these amusement areas, a shoreside complex that's complete with restaurants, bars and clubs, souvenir sellers, surreys, saltwater taffy vendors, and shops. When the lights go on after sunset, the mood is festive—the stage is set for plentiful diversions and a romantic stroll. For information on events call the **Board-Walk entertainment hotline** (☎ 407/939–3492 or 407/939–2444).

Atlantic Dance Hall. This club started out as a hypercool room recalling the Swing Era, with martinis, cigars, and Sinatra sound-alikes, but that didn't last, so it reopened as a Latin club. That didn't last either, so now it is a typical Top 40 dance club with a DJ Dance Party Tuesdays through Saturdays. How long will this last? Who knows? Next it may become an American Legion hall. You must be 21 to enter. ☎ *407/939–2444 or 407/939–2430* 🖃 *No cover* ☉ *Tues.–Sat. 9 PM–2 AM.*

Big River Grille & Brewing Works. Disney World's first brew pub, Big River, has warm wood surfaces and intimate tables where brewmasters tend to their potions, adding to the charm of this retreat. Inside, stainless steel vats brew a variety of beers, the most popular being Rocket Red Ale. But if you're not sure what you'd like best, order a $5 sampler that includes up to six 4-ounce shots of whatever they have on tap that day, from the Red Rocket, Southern Flyer Light Lager, Gadzooks Pilsener, and Tilt Pale Ale to Sweet Magnolia Brown and Irish Red Lager. Pub grub, sandwiches, and cigars round out the offerings, and the brewery's sidewalk café is a great place for people-watching and good conversation. ☎ *407/560–0253* 🖃 *No cover* ☉ *Daily 11:30 AM–12:30 AM.*

ESPN Club. As with all themed things at Disney, the sports motif here is carried into every nook and cranny. The main dining area looks like a sports arena, with a basketball-court hardwood floor and a giant score-board that projects the big game of the day. Sportscasters originate pro-grams from a TV and radio broadcast booth, and there are more than 100 TV monitors throughout the facility, even in the rest rooms. If you want to watch NFL on Sunday, get here about two hours before kick-off, because the place is packed for back-to-back games. On special game days, like those of the World Series or Super Bowl, count on huge crowds and call in advance to see if special seating rules are in effect. ☎ *407/939–1177* 🖃 *No cover* ☉ *Sun.–Thurs. 11:30 AM–1 AM, Fri. and Sat. 11:30 AM–2 AM.*

Jellyrolls. In this rugged, rockin', and boisterous piano bar, comedians act as emcees and play dueling grand pianos nonstop. In a Disney ver-sion of "Stump the Band," they promise "You Name It. We Play It." You may have gone to piano bars before, but the steady stream of con-ventions at Disney makes this the place to catch CEOs doing the conga to Barry Manilow's "Copacabana"—if that's your idea of a good time. You must be 21 to enter. ☎ *407/560–8770* 🖃 *$8 cover after 7 PM* ☉ *Daily 7 PM–2 AM.*

Downtown Disney

West Side

Disney's West Side is a hip outdoor complex of shopping, dining, and entertainment with the main venues being the House of Blues, Dis-neyQuest, and Cirque du Soleil. Aside from this trio, there are no cover charges. Whether you're club hopping or not, the West Side is worth a visit for its waterside location, wide promenade, and diverse shopping and dining. Opening time is 11 AM, closing time around 2 AM; crowds vary with the season, but weeknights tend to be less busy. For entertainment times and more information, call 407/824–4500 or 407/824–2222.

Bongos Cuban Café. Latin rhythms provide the beat at this enterprise owned by pop singer Gloria Estefan. Although this is primarily a restaurant, you may get a kick out of the pre-Castro Havana interior, the three bars, and the Latin band that plays *muy caliente* music every Friday and Sat-urday evening. Samba, tango, salsa, and merengue rhythms are rolling throughout the week. Drop by for a beer and a "babalu." ☎ *407/828–0999* ☉ *Daily 11 AM–2 AM.*

Fodor'sChoice **Cirque du Soleil–***La Nouba***.** This surreal show by the world-famous cir-
★ cus company starts at 100 mph and accelerates from there. Although the ticket price is high compared with those for other local shows, you'd be hard-pressed to hear anyone complain. The performance is 90 minutes of extraordinary acrobatics, avant-garde stagings, costumes, choreography, and a thrilling grand finale that makes you doubt New-ton's law of gravity. The story of *La Nouba*—derived from the French phrase *faire la nouba* (which translates to "live it up")—is alternately mysterious, dreamlike, comical, and sensual. A cast of 72 international performers takes the stage in this specially constructed, 70,000-square-foot venue. The original music is performed by a live orchestra that you might miss if you don't scrutinize the towers on either side of the stage,

which is a technical marvel in itself, with constantly moving platforms and lifts. A couple of hints: call well in advance for tickets to improve your chances of getting front row seats (there are three levels of seating) and hire a babysitter if necessary—admission is charged for infants. ☎ *407/939–7600 reservations* ⊕ *www.cirquedusoleil.com* ✉ *Premium seats (center section) $87 adults, $65 children under 10; Category 2 seats (to the side and the back) $75 adults, $56 children under 10; Category 3 seats (to the far sides and very back) $59 adults, $44 children under 10* ⊙ *Performances Tues.–Sat. 6 and 9 PM.*

DisneyQuest. Inside an enclosed five-floor video–virtual reality minitheme park, they've figured out that some suckers—er, guests—will pay big bucks to play video games. To be fair, once you've shelled out the considerable cover, you can play all day. There are some cutting-edge games here, but save your money if you think you'll quickly tire of electronic arcade noises. ☎ *407/828–4600* ✉ *$34 adults, $28 children 3–9, including tax* ⊙ *Sun.-Thurs. 11:30 AM–11 PM, Fri.-Sat. 11:30 AM–midnight.*

Fodor's Choice **House of Blues.** The restaurant hosts cool blues nightly (alongside its rib-
★ sticking Mississippi Delta cooking), but it's the HOB's concert hall next door that garners the real attention. The hall has showcased local and nationally known artists including Aretha Franklin, David Byrne, Steve Miller, Los Lobos, the Backstreet Boys, and *NSync. From rock to reggae to R&B, this is arguably the best live-music venue in Orlando, and standing a few feet from your guitar heroes is the way music should be seen and heard. ☎ *407/934–2583* ✉ *Covers vary* ⊙ *Daily, performance times vary.*

Downtown Disney Marketplace
Although the Marketplace offers little in the line of typical nightlife, there is hardly a more enjoyable place for families to spend a quiet evening window shopping, enjoying ice cream at a courtyard café, or strolling among eclectic Disney stores.

Cap'n Jack's Restaurant. Swing by to gulp down some oysters or sip on a huge strawberry margarita made with strawberry tequila. It's not a lively joint, but it's a nice spot for a quiet evening beside the waterfront. ☎ *407/828–3971* ⊙ *Daily 11:30–10:30.*

Pleasure Island
Pleasure Island was Disney's first foray into a nighttime complex, and judging by the crowds, the combination of clubs, stores, and entertainment remains an attractive mix. The 6-acre park has seven jam-packed clubs—all of which can be accessed with a single admission. Pleasure Island is packed with an across-the-board mix of college kids, young married couples, middle-age business folk, world travelers, and moms and pops sneaking out for an evening. Even kids (with an accompanying adult) are allowed in each club, except Mannequins and BET Sound-Stage Club. Weekends are the busiest, although Thursday hops with Disney World cast members itching to blow their just-issued paychecks.

At the West End Stage, the mistress of ceremonies at a popular disco/rock n' roll stage show lets you know that the Island's theme is a nightly New

Year's Eve party. She leads you through this storyline: to avoid a midnight curfew, dancers—and this is no joke—need to shimmy like maniacs in an energetic effort to disable the evil computer that enforces the deadline. Surprisingly, the audience buys it. When asked to help the cause by shouting "Par-tay!" they do so with passion and gusto. Don't worry, dancers never fail to add two extra hours of "partay"-ing by simply boogie-ing that rotten old computer into submission. ⊠ *Off Buena Vista Dr.* ☎ *407/ 934–7781 or 407/824–2222* ✉ *$18 for entire park, access to shops, clubs, and restaurants free* ☾ *until 7 PM when cover charge takes effect. Clubs daily 7 PM–2 AM; shops and restaurants daily 10:30 AM–2 AM.*

Adventurers' Club. Like those of a private 1930s cabaret, the clubroom walls here are practically paved with memorabilia from exotic places. Servers entertain you with their patter, and several times a night character explorer–actors share tall tales of the adventures they encountered on imaginary expeditions. Stop in for a drink and enjoy the scenery, or visit the Library for a slapstick show. With all its props and comedy, this is a good option if you're here with kids—who love shouting the club's rallying cry, "Kungaloosh!" ☎ *407/824–2222 or 407/824–4500.*

BET SoundStage Club. Backed by Black Entertainment Television, this club pays tribute to all genres of black music through videos, live performances, and shows by BET's own dance troupe. As the evening progresses, sounds shift from BET's Top 10 to old R&B to hip-hop—a blend that's attracted legions of locals who proclaim this the funkiest nightspot in Central Florida (perhaps also the loudest). Even if you're dance-challenged, you might find it hard to resist shakin' your groove thang to the beat-rich music. Go on, Spaulding. Bust a move. You must be at least 21 to enter. ☎ *407/934–7666.*

Fodor'sChoice **Comedy Warehouse.** At one of the island's most popular clubs, gifted co-
★ medians perform various improv games, sing improvised songs, and create off-the-cuff sketches based largely on suggestions from the audience. Each of the evening's five performances is different, but the cast is usually on target. Lines for the free shows start forming roughly 45 minutes before curtain, so get there early for a good seat. It's well worth the wait to watch a gifted comedy troupe work without profanity. ☎ *407/828–2939.*

8TRAX. In case the lava lamps and disco balls don't tip you off, the '70s are back at this glittering club. Slip on your bell-bottoms, strap on your platform shoes, and groove to Chic, the Village People, or Donna Summer on disk. After a while, it might seem like you're in your own Quentin Tarantino film. Swing by on Thursdays when the calendar fast-forwards to the 1980s to celebrate the music of that not-so-long-gone era. ☎ *407/934–7160.*

Mannequins. You can expect over-the-top floor shows complete with suggestive bump-and-grind moves at this New York–style dance palace. Twentysomethings rule on the revolving dance floor, and the club also welcomes a gay clientele. Everyone grooves to Top 40 hits, elaborate lighting, and special effects like bubbles and snow. You must be at least 21 to be admitted. ☎ *407/934–6375.*

Motion. The latest arrival to the Pleasure Island mix, Motion offers a play list of dance music from Zoot Suit Riot to the latest techno hits. This mix of music means that it attracts a cross-section of people who (eventually) hear at least one song they like. The two-story warehouse-like club is stark, emphasizing the dance floor and the club's twirling lights and thumping sound system. Motion hits the right tone to attract a young and hip clientele. Doors open nightly at 9 PM (and stay open until 2 AM). ☎ 407/827–9453.

Rock & Roll Beach Club. This three-tier bar is always crowded and throbbing with rock music from the '50s to the '80s. With most clubs playing machine-produced music, it's a treat to hang out where the tunes were created by humans. The live band and disc jockeys never let the action die down, and the sounds attract a slightly older (thirties) crowd. The friendly and fun feel of a neighborhood bar is sustained by the pool tables, pinball machines, Foosball, darts, and video games. ☎ 407/934–7654.

Hotel Bars

Disney-Owned Hotels in Walt Disney World

With more than a dozen resort hotels on Walt Disney World property, the hotel-bar scene is understandably active. Depending on whether the resort is geared toward business or romance, the lounges can be soothing or boisterous—or both. You do not have to be a resort guest to visit the bars and lounges, and a casual tour of them may well provide an evening's entertainment. To reach any of these hotel bars directly, you can call the Disney operator at 407/824–4500 or 407/824–2222.

Ale and Compass Lounge. This tiny, serene, nautical-theme cappuccino-coffee bar also serves ales and spirits. ⊠ *Yacht Club Resort* ☉ *Daily 4 PM–midnight.*

Belle Vue Room. Settle back in this lovely 1930s-style sitting room to escape the crowds, play board games, savor a quiet drink, and listen to long-ago shows played through old radios. Step out onto the balcony for a soothing view of the village green and lake. ⊠ *Boardwalk Inn* ☉ *Daily 5 PM–midnight.*

California Grill. High atop the Contemporary Resort, this restaurant-lounge offers a fantastic view of the Magic Kingdom, especially when the sun goes down and the tiny white lights on Main Street start to twinkle. Add nightly fireworks (usually at 10 PM), and there's no better place to order a glass of wine and enjoy the show. An observation deck, which extends to the end of the hotel, adds a breezy vantage point from which to see all this, plus surrounding Bay Lake. In high season, you may need dinner reservations to gain access to the observation deck. ⊠ *Contemporary Resort* ☉ *Daily 5:30 PM–midnight, dinner 6 PM–10 PM.*

Banana Cabana. Befitting its location in Old Port Royale, the cabana serves tropical drinks, beer, wine, and cocktails. It may not be Margaritaville, but it's close enough. ⊠ *Caribbean Beach Resort* ☉ *Daily 5 PM–10 PM.*

Citrico's. Another Grand Floridian lounge, this one is attached to the eponymous hip and classy restaurant. If you can't make it to Tuscany, Provence, or the Spanish Riviera, this intimate lounge will take you there in spirit. ⊠ *Grand Floridian* ⊙ *Wed.–Sat. Daily 5:30 PM–11 PM.*

Copa Banana. Karaoke, specialty drinks, and a DJ keep the clientele entertained and tipsy. Because the Dolphin is a business hotel, count on sharing a fruit slice–shape table with after-hours suits. If you're annoyed by Peterson from accounting, the large-screen TV may provide a diversion. Although it's on-property, the Dolphin is not a Disney hotel. ⊠ *Dolphin Hotel* ⊙ *Daily 8 PM–2 AM.*

Francisco's Lounge. Disney added this bar to the sprawling Southwestern-theme Coronado Springs Resort to slake the thirst of conventioneers. At the open-air cantina near the convention hall entrance, cool tile floors and umbrellas are a backdrop for house-specialty margaritas. Bottoms up! ⊠ *Coronado Springs Resort* ⊙ *Weekdays 1 PM–midnight, weekends noon–1 AM.*

Martha's Vineyard Lounge. This is a cozy, refined hideaway where you can sit back and sip domestic and European wines. Each evening 18 wines are poured for tasting. After facing the madding crowd, it's worth a detour if you're looking for a quiet retreat and a soothing glass of zinfandel. ⊠ *Beach Club Resort* ⊙ *Daily 5:30 PM–10 PM.*

Mizner's. At the stylish Grand Floridian, a refined alcove is tucked away at the far end of the second-floor lobby. Even on steroids, this place wouldn't approach rowdy—it's a tasteful getaway where you can unwind with ports, brandies, and mixed drinks while overlooking the beach and the elegance that surrounds you. ⊠ *Grand Floridian* ⊙ *Daily 5 PM–1 AM.*

Narcoossee's. Inside the restaurant is a bar that serves ordinary beer in expensive yard glasses, but the porch-side views of the Seven Seas Lagoon (and the nightly Electrical Water Pageant) are worth the premium you pay. Find a nice spot and you can also watch the Magic Kingdom fireworks. ⊠ *Grand Floridian* ⊙ *Daily 5 PM–10 PM.*

Tambu Lounge. Beside 'Ohana's restaurant at the Polynesian Resort, Disney bartenders ring up all the variations on rum punch and piña coladas. Festooned with South Seas–style masks, totems, and Easter Island head replicas, this place is exotic—with the exception of the large screen TV. ⊠ *Polynesian Resort* ⊙ *Daily 1 PM–midnight.*

Territory Lounge. Nestled within a carbon copy of the magnificent Yellowstone Lodge, this lounge is a frontier-theme hideout that pays tribute to the Corps of Discovery (look overhead for a Lewis and Clark expedition trail map). In between drinks, check out the props on display: surveying equipment, daguerreotypes, large log beams, parka mittens, maps, and what the lounge claims is a pair of Teddy Roosevelt's boots. ⊠ *Wilderness Lodge* ⊙ *Daily 4 PM–midnight.*

Victoria Falls. The central lounge at the extraordinary Animal Kingdom Lodge is a second-floor retreat that overlooks the Boma restaurant. The exotic feel of an obligatory safari theme extends to leather directors' chairs, native masks, and the sounds of a stream flowing past. Across the hall near the front desk, a small alcove beckons. Although no drinks are served in the sunken den called the Sunset Overlook—with artifacts and photos from 1920s safaris of Martin and Osa Johnson—it is a popular spot for late-night conversation. ⊠ *Animal Kingdom Lodge* ⊗ *Daily 5:30 PM–midnight, dinner 6 PM–10 PM.*

Other Hotels in Walt Disney World

Non-Disney–owned hotels on Walt Disney World property, most near Downtown Disney and Lake Buena Vista, also offer a slew of nightlife venues. Two of the best of these clubs are at the Wyndham Palace Resort & Spa.

Laughing Kookaburra. Lively entertainment and good drink specials draw an energetic young crowd of Disney cast members to the Palace's casual nightspot. The "good time" music you'll hear is a mix of Latin, disco, rock n' roll, and '80s tunes. Friday brings the Birthday Bash (if your birthday falls this day or in the previous six days, you drink free). All ages are allowed in until 8 PM, when you'll need to be 21 to stay. ⊠ *Wyndham Palace Resort & Spa, Lake Buena Vista* ☎ *407/827–3722* ⊗ *Daily 7 PM–2 AM.*

Top of the Palace Lounge. The polar opposite of the ground-floor "Kook," this casual 27th-floor lounge offers a dazzling view of the Disney empire plus a free champagne toast at sunset each evening—a clock in the lobby lets you know when that is. Considering that this is the highest vista at WDW, file this one away under "worth a detour"—it's a pleasant precursor to dinner at the stylish Arthur's 27 next door. ⊠ *Wyndham Palace Resort & Spa, Lake Buena Vista* ☎ *407/827–3591* ⊗ *Daily 5 PM–1 AM.*

Disney's Wide World of Sports

Official All-Star Cafe. Disney's Wide World of Sports Complex is suspiciously empty when no games are being played, but when the games begin there's plenty of action over at this sports bar. Within this stadium-size space are a restaurant and souvenir equipment donated by Andre Agassi, Monica Seles, Tiger Woods, Lou Holtz, and company. For a drink, skip the restaurant and head to the bar in front, and afterward check out the huge billiard room in back. If you subscribe to 48 premium sports channels, then this place is a must-see. Otherwise, just take a look if you're here on game day. ⊠ *690 S. Victory Way* ☎ *407/824–8326* ⊗ *Daily 11–11, bar until midnight.*

Celebration

It may not be "nightlife" per se, but there is a quaint cluster of shops, restaurants, and a movie theater in the Utopian community of Celebration, a few minutes down the road from the rest of Disney. Although Celebration's artificial perfection recalls an episode of the *Twilight Zone,* at night everything seems almost real and you can walk around and check out the Celebration Town Tavern, Columbia Restaurant, Barnie's Coffee & Tea Co., bookstores, boutiques, toy shops, and the two-screen AMC Theatre (☎ 407/566–1403).

Dinner Shows

★ **Hoop-Dee-Doo Revue.** Staged at Fort Wilderness's rustic Pioneer Hall, this show may be corny, but it's also the liveliest dinner show in Walt Disney World. A troupe of jokers called the Pioneer Hall Players stomp their feet, wisecrack, and sing and dance, while the audience chows down on barbecued ribs, fried chicken, corn on the cob, strawberry shortcake, and all the fixin's. There are three shows nightly, and the prime times sell out months in advance in busy seasons. But you're better off eating dinner too early or too late rather than missing the fun altogether—so take what you can get. If you arrive in Orlando with no reservations, try for a cancellation. ⊠ *Fort Wilderness Resort* ☎ *407/939–3463 advance tickets, 407/824–2803 day of show* ☜ *$50.22 adults, $25.43 children 3–11, including tax and gratuity* ☉ *Daily 5, 7:15, and 9:30.*

Spirit of Aloha. Formerly the Polynesian Luau, this show is still an outdoor barbecue with entertainment in line with its colorful South Pacific style. Its fire jugglers and hula-drum dancers are entertaining for the whole family, if never quite as endearing as the napkin twirlers at the Hoop-Dee-Doo Revue. The hula dancers' navel maneuvers, however, are something to see. You should try to make reservations at least a month in advance. ⊠ *Polynesian Resort* ☎ *407/939–3463 advance tickets, 407/824–1593 day of show* ☜ *$50.22 adults, $25.43 children 3–11, including tax and gratuity* ☉ *Tues.–Sat. 5:15 and 8.*

Fireworks, Light Shows & Parades

Both in the theme parks and around the hotel-side waterways, Walt Disney World offers up a wealth of fabulous sound-and-light shows after the sun goes down. In fact WDW is one of the earth's largest single consumers of fireworks—perhaps even rivaling mainland China. Traditionally, sensational short shows have been held at the Magic Kingdom at 10. Starting times vary throughout the year, but you can check them at Guest Services. You can also find fireworks at Pleasure Island as part of the every-night-is-New Year's Eve celebrations—an event that's worth the wait into the wee hours.

Fireworks are only part of the evening entertainment. Each park hosts shows staged with varying degrees of spectacle and style. For the best of the best, head to Epcot, which hosts visiting shows that are free with admission. Regular performers include a Beatles sound-alike group in the United Kingdom, acrobats in China, mimes in France, musicians in a smaller African kiosk, and rock-and-roll bagpipers in Canada. Catching any of these parades and/or performances easily soothes the sting of what you may feel is an overpriced admission.

Electrical Water Pageant

One of Disney's few remaining small wonders is this 10-minute floating parade of sea creatures outlined in tiny lights, with an electronic score highlighted by Handel's *Water Music*. Don't go out of your way, but if you're by Bay Lake and the Seven Seas Lagoon, look for it from the beaches at the Polynesian (at 9), the Grand Floridian (9:15), Wilderness Lodge (9:35), Fort Wilderness (9:45), the Contemporary (10:05), and, in busy seasons, the Magic Kingdom (10:20). Times occasionally vary, so check with Guest Services.

Fantasmic!

★ Disney–MGM's blockbuster after-dark show is held once nightly (twice on weekends and in peak seasons) in a 6,500-seat amphitheater. The throngs of people filing into the Hollywood Bowl–style amphitheater give you the distinct sense that you're in for something amazing. The special effects are superlative indeed, as Mickey Mouse in the guise of the Sorcerer's Apprentice emcees a revue full of song and dance, pyrotechnics, and special effects. Several scenes from Disney films and historic events are staged amid music, special lighting, and fireworks. Arrive an hour in advance for the best seats, 20 minutes if you don't mind sitting to the side of the stage. Or, make dinner reservations at either the Studio's Brown Derby, Hollywood & Vine, or Mama Melrose.

IllumiNations: Reflections of the Earth

Fodor's Choice   It's worth sticking around until dark to see Epcot's light and fireworks
★ show, which takes place over the reflective World Showcase lagoon. As orchestral music fills the air, accompanied by the whoosh and boom of lasers and pyrotechnic bursts, a 30-foot globe on a barge floats across the lagoon, revealing the wonders of the seven continents on its curved LED screens. Meanwhile, each of the World Showcase pavilions is illuminated with more than 26,000 feet of lights. Check the wind direction before staking a claim, since smoke can cloak some views. Some of the better vantage points are the Matsu No Ma Lounge in the Japan pavilion, the patios of the Rose and Crown in the United Kingdom pavilion, and Cantina de San Angel in Mexico. Another good spot is the World Showcase Plaza between the boat docks at the Showcase entrance, but this is often crowded with those who want to make a quick exit after the show. If you decide to join them here, claim your seat at least 45 minutes in advance. It's worth waiting to see this spectacle.

SpectroMagic

Fodor's Choice   This splendidly choreographed parade of lights is one of the Magic King-
★ dom's don't-miss attractions. It's a colorful, flickering, luminescent parade with cartoonish floats and a complete lineup of favorite Disney characters. Times vary, so check the schedule before you set out, or ask any Disney staffer while you're in the park. The early showing is for parents with children, while the later ones attract night owls and others with the stamina and the know-how to enjoy the Magic Kingdom's most pleasant, least-crowded time of day.

Wishes

★ In late 2003 Disney retired the long-running Fantasy in the Sky fireworks show at the Magic Kingdom to premiere the even more elaborate and longer Wishes show. Fireworks are launched from 11 locations around the park to the accompaniment of Disney melodies, as Jiminy Cricket reminds you that "anything your heart desires" can come true. The fireworks and music recall scenes from Disney films in which a fairytale character did indeed get his or her wish. The best place to watch the show is on Main Street—try to snag the few seats on the second floor of the Walt Disney World train station.

Movies

Some nights, your feet won't walk even one more step. Try the **AMC 24 Theatres** (⊠ Downtown Disney West Side ☎ 407/827–1309 ticket office, 407/298–4488 show times). The cinema is state-of-the-art and plays the latest films.

UNIVERSAL ORLANDO

At Universal, the after-hours action has seeped out of the parks and into CityWalk, an eclectic and eccentric 30-acre pastiche of shops, restaurants, clubs, and concert venues. CityWalk's attitude is as hip and sassy as anywhere in the Universal domain.

Universal Orlando's CityWalk

CityWalk. Armed with a catchy headline ("Get a Nightlife"), CityWalk met the challenge of diverting the lucrative youth market from Disney and downtown Orlando. It did so by creating an open and airy gathering place that includes clubs ranging from quiet jazz retreats to over-the-top discotheques. On weeknights the crowd is a mix of families and conventioneers; weekends draw a decidedly younger demographic who are still arriving into the wee hours.

Although clubs have individual cover charges, it's far more economical to pay for the whole kit and much of the caboodle. You can buy a Party Pass (a one price–all clubs admission) for $9.95; or a Party Pass-and-a-Movie for $13. Making these deals even better is the fact that after 6 PM the $8 parking fee drops to nothing. It is, however, a long walk from the parking garage to CityWalk (even longer when you stumble out at 2 AM and realize it's a ¼-mi walk to your car). Then again, you shouldn't be driving in this condition, so have a good time and call a cab. Taxis run at all hours (⇨ Taxis *in* Smart Travel Tips A to Z). ☎ 407/224–2692, 407/363–8000 *Universal main line* ⊕ *www.citywalkorlando.com.*

Loew's Universal Cineplex. Why spend your time watching a movie when you're on vacation? Who cares? It's your vacation. The 20-screen, 5,000-seat, bilevel theatre offers an escape from the crowds. You can purchase tickets in advance by telephone. ☎ *407/354–5998 recorded information and tickets, 407/354–3374 box office.*

★ **Bob Marley—A Tribute to Freedom.** The beauty of this place is that even if you can't dance, you can pretend you can by simply swaying to syncopated reggae rhythms. The museum-club is modeled after the "King of Reggae's" home in Kingston, Jamaica, complete with intimate low ceilings and more than 100 photographs and paintings reflecting pivotal moments in Marley's life. Off the cozy bar is a patio area where you can be jammin' to a (loud) live band that plays from 8 PM to 1:30 AM nightly. You must be 21 or over to be admitted on Friday and Saturday after 10 PM. ☎ 407/224–2692 ⊠ $5 after 8 PM ⊙ Weekdays 4 PM–2 AM, weekends 2 PM–2 AM.

the groove. The very sound of this place can be terrifying to the uninitiated: images flicker rapidly on several screens and the combination of music, light, and mayhem appeals to a mostly under-thirty crowd. Within the cavernous hall, every nook and cranny is filled with techno pop. If you need to escape, the dance floor leads to three rooms: the '70s-style Green Room, filled with beanbag chairs and everything you threw out when Duran Duran hit the charts; the sci-fi Jetson-y Blue Room; and the Red Room, which is hot and romantic in a bordello sort of way. Prepare yourself for lots of fog, swirling lights, and sweaty bodies. ☎ 407/224–2692 ⊠ $5 ⊙ Daily 9 PM–2 AM.

Hard Rock Cafe. This Hard Rock Cafe is the largest on earth, and the one that seems to play the loudest music. The best objects adorn a room on the second floor: Beatles rarities such as cutouts from the *Sgt. Pepper* cover, John Lennon's famous "New York City" T-shirt, Paul's original lyrics for "Let It Be," and the doors from London's Abbey Road studios. Buddy Holly's Boy Scout booklet and favorite stage suit are also here. Wow. Start with dinner and stay for the show, since much of the attraction here is at the adjoining **Hard Rock Live.** The concert hall's exterior resembles Rome's Colosseum, and almost every evening an entertainer performs here; occasionally it's one you recognize (Ringo Starr, Elvis Costello, Jerry Lee Lewis, etc.). Although the seats are hard and two-thirds don't face the stage, it's one of Orlando's top venues. Cover prices vary. Warning: you can't bring large purses or bags inside and there are no lockers at CityWalk, so leave big baggage in your car. ☎ 407/224–2692 ⊕ www.hardrocklive.com ⊙ Daily from 11 AM, with a varying closing time, generally around midnight.

★ **Jimmy Buffett's Margaritaville.** Jimmy Buffett may be the most savvy businessman in America. He took a concept, wrapped it up in a catchy tune, and parlayed it into books, clothing, musicals, and a hot club at Universal. It seems that Florida law requires residents to play Buffett music 24 hours a day, but if you're from out of state you might still not be over "Cheeseburger in Paradise." Attached to the restaurant are three bars (Volcano, Land Shark, and 12 Volt). There's a Pan Am Clipper suspended from the ceiling, music videos projected onto sails, limbo and Hula-Hoop contests, a huge margarita blender that erupts "when the volcano blows," live music nightly, and all the other subtleties that give Parrotheads a place to roost. ☎ 407/224–2692 ⊕ www.margaritaville.com ⊠ $5 after 10 PM ⊙ Daily 11:30 AM–2 AM.

Latin Quarter. This tribute to Latin music and dance is especially popular with local Hispanics. It's easy to overlook the restaurant here, as most attention is paid to the nightclub, which is crowded with party-goers in eye-catching clothing. The club feels like a 21st-century version of Ricky Ricardo's Tropicana, although the design is based on a mix of Aztec, Inca, and Maya architecture. There's even an Andes mountain range, complete with waterfalls, around the dance floor. If you can get your hips working overtime, pick a rhumba from 1 to 10 and swivel . . . and tango and merengue and salsa . . . ☎ 407/224–2692 ⊕ *www. thelatinquarter.com* ✉ *$5; price may vary for certain performances* ⊙ *Mon.–Thurs. 5 PM–2 AM, Fri. and Sat. noon–2 AM.*

Pat O'Brien's. A legend in New Orleans, this exact reproduction of the original is doing all right in Orlando, with its flaming fountain, dueling pianists, and balcony that re-creates the Crescent City. The draw here is the Patio Bar, where abundant tables and chairs allow you to do nothing but enjoy a respite from the madding crowd—and drink a potent, rum-based hurricane. ☎ 407/224–2692 ⊕ *www.patobriens.com* ✉ *$5 after 9 PM* ⊙ *Patio Bar daily 4 PM–2 AM; Piano Bar daily 6 PM–2 AM.*

ORLANDO

For several years, downtown Orlando clubs had a monopoly on nighttime entertainment—which they lost when Disney and Universal muscled their way in. Most of the few clubs left are on Orange Avenue, alongside grungy tattoo and piercing parlors that make the downtown area look tired and seedy. Outside downtown, the neighborhood of Thornton Park and the community of Winter Park have clusters of chic bars and restaurants, though no serious dance clubs.

The Arts

When the fantasy starts wearing thin, check out the Orlando arts scene in the *Orlando Weekly* (⊕ www.orlandoweekly.com), a local entertainment and opinion newspaper that accurately tracks Orlando culture, lifestyles, and nightlife. Perhaps your best source of up-to-the-week information is in Friday's *Orlando Sentinel* (⊕ www.orlandosentinel.com). In it, the handy "Calendar" section carries reviews of plays, nightclubs, live music venues, restaurants, and attractions, and also contains a few tourist-oriented coupons.

The Orlando area has a fairly active agenda of dance, classical music, opera, and theater, much of which takes place at the multiple venues known collectively as the **Orlando Centroplex** (✉ 600 W. Amelia St., Orlando ☎ 407/849–2000 ⊕ www.orlandocentroplex.com). The **Carr Performing Arts Centre** (✉ 401 W. Livingston St., Orlando ☎ 407/849–2577) hosts the Broadway Series, which brings top-notch touring shows such as *Beauty and the Beast, Fame,* and *Fosse* to town. The **TD Waterhouse Centre** (✉ 600 W. Amelia St., Orlando ☎ 407/849–2020) is the home of the Orlando Magic, and also where wrestling matches are held and A-list rock acts play.

During the school year, the Bach Festival organization at **Rollins College** (✉ Winter Park ☎ 407/646–2233) throws a thoroughly enjoyable three-part concert series that is open to the public, usually for free. The choral series is held at Rollins's Knowles Memorial Chapel. The second part, the visiting-artists series at the Annie Russell Theater, showcases internationally celebrated artists who have performed at venues such as

Carnegie Hall. During the last week in February internationally recognized artists appear at the **Bach Music Festival** (☎ 407/646–2182 ⊕ www.bachfestivalflorida.org), a Winter Park tradition since 1936. The festival is held at the Annie Russell Theater and the Knowles Memorial Chapel and culminates on Sunday afternoon with "Highlights," which includes short performances by several of the artists who appeared during the week. While at Rollins, contact the **Annie Russell Theater** (☎ 407/646–2501) for information about its regular series of student productions.

Downtown Orlando Clubs & Bars

Club Paris. Socialite Paris Hilton lent her name and abundant business talents to this new nightclub, which premiered in late 2004. Three million dollars helped refurbish what was the Orchid Garden ballroom of the defunct Church Street Station. Now, a South Beach courtyard sets the tone for entry and the floor is monitored by 'fashion police' who award the trendiest patrons a free bar tab for the evening. There's plenty of room to dance (20,000 square feet) to New York–style DJ noise, as well as varied music on themed nights: Latin, Ladies, Fashion, and '80s. If you're considered worthy or are willing to pay an added admission, then you can go upstairs to the VIP club. As of now, this may be the hottest club in Orlando. Isn't life wonderful? ⊠ *122 W. Church St.* ☎ *407/ 832–7409* ⊕ *www.clubparis.net* ✉ *$5–$20* ☉ *Mon.–Sat. 8 PM–2 AM.*

★ **Sak Comedy Lab.** Refreshingly free of stand-up comedians, this stage show stars Orlando's most popular improv comedy troupe. The regular cast performs the Duel of Fools show and the late-night Fool Jam; the Sak Comedy Lab Rats are apprentices with potential, and the Generation S show spotlights Lab Rat with promise. Each show, consisting of experimental comedy, improv challenges, and audience participation, lasts approximately 90 minutes. Sak is family-friendly with most material at the PG-13 level. To make someone in your group the star of the show, for $100 you can surprise them with a "Slice of Life" scene based on their work, hobbies, and personality. Call in advance for the questionnaire. Emmy-winning Wayne Brady got his start here. ⊠ *380 W. Amelia Ave.* ☎ *407/648–0001* ⊕ *www.sak.com* ✉ *Lab Rats and Generation S, $5; Duel of Fools, $10–$13* ☉ *Lab Rats, Tues. 9 PM; Generation S, Wed. 9 PM; Duel of Fools, Thurs.–Sat. 9 PM.*

Social. Perhaps the favorite live-music venue of locals, Social is a great place to see touring and local musicians. It serves full dinners Wednesday through Saturday and offers up live music seven nights a week. You can sip trademark martinis while listening to anything from alternative rock to rockabilly to undiluted jazz. Several now-national acts got their start here, including Matchbox Twenty and Seven Mary Three. ⊠ *54 N. Orange Ave.* ☎ *407/246–1419* ⊕ *www.orlandosocial.com* ✉ *$5–$18, depending on entertainment* ☉ *Sat.–Thurs. 8 PM–2 AM, Fri. 5 PM–2 AM.*

Wally's. One of Orlando's oldest bars, this longtime local favorite is a hangout for a cross section of cultures and ages. Some would say it's a dive, but that doesn't matter to the students, bikers, lawyers, and barflies who land here to drink surrounded by the go-go dancer wallpaper and '60s-era interior. Just grab a stool at the bar to take in the scene and down a cold one. ✉ *1001 N. Mills Ave.* ☎ *407/896–6975* ☉ *Daily 7:30 PM–1 AM.*

Clubs & Bars Around I-Drive

International Drive embodies all the stereotypes of mass-market tourism: T-shirt shops, discount ticket kiosks, and a clutter of chain restaurants and strip malls. It's certainly not the most picturesque spot in town, but if you're in the neighborhood, there are countless retreats where you can watch a game and drink a brew.

Cricketers Arms. This prototypical American pub, in the Mercado shopping complex, has 17 hand-drawn beers and ales on tap. Locals crowd in to hear Florida bands. Tables are small and closely packed inside, but you can always grab one outside on the sidewalk or go to the back patio. Satellite-fed soccer and rugby games sometimes are aired in the afternoon. ✉ *In the Mercado, 8445 International Dr.* ☎ *407/354–0686* ⊕ *www.cricketersarmspub.com* ✆ *No cover except for televised soccer matches ($10)* ☉ *Daily 11 AM–2 AM; later when games are played.* ⊟ *AE, MC, V.*

Dan Marino's Town Tavern. He never won a Super Bowl, but Miami Dolphin quarterback Dan Marino has had better luck with this combination restaurant and lounge. More sophisticated than a locker room, it has secluded booths and an oblong, football-shape bar that seems to have struck a chord with locals who linger over the Marino Margaritas (no, they don't contain Gatorade). This is more restaurant than bar— until around 9 PM, when the bar comes to life. It's not wild, just a calming place for a quiet drink. Be sure to have your server validate your parking ticket. ✉ *Pointe*Orlando, 9101 International Dr.* ☎ *407/363–1013* ✆ *No cover; parking $2, free with validation* ☉ *Sun.–Thurs. 11 AM–midnight, Fri. and Sat. 11 AM–1 AM* ⊟ *AE, MC, V.*

Friday's Front Row Sports Grille & Restaurant. Friday's national empire explains how it could afford to build a sports bar the size of Delaware. You enter on an incline, giving you the sense that you're walking into a sports stadium. To the right is the dining area; if you're here for drinks, walk past the bleachers toward the back and join the locals, who come here to play trivia games, eat the bar food, talk stats, and ogle autographed pictures. The fun continues upstairs, and upstairs beyond that. ✉ *8126 International Dr.* ☎ *407/363–1414* ✆ *No cover* ☉ *Daily 11 AM–2 AM* ⊟ *AE, D, DC, MC, V.*

JB's Sports Bar & Restaurant. Here since 1987, JBs survives on sports-minded locals, Universal employees, and Disney cast members. Weeknights are fine, but on weekends and during big games the place is like a frat-house party, with 28 TVs broadcasting the action and beer flowing nonstop. You can shoot some darts during commercials. JB's is in a shopping plaza, and its appearance is as basic as its bar food: hot dogs, wings, and sandwiches. Head for the enclosed patio if you need a break from the noise. ✉ *4880 S. Kirkman Rd.* ☎ *407/293–8881*

✍ No cover except for special pay-per-view events ⊙ Daily 11 AM–2 AM ▭ AE, D, DC, MC, V.

Matrix and Metropolis. In addition to Dan Marino's and a standard-issue Hooter's, also located at Pointe*Orlando are these two clubs in one. Together they offer 30,000 square feet of dazzling dance rooms. The Metropolis side is decorated in a decadent Moulin Rouge style, while the Matrix is futuristic and industrial-looking. You can expect to hear Top 40, techno, euro-trance, break-out, and other musical styles you've never heard of. Complementing the noise are a 13-foot video wall and several 27-inch televisions. Call to find out about special theme nights (e.g., Latin, hip-hop, or African). You must be 18 to enter the Matrix and 21 to enter the Metropolis. ⊠ Pointe*Orlando, 9101 International Dr. ☎ 407/370–3700 ✍ Cover varies ⊙ Metropolis Thurs.–Sun. 9 PM–2 AM, Matrix Tues. and Thurs.–Sun. 9 PM–2 AM ▭ AE, D, DC, MC, V.

Orlando Ale House. Across the street from the entrance to Universal Orlando, the Ale House is a nice retreat for a beer (and would be even nicer if it weren't in a strip mall). Still, it's very pleasant inside, with cozy booths, brass rails, pool tables, dart boards, and TV screens. There's a raw bar, and you can order sandwiches, burgers, pastas, and fried foods. Beer is the big seller here, especially on Monday and Thursday, when you can buy a pitcher for $5. During the weekday 11 AM to 7 PM happy hour, draft beers and margaritas are $1. ⊠ 5573 S. Kirkman Rd. ☎ 407/248–0000 ✍ No cover ⊙ Daily 11 AM–2 AM ▭ AE, D, MC, V.

Samba Room. Although it's really a restaurant, the Samba Room has attracted a steady and loyal nightclub clientele thanks to its warm, Latin-flavored interior and the steady boom-boom-boom of Cuban and Brazilian music. That said, Thursday through Saturday the entrées are only an appetizer for tunes that'll get you up and dancing to live bands playing Brazilian jazz, tropical salsa, and merengue. ⊠ 7468 W. Sand Lake Rd. ☎ 407/226–0550 ✍ $10 cover for nightclub, waived if you dine ⊙ Dancing Thurs.–Sat. 8 PM–2 AM ▭ AE, D, MC, V.

Dinner Shows

Dinner shows are an immensely popular form of nighttime entertainment around Orlando. For a single price, you get a theatrical production and a multicourse dinner. Performances run the gamut from jousting to jamboree tunes, and meals tend to be better than average; unlimited beer, wine, and soda are usually included, but mixed drinks (and often *any* drinks before dinner) cost extra. What the shows lack in substance and depth they make up for in grandeur and enthusiasm. The result is an evening of light entertainment, which youngsters in particular enjoy. Seatings are usually between 7 and 9:30, and there are usually one or two performances a night, with an extra show during peak periods. You might sit with strangers at tables for 10 or more, but that's part of the fun. Always reserve in advance, especially for weekend shows, and always ask about discounts.

If you're in Orlando off-season, try to take in these dinner shows on a busy night—a show playing to a small audience can be uncomfortable.

Be on the lookout for discount coupons: you can find them in brochure racks in malls, in hotels, and at the Orlando/Orange County Convention & Visitors Bureau. Since performance schedules can vary depending on the tourist season, it's always smart to call in advance to verify show times. When buying tickets, ask if the cost includes a gratuity—servers anxious to pocket more cash may hit you up for an extra handout.

Orlando

★ **Dolly Parton's Dixie Stampede Dinner & Show.** For real old-fashioned family entertainment, Dolly's show can't be beat. The evening begins in a preshow area featuring a singing cowboy who also has the interesting ability to rip, tear, and snap small objects to bits with a lightning-fast bullwhip. Next, in the main arena—an antebellum-style auditorium—you sit on either the North or South side and cheer on your teams as they engage in such competitions as ostrich and pig races. Expect lots of singing, dancing, comedy, and fast-paced acrobatic horsemanship with 32 magnificent horses. A four-course feast and plenty of audience participation make this show stand out above the others. The patriotic grand finale was written by Dolly Parton. Stick around after the show and you can meet the horses and performers. ⊠ *8251 Vineland Ave., Lake Buena Vista Area* ☎ *407/238–4455 or 866/443–4943* ⊕ *www. dixiestampede.com* 🍽 *$47 adults, $20 children 3–11* ☉ *Shows usually daily at 7* PM, *but hrs may vary in high season and during holidays* 🖃 *AE, D, MC, V.*

Sleuths Mystery Dinner Show. If Sherlock Holmes has always intrigued you, head on over for a four-course meal served up with a healthy dose of conspiracy. There are nine rotating whodunnit performances staged throughout the year, and each stops short of revealing the perpetrator. The show begins at a wedding, class reunion, anniversary party, etc., and over appetizers the short play you're watching ends in murder. Discuss the clues over dinner, question the still-living characters, and solve the crime during dessert. Did the butler do it? There are three theaters, which accounts for the frequent performances. ⊠ *7508 Universal Blvd.* ☎ *407/363–1985 or 800/393–1985* ⊕ *www.sleuths.com* 🍽 *$47 adults, $24 children 3–11* ☉ *Weekdays 7:30, sometimes 8:30, Sat. 6, 7:30, and 9, Sun. 7:30* 🖃 *AE, D, MC, V.*

Kissimmee

Arabian Nights. An elaborate palace on the outside, this arena has seating for more than 1,200 on the inside. Its 25-act dinner show centers around the quest for an Arabian princess to find her true love, and includes a buffoonish genie who may or may not be amusing, a chariot race, an intricate western square dance on horseback, and 60 fabulous horses that perform in such acts as bareback acrobatics by gypsies. Dinner is served during the show, so you might end up not paying much attention to the food—which is not a bad idea since the meal of prime rib or vegetable lasagna is functional, not flavorful. Extra shows are added in summer. Fans of equestrian displays will get the most out of this show. Make reservations in advance and ask about discounts, which are also available when booking online. ⊠ *6225 W. Irlo Bronson Memorial Hwy., Kissimmee* ☎ *407/239–9223, 800/553–6116, 800/533–3615 in Canada*

⊕ *www.arabian-nights.com* ⊠ *$47 adults, $29 children 3–11* ⊙ *Shows nightly, times vary* ⊟ *AE, D, MC, V.*

Capone's Dinner and Show. This show brings you back to the era of 1931 gangland Chicago, when mobsters and their dames were the height of underworld society. The evening begins in an old-fashioned ice-cream parlor, but say the secret password and you are ushered inside Al Capone's private Underworld Cabaret and Speakeasy. Dinner is an un-limited Italian buffet that's heavy on pasta. ⊠ *4740 W. Irlo Bronson Memorial Hwy.* ☎ *407/397–2378* ⊕ *www.alcapones.com* ⊠ *$39.95 adults, $23.95 children 4–12* ⊙ *Daily 7:30* ⊟ *AE, D, MC, V.*

Medieval Times. In a huge, ersatz-medieval manor house, this evening out presents a tournament of sword fights, jousting matches, and other games on a good-versus-evil theme. No fewer than 30 charging horses and a cast of 75 knights, nobles, and maidens participate. Sound silly? It is. But it is also a true extravaganza. That the show takes precedence over the meat-and-potatoes fare is obvious: everyone sits facing forward at long, narrow banquet tables stepped auditorium-style above the tour-nament area. Additional diversions include tours through a dungeon and torture chamber and demonstrations of antique blacksmithing, wood-working, and pottery making. ⊠ *4510 W. Irlo Bronson Memorial Hwy.* ☎ *407/239–0214 or 800/229–8300* ⊕ *www.medievaltimes.com* ⊠ *$45.95 adults, $29.95 children 3–11* ⊙ *Castle daily 9–4, village daily 4:30–8, performances usually daily at 8 but call ahead* ⊟ *AE, D, MC, V.*

Movies

Muvico Pointe 21. In addition to the theatres at Downtown Disney and CityWalk, check out the impressive theater at Pointe*Orlando. It has 21 screens and stadium seating. ⊠ *Pointe*Orlando, 9101 International Dr., Orlando* ☎ *407/903–0555* ⊠ *$8 after 6 PM, $5 children, $6 for matinees.*

The Space Coast

FODOR'S CHOICE

Kennedy Space Center Visitor Complex, *in Titusville*
Merritt Island National Wildlife Refuge, *in Titusville*
Ron Jon Surf Shop, *in Cocoa Beach*
Surfing off Cocoa Beach

Updated by
Gary
McKechnie

ONE SMALL STEP FROM ORLANDO; one giant leap from Toledo. The most direct route from Greater Orlando to the coast, the Beeline Expressway (Route 528), is arrow-straight, cut through forests of long-needle pine and laid across the yawning savannas at the very southern tip of the south-to-north St. Johns River, which begins life as a tiny stream in a place called Hell and Blazes, Florida. In this extremely flat countryside of cedars, red maples, and palmettos, American egrets, blue herons, and shy limp-kins wade and fish for dinner; ibises tend their chicks; and graceful an-hingas perch where they can, spreading their wings to dry. High above watery prairies, hawks hunt and ospreys soar over their nests crowning stately sabal palms, Florida's official tree. It feels a million miles from the artificial worlds of the theme parks, and it's one good reason to make the one-hour trip from Orlando directly east to the coast.

The laid-back little towns and beach communities from Cocoa Beach north to New Smyrna Beach are another reason to venture out of Orlando in this direction. Don't expect much in the way of picturesque towns and villages, however. The constant seaspray and baking sun take their toll on housepaint, lawns, and landscaping. Then again, you don't need lush grass to enjoy the area's most popular tourist attraction: the beach. The best sands are on Cocoa Beach, a narrow five-mile long bar-rier island. In addition to great beaches and plentiful lodging, Cocoa Beach offers about a dozen surf shops, a few hundred restaurants and, believe it or not, four tanning salons. Go figure.

Another popular attraction is the Kennedy Space Center, located a few miles north near Titusville. There's talk that following the tragic accident that befell the *Columbia* in 2003, the space shuttle fleet may soar again. Whether that happens or not, NASA will continue to launch rockets such as Delta II's and Titans. To find out when to look east for a launch, call the NASA Launch Hotline at ☎ 800/572–4636. For the closest access pos-sible, you can purchase tickets in advance for space shuttle launches by calling ☎ 321/449–4444 or visiting ⊕ www.kennedyspacecenter.com.

10

If you have
2 days

For a reprieve from Disney, take this surf-and-turf tour of the Space Coast. From Orlando, drive the Beeline Expressway (Route 528) east. Just past mile marker 30, take the exit for Route 520 and head east. Be advised that this is a very narrow two-lane road, and the danger increases after dark. From the exit off the Beeline, it's about 9½ mi to the **Lone Cabbage Fish Camp.** Stop in for a touch of real down-home Florida. Here you can fish from the dock, get some gator tail for lunch, and take an airboat ride—a genuine Florida experience. Continue east on 520 through city traffic to reach **Cocoa Village,** a restored neighborhood, with more than 50 shops and restaurants, on the west side of the Intracoastal Waterway. If you want to shop, it's best to come here sometime between midmorning and midafternoon. On Sunday many of the shops are closed. To explore the entire Cocoa Village area, allow at least an hour; triple that if you plan to do some serious browsing in the shops.

Proceed farther east on 520 to **Cocoa Beach.** 520 deadends in A1A, the coastal highway known as Atlantic Avenue in Cocoa Beach. When you take a right (south) here, almost immediately on your left is the **Ron Jon Surf Shop.** It's a two-story display of all the surfing and beach gear you could ever use, and it's open 24 hours a day. Check into your hotel and spend the rest of the day soaking up the sun.

On your second day head north on A1A to the **Kennedy Space Center Visitor Complex.** Follow the signs to 528 (Orlando) and take the exit for Route 3 (heading north). From here, it's about a 20-minute drive. Spend the day learning the story of America's exploration of space. Be sure to include a stop at the **United States Astronaut Hall of Fame.** It's one of the few places where you can test your skills landing a shuttle on a simulator. On your way back, retrace your route; at the end of Route 528, follow the signs for **Port Canaveral.** You're likely to see several giant cruise ships at dock, and you get another good view of Kennedy Space Center's launchpads.

If you have
4 days

Allowing yourself that extra day or two will give you an opportunity to explore at a more leisurely pace. This itinerary picks up on Day 3—your day to get back to nature. From the beach head north on A1A to U.S. 1 on the mainland and go north to Route 406. Turn east on Route 406 and then right on Route 402 and look for signs to the **Merritt Island Wildlife Refuge.** Take a drive through the refuge (just continue on Route 402) and then either head to Playalinda Beach, the southernmost beach of the **Canaveral National Seashore,** where you can get great views of the launchpads, or retrace your drive back to U.S. 1 and head north to New Smyrna Beach. Follow the signs to A1A and stop at the public beach or drive on down to one of the northern beaches at the **Canaveral National Seashore.** There's a northern and southern entrance to the national seashore, but these two roads don't connect, so you'll need to head back to U.S. 1 to return to Cocoa Beach for your fourth day on the Space Coast. Jumpstart the day with a brisk walk or jog along the beach to witness a spectacular sunrise. When you've had enough sun and sand, head for the low-key shops and restaurants of **Cocoa Beach Pier.**

Beyond the shuttle, there was another tragedy, albeit a natural one, in 2004. Courtesy of Florida's active hurricane season, the Space Coast bore the brunt or side effects of three of the four hurricanes that stormed across the state (Charley, Francis, and Jeanne). Despite the multiple hits, residents proved resilient and you'd be hard pressed to find any broken windows or missing shingles by the time you visit. The area also offers water sports, fishing, golf, nature, nightlife, a great zoo, some distinctive shopping, and Caribbean cruises sailing from Port Canaveral. Matching this overwhelming slate of activities is the daunting geography of the area. Stretching from near Vero Beach in the south to New Smyrna Beach near Daytona, the Space Coast is an area *115 miles* long and to see it all in one visit is virtually impossible. So be judicious in selecting what interests you, swab on the tanning butter, and get the most out of the coast.

Exploring the Space Coast

Although just 50 mi separate the Space Coast and Orlando, they're a world apart. In the small oceanfront towns of Cocoa Beach, Titusville, New Smyrna Beach, and Cape Canaveral you won't find a lot of glitz, glamour, or giddy attractions. Mainly, it's sun, sand, and surf.

Besides the beach, there's one major attraction in the area: Kennedy Space Center Visitor Complex. The other sights tend to be rather low-key, funky, and offbeat. Still, there's plenty to see and do—or not do.

If you have the time, the best plan is to set aside two or three days to enjoy the area. But the Space Coast can also be enjoyed as a one- or two-day trip from Orlando.

About the Restaurants & Hotels

The Space Coast area is dotted with casual eateries with a heavy emphasis on fish and shellfish. There are a few upscale dining establishments in Cocoa, Cocoa Beach, and New Smyrna Beach, but for the most part the eatin' is easy.

Most lodging is on Route A1A. Hotel prices spike seriously in peak season (February through April and Memorial Day through Labor Day), especially when a NASA space shuttle is scheduled to launch. A room that may be $130 in low season can go to $180 or $200 in high season.

WHAT IT COSTS				
$$$$	**$$$**	**$$**	**$**	**¢**
RESTAURANTS over $30	$20–$30	$15–$19	$10–$14	under $10
HOTELS over $220	$140–$220	$100–$139	$80–$99	under $80

Restaurant prices are per person for a main course at dinner. Hotel prices are for a standard double room, excluding 6% sales tax (more in some counties) and 1%–4% tourist tax.

Beaches On Florida's mid-Atlantic coast, stretching from New Smyrna Beach and Canaveral National Seashore south to Sebastian Inlet, there are about 120 miles of wide, sandy beaches. Although the winter season alone counts about 650,000 vacationers, the area's beaches are much less densely developed than Daytona's. From New Smyrna Beach south to Satellite, the offshore incline is gentle and waters are shallow for some distance out, and bottoms are smooth. Below Satellite Beach, beaches tend to be rocky, with an uneven bottom. Remember: there *are* sharks off Florida's coast. Ask lifeguards or local residents about shark activity before deciding whether or not to swim. More of a danger than sharks, however, are rip currents. When the receding waves break through a sandbar, the current can pull you out to sea. If you're caught in a riptide, stay calm and swim parallel to the shore until you're out of the force of the flow before trying to swim to shore. Again, ask locals and lifeguards about the water conditions before going in.

10

Casting Your Line From trolling on the marsh flats to hitting the open water, the Space Coast is a great place to get hooked. There's big bass in the St. Johns River; giant redfish, trout, and snook in the Indian River Lagoon; and excellent deep-sea sites for dolphinfish, grouper, king mackerel, wahoo, blue and white marlin, sailfish, tuna, and snapper offshore in the Atlantic. You can also surf-cast for bluefish, pompano, sea bass, and flounder; success is mixed and depends on the season. Or try your hand at pier fishing for mackerel, trout, sheepshead, and tarpon. Most major beach towns have lighted piers, and admission is usually $1 to $4. Because it's on the Intracoastal Waterway rather than the Atlantic, the Titusville pier has good shrimping, too. Check *Florida Today,* the local newspaper, or bait-and-tackle shops to find out what's biting where. Approximately 40 charter captains offer trips from Cape Canaveral, and they are all licensed, insured, and experienced. You can find a complete listing of the hale and hearty skippers of the Canaveral Charter Captains organization at ⊕ www.fishingspacecoast.org, or their peers at the Indian River Guides Association at ⊕ www.irga.org. Check individual charter listings for prices and hours.

Surfing Cocoa Beach is the self-proclaimed Small Wave Capital of the World—an unusual title, yet one the locals hold in high regard. Those who like to hang 10 in the Pacific, however, will find the waves here quite tame. Of course, when there's a major storm or hurricane a-brewing, then you can catch quite a wave. Cocoa Beach's main tourist attraction, the collection of Ron Jon Surf Shops, is a tribute to the town's principal claim to fame. New Smyrna Beach also is popular with surfers, and there's a cluster of surf shops at the main entrance to the beach.

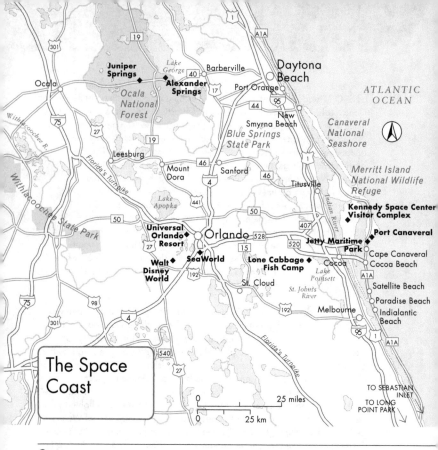

The Space Coast

Cocoa

50 mi east of downtown Orlando, 60 mi east of WDW.

Not to be confused with the seaside community of Cocoa Beach, the small town of Cocoa sits smack dab on mainland Florida and faces the Intracoastal Waterway, known locally as the Indian River. Aside from the dense concentration of shops in the village, most of the area is sprawling and it is several miles between sights. A comprehensive visit involves plenty of driving and some backtracking.

Perhaps Cocoa's most interesting feature is restored **Cocoa Village** (⊕ www.cocoavillage.com). Within the cluster of restored turn-of-the-20th-century buildings and cobblestone walkways are several restaurants, indoor and outdoor cafés, snack and ice-cream shops, and almost 50 specialty shops and art galleries. To get to Cocoa Village, head east on Route 520—named King Street in Cocoa—and when the streets get narrow and the road curves, make a right onto Brevard Avenue; follow the signs for the free municipal parking lot. Folks in a rush to get to the beach tend to overlook this Victorian-style village, but it's definitely worth a stop.

On the campus of Brevard Community College is the **Astronaut Memorial Planetarium and Observatory.** If you're a true space enthusiast and have exhausted the displays at the Kennedy Space Center, you may want to stop by one afternoon to see the **Science Quest Demonstration Hall,** which features hands-on exhibits, including scales calibrated to other planets. On the moon, big Vegas Elvis would have weighed just 42 pounds. The planetarium has two theaters, one showing a changing roster of nature documentaries, the other hosting laser and planetarium shows. The **Astronauts Hall of Fame** (not to be confused with the one near the Kennedy Space Center) displays exhibits on space travel. It's a rather long ride to reach the campus from the main tourist area on Cocoa Beach, but if you decide to make the visit at night you'll have the chance to see the solar system and deep space in one of the largest observatories in Florida. Hours vary, so call ahead. From Cocoa Village, take U.S. 1 north about three miles to Michigan Avenue, turn left and look for the campus on your left. ✉ *1519 Clearlake Rd.* ☎ *321/433–7373* ⊕ *www.brevard.cc.fl.us/planet* ✆ *Observatory and exhibit hall free; film or planetarium show $6 adults, $4 children 12 and under; both shows $10 adults, $6 children; laser show $6; planetarium, movie, laser show combination $14 adults and children* ⊙ *Call for current schedule.*

Just a quarter mile from the planetarium is the **Brevard Museum of History and Natural Science.** An average museum for the most part, one particularly interesting display is the **Windover Archaeological Exhibit.** In 1984 a developer was draining a shallow pond in Titusville and discovered preserved in the muck the 7,000-year-old bodies of more than 200 indigenous people. To the surprise of archaeologists, the peat had preserved the bones and brains of the ancient tribe, and each was buried in an identical manner, revealing the care, formality, and respect the tribe afforded the deceased. Also on display is a collection of Victoriana and a 22-acre **nature center** that encompasses three distinct ecosystems—sand pine hills, lake lands, and marshlands. ✉ *2201 Michigan Ave.* ☎ *321/632–1830* ⊕ *www.brevardmuseum.com* ✆ *$5.50 adults, $3.50 children under 17; trails free* ⊙ *Mon.–Sat. 10–4, Sun. noon–4.*

About 20 miles east of the Atlantic Ocean on the banks of the St. Johns River, the **Lone Cabbage Fish Camp** is a strange old Florida riverfront restaurant and attraction. There's a dock where you can buy bait and fish, and there's a Florida Cracker restaurant. If you want to see the river's wildlife up close, there are airboat rides, including specially arranged nighttime tours as well as longer and more thrilling rides aboard shorter and more nimble watercraft. Naturally, there are souvenir T-shirts to memorialize your visit. The camp is about 9 mi west of Cocoa's city limits, 4 mi west of I–95. ✉ *8199 Rte. 520* ☎ *321/632–4199* ⊕ *www.twisterairboatrides.com* ✆ *Airboat ride $18 adults, $10 children under 12* ⊙ *Airboat rides daily 10–6.*

Due to the the gentle climate, the Banana River (actually a lagoon) is one of the most biodiverse waterways in America, with more than 4,200 types of plants, animals, and fish living here. To see it and the

Thousand Islands section of the lagoon, the **Island Boat Lines Nature Tour** heads out for a two-hour tour aboard a sturdy and whistle-clean pontoon boat. The narrator/naturalist will fill you in on the fish and fowl you'll see—usually a lot of anhingas and bottlenose dolphins. Manatees may reveal themselves in winter, but primarily when the water temperature's above 68 degrees. You'll also see plenty of snowbirds roosting on the patios of their waterfront condos. ⊠ *1891 E. Merritt Island Causeway (Cactus Flower restaurant) Merritt Island* ☎ *321/302–0544 or 321/454–7414* ⊕ *www.islandboatlines.com* 🖃 *$20 adults, $18 children* ⊗ *Regularly scheduled tours daily at 10 am, 1 pm, and two hours before sunset.*

Few people link Florida with the frontier, but before there were tourists, there were cowboys and cattle. From the 25-acre **Ace of Hearts Ranch & Equestrian Center,** you head out to explore the surrounding 80 acres of wooded trails lined with pine scrub, oak hammock, and wetlands. The ranch also arranges overnight trips, campfires, hayrides, barbeques, and even beach rides for experienced adults. This is ecotourism at its finest. ⊠ *7400 Bridal Path La. Port St, John (between Cocoa and Titusville)* ☎ *321/638–0104* ⊕ *www.aceofheartsranch.com* 🖃 *$25 for one-hour horseback ride* ⊗ *Daily.*

Where to Stay & Eat

$$$ ✕ **Café Margaux.** In a quiet courtyard at the entrance of Cocoa Village is this cute and cozy indoor/outdoor restaurant. The setting plus the eclectic, creative mix of French and Italian cuisine is reminiscent of a café on the Riviera. The lunch menu features black sesame–coated chicken over mesclun greens, as well as lump crab cakes over pancetta and roasted corn relish. Dinners are equally exotic, with pork loin stuffed with duck liver paté, veal loin chop with lobster shrimp risotto, and a lollipop pork chop on crab-and-pea risotto. ⊠ *220 Brevard Ave.* ☎ *321/639–8343* ⊕ *www.margaux.com* 🖃 *AE, DC, MC, V* ⊗ *Closed Sun. and Tues.*

$$–$$$ ✕ **Black Tulip Restaurant.** Two intimate dining rooms invite romance at this Cocoa Village bistro, which takes pride in its 50-plus-label wine menu. Appetizers include tortellini with meat sauce and crab-stuffed mushrooms. Entrées include fettuccine primavera Alfredo; pork loin sautéed with apples, brandy, and cream; and filet mignon medallions with artichoke sauce. Tulip Crisp Roast Duckling is their signature dish: a Long Island duck, double roasted then drizzled with a not-too-sweet sauce made of apples, cashews, and red wine. Lighter lunch selections include sandwiches, salads, and quiches. For dessert, try the chocolate mousse pie and warm apple strudel. ⊠ *207 Brevard Ave.* ☎ *321/631–1133* ⊕ *www.blacktulip.com* 🖃 *AE, DC, MC, V.*

¢–$$ ✕ **Paradise Alley Cafe.** The small and active eatery in the heart of Cocoa Village looks a little like Margaritaville, and the menu follows suit. There are tropical kebabs, blackened seafood, jerked chicken, gumbo, and other dishes taken from the deep South, Caribbean, and South and Central America. One of the more casual restaurants in the village, it's a nice place to stop for lunch in the midst of a shopping spree. ⊠ *234 Brevard Ave.* ☎ *321/639–2515* 🖃 *AE, MC, V* ⊗ *Closed Sun.*

¢–$ ✕ **Lone Cabbage Fish Camp.** This down-home, no-nonsense eatery oc-
cupies a rustic spot on the St. Johns River. Opened as a bait shop in the
1950s, the fish camp has evolved as a port for airboats and a destination for diners seeking plates of catfish, frogs' legs, and alligator meat
(as well as the more pedestrian burgers and hot dogs). There's a fish fry
and country-western hoedown every Sunday. If you want to see real
Florida, this is it. ⊠ *8199 Rte. 520* ☎ *321/632–4199* ▤ *AE, MC, V.*

¢ ✕ **Ossorio.** Part of the appeal of this village bistro is its design: it seems
like an open-air living room with couches, tables, and even a small library in back. Order wood-roasted flat-bread pizza, oven-roasted coffee, homemade ice cream, pastries, salads, soups, or crepes and enjoy
the opportunity to relax in a nice, unhurried setting. Beer and wine are
also served. ⊠ *316 Brevard Ave.* ☎ *321/639–2423* ▤ *AE, MC, V.*

Nightlife & the Arts

The **Cocoa Village Playhouse** (⊠ 300 Brevard Ave. ☎ 321/636–5050) has
an interesting pedigree. In 1918 this building was a Ford dealership that
sold Model Ts. After that, it became a vaudeville house called the Aladdin Theater, and then it did a turn as a movie theater before being
purchased by Brevard Community College. Today this is the area's
community theater, with performances starring local talent scheduled
September through June, and performances by touring professional
productions the rest of the year.

Dog n' Bone British Pub (⊠ 300 Brevard Ave. ☎ 321/636–2828 ⊕ www.
thedognbone.com) is a smart-looking pub with all the little touches that
make it feel like a neighborhood favorite. Couches, a fireplace (fake),
darts, a chess board, cribbage, a pool table, British football jerseys, and
plenty of pictures of the Beatles will put you at ease. Drink specials like
$5 liter beers make things even better. It's open daily noon to 2 AM. Up-
stairs from the Dog n' Bone, there's another hangout: the **9 Stone Club**
(⊠ 300 Brevard Ave. ☎ 321/636–2828), which has a full liquor bar and
hosts live bands, karaoke nights, and dance parties. It's open Wednesday through Sunday from 9 PM to 2 AM.

Although it's really more of a restaurant, **Bankers Bar & Grill** (⊠ 114 Harrison St. ☎ 321/635–8002) also features a full liquor bar. The name makes
sense when you see that it's within the marble-rich confines of an early-
20th-century bank. There are nice large booths where your group can
converse, or sit at the bar where tellers once cashed checks. Menu items
reflect a nice mix of pork chops, porterhouse, and filet mignon balanced
by nachos, salads, wings, and burgers. It's open daily 11 AM to 10 PM.

When you're bored to death by Buffett, dig some real blues at **Big
Daddy's Jazz and Blues Club** (⊠ 105 Harrison St. ☎ 321/638–1370,
⊕ www.bigdaddydaves.com). Tucked away on a side street in the village, the highlight here is live bands playing Thursday through Saturday from 5 PM to 2 AM. During the week, you can also get gritty with
jazz jams, R&B jams, and ladies nights. It has a surprisingly full slate
of local blues soloists and groups.

Shopping

For visitors, Cocoa Village is what Cocoa's all about. For blocks east of the Indian River you'll find wonderful boutiques, quiet lanes, neat pubs and fantastic restaurants. For a map and more information, visit the cleverly hidden **Cocoa Village Welcome Center,** (⊠ 216 Florida Ave. ☎ 321/433–0362) a few blocks east of Brevard Avenue. In addition to the shops and restaurants, this is the heart of local activity and it's where you'll find art shows, craft fairs, Oktoberfest, Christmas festivals, and New Year's celebrations.

The main line of stores is along Brevard Avenue (parallel with the river) where, thankfully, there doesn't seem to be a chain store in sight. Most are open daily, with shorter hours on Sunday. Among the standouts are **Season Tickets** (⊠ 301 Brevard Ave. ☎ 321/690–1919), a ladies boutique with nouveau retro clothing and accessories. **Mango's** features fruit-flavored tropical clothes; the type of loose, soft pastels that are great when you crave a tropical look. A block west, the **Village Gourmet** (⊠ 19 Stone St. ☎ 321/636–5480 ⊕ www.cocoavillagegourmet.com) has been here since the mid-'70s selling a huge selection of kitchen and cooking items—handsome ceramic bowls, colorful glassware, regional cookbooks, exotic soup mixes, gourmet ingredients, and wines from South America, Europe, and California.

Kids may enjoy the array of simple (read: few high-tech) toys at **Annie's Toy Chest** (⊠ 403 Brevard Ave. ☎ 321/632–5890 ⊕ www.anniestoychest. com), a good spot to find Ty, LEGO, Madame Alexander, and company. A few doors down, the **Bath Cottage** (⊠ 425 Brevard Ave. ☎ 321/690–2284 ⊕ www.bathcottage.com) carries just about everything for the bathroom, from fine soaps to aromatherapy candles, plush towels, and elegant shower curtains. It also has one-of-a-kind accessories for the home, including colorful blown-glass balls, drawer pulls, and table lamps. Across the street, the **Threadneedle Street Mall** (⊠ 404 Brevard Ave.) is a short open-air promenade featuring a few boutiques, gift shops, and art galleries.

> **need a break?** If all this shopping's worn you down, take a break from the heat with a hand-packed ice-cream cone from the **Village Ice Cream & Sandwich Shop** (⊠ 120 Harrison St. ☎ 321/632–2311).

Cocoa Beach

65 mi east of Orlando, 70 mi east of WDW.

After crossing a long and high bridge just east of Cocoa Village, you'll be dropped down upon a barrier island. A few miles farther at Route A1A you'll reach the Atlantic Ocean and picture-perfect **Cocoa Beach.** This is one of the Space Coast's nicest beaches, with many wide stretches that are excellent for biking, jogging, power walking, or leisurely strolling. In some places there are dressing rooms, showers, playgrounds, picnic areas with grills, snack shops, and surfside parking lots. Beach vendors offer necessities, and guards are on duty in summer. Cocoa Beach is considered the capital of Florida's surfing community, dude.

As you drive south along the coast on A1A, you'll notice three things: the homes and businesses become progressively less appealing, you'll drive through a long stretch of nothing as you pass through Patrick Air Force Base, and you'll spy short avenues leading from the road to nearly private entrances to the beach. Remember these locations. On these short side streets you can park your car and enjoy relative seclusion far from the densely packed beaches several miles north.

Stretching far over the Atlantic, the **Cocoa Beach Pier** (⊠ 401 Meade Ave. ☎ 321/783–7549 ⊕ www.cocoabeachpier.com) is a local gathering spot as well as a beachside grandstand for space-shuttle launches. There are several souvenir shops, bars, and restaurants, as well as a bait-and-tackle shop. It costs $3 to park here, and another $1 for access to the fishing part of the pier that dangles 800 feet out into the Atlantic. Don't expect pristine Disney cleanliness here; this is a weather-beaten, sandy hangout for people who love the beach. When the children have had enough of the beach, take them to **Jungle Village Family Fun Center** to tire them out. There are 70-plus video games, 36 holes of mini-golf, mazes to climb around and get lost in, three tracks of go-carts for children and adults, a "soft play" playground, batting cages for both softball and hard ball, and laser tag. Don't go in the middle of the day in summer; you could wilt from the sweltering heat. Evenings are active—especially when there's a cruise leaving the next day and passengers staying the night at nearby hotels drop in. ⊠ Rte. A1A, 2½ mi north of Rte. 520 ☎ 321/783–0595 ⊠ Park free; go-carts $6.50 for pro track, $4.75 for family track, $4.50 for junior track; miniature golf and laser tag $5 for adults and children; call for off-season price specials ⊗ Sun.–Thurs. 10 AM–10 PM, Fri. and Sat. 10 AM–midnight.

Where to Stay & Eat

★ $$–$$$$ ✕ **Mango Tree Restaurant.** Candles, fresh flowers, and rattan basket chairs set a romantic mood in the intimate dining room, designed to evoke the feel of a South Pacific plantation, which is quite a feat since the restaurant is in a small converted home. *Lobsterocki* (Maine lobster wrapped in bacon with teriyaki cream sauce), baked Brie, or rare seared tuna are good appetizer choices. For a main course, try the Indian River crab cakes, coq au vin, or veal Française (scallopini with mushroom sauce). Wine lovers will appreciate their extensive selection of vintages, which includes domestic and European red, white, blush, and dessert wines. ⊠ 118 N. Atlantic Ave. ☎ 321/799–0513 ⊕ www.themangotreerestaurant.com ⊟ AE, MC, V ⊗ Closed Mon. No lunch.

★ $$–$$$ ✕ **Bernard's Surf.** Opened in 1948, Bernard's was here to welcome the *Mercury* 7 astronauts and remains a special gathering place for locals, astronauts, reporters, politicians, and celebrities from around the world. The restaurant is a family operation supported by its own fleet of boats. The menu focuses on fresh seafood, such as swordfish, cobia, popano, lobster, and shrimp, although you also find pork chops and steak. You might start with jumbo coconut-fried shrimp with orange dipping sauce and continue with the house specialty: snapper in cream sauce. Save room for the unbeatable cheesecake, topped with raspberries and chocolate. Also located within Bernard's is **Fischer's Bar and Grill.** This is a fine place to wind down after a tough day at the beach. Although complete dinners are available, diners tend to come for simpler fare such as salads, pastas, burgers, and platters of tasty fried shrimp. Happy hour is from 4 to 7. ⊠ *2 S. Atlantic Ave.* ☎ *321/783–2401* ⊕ *www.bernardssurf. com* ⊟ *AE, D, DC, MC, V* ⊙ *No lunch.*

$$–$$$ ✕ **Heidelberg.** As the name suggests, the cuisine here is definitely German, from the sauerbraten served with potato dumplings and red cabbage to the beef Stroganoff and spaetzle to the classically prepared Wiener schnitzel. All the soups and desserts are homemade; try the apple strudel and the rum-zapped almond-cream tortes. The atmosphere is elegant, with crisp linens and fresh flowers. Next door is Heidi's Jazz Club, where there's live music every day but Monday. ⊠ *7 N. Orlando Ave., opposite City Hall* ☎ *321/783–6806* ⊕ *www. heidisjazzclub.com* ⊟ *AE, MC, V* ⊙ *Closed Mon. No lunch Sun.*

$–$$$ ✕ **Atlantic Ocean Grille.** Five hundred feet over the water in the shopping, dining, and entertainment complex on Cocoa Beach Pier, this restaurant has floor-to-ceiling windows that overlook the ocean. The setting is typical of most Florida seafood restaurants: very large, family-oriented, and with a nautical theme. Among the excellent fresh-fish options are mahimahi and grouper, which you can order broiled, blackened, grilled, or fried. ⊠ *401 Meade Ave.* ☎ *321/783–7549* ⊟ *AE, D, DC, MC, V.*

¢–$ ✕ **The Boardwalk.** Finger food reigns at this popular open-air bar on Cocoa Beach Pier. You can count on live entertainment Monday, Wednesday, and Friday through Sunday evenings. At the very popular Friday-night Boardwalk Bash there are $7 lobsters and $2 ribs. ⊠ *401 Meade Ave.* ☎ *321/783–7549* ⊕ *www.cocoabeachpier.com* ⊟ *AE, D, DC, MC, V.*

¢–$ ✕ **Oh, Shucks!** Oysters served on the half shell are the main menu item at this open-air bar on the beach. You can also find burgers and fries, and there's live entertainment on Friday and Saturday. ⊠ *401 Meade Ave.* ☎ *321/783–7549* ⊟ *AE, D, DC, MC, V.*

$$$–$$$$ ▥ **Cocoa Beach Hilton Oceanfront.** At seven stories this hotel is one of the tallest buildings in Cocoa Beach, although its height helped it catch gusts from three hurricanes in 2004. Repairing led to remodeling and as of early 2005 most rooms have new tropical furniture and windows that have been expanded to reveal more ocean views. The hotel is popular with businesses, but leisure travelers come, too, for the good beach access and cool poolside retreat. ⊠ *1550 N. Atlantic Ave., 32931* ☎ *321/799–0003 or 800/889–4787* 🖷 *321/799–0344* ⊕ *www. cocoabeachhilton.com* ⇥ *296 rooms* ⌂ *Restaurant, cable TV, pool, beach, bar, video game room, babysitting, conference center* ⊟ *AE, D, DC, MC, V.*

$$$–$$$$ ▥ **Doubletree Oceanfront Hotel.** Conveniently located across from the Banana River Square shopping center, the Doubletree has light and airy rooms furnished with blond rattan and pastel prints. Many of the rooms have superb water views and private balconies. This well-maintained five-story hotel is popular with families and is also a favorite of Orlandoans as a weekend getaway, perhaps due to the swanky Three Wishes restaurant and its great view of the ocean. ⊠ *2080 N. Atlantic Ave.,*

32931 ☏ *321/783–9222 or 800/552–3224* 🖨 *321/783–6514* ⊕ *www. cocoabeachdoubletree.com* ⇥ *138 rooms, 10 suites* ⚫ *Restaurant, cable TV, 2 pools, wading pool, gym, bar* ☰ *AE, DC, MC, V.*

★ **$$–$$$$** 🖾 **Inn at Cocoa Beach.** Although from the outside it looks like an office building surrounded by boxy condos, this inn has charming individually decorated rooms with four-poster beds, upholstered chairs, balconies or patios, and ocean views. Deluxe rooms are much larger, with a king-size bed, sitting area, and sometimes a dining table. Other special rooms have Jacuzzis or fireplaces. Included in the rate are evening wine and cheese and a sumptuous continental breakfast. ⊠ *4300 Ocean Beach Blvd., 32931* ☏ *321/799–3460, 800/343–5307 outside Florida* 🖨 *321/ 784–8632* ⊕ *www.theinnatcocoabeach.com* ⇥ *50 rooms* ⚫ *Dining room, cable TV, pool, gym, beach* ☰ *AE, D, MC, V* ❚◉❙ *BP.*

$$$ 🖾 **Courtyard by Marriott.** To justify its name, this hotel preserved a few of the native trees, which has helped give it a fairly secluded feel. A light Spanish theme is carried through the lobby and into guest rooms, each of which comes with an appealing accent: a balcony that opens up to generous ocean views. More meeting space was added in early 2005 and that, plus free high-speed Internet and a slew of business magazines and newspapers, make this a good bet for business travelers. ⊠ *3435 North Atlantic Ave., 32931* ☏ *321/784–4800, 800/321–2211* 🖨 *321/784–4812* ⊕ *www.courtyardcocoabeach.com* ⇥ *131 rooms* ⚫ *Lounge, cable TV, pool, fitness center, beach, laundry services* ☰ *AE, D, MC, V.*

$$–$$$ 🖾 **Hampton Inn.** Facing the neighboring Courtyard by Marriott and owned by the same family, the two hotels share similar amenities, namely comfortable rooms with balconies. On each bed is a handy, padded laptop writing desk, and you also get free high-speed Internet access, a microwave, fridge, coffeemaker, and a large bath with double sinks. All rooms have a king bed and pullout sofa, or two queen beds. ⊠ *3425 N. Atlantic Ave., 32931* ☏ *321/799–4099 or 877/492–3224* 🖨 *321/ 799–4991* ⊕ *www.hamptoninncocoabeach.com* ⇥ *149 rooms* ⚫ *Refrigerators, microwaves, cable TV, pool, gym, beach, laundry facilities* ☰ *AE, DC, MC, V.*

★ **$$–$$$** 🖾 **Holiday Inn Cocoa Beach Resort.** What a history: this is where the first astronauts stayed in the early 1960s. Today public rooms are plush, modern, and designed in bright tropical colors. Lodging options include standard and king rooms; oceanfront suites, which have a living room with sleeper sofa; villas; or bilevel lofts. KidsSuites are rooms with an adult area and a kids' playroom. Outside a water play area modeled like a pirate ship is a great place for kids to play and splash. A nice bar with a second-story observation deck opens up even larger views of the ocean and, even if you may not use it, adjacent to the hotel is Lori Wilson Park, one of the nicest parks around. A boardwalk, picnic pavilions, a playground, and beach access are wrapped within a wooded hammock and coastal scrub that's a migratory stop for songbirds, scrub-jays, shorebirds and seabirds. ⊠ *1300 N. Atlantic Ave., 32931* ☏ *321/783–2271 or 800/206–2747* 🖨 *321/784–8878* ⊕ *www.holidayinnsofcentralflorida.com* ⇥ *500 rooms, 119 suites* ⚫ *2 restaurants, snack bar, cable TV, 2 tennis courts, pool, hair salon, shuffleboard, volleyball, 2 bars, babysitting, children's programs (ages 3–12), laundry facilities* ☰ *AE, DC, MC, V.*

★ **$$–$$$**   🏨 **Wakulla Suites Resort.** This popular two-story motel is clean and comfortable and just off the beach. Although it doesn't look like much from the outside, along the courtyard between the facing wings it's a tropical paradise—circa 1950. It's kitsch and cute, with long-term guests creating a second home in the units with a large living room, two bedrooms, and a fully-equipped kitchenette. This is a great choice for families, with a palpable feeling of camaraderie. After playing on the beach, splash in the pool, play shuffleboard, or grill dinner along the courtyard. ✉ *3550 N. Atlantic Ave., 32931* ☎ *321/783–2230 or 800/992–5852* 🖷 *321/783–0980* ⊕ *www.wakulla-suites.com* 🛏 *116 suites* ᗐ *2 pools, cable TV, shuffleboard, grills* ▭ *AE, D, DC, MC, V.*

Nightlife

The **Cocoa Beach Pier** (✉ 401 Meade Ave. ☎ 321/783–7549) is for locals, beach bums, surfers, and people who don't mind the weatherworn wood and sandy, watery paths. At the Mai Tiki they claim that "No Bar Goes This Far, " which is true, considering it's at the end of the 800-foot pier. Come to the Boardwalk Friday night for the Boardwalk Bash, with live acoustic and rock-and-roll music; drop in Saturday for more live music; and come back Wednesday evening to catch the reggae band. Oh, Shucks! has live bands Friday and Saturday nights.

Coconuts on the Beach (✉ 2 Minuteman Causeway ☎ 321/784–1422 ⊕ coconutsonthebeach.com), a beachfront hangout that's long been the local party place, is popular with the younger crowd. It's several miles south of the main beach area, in downtown Cocoa. There are karaoke nights, ladies' nights, 25¢-beer nights, bikini contests every Saturday at 3, volleyball tournaments, plus live music on Thursday, Friday, and Saturday. Burgers, salads, and sandwiches are on the menu.

For some great live jazz, head to **Heidi's Jazz Club** (✉ 7 N. Orlando Ave. ☎ 321/783–4559 ⊕ www.heidisjazzclub.com). Local and nationally known musicians play Tuesday through Sunday, with showcase acts usually appearing on weekends.

Sports & the Outdoors

The **Space Coast Office of Tourism** (☎ 321/637–5483 or 877/572–3224 ⊕ www.space-coast.com) publishes a lengthy, detailed, and extensive listing of outdoor adventures, from horseback rides to airboat rides to sea-turtle walks. It also lists surfing and sailing schools and fishing charters.

BIKING   Although there are no bike trails as such in the area, cycling is allowed on beaches and the Cocoa Beach Causeway. Bikes can be rented hourly, daily, or weekly at **Ron Jon Surf Shop** (✉ 4151 N. Atlantic Ave., Rte. A1A ☎ 321/799–8888). The rates are $5 for two hours, $10 for eight hours, $15 for 24 hours, $30 for three days, and $50 for a week; there's also a $10 deposit for each bike. Locks are included.

FISHING   Although it's free to see most of the pier, there's a $1 charge to enter the fishing area at the end of the 800-foot-long boardwalk at the **Cocoa Beach Pier** (✉ 401 Meade Ave. ☎ 321/783–7549). After that, it won't cost much more to enjoy a real Florida thrill: renting a rod and reel for a nominal $3.50 and spending a few hours casting for fresh seafood from the pier. Maybe you'll catch dinner.

SURFING If you can't tell a tri-skeg stick from a hodaddy shredding the lip on a gnarly tube, then you may want to avail yourself of the **Cocoa Beach Surfing School** (✉ 150 E. Columbia La. ☎ 321/868–1980). They transform grommets (dudes) and gidgets (chicks) from sandspiders into waveriders. All ages have learned to surf here. Rates are $50 for a one-hour private lesson and $40 for a one-hour semiprivate (two people). For a three-hour lesson rates are $75 for a semi-private and $50 for a group of three or more. No credit cards; cash and traveler's checks only.

Shopping
Heading into Cocoa from Orlando on Rte. 520, you'll pass the **Merritt Square Mall** (✉ 777 E. Merritt Island Causeway, Rte. 520, Merritt Island ☎ 321/452–3272 ⊕ www.merrittsquaremall.com), the area's only major shopping mall. Stores include Burdines, Dillard's, JCPenney, Sears Roebuck, Bath & Body Works, Foot Locker, Waldenbooks, and roughly 100 others. There's a six-screen multiplex, as well as a 16-screen theater, plus a food court and several popular restaurant chains. If you're staying on the beach, it's about a 20-minute ride. ☉ *Mon.–Sat. 10 AM–9 PM, Sun. noon–6.*

FodorśChoice It's impossible to miss the **Ron Jon Surf Shop** (✉ 4151 N. Atlantic Ave.,
★ Rte. A1A ☎ 321/799–8888 ⊕ www.ronjons.com). With a giant surfboard and an aqua, teal, and pink art-deco facade, Ron Jon takes up nearly two blocks along A1A. What started in 1963 as a small T-shirt and bathing-suit shop has evolved into a 52,000-square-foot superstore that's open every day 'round the clock. The shop has water-sports gear as well as chairs and umbrellas for rent, and sells every kind of beachwear and surf wax, plus the requisite T-shirts and flip-flops. For up-to-the-minute surfing conditions, call the store and press 3 and then 7 for the **Ron Jon Surf and Weather Report. Ron Jon Watersports** (✉ 4151 N. Atlantic Ave. ☎ 321/799–8888) features the latest in surfing rentals, including glass and foam surfboards, body boards, scuba equipment, and kayaks. Tip: Don't buy anything until you've snagged one of the plentiful 15%-off coupons available at nearly every hotel and attraction. After the store, go next door to the **East Coast Surfing Hall of Fame Museum** (☎ 321/799–8840), which features a collection of vintage surfing magazines, surfboards and assorted memorabilia that celebrate surfing's roots and its hottest celebrities.

Sebastian

22 mi south of Melbourne.

One of only a few sparsely populated areas on Florida's east coast, this little fishing village has as remote a feeling as you're likely to find anywhere between Jacksonville and Miami Beach.

The 578-acre **Sebastian Inlet State Recreation Area** is so popular that it's the only Florida state park open 24 hours a day, 365 days a year. Popular doesn't mean crowded, thankfully, just blessed with a wide range of activities. It offers 3 mi of beach that's good for swimming, surfing, and snorkeling, although the sand is coarser than elsewhere along the coast, and the underwater drop-off is often sharp. It's fun for treasure hunters, because storms occasionally wash up coins from the area's ancient Spanish shipwrecks. Sebastian is also a favorite destination for Florida anglers. Warning: bring mosquito repellent. The park has a bathhouse, a concession, a fishing jetty, a boat ramp, and campsites that cost $23 per night, with additional fees for electricity and pets. Reservations can be made by calling **Reserve America** at ☎ 800/326–3521. ✉ *9700 S. Rte. A1A, Melbourne Beach* ☎ *321/984–4852* ⊕ *www.dep.state.fl.us/ parks* ✉ *$5 per carload* ☉ *Daily 24 hrs, bait-and-tackle shop daily 8–6, concession stand daily 9–5.*

At the southern tip of Sebastian Park, across the border in the city of Vero Beach, is the **McLarty Treasure Museum**, built to commemorate the loss of a fleet of Spanish treasure ships in a hurricane. Don't miss the dramatic movie *The Queen's Jewels and the 1715 Fleet*. Filmed by the Arts & Entertainment television network, it's a riveting tale of the 11 ships that sank in one devastating hurricane in 1715. These ships are the source of most of the treasure that still washes ashore along this part of the Florida coastline. You'll have to pay the park admission before you can reach the museum. If you find a doubloon, you're covered. ✉ *13180 N. Rte. A1A* ☎ *772/589–2147* ✉ *$1 ages 6 and older* ☉ *Daily 10–4:30.*

Port Canaveral

5 mi north of Cocoa.

This once-bustling commercial fishing area is still home to a small shrimping fleet, charter boats, and party fishing boats, but its main business these days is as a cruise-ship port. Cocoa Beach itself isn't the spiffiest place around, but what *is* becoming quite clean and neat is the north end of the port where the Carnival, Disney, and Royal Caribbean cruise lines put to sea. Port Canaveral is now Florida's second-busiest cruise port, which makes this a great place to catch a glimpse of these giant ships even if you're not boarding one.

Jetty Maritime Park serves a wonderful taste of the real Florida. It's a campground, fishing point, and much more. At Port Canaveral's south side, there are assorted restaurants and marine shops, a 4½-acre beach, more than 150 campsites for tents and RVs, picnic pavilions, and a 1,200-foot-long fishing pier that doubles as a perfect vantage point from which to watch a lift-off of the space shuttle. A jetty constructed of giant boulders adds to the landscape, and a walkway that crosses it provides access to a less-populated stretch of beach. Real and rustic, this is Florida without the theme-park varnish. For kicks, be here when the big ships head to sea. ✉ *400 E. Jetty Rd., Cape Canaveral* ☎ *Campground 321/783–7111* ✉ *$5 per car, $7 for RVs, for either fishing or beach: Camping $24 for basic, $28 with water–electric, $31 full hookup* ☉ *Daily 7 AM–9 PM.*

Where to Stay & Eat

$$–$$$ ☒ **Radisson Resort at the Port.** A few blocks from the port, there's a casual and comfortable Bahamian feel here. Rooms have wicker furniture, colorful wallpaper, coffeemakers, ceiling fans, and beds that can be adjusted for firmness or flexibility. The pool has a 95-foot waterfall and is surrounded by tropical landscaping. Parking is free, and the hotel provides complimentary transportation to the beach, Ron Jon Surf Shop, and the cruise ship terminals at Port Canaveral. ⊠ *8701 Astronaut Blvd., 32920* ☎ *321/784–0000 or 800/333–3333* ⊟ *321/784–3737* ⊕ *www. radisson.com* ☞ *284 rooms* ⚘ *Restaurant, cable TV, 2 tennis courts, 2 pools, health club, hot tub, playground, laundry service, business services, convention center, airport shuttle* ⊟ *AE, DC, MC, V.*

¢–$$$ ✗ **Rusty's Seafood & Oyster Bar.** Oysters, prepared raw, steamed, or casino style, are just one of the draws at this casual eatery with a Hooters motif—waitresses are dressed in very short shorts. Other popular menu items include seafood gumbo, spicy wings, steamed crab legs, burgers, and baskets of fish-and-chips, clam strips, or fried calamari. It's a popular spot with the locals. ⊠ *628 Glen Cheek Dr., Port Canaveral* ☎ *321/783–2033* ⊕ *www.rustysseafood.com* ⊟ *AE, D, DC, MC, V.*

Sports & the Outdoors

For a complete listing of boats heading out to sea, check the Web site of the **Canaveral Charter Captains Association** (⊕ www.fishingspacecoast. org). Prices vary from around $50 for a chance to fish with a dozen other people to around $1,000 to share a boat with a few friends for a day. Similar services are offered by the **Indian River Guides Association** (⊕ www. irga.org).

Cape Marina (⊠ 800 Scallop Dr. ☎ 321/783–8410 or 321/634–5792 ⊕ www.capemarina.com) books 8-, 10-, and 16-hour fishing charters in search of the elusive wahoo, tuna, dolphin, mackerel, snapper, grouper, amberjack, marlin, and sailfish.

Titusville

17 mi north of Cocoa.

It's unusual that such a small, easily overlooked community could accommodate what it does, namely the Kennedy Space Center, the nerve center of the U.S. space program, and the magnificent Merritt Island National Wildlife Refuge. Although the town isn't much, the attractions are. Discounts are usually available, particularly if you're active or retired military.

Fodor'sChoice ★ The must-see **Kennedy Space Center Visitor Complex,** just southeast of Titusville, is one of Central Florida's most popular sights. Following the lead of the theme parks, they've switched to a one-price-covers-all admission. To get the most out of your visit to the space center, take the bus tour (included with admission), which makes stops at several facilities. Buses depart every 15 minutes, and you can get on and off any bus whenever you like. As you approach the Kennedy Space Center grounds, tune your car radio to AM1320 for attraction information.

The first stop on the tour is the **Launch Complex 39 Observation Gantry,** which has an unparalleled view of the twin space-shuttle launch-pads. At the **Apollo Saturn V Center,** don't miss the presentation at the Firing Room Theatre, where the launch of America's first lunar mission, 1968's *Apollo VIII,* is re-created with a ground-shaking, window-rattling lift-off. At the **Lunar Surface Theatre,** recordings from *Apollo XI* offer an eerie and awe-inspiring reminder that when Armstrong and Aldrin landed, they had less than 30 seconds of fuel to spare. In the hall it's impossible to miss the 363-foot-long *Saturn V* rocket. A spare built for a moon mission that never took place, this 6.2-million-pound spacecraft has enough power to throw a fully loaded DC-3 all the way to the sun and back!

Exhibits near the center's entrance include the **Early Space Exploration** display, which highlights the rudimentary yet influential Mercury and Gemini space programs; **Robot Scouts,** a walk-through exhibit of unmanned planetary probes; and the **Exploration in the New Millennium** display, which offers you the opportunity to touch a piece of Mars (it fell to the Earth in the form of a meteorite). Don't miss the outdoor **Rocket Garden,** with walkways winding beside spare rockets from early Atlas spacecraft to a Saturn 1. There's also a museum filled with exhibits on spacecraft that have explored the last frontier, and a theater showing several short films. A full-scale reproduction of a space shuttle, *Explorer,* is displayed and you can walk through the payload bay, cockpit, and crew quarters. Children love the space playground, with a one-fifth-scale space shuttle–space station gym.

The most moving exhibit is the **Astronauts Memorial,** a tribute to those who have died while in pursuit of space exploration. A 42½-foot-high by 50-foot-wide "Space Mirror" tracks the movement of the sun throughout the day, using reflected sunlight to brilliantly illuminate the names of the 24 fallen astronauts that are carved into the monument's 70,400-pound polished granite surface.

During the **Astronaut Encounter,** in a pavilion near the center's entrance, an astronaut who's actually flown in space hosts a daily Q&A session to tell visitors about life in zero gravity, providing insights to an experience only a few hundred people have ever shared. If you'd like to have a closer encounter with an astronaut, you can purchase a special ticket option to **Lunch with an Astronaut** for $20 for adults and $13 for kids—which includes your regular KSC admission. No, it's not freeze-dried food and Tang. For an added fee and a more in-depth experience ($22 adults, $16 children 3–11), take the **NASA Up Close** tour, which brings visitors to sights seldom accessible to the public, such as the NASA Press Site Launch Countdown Clock, the Vehicle Assembly Building, the shuttle landing strip, and the 6-million-pound crawler that transports the shuttle to its launchpad.

The only back-to-back twin **IMAX theater complex** in the world is in the complex, too. *The Dream Is Alive,* an awesome 40-minute film narrated by Walter Cronkite and shot mostly by the astronauts, takes you from astronaut training and a thundering shuttle launch to an astronaut's-eye view of life aboard the shuttle while in space. **Space Station IMAX 3-D** follows astronauts and cosmonauts on their missions, with the 3-D effects putting you in space with them. ⊠ *Rte. 405, Kennedy Space Center* ☎ *321/449–4400 or 800/572–4636 (launch hotline)* ⊕ *www. kennedyspacecenter.com* ☲ *General 1-day admission includes bus tour and IMAX movies, $30 adults, $20 children 3–11; Maximum Access Badge, valid for 2 days, includes bus tour, IMAX movies, and the Astronaut Hall of Fame, $37 adults, $27 children 3–11; NASA Up Close Tour: $22 plus admission* ☉ *Space Center daily 9–5:30, last regular tour 3 hrs before closing; closed certain launch dates; IMAX I and II Theaters daily 10–5:40.*

The original Mercury 7 team and the later Gemini, Apollo, Skylab, and shuttle astronauts contributed to make the **United States Astronaut Hall of Fame** the world's premium archive of astronauts' personal stories. Authentic memorabilia and equipment from their collections tell the story of human space exploration. You'll watch videotapes of historic moments in the space program and see one-of-a-kind items like Wally Schirra's relatively archaic Sigma 7 Mercury space capsule, Gus Grissom's spacesuit (colored silver only because NASA thought silver looked more "spacey"), and a flag that made it to the moon. The exhibit **First on the Moon** focuses on crew selection for *Apollo 11* and the Soviet Union's role in the space race. Definitely don't miss the **Astronaut Adventure,** a hands-on discovery center with interactive exhibits that help you learn about space travel. One of the more challenging activities is a space-shuttle simulator that lets you try your hand at landing the craft— and afterward replays a side view of your rolling and pitching descent. If that gets your motor going, consider enrolling in **ATX (Astronaut Training Experience).** Held at the Hall of Fame, this is an intense full-day experience where you prepare for a launch, feel the g-force of take-off, and take the controls of a pseudo space shuttle. Veteran NASA astronauts helped design the program, and you'll hear first-hand from them as you progress through your training, which includes a full-scale space shuttle mission simulation. Space is limited (no pun intended), so call well in advance. Included in the $225 program is your astronaut gear, lunch, and a VIP tour of the Kennedy Space Center. ⊠ *6225 Vectorspace Blvd., off Rte. 405* ☎ *321/452–2121 or 800/572–4636, 321/ 449–4400 for ATX* ⊕ *www.kennedyspacecenter.com* ☲ *AHOF only: $17 adults, $13 children 6–12; Maximum Access Pass, valid for 2 days, combines the Kennedy Space Center Visitor Complex and the Astronaut Hall of Fame, $37 adults, $27 children 3–11* ☉ *Daily 9–6.*

The **American Police Hall of Fame and Museum,** opened in late 2003, is adjacent to the Astronaut Hall of Fame and, in its own way, is just as impressive. In addition to memorabilia like the Robocop costume and Blade Runner car from the eponymous films, there are informative displays on what cops face every day: drugs, homicides, and criminals who can create knives from dental putty and guns from a bicycle spoke (really). At times, it can be a gruesome chamber of horrors with autopsy photos of criminals and chilling mock-ups of prison cells, gas chambers, and an electric chair. An eerie example of law enforcement memorabilia is a piece of one of the World Trade Center towers fused with the plane that hit it. Other historical exhibits include invitations to hangings, crime-scene evidence kits, and, most importantly, a rotunda where more than 7,000 names are etched in marble to honor police officers who have died in the line of duty. Cops, gun nuts, and curious tourists are taken by the 24-lane shooting range that provides rental guns. Give it a shot. ⊠ *6350 Horizon Dr.* ☎ *321/264–0911* ⊕ *www.aphf.org* ⌨ *$12 adults, $8 children 4–12* ☉ *Daily 10–6; shooting range weekdays noon–7, weekends noon–5.*

Although its exterior looks sort of squirrelly, what's inside the **Valiant Air Command Warbird Air Museum** is certainly impressive. Aviation buffs won't want to miss memorabilia from both world wars, Korea, and Vietnam, as well as extensive displays of vintage military flying gear and uniforms. There are posters used to identify Japanese planes, plus there's a Huey helicopter and the cockpit of an F-106 that you can sit in (but can't start). In the north hangar it looks like activity day at the senior center as a volunteer team of retirees busily restores old planes. It's an inspiring sight, and a good place to hear some war stories. In the lobby gift shop they sell real flight suits ($40), old flight magazines, bomber jackets, books, and T-shirts. ⊠ *6600 Tico Rd.* ☎ *321/268–1941* ⊕ *www.vacwarbirds.org* ⌨ *$9 adults, $5 children 4–12* ☉ *Daily 10–6.*

★ The 57,000-acre **Canaveral National Seashore** is on a barrier island that's home to more than 1,000 species of plants and 300 species of birds and other animals. The unspoiled area of hilly sand dunes, grassy marshes, and seashell-sprinkled beaches is a large part of NASA's buffer zone. Surf and lagoon fishing are available, and a hiking trail leads to the top of a Native American shell midden at Turtle Mound. A visitor center is on Route A1A. Weekends are busy, and parts of the park are closed before launches, sometimes as much as two weeks in advance, so call ahead.

Part of the national seashore, remote **Playalinda Beach** has pristine sands and is the longest stretch of undeveloped coast on Florida's Atlantic seaboard. Its isolation explains why a remote strand of the beach is popular with nude sunbathers. Aside from them, hundreds of giant sea turtles come ashore here May through August to lay their eggs. There are no lifeguards, but park rangers patrol. Eight parking lots anchor the beach at 1-mi intervals. Take bug repellent in case of horseflies. To get here, follow U.S. 1 north into Titusville to Route 406 (I–95 Exit 80), follow Route 406 east across the Indian River, and then take Route 402 east for 12 mi. ⊠ *Southern end: Rte. 402* ☎ *321/267–1110* ⌨ *Northern end: 7611 S. Atlantic Ave., New Smyrna Beach* ☎ *386/428–3384* ⊕ *www.nps.gov/cana* ⌨ *$5 per car* ☉ *Apr.–Oct., daily 6 AM–8 PM; Nov.–Mar., daily 8 AM–6 PM.*

If you prefer wading birds over waiting in line, don't miss the 140,000-acre **Merritt Island National Wildlife Refuge,** which adjoins the Canaveral National Seashore. It's an immense area dotted by brackish estuaries and patches of land with coastal dunes, scrub oaks, pine forests, and

FodorsChoice
★

palm and oak hammocks. You can borrow field guides and binoculars at the visitor center to track down various types of falcons, osprey, eagles, turkeys, doves, cuckoos, loons, geese, skimmers, terns, warblers, wrens, thrushes, sparrows, owls, and woodpeckers. A 20-minute video about refuge wildlife and accessibility—only 10,000 acres are developed—can help orient you. You might take a self-guided tour along the 7-mi **Black Point Wildlife Drive.** The dirt road takes you back in time, where there are no traces of encroaching malls or mankind and it's easy to visualize the Indian tribes who made this their home 7,000 years ago. On the **Oak Hammock Foot Trail,** you can see wintering migratory waterfowl and learn about the plants of a hammock community. If you exit the north end of the refuge, look for the **Manatee Observation Area** just north of the Haulover Canal (maps are at the visitor center). They usually show up in spring and fall. There are also fishing camps scattered throughout the area. The refuge is closed four days prior to a shuttle launch. ⊠ *Rte. 402, across Titusville causeway* ☎ *321/861–0667* ⊕ *merrittisland.fws.gov* ⊡ *Free* ⊗ *Daily sunrise–sunset, visitor center open weekdays 8–4:30, Sat. 9–5.*

Bringing people closer to nature since the early 1980s, **Space Coast Nature Tours** sets sail on the Indian River, using stable pontoon boats, quiet electric motors, and knowledgeable guides to enhance the experience. The true nature of the coast is revealed when you skim in close to bird rookeries, past manatees, and alongside dolphins on the 90-minute cruise. On the journey, you'll also spy wading birds, shore birds, birds of prey, migratory birds, alligators, and the massive space shuttle launch pads just 7 miles away. ⊠ *451 Marina Road (Titusvilee Municipal Marina, slip A-23)* ☎ *321/267–4551* ⊕ *www.spacecoastnaturetours.com* ⊡ *$17 adults, $15 children* ⊗ *Regularly scheduled tours daily except Sun. at 10:30 AM and 1:30 PM.*

Where to Eat

$$–$$$ ✕ **Paul's Smokehouse.** On the shores of the Indian River right across from the Kennedy Space Center, this family-owned restaurant open since 1975 has one of the best views in America. The huge dining room opens to the river—a perfect setting for dining on shrimp, scallops, swordfish, oysters, and lobster tails, all of which can be broiled, blackened, sautéed, or grilled. Beef is well represented, with filet mignon and New York strip steaks. Less elaborate meals are served in the lounge, where you'll also find well drinks, draft and bottled beer, and name-brand liquors. Where else can you eat lunch and watch a launch? ⊠ *3665 U.S. 1* ☎ *321/267–3663* ⊗ *Closed Mon.* ▭ *AE, DC, MC, V.*

★ ¢–$$$ ✕ **Dixie Crossroads.** This sprawling restaurant is always crowded and festive. Part of the attraction is the fishpond, the plentiful memorabilia reflecting the dawn of the Space Age and natural attributes of the coast, and a stunning 160-foot-long mural commissioned by the environmentally friendly owner. The artwork shares the stage with Dixie's specialty: the difficult-to-cook rock shrimp, which is served fried or broiled. Other standouts include the clam strips, snow crab legs, all-you-can-eat catfish, and the free sugared corn fritters, which are absolutely sinful. Often the wait for a table can last 90 minutes, but if you don't have time to wait, you can order takeout or eat in the bar area. If you have one night to dine on the coast, consider this true Florida favorite. ⊠ *1475 Garden St., 2 mi east of I–95 via Exit 80* ☎ *321/268–5000* ⚙ *Reservations not accepted* ▤ *AE, D, DC, MC, V.*

¢–$ ✗ **El Leoncita.** Despite the cheesy 1960s south-of-the-border décor, this is one of a few local Mexican restaurants so it gets a lot of traffic from locals, including NASA employees and astronauts. The standard line-up of dishes includes arroz con pollo, chile relleno, enchiladas, and tacos. You can also head to Cuba with *palomilla* (sirloin steak Old Havana-style) and *chuletas de puerco*—known by most customers as pork chops with *mojo* sauce, a marinade made with garlic, olive oil, orange juice, lemon juice, cumin, salt, and black pepper. Early dinner specials are offered from 3 to 6 PM. ⊠ *3800 U.S. 1* ☎ *321/267–1159* ▤ *AE, D, DC, MC, V.*

Sports & the Outdoors

One of the most spectacular events on the coast is the laying and hatching of rare loggerhead sea turtles. The **Sea Turtle Preservation Society** (☎ 321/676–1701, ⊕ www.seaturtlespacecoast.org) leads beach tours from dusk to midnight from May through September, so you can witness the nesting, birth, and survival of these lumbering creatures. Best experienced during a full moon, you'll see 300-pound turtles lumber ashore, dig their nest in the soft sand, and lay an average of 100 eggs. About two months later, the baby sea turtles hatch and return to the sea—and you can be there to witness it. Guided walks begin at 9 PM Wednesday through Saturday.

Shopping

Space Coast Frontenac Flea Market. On any weekend you can find bushels of farm-fresh produce and acres of new and used toys, tools, watches, clocks, CDs, clothing, birds, pets, silk plants and trees, framed pictures and paintings, and eleven million other items. If you like browsing at flea markets, this is one of the best on the coast. ⊠ *5605 N. U.S. 1, south of Titusville, Frontenac* ☎ *321/631–0241* ⊕ *www.spacecoastfleamarket. com* ⊙ *Fri.–Sun. 7–5.*

New Smyrna Beach

35 mi north of Titusville, 70 mi north of Cocoa Beach

This small town has a long dune-lined beach that abuts the north end of the Canaveral National Seashore. Behind the dunes sit beach houses, small motels, and an occasional high-rise. Canal Street, on the mainland, and Flagler Avenue, home to many beachside shops and restaurants, have both been "street-scaped" and are now lined with wide, brick sidewalks and stately palm trees. The town is also known for its internationally recognized artists' workshop.

Changing every two months, the gallery exhibits at the **Atlantic Center for the Arts** feature the works of internationally known artists—sculpture, mixed media, video, drawings, prints, and paintings. Intensive three-week workshops are periodically run by master visual, literary, and performing artists; faculty have included playwright Edward Albee, the late poet and author James Dickey, and sculptor Beverly Pepper. ⊠ *1414 Art Center Ave.* ☎ *386/427–6975* ⊕ *www.atlanticcenterforthearts.org* 🗺 *Free* ☉ *Weekdays 9–5, Sat. 10–2.*

Smyrna Dunes Park is on the northern tip of its barrier island. Here 1½ mi of boardwalks crisscross sand dunes and delicate dune vegetation as they lead to beaches and a fishing jetty. Botanical signs identify the flora, and there are picnic tables and an information center. ⊠ *N. Peninsula Ave.* 🗺 *$3* ☉ *Daily 7–sunset.*

The town's **public beach** extends 7 mi from the northernmost part of the barrier island south to the Canaveral National Seashore. It's mostly hard-packed white sand, and at low tide can be stunningly wide. The beach is lined with heaps of sandy dunes, but please don't disturb them. The dunes are endangered, and it's against the law to walk or play on them or to pick the sea grass that helps to stabilize the dunes. Be aware that from sunrise to sunset cars are allowed on certain sections of the beach (speed limit: 10 mph).

★ The entrance to the north end of the **Canaveral National Seashore** begins at the south end of the public beach. ⊠ *7611 S. Atlantic Ave.* ☎ *386/ 428–3384* 🗺 *$5 per car* ☉ *Apr.–Oct., daily 6 AM–8 PM; Nov.–Mar., daily 6 AM–6 PM.*

Where to Stay & Eat

¢–$$$$ ✕ **Norwood's.** Since 1946, this seafood restaurant has been one of the area's most popular places, thanks to its fresh fish (prepared any style), Angus beef, fresh oysters and scallops, and decadent desserts. Another attraction is its impressive selection of wines, with more than 30,000 bottles of 1,400 different wines in stock. Credit Southern hospitality honed over a half century for the exemplary service. ⊠ *400 E. 2nd Ave.* ☎ *386/428–4621* ▤ *AE, MC, V.*

$–$$$ ✕ **New Smyrna Steakhouse.** Locals and visitors flock to this dark and busy spot to dine on giant steaks, spicy ribs, and juicy cheeseburgers. Try the 12-ounce New York strip or sirloin, the 20-ounce porterhouse, the 8-ounce filet mignon, or a rack of tender ribs. Other good choices are the Cajun pizza, shrimp Caesar salad, and mesquite chicken. Booths are lit by individual, low-hanging lamps that provide intimacy but still enough light to read the menu. ⊠ *723 3rd Ave.* ☎ *386/424–9696* ▤ *AE, MC, V.*

$–$$$ ✕ **Spanish River Grill.** Chef-owners Michelle and Henry Salgado preside over this first-rate Cuban spot, where everything is made from scratch. Start with fried green plantains or black-bean soup, then move on to a tender rib-eye steak stuffed with chorizo, incredibly fresh grilled fish, or the roasted sour-orange chicken. The wine list includes many reasonably priced selections. Ocher walls, crisp table linens, and romantic lighting provide an intimate setting. ⊠ *737 E. 3rd Ave.* ☎ *386/424–6991* ▤ *AE, MC, V* ☉ *Closed Mon.*

$$–$$$ ✕ **Chase's on the Beach.** Dine indoors or eat on an outdoor deck beneath the stars, resting easy by the ocean and the pool. Popular day and night,

it's where barefoot beachgoers wander up for beverages, hamburgers, and salads during the day (shoes required inside), and an evening crowd arrives for fried shrimp, grouper sandwiches, and weekend entertainment like live music by the pool. The epitome of a Florida beach bar. ⊠ *3401 S. Atlantic Ave.* ☎ *386/423–8787* ▭ *AE, MC, V.*

¢ ✕ **Toni and Joe's.** This longtime, ultracasual favorite (no shoes required) opens right onto the beach and has a large terrace perfect for people-watching. Head for the famous hoagies: long rolls of fresh bread stuffed with steak slices, cheese, sweet peppers, and onions and heated until the cheese is perfectly melted. ⊠ *309 Buenos Aires* ☎ *386/427–6850* ▭ *No credit cards* ⊘ *Closed Mon. No dinner.*

★ **$$–$$$** ▦ **Night Swan.** This inn on the Intracoastal Waterway was created from a grand, three-story 1906 home. Inside, a central fireplace sets a relaxing tone, which is matched by the indulgent pleasure of doing nothing while sitting on the porch and watching the river roll past. Inside, 15 guest rooms are decorated with plush queen or king beds. Some rooms have large whirlpool tubs and showers. Catered dinners, in-room massages, and sweetheart packages are available, too. A full breakfast is served in the dining room, on the porch, or in your room. ⊠ *512 South Riverside Dr., 32168* ☎ *386/423–4940 or 800/465–4261* ⊕ *www.nightswan.com* ⬎ *15 rooms* ⼂ *Cable TV, bicycles* ▭ *AE, D, DC, MC, V.*

$$–$$$ ▦ **Riverview Hotel & Spa.** Built in 1886, this pink B&B is set back from the Intracoastal Waterway. Individually furnished rooms open out to plant-filled verandas and balconies with views of water or a private courtyard and pool. Most rooms are around $120, but champagne in the Executive Suites bumps the prices. A complimentary continental breakfast is served in your room. The full-service spa offers facials, manicures, massages, and other treatments. ⊠ *103 Flagler Ave., 32169* ☎ *386/428–5858 or 800/945–7416* ⊟ *386/423–8927* ⊕ *www.riverviewhotel.com* ⬎ *18 rooms* ⼂ *Restaurant, cable TV, pool, bicycles, wireless Internet* ▭ *AE, D, DC, MC, V* ⼌ *CP.*

THE SPACE COAST A TO Z

To research prices, get advice from other travelers, and book travel arrangements, visit www.fodors.com.

AIR TRAVEL

The nearest major airport is Orlando International Airport, a one-hour ride from the Space Coast. The Cocoa Beach Shuttle provides transportation to and from the airport; reservations are required. American Eagle, Continental, Delta, Spirit, and US Airways provide some service to Melbourne International Airport, approximately a half-hour drive from Cocoa. Melbourne Airport Shuttle and Taxi ferries arriving and departing passengers.

▶ Airport Information **Cocoa Beach Shuttle** ☎ 321/784–3831. **Melbourne Airport Shuttle and Taxi** ☎ 321/724–1600. **Melbourne International Airport** ☎ 321/723–6227 ⊕ www.mlbair.com. **Orlando International Airport** ☎ 407/825–2001.

BUS TRAVEL

Chances are that you'll never ride a bus when you're here, but if you do, the Space Coast Area Transit is the provider of local bus service. The fare is $1 for adults, 50¢ for senior citizens, people with disabilities, or students with valid ID cards. Route 9 goes up and down A1A, and Route 4 rides from the terminal in Cocoa to the Merritt Square Mall and east on 520 to A1A. An in-depth map of all routes is available on their website.

🚍 Bus Information **Space Coast Area Transit** ☎ 321/633-1878 ⊕ www.ridescat.com.

CAR TRAVEL

The Beeline Expressway (Route 528) is accessible from either I–4 or Florida's Turnpike. Tolls for the trip from Orlando add up to $3 for a car. If you take the Beeline directly to the coast, you'll end up in Port Canaveral, about 6 mi north of Cocoa Beach, where the road changes names to Route A1A and drops south along the coast to the main tourist areas. The coast is about 90 minutes from WDW and 60 minutes from Orlando.

Route 520, which is reached from the Beeline—take Exit 31 just past mile marker 30—is a slightly less direct but more scenic route, at least until you hit the pit of Cocoa and its strip malls and unchecked growth. Continuing east on Route 520 past Cocoa, you'll reach the beach and Route A1A, the beach's main artery.

Route 50, known in Orlando as Colonial Drive, is also a straight shot to the coast. You have to get through some dense city traffic at first, but once you're on the outskirts of Orlando it's smooth sailing as long as it's not during the morning or evening rush hour. Route 50 dead-ends at A1A in Titusville, north of the access road to the Kennedy Space Center Visitor Complex. If you're going to the center for the day, Route 50 is actually a more direct route than the Beeline.

If your destination is New Smyrna Beach, follow the Beeline Expressway to Route 407. Take Route 407 to I–95 north to Exit 249 (State Rd. 44) and go east 5 mi. The trip takes about 75 minutes from Orlando and about 95 minutes from WDW.

The Space Coast is easy to navigate. On the beach, the main thoroughfare is A1A, known as Atlantic Avenue in Cocoa Beach and in New Smyrna Beach, and by other names in some beach towns. The area around the intersection of A1A and Route 520 in Cocoa Beach tends to be congested at almost all hours. In general, however, traffic here can be somewhat lighter than in other towns along the coast. The principal route on the "mainland" is U.S. 1, which goes by various local names, such as Dixie Highway, and is generally not traffic-clogged except in the middle of towns.

EMERGENCIES

Dial **911** for police, fire, or ambulance.

🏥 Hospitals **Bert Fish Medical Center** ⊠ 401 Palmetto St., New Smyrna Beach ☎ 386/424-5000. **Cape Canaveral Hospital** ⊠ 701 W. Cocoa Beach Causeway, Rte. 520, Cocoa Beach ☎ 321/799-7111.

VISITOR INFORMATION

The best first source for rocket launch and area information is the Space Coast Office of Tourism. The Cocoa Beach Area Chamber of Commerce also offers information about lodging and dates for rocket launches.

🗷 **Cocoa Beach Area Chamber of Commerce** ⊠ 400 Fortenberry Rd., Merritt Island 32952 ☎ 321/459-2200 ⊕ www.visitcocoabeach.com. **Cocoa Village Association** ⊠ Brevard Ave., south of Rte. 520, Box 1, Cocoa Village, Cocoa 32923 ☎ 321/631-9075 ⊕ www.cocoavillage.com. **Melbourne/Palm Bay Area Chamber of Commerce** ⊠ 1005 E. Strawbridge Ave., Melbourne 32901 ☎ 321/724-5400 ⊕ www.melpb-chamber.org. **Southeast Volusia Chamber of Commerce** ⊠ 115 Canal St., New Smyrna Beach 32168 ☎ 386/428-2449. **Space Coast Office of Tourism** ⊠ 2725 Judge Fran Jamieson Way, Viera 32940 ☎ 321/637-5483 or 877/572-3224 ⊕ www.space-coast.com. **Titusville Area Chamber of Commerce** ⊠ 2000 S. Washington Ave., Titusville 32780 ☎ 321/267-3036 ⊕ www.titusville.org.

INDEX

NOTES

NOTES

NOTES

NOTES

FODOR'S KEY TO THE GUIDES

AMERICA'S **GUIDEBOOK LEADER** PUBLISHES GUIDES FOR **EVERY KIND OF TRAVELER**. CHECK OUT OUR MANY SERIES AND FIND YOUR **PERFECT MATCH**.

FODOR'S GOLD GUIDES
America's favorite travel-guide series offers the most detailed insider reviews of hotels, restaurants, and attractions in all price ranges, plus great background information, smart tips, and useful maps.

COMPASS AMERICAN GUIDES
Stunning guides from top local writers and photographers, with gorgeous photos, literary excerpts, and colorful anecdotes. A must-have for culture mavens, history buffs, and new residents.

FODOR'S 25 BEST / CITYPACKS
Concise city coverage in a guide plus a foldout map. The right choice for urban travelers who want everything under one cover.

FODOR'S AROUND THE CITY WITH KIDS
Up to 68 great ideas for family days, recommended by resident parents. Perfect for exploring in your own backyard or on the road.

SEE IT GUIDES
Illustrated guidebooks that include the practical information travelers need, in gorgeous full color. Perfect for travelers who want the best value packed in a fresh, easy-to-use, colorful layout.

FODOR'S FLASHMAPS
Every resident's map guide, with 60 easy-to-follow maps of public transit, parks, museums, zip codes, and more.

FODOR'S LANGUAGES FOR TRAVELERS
Practice the local language before you hit the road. Available in phrase books, cassette sets, and CD sets.

THE COLLECTED TRAVELER
These collections of the best published essays and articles on various European destinations will give you a feel for the culture, cuisine, and way of life.